T0185365

More information about this series at http://www.springer.com/series/7899

Shekhar Verma · Ranjeet Singh Tomar
Brijesh Kumar Chaurasia · Vrijendra Singh
Jemal Abawajy (Eds.)

Communication, Networks and Computing

First International Conference, CNC 2018
Gwalior, India, March 22–24, 2018
Revised Selected Papers

Springer

Editors
Shekhar Verma
Indian Institute of Information Technology
Allahabad
India

Ranjeet Singh Tomar
ITM University
Gwalior
India

Brijesh Kumar Chaurasia
ITM University
Gwalior
India

Vrijendra Singh
Indian Institute of Information Technology
Allahabad
India

Jemal Abawajy
School of Information Technology
Deakin University
Burwood, VIC
Australia

ISSN 1865-0929   ISSN 1865-0937   (electronic)
Communications in Computer and Information Science
ISBN 978-981-13-2371-3   ISBN 978-981-13-2372-0   (eBook)
https://doi.org/10.1007/978-981-13-2372-0

Library of Congress Control Number: 2018953421

This Springer imprint is published by the registered company Springer Nature Singapore Pte Ltd.
The registered company address is: 152 Beach Road, #21-01/04 Gateway East, Singapore 189721, Singapore

Preface

The book focuses on communication, networks, and computing to simplify the real-time problems occurring in different domains of communication, networks, and computing. Presently, research is entering a new era of convergence of these domains wherein the established models and techniques are being challenged. New ideas are being proposed and established ideas are being retested. Evaluating the performance of emerging smart technologies, however, poses a huge challenge.

The book includes high-quality papers presented at the International Conference on Communication, Networks, and Computing (CNC 2018), organized by ITM University Gwalior, India. Offering significant insights into this domain for academics and industry alike, the book inspires more researchers to work in the field of intelligent networks for communication systems. The theme of the conference was "Intelligent Networks for Communication Systems." This theme covers the exciting new areas of wired and wireless communication systems, high-dimensional data representation and processing, networks and information security, computing techniques for efficient networks design and electronic circuits for communication systems that promise to make the world a better place to live in.

ITM University Gwalior, India, is a multidisciplinary university with an international reputation for the quality of its research and teaching across the academic spectrum. The university has received more than 20 awards and has been ranked in the top category by a number of governmental and other agencies. The university is ranked 32nd in management and 58th in engineering in 2016 by the National Institutional Ranking Framework, Ministry of HRD, Government of India. The university is approved by the regulatory bodies required to run courses in engineering, management, pharmacy, commerce, agriculture, architecture, computer applications, teacher education, art and design, physical education, sciences, law, India and South Asia studies, journalism, nursing etc. It is at the forefront of learning, teaching, and research and the leader in different fields. It seeks to sustain and enhance its excellence as an institution of higher learning through outstanding teaching and world-class societies it serves.

The ITM School of Engineering and Technology is one of the flagship and leading schools of central and north India. The school is unique in that it tries to assimilate cutting-edge ideas in engineering and technology through a variety of projects in association with industry. In addition, prominent industries directly contribute to the knowledge and skill sets of students through various augmentation programs customized for students of ITM University. A mix of lectures, tutorials, laboratory studies, seminars, and projects are used to groom the conceptual and analytical abilities of students. For the first time in India, ITM University Gwalior has taken the initiative to introduce activity-based continuous assessment (ABCA) in order to increase the employability of students.

This conference was successful in facilitating academics, researchers, and industry professionals to deliberate upon the latest issues, challenges, and advancements in

Publicity Chairs

Pallavi Khatri   ITM University Gwalior, India
Shashikant Gupta   ITM University Gwalior, India

Workshop/Tutorial Chairs

Arun Kumar Yadav   ITM University Gwalior, India
Rajendra Singh Kushwah   ITM-GOI, Gwalior, India
R. Jenkin Suji   ITM University Gwalior, India

Hospitality Chairs

Mukesh Kumar Pandey   ITM University Gwalior, India
Rishi Soni   ITM-GOI, Gwalior, India

Local Organizing Committee

Ratan Kumar Jain   ITM University Gwalior, India
Geetanjali Surange   ITM University Gwalior, India
Deepak Motwani   ITM University Gwalior, India
Kapil Govil   ITM University Gwalior, India
Anshul Agarwal   ITM University Gwalior, India
Shailendra Singh Ojha   ITM University Gwalior, India
Ashish Garg   ITM University Gwalior, India
Kapil Sharma   ITM University Gwalior, India

Organizing Secretariat

Sumit Mohanti   ITM University Gwalior, India
Mayank Shastri   ITM University Gwalior, India

Contents

Wired and Wireless Communication Systems

Properties and Performance of Linearly Extensible Multiprocessor
Interconnection Networks.................................... 3
    Savita Gautam and Abdus Samad

An Analysis on Improvement of Lifetime in Wireless Sensor Network 13
    Shubhi Malhotra, Shushant Kumar Jain, and Vineet Shrivastava

A Novel Solution for Cloud Enabled E-Governance Using Openstack:
Opportunities and Challenges 24
    Bhushan Jadhav and Archana B. Patankar

Frequency of Meeting with Node and Visit to Physical Location
Based on Mobility Pattern 37
    Binod Kumar, R. R. Suman, and Binod Kumar Singh

A New Lightweight Approach for Multiuser Searchable Encryption
in the Cloud... 49
    Nitish Andola, Sourabh Prakash, Raghav, S. Venkatesan,
    and Shekhar Verma

Performance Evaluation of Multi-functional Defected Ground Structure
Embedded with Microstrip Patch Antenna for ISM
Band Wireless Communications 64
    Guru Prasad Mishra, Sumon Modak, Madhu Sudan Maharana,
    and Biswa Binayak Mangaraj

Evaluation of Character Recognition Algorithm Based
on Feature Extraction. 76
    Bishakha Sharma and Arun Agarwal

A High Performance BPSK Trans Receiver Using Level Converter
for Communication Systems.................................. 89
    Akula Rajesh, B. L. Raju, and K. Chenna Kesava Reddy

Connectivity Analysis of Mobile Ad Hoc Network Using Fuzzy
Logic Controller 99
    Poonam Rathore and Laxmi Shrivastava

Improved Election of Cluster Head Using CH-PSO for Different
Scenarios in VANET... 110
   Bhairo Singh Rajawat, Ranjeet Singh Tomar,
   Mayank Satya Prakash Sharma, and Brijesh Kumar Chaurasia

Utilizing Clustering Techniques for Improving the Boxplots............. 121
   Kalpak Patil, Naresh Kumar Nagwani, and Sarsij Tripathi

Mathematical Model for Sink Mobility (MMSM) in Wireless Sensor
Networks to Improve Network Lifetime........................... 133
   Mohit Kumar, Dinesh Kumar, and Md. Amir Khusru Akhtar

Detection of High Transmission Power Based Wormhole Attack
Using Received Signal Strength Indicator (RSSI) 142
   Prachi Sharma and Rajendra Kumar Dwivedi

Effective Data Storage Security with Efficient Computing in Cloud........ 153
   Manoj Tyagi, Manish Manoria, and Bharat Mishra

Privacy Preserving Multi Keyword Ranked Search with Context Sensitive
Synonyms over the Encrypted Cloud Data......................... 165
   Anu Khurana, Rama Krishna Challa, and Navdeep Kaur

An Optimized High Gain Microstrip Patch Array Antenna
for Sensor Networks 181
   Chandra Shekhar

An Efficient Data Aggregation Algorithm with Gossiping for Smart
Transportation System 191
   Sudhakar Pandey, Ruchi Jain, and Sanjay Kumar

Lane Change in Roundabout for Reduced Trip Time.................. 201
   Hitender Vats and Ranjeet Singh Tomar

High Dimensional Data Representation and Processing

Fundamental Survey of Map Reduce in Bigdata
with Hadoop Environment 215
   Maulik Dhamecha and Tejas Patalia

Improve Tampered Image Using Watermarking Apply
the Distance Matrix.. 223
   Nisha Chauhan and Arun Agarwal

A Novel Approach for Image Fusion with Guided Filter
Based on Feature Transform.................................... 235
   Krishnavijay Tripathi and Ashutosh Sharma

Networks and Information Security

Man in the Middle Attack on NTRU Key Exchange 251
Vijay Kumar Yadav, S. Venkatesan, and Shekhar Verma

Information Theoretic Analysis of Privacy in a Multiple Query-Response
Based Differentially Private Framework 262
Bodhi Chakraborty, Debanjan Sadhya, Shekhar Verma,
and Krishna Pratap Singh

Security in MQTT and CoAP Protocols of IOT's Application Layer 273
Anup Burange, Harshal Misalkar, and Umesh Nikam

Forensic Analysis of a Virtual Android Phone 286
Aman Sharma, Animesh Kumar Agrawal, Bhupendra Kumar,
and Pallavi Khatri

Implementation of Security Algorithm and Achieving Energy Efficiency
for Increasing Lifetime of Wireless Sensor Network 298
Harshal Misalkar, Umesh Nikam, and Anup Burange

Secure Portable Storage Drive: Secure Information Storage 308
Ashish Dhiman, Vishal Gupta, and Damanbir Singh

Performance Evaluation of Facenet on Low Resolution Face Images 317
Monika Rani Golla and Poonam Sharma

Computing Techniques for Efficient Networks Design

Grading and Defect Detection in Potatoes Using Deep Learning 329
Nikhil Pandey, Suraj Kumar, and Raksha Pandey

Rough Fuzzy Technique for Giant Cell Tumor Detection 340
Krupali Mistry, Sweta Dargad, and Avneet Saluja

Face Recognition in Surveillance Video for Criminal Investigations:
A Review 351
Napa Lakshmi and Megha P. Arakeri

Prototype to Control a Robot by Android System Remote Controller 365
Tanvir Rahman, Fazal Mahmud Hassan, Shamma Binte Zakir,
Md. Ashraful Alam, Bir Ballav Roy, and Hasib Ahmed

Plane-Wise Encryption Based Progressive Visual Cryptography
for Gray Image 373
Suresh Prasad Kannojia and Jasvant Kumar

An Advanced Throttled (ATH) Algorithm and Its Performance Analysis
with Different Variants of Cloud Computing Load Balancing Algorithm   385
    Saurabh Gupta, Nitin Dixit, and Pradeep Yadav

Role of Cache Replacement Policies in High Performance Computing
Systems: A Survey   400
    Purnendu Das

Edge Detection Techniques in Dental Radiographs
(Sobel, T1FLS & IT2FLS)   411
    Aayushi Agrawal and Rosepreet Kaur Bhogal

Review of Deep Learning Techniques for Object Detection
and Classification   422
    Mohd Ali Ansari and Dushyant Kumar Singh

Improved Symmetric Key Technique Using Randomization   432
    Anshu Chaturvedi and Hirendra Singh Sengar

An Interpretable SVM Based Model for Cancer Prediction
in Mammograms   443
    Abhishek Verma, Prashant Shukla, Abhishek, and Shekhar Verma

DPVO: Design Pattern Detection Using Vertex Ordering a Case
Study in JHotDraw with Documentation to Improve Reusability   452
    Arti Chaturvedi, Manjari Gupta, and Sanjay Kumar Gupta

Intelligent Aggregation for Ensemble LSTM   466
    Ashima Elhence, Abhishek, and Shekhar Verma

Optimal Low Rank Tensor Factorization for Deep Learning   476
    Antra Purohit, Abhishek, Rakesh, and Shekhar Verma

Performance Analysis of Naive Bayes Computing Algorithm
for Blood Donors Classification Problem   485
    Anil Kewat, P. N. Srivastava, and Arvind Kumar Sharma

Electronic Circuits for Communication Systems

Design of a Single-Ended 8T SRAM Cell for Low Power Applications   499
    S. R. Mansore, R. S. Gamad, and D. K. Mishra

Y-Shaped Cantilever Beam RF MEMS Switch for Lower
the Actuation Voltage   509
    Aamir Saud Khan and T. Shanmuganantham

Concentric Circular Ring Arc Antenna at Dual Band
for Ku Band Applications 518
T. Srinivasa Reddy, S. K. Nannu Saheb, P. Koteswara Rao,
and Ashok Kumar Balijepalli

Design of Spider Shaped Microstrip Patch Antenna for IoT Application. 528
S. K. Vyshnavi Das and T. Shanmuganantham

Design of Microstrip Polygon Shaped Patch Antenna for IoT Applications. . . 538
S. K. Vyshnavi Das and T. Shanmuganantham

A Novel Microstrip Patch Antenna with Single Elliptical CSRR
for Multiband Applications. 548
V. Priyanka, T. Shanmuganantham, and Daisy Sharma

Analysis of Circular Ring Patch Antenna for Enhancement of Wide
Bandwidth with Defected Ground Structure 557
T. Srinivasa Reddy, Ashok Kumar Balijepalli, P. Koteswara Rao,
and S. K. Nannu Saheb

The Analysis of U Slotted Rectangular Patch with Geometric Series DGS
for Triple Band Applications 568
T. Srinivasa Reddy, P. Koteswara Rao, Ashok Kumar Balijepalli,
and S. K. Nannu Saheb

A Dual Band Coplanar Concentric Ring Patch Antenna for Ku
Band Applications. 579
T. Srinivasa Reddy, Ashok Kumar Balijepalli, S. K. Nannu Saheb,
and P. Koteswara Rao

Optimal Design of CMOS Amplifier Circuits Using Whale
Optimization Algorithm 590
M. A. Mushahhid Majeed and Patri Sreehari Rao

Reliability Analysis of Comparator: NBTI, PBTI, HCI, AGEING 606
Seelam V. Sai Viswanada Prabhu Deva Kumar and Shyam Akashe

Sag Calculations in Transmission Line with Different Case Studies 620
Sandeep Gupta and Shashi Kant Vij

Dual Band Slotted Patch Microstrip Antenna Array Design for K
Band Application 632
Ritesh Kushwaha and R. K. Chauhan

A 6-Bit Low Power SAR ADC. 642
K. Lokesh Krishna, K. Anuradha, and Alfakhri M. Murshed

Author Index 653

Wired and Wireless Communication Systems

Properties and Performance of Linearly Extensible Multiprocessor Interconnection Networks

Savita Gautam and Abdus Samad[✉]

F/O Engineering and Technology, University Women's Polytechnic,
Aligarh Muslim University, Aligarh, India
savvin2003@yahoo.co.in, abdussamadamu@gmail.com

Abstract. Interconnection networks arise as the basic bone of research related to parallel computing, high-performance system design, distributed computing or computer networks. There has been a strong interest in the design of modern interconnection topologies to achieve the desired performance. This paper presents the performance study of a new class of parallel architectures known as linearly extensible multiprocessor architectures. It describes the properties and parameters to evaluate the performance of newly designed interconnection networks. The comparative study is carried out which shows that the proposed class posses the desirable topological properties of hypercube as well as tree type topologies. The performance of these architectures is also evaluated in terms of load balancing by applying standard scheduling algorithm on them. The simulation results show that the proposed architectures are performing on equal footing and their performance are compatible with standard hypercube architecture. The comparative study implies the various aspects while designing and efficient multiprocessor interconnection network.

Keywords: Linearly extensible network · Diameter · Load balancing accuracy
Scheduling algorithm · Interconnection network topology · Hypercube

1 Introduction

The study of interconnection networks is an emerging research area in the design of high performance parallel system, computer networks and also in distributed computing environment. To satisfy the requirements of modern ICT technologies and to take services of massively parallel systems, computer architects have always strived to increase the performance of their architectures by designing high quality networks. It is anticipated that large parallel applications shall be deployed on next generation High Performance Computing systems [1, 2]. Therefore, it is apparent that low cost, efficient and scalable architectures design has a deep concern while working with parallel applications.

There are several challenges while designing an interconnection networks. The most important are scalability, simple and cost effective topology. Meshes and hypercube based topologies have been utilized extensively in the design of parallel computers in the recent years [3]. As the density of processor package increases, scalability and extensibility is becoming a critical issue in the design of interconnection

© Springer Nature Singapore Pte Ltd. 2019
S. Verma et al. (Eds.): CNC 2018, CCIS 839, pp. 3–12, 2019.
https://doi.org/10.1007/978-981-13-2372-0_1

networks. The primary objective of any interconnection network is to maintain the appealing topological properties of both, hypercube and tree type architectures. Several interconnection topologies have been investigated with many attractive properties such as small diameter, constant node degree, lesser complexity and cost. Cube-based architectures are one of major class of such architectures [4–6]. However, purely cube-based architectures suffer from a common drawback of complexity when extended to higher levels. Another major disadvantage of cube-based systems is difficulty of its VLSI layout [7, 8].

Recently a new class of multiprocessor interconnection network has been reported which preserves most of the desirable properties of hypercube as well considered to be cost effective. The important characteristic of these networks is the accommodation of more number of processing elements with lesser complexity and interconnection hardware. They do not suffer from exponential expansion which has always been a major drawback of hypercube networks [9–11]. This paper describes the various topological properties of linearly extensible networks. A comparative study is carried out to demonstrate their advantages and limitations.

The performance measure is essential to monitor the efficiency of a particular multiprocessor network with appropriate routing algorithm. The efficiency of such system depends upon the effective and efficient utilization of processing elements (nodes). The process of assigning the load to various processors in the network and making the optimal use of resources is called scheduling. In the present paper the performance evaluation of the proposed class of networks is also discussed by applying standard scheduling algorithm on them.

The rest of the paper is organized as follows: Sect. 2 gives a background of linearly extensible multiprocessor interconnection networks. Section 3 identifies the various topological properties and a comparative study is carried out. In Sect. 4 standard scheduling algorithm with performance parameter is discussed and results have been presented. Finally the conclusion is drawn in Sect. 5.

2 Background and Related Work

The interconnection network allows computer nodes to interchange messages in terms of tasks with high throughput and low communication latency. High throughput is a key element of massively parallel systems and communication latency has a definite impact on the overall execution time of parallel applications. Delay, if found by the messages traveling through the network will significantly affect the execution time. This is the reason why we should not decide lightly while designing an interconnection network that interconnects computing elements and work in coordination in a high performance system. The evaluation of an interconnection network is a difficult task that requires deep knowledge about how parallel applications make use of the network. Prior to the evaluation of the considered topologies for performance parameter an analytical comparison of their properties is carried out.

The binary tree is the basic architecture which is considered as scalable architecture having constant node degree and bisection width. At n-level complexity the binary tree is having $N = 2^n - 1$ nodes with diameter $2(n - 1)$. Several variations of binary tree are reported in the literatures which possess desirable topological properties. Some examples are FAT Tree, Linearly Extensible Tree (LET), Linearly Extensible Triangle (LEΔ), Chain Cubic Tree (CCN) etc. [12–14].

Fat-tree interconnection network is a general purpose scalable network having simple topology. It has the structure of a tree network, however, its links have different bandwidth at each level. The larger bandwidth could be obtained by placing the link closer to root. Intermediate switches are used to communicate messages to nodes located at the leaf. The important feature of Fat-tree network is that any network can be embedded with this on the same chip [13]. The LET network is based on binary tree, however, in a binary tree, the number of nodes at level n is 2^n whereas in LET network the number of nodes is (n + 1). The LET network combines the properties of linear extensibility with small number of nodes per extension [9]. Figures 1 and 2 demonstrate the FAT and LET architectures respectively.

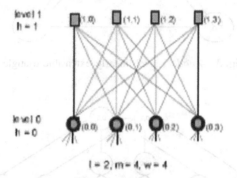

Fig. 1. *16-node* two-level FAT tree.

The triangle-based multiprocessor network known as Linearly Extensible Triangle (LEΔ) is basically having the concept of simple geometry and is designed using the concept of isosceles triangle shown in Fig. 3. The links between nodes could easily be

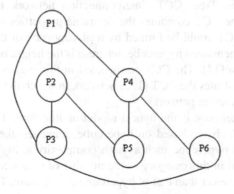

Fig. 2. *6-node* 1-level linearly extensible tree.

obtained by forming two isosceles triangles and joining their corresponding vertices. The main attraction of this architecture is having the properties of a linearly extensible multiprocessor architecture and it can easily be extended to higher levels without increasing the complexity of network [12].

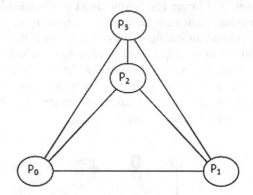

Fig. 3. *4-node* 1-level linearly extensible triangle.

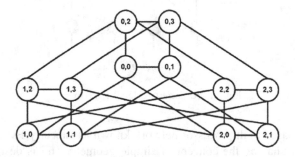

Fig. 4. *12-node* 1-level chained-cubic tree.

The Chained-Cubic Tree (CCT) interconnection network topology is recently proposed topology. The CCT combines the desirable properties of the hypercube and tree topologies. The CCT could be formed by replacing each of the $2^{h+1} - 1$ nodes of the tree (T_h) by a d-dimensional hypercube, where h is the height of the tree and d is the hypercube's dimension [14]. The CCT constructed in this way is represented as CCT (h, d). Figure 4 demonstrates the CCT (1, 2) network in which the tree's height is 1 and it consists of 2-D hypercube networks.

Another class of network is the hybrid model architecture. This type of architectures are like CCT which are based on hypercube, however, they overcome the undesirable properties of hypercube such as high complexity at higher levels. The CCT may also be considered in this category as the number of nodes could be arranged in a number of dimensions fewer than that of hypercube architecture. These networks shape

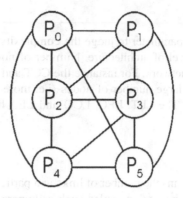

Fig. 5. *6-node* linearly extensible cube.

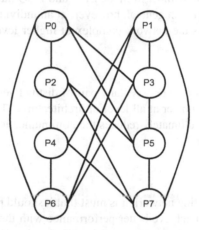

Fig. 6. *8-node* linear crossed cube.

are like cube-based architecture, but they posses the properties of linearly extensible architectures. The two famous topologies are linearly Extensible Cube (LEC) and Linear Cross Cube (LCQ) [10, 11] shown in Figs. 5 and 6 respectively.

3 Comparative Study

The performance of various interconnection networks could be evaluated analytically by considering various topological parameters and experimentally by applying appropriate scheduling scheme on them. In this section the topological properties of linearly extensible multiprocessor networks are described. The performance based on simulation is discussed in the next section.

3.1 Number of Nodes

One of the most important parameter to judge the complexity of network is number of nodes allowed at higher level of architecture. Number of nodes also plays significant role in the performance of network. For instance the CCT and FAT networks consumes lesser execution time with large number of nodes (i.e. more than 64) however, at the cost of greater complexity. The LET, LEC, LCQ and LEΔ has reasonable number of processors at higher levels.

3.2 Node Degree

The degree of a network means the number of links at a particular node. Larger number of links may also make the network complex such as hypercube. In order to make the network simple and to reduce complex routing, small node degree is desirable. In CCT, effort is made to reduce the number of links. LEC and LCQ have constant node degree of 4. LEΔ has smaller degree in general, however, at an individual node it is increasing at each level which makes the network complex at higher levels.

3.3 Diameter

It is the maximum shortest path between any pair of distinct vertices. Interestingly LEΔ has a constant value of diameter at all level of architectures. The LET, LEC and LCQ has lower diameter which ultimately reduces the communication cost. The CCT has an average value of diameter.

3.4 Extensibility

In order to extend the existing network it is must that it should preserve all the desirable topological properties and achieve better performance with the increase in the number of nodes in it. Cube-based networks have a common drawback of exponential expansion. Since FAT and CCT are more closer to cube, they result high complexity at higher level. LEC has a constant expansion with 2 nodes at a level and LET and LEΔ has linear expansion. The summary of parameters is demonstrated in Table 1.

Table 1. Topological parameters of linearly extensible networks

Name of architectures	Number of nodes	Degree	Diameter	Cost
LET	N $N = \sum\limits_{k=1} k$	4	$\sqrt{N}$	$4\sqrt{N}$
LEC	$N = 2 * n$	4	$\lfloor N \rfloor$	$4 \lfloor N \rfloor$
LCQ	$\sum k$	4	$(\lfloor\sqrt{N}\rfloor)$	$4(\lfloor\sqrt{N}\rfloor)$
LEΔ	N $N = \sum\limits_{k=3} k$	$N-1$	2	$2(N-1)$

3.5   Cost

Cost can be measured in different ways. When simulating a network cost may represent number of communication steps. However, the overall communication depends upon the topological characteristics of a network. The most effective parameters for cost are diameter and degree. Taken these parameters into consideration the cost of similar architectures is evaluated and depicted in Fig. 7. The results in the given graph demonstrate similar behavior of increments in cost when architectures are extended to higher levels.

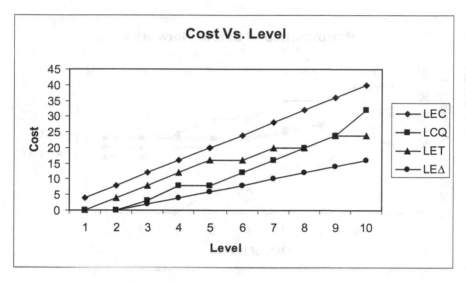

Fig. 7. Cost analysis of different interconnection networks.

4   Performance Evaluation

Task scheduling has an important role to assess the performance of parallel systems. An efficient task scheduling is the key of effective utilization of nodes to execute parallel applications. The literature is full with enormous work related the problem of scheduling. The scheduling problem has been tackled using different approaches on different architectures/topologies [15–17, 19]. In general problem of task scheduling on tree type architectures is NP-hard. As a solution to the scheduling problem on linearly extensible networks the Two Round Scheduling (TRS) scheme is taken into consideration [18, 20]. The TRS algorithm is based on minimum distance property; however, it covers the entire network for exchanging the tasks with two hopes by considering one intermediate node in communication. Although it requires traveling one extra hop by the tasks still this mechanism helps in reducing the load imbalance. The performance of various linearly extensible networks studies in this paper is evaluated in terms of load balance accuracy when TRS algorithm is applied on them. To calculate load balance accuracy the average load on the network is evaluated first. The average load is calculated as T/N, where T is the total number of tasks at a particular level and N is the number of nodes available in the network. Keeping the network size same the simulation is carried out in order to compare the accuracy of load balance.

Figure 8 shows a comparison of load balance accuracy of various networks against different set of tasks represented by levels. In general the performance of parallel scheduling when applied on tree is limited to certain range beyond which the cost increases due to more distance between under loaded and over loaded nodes. On the other hand cube-based networks consume lesser steps for load migration since the same numbers of processors are arranged in fewer dimensions.

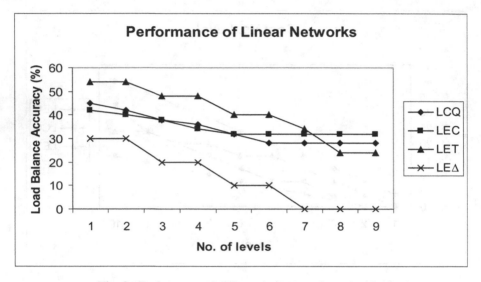

Fig. 8. Performance of different interconnection networks.

The attained results are depicted in Fig. 8, which make it evident that approximately the similar accuracy is achieved by both tree type networks as well as hybrid networks. This refers to the fact that hybrid networks inherit the properties of tree type architectures. In particular the LEΔ network has fast rate of balancing and produces better results at higher stages of task structure. This is due to increasing node degree in LEΔ at higher levels. The CCT and FAT networks are not taken into consideration as they consist of larger number of nodes at first level of architecture.

5   Conclusion

A new class of interconnection topology knows as linearly extensible network has been studied and discussed. These networks inherit the desirable properties of tree architectures as well as cube-based architectures. The major advantage of these networks is their simple structure when extended to higher levels. The effectiveness of these networks is approved in this paper by carrying out analytical study.

The performance, however, is evaluated experimentally by applying appropriate scheduling algorithm on them. The TRS scheme which is originally designed for such networks is considered and applied on different linearly extensible architectures and load balance accuracy is evaluated to judge the performance of these networks. Simulation results show that same degree of accuracy is achieved on both tree type architectures as well as on those which have more characteristics of cube-based architectures. For better results a new algorithm could be investigated particularly for linearly extensible networks.

References

1. Koibuchi, M., Fujiwara, I., Matsutani, H., Casanova, H.: Layout-conscious random topologies for HPC off-chip interconnect. In: 19th International Conference on High-Performance Computer Architecture (HPCA), pp. 484–495 (2013)
2. Le, N.T., Nguyen, V.K.: Interconnection networks with efficient custom routing, exploiting small-world effect. In: IEEE International Conference on Computing and Communication Technologies-Research, Innovation, and Vision for the Future (RIVF), pp. 41–46 (2013)
3. Prasad, N., Mukkherjee, P., Chattopadhyay, S., Chakrabarti, I.: Design and evaluation of ZMesh topology for on-chip interconnection networks. J. Parallel Distrib. Comput. **113**, 17–36 (2018)
4. Monemizadeh, M., Azad, H.S.: The necklace-hypercube: a well scalable hypercube-based interconnection network for multiprocessors. In: ACM Symposium on Applied Computing, pp. 729–733 (2005)
5. Mohanty, S.P., Ray, B.N., Patro, N.S., Tripathy, A.R.: Topological properties of a new fault tolerant interconnection network for parallel computer. In: Proceeding of ICIT International Conference on Information Technology, pp. 36–40 (2008)
6. Khan, Z.A., Siddiqui, J., Samad, A.: Topological evaluation of variants hypercube network. Asian J. Comput. Sci. Inf. Technol. **3**(9), 125–128 (2013)
7. Alam, M., Varshney, A.K.: A comparative study of interconnection network. Int. J. Comput. Appl. (0975-8887) **127**(4), 37–43 (2015)
8. Patelm, A., Kasalik, A., McCrosky, C.: Area efficient VLSI layout for binary hypercube. IEEE Trans. Comput. **49**(2), 160–169 (2006)
9. Khan, Z.A., Siddiqui, J., Samad, A.: Performance analysis of massively parallel architectures. BVICAM's Int. J. Inf. Technol. **5**(1), 563–568 (2013)
10. Samad, A., Rafiq, M.Q., Farooq, O.: LEC: an efficient scalable parallel interconnection network. In: Proceeding of International Conference on Emerging Trends in Computer Science, Communication and Information Technology, Nanded, India, pp. 453–458 (2010)
11. Khan, Z.A., Siddiqui, J., Samad, A.: Linear crossed cube (LCQ): a new interconnection network topology for massively parallel architectures. Int. J. Comput. Netw. Inf. Sci. (IJCNIS) **7**(3), 18–25 (2015). ISSN/ISBN NO: 2074-9090
12. Manullah: A Δ-based linearly extensible multiprocessor network. Int. J. Comput. Sci. Inf. Technol. **4**(5), 700–707 (2013)
13. Ding, Z., Hoare, R.R., Jones, K.A.: Level-wise scheduling algorithm for fat tree interconnection networks. In: Proceedings of the 2006 ACM/IEEE SC|06 Conference (SC 2006), pp. 9–17 (2006)
14. Mahafzah, B.A., Jaradat, B.A.: The hybrid dynamic parallel scheduling algorithm for load balancing on chained-cubic tree. J. Supercomput. **52**, 224–252 (2010)

15. Dutot, P.: Complexity of master-slave tasking on heterogeneous trees. Eur. J. Oper. Res. **164** (3), 690–695 (2005)
16. Haung, K., Wang, Z., Weng, X., Lin, W.: A scheduling algorithm on heterogeneous star and tree grid computing platform. In: International Conference on Convergence Information Technology, pp. 347–351. IEEE (2007). https://doi.org/10.1109/icct.2007.275
17. Birmpilis, S., Aslanidis, T.: A critical improvement on open shop scheduling algorithm for routing in interconnection networks. Int. J. Comput. Netw. Commun. (IJCNC) **9**(1), 1–19 (2017)
18. Samad, A., Khan, Z.A., Siddiqui, J.: Optimal dynamic scheduling algorithm for cube based multiprocessor interconnection networks. Int. J. Control Theory Appl. **9**(40), 485–490 (2016)
19. Mohammad, S.B., Ababneh, I.: I Improving system performance in non-contiguous processor allocation for mesh interconnection networks. Int. J. Simul. Model. Pract. Theory **80**, 19–31 (2018)
20. Samad, A., Rafiq, M.Q., Farooq, O.: Two round scheduling (TRS) scheme for linearly extensible multiprocessor systems. Int. J. Comput. Appl. **38**(10), 34–40 (2012)

An Analysis on Improvement of Lifetime in Wireless Sensor Network

Shubhi Malhotra$^{(\boxtimes)}$, Shushant Kumar Jain, and Vineet Shrivastava

Department of Electronics and Communication Engineering,
Institute of Technology and Management Gwalior, Gwalior, M.P., India
shubhimalhotra@rocketmail.com,
shushant.or.jain@gmail.com,
mr.veenit.shrivastav@itmgoi.in

Abstract. Wireless sensor networks (WSNs) are uncommon networks wherein nodes are furnished to study the tangible world by abundant minute, economical and intelligent sensor nodes(junction) scattered across required field of interest. All of sensor nodes are independently self-reliant in detecting, strategy and wirelessly specific surroundings situations at the base station (BS). Clustering is the form of grouping nodes into clusters and LEACH is mainly used in cluster formation in which it regularly change the cluster head to send the data towards destination. MTE algorithm is also useful in multihop environment for transmitting data from one cluster head to another and distance is calculated to send the data accurately. In the existing approach, they used hybrid technique like multi-hop and clustered routing technique to diminish energy consumption this is based totally on LEACH and minimum transmission energy (MTE) protocols for distributing facts to the BS. In our proposed work, we improve the network performance by forwarding the data to the nearby Cluster Head (CH). This get better the consumption of energy at each node if the distance of the node is larger to transmit it towards the BS.

Keywords: WSN · Base station · Node · Energy
Cluster based routing algorithm · Cluster head · LEACH and MTE

1 Introduction

WSNs are unrecognized correspondence shape that makes utilization of a massive variety of self competent sensor nodes, to shape a network. Every node in a WSN is prepared for detecting environment, processing locally the records and sending it to one or more prominent assortment of goals through a wireless link (Fig. 1).

WSNs or sensors are hardware devices that are small in length, utilize low energy, feature in excessive densities, are self reliant and trademark dismissed, and are robust to the climate. The chronic analog sign got from the sensors is changed over through method for an analog-to-digital converter into digitized sign and sent to controllers for in like manner dealing with [1]. There are various other networks which have different security requirements and challenges to overcome the problems [2].

© Springer Nature Singapore Pte Ltd. 2019
S. Verma et al. (Eds.): CNC 2018, CCIS 839, pp. 13–23, 2019.
https://doi.org/10.1007/978-981-13-2372-0_2

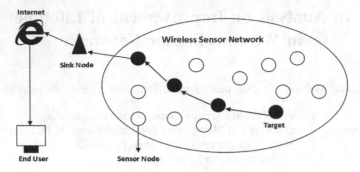

Fig. 1. WSN architecture

2 Classification of Custer Based Routing Algorithm in WSNs

Clustering algorithms play a pivotal role in reaching software specific goals. Cluster based routing algorithms are characterized into 3 wide classes as appeared in Fig. 2. The protocols mentioned underneath schemes are in brief discussed in this text [14].

(a) *Block Cluster based Routing Algorithms*
(b) *Grid Cluster based Routing Algorithms.*

3 Leach (Low Energy Adaptive Clustering Hierarchical Routing Protocol)

LEACH is oneself- devise with reconstructable cluster grounded routing protocol. This uses hierarchical procedure to pass on the data. Data is grouped and sended to the BS. Each and every one of the points is confined to the groups of invariant size and the CH

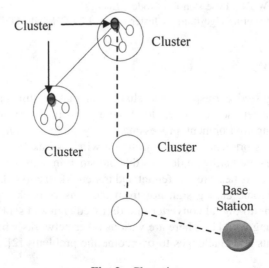

Fig. 2. Clustering

is investigated each group [3]. All junctions gather the real data and sent to its specific CH utilizing TDMA motivation [4].

CHs will other than propagate the data to the BS. Vitality will be depleted, if a proximity junction will holdout the CH and that CH junction will fail miserable which will decrease the life being of the network. T + o stay away from this kind of condition a substitute center point is picked as a CH after each cycle of working and criticalness will be stabilized. LEACH settlement has below fundamental operations:

- Framework building stage
- Data correspondence stage
- Building stage: In the building stage neighbour junctions form a group consistently and a CH is chosen randomly from that group of junctions for each cluster. In this stage a number in between 0 and 1 is picked arbitrarily, while building groups and the very same is separated and a limit, t(s). The junction is called as a CH in the ongoing cycle, if picked esteem < t(s); something other than what's expected, the node stays as a member node. The limit t(s) is enrolled by utilizing condition [5–7].

4 Literature Survey

Nayak et al. in this study, WSNs have been utilized as a part of numerous zones like health care, agriculture, defense, military, disaster hit areas and so on [8].

Sharma et al. this paper proposes another methodology i.e. manufactured artificial bee colony is an swarm based totally optimization technique for energy efficient routing algorithm and the compressive sensing is likewise used to growth the energy rate or overall performance [9].

Singh et al. this paper proposes a new procedures i.e. artificial bee colony is an swarm fundamentally based optimization procedure for energy efficient routing algorithm and the compressive sensing is likewise used to increase the energy rate or overall performance [10].

Dayanand et al. in this study, another hybrid algorithm is proposed which fuses each allotted and centralized algorithms for determination of the cluster head (CH) [11].

Baroudi et al. on this work, they propose a realistic system, suggested as wirelessly energy - charged WSN (WINCH), for battery upkeep; it includes energizing. This structure coordinates a routing process in which the CHs are chosen ideally [12].

Sharma et al. in this study, they have considered traffic heterogeneity, and analyzed its impact on well known hierarchical clustering based routing algorithm in the area. Also, they've got proposed a stepped forward CH selection mechanism beneath the traffic heterogeneous scenario [13].

5 Proposed Work

The formation of clusters in WSNs is a proficient planning toward the arrangement of nodes in the sensor n/w effectively. LEACH will permit efficient stability which is ordinarily used clustering protocol in which CHs and their appended starting nodes are irregularly changed. On the other hand, LEACH entails all starting nodes to passing their information to the related CHs at once which influence energy of starting nodes due to the tremendous fee for lengthy distance transmissions. Consequently, source nodes which are at from the CH deplete their power rapidly than different nodes. To determine the constraint of energy, they planned the method which utilized multiple hop for inter-nodes conversation the usage of minimum transmission energy (MTE) algorithm in which starting nodes ahead their data to the CHs through midway nodes inner every cluster. Every starting node inside the cluster forwards. Its message to the connecting node while in transit to the CH so as to decrease the energy of transmission. In the present approach, the MTE algorithm used to produce a cluster with straight direction among nodes right down to their CH till the data reached to destination. This route is designed the use of Dijkstra's straight route routing algorithm and nodes deliver their observed information to the CH with propagation for multiple hop. Each non-CH node needs to communicate their data to its near successor inside the route to arrive at his CH. Correspondence is the aim of the critical exhaustion of battery's energy, because of reality that SN (Sensor Nodes) consumes a lot of its vitality in transmission and gathering of data. The MTE algorithm used to generate a cluster with smallest direction between nodes all the way down to their CH till the packet arrived at to BS. This route is designed the use of Dijkstra's shortest route dispel (routing) algorithm and nodes deliver their suspected information to the CH with multi-hop propagation. Every non-CH junction have to spread its packet to its proximity inheritor in the course to attain his CH. disclosure is the principle motive of the sizeable depletion of battery's strength, due to the reality that junction node waste a large quantity of its energy in information communication and receipt.

Unlike communique, data processing uses smaller quantity energy. For this purpose, every node accepts data packet from its inheritor. Inside the manner to perform the data blend and condenses the packet earlier than sending it to the next node in line till it arrives at the CH. When a CH gets statistics from all other junction nodes, it plays numerous crucial signal handling skills on the data to clump and reduce it. In this phase, the junctions gather and transmit discovered data to the CH. The CH sent the obtained data straightly in the direction of BS. We improved forward the above drawback with our proposed method and enhance the energy utilization of nodes to augment the time being of the network (Fig. 3).

Proposed Algorithm

Step:1 Start
Step:2 Initialize the network
Step:3 Place the sensor junctions randomly in the network
Step:4 Divide the whole network into 4 grids of similar size

Step:5 Consider the grid area as cluster of nodes
Step:6 Select CH by using the two parameters such as:

    a. Energy of the node
    b. Distance from BS

Step:7 Now group members compile the data to the cluster head
Step:8 CH propagate the data to the another CH which is close to BS
Step:9 Then data reached to BS from the nearby CH
Step:10 Exit.

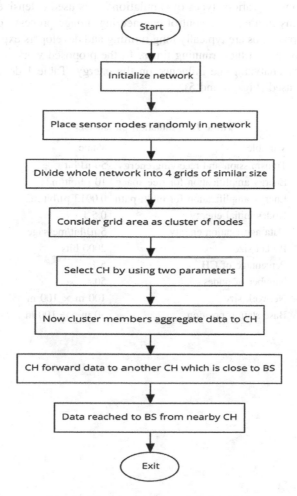

Fig. 3. Flowchart of proposed algorithm

6   Result Analysis

We used MATLAB tool for the simulation for the node deployment. MATLAB makes utilization of in wide assortment of capacities, together with signal and image handling, correspondences, control configuration, test and size, financial modeling and analysis, computational science and parallel preparing. The present PC systems have tremendous registering force as customary CPU centers and also throughput-situated quickening agents, for example, pix processing units (GPUs). MATLAB programs are declarative and naturally express data-level parallelism as the language provides several high-level operators that work directly on arrays. Traditionally, MATLAB is used as programming language to write various types of simulations. It is used extensively to simulate and design systems in areas like control engineering, image processing and communications. These programs are typically long running and developers expend significant effort in trying to shorten their running times. In the proposed work, we estimate the whole network by analyzing the influence on the energy. Table 1 demonstrates simulation variables used (Figs. 4 and 5).

Table 1. Simulation parameters

Variables	Value
Transmission and receiving energy	50 nJ/bit
Energy amplification for free space	10 pJ/bit/m2
Energy amplification for multi path	0.0013 pJ/bit/m2
Nodes initial energy	0.5 J
Data aggregation energy	5 nJ/bit/message
Packet size	2000 bits
Percentage of CH	5%
Number of nodes	50
Network size	100 m × 100 m
Base station position	50 m × −100 m

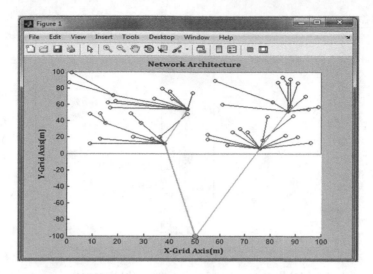

Fig. 4. Initial network architecture

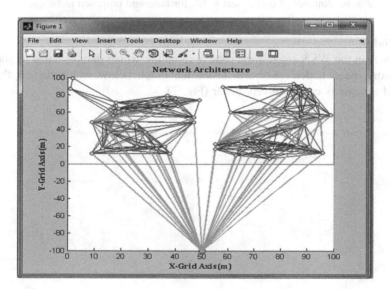

Fig. 5. Data communication among node

Packet Sent

Gross packets sent to the BS are evaluated to show that the proposed scheme is comparatively better than the base scheme (Fig. 6).

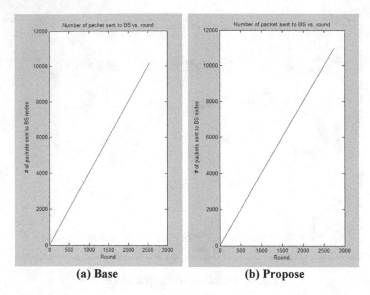

(a) Base   (b) Propose

Fig. 6. Number of packet sent to BS for base and proposed technique

Dead Nodes

Dead nodes in the WSN suggest the passive in nature which demonstrates its status in the network. dead nodes are shown inside the graph below which depicts that the proposed scheme is comparatively better (Fig. 7).

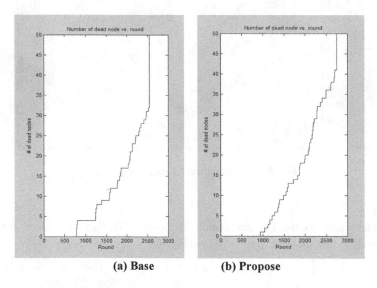

(a) Base   (b) Propose

Fig. 7. Number of dead nodes for base and proposed technique

Energy of Nodes

Energy of the nodes is taken on the x-axis and cycles on the y-axis within the graph indicating that the strength of nodes is comparatively better in our work (Fig. 8 and Table 2).

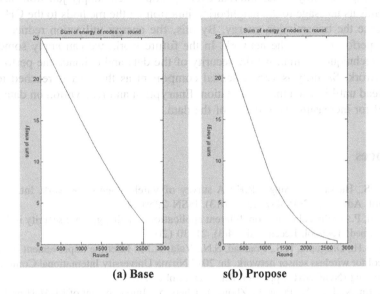

(a) Base   s(b) Propose

Fig. 8. Sum of energy of nodes for base and proposed technique

Table 2. Comparison between base and proposed approaches

Protocol	Metric			
	First node dead	Half node dead	Last node dead	Total packet sent
Base approach	786	2213	2540	10160
Proposed approach	900	2030	2751	11004

7 Conclusion and Future Scope

WS Node are normally fuelled through confined restrict batteries which substitution is delicate in renounced condition in which masses of nodes are capriciously passed on. Routing algorithm is of fundamental monstrosity in optimizing energy utilization in WSN. In this paper, we proposed a multi-hop cluster based completely routing system to decorate LEACH protocol through lessening the quality utilization and broadening the sensor arrange lifetime. The executed method is develop absolutely in light of a total of LEACH and MTE protocol. Wireless sensor nodes are ordinarily controlled

A Novel Solution for Cloud Enabled
E-Governance Using Openstack:
Opportunities and Challenges

Bhushan Jadhav[✉] and Archana B. Patankar[✉]

Thadomal Shahani Engineering College, University of Mumbai,
Mumbai 400050, India
{bhushan.jadhav,archana.patankar}@tsec.edu

Abstract. The rapid development in internet and related computing technologies have urged many businesses and governments to go for technology upgradation of their applications running on the web. The E-governance is an application of information and communication technology (ICT) that enable governments across the world to provide the information access and other service through web to their various stakeholders. Because of increasing internet literacy the demand for using E-governance is also increasing and the traditional computing solutions used are also becoming incapable to fulfill the current requirement of user access. The other technical challenges faced by E-government are difficulty in storing and processing of huge data, lack of scalability, degraded performance due to limited infrastructure, absence of disaster recovery etc. So the emerging technology like Cloud computing accept these challenges and overcome them using a modern approach for computing. The objective of this paper is to presents a theoretical and practical perspective on cloud enabled E-governance and propose the model by integrating cloud computing to an E-governance using open stack cloud platform.

Keywords: E-governance · Cloud computing · Openstack · Datacenter

1 Introduction

The evolution in web and internet technologies have attracted many businesses and governments across the world to opt them because of their popularity amongst people. At the initial stage of governance, the government used to provide their services manually that involve lot of paper works with procedures and formalities [17]. Upon popularity of internet, governments across the world have come together, understood the importance of web and started delivering their services through the internet called "E-Governance". Today, the usage of E-governance is massive because of its popularity among its various stakeholders. The increased access to services by citizens brings more expectations from government to offer them in optimized manner by applying effective IT innovations [7].

At the beginning of this paper the E-governance and cloud computing are discussed in detail. The later part explains the Openstack cloud architecture along with the proposed model for Cloud integrated E-governance based on Openstack.

© Springer Nature Singapore Pte Ltd. 2019
S. Verma et al. (Eds.): CNC 2018, CCIS 839, pp. 24–36, 2019.
https://doi.org/10.1007/978-981-13-2372-0_3

2   E-Governance

The E-Governance is developed to improve the transparency in public administration, efficiency, accountability and effectiveness in the government services by using information and communication technologies. It makes communication by exchanging information, providing services and transactional exchange within government organizations, citizens and businesses through internet technologies [1, 5, 17]. The benefits of E-governance are cost reduction in service delivery, increased transparency, less corruption, greater convenience and revenue growth [3].

2.1   Models of E-Governance

The applications in E-Governance are categorized based on its interaction with various stakeholders. The E-Governance is categorized in to following three models [1, 3, 16, 17].

(a) **Government to Citizens (G2C)**

The G2C model makes the interaction between Government and citizens by means of providing different governments services designed for citizens. Some of the popular G2C Services are identity services, revenue services, agricultural services and land services etc.

(b) **Government to Business (G2B)**

The G2B model makes the communication between the government and business organizations by means of various services like payment of taxes, auditing, security, contract management, renewing and obtaining licenses, registration of companies etc.

(c) **Government to Government (G2G)**

In this model the communication happens between the government and other governments. It provide intergovernmental services like revenue management, decision making, fund transfer, resource sharing and law enforcement within the different departments of government.

2.2   Traditional Architecture of E-Governance

The architecture of E-governance is a layered architecture where each layer performs a specific function and provide services to its upper layer. The traditional architecture of E-governance has four layers namely Infrastructure, E-business, E-government and Access layers as shown in Fig. 1 [2].

The first layer is Infrastructure layer which is responsible for providing various infrastructural components like hardware, software or network resources for running E-governance portals and applications. The second layer is E-business layer that runs an E-governance applications like CRM, ERP, EAI etc. over the core infrastructure layer and does information storage and processing. It is also responsible for storing and retrieving government data from data warehouse by means of various database management systems and integrates various IT applications together running inside and outside the organization boundary. The third layer is E-governance layer which is

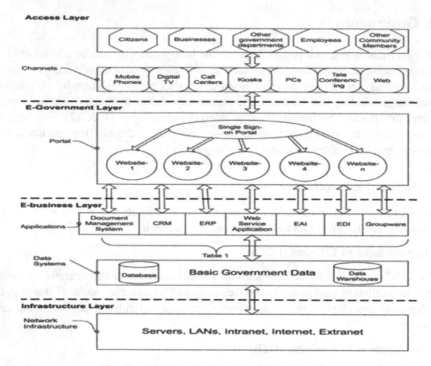

Fig. 1. Traditional architecture of E-governance

responsible for providing various government portals or websites. This layer provide access to various portals of E-governance by using Single-Sign on feature. The fourth layer of E-governance architecture is an access layer which provide different channels through which various stakeholders of E-governance can access the government services seamlessly over the internet.

2.3 Technical Challenges of Traditional E-Governance

Although the architecture of E-governance is looks like simple but has many technical challenges associated with it. Some of the Challenges associated with traditional E-governance architecture are explained as follows [3, 6, 16].

(a) **Scalability:** The traditional architecture has lack of scalability because the infrastructural components used in the architecture has fixed capacity and cannot be scaled beyond certain limit.

(b) **Disaster recovery:** The traditional architecture of E-governance does not have a feature like disaster recovery. Therefore any failure may result into loss of data and services.

(c) **Application Complexities:** In traditional setup the E-business integrates various components together which may generate inter application complexities.

(d) **Software Licensing:** The implementation of traditional architecture involve purchasing of very expensive Software and application licenses that put extra financial burden on government.

(e) **Expensive implementation:** The implementation of E-governance involve purchasing of servers, softwares, infrastructure, manpower and maintenance which makes it very expensive.

Apart from that there are many more challenges like lack of performance, limited infrastructure, difficulties in managing and monitoring the infrastructure, stoppage of services due to insufficient bandwidth, no prediction of number of access requests, cost overhead due to management and maintenance of resources etc.

3 Cloud Computing

The Cloud Computing is an emerging technology, which become popular because of its eminent features over the existing computing architectures.

According to National Institute of Standards and Technology (NIST), one of the most accepted definition of cloud computing is "It is a model for enabling ubiquitous, convenient, on-demand network access to a shared pool of configurable computing resources (e.g., networks, servers, storage, applications, and services) that can be rapidly provisioned and released with minimal management effort or service provider interaction" [15, 18].

3.1 Cloud Deployment Models

The cloud computing is classified based in to four deployment models based on its functionality and accessibility [9, 16].

The Public cloud runs over the internet and exclusively managed by Cloud service providers (CSP). The users of public cloud do not have to worry about infrastructure and their maintenance as it is fully managed by CSP. This model follows utility computing where services are available on either subscription or pay-per-use basis. The disadvantage of public cloud is lack of security. Some of the popular public cloud platforms are Amazon web services, Microsoft azure, Google cloud platform, Salesforce etc.

The private cloud is also called in house cloud where services are hosted on internal servers. Therefore the infrastructure of private cloud is completely managed and fully maintained by the organization itself. The private cloud is highly secure than public cloud as local administrators used to write their own security policies for protecting users data and access. The disadvantage of private cloud is huge capital expenditure. Some of the most popular private cloud platforms are Openstack, Eucalyptus, VMware VCloud, Apache Cloud stack, Open Nebula etc.

The Hybrid cloud is made up of two or more private and public clouds which provide benefits of both the clouds. Hybrid Cloud architecture has both on-premises and off-premise servers. The best example of hybrid cloud platform is eucalyptus with Amazon web services [16].

(6) **Horizon (Dashboard)**

Horizon is an entry point to the Openstack cloud. It has web-based self-service portal to give access to all Openstack services. It allows users and administrators to manage, automate and provision the instances and other OpenStack services through a customized web portal.

(7) **Keystone (Identity Service)**

Keystone is an Identity service for Openstack cloud which provides authentication and authorization for other OpenStack services. Each Openstack service has an endpoint whose catalog is managed by keystone. It supports multiple authentication mechanisms based on tokens and credentials for accessing the services.

(8) **Ceilometer (Telemetry or metering service)**

Ceilometer is a metering or telemetry service. It collects the data from various components of Openstack and monitors or meters them for billing, scaling and statistical purposes.

(9) **Heat (Orchestration service)**

Heat is used for orchestrating the multiple composite cloud applications by using either native template format or the AWS CloudFormation template format. It supports both REST APIs and a CloudFormation-compatible Query API.

(10) **Trove (Database as a service)**

Trove is a Database as a service in OpenStack cloud platform that has provision to scale and manage the multiple database instances as required by the user. It allows users to create and run relational or non-relational databases without taking the burden of database management.

(11) **Sahara (Hadoop service)**

The Sahara service is used for big data analytics over Openstack cloud. It provides different data processing frameworks like Apache Hadoop, Apache Spark and Apache Storm to process the big data. It can easily and rapidly provision the Hadoop clusters and supports Map-Reduce for processing a huge data sets which can read from or write on to Hadoop distributed file system.

(12) **Ironic (Bare metal provisioning service)**

Ironic is a bare metal provisioning service which is integrated in OpenStack to provision the bare metal machines instead of virtual machines.

5 Proposed Openstack Architecture for E-Governance

The Openstack is a highly customized cloud platform with wide variety of components. It allows to modify the functionality of each component as per the requirement. Therefore it is been selected for implementing the proposed architecture because of its uniqueness as compared to other cloud platforms. The proposed architecture for E-governance is categorized in to five distinct layers. It uses Bottom Up approach where each underlying layer provide services to its upper layer (Shown in Fig. 3). The functionalities accumulated in each layer directly benefits the E-governance solution with new features which make it more appealing than the other architectures. The layers of proposed architecture are explained as follows.

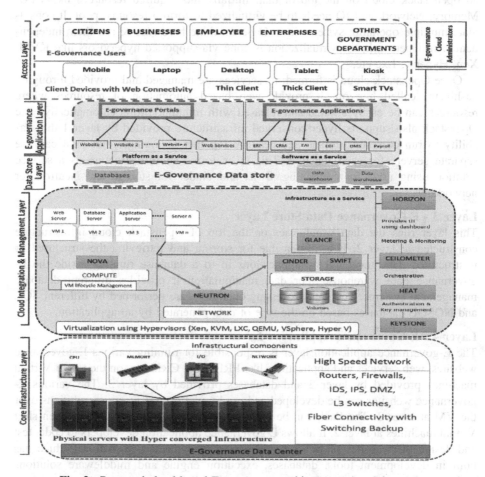

Fig. 3. Proposed cloud based E-governance architecture using Openstack

Layer 1 - Core Infrastructure Layer

The Bottom layer of proposed architecture is Core Infrastructure Layer that deals with managing and providing infrastructural components like CPU, Memory, Io, network etc. to the cloud integration and management layer for Virtualization. The foundation component of this layer and proposed architecture is a Datacenter [12]. The Datacenter is a massive infrastructure where infrastructural components like compute (CPU & Memory), Storage and networking equipments are installed at a centralized location for the purpose of acquisition, storage and processing a large amount of distributed data along with computations over the network [13]. The network devices like Firewalls, routers, L2/L3 switches, IDS, IPS, and DMZ etc. are massively used for providing high speed fiber connectivity within and outside the data center.

Layer 2 - Cloud Integration and Management Layer
This layer is responsible for acquiring the resources from infrastructure layer to build an open stack cloud on the top of that. Initially the acquired resources like CPU, Memory, Network and IO needs to be virtualized to form a resource pool. It consolidate multiple operating systems in a single machine hardware & run them independently. In Openstack, the virtualization is done via supported hypervisors like KVM, Xen, Hyper v, Lxc etc.

Once Openstack cloud is formed, its services are managed and provided through a dashboard called horizon. It provide web based automation of resources where resources can be easily allotted and released with minimal efforts automatically. The Openstack also supports hyper converged infrastructure provided by layer 1 that has ability to run compute, storage and network together in a single box or it can use separate servers for each function. This layer forms an Infrastructure as a service solution using nova for computing, Swift and cinder for storage and Neutron for networking.

Layer 3 - E-Governance Data Store Layer
This layer runs the data warehouses on the top of Openstack cloud infrastructure constructed at layer 2. It is responsible for storing and retrieving the structured or unstructured data generated by applications in to a database running inside the E-governance data warehouse. For data manipulation it provides different database management systems. The data processing operations are performed by different SQL and NOSQL databases based on the type of data generated by an application.

Layer 4 - E-Governance Application Layer
The E-governance application layer is responsible for running various E-governance websites, web services and applications like ERP, EDI, CRM etc. on the top of Virtual machines provided by layer 2 and databases provided by layer 3. The various E-governance websites can be developed and run by platform as a service solutions over the VM at layer 2. The PaaS can be built by deploying cloud foundry or open shift Virtual machines at layer 2. It allows E-governance application developers to code, test and design the websites or web services over a readymade web platform which has built in development tools, databases, execution engine and middleware solutions without any hassle to install and manage them locally.

The applications of E-governance are managed by centralized Software as a service solutions that provides on demand application delivery over the network. It allow run E-governance applications like ERP, EDI, CRM etc. remotely without installing them in a local machine. The abstraction provided by SaaS make it more secure and fast such that although it runs remotely but appears to be a local. This layer gives the access to application and services to layer 5 through a cloud based APIs.

Layer 5 - Access Layer

This layer deals with providing access to E-governance websites, applications and services to the various stakeholders like citizens, businesses, other governmental departments or government employees through a secure cloud interface. It provide access on various cloud supported devices like mobile, laptop, pc, thin client etc.

The functionality of proposed architecture is controlled and managed by Horizon that allows E-governance cloud administrators to manage the virtual machines, OS images, cloud resources, storage volumes, network services etc. The Keystone is used for securing the access to the applications and websites using multiple authentication mechanisms as well as provide end to end encryption with private/public key management. The accountability for Openstack is provided by Ceilometer which measures the cloud usage and monitor the services.

The proposed architecture is advantageous over the traditional architecture by means of various features. The comparison between traditional and proposed E-governance architecture is given in Table 1.

Table 1. Comparison between traditional and proposed E-governance architecture

Sr. no.	Features	Traditional architecture	Proposed architecture
1	Scalability	Limited	Very high
2	Security	Less secure	Most secure
3	Performance	Low to medium	Very high
4	Reliability	Medium	High
5	Upfront cost	Very high	Low to medium
6	Mobility	Absent	Present
7	Disaster recovery	Absent	Present
8	Availability	Medium	High

5.1 Opportunities Provided by Proposed Architecture

The proposed architecture overcomes the technical challenges of traditional E-governance architecture by integrating the cloud layer. The propose architecture address the scalability issue by providing a resource pool which fulfills the requirement of applications, the built-in disaster recovery in cloud computing allows to recover data and services in case of failure due to natural disaster, the software license cost is reduced due to the virtualization of software resources and application complexities are reduced with independent implementations. Apart from that, there are many opportunistic services offered by proposed architecture which were not there in its existing implementations. Those services are collectively called as XaaS [14]. The Featured services provided by proposed system are given as follows.

(1) **Infrastructure as a Service (IaaS):** For E-governance this service can provide compute, storage and network resources for running the virtual machine instances with no limit.

(2) **Platform as a service (PaaS):** This service allows E-governance developers to host or run their websites, web services, databases and middleware solutions on readymade cloud platform without installing them in local machine.

(3) **Software as a service (SaaS):** This service allows E-governance providers to use on demand application delivery. It allows to host their Softwares like ERP, EDI, CRM solutions on cloud server and deliver them remotely.

(4) **Database as a Service (DBaaS) using Trove:** It allows E-governance developers to use readymade structured and unstructured databases for their various applications.

(5) **Big data as a service (BDaaS) using Sahara:** This service provides a readymade Hadoop clusters to store, process and analyze a Big data using HDFS and map reduce.

(6) **Load balancing as a Service (LBaaS) using neutron:** Load balancing as a Service can be used in E-governance to improve the performance and speed of access by equally distributing the tasks or load across multiple servers or virtual machines running inside the data center.

(7) **Benchmarking-as-a-Service (BaaS):** In E-governance this service can be used to test the performance of various components in open stack environment. It uses Rally tool for benchmarking the various resources.

(8) **Security as a service (SECaaS):** This service allows to protect the E-governance applications and services by means of built-in security mechanisms like Identity and access management, authentication, authorization, encryption, cloud based anti-virus, anti-malware/spyware, built in intrusion detection tools, Cloud firewalls, Penetration testing tools and security event management Softwares.

(9) **Networking as a Service (NaaS):** It allows E-governance to use basic networking services like IPTables, NAT, Firewall, Routing plus advance features like Network functions Virtualization (NFV), Software defined network (SDN) and Open flow over the Openstack cloud platform.

(10) **Disaster Recovery as a service (DRaaS):** Disaster Recovery as a Service (DRaaS) for OpenStack Provides protection for applications and services (VMs, images, volumes, etc.) in case of failure due to the natural disasters like flood, earthquake etc.

(11) **Monitoring as a Service (MaaS):** This feature allows E-governance to monitor the cloud services using monitoring tools like Ganglia, Zabbix, Nagios and Ceilometer

(12) **Devops:** Devops provides integrated tools for software development and operations under one roof. Openstack supports wide variety of open source Devops tools like Docker, Ansible, puppet, chef, vagrant, Jenkins, Nagios etc. Devops integrated Openstack will be a biggest gain for E-governance that allows their application developers and operation teams to work together for faster building, deploying and monitoring of applications over the cloud.

(13) **Autos scaling:** The auto scaling feature of Openstack allows E-governance applications to be scaled automatically when load increases to avoid the stoppage of services. The autos calling is provided by heat which scales up when number of user hit increases and scales down when there is no load on servers.

(14) **Supports Software defined data center (SDDC):** The Openstack cloud supports concept of Software defined data center that allows E-governance implementers to virtualize the whole infrastructure and delivers as a service. It virtualize the resources and automate all data center operations through a software interface that involves abstraction, pooling, and automation of resources.

(15) **Supports Hyper converged Infrastructure:** The Openstack can run on commodity hardware as well as it can run on hyper converged Infrastructure. The hyper converged infrastructure allows E-governance implementers to tightly integrate compute, storage and network resources of Openstack together in a single servers to minimize the hardware compatibility issues, reduce cost and simplify the management.

5.2 Challenges of Proposed Architecture

With some opportunities, there are some challenges exists in proposed architecture which are given as follows.

(1) **Complex Architecture:** The Openstack poses a complex architecture as it has too many components in its architecture. The functionality of each component is dependent on other components that makes it more complex.

(2) **Required proficient administrator for Management:** The Openstack requires a proficient administrator to manage and administrate the cloud services.

(3) **Required expert for customization:** In Openstack, the customization of services is not an easy task. It can only be done by experts who understands the core functionality of each component.

(4) **Difficult to understand for novice:** The Openstack is very difficult to understand to the novice users who don't know have knowledge of Linux operating system and its services.

(5) **Rely on Community support:** Sometime the developers have to rely on community and forums for support if they stuck somewhere.

6   Conclusion

This research paper has covered the basics of E-governance along with the challenges in traditional E-governance architecture. The cloud computing is an emerging technology which can be used to address those challenges by its integration in existing system. There are many cloud platforms are available but openstack is chosen in proposed model because of its key advantages over other platforms. The proposed openstack based cloud enabled E-governance model has five layer that address the challenges in E-governance like scalability, application complexity, disaster recovery, software licensing, cost overhead etc. This paper has also described the opportunistic services in proposed model like LBaaS, DBaaS, DRaaS, SECaaS, NaaS, and MaaS etc. along with the challenges in proposed architecture.

References

1. Dash, S., Pani, S.K.: E-governance paradigm using cloud infrastructure: benefits and challenges. In: International Conference on Computational Modeling and Security, pp. 843–855. Elsevier (2016). https://doi.org/10.1016/j.procs.2016.05.274
2. Ebrahim, Z., Irani, Z.: E-government adoption: architecture and barriers. Bus. Process Manag. J. **11**(5), 589–611 (2005)
3. Varma, V.: Cloud Computing for E-Governance. A white paper, IIIT, Hyderabad (2010)
4. Kang, M., Kang, D.-I., Walters, J.P., et al.: A comparison of system performance on a private Openstack cloud and Amazon EC2. In: 10th International Conference on Cloud Computing, pp: 311–317. IEEE (2017)
5. Tripathi, A., Parihar, B.: E-governance challenges and cloud benefits. In: International Conference on Computer Science and Automation Engineering, pp. 351–354. IEEE (2011)
6. Smitha, K.K., Chitharanjan, K.: Security of data in cloud based e-governance system. Int. J. Comput. Appl. **0975-8887**, 1–6 (2012)
7. Mohammed, F., Ibrahim, O., Nilashi, M., Alzurqa, E.: Cloud computing adoption model for e-government implementation. Inf. Dev. **33**(3), 303–323 (2016)
8. Sha, L., Ding, J., et al.: Performance modeling of Openstack cloud computing platform using performance evaluation process algebra. In: International Conference on Cloud Computing and Big Data. IEEE (2015)
9. Wang, Q., Ye, X.D., Chen, W.D., Xu, Y.F.: A study of cloud education environment design and model construction, pp. 3082–3085. IEEE (2012)
10. Awasthi, S., Pathak, A., Kapoor, L.: Openstack-paradigm shift to open source cloud computing & its integration. In: International Conference on Contemporary Computing and Informatics. IEEE (2016)
11. Openstack Mitaka. https://docs.openstack.org/mitaka/install-guide-rdo/common/get_started_conceptual_architecture.html
12. E-governance Infrastructure. http://meity.gov.in/content/e-governance-infrastructure
13. Data Center. https://www.gartner.com/it-glossary/data-center
14. Duan, Y., Fu, G., Zhou, N., Sun, X.: Everything as a service (XaaS) on the cloud: origins, current and future trends. In: International Conference on Cloud Computing. IEEE (2015)
15. Mell, P., Grance, T.: The NIST Definition of Cloud Computing. NIST Special Publication 800-145 (2011)
16. Jadhav, B., Patankar, A.: Opportunities and challenges in integrating cloud computing and big data analytics to e-governance. Int. J. Comput. Appl. **180**(15), 6–11 (2018)
17. Smitha, K.K., Thomas, T., Chitharanjan, K.: Cloud based e-governance system: a survey. In: International Conference on Modeling, Optimization and Computing, pp. 3816–3823. Elsevier (2012). https://doi.org/10.1016/j.procs.2016.05.274
18. Almarabeh, T., Majdalawi, Y.K., Mohammad, H.: Cloud computing of e-government. Int. J. Commun. Netw. **08**(01), 1–8 (2016). https://doi.org/10.4236/cn.2016.81001. Article ID 63540

Frequency of Meeting with Node and Visit to Physical Location Based on Mobility Pattern

Binod Kumar[✉], R. R. Suman, and Binod Kumar Singh

Department of CSE, NIT Jamshedpur, Jamshedpur, India
bkumar0595@gmail.com,
{rrsuman.cse, bksingh.cse}@nitjsr.ac.in

Abstract. Communicating the information between different people distributed over various geographical locations is a very difficult task, especially in sparse and highly crowded areas. Sparse areas lack regular network and follow highly intermittent connectivity, whereas overcrowded areas contain overlapped bandwidth. Opportunistic network (Oppnet) has the solution to all the above problem. In oppnet to overcome the problem node does not have to depends on the regular network. Source node who want to send the message to the destination forward the message to the node who have similar mobility patterns like that of source and destination. We design small routing protocol based mobility pattern that helps in control the message generation, message deletion, aborting of the message and save the network with the overcrowded message. It also helps in quick transfer of the message. This is implemented over the One simulator.

Keywords: Meeting pattern · Geographical location visiting pattern
Mobility pattern · Sparse area

1 Introduction

Oppnet stands for opportunistic network. It is very effective over the irregular network When the network is weak or there is no network, Oppnet helps in perform the communication. The different geographical areas such as north/south pole, desert, village etc. have a very low probability of communication because there is no dedicated path exist between source and destination. It fails to deliver the message using traditional routing such as DSDR, AODV, DSDV etc. In mobile ad hoc network, all the nodes are not stable, they are roaming, so implementing routing over that is a very tough challenge. In this paper, a new routing protocol is presented by using the mobility pattern by following meeting frequency and physical location visiting frequency.

Using propose routing protocol establish the communication between two sparse places such village1 and village2. Conventional routing protocol named as epidemic routing uses flooding in the absence of network for communication that unnecessarily overloads the network. Propose routing protocol includes the only limited number of message for communication. Every node uses a timer to find out the position of the node. If the timer value is large then the destination is at a very large distance from the source and if the value of the timer is small, then the destination is very near to the source. Move vector is used to calculate the future location that uses the velocity and adjacent node to calculate the nearest node beside the destination. After knowing the distance and physical location of the destination, it's time to find out the availability of the path between source and destination. By analyzing the meeting frequency and physical location visiting frequency of different nodes, it is easy to determine whether a path is available or not. If the path is available, then forward the message by assigning priority to it. The higher priority assigned to the newly created message and lower priority to the older message. At the destination side message that contains high priority accepted by the destination, lower priority message deleted from the destination side to make the space free for the newly arrived message.

This routing protocol seems to be complex but it works very fine for the intermittent network. It helps in reduce burden over the network and save the network bandwidth, control the relay of the message, control the aborting of the message. The whole procedure is the part of partially context-aware routing. It is implemented over the one sim.

2 Related Work

Earlier it was very difficult to perform practical life activity task such as perform bank transaction, business transaction, read books etc. while roaming. It is now possible with the help of wireless technology [1]. When the network is either wireless or connected is intermittent, it is very difficult to exchange the data between them. In MANETs, nodes can directly communicate with each other if they enter each other's communication range [2]. For performing the communication and sending the message between different node we must consider the context information which plays very important role in the discovery of the route to forward it [3]. Epidemic routing protocol helps in forwarding the information using flooding. but it also used to minimize message latency and the total number of resources [4]. In the spray and focus routing authors worked on the single copies based utilities scheme. This helps to overcome the overpopulated network because it distributes only a small number of copies of the message to the destination [5]. Also to overcome the flooding problem, we use the Randomized protocol that helps in reduction of the number of messages in the network [6]. After deciding the number of messages sent from source to destination using the prophet routing helps to decide the interval for message forwarding [7]. Source node forwards the message to the intermediate node which has similar mobility pattern as that of it also, it enables informed message passing [8]. Max prop is used to synchronize the message transmission by assigning priority to the message transmission and message deletion [9]. After synchronization implementing the security while transmission through mobility casting. Here, casting means perform the communication between similar type of nodes. Working of the proposed algorithm and their analysis is given below through the different graphs.

3 Key Factors

We have combined the property of predefined routing protocols to make a complete algorithm that helps in establish the communication between two different geographical locations that follows intermittent routing network. Below is the description of some predefined protocols that affects working of the algorithm (Fig. 1).

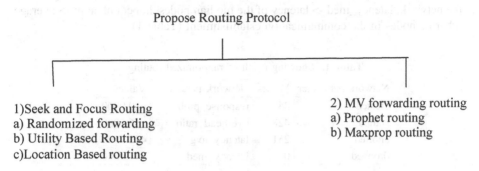

Propose Routing Protocol

1)Seek and Focus Routing
a) Randomized forwarding
b) Utility Based Routing
c)Location Based routing

2) MV forwarding routing
a) Prophet routing
b) Maxprop routing

Fig. 1. Showing the hierarchy of the protocols

3.1 Seek and Focus Routing

As we know the epidemic routing protocol used the flooding to spread the message on the network to perform the communication. This flooding increases the overhead to the transmission in the network. To reduce the network overhead. It uses the concept of the spray and Focus where it sprays only fixed number of copies in the network. Further, it uses the equation to reduce the number of copies in the network. It helps in overcoming the slow-sow, start problem. It is the impure algorithm. It combines the features of Randomized routing and Utility based routing [10].

3.1.1 Randomized Routing

As we know flooding creates the burden over the network. The network is over populated due to redundant copies of the message. A very effective algorithm that proposes the concept to route one copy of the message rather than the huge number of redundant copies. It is derived from the direct routing protocol. Here a node P performs the message forwarding to the node Q only if Q has the higher probability of transferring the message than P. Here last contact information is used for finding out the probability and this is calculated using a specific timer [10].

Here is the result of the simulation of the Randomized routing:
Suppose,

P=. 06
Q=. 07
R. .08

P

Q

$P > Q$

Simulation Result in the form of Table

Here Sim time is showing the total time taken in the simulation. Created -> total number of nodes created, Started -> It is showing the simulation starting time. Aborted -> time when it is aborted, dropped -> showing total number message dropped, removed -> number of nodes removed from the buffer, hopecount_med -> total number of intermediate nodes, response_prob -> response probability of different nodes, overhead_ratio -> represent the overhead in the network, latency_avg -> average delay in the network, latency_med -> latency of the median nodes, hopcount_avg: -> average number of nodes in the communication establishment (Table 1).

Table 1. Showing result of randomized routing

Network parameter	Values	Network parameter	Values
created	34	response_prob	0.0000
started	428	overhead_ratio	86.5000
aborted	251	latency_avg	443.9500
dropped	0	latency_med	741.9000

3.1.2 Utility Based Routing

To find out the position of the node we take last encountered time of every other node and as we know this timer is represented by maintaining the timer at every other node. But we do not consider its absolute value. Visiting at the physical time also depends on the speed of the node and mobility pattern of the node. Here we show that if the value of the timer is small then it is very near and if the value of the time is large then it has very large distance from the source. A function is used by each node called Utility for nodes in the network [10]. For example,

$U_x(Y)$ = probability of transferring messages from node X to Here P node transfer the packet to the node Q.

$$UP(R) > UQ(R).$$

- Problem:
  With the utility Based routing: As we know there may be large distance from source to destination, node between these two may or may not have detail about destination node. In that case intermediate nodes take lots of time in finding out the node with larger utility value.
  It is affected by the slow start and initial phase problems.
  Solution:
  lies in the combining of Randomized with Utility Based routing (Table 2):
  Here is the analysis is represented as

Table 2. Representing the modified solution of the utility based routing

Simulation	Result	Simulation	Result
created	851	delivery_prob	0.2174
started	3416	response_prob	0.0000
relayed	1424	overhead_ratio	97.6324
aborted	1592	latency_avg	4241.3162
dropped	1781	latency_med	2981.4000

3.1.3 Location Based Forwarding

In the location based routing source will forward the message to the node which have location very close to the Destination. Here moves vector is used to calculate the future location that uses the velocity and adjacent node to calculate the nearest node beside the destination.

In the location-based forwarding approaches, nodes Interrogation based relay routing here nodes required to hold their data for the same period until it gets required opportunity to transfer the data. Here figure showing the exact representation of the simulation [2] (Fig. 2).

Here showing the Physical location between 1, 5.

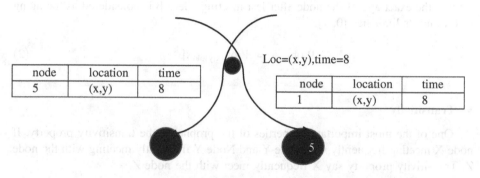

Fig. 2. Showing the how to remember the location of different places

3.2 MV Forwarding

It is the improvement over the epidemic routing protocol. It does not blindly flood the network. Instead of flooding it uses the analyzed or observed data for calculating the probability of meeting and a visit to the physical location of different nodes in the network. Small Table example is showing the detail about location visited by the particular node in a day. After analyzing the data, we can take the right decision whether or not our message will be forwarded in the right direction and in quick time [10].

3.2.1   PROPHET (Probabilistic Routing Protocol Using History of Encounters and Transitivity)

Epidemic routing is the worst for the network. Researchers used the extended form of the epidemic routing (delivery probability + epidemic routing). To deliver the message to the destination, it very much depends on the predicting delivery probability.

> If (x visited 10 times in a day z campus rather than other places)
> Then,
> (It is most likely that x will visit the campus again in a day)

After analyzing the node and its meeting behavior it is used as context information to overcome the narrow performance of the routing. So all the node in the network maintains the metric for every destination called delivery probability metric PP $(a, b) \varepsilon \{0, 1\}$. Three equations help in the computing delivery probability that is given below [10].

$$Prob_{(x,y)} = Prob_{(x,y)old} + (1 - Prob_{(x,y)old}) \times Prob_{int} \qquad (1)$$

Where Probint $\varepsilon \{0, 1\}$.

Now Question arises about the Good forwarder and Bad forwarder. Good forwarder are the nodes that meet with each other regularly in predetermined time. Bad forwarder fails to maintain regular meeting. Aging Factor (Y): Ageing factor helps in finding out what is the exact age of the node after last meeting. Here β is considered as the aging factor and its limit lies [0, 1].

$$Prob_{(x,y)} = Prob_{(x,y)old} \times \beta^k \qquad (2)$$

- **Transitivity:**

One of the most important properties of the prophet is the transitivity property. If node X meeting frequently with node Y and Node Y frequently meeting with the node Z. Transitivity property say X frequently meet with the node Z.

Given equation for transitivity:

$$Prob(x,z) = Prob(x,z) + (1 - Prob(x,Z)old) \times Prob(x,y) \times Prob(y,z) \times a \qquad (3)$$

A table showing the Simulation result (Table 3):

Table 3. Showing the result of the simulation of prophet

Simulation	Result	Simulation	Result
created	1455	delivered	740
started	1614	delivery_prob	0.5086
relayed	1556	response_prob	0.0000
aborted	5821	overhead_ratio	2102.5392
dropped	15497	latency_avg	835.2546

3.2.2   Prioritized Epidemic Routing

The maxprop protocol work on the scheduling of the message. It assigns priority to the message at the time of transmission and deletion of the message. Newly created message assigned high priority, older message stored in buffer at the destination assigned lower priority. These priorities are based on the likelihood of paths to peers, based on historical data and also on several complementary mechanisms, including acknowledgments, a head start for new packets, and lists of previous intermediaries.

When considering load, delivery ratio, network connectivity, then PREP routing, perform well and give very good results. PREP is divided into two categories, one for estimating cost and second assign the priority to the transmission. All the category is shown below.

- **Packet drop and transmit priority:**
  It helps in overcoming the network congestion and rescheduling of the packet. It works on following two ways to assign priority to the packet that helps to maintain the network. Both parameters are given below.
- Pt-transmit priority:
  Will assign the priority of the packet when the packet is transmitted to the node buffer.
- Pd-drop priority:
  Will assign the drop priority of the packet, the lower priority packet will drop first when the new high priority packet comes to the node buffer.

Max always known for the complete utilization of the resources. And work very fine on the highly intermittent network where it is very rare chances to utilize the network resources in limited time constraint (Table 4).

Table 4. Showing the result of the simulation of the prioritized epidemic routing

Simulation	Result	Simulation	Result
sim_time	8024.9000	delivered	51
created	270	delivery_prob	0.1889
started	9703	response_prob	0.0000
relayed	4951	overhead_ratio	96.0784
aborted	4749	latency_avg	2274.4882
dropped	4099	latency_med	1901.8000

4 Experiment and Analysis

Performing communication in the oppnet is the very difficult task. With the help of propose routing protocol, we can establish the communication between two different geographical area named as A and B.

Area A contains two localities named as locality1 and locality2, Area B also contains two locality B3 and B4. For establishing communication, we require calculating two forwarders named as the local forwarder and global forwarder by using meeting behavior and physical location visiting behavior.

- Local forwarder is created based on finding the probability of the node based on the meeting pattern.
- Global forwarder is created based on finding the probability of the node using the visiting pattern of the different places.

5 Working Procedure

Step by step working procedure of the algorithm is given below (Fig. 3):

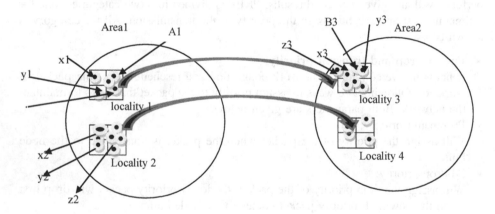

Fig. 3. Showing the communication between two sparse area

First, we need to find the local forwarder based on the meeting probability of a node to the other nodes. Source node who want to forward the message find the local forwarder and hand over the message to it. The table below showing how to find the local forwarder of the messages. Here as given in the figure, Node A1 meet with four different node name as "w1, x1, y1, z1" with the different probability. W1 meet number of time with node A1. Hence, w1 is declared as a good local forwarder of the message (Table 5).

- Table showing the way of finding the local forwarder of the node based the frequency of meeting with different node in locality1:

Table 5. Showing the frequency of meeting with the different nodes

Name	Node A1	Freq
w1	10	1/10
x1	5	1/5
y1	8	1/8
z1	8	1/6
$\sum =$	(1/10 + 1/5 + 1/8 + 1/6)	0.5916

- After finding the local forwarder, now it's time to find the global forwarder of the of Area1. We can find out global forwarder with the help of visiting frequency of node to the different geographical location. Table below shows four best global forwarders. Here node named as "w1" contain high frequency to visit the locality 3. So, it is best global forwarder of information in the form of the message (Table 6).

Table 6. Showing the frequency of visiting the different locations

Name	Place2 (locality 2)	Freq	Place3 (locality3)	Freq
w2	5	1/5	9	1/9
x2	4	1/4	0	0
y2	3	1/3	0	0
z2	8	1/8	7	1/7
$\sum =$	(1/5 + 1/4 + 1/3 + 1/8)	0.905	(1/7 + 1/9)	0.2538

Here,

If $w2_{prob} > A1_{prob}$ then {message forwarded successfully}

- After finding out local and global forwarder its time to forward the message. To forward the message it requires the path between two different geographical locations. With the help of a modified Dijkstra algorithm we can find the shortest path [6].
- After finding the path Node "w1" now reached in the locality B3. Here if it finds Destination node B3 then it forwards the message directly otherwise it finds next suitable node which is very close to the Destination, after analyzing the table given below. Here table shows that there are different nodes available in the locality3. But "w1" meet "" more number of times with w3. Also, "w3" meet more number of times with Node B3. Hence w3 is the good forwarder (Table 7).

Table 7. Showing the frequency of meeting between different locations

Name	w1	Freq	Node B3	Freq
w3	8	1/8	7	1/7
x3	5	1/5	3	1/3
y3	6	1/6	3	1/3
z3	2	1/2	5	1/5
$\sum =$	(1/8 + 1/5 + 1/6 + 1/2)		(1/7 + 1/3 + 13 + 1/5)	

Finally, "w1" forward the message to the w3. w3 transfers the message to Node B3 successfully. And acknowledgment is sent from destination B3 to source A1 using the same procedure.

5.1 Some Important Key Points

Node transfer message up to one node maximum otherwise it directly transfers the message to the destination. Exchange of the message contain following Steps. Every node maintains the buffer for storing the message, and maintain the following property as:

(1) Unlimited buffered space for their own messages.
(2) But limited buffered space for other nodes.

When the message comes, it stores the message in the buffer after checking the priority. If the priority of the message is greater than the priority of the stored message, then the message is accepted by the buffer by discarding the previous low priority message. Otherwise the message is discarded by the buffer. Each node maintains two levels, one is called high water mark and second is called low water mark. Above prioritized message is accepted between these markers.

Final simulation of the result is shown in the table (Table 8).

Table 8. Proposes routing protocols result

Simulation	Result	Smulation	Result
started	9046	response_prob	0.0000
relayed	4148	overhead_ratio	53.5789
dropped	3347	latency_med	2604.7000
removed	0	hopcount_avg	2.9079
delivered	76	buffertime_med	886.9000

5.2 Experiment and Result

Below is the detail description of the result which is shown through different graphs and figures.

5.2.1 Message Relay v/s Drop v/s Abort

Here, the result shows that relaying of the frame is very much controlled which means the message is generated in a very controlled manner. Also, message dropped is reduced, unnecessary message, abort is controlled. Below graph shows the expected output of the proposed, protocol. Here, Y axis shows the transmission of the message per second. X axis shows the proposed protocol and different network protocols. Blue bar shows the relay of the messages, green bar shows the message dropped per second, and Yellow bar shows the Message aborted per second (Fig. 4).

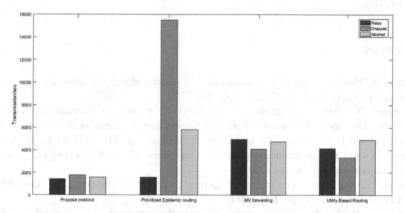

Fig. 4. Showing the relaying, dropping and aborting of the message (Color figure online)

5.2.2 Message Relay v/s Buffered

Before, delivering the message we need to buffer the message, here graph showing the result of buffered v/s total number of message delivered to the destination. Black line shows initially there is lots of message buffered and red line shows message delivery started from scratch (Fig. 5).

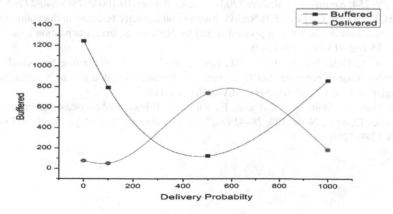

Fig. 5. Showing the buffered v/s delivered (Color figure online)

6 Conclusion

Establishing communication in the oppnet is a difficult task because of its intermittent connectivity. Proposed solution helps in not only establishing the communication, but also to overcome the problem of lack of resource, improper channel use and lazy transmission. The propose algorithm helps in reduce number of message relay. As an effect of this less number of packets dropped and aborted and delivery probability is also improved. This also helps in obtain synchronization between message relay and message delivery. Thus, overall solution gives the improved result in the partial context aware routing.

References

1. Kumar, S., Paul, S., Amar, A.K.: Communication in vehicular cloud network using ns-3. Int. J. Control Theory Appl. **10** (2017). ISSN 974-5572
2. Lindgren, A., Doria, A., Schelén, O.: Probabilistic routing in intermittently connected networks. Division of Computer Science and Networking, Department of Computer Science and Electrical Engineering, Lule University of Technology, SE - 971 87 Luleå, Sweden. Electronics and Telecommunications Research Institute (ETRI), 161 Gajeong-don, Yuseong-GU, Daejeon 305-350, Korea (2003)
3. Verma, A., Srivastava, D.: Integrated routing protocol for opportunistic networks. Int. J. Adv. Comput. Sci. Appl. **2**(3) (2011)
4. Vahdat, A., Becker, D.: Epidemic routing for partially-connected ad hoc networks. Technical report CS-200006, Duke University, April 2000
5. Spyropoulos, T., Psounis, K., Raghavendra, C.S.: Spray and focus: efficient mobility-assisted routing for heterogeneous and correlated mobility. In: Proceedings of the Fifth Annual IEEE International Conference on Pervasive Computing and Communications Workshops (PerComW 2007) 0-7695-2788-4/07 (2007)
6. Woungang, I., Dhurandher, S.K., Anpalagan, A., Vasilakos, A.V.: Routimg in opportunity networks. https://doi.org/10.1007/978-1-4614-3514-3. ISBN 978-1-4614-3513-6
7. Lindgren, A., Doria, A., Schelén, O.: Probabilistic routing in intermittently connected networks. In: Dini, P., Lorenz, P., de Souza, J.N. (eds.) SAPIR 2004. LNCS, vol. 3126, pp. 239–254. Springer, Heidelberg (2004). https://doi.org/10.1007/978-3-540-27767-5_24
8. Burns, B., Brock, O., Levine, B.N.: MV routing and capacity building in disruption tolerant networks. This research was supported in part by National Science Foundation award. ANI-0133055 and EIA-0080199 (2005)
9. Burgess, J., Gallagher, B., Jensen, D., Levine, B.N.: MaxProp: routing for vehicle-based disruption-tolerant networks. DARPA contract C-36-B82-S1 and in part by National Science Foundation awards CNS-0519881, EIA-0080199 (2006)
10. Costantino, G., Maiti, R., Martinelli, F., Santi, P.: Private mobility-cast for opportunistic networks. Comput. Netw. **120**, 28–42 (2017). https://doi.org/10.1016/j.comnet.2017.04.010. ISSN 1389-1286

A New Lightweight Approach
for Multiuser Searchable Encryption
in the Cloud

Nitish Andola$^{(\boxtimes)}$, Sourabh Prakash, Raghav, S. Venkatesan,
and Shekhar Verma

Department of Information Technology,
Indian Institute of Information Technology, Allahabad,
Allahabad 211012, U.P., India
{pcl2014004,sverma}@iiita.ac.in, sprakash13@gmail.com

Abstract. Recently the concept of storing data at the cloud server is becoming more and more popular, where the users can store their large amount of data at the cloud server very conveniently. Also concept of searchable encryption is gaining a lot of attention for the data transmission, which allows cloud to perform searching operations on encrypted data, whereas on the other hand the workload in the cloud server increases significantly. To overcome this issue, we propose a new scheme which provides searchable encryption, while reducing the burden in cloud remarkably. The third party manager is introduced here, which takes most of the workload on his side, while we make sure to keep him away from any sensitive data. Which results in better workload management while maintaining desired privacy. Proper security proofs and analysis is given for the proposed scheme. The results indicates the practicality of the proposed scheme, with reduced load in cloud server.

Keywords: Cloud storage service · Searchable encryption
Bilinear pairing · Data security

1 Introduction

In present days, Cloud Service Provider (CSP) is becoming increasingly popular for putting away information in the IT Enterprise. They give a negligible cost plan for storing, accessing and sharing information. For example, a few renowned cloud service providers CSP offer some free distributed storage space to clients including iCloud, Google Drive, Drop-box, MEGA, Microsoft Skydrive and Amazon S3. Be that as it may, clients can't acknowledge whether their information put away in these CSP's are sufficiently protected. For CSP to be secure we ought to look after Confidentiality, Integrity and Availability (CIA), which are the most essential security issues for cloud service. To accomplish secrecy data owners must encode the records before outsourcing them to the cloud, which leads to accomplish a viable hunt on the encrypted data.

© Springer Nature Singapore Pte Ltd. 2019
S. Verma et al. (Eds.): CNC 2018, CCIS 839, pp. 49–63, 2019.
https://doi.org/10.1007/978-981-13-2372-0_5

We proposed a new approach, in which another entity named as manager (*Mng*) is introduced, who will be incharge of putting away each trapdoor with a random number which is sent by the data owners. Nonetheless, the manager can't understand the content of the trapdoor. To avoid the Keyword Guessing Attack by the manager we have used the algorithm inspired from [1].

1.1 Related Work

Searchable Encryption is a technique which enables the legitimate users to search over the encoded information and locate the fitting reports containing the desired keywords. The first constructive scheme of keyword searching on encrypted database, in which the user execute searches on encrypted text files without revealing any facts about the plaintext. The non trustworthy server cannot get the hang of anything about the file contents [2]. A scheme [3] permits searches over encrypted data by building a secure index based on bloom filter technique. Goh's scheme decreases storage cost in searchable encrypted data scheme. All the previously mentioned schemes rely upon secret keys however, it enables a solitary client to access or share keys among a grup of approved clients. The notions of PKES was first presented [4] in which a public private key pair was introduced. It enables clients to utilize Public Key Encryption (PKE) scheme to encrypt its data. Only validated clients containing the private key are permitted to look and decode the data. However, secure channel is required in this scheme.

The current scheme has certain resistance towards the updation of exiting dataset. In our proposed scheme Data Owners can do update operations, ie. modification, insertion, deletion. Further, algorithms for encryption and decryption in proposed work discovered motivation from [5] scheme.

1.2 Our Contribution

Our contribution is as follows:

1. We managed to reduce the workload on the cloud.
2. In our scheme, we reduce the *communication overhead* between the Users and the cloud server by addition of a Manager *Mng*.
3. Unlike the existing schemes, where either the data owner is involved in every file retrieval query, else otherwise they lack security, in our scheme, Data owner is not involved for every file retrieval query, i.e. users will directly contact to the manager, and further manager will request cloud to send the document for the specific query to the respective user.
4. We have removed the weakness in Rhee's dPEKS scheme and used a improved dPEKS scheme for the secure transmission of data.
5. We maintain the same existing level of security while achieving the burden reduction goal.

2 Preliminaries

2.1 Definition of Traditional Public Key Encrytion

In Traditional Public Key Encryption (TE), there are two participants, a receiver and a sender. The defination is well stated in following phases:

1. TE.Setup(k): This algorithm takes a security parameter k as input, and outputs the system parameter SP.
2. TE.KeyGen(SP): This algorithm takes the system parameter SP as input, and outputs the public/private key pair R_{pub}, R_{priv}.
3. TE.Encrypt(SP, R_{pub}, M): This algorithm takes the system parameter SP, the public key R_{pub} and a message M as inputs, and forms the ciphertext C.
4. TE.Decrypt(SP, R_{priv}, C): This algorithm takes the system parameter SP, the private key R_{priv} and a ciphertext C as inputs, and retrieves the message M.

Ciphertext Indistinguishability Against Adaptive Chosen CiphertextAttack ($IND-CCA2$). Let C be a challenger and $\mathcal{A}$ be a probabilistic polynomial time adversary. The security game for IND-CCA2 works between $\mathcal{A}$ and C as follows.

1. Setup: TE.Setup and TE.KeyGen are run by C, and then the system parameters SP and a public key R_{pub} are returned to $\mathcal{A}$. Note that R_{priv} is kept secretly.
2. Phase 1: $\mathcal{A}$ queries Decrypt oracle to C. A message M which is retrieved form a ciphertext C for $\mathcal{A}$'s queries will be returned.
3. Challenge: $\mathcal{A}$ selects two messages $M_0{}^*, M_1{}^*$ for challenge. C picks $b \in \{0,1\}$ randomly and outputs a challenge ciphertext $C^* = $ TE.Encrypt($SP, M_b{}^*, R_{pub}$ to $\mathcal{A}$.
4. Phase 2: $\mathcal{A}$ can query Decrypt oracle as long as $C \neq C*$.
5. Guess: $\mathcal{A}$ outputs $b' \in \{0,1\}$. If $b = b'$ then $\mathcal{A}$ wins the game.

   The advantage of $\mathcal{A}$ to break a TE scheme is denoted by $Adv_{\mathcal{A}}, TE^{IND-CCA2}(k) = |Pr[b = b'] - \frac{1}{2}|$.

   Definition 1 If $Adv_{\mathcal{A}}, TE^{IND-CCA2}(k)$ is negligible for any probabilistic polynomial time adversary $\mathcal{A}$, we say that the TE scheme meets $IND-CCA2$.

2.2 Definition of Identity Based Encryption (IBE)

In IBE, there is a Trust Agency (TA) which takes its master private key and a user's identity ID to generate the user's private key. The formal definition of IBE scheme is as follows.

1. IBE.setup(k): This algorithm is run by the TA. It takes a security parameter k as input, the master public/private key pair P_{pub}, P_{priv} and an identity space ID are included in system parameter SP.

2. IBE.Extract(SP, ID, P_{priv}): This algorithm takes the system parameter SP, an identity ID and the master private key P_{priv} as inputs, generates the user's private key U_{priv}.
3. IBE.Encrypt(SP, M, ID): This algorithm takes the system parameter SP, a message M and the receiver's ID as input, ouputs C as the ciphertext.
4. IBE.Decrypt(SP, U_{priv}, C): This algorithm takes the user's private key and a ciphertext C as inputs, retrieves the message M.

3   Improvement of Rhee's dPEKS Scheme

Here we first discuss the dPEKS scheme and then the security problem in this scheme.

3.1   Definition

In this section, we will revise the Rhee's dPEKS scheme [5] and discuss the security problem in it.

1. GlobalSetup(k): The input to this algorithm is a security parameter k, and the output is System Parameter SP.
2. dKeyGen(SP): The input to this algorithm is SP. It runs TE.KeyGen to generate R_{pub}, R_{priv} and the ouptputs $S_{pub} = R_{pub}$ and $S_{priv} = R_{priv}$.
3. rKeyGen(SP): The input to this algorithm is SP, the algorithm runs IBE.Setup to generate A_{pub}, A_{priv} and the ouptputs $P^y = P_{pub}$ and $y = P_{priv}$.
4. dPEKS($SP, W_i, A_{pub}, S_{pub}$): Bob with the help of Alice's public key and keyword $W \in \mathcal{W}$ generates a searchable ciphertext C. Now Bob sends n such searchable ciphertexts along with a encyrpted message $\bar{M}$, where $\bar{M}$ is the traditional encryption of real message $M \in \mathcal{M}$ with the help of Alice's public key.
5. Trapdoor($SP, W', A_{priv}, S_{pub}$): Alice with the help of her private key and a keyword $W' \in \mathcal{W}$ generates a *trapdoor* T and sends it to the server.
6. Test(SP, C, T, S_{priv}): The input to the algorithm is server's private key S_{priv} and the output is 1 if $W' = W$ else 0.

3.2   Security Problem

Here, we discuss the security problem in dPEKS scheme.

Given a trapdoor a malicious server can find the keyword used for generating the trapdoor, ie the trapdoor is distinguishable when the server is malicious.

The trapdoor T outputted from Trapdoor algorithm is $T = $ TE.Encrypt (SP, T', S_{pub}), where $T' = yH_1(W')$.

After receiving T from the receiver, the malicious server first decrypts T with its private key S_{priv} to recover T', and then performs the following steps to guess the keyword W':

1. Choses a keyword W, then computes $H_1(W)$.
2. Check whether or not e(P, T') = e($A_{pub}, H_1(W)$). If $W = W'$, then the output is 1, else 0.

3.3   Improvement in dPEKS Scheme

We managed to find a solution for the above mentioned scheme, as we can see that the malicious server performs keyword guessing attack to recover the receiver's keyword, as it is assumed that the entropy of keywords is low. So in our improved scheme we introduced a nonce based approach in which a random number is padded with the keyword before it is encrypted, thereby increasing its entropy, now the server cannot perform the keyword guessing attack, hence the scheme is not secure from the malicious server.

4   Proposed Scheme

In this proposed scheme, there are four entities involved:

Data Owners (DO), Cloud Service Provider (CSP), Users (U_{id}) and Manager (Mng).

The main idea for the scheme is as follows:

Here we supposed that in an organisation there are data owners who store their data in cloud. Users/clients of the organisation who act as Users and wants to get access to data of DO.

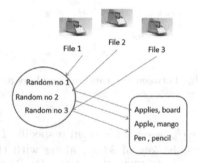

Fig. 1. Mapping between the files, keywords and random numbers

Data Owner (DO): The primary job of the DO is to generate a nonce. He then extract keywords from a file F_i, then encrypt the file using symmetric encryption technique with the nonce which he has generated and linked the encrypted file with a random number $\Re$. Now DO sends the nonce to a set of users via a secure channel so that they can decrypt the encrypted file after receiving it. For authentication purpose the encrypted keywords corresponding to each file are attached to a list of authenticated users i.e. these users have permission to access the file corresponding to these encrypted keywords.

Another job of DO is to encrypted keywords corresponding to every file. He encrypt the keywords using the same nonce which he earlier used for encrypting the files, DO further generates different random numbers, where each random number is associated with a specific file. Now it maintains mapping list in which the encrypted file's F identifier, random number for the specific file and encrypted keywords for that particular file are linked with each other as mentioned in Fig. 1. After that DO sends the encrypted file F_i and a linked random number $\Re$ as mentioned in Fig. 2 to (CSP). All encrypted keyword $(w_1, w_2 \ldots \ldots w_n)$ linked with random number as mentioned in Fig. 3 are then sent to the Mng.

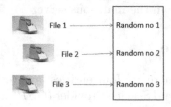

Fig. 2. Mapping between the files and random numbers

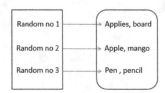

Fig. 3. Mapping between the random numbers and keywords

Users: Whenever a User U_{id} want a file from a specific DO, the User will take the public key of DO, public key of Mng, along with the nonce provided by DO to compute a ciphertext C. This C and the User's ID U_{id} will be send to Mng for further computation. Also, after receiving encryptrd file F_i, user can now decrypt the file by using its Symmetric key, which was given by the DO.

Manager(Mng): After getting $(T_{W\prime})$ along with the user id (U_{id}) from the user, Mng can test whether the request matches some ciphertext. If required ciphertext is found, then Mng checks whether the concerned user id is present in the list of approved clients corresponding to the matched keyword. In the event that the user is legitimate then Mng sends the user's id and the random number relating to the matched keyword to the CSP.

Cloud Service Provider (CSP): After getting the random number and the user id from Mng, CSP will look through the encrypted record related with the random number, if found, then the CSP will again encrypt the encrypted record utilizing Traditional Encryption sent to the User id U_{id}.

4.1   Definition

1. **Setup(k)**: This algorithm takes a security parameter k as an input and the outputs a public parameter SP. We take two cyclic groups G_1 and G_2 of prime order q, and the bilinear pairing function e: $G_1 * G_1 \rightarrow G_2$. The hash functions used are defined as H:$\{0,1\}^* \rightarrow G_1$ which maps to group G_1. The random generator $P \in G_1$ is chosen.

2. **KeyGen1(SP)**: This algorithm will be run by manager Mng and the input to this algorithm is SP and the output is a public/private key pair (sk_m, pk_m).

3. **KeyGen2(SP)**: This algorithm will be run by Data owners $DO(1 \leq i \leq M)$ to generate its own public/private key pair (sk_{do}, pk_{do}).

4. **KeyGen3(SP)**: This algorithm will be run by the Users ($1 \leq i \leq N$) to generate the public-private key pair ($sk_{U_{id}}, pk_{U_{id}}$).

5. **fGen**: (ξ) $\rightarrow nonce$ This algorithm takes ξ and outputs a random nonce.

6. **Trapdoor**: ($sk_{do}, pk_m, W_i, nonce$) $\rightarrow T_{W_i}$
   Data Owner (DO) run this algorithm and sets the trapdoor for every keyword by computing T_{W_i}. The input to this algorithm is a random number $nonce$ private key of the data owner sk_{do}, public key of the manager pk_m and the list of keywords W_i, where ($0 < i <= k$), and its assumed that there are fixed k number of keywords in every file . And the output to this algorithm is Trapdoor $= T_{W_i}$. For each and every keyword there will be a trapdoor, which will be sent to the Mng for Users search later. Where W is a keyword.

7. **dPEKS**: ($pk_m, pk_{do}, W', nonce$) $\rightarrow \{U, V\}$
   This algorithm is run by User, who wish to access the document of certain DO. The U_{id} adopts $nonce$, Mng public key pk_m and DO public key pk_{do}, in order to compute the $dPEKS$ cipher-text. The input to this algorithm is $nonce$, Mng public key pk_m, DO public key pk_{DO} and a keyword W'. And the output is $C = (U, V)$ Then the ciphertext C and the Users ID U_{id} is sent to Mng for further computation.

8. **Test**: ($C, sk_m, T_{W'}$) $\rightarrow$ Random Number($\Re$)
   This algorithm is run by Mng for searching a ciphertext C sent by the User. Once Mng receives the ciphertext C from the User, then Mng is able to test whether the keyword W' exists in some Trapdoor $T_{W'}$ or not. If found then the Mng will send the random number to the Cloud service provider CSP for further authentication.

9. **Search**: (U_{id}, Random Number($\Re$)) $\rightarrow$ Encrypted File(F)
   This algorithm is run by Cloud service provider, the input to this algorithm is random number($\Re$) and a User ID U_{id} which was sent by the Mng, and the output to this algorithm is a encrypted file F.

10. **Encrypt**: (SP, F, pk_{do}) $\rightarrow \bar{F}$
    The input to this algorithm is public parameter SP, file F, public key of data owner pk_{do} and the output is an encyypted file $\bar{F}$.

11. **Decrypt**: ($SP, \bar{F}, sk_{do}$) $\rightarrow F$
    The input to this algorithm is public parameter SP, encypted file $\bar{F}$, private key of data owner pk_{do} and the output is a decrypted file F.

5   Security Models

Before presenting the security models, we show following four oracles, Trapdoor, Test, Decrypt and dPEKS. We assume $\mathcal{A}$ to be an adversary.

1. Trapdoor: $\mathcal{A}$ sends a keyword W' to given oracle. A trapdoor T is generated and sent back in return.
2. Test: A searchable ciphertext C and a trapdoor T is provided to the oracle by $\mathcal{A}$. If $W = W'$, it outputs 1 else 0.
3. Decrypt: A ciphertext $\bar{C}$ is given to oracle by $\mathcal{A}$. Encrypted message $\bar{M}$ is sent back in return.
4. dPEKS: $\mathcal{A}$ sends a keyword $W' \in \mathcal{W}$ to given oracle. It returns a searchable ciphertext C for this keyword W'.

5.1   Security Models for SC-IND (Searchable Ciphertext Indistinguishability)

In this security model, the adversary $\mathcal{A}$ acts as a malicious manager or a data owner. SC-IND guarantees that the searchable ciphertexts formed by the two keywords W_0^* and W_1^* are indistinguishable for an adversary. The security model for SC-IND is the following game between $\mathcal{A}_1$ and a challenger $\mathcal{C}$.

Game 1: (SC-IND1) Let $\mathcal{A}_1$ be malicious manager. The game is performed as follows.

1. Setup: $\mathcal{A}_1$ generates its public and private keys as (pk_m, sk_m) respectively and sends pk_m to $\mathcal{C}$. $\mathcal{C}$ also generates its public and private keys as $(pk_{U_{id}}, sk_{U_{id}})$ respectively and sends $pk_{U_{id}}$ to $\mathcal{A}_1$.
2. Phase 1: $\mathcal{A}_1$ can send a keyword $W \in \mathcal{W}$ to trapdoor oracle and the dPEKS oracle. In response trapdoor oracle returns a trapdoor T and dPEKS oracle returns a searchable ciphertext C.
3. Challenge: $\mathcal{A}_1$ sends two keywords W_0^*, W_1^* for challenge to $\mathcal{C}$. But condition here is that W_0^*, W_1^* should not have been queried to trapdoor oracle. In return, $\mathcal{C}$ forms a searchable ciphertext C^* with for the keyword W_b^* where $b \in \{0, 1\}$ is randomly chosen.
4. Phase 2: $\mathcal{A}_1$ is again allowed to query to trapdoor and dPEKS oracles with a condition that the keywords W_0^*, W_1^* should not be queried.
5. Guess: Finally, $\mathcal{A}_1$ outputs its result as $b' \in \{0, 1\}$. $\mathcal{A}_1$ succeeds if $b = b'$.

The advantage of $\mathcal{A}_1$ to break our scheme is $Adv_{\mathcal{A}_1}{}^{SC-IND}(k) = \left| Pr[b = b'] - \frac{1}{2} \right|$.

Definition 1. With respect to adaptive chosen keyword attack, our scheme is secure if $Adv_{\mathcal{A}_1}{}^{SC-IND}(k)$ is negligible for any PPT adversary $\mathcal{A}_1$.

5.2 Security Model for TD-IND (Trapdoor Indistinguishablity)

In these security models, the adversary $\mathcal{A}$ acts as outsider or a malicious manager. TD-IND guarantees that the trapdoors formed by the two keywords W_0^* and W_1^* are indistinguishable for an adversary. The security model for TD-IND is the following games between $\mathcal{A}_2$ (or $\mathcal{A}_3$) and a challenger $\mathcal{C}$.

Game1 (TD-IND1): Let $\mathcal{A}_2$ be an outsider. The game is performed as follows.

1. Setup: $\mathcal{C}$ runs GlobalSetup(k), KeyGen1(SP) and KeyGen2(SP), and then gets (pk_m, sk_m) and (pk_{do}, sk_{do}). It will keep (sk_m, sk_{do}) secret and gives (pk_m, pk_{do}) to $\mathcal{A}_2$.
2. Phase 1: $\mathcal{A}_2$ is allowed to access the trapdoor oracle, dPEKS oracle as well as test oracle for a keyword $W \in \mathcal{W}$.
3. Challenge: $\mathcal{A}_2$ sends two keywords W_0^*, W_1^* for challenge to $\mathcal{C}$. But condition here is that W_0^*, W_1^* should not have been queried to trapdoor oracle. In return, $\mathcal{C}$ forms a trapdoor T^* with for the keyword W_b^* where $b \in \{0,1\}$ is randomly chosen.
4. Phase 2: $\mathcal{A}_2$ is again allowed to query trapdoor oracle, dPEKS oracle and Test oracle with the condition that W_0^*, W_1^* are not allowed to access these oracles.
5. Finally, $\mathcal{A}_2$ outputs its result as $b' \in \{0,1\}$. $\mathcal{A}_2$ succeeds if $b = b'$.

Game2 (TD-IND2): Let $\mathcal{A}_3$ be the malicious manager. This game is performed as follows.

1. Setup: $\mathcal{A}_3$ generates its public and private keys as (pk_m, sk_m) respectively and sends pk_m to $\mathcal{C}$. $\mathcal{C}$ also generates its public and private keys as (pk_{do}, sk_{do}) respectively and sends pk_{do} to $\mathcal{A}_3$.
2. Phase 1: $\mathcal{A}_3$ can send a keyword $W \in \mathcal{W}$ to trapdoor oracle and the dPEKS oracle. In response trapdoor oracle returns a trapdoor T and dPEKS oracle returns a searchable ciphertext C.
3. Challenge: $\mathcal{A}_3$ sends two keywords W_0^*, W_1^* for challenge to $\mathcal{C}$. But condition here is that W_0^*, W_1^* should not have been queried to trapdoor oracle. In return, $\mathcal{C}$ forms a trapdoor T^* with for the keyword W_b^* where $b \in \{0,1\}$ is randomly chosen.
4. Phase 2: $\mathcal{A}_3$ is again allowed to query to trapdoor and dPEKS oracles with a condition that the keywords W_0^*, W_1^* should not be queried.
5. Guess: Finally, $\mathcal{A}_3$ outputs its result as $b' \in \{0,1\}$. $\mathcal{A}_3$ succeeds if $b = b'$.

The advantage of $\mathcal{A}_2$ or $\mathcal{A}_3$ to break our scheme is $Adv_{\mathcal{A}_2 or \mathcal{A}_3}{}^{TD-IND}(k) = \left| Pr[b = b'] - \frac{1}{2} \right|$.

Definition 2. With respect to adaptive chosen keyword attack, our scheme is secure if $Adv_{\mathcal{A}_2 or \mathcal{A}_3}{}^{TD-IND}(k)$ is negligible for any PPT adversary $\mathcal{A}_i(i = 2, 3)$.

6   The Concrete Scheme

1. **Setup(k):** This algorithm takes a security parameter k as an input and the outputs a public parameter SP. We take two cyclic groups G_1 and G_2 of prime order q, and the bilinear paring function $e : G_1 * G_1 \to G_2$. The hash functions used are defined as H:$\{0,1\}^* \to G_1$ which maps to group G_1. The random generator $P \in G_1$ is chosen.
2. **KeyGen1(SP):** This algorithm will be run by Manager Mng and the input to this algorithm is SP and the output is a public/private key pair (sk_m, pk_m), where $pk_m = g^{(1/sk_m)}$.
3. **KeyGen2(SP):** This algorithm will be run by Data owners $DO(1 \leq i \leq D)$ to generate its own public/private key pair (sk_{do}, pk_{do}), where $pk_{do} = g^{(1/sk_{do})}$.
4. **KeyGen3(SP):** This algorithm will be run by the Users $(1 \leq i \leq N)$ to generate the public-private key pair $(sk_{U_{id}}, pk_{U_{id}})$, where $pk_{U_{id}} = g^{(1/sk_{U_{id}})}$.
5. **fGen:** $(\xi) \to nonce$
   A random nonce is chosen from Nonce space ξ.
6. **Trapdoor:** $(sk_{do}, pk_m , W_i, nonce) \to T_{W_i}$
   Firstly, the input is a keyword W_i, along with $nonce$, and the output is computed as $\bar{W}_i = W_i \| nonce$
   Now from the extracted keyword the DO will set the trapdoor by computing $T_{\bar{W}_i}$ for each and every keyword.
   $\hat{T} = (T_1, T_2) = \{P^r, H(\bar{W}_i)^{\frac{1}{sk_{do}}} \cdot H(pk_m)^r\}$. And returns $T = TE.Encrypt(\hat{T})$
7. **dPEKS:** $(pk_m, pk_{do}, W, nonce) \to \{U, V\}$
   The input to first phase is a keyword $W, nonce$, and the output is computed as $W' = W \| nonce$ When the authorized User propose to process the search task for keyword (W'), he has to generate a $dPEKS$ ciphertext C. The User (U_{id}) adopts Mng public key (pk_m) and DO public key (pk_{do}), in order to compute the $dPEKS$ ciphertext C.
   $\hat{C} = (U, V)' = (pk_m^{r^1}, H(e(pk_{do}, H(W^{1^{r^1}}))))$. And returns $C = U, V = TE.Encrypt((U, V)')$. Where $r^1 \in Z_p$ is randomly chosen. User will send this ciphertext C and User's ID U_{ID} to the Mng for further computation.
8. **Test:** $(C, sk_m , T_W) \to$ Random Number($\Re$)
   After receiving the C from the User U_{id}, the Mng tests whether the keyword W' exist in some of the Trapdoors $T_{W's}$ or not.
   First, Mng computes $\hat{C} = TE.Decrypt(C)$, $\hat{T} = TE.Decrypt(T)$ and $T_3 = \frac{T_2}{H(T_1^{sk_m})}$.
   Second, the Mng checks if $H(e(U, T_3^{sk_m}))$ is equal to V. If yes, then Mng checks whether the concerned user id is present in the list of authorized users corresponding to the matched keyword. If the user is authorized then Mng sends the user id and the random number corresponding to the matched keyword to the CSP.
9. **Search:** $(U_{id},$ Random Number($\Re$)) $\to$ Encrypted File(F)
   This algorithm is run by Cloud service provider, the input to this algorithm

is random number($\Re$) and a User ID U_{id} which was sent by the Mng, and the output to this algorithm is an encrypted file F.

10. **Encrypt:** $(SP, F, pk_{do}) \rightarrow \bar{F}$

This algorithm is run by Cloud service provider, the input to this algorithm is SP, a file F which is assumed to be encrypted by symmetric encyption, and data owner's public key pk_{do} and the output is computed as $\bar{F} =$ TE.Encrypt(SP, pk_{do}, F).

11. **Decrypt:** $(SP, \bar{F}, sk_{do}) \rightarrow F$

This algorithm is run by data owner, the input to this algorithm is SP, an encrypted file $\bar{F}$, and data owner's private key sk_{do} and the output is computed as $F =$ TE.Decrypt($SP, sk_{do}, \bar{F}$).

6.1 Security Analysis

We provide the security models for our proposal.

Theorem 1. Our scheme gives security for SC-IND as well as TD-IND.

We provide Lemmas 6.1–6.3 to support the above theorem. In the proof mentioned below, we represent adversary of our scheme as $\mathcal{A}_i$ for Game i(i = 1, ..., 3) $\mathcal{B}$ for IBE, $\mathcal{F}$ for TE $\mathcal{C}$ as the challenger.

Lemma 6.1. We assume that $\mathcal{A}_1$ breaks SC-IND with advantage $Adv_{\mathcal{A}_1}{}^{SC-IND}(k)$, then their exists another adversary $\mathcal{B}$ which breaks the ANON-sID-CPA [6] of IBE.

Proof. Here the adversary $\mathcal{B}$ will simulate the adversary $\mathcal{A}_1$ for breaking the ANON-sID-CPA of IBE.

1. Setup: $\mathcal{A}_1$ generates its public and private keys as pk_m, sk_m respectively and sends pk_m to $\mathcal{C}$. $\mathcal{C}$ also generates its public and private keys as (pk_{do}, sk_{do}) respectively and sends pk_{do} to $\mathcal{A}_1$.
2. Phase1: $\mathcal{A}_1$ is allowed to send a trapdoor query. Whenever $\mathcal{A}_1$ sends a trapdoor query for keyword $W \in \mathcal{W}$ to $\mathcal{B}$, $\mathcal{B}$ after receiving W sends ID = W to IBE. Extract and recovers U_{priv} of ID. Now $\mathcal{B}$ generates trapdoor $T =$ TE.Encrypt(SP, pk_m, U_{priv}) and sends it to $\mathcal{A}_1$.
3. Challenge: $\mathcal{A}_1$ sends two keywords $W_0{}^*, W_1{}^*$ for challenge to $\mathcal{B}$. But condition here is that $W_0{}^*, W_1{}^*$ should not have been sent as Trapdoor query. Now $\mathcal{B}$ sends $ID_0{}^* = W_0{}^*, ID_1{}^* = W_1{}^*$ for challenge to $\mathcal{C}$.In return, $\mathcal{C}$ forms a searchable ciphertext C^* with for the keyword $W_b{}^*$ where $b \in \{0, 1\}$ is randomly chosen and sends C^* to $\mathcal{B}$. Again, $\mathcal{B}$ sends this C^* to $\mathcal{A}_1$.
4. Phase 2: $\mathcal{A}_1$ is again allowed to send trapdoor query with a condition that the keywords $W_0{}^*, W_1{}^*$ should not be queried.
5. Guess: Finally, $\mathcal{A}_1$ outputs its result as $b' \in \{0, 1\}$. $\mathcal{A}_1$ succeeds if $b = b'$. and hence $\mathcal{B}$ also succeeds Game $ANON - SID - CPA$.

We assume that A_1 succeeds the game in polynomial time. But B simulates A_1 and therefore B breaks the ANON-sID-CPA in polynomial time. Hence, $Adv_{A_1}{}^{SC-IND}(k) \leq Adv_{B.IBE}{}^{ANON-sID-CPA}(k)$ and that $Adv_{A_1}{}^{SC-IND}(k)$ is equivalent to $Adv_{B.IBE}{}^{ANON-sID-CPA}(k)$.

We conclude that the proof of the lemma is completed.

Lemma 6.2. We assume that A_2 breaks TD-IND with advantage $Adv_{A_2}{}^{TD-IND}(k)$, then their exists another adversary F which breaks the IND-CCA [7] of TE.

Proof. The adversary F will simulate the adversary A_2 for breaking the IND-CCA of TE.

1. Setup: C runs GlobalSetup(k), KeyGen1(SP), and KeyGen2(SP), and then gets(pk_m, sk_m) and (pk_{do}, sk_{do}) It will keep sk_{do} and sk_m secret. It will send pk_m, pk_m to A_2.
2. Phase 1: A_2 is allowed to send a trapdoor query to F. In return F generates a trapdoor $T = TE.Encrypt(SP, pk_m, IBE.Extract(SP, P_{priv}, W))$ and returns it to A_2. Also, A_2 is allowed to send as Test query for (C, T) as input to F. Now F sends C and T to TE.Decrypt(SP, C, sk_m) and TE.Decrypt(SP, T, sk_m) respectively and recovers $\hat{C}$ and $\hat{T}$, further performing IBE.Decrypt$(SP, \hat{C}, \hat{T})$ and outputs 1 if equation holds else 0.
3. Challenge: A_2 sends two keywords W_0^*, W_1^* for challenge to F, but the condition here is that C and T^* for W_0^*, W_1^* must not have been queried in phase 1. Now F sends W_0^*, W_1^* for challenge to C. In return, C forms a trapdoor T^* for the keyword W_b^* where $b \in \{0,1\}$ is randomly chosen and sends to F. Again, F sends this T^* to A_2.
4. Phase 2: A_2 is allowed to send trapdoor queries as in phase 1 but with a condition that keyword chosen should not be W_0^*, W_1^*.
5. Guess: Finally, A_2 outputs its result as $b' \in \{0,1\}$. A_2 succeeds if $b = b'$. Hence F also succeeds Game IND-CCA.

We assume that A_2 succeeds the game in polynomial time. But F simulates A_2 and therefore F breaks the IND-CCA in polynomial time. Hence $Adv_{A_2}{}^{TD-IND}(k) \leq Adv_{F.TE}{}^{IND-CCA}(k)$ and that $Adv_{A_2}{}^{TD-IND(k)}$ is equivalent to $Adv_{F.TE}{}^{IND-CCA}(k)$.

We conclude that the proof of the lemma is completed.

Lemma 6.3. We assume that A_3 breaks TD-IND with advantage $Adv_{A_3}{}^{TD-IND}(k)$, then their exists another adversary B which breaks the ANON-sID-CPA of IBE.

Proof. The adversary B will simulate the adversary A_3 for breaking the ANON-sID-CPA of IBE.

1. Setup: A_3 generates its public and private keys as pk_m, sk_m respectively and sends pk_m to C. C also generates its public and private keys as pk_{do}, sk_{do} respectively and sends pk_{do} to A_3.

2. Phase1: $\mathcal{A}_3$ is allowed to send a trapdoor query. Whenever $\mathcal{A}_3$ sends a trapdoor query for keyword $W \in \mathcal{W}$ to $\mathcal{B}$, $\mathcal{B}$ after receiving W sends ID = W to IBE.Extract and recovers U_{priv} of ID. Now $\mathcal{B}$ generates trapdoor $T = $ TE.Encrypt(SP, pk_m, U_{priv}) and sends it to $\mathcal{A}_3$.
3. Challenge: $\mathcal{A}_3$ sends two keywords $W_0{}^*, W_1{}^*$ for challenge to $\mathcal{B}$. But condition here is that $W_0{}^*, W_1{}^*$ should not have been sent as Trapdoor query. Now $\mathcal{B}$ sends $ID_0{}^* = W_0{}^*, ID_1{}^* = W_1{}^*$ for challenge to $\mathcal{C}$. In return, $\mathcal{C}$ forms a trapdoor T^* for the keyword $W_b{}^*$ where $b \in \{0, 1\}$ is randomly chosen and sends to $\mathcal{B}$. Again, $\mathcal{B}$ sends this T^* to $\mathcal{A}_3$.
4. Phase 2: $\mathcal{A}_3$ is again allowed to send trapdoor query with a condition that the keywords $W_0{}^*, W_1{}^*$ should not be queried.
5. Guess: Finally, $\mathcal{A}_3$ outputs its result as $b' \in \{0, 1\}$. $\mathcal{A}_3$ succeeds if $b = b'$. and hence $\mathcal{B}$ also succeeds Game $ANON - sID - CPA$.

We assume that $\mathcal{A}_3$ succeeds the game in polynomial time. But $\mathcal{B}$ simulates $\mathcal{A}_3$ and therefore $\mathcal{B}$ breaks the ANON-sID-CPA in polynomial time. Hence $Adv_{\mathcal{A}_3}{}^{SC-IND}(k) \leq Adv_{\mathcal{B}.IBE}{}^{ANON-sID-CPA}(k)$ and that $Adv_{\mathcal{A}_3}{}^{SC-IND}(k)$ is equivalent to $Adv_{\mathcal{B}.IBE}{}^{ANON-sID-CPA}(k)$.

We conclude that the proof of the lemma is completed.

7   Experiments

In order to assess the representation of our scheme, we have achieve our construction using $SageMathTool$ [8] for implementation of a type-1 curve. We have performed all experiments on an Intel(R) Core(TM) $i3$-3220 CPU @ 3.30 GHz with 2 GB RAM running Ubuntu 14.04 LTS with 3.13.X kernel version. The disk of the our machine has the capacity of 200 GB. We run all the experiments single-threaded on the machine.

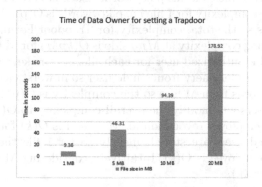

Fig. 4. Execution time for setting a trapdoor

In our experiments, we take a real world data. The data set was taken from the Enron emails [9], we derive a subset of emails as file collections. Figure 4

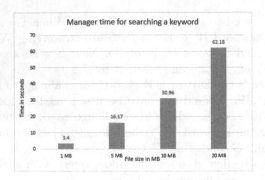

Fig. 5. Execution time for matching a keyword

shows the results of the *Trapdoor* algorithm, which takes the most of the time of our scheme. Note that before sending *DO* files to the cloud service provider the *Trapdoor* algorithm is executed first. Figure 5 gives the time required for the manager *Mng* to perform a match, given a ciphertext *C* by any User.

7.1 Complexity

Let us assume their are N employees where EMP is set of all the employees in an organization, $EMP = (e_1, e_2, \ldots e_N)$. And their are total M files stored at the cloud server which are owned by some *DO*, where F is set of total files. $F = (F_1, F_2, \ldots F_M)$ and each file contains p keywords, where W is a set of all keywords in the file, $W = (w_1, w_2, \ldots w_p)$. Also we assume that their are k authorised users having access for a specific file.

1. The space complexity for forming trapdoor at *DO* side is $O(pM)$. As their are M files and each file contains p keywords. Each keyword requires 1 pairing operation so the complexity for 1 file i.e. p keywords is O(p). As in our scenario there are M files so the total complexity for Trapdoor Formation is O(Mp).
2. Keyword matching complexity at *Mng* side is $O(kpM)$ for M files. As their are p keywords and k authorized user for each file. As the keywords are linearly stored so if we consider query from single user so in worst case *Mng* will have to match p keywords from M files so the complexity is O(pM) for single user, now having k users will modify the overall complexity to O(kpM).
3. Complexity for employee revocation at *Mng* end is $O(k)$ for one file. As the list of authorized users are stored linearly so for 1 file the complexity for revocating the employee is O(k). Intuitively considering M files, the overall complexity is O(Mk).

8   Conclusion

The proposed scheme introduced a concept of manager, which manages the job of handling the file retrieval queries, thereby reducing the additional workload of the cloud server. Their is no information leakage neither in the cloud server nor in the manager side. To prevent the keyword guessing attack by the manager, we used a new nonce based dPEKS approach. The results and security models concludes that the scheme is fully secure as well as practical. We limit the feasibility of our scheme to an organization where the number of users are assumed to be limited.

References

1. Andola, N., Prakash, S., Venkatesan, S., Verma, S.: Improved secure server-designated public key encryption with keyword search. In: Proceedings of the Conference on Information and Communication Technology. IEEE (2017)
2. Song, D.X., Wagner, D., Perrig, A.: Practical techniques for searches on encrypted data. In: IEEE Symposium on Security and Privacy, pp. 44–55 2000. citeseer.ist.psu.edu/song00practical.html
3. Goh, E.: Secure indexes, cryptology eprint archive, in Report 2003/216 (2003)
4. Boneh, D., Di Crescenzo, G., Ostrovsky, R., Persiano, G.: Public key encryption with keyword search. In: Cachin, C., Camenisch, J.L. (eds.) EUROCRYPT 2004. LNCS, vol. 3027, pp. 506–522. Springer, Heidelberg (2004). https://doi.org/10.1007/978-3-540-24676-3_30
5. Rhee, H.S., Park, J.H., Susilo, W., Lee, D.H.: Trapdoor security in a searchable public-key encryption scheme with a designated tester. J. Syst. Softw. 83(5), 763–771 (2010). https://doi.org/10.1016/j.jss.2009.11.726
6. Boyen, X., Waters, B.: Anonymous hierarchical identity-based encryption (without random oracles). In: Dwork, C. (ed.) CRYPTO 2006. LNCS, vol. 4117, pp. 290–307. Springer, Heidelberg (2006). https://doi.org/10.1007/11818175_17
7. Rackoff, C., Simon, D.R.: Non-interactive zero-knowledge proof of knowledge and chosen ciphertext attack. In: Feigenbaum, J. (ed.) CRYPTO 1991. LNCS, vol. 576, pp. 433–444. Springer, Heidelberg (1992). https://doi.org/10.1007/3-540-46766-1_35
8. Stein, W., et al.: Sage: Open Source Mathematical Software, 7 December 2009 (2008)
9. Cohen, W.W.: Enron email dataset (2009). http://www.cs.cmu.edu/enron. Accessed 15 Feb 2017

Performance Evaluation of Multi-functional Defected Ground Structure Embedded with Microstrip Patch Antenna for ISM Band Wireless Communications

Guru Prasad Mishra[1(✉)], Sumon Modak[2], Madhu Sudan Maharana[1], and Biswa Binayak Mangaraj[1]

[1] Veer Surendra Sai University of Technology, Burla, Odisha, India
guruprasadmishra5@gmail.com,
madhusudan.maharana@gmail.com, bbmangaraj@gmail.com
[2] Sambalpur University Institute of Information Technology,
Burla, Odisha, India
sumon.ssmodak@gmail.com

Abstract. This article evaluates the multi-functional characteristics of dumbbell-shaped Defected Ground Structure (DGS) embedded with microstrip patch antenna for various wireless applications. To validate the effects of DGS like antenna size reduction and higher order harmonics suppression, the ground plane defects distinctly at different positions beneath the substrate, and later the structure is optimized. Finally, different design parameters of DGS are varied separately over a wide range to find control over the performance of DGS. All the antennas are designed to operate at 2.4 GHz frequency on a Rogers RT/duroid 5880 (tm) substrate material with a dielectric constant of 2.2 and a height of 1.5 mm. All the structures are designed using ANSYS HFSS, and their performance parameters are evaluated and analyzed in terms of return loss, VSWR, gain and radiation patterns. The proposed DGS antennas and its array can find extensive application in ISM band wireless communications.

Keywords: Defected Ground Structure (DGS) · Patch antenna
Size reduction · Harmonic suppression · ISM band

1 Introduction

In this modern communication era, the use of personal phones, tablets, laptops, GPS radio navigators and other wireless handheld devices are increasing moderately day by day. They are also connected among themselves to exchange high-quality data or information without any interruption through wireless channels. In this type of communications, antenna plays a key role at both transmission and reception ends. Due to the huge usage of these communication devices, the demand of small size antennas like Microstrip Patch Antenna (MPA) has become the most suitable candidate for these purposes [1]. However, conventional patch antennas suffer from a number of drawbacks such as a single band of operation, narrow bandwidth, low power handling

© Springer Nature Singapore Pte Ltd. 2019
S. Verma et al. (Eds.): CNC 2018, CCIS 839, pp. 64–75, 2019.
https://doi.org/10.1007/978-981-13-2372-0_6

capacity, higher mode harmonics, large dimension at a low frequency of operation, etc. [2]. Several methods have been suggested by different researchers to overcome these demerits of the simple patch antenna. Most effortless and accepted technique concerning the size reductions and harmonics suppression of the patch antenna include in defecting the ground plane with different shaped structures [3]. Group of geometrical shapes is composed of a single elementary shape, and the shape is etched from the ground plane to form DGS antennas. Among different geometries, dumbbell-shaped, spiral headed, arrow-headed, H-shaped DGSs are most popular and anticipate the fruitful design of highly efficient patch antennas [4, 5].

Many articles are found on the application of DGS to patch antennas. In [6], three kinds of Periodic Defected Ground Structures are analyzed using finite element method along with periodic boundary conditions to assess their effects on surface and leaky waves. A wideband microstrip filter is designed in [7], which is composed of split-ring resonator DGS having a passband from 1 GHz to 2.4 GHz. A circular polarized MPA has designed in [8] to resonate at three different bands with DGS for various wireless applications. Three different DGS are tested in three different antennas and compactness above 20% is achieved in all three cases. Ujjal Chakraborty et al. [9], has developed a miniaturized frequency tunable rectangular MPA embedded with T-shaped DGS. Antenna size reduction of about 80% is achieved with parametric analysis of the DGS, and the antenna can be tuned from 1.80 GHz to 3.188 GHz frequency with more than 4% bandwidth. After designing antennas along with DGS, all the structures need to be optimized to achieve desirable and improved performances characteristics at the resonant frequency. A linear antenna array is optimized in [10], to achieve high gain in a particular direction with minimal element separations. A comparison is made between two optimization techniques, Taguchi method and Cuckoo Search method regarding the time required to optimize the array structure to achieve desired performance characteristics. From the experiment, it can be observed that Taguchi method seems to be taking less time than Cuckoo search method in the process of array optimization. B. B. Mangaraj et al. has optimized a Yagi-Uda array in [11], using bacteria foraging algorithm. The effects of DGS on patch antennas are briefly discussed with optimization by all the literature cited here. However, they are concentrating on any single DGS effect at a time and also as far as the knowledge of the author, the effect of individual design parameter of DGS is not analyzed over the performance of DGS integrated MPA.

The presented work is focused on the performance evaluation of DGS on MPA for ISM band wireless applications. At first, a dumbbell-shaped DGS is positioned at different places underneath the substrate to improve the performance of the patch antenna. Then the design parameters of DGS are varied over a wide range to examine the effect of the DGS, embedded to patch antenna. The remainder part of the article is organized as follows. The optimal design of the proposed antenna is shown in Sect. 2. Section 3 presents applications of DGS to MPA at different places of the ground plane below the substrate. All optimized simulation results of the patch antenna with and without DGS are discussed in Sect. 4. Also, this section discussed the effect of parameter variations on MPA. Eventually, the paper is concluded in Sect. 5.

2 Patch Antenna Design

Nowadays, wireless communications set a challenge for antenna engineers to develop compact sized antennas having high-performance parameters with low cost and simple fabrication processes. Antenna performance mainly depends on the feeding mechanism and the optimum feeding location. Among different feeding techniques, inset feed, strip line feed, edge feed and coaxial feed are very popular for single layered patch antennas [1]. In this antenna design, due to simplicity and ease of analysis, microstrip edge feed is adopted. To achieve impedance matching condition in feeding network, a quarter wavelength matching line is used between the feed and edge of the patch. By keeping in view of the moderate use of ISM band wireless communication, all antenna and array structures are designed at the center frequency (f_0) of 2.4 GHz. All the patches are placed on the Rogers RT/duroid 5880 (tm) substrate with a relative permittivity (ε_r) of 2.2 and the substrate height (h) of 1.5 mm. Considering these three parameters f_0, ε_r, and h as basic elements, the dimension of the MPA is calculated using transmission line equations [2].

After designing the proposed antenna shown in Fig. 1, a mismatch is found between the theoretical predictions and simulation results. So to avoid this mismatch and to improve the performances of MPA, optimization of the antenna structure is highly essential. Optimization of all the design parameters are conducted in HFSS and are listed in Table 1. However, after the optimal design of the MPA, size of the structure can be further reduced using DGS concept. Along with this, DGS can be used in the suppression of higher order harmonics as discussed in the next section.

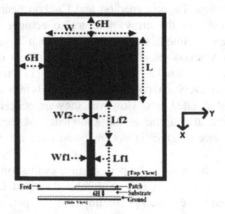

Fig. 1. Layout of simple patch antenna at 2.4 GHz (Both top and side view).

3 Application of DGS to Microstrip Patch Antenna

Recently, there has been an increasing demand for highly efficient small sized patch antenna to be used in modern wireless applications. However, a simple patch antenna can't fulfill all the need of communications, for which some modifications must be

Table 1. Optimized design parameters for single patch antenna at 2.4 GHz.

Parameters	Value (In mm)	Parameters	Value (In mm)
L	40.28	Lf1	22.35
W	49	Lf2	23.12
Wf1	4.622	H	1.5
Wf2	1.179	ε_r	2.2

made to the antenna to make it compact and highly efficient for all purposes. Different periodic structures like Photonic Band Gap structure (PBGs), Defected Ground Structure (DGS), etc. are integrated with the patch antenna to achieve desired performance parameters. Among the above periodic structures, DGS is adopted by many researchers due to its simple design and ease of control by the equivalent circuit parameters. Some periodic structures like dumbbell-shaped, circular-head shaped, rectangular-head shaped DGS are commonly used with patch antennas. Figure 2 shows the equivalent R-L-C resonance circuit of a dumbbell-shaped DGS integrated with a microstrip line over the substrate. However, the same circuit can be used here to approximate the effect of DGS over the patch antenna. The reactance (L) and the capacitance (C) can be found out from these two (1–2) equations as described in [12].

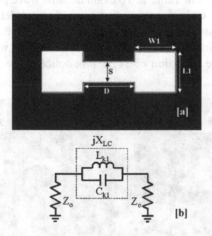

Fig. 2. (a) Layout of Dumbbell-shaped DGS and its (b) RLC circuit equivalence.

$$C = \frac{\omega_c}{2Z_0(\omega_0^2 - \omega_c^2)} \tag{1}$$

$$L = \frac{1}{4\pi^2\omega_0^2 C} \tag{2}$$

Where ω_c is 3 dB cutoff angular frequency, ω_0 is angular resonance frequency, and Z_0 is characteristic impedance of the strip line. All these parameters can be easily found out from the band response diagram of the DGS. This dumbbell-shaped DGS is placed in different positions for all two cases to achieve a compact size of the antenna and harmonics suppression at higher frequencies.

3.1   Antenna Size Reduction

Several techniques have been used to reduce the size of the antenna, such as shorting pins, shorting walls, high dielectric constant, etc. Defecting of the ground plane is a new technique to reduce the antenna size. By embedding the DGS section at the ground, it is observed that the resonant frequency of the MPA is significantly dropped, which can lead to a huge amount of size reduction for a fixed frequency operation. For this case, the DGS is placed exactly center of the patch beneath the substrate symmetrical to both x-axis and y-axis as shown in Fig. 3. The defect on the ground plane of MPA provides additional effective inductive (L) component, which introduces a slow-wave characteristic in the antenna structure. The resultant electrical length of the microstrip antenna with DGS is longer than that of the conventional MPA for the same physical length. This extra electrical length helps in reduction of the size of the structure at the same resonant frequency. All the optimal design parameters of both antenna and DGS are listed in Table 2. To evaluate slow wave property of the DGS, an MPA is designed at the 3 GHz resonating frequency. Later, a defect is introduced to the ground plane, and the structure is optimized to operate at 2.4 GHz resonance frequency. Finally, conventional 2.4 GHz MPA and 3 GHz MPA with DGS are compared regarding size, and a size reduction of 31.53% is noticed.

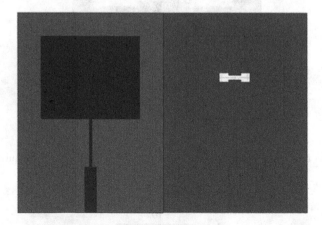

Fig. 3. Patch and DGS position for antenna size reduction (Both top and bottom view).

3.2   Higher Order Harmonics Suppression

A simple antenna resonating at a lower frequency is quite useful for many wireless applications. However, when we increase the frequency range of the same for

Table 2. Structural dimension of antenna along with DGS used for size reduction.

Parameters	Value (In mm)	Parameters	Value (In mm)
L	32	Lf1	17.75
W	38.4	L1	4
Wf2	1.212	W1	8.29
Lf2	18.36	S	1.867
H	1.5	D	4.668
Wf1	4.622	ε_r	2.2

analyzation, some higher order harmonics are introduced. The effect of these harmonics can't be neglected, and they must be suppressed to increase the efficiency of the antenna. Hence, in this work, a dumbbell-shaped DGS is proposed to suppress the harmonics, and it is placed exactly under the feed, symmetry to the x-axis as shown in Fig. 4. An etched defect in the ground plane disturbs the current distribution in the ground plane. This disturbance can change characteristics of the patch antenna in terms of capacitance and inductance. The proposed dumbbell-shaped DGS consists of narrow and wide etched areas in backside metallic ground plane as shown in the figure, which gives rise to increasing the effective capacitance and inductance of the MPA, respectively. Thus, an LC equivalent circuit same as a low pass filter (LPF) can represent the proposed periodic DGS circuit. Hence, DGS can act as an LPF and rejects the higher order harmonics introduced by the structure.

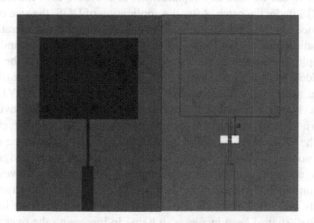

Fig. 4. Patch and DGS position for harmonic suppression (Both top view and bottom view).

Here, the same MPA as discussed in Sect. 2, resonating at 2.4 GHz is considered, and the structure is simulated in HFSS over a range of 1 GHz to 10 GHz. Then, by introducing DGS to MPA, the 2nd, 3rd, 4th, and 5th harmonics at 4 GHz, 6.34 GHz, 8.26 GHz, and 9.28 GHz, are suppressed. All the optimal design parameters of DGS integrated MPA are listed in Table 3. A detail investigation on the effect of variation of parameters related to DGS is carried out and discussed in detail in the next section.

Table 3. Structural dimension of antenna along with DGS used for harmonics suppression.

Parameters	Value (In mm)	Parameters	Value (In mm)
L	40.28	W1	4
W	48.4	L1	4
Wf1	4.622	D	1.6
Wf2	1.179	S	0.8
Lf1	22.35	H	1.5
Lf2	23.12	ε_r	2.2

4 Results and Discussion

All the DGS integrated MPAs are designed and analyzed using Finite Element Method (FEM) computation based ANSYS HFSS (High-Frequency Structural Simulator) software. After the successful simulation of the structures, all the performance data are exported to MATLAB to visualize them in a single graph for better comparison. A 64-bit based Personal Computer with 16 GB RAM and Intel(R) Core(TM) i7-7400 U CPU @ 2.70 GHz processor is used for conducting the whole process.

In this work, at first a simple 2.4 GHz MPA is designed, and then DGS is placed at proper locations to verify different effects of DGS over patch antenna and its array. Figure 5 shows S11 characteristics of MPA with and without DGS over a frequency range for size reduction case. From the figure, it can be observed that an antenna designed at 3 GHz can be used as a replacement of 2.4 GHz conventional antenna by only using a DGS under the patch. After the application of DGS, the size of the antenna structure is reduced by 31.53% for the same 2.4 GHz frequency of operation. Figure 6 shows the radiation patterns for both E-Plane and H-Plane with co and cross polarization for simple 2.4 GHz antenna, antenna design at 3 GHz, and the reduced size antenna embedded with DGS structure. After the successful reduction of the antenna size at 2.4 GHz, a study on variations of DGS design parameters (L1, W1, S, and D) is also carried out. Figure 7 describes the resonant frequencies of respective MPAs with DGS w.r.t. variations of all the above four parameters. As a slight change in the dimension of the DGS affect in equivalent inductance and capacitance of the whole structure, the resonant frequency changes with a change in all these design parameters. All four parameters seem to affect antenna frequency of operation. However, 'W1' has a strong effect on all, as its resonant frequency curve has a steep downward path over the change in its dimension. This effect can be well predicted from the fact that as the width of dumbbell-shaped head increases, it helps in increasing the overall inductance of the structure. This increased inductance give rise to generate a lower resonant frequency for MPA.

Similar to the above case, DGS can also be used as an LPF, if placed below the feed, to suppress higher order harmonics to increase the efficiency of the antenna. Figure 8 shows the S11 characteristics of MPA with and without DGS for harmonics suppression case. To verify, this property of DGS, at first a simple antenna is designed at 2.4 GHz frequency, and later the frequency range is increased to 10 GHz to analyze higher order harmonics. From the S11 curves, it can be observed that the MPA without

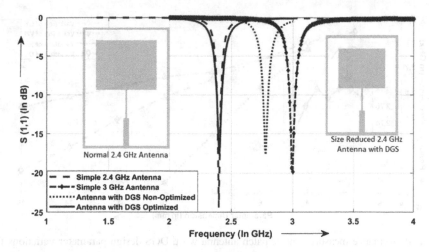

Fig. 5. S (1, 1) vs. frequency characteristic of antenna with and without DGS for size reduction case.

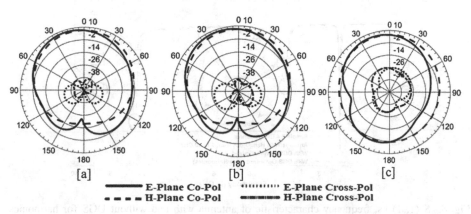

Fig. 6. Simulated Co-Pol and Cross-Pol radiation patterns for size reduction case, [a] Simple 2.4 GHz antenna, [b] antenna at 3 GHz, and [c] antenna with DGS.

DGS has four harmonics at 4 GHz, 6.34 GHz, 8.26 GHz, and 9.28 GHz respectively. A defect is made exactly below the feedline to suppress these harmonics. However, by carefully adjusting the distance between the DGS and the edge of the patch (a), all four harmonics are suppressed to an acceptable level. For un-optimized and optimized DGS antenna structure, 'a' is taken as 11 mm and 17 mm respectively. Co and cross polarization radiation patterns of MPA with and without DGS, are displayed in Fig. 9 for harmonics suppression case.

Same as the previous case, here also the effect of DGS parameter variation is tested. Among all parameters, only the distance between DGS and edge of the patch (a), the distance between DGS heads (D) have a better effect on the performance of MPA. Total number of harmonics over the change in these two parameters ('a' and 'D') are

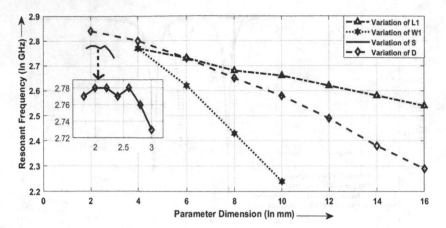

Fig. 7. Performance measurement of patch antenna w.r.t. DGS design parameter variations for size reduction case.

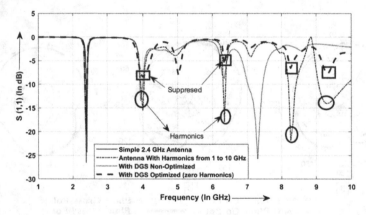

Fig. 8. S (1, 1) vs. frequency characteristic of antenna with and without DGS for harmonics suppression case.

shown in Figs. 10 and 11, respectively. From these two figures, one can predict that the variation of these parameters has an effect on the stop band characteristics of the DGS over a wide range. Different values of 'a' and 'D' can be adjusted carefully to control the harmonics of the DGS integrated MPA for application at different wireless applications.

All the optimal performance parameter of MPA, with and without DGS are characterized in Table 4 for all two cases. The table also includes the real and imaginary part of impedance at the resonant frequency to consider all MPAs with DGS for different practical applications. From the table, it can be observed that all antennas are designed with all acceptable performance parameters to operate at 2.4 GHz ISM band wireless communications. This work is purely focused on the theoretical predictions of defected ground plane and variation of its parameters on the performance of patch

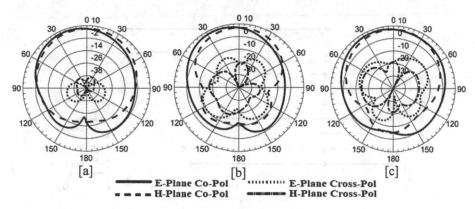

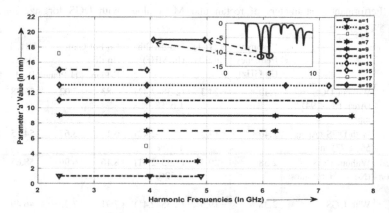

Fig. 9. Simulated Co-Pol and Cross-Pol radiation patterns for harmonic suppression case, [a] Simple 2.4 GHz antenna, [b] 2.4 GHz antenna with harmonics, and [c] antenna with DGS without harmonics.

Fig. 10. Performance measurement of patch antenna w.r.t. DGS distance variations from edge of patch (a) for harmonics suppression case.

antenna. However, the antennas with DGS can be fabricated physically and the measured results can be compared with the simulates ones to validate these theoretical predictions. As the modification done here to the ground plane is not very complex, a perfect matching is expected in the performance parameters of simulated and fabricated ones.

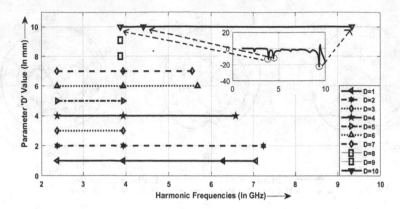

Fig. 11. Performance measurement of patch antenna w.r.t. DGS design parameter variation (D) for harmonics suppression case.

Table 4. Performance parameters of rectangular MPA along with DGS for size reduction, harmonic suppression.

Different cases		Resonant frequency (In GHz)	S (1, 1) (In dB)	Bandwidth (In MHz) (%)	Co-Pol Gain (In dB)		Z(1, 1) (In Ω)	
					E-Plane	H-Plane	Real	Imag
Size reduction	Without DGS (Area: 67 × 94) mm²	2.40	−24.3	(2.38–2.42) 1.67%	7.83	7.02	56.38	−1.1
	With DGS (Area: 56 × 77) mm²	2.40	−17.5	(2.38–2.42) 1.67%	6.19	5.67	54.65	13.9
Harmonic suppression	Without DGS (No. of Harmonics: 4)	2.38	−20.5	(2.35–2.41) 2.52%	8.16	6.96	58.65	5.40
	With DGS (Harmonics Suppressed: 4)	2.38	−19.5	(2.35–2.41) 2.52%	7.91	7.22	46.49	-9.6

5 Conclusion

This article presents the design and simulation of different patch antennas with dumbbell-shaped Defected Ground Structure (DGS). DGS is placed at different positions like exactly under the patch, under the feed line to achieve two main characteristics like; antenna size reduction and harmonics suppression, respectively. It is also clear that the application of DGS in MPA shows an improved performance of the system. A 31.52% of antenna size reduction is obtained in case of DGS integrated MPA. The suppression of unwanted frequencies makes the antenna to concentrate on a particular application without any interferences. With the help of DGS and some optimization, four higher order harmonics are suppressed. Finally, the effects of all design parameters of DGS are verified over the performance of the antenna and array. After going through the various sections of this article, the readers can get a good insight into the properties of DGS when applied to an antenna structure. The proposed DGS antennas and its array can find extensive application in ISM band wireless communications like fixed mobile communications, satellite broadcasting (from Space to earth), radio navigation for different government and private organizations.

References

1. Garg, R., Bhartia, P., Bahl, I., Ittipiboon, A.: Microstrip Antenna Design Handbook. Artech House, Norwood (2000)
2. Balanis, C.A.: Antenna Theory: Analysis and Design, 2nd edn. Wiley, New York (1997)
3. Guha, D., Biswas, S., Antar, Y.M.M.: Defected Ground Structure for Microstrip Antennas, in Microstrip and Printed Antennas: New Trends, Techniques and Applications. Wiley, London (2011)
4. Ahn, D., Park, J.-S., Kim, C.-S., Kim, J., Qian, Y., Itoh, T.: A design of the low-pass filter using the novel microstrip defected ground structure. IEEE Trans. Microw. Theory Tech. 49 (1), 86–93 (2001)
5. Saha, P., Singh, A., Pandey, V.K., Kanaujia, B.K., Khandelwal, M.K.: Design and analysis of UWB circular ring two element microstrip patch antenna array with notched band for modern wireless applications. Microw. Opt. Technol. Lett. 57(9), 2067–2072 (2015)
6. Oskouei, H.D., Forooraghi, K., Hakkak, M.: Guided and leaky wave characteristics of periodic defected ground structures. Prog. Electromagn. Res. 73, 15–27 (2007)
7. Hou, Z.-Z.: Novel wideband filter with a transmission zero based on split-ring resonator DGS. Microw. Opt. Technol. Lett. 50(6), 1691–1693 (2008)
8. Khandelwal, M.K., Kanaujia, B.K., Dwari, S., Kumar, S., Gautam, A.K.: Triple band circularly polarized compact microstrip antenna with defected ground structure for wireless applications. Int. J. Microw. Wirel. Technol. 8(6), 943–953 (2015)
9. Chakraborty, U., Chowdhury, S.K., Bhattacharjee, A.K.: Frequency tuning and miniaturization of square microstrip antenna embedded with 'T'-shaped defected ground structure. Microw. Opt. Technol. Lett. 55(4), 869–872 (2013)
10. Mohanty, S. Ku., Mishra, G. P., Mangaraj, B. B.: Implementing Taguchi and cuckoo search to optimize LAA. In: IEEE Annual India Conference (INDICON), Pune, Maharashtra, India, pp. 1–5 (2014)
11. Mangaraj, B.B., Mishra, I.S., Sanyal, S.K.: Application of bacteria foraging algorithm for the design optimization of multi-objective Yagi-Uda array. Int. J. RF Microw. Comput. Aided Eng. 21(1), 25–35 (2011)
12. Lim, I.S., Lee, B.S.: Design of defected ground structures for harmonics control for active microstrip antenna. In: Proceedings of the IEEE AP-S International Symposium, vol. 2, pp. 852–855 (2002)

Evaluation of Character Recognition Algorithm Based on Feature Extraction

Bishakha Sharma[✉] and Arun Agarwal

ITM Group of Institutions, Gwalior, MP, India
bishakhasharmajmp@gmail.com, arun.agarwal@itmgoi.in

Abstract. At display circumstance there is creating enthusiasm for the item system to see characters in a PC structure when information is investigated paper records. This paper presents point by point review in the field of Optical Character Recognition. Diverse methods are settled that have been proposed to comprehend the point of convergence of character affirmation in an optical character affirmation structure. Decision and feature extraction in light of Optical Character Recognition (OCR). By using the OCR, we can change the information of picture into the information of substance which is definitely not hard to control. In our proposed method, Select the any particular number and crop the selected image and then extract the feature. The text from the OCR process will be compared with the selected number from the loaded image. The overall accuracy of the proposed method is 92%.

Keywords: Image processing · Optical Character Recognition
Feature extraction

1 Introduction

A piece of software through which printed text and images can be converted into digitized form such that it can be manipulated by machine is known as character recognition system. The human brain which has the capability to very easily recognize the text/characters from an image, but machines have not enough capability to perceive image information. Therefore, a large number of research efforts have been put forward that attempts to transform a document image to format understandable for machine.

OCR is a mind boggling issue in light of the assortment of dialects, scholarly styles and styles in which substance can be made, and the versatile tenets of tongues and so on. Thusly, frameworks from various solicitations of programming outlining (i.e. picture dealing with, design depiction and trademark vernacular arranging and so forth are utilized to address grouped difficulties. This paper acclimates the peruser with the issue. It enlightens the reader with the historical perspectives, applications, challenges and techniques of OCR. [1]

Optical Character acknowledgment has been a subject of research. Example acknowledgment has three fundamental advances: perception, design division, and example arrangement. Optical Character Recognition (OCR) frameworks is changing substantial measure of records, either printed letters in order or transcribed into machine encoded content with no change, tumult, affirmation blends and different segments.

At the point when all is said in done, handwriting affirmation is portrayed into two sorts as offline and On-line character recognition. Offline recognition includes programmed change of content into a picture into letter codes which are usable inside PC and content preparing applications. Offline recognition is more troublesome, as different people have assorted handwritten styles. Be that as it may, in the on-line framework, On-line character acknowledgment manages an information stream which originates from a transducer while the client is composing.

The normal equipment to gather information is a digitizing tablet which is electromagnetic or weight delicate. At the point when the client composes on the tablet, the progressive developments of the pen are changed to a progression of electronic flag which is remembered and investigated by the PC. Optical Character Recognition (OCR) is a field of research in design acknowledgment, manmade brainpower and machine vision, signal processing. It is additionally aforementioned that Optical character recognition (OCR) is reffered to as associate Off-line character recognition system during which system scans and static image of the characters ought to be recognized. It alludes to the mechanical or electronic interpretation of pictures of manually written character or printed content into machine code with no variation [2] (Fig. 1).

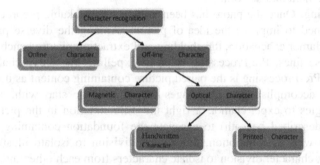

Fig. 1. Character recognition system

OCR comprises of many stages, for example, Pre-handling, Segmentation, Feature Extraction, Classifications and Recognition. The contribution of one stage is the yield of subsequent stage. The undertaking of preprocessing identifies with the evacuation of clamor and variety in written by hand. A few region where OCR utilized including mail arranging, bank preparing, record perusing and postal address acknowledgment require Off-line character recognition systems, design acknowledgement (Fig. 2).

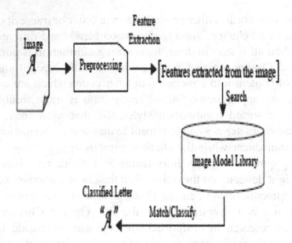

Fig. 2. Periods of general character recognition system

1.1 Using Techniques

The process of OCR is a composite activity comprises different phases. These stages are as per the following: Image securing: To catch the picture from an outer source like scanner or a camera and so forth.

Preprocessing: Once the photo has been gotten, unmistakable preprocessing steps can be performed to improve the idea of picture. Among the diverse preprocessing strategies are clamor evacuation, thresholding and extraction picture benchmark and so on. Along these lines, Pre-Processing helps in expelling the above challenges. The outcome after Pre-Processing is the paired picture containing content as it were. Along these lines, to accomplish this, few stages are required, to start with, some picture upgrade strategies to expel clamor or right the differentiation in the picture, second, thresholding (described beneath) to evacuate the foundation containing any scenes, watermarks as well as commotion, third, page division to isolate illustrations from content, fourth, character division to isolate characters from each other and, at long last, morphological preparing to improve the characters in situations where thresholding or potentially other pre-handling methods disintegrated parts of the characters or added pixels to them. This technique is utilized generally in different character acknowledgment usage.

Thresholding: Thresholding is a methodology of changing over a grayscale input picture to a bi-level picture by using a perfect farthest point. The motivation behind thresholding is to extricate those pixels from some picture which speak to a protest (either message or other line picture information, for example, diagrams, maps). In spite of the fact that the data is paired the pixels speak to a scope of forces. In this way the goal of binarization is to check pixels that have a place with genuine frontal area districts with a solitary force and foundation areas with various powers (Fig. 3).

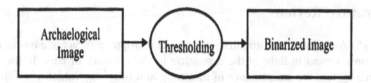

Fig. 3. Thresholding process

For a thresholding calculation to be extremely successful, it should protect legitimate and semantic substance. Different types of thresholding algorithms are as follows.

1. Global thresholding calculations
2. Neighborhood or flexible thresholding counts

In overall thresholding, a lone farthest point for all the photo pixels is used. At the point when the pixel estimations of the segments and that of foundation are genuinely predictable in their individual esteems over the whole picture, global thresholding could be used. [3]

Character segmentation: In this progression, the characters in the picture are isolated to such an extent that they can be passed to acknowledgment motor. Among the least difficult systems are associated segment examination and projection profiles can be utilized. However in complex circumstances, where the characters are covering/broken or some clamor is available in the picture. In these circumstances, propel character division strategies are utilized. In this progression, the picture is sectioned into characters before being passed to characterization stage.

The division can be performed expressly or verifiably as a side-effect of grouping stage [2]. Also, alternate periods of OCR can help in giving logical data valuable to division of picture.

Feature extraction: The fragmented characters are then procedures to separate diverse highlights. In light of these highlights, the characters are perceived. Different types of features that can be used extracted from images are moments etc. The removed features should be capably measurable, restrain intra-class assortments and lifts between class assortments.

Character classification: This step maps the features of segmented image to different categories or classes. There are distinctive kinds of character order systems. Basic characterization procedures depend on highlights removed from the structure of picture and uses diverse choice guidelines to group characters. Statistical pattern classification methods are based on probabilistic models and other statistical methods to classify the characters.

Post processing: After classification, the results are not 100% correct, especially for complex languages. Post planning methodologies can be performed to upgrade the precision of OCR systems. These systems uses normal dialect handling, geometric and semantic setting to redress blunders in OCR comes about. For instance, post processor can utilize a spell checker and lexicon, probabilistic models like Markov chains and n-grams to enhance the exactness. The time and space multifaceted nature of a post processor ought not be high and the use of a post-processor ought not cause new blunders [4].

2 Literature Review

Jain et al. [5] As of late the distinguishing proof and stopping of vehicle has turned into a troublesome errand in light of the expansion in the quantity of cars. In the existing surveillance system the maintenance of incoming and outgoing vehicles is difficult. To determine this issue various strategies can be utilized out of which Optical Character Recognition (OCR) is most the appropriate innovation. OCR has been the subject of research for more than decades. OCR is characterized as the change of examined pictures into machine encoded content. The proposed system is implementing the OCR technology to park the vehicles in smart way and keep the track of the vehicles which are entering and leaving. The framework will catch the picture of number plate of the vehicle utilizing the OCR procedure and will in a flash refresh the database.

Badwaik et al. [6] as more and more learners are opting for online learning, e-learning industry is working on improving learning experience of online user by providing relevant substance and part of extra references. Since online students generally incline toward video instructional exercises, recognizing real subjects and sub-topics canvassed in video instructional exercise is a major test. As of late, for productive information sharing and interoperability over web parcel of consideration is given to semantic web. In this paper, we propose a semantic electronic structure for programmed subject ID from video instructional exercises so as to recognize the ideas and their related semantically significant resources. Our system distinguishes pertinent theme utilizing disambiguation in e-learning asset which helps students in more engaged examination.

Chiron et al. [7] In this paper, we plan to assess the effect of OCR mistakes on the utilization of a noteworthy online stage: i.e. Gallica digital library from the National Library of France. It accounts for more than 100M OCRed documents and receives 80M search queries every year. In this uncommon situation, we show two basic obligations. Initial, an exceptional corpus of OCRed records made out of 12M characters near to the differentiating most bewildering quality level is shown and given, with an equivalent offer of English- and French-written documents. Next, statistics on OCR errors have been computed thanks to a novel alignment method introduced in this paper. Making utilization of all the client inquiries submitted to the Gallica entrance more than 4 months, we exploit our blunder model to propose a marker for anticipating the relative hazard that questioned terms confound focused on assets because of OCR mistakes, underlining the basic degree to which OCR quality effects on computerized library get to.

Xiaoxiao et al. [8] Another strategy for computerized number acknowledgment for mechanical advanced meters in substation is clarified in this paper, which acknowledge straight SVM unending supply of Oriented Gradients (HOG) highlights. The grids of Histograms of Oriented Gradient descriptors considerably exceed for feature detection of the gray image which has more information than binary image. A unique approach with division of locale of character picture is proposed in this paper, which is critical to the further HOG include location. SVM classifier is utilized as a part of the recognition parade and result demonstrates that HOG has better execution on digit arrangement in the substation examination robot instrument recognition.

Lusa et al. [9] Programmed activity sign acknowledgment by PCs is winding up broadly attractive actually. Techniques for programmed movement sign discovery are utilized as a part of the car business, in models of car autos, as well as in mass-created models and cell phones. In this paper, a two-stage calculation in view of key focuses include locators to identify and perceive street signs will be exhibited. The principal phase of the calculation finds objects show in the scene and decides their shape in light of geometric properties. In order to reduce the number of found objects first phase includes two additional steps to remove too large and too small objects, and to merge objects of the same shape found in a similar area of the scene into one object. The second stage includes appropriate examination of recognized question with street signs from the information database in light of distinguished keypoints.

Cho [10] This paper gives a novel scene content location calculation, Canny Text Detector, which takes advantage of the contrast between picture edge and content for viable content limitation with enhanced review rate. As closely associated edge pixels construct the structural information of an object, we observe that consistent characters compose a meaningful word/sentence which can shared a parallel properties such as spatial location, size, color, and stroke width in spite of language. In any case, regular scene content discovery approaches have not completely used such likeness, but rather generally depend on the characters characterized with high certainty, can lead to a low review rate. With a specific end goal to rapidly and heartily confine an assortment of writings we can misuse a correlation. By the utilization of unique Canny edge indicator, our calculation makes utilization of twofold limit and hysteresis following to recognize writings of low certainty. As indicated by exploratory outcomes on open datasets we can show that our calculation beats the state-of the-art scene content identification techniques in wording of detection rate.

Hengel et al. [11] This paper communicated the detail study and examination of different character acknowledgment techniques and methodologies: in subtle elements like as stream and kind of moved toward procedure was utilized, sort of calculation has worked with help of innovation has actualized foundation of the proposed system and development best outcomes stream for the every system. This paper and furthermore communicated the primary destinations and philosophy of different OCR calculations, as neural systems calculation, auxiliary calculation, bolster vector calculation, factual calculation, format coordinating calculation alongside how they classified, recognized, govern shaped, surmised for acknowledgment of characters and pictures.

Chopra et al. [12] This paper shows a straightforward, proficient, and ease way to deal with develop OCR for perusing any record that has settle text dimension and penmanship style. Optical Character Recognition in this paper utilizes database to perceive English characters which makes this OCR extremely easy to oversee which accomplishes proficiency and less computational cost. The component extraction advance of optical character acknowledgment is the most imperative. It can be utilized with other existing OCR techniques with the end goal of English content acknowlededgment. This system offers an upper edge by having an advantage i.e. its scalability, i.e. in spite of the fact that it is arranged to peruse a predefined set of report designs, as proposed in this paper for English records, it can be arranged to perceive new composes.

3 Propose Work

In this paper propose work define that how to extract feature from the image using various steps and technique, we will define propose work using flow chart that will define in below (Fig. 4).

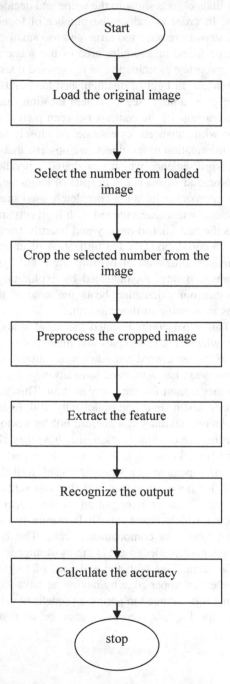

Fig. 4. Flow chart of propose work

Propose Algorithm-
Step 1- first we takes an original image.
Step 2-After choosing an image now select the number from the image.
Step 3-after selecting the number crop the selected number.
If (RGB)
Cropping=rgb2gray
Else
Gray=gray
Step 4-after crooping the number prepocess the cropped gray image.
Step 5- Extract the feature from the preprocessed image.
Step 6- after feature extraction we can recognize the output.
Step 7-the last step calculate the accuracy.

4   Result Analysis

See Figs. 5, 6, 7, 8, 9, 10, 11, 12 and Table 1.

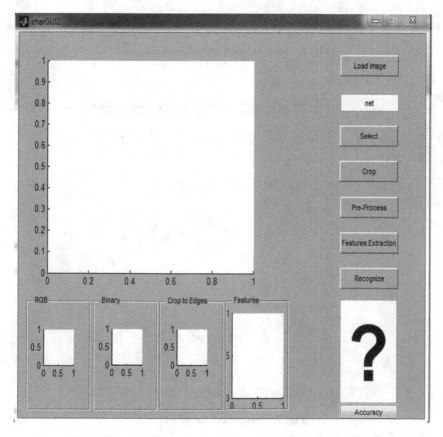

Fig. 5. First run the our code than we obtain this type of figure.

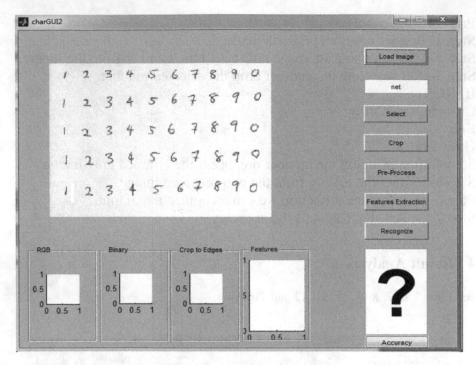

Fig. 6. Now browses the original image.

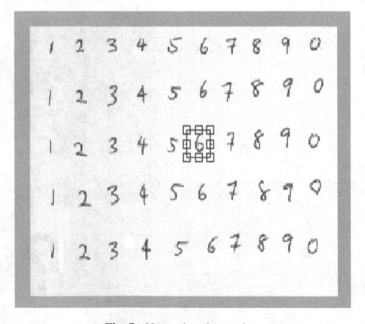

Fig. 7. Now select the number.

Fig. 8. Now crop the selected number.

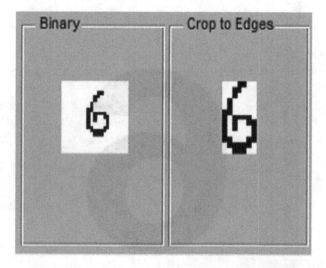

Fig. 9. now preprocesses the cropped image.

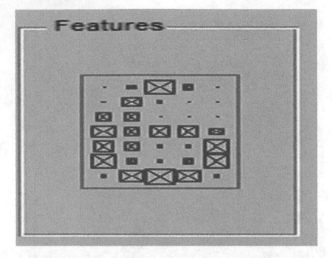

Fig. 10. Now extract feature from the preprocessed image.

Fig. 11. Finally analysis the image.

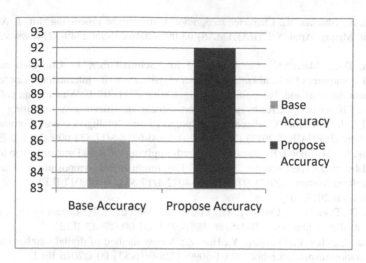

Fig. 12. Comparison on base accuracy and propose accuracy

Table 1. Comparison on base accuracy and propose accuracy

Base accuracy	Propose accuracy
86	92

5 Conclusion

In this paper, we have described the methodology of the Selection and feature extraction based on OCR. The experimental setting is done by capturing 1 image from several website. The outcomes demonstrated that our proposed technique can altogether transpose the choice and highlight extraction. The general precision of the proposed strategy is 92%. Beside, this method can use directly in the other captured image types such as scanned image and photography images etc.

Future work includes comparisons by using other distance measures with the best meta-heuristic -the considered computationally cheaper-, found in this work, in order to determine if the convergence of the algorithm is improved according the cost function used.

References

1. Islam, N., Islam, Z., Noor, N.: A survey on optical character recognition system. J. Inf. Commun. Technol.-JICT **10**(2) (2016). ISSN 2409-6520
2. Bhatia, E.N.: Optical character recognition techniques: a review. Int. J. Adv. Res. Comput. Sci. Softw. Eng. **4**(5) (2014). ISSN 2277 128X

3. Sharma, S., Sharma, R.: Character recognition using image processing. Int. J. Adv. Eng. Technol. Manag. Appl. Sci. (IJAETMAS) **03**(09) (2016). ISSN 2349-3224. www.ijaetmas. com
4. Ciresan, D.C., Meier, U., Gambardella, L.M., Schmidhuber, J.: Convolutional neural network committees for handwritten character classification. In: International Conference on Document Analysis and Recognition, Beijing, China, 2011. IEEE, Washington, D.C. (2011)
5. Jain, K., Choudhury, T., Kashyap, N.: Smart vehicle identification system using OCR. In: 3rd IEEE International Conference on Computational Intelligence and Communication Technology (IEEE-CICT 2017) (2017). 978-1-5090-6218-8/17/$31.00 ©2017 IEEE
6. Badwaik, K., Mahmood, K., Raza, A.: Towards applying OCR and semantic web to achieve optimal learning experience. In: 2017 IEEE 13th International Symposium on Autonomous Decentralized Systems (2017). 978-1-5090-4042-1/17 $31.00 © 2017 IEEE. https://doi.org/ 10.1109/isads.2017.40
7. Chiron, G., Doucet, A., Coustaty, M., Visani, M., Moreux, J.-P.: Impact of OCR errors on the use of digital libraries. 978-1-5386-3861-3/17/$31.00 ©2017 IEEE
8. Xiaoxiao, C., Hua, F., Guoqing, Y., Hao, Z.: A new method of digital number recognition for substation inspection robot" 978-1-5090-3228-0/16/$31.00 ©2016 IEEE
9. Lusa, M.: Recognition of multiple traffic signs using keypoints feature detectors. In: 2016 international Conference and Exposition on Electrical and Power Engineering (EPE 2016), 20–22 October, Iasi, Romania (2016)
10. Cho, H., Sung, M., Jun, B.: Canny text detector: fast and robust scene text localization algorithm. In: 2016 IEEE Conference on Computer Vision and Pattern Recognition (2016)
11. Hengel, S.K., Rama, B.: Comprative study with analysis of OCR algorithms and invention analysis of character recognition approached methodologies. 1st IEEE International Conference on Power Electronics. Intelligent Control and Energy Systems (ICPEICES-2016), 978-1-4673-8587-9/16/$31.00 ©2016 IEEE
12. Chopra, S.A., Ghadge, A.A. Padwal, O.A. Punjabi, K.S., Gurjar, G.S.: Optical character recognition. Int. J. Adv. Res. Comput. Commun. Eng. **3**(1) (2014)

A High Performance BPSK Trans Receiver Using Level Converter for Communication Systems

Akula Rajesh[1], B. L. Raju[2(✉)], and K. Chenna Kesava Reddy[3]

[1] JNTU, Hyderabad, India
rajeshakula07@gmail.com
[2] ACE Engineering College, Hyderabad, India
blraju2@gmail.com
[3] JNTU College of Engineering, Jagityal, India
kesavary@yahoo.com

Abstract. The Earlier design of VLSI Systems focused on optimizing Area, rather than Power Consumption in order to perform real time functions. Mobile Communication Market utilizing the wireless technology has developed many portable devices whose primary requirement is power consumption. The primary parameter to be considered is to reduce the total power consumed in the system with secondary parameter to be considered is reduction of size, improvement in battery life. In the design of System on Chip, low power design is the predominant parameter for portable devices. Dual supply voltage is used to reduce the power consumed without degrading the performance in an VLSI circuit (IC). The Designed Logic Level Converter power consumption is compared with the Existing Level Converter. Transreceiver is designed with Dual Vdd and multi Vth using various Level Converters. The Transreceiver is analysed for power consumption with different Level Converters. The impact of process variations is also examined; the effect of temperature on process parameters is analyzed using Cadence Tools. This work provides different methods of designing Level Converters and the power consumption of Low Power Tran receivers circuit using Level Converters.

Keywords: Dynamic power · Dual supply voltages · Multi Vth
Level converters · Transreceiver

1 Introduction

For designing a Complex VLSI Chip, the Various Entities to be considered in designing are Speed, Area, Power Consumption, Cost and Performance. These are optimized as Low Area, High Performance (decided by the speed which is a design constraint), Low Cost and High Reliability. The Major Parameter Customer prefers is battery life i.e. Power Consumed by the product. This issue is solved by providing improved battery capacity (which leads to dissipation of heat and consumes more area) or using alternate logics of design which consume low power. Logic Network and Clock distribution network both consume proportionate amount of power depending on

© Springer Nature Singapore Pte Ltd. 2019
S. Verma et al. (Eds.): CNC 2018, CCIS 839, pp. 89–98, 2019.
https://doi.org/10.1007/978-981-13-2372-0_8

the design. The high clock frequency used and scaled transistor size and supply voltage lead to high density of transistors but in turn causes environment parameters to affect on the characteristics of the design. The power consumed by the clock is proportionate to that of the total power. The clock requires driving large load capacitance and it needs to switch as many times which increases dynamic power consumption. Any communication system consists of a transmitter section and a receiver section. If the information is transmitted as EM waves via wireless medium, digital communication technique is noise free and fidelity compare to an analog communication. Among Digital Communication Techniques, BPSK modulation techniques is the best method and consume less signal power [1].The Total Power Dissipation is the power used to charge and discharge the output capacitance in the circuits.

$$P = \text{freq} \, C_{\text{Load}} \, V_{\text{dd}}^2.$$

Where freq is the Operating Clock Frequency, C_{Load} is the Effective Capacitance, Vdd - the operating voltage.

In today's innovative world, any kind of VLSI design has to consider less area, delay and power consumption. The main objective of designing Level shifter is to minimize the power, area and delay requirements to design a multi thresholding and supply voltage conversion circuits. An SOC Voltage conversion has two stages that are voltage reference stage and buffer stage. With this technique VddL to VddH conversion VLSI circuit has been implemented [2]. Another kind of Level shifter for conversion of supply voltage from VddL to VddH has been implemented with 0.18-µm CMOS process. The typical values of VddL range from 0.9 to 1.5 V and VddH range from 1.8 V to 2.5 V. The supply voltage VDD can be reduced even below 1.0 V [3]. Low power application can be implemented by using one supply level converter by using supply level converter. With this complexity can be reduced but not suitable for high power applications [4]. In CMOS technology power reduction is mainly depends on channel area and threshold values of the system [5]. This can be achieved by using Simultaneous voltage scaling and gate sizing, with this power consumption has been minimized [6].

In Data salvaging technique, domain selection and directory-based error detection has minimized the power consumption of the design [7]. Today's technology focuses in reducing the power consumption of design which can increase the performance of the system and can extend battery life. In a large design, some circuits in the system requires very high voltage as compared other blocks [8]. To provide required voltage level, a new power efficient voltage level shifting architecture has been implemented. This circuit design has reduced the transition time of the output signals [9]. This conversion makes extremely challenging task in the design of any kind of VLSI circuit. To conquer this, clock synchronization and low swing inverter has been introduced to design static and dynamic converters for low threshold logics [10]. There are various kinds of the level shifters were implemented with CMOS technology and has been analyzed for power consumption of the circuits [11]. Here considered three kinds of the level shifters such as modified single supply, modified conventional, and modified contention mitigated. The power consumption of all the three kinds of proposed circuits has been reduced.

A Multiple voltage supply system has got very much importance in any kind of CMOS circuit design with less power consumption. The integrated chip has been divided into various regions according to their operating voltages. Here a novel high performance level converter has been implemented on Cadence Virtuoso tool with UMC 180 nm CMOS technology [12]. Several kinds of level shifter have been designed and comparison has been done by considering the parameters such as output voltage, delay and power consumption of the shifter [13]. The all above methods have consuming more power, delay and area, still these have to be minimized [14].

The main aim of the research work is to design a Multi threshold level converter based transceiver for low power high efficiency communication applications. To achieve the main objective, the following are sub-objectives:

1. To develop a Optimized Transmitter and Receiver using multi threshold voltage based Level Converter. To design a Tran receiver with Low Power utilization with Level Converter and compare it with a Transreceiver without Level Converter.
2. To design different Level Converters using Dual Vdd and Multi Vth and compare the Power consumption of Transreceivers among them.
3. To evaluate the performance of the proposed schemes through simulations in Cadence Tools and compare with the existing schemes.

The proposed method has introducing a novel power as well as area efficient voltage level shifter in the transceiver system to reach the optimized consumption of the resources and also various thresholding levels are achieved using level shifter.

2 Proposed Methodology

In proposed method we have introduced a multi threshold level shifter in transceiver system for optimized power consumption. The transmitter of the system consists of analog to Digital converter (DAC), NRZ Encoder, BPSK Modulator, Ring Oscillator (VCO), level shifter and receiving section has phase detector and integrator, Digital to Analog converter (ADC) as shown in the Fig. 1. A level shifter is a digital logic, which converts digital signals from one logic level to another logic level. It is also called a translator.

The analog message signal (low frequency) x(t) is given to ADC converter which is digitized (1's & 0's) and is fed serially to NRZ Converter by using a Serial to Parallel Converter(Multiplexer). The NRZ Converter stands for Non Return to Zero (1 is encoded as +1 and 0 is encoded as −1. This is given as input to BPSK Modulator (CMOS Multiplier) which has two inputs low frequency message signal and high frequency carrier signal. The modulated output is a BPSK (Binary Phase Shift Keying). It means for +1 data the carrier is same but for −1. The carrier is given a phase shift of 180'phase shift. This is further boosted in the next stage and transmitted through an antenna. The Ring Oscillator will generate high frequency carrier signal with specified phase, this signal is applied to the level shifter to get the required level of the signal for modulation. The multiplier will give the modulated output by performing multiplication on the NRZ output and level shifter output as we can see in the Fig. 1. ADC stands for Analog to Digital Converter where the input analog signal. Compared with a

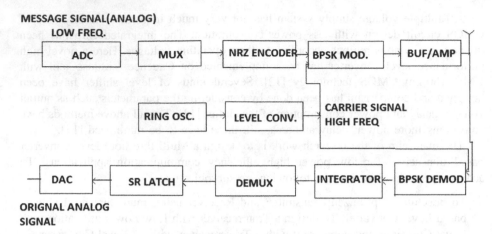

MESSAGE SIGNAL(ANALOG)
LOW FREQ.

ADC → MUX → NRZ ENCODER → BPSK MOD. → BUF/AMP

RING OSC. → LEVEL CONV. → CARRIER SIGNAL HIGH FREQ

DAC ← SR LATCH ← DEMUX ← INTEGRATOR ← BPSK DEMOD.

ORIGNAL ANALOG
SIGNAL

Fig. 1. Block diagram of the transceiver

reference voltage using a comparator and produces a digital output. In this design FLASH ADC is used. It consists of a voltage ladder with different reference voltage created by resistors. A flash converter requires $2^n - 1$ comparators for an n-bit conversion (Fig. 2).

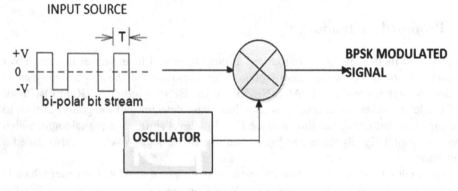

INPUT SOURCE

+V
0
-V
bi-polar bit stream

OSCILLATOR

BPSK MODULATED SIGNAL

Fig. 2. BPSK modulation

The high frequency carrier signal is modulated with respect to the message signal from information source. For +V of bit stream the output of BPSK Modulator is a high frequency signal with same phase. wheareas −V of bit stream the output of BPSK Modulator is a 180' phase shift of original signal

In the receiver section, the modulated BPSK signal and output of the level shifter is applied to the Demodulator to get the original signal. Depending on the phase difference the data is reconstructed and given to loop filter, which removes unwanted high frequency component. The output of the filter is given to the integrator to obtain the estimated data at the end of the receiving section and is converted back to analog form with DA converter. The high frequency carrier signal is demodulated to retrieve the message signal from modulated signal. For signal of same phase the output of BPSK demodulator is a +V Level. wheareas a signal of 180' phase is demodulated as −V bit stream (Fig. 3).

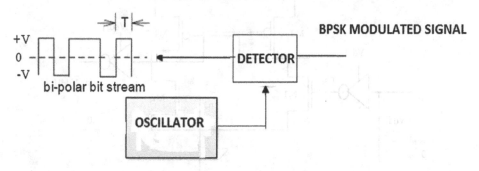

Fig. 3. BPSK demodulation

A Ring oscillator is designed as odd number of inverters where output of the last inverter drives the first inverter. Inverter is basically a NOT gate (Fig. 4).

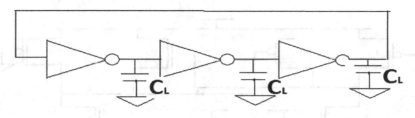

Fig. 4. Ring oscillator

The design is simulated with an existing Level Converter and a proposed Level Converter.

The Level Converter is used to shift the level of the input from VddL to VddH and Viceversa. The standard Level Converter consists of two nmos devices M1 and M2 whose pullup consists two pmos devices which are cross coupled i.e. output of one nmos device (M2) is driving the opposite pmos (M3). Similarly, the output of nmos device (M1) is driving the opposite pmos (M4). This Level Converter has a drawback of static dc current which occurs when a low voltage swing signal is driving a gate with high supply voltage.

Similarly a standard Level Converter (HL) can be designed by applying voltage as VddL to VddH and viceversa. It converts the signal from a Higher voltage range of gnd to VddH to a Lower voltage range of gnd to VddL.

In the proposed Level Converter the Level Shift is done from VddL to VddH V and Vice Versa. The static dc current is solved by designed P6 transistor with high threshold voltage. Thereby the design consists of mosfets with multi threshold voltage to reduce power consumed (Figs. 5 and 6).

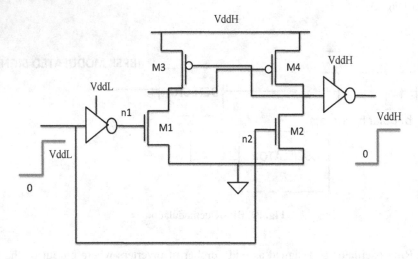

Fig. 5. Standard level converter

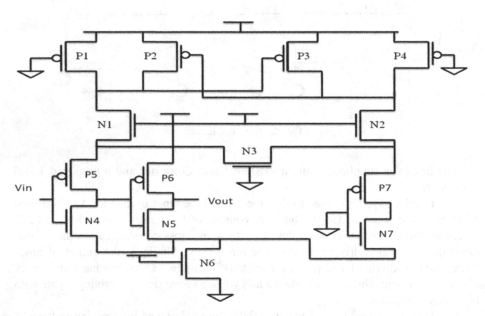

Fig. 6. Proposed level converter

3 Results

The design is implemented using Cadence tools which consists of Cadence Virtuoso Schematic Editor to generate a schematic and simulation is done using Analog Design Environment spectre simulator.

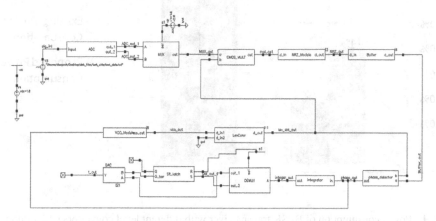

Fig. 7. Block diagram of BPSK transreceiver with level converter

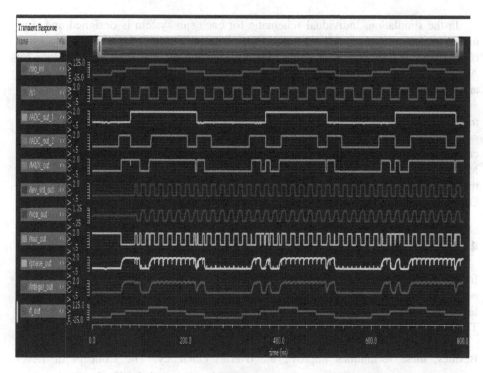

Fig. 8. Simulation results of BPSK transreceiver with level converter

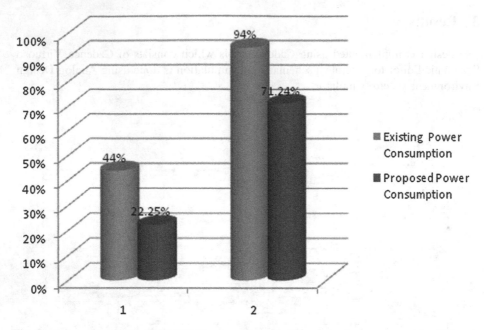

Fig. 9. Power consumption of BPSK transreceiver with different level converters under different temperatures.

In the simulation, Individual schematic for each sub system is designed and simulated according to the requirements and the parameters chosen for active and passive components and symbol is created in Virtuoso and saved. The simulation is done by ADEL and results are viewed in spectre simulator. The various analyses done in ADEL are DC Analysis, AC Analysis and Transient Analysis.

The Top module is designed by instantiating the sub modules in Virtuoso Schematic and Editor and is Simulated using Transient Analysis. The Results are verified with theoretical data. Transreceiver is designed with and without Level Converter and corresponding Power dissipation/consumption is verified & compared. In this paper Multi threshold BPSK Transreceiver is designed using Cadence Tools. The Figures are the design of sub systems of BPSK Transreceiver with Level Converter & Simulation Design of BPSK Transreceiver with level converter.

4 Conclusion

In this research work, a "Multi-Threshold Level Converter based transceiver for low power high efficiency Communication Applications" is developed by using various level converters. Comparison with Transreciever without Level Converters is done. The various Level Converters are analyzed with respect to Power reduction.

These techniques are used for yielding better throughput with reduced delay. Besides, these techniques improve the overall efficiency. The Concept of Level

Conversion can be used in system designed with multi Vdd and multi Vth and thus reduce power consumed instead of using single power supply (Figs. 7 and 8).

The "Multi-Threshold Level Converter based transceiver for low power high efficiency Communication Applications is evaluated by varying sources, such as Analog Data and Digital Data, transmission rates and arrival rates by measuring throughput and delay. The Multi-Threshold Level Converter based transceiver achieves improved Power consumption with compromise in area and speed as the density of transistors increases compared with "Transreceiver without Level Converters and Single threshold devices."

In most cases, Optimized Level Converter can be used for reducing the power consumed in the Transreceiver. Therefore, the Transreceiver without and with Level Converters can be designed as multi vdd systems. Instead of a bpsk transreceiver, the concept of multi vdd and multi Vth can be extended to QPSK and M-PSK modulator and demodulator. The system on chip designed can further be handled for power consumption using the concept of multi vdd and multi vth. The Proposed method have power consumption less than the existing techniques and temperature effect is shown in Fig. 9.

References

1. Chang, I.J., Kim, J.-J., Roy, K.: Robust level converter design for sub-threshold logic. In: Proceedings of the 2006 International Symposium on Low Power Electronics and Design. ACM (2006)
2. Chu, K., Pulfrey, D.: Design procedures for differential cascode voltage switch circuits. IEEE J. Solid Circuits 21(6), 1082–1087 (1996)
3. Taur, Y., Ning, T.H.: Fundamentals of Modern VLSI Devices. Cambridge University, Cambridge
4. Kang, S.M., Leblebici, Y.: CMOS Digital Integrated Circuits: Analysis and Design, 3rd edn. MCGraw-Hill, New York
5. Chen, C., Sarrafzadeh, M.: Simultaneous voltage scaling and gate sizing for low-power design. IEEE Trans. Circuits Syst. II: Analog Digital Signal Process. 49(6), 400–408 (2002)
6. Kulkarni, S.H., Sylvester, D.: High performance level conversion for dual VDD design. IEEE Trans. Very Large Scale Integr. (VLSI) Syst. 12(9), 926–936 (2004)
7. Zimmermann, R., Fichtner, W.: Low Power logic styles: CMOS versus pass transistor logic. IEEE J. Solid State Circuits 31(6), 792–803 (1996)
8. Thakur, S., Mehra, R.: CMOS design and single supply level shifter using 90 nm technology. In: Conference on Advances in Communication and Control Systems (2013)
9. Schultz, K.J., Francis, R.J., Smith, K.C.: Ganged CMOS. IEEE J. Solid State Circuits 25(3), 870–873 (1990)
10. Hamada, M., et al.: A top-down lowpower design technique using clustered voltage scaling with variable supply-voltage scheme. In: Proceedings of the IEEE Custom Integrated Circuits Conference, pp. 495–498, May 1998
11. Han, Y., Wang, Y., Li, H., Li, X.: Enabling near-threshold voltage (NTV) operation in multi-VDD cache for power reduction. In: 2013 IEEE International Symposium on Circuits and Systems (ISCAS). IEEE (2013)
12. Bellaouar, A., Elmasry, M.I.: BiCMOS nonthreshold logic for high-speed low-power. IEEE Solidcircuits

13. Heller, L., Griffin, W., Davis, J., Thomas, N.: Cascode voltage switch logic: a differential logic family. In: Proceedings of IEEE International Solid State Circuits Conference, pp. 16–17 (1984)
14. Wang, W.-T., et al.: Level shifters for high-speed 1 V to 3.3 V interfaces in a 0.13/spl mu/m Cu-interconnection/low-k CMOS technology. In: 2001 International Symposium on VLSI Technology, Systems, and Applications. Proceedings of Technical Papers. IEEE (2001)
15. Revathi, L., Deepika, P.: Design of low power VLSI circuits using cascode logic style, 41–47
16. Lau, K.T.: On-chip MOS supply voltage converter. School of Electrical and Electronic Engineering Nanyang Technological Institute Singapore. IEEE (1989)
17. Hosseini, S.R., Saberi, M., Lotfi, R.: An energy-efficient level shifter for low-power applications. In: 2015 IEEE International Symposium on Circuits and Systems (ISCAS). IEEE (2015)
18. Kumar, M., Arya, S.K., Pandey, S.: Level shifter design for low power applications. arXiv preprint arXiv:1011.0507 (2010)
19. Ahmad, G., Kumar, Y., Sahu, P.K.: High performance multi threshold voltage level converter for multi-VDD systems. In: 2013 Students Conference on Engineering and Systems (SCES). IEEE (2013)
20. Gupta, S., Kumar, M.: CMOS voltage level-up shifter–a review. In: Proceedings of 2nd International Conference on Emerging Trends in Engineering and Management. ICETEM (2013)
21. Zhou, J., Wang, C., Liu, X., Zhang, X., Je, M.: An ultra-low voltage level shifter using revised wilson current mirror for fast and energy-efficient wide-range voltage conversion from sub-threshold to I/O voltage. IEEE Trans. Circuits Syst. I Regul. Pap. 62(3), 697–706 (2015)
22. Lanuzza, M., Corsonello, P., Perri, S.: Low-power level shifter for multi-supply voltage designs. IEEE Trans. Circuits Syst. II Express Briefs 59(12), 922–926 (2012)

Connectivity Analysis of Mobile Ad Hoc Network Using Fuzzy Logic Controller

Poonam Rathore[✉] and Laxmi Shrivastava

Department of Electronics and Communication, Madhav Institute of Technology and Science, Gwalior, India
poonamrathore476@gmail.com, lselex@yahoo.com

Abstract. Nowadays, efficient and fast communication network is a necessity for various real life scenarios, as network connectivity problem is frequent in wireless ad hoc network. Various network parameters provide measures to ensure ideal network performance leading towards better QoS. This research paper focuses on the development of easier approach towards level of node connectivity using fuzzy logic for betterment of the ad hoc network performance, and, also evaluates an ideal transmission range which would ensure perfect node connectivity for a given number of nodes. Hence, ideal transmission range can be easily evaluated for given number of nodes, in such a way, that sure connectivity is achieved, using the easier method of fuzzy logic, as compared to that of the conventional method. Network simulations are performed using QualNet 6.1.

Keywords: Mobile ad hoc network · Network connectivity
AODV routing protocol · MATLAB · Fuzzy logic · QualNet 6.1

1 Introduction

A mobile ad-hoc network (MANET) is defined as a wireless network which consists of number of mobile nodes in an infrastructure-less environment. A wireless ad hoc network has dynamic topology, and node connectivity depends upon the device behavior, mobility pattern, distance between them, etc. Infrastructure-less networks lack any central controller for the nodes, therefore the nodes of such networks possess highly dynamic nature and interconnections of nodes vary continuously. Thus, such wireless ad-hoc networks communicate with the help of routing protocols, which provide routing paths between nodes [1]. In routing process, each node transmits data to other nodes such that the routes are discovered dynamically on a continuous basis, with the help of routing protocols. The main function of any routing protocol is to establish routing path between nodes, which provide efficient transmission of data with minimum delay, expense and bandwidth consumption [2].

QoS (Quality of Service) is defined as the set of parameters, which needs to be fulfilled by mobile ad-hoc networks (MANET) in order to ensure efficient and faster communication between the source and destination nodes. These parameters vary according to the different networking layer. Most commonly used QoS parameters for performance analysis of ad-hoc networks are bandwidth, delay and jitter. Improving

© Springer Nature Singapore Pte Ltd. 2019
S. Verma et al. (Eds.): CNC 2018, CCIS 839, pp. 99–109, 2019.
https://doi.org/10.1007/978-981-13-2372-0_9

QoS parameters for mobile ad-hoc networks is very crucial due to the dynamic nature of MANET topology and decentralization [3].

In this research paper, AODV routing protocol is employed by mobile ad-hoc networks for performance analysis in different environments. Ad-hoc On Demand Distance Vector (AODV) routing protocol is a reactive routing protocol which establishes routes on-demand. Thus, the transmission of topology information by nodes occurs only on demand. AODV uses routing tables with one entry per destination. Every node maintains two route entries i.e. (a) broadcast_id which increases each time the source broadcasts a route request packet (b) sequence number to prevent routing loops and to eliminate old, broken routes. Routes are maintained in AODV with the help of RREQ (route request), RREP (route reply) and RERR (route error) control messages [4].

2 Network Connectivity

In mobile ad hoc networks, connectivity differs due to the continuous node movement because of their dynamic property, causing network partition. Connectivity Management is difficult due to dynamic network topology, frequent link occurrence and nodes failure via interference, radio channel effects, and mobility and battery limitation. Hence, Connectivity is a major issue in mobile ad hoc network. The reasons behind failure in the network that divides the network into two or more parts and can obliterate end-to-end connectivity are classified into the following as given below:

2.1 Network Connectivity Issues

Node Failure. This happens when an intermediate node working as router is unavailable because of hardware and software failure, and, secondly, when the node is not in communication range of the network. It is also known as Device Failure.

Critical Point. In a topology such points are nodes and links which fail and cause network division into two or more parts. It is also known as Weak Point.

Link Failure. Link failure happens because of many factors such as link obstacle among communicating nodes, node mobility, fading and high interference. It is also known as Edge Failure.

Power Failure. Power failure happens when the node battery is very low, and hence the node cannot work as router. It is also known as Battery Failure [5].

2.2 Literature Review

Node connectivity was first defined by Cheng and Robertazziin in 1989. They studied the effect of node density and node's broadcast transmission range in a multi hop radio network followed by spatial Poisson method. They prescribed that for transmission range optimization, its value must be low bounded to achieve ideal network connectivity. But, this method is difficult to implement practically [6]. Based on previous work, this research paper studies the Poisson distributed nodes disconnection. It gives comparison between node's critical coverage range and critical transmission range in a square area based on Poisson fixed density [7]. This issue is studied for one dimensional segment which provides critical range of transmission for Poisson distributed nodes in given area of square. But, these researches were difficult to implement in real situation, since, in Poisson process deployed nodes are originally random variable and only its average value can be determined [8].

2.3 Definition

Connectivity is the route directness between nodes in a network topology. For a given network with $|N|$ nodes, where $N = \{n1, n2, n3....n|N|\}$, and the degree of node (n_j) is deg (n_i), then connectivity is defined as:

$$\text{Connectivity (NW)} = \sum_{i=1}^{|N|} \frac{\deg(n_i)}{\binom{|N|}{2}}. \tag{1}$$

Where, $\binom{|N|}{2} = |N|^2 - |N|$

A Network has full connectivity when the Connectivity of the Network Connectivity (NW) is 1. The necessary condition for full connectivity is described as:

$$\sum_{i=1}^{|N|} \deg(n_i) = ||N|^2 - |N| \tag{2}$$

Full connectivity implies that the transmission range of a network is more than or equal to the longest distance between any given node pair in the network and the node degree is $|N| - 1$. The nodes in this network are capable of transferring data. But, the required transmission range is higher. This network topology results into high channel interference, which lowers the network QoS due to very high transmission range.

Each node has a definite maximum transmission power range P_{MAX}. P_a is the transmission power of node a. α is the path loss exponent and τ is the minimum average SNR required for decoding received data. d_{ab} is the distance between node a and node b. For a source node i to communicate with node j in a given straight line as shown in Fig. 1, it should follow [9]

$$P_a(d_{ab}) - \alpha \geq \tau \tag{3}$$

Where, $P_a \leq P_{MAX}$.

3 Fuzzy Logic

MATLAB which refers to Matrix Laboratory is ideal software for high level language programming in diverse environments, basically science and technology, which may include fuzzy logic, DSP system, instrument control, econometrics and lots more.

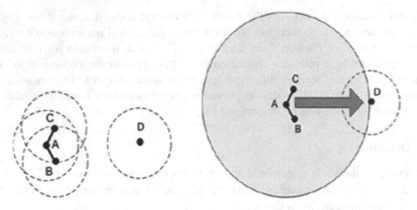

Fig. 1. Effect of transmission range on network connectivity

MATLAB provides easy approach towards intricate problems through simple programming, separate toolboxes and also GUI.

In this research paper, MATLAB software is utilized to embed the concept of fuzzy logic, in order to provide an easier and feasible approach towards perfect network connectivity for a given transmission range and number of nodes in a wireless ad hoc network, thereby, ensuring efficient network performance by improving QoS. In MATLAB's Fuzzy Logic Toolbox, FIS editor is provided for fuzzy inference system development. Mamdani's fuzzy inference system is taken in this research paper. The block description of mamdani's fuzzy inference system is given in Fig. 2 [10].

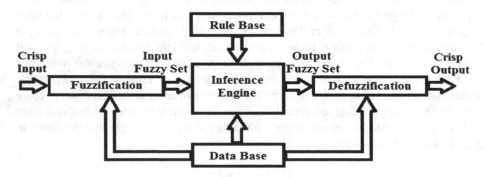

Fig. 2. Block description of fuzzy inference system

The crisp inputs are transformed generating input fuzzy set through fuzzification. After that, the inference engine computes the output fuzzy set with the help of knowledge base which comprises of fuzzy if-then rules in rule base and knowledge about linguistic functions to map called membership functions of the I/O fuzzy set in data base. Finally, the output fuzzy set is transformed generating crisp outputs. Fuzzy Logic is analogous to the human brain functioning, thus enabling feasible computational learning [11].

3.1 Proposed Work

The implemented fuzzy inference system is given in Fig. 3. It consists of two inputs, i.e., number of nodes having membership functions {Low, Medium, High} and transmission range having membership functions {Low, Medium, High} and one output, i.e., network connectivity having membership functions {Poorly-Connected, Surely-Connected}. The Input-Output variables associated with FIS are given in Figs. 4, 5 and 6, retrieved from MATLAB fuzzy logic toolbox.

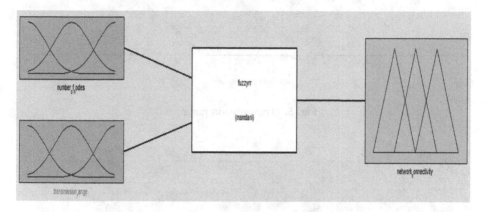

Fig. 3. Fuzzy inference system

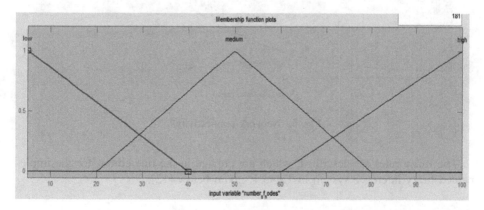

Fig. 4. Number of nodes

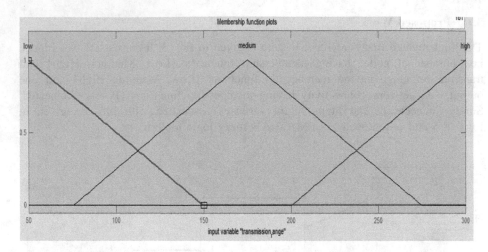

Fig. 5. Transmission range

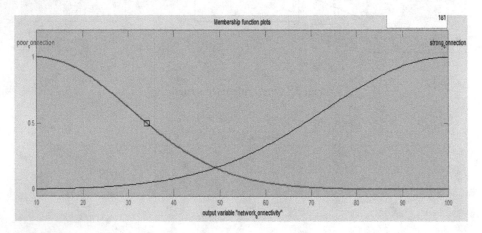

Fig. 6. Network connectivity

The fuzzy rules are described, which are created in the rule editor, for the implemented fuzzy inference system in Table 1, given below [12]:-

Table 1. Fuzzy rule base

Number of nodes Transmission range	Low	Medium	High
Low	Poor connection	Poor connection	Poor connection
Medium	Strong connection	Strong connection	Strong connection
High	Strong connection	Strong connection	Strong connection

The output consequent to given set of inputs can be obtained using rule viewer, which is graphically depicted using surface viewer. Figure 7 represents the snapshot of FIS rule viewer and Fig. 8 represents the FIS surface viewer, given below:-

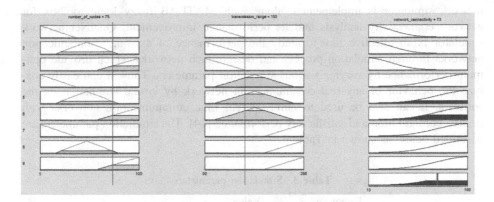

Fig. 7. Snapshot of FIS rule viewer

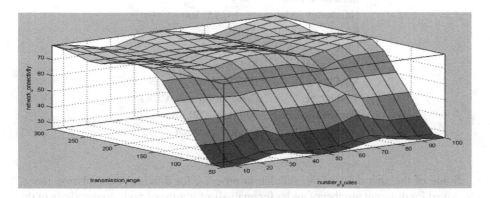

Fig. 8. FIS surface viewer

In Fuzzy Simulation, estimation of network connectivity is being done on the basis of number of nodes and transmission range, which are given in Table 2, as shown below:

Table 2. Fuzzy based simulation parameters

Transmission range, dBm	100	150	250
Number of nodes			
25	49.2	73.8	73.8
50	47.5	77.4	74.8
75	50.6	73	73
100	47.5	77.4	74.8

4 Simulation Environment and Parameters

In earlier research papers, network connectivity analysis has been done using NS 2 network simulator in its older software versions. In this research paper, QualNet 6.1 network simulator is implemented, along with MATLAB fuzzy logic toolbox for network connectivity analysis and its performance improvement. QualNet network simulator is an effective tool to study the performance of existing communication networks through simulation process and design such networks which provide optimum performance by varying various simulation parameters. Thus, it can easily analyze the behavior of any real communication network by virtual simulation on the software. It can also be used to build up real time communication networks with desired configuration and satisfactory performance [14]. The simulation parameters are described below as shown in Table 3:

Table 3. Simulation parameters

Parameters	Value
Simulation area	$1000 \times 1000 \text{ m}^2$
Simulation time	300 s
Number of nodes	25, 50, 75, 100
Routing protocol	AODV
CBR	5, 10, 15, 20
Packet size	512 bytes
MAC layer	IEEE 802.11
Traffic type	Constant bit rate (CBR)
Transmission range	100, 150, 250 dBm
Antenna model	Omni directional

Some of the snapshots of the simulation process, for different transmission range, employed for different number of nodes for analysis of improved node connectivity of the network, are shown below, retrieved from QualNet network simulator (Figs. 9 and 10):

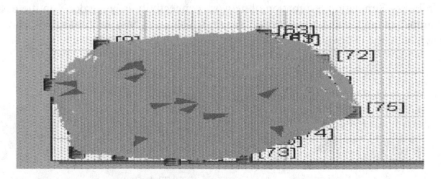

Fig. 9. Snapshot of 75 nodes during simulation employing 150 dBm transmit range

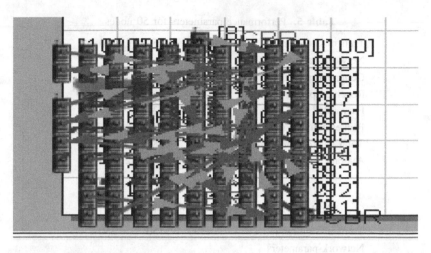

Fig. 10. Snapshot of 100 nodes during simulation employing 100 dBm transmit range

5   Results and Analysis

The performance parameters regarding measure of network connectivity are computed for various numbers of nodes ranging from 25 to 100 nodes using varying transmission range, namely 100, 150, 250 dBm. These performance parameters include generated packet, received packet, forwarded packet, packet delivery ratio, total packets dropped and average end-to-end delay. The respective performance parameters tables for various nodes are shown below (Tables 4, 5, 6 and 7):

Table 4. Performance parameters for 25 nodes

Transmission range	100	150	250
Network parameters			
Generated packet	126	152	154
Received packet	48	116	111
Forwarded packet	0	53	92
Packet delivery ratio	0.5	0.95	0.97
Total packets dropped	5	16	67
Average end to end delay (ms)	11.104	109.8	57.714

Table 5. Performance parameters for 50 nodes

Transmission range	100	150	250
Network parameters			
Generated packet	158	254	289
Received packet	116	176	270
Forwarded packet	60	121	151
Packet delivery ratio	0.5	0.98	0.97
Total packets dropped	10	38	76
Average end to end delay (ms)	20.083	729.832	188.52

Table 6. Performance parameters for 75 nodes

Transmission range	100	150	250
Network parameters			
Generated packet	246	334	395
Received packet	173	182	250
Forwarded packet	97	119	161
Packet delivery ratio	0.2	0.8	0.95
Total packets dropped	18	43	105
Average end to end delay (ms)	20.943	659.142	170.606

Table 7. Performance parameters for 100 nodes

Transmission range	100	150	250
Network parameters			
Generated packet	263	371	425
Received packet	172	193	278
Forwarded packet	127	134	159
Packet delivery ratio	0.2	0.9	0.96
Total packets dropped	46	58	10.6
Average end to end delay (ms)	45.977	906.055	304.553

From above performance parameters tables, it can be concluded that in case of 150 dBm, there are fewer packets generated and average end to end delay increases while packet delivery ratio drops, as compared to that of 250 dBm, in all the cases of nodes, namely from 25 to 100 nodes. For transmission range 100 dBm, although packets are generated in all cases, they are not being forwarded to the desired destination. Hence, 250 dBm transmission range is best suited for sure connectivity in given networks containing defined number of nodes.

6   Conclusion

With the help of this research paper, performance of mobile ad-hoc networks can be enhanced using network connectivity improvement, through transmission range and number of nodes in a fuzzy based approach, thereby, improving QoS. With the help of the fuzzy approach, it can be concluded that better QoS through sure connectivity is achieved in given networks of defined number of nodes through 250 dBm transmission range.

References

1. Bakshi, A., Sharma, A.K., Mishra, A.: Significance of mobile AD-HOC networks (MANETS). Int. J. Innov. Technol. Explor. Eng. (IJITEE) 2(4), 1–5 (2013). ISSN 2278-3075
2. Alslaim, M.N., Alaqel H.A., Zaghloul, S.S.: A comparative study of MANET routing protocols. In: Third International Conference on e-Technologies and Networks for Development (ICeND), pp. 178–182. IEEE, Beirut (2014)
3. de Gouveia, F.C., Magedanz, T.: Quality of service in telecommunication networks. In: Bellavista, P. (ed.) Telecommunication Systems and Technologies, 1st edn, vol. 2, pp. 77–97. Encyclopedia of Life Support Systems (EOLSS) (2009)
4. Perkins, C., Belding-Royer, E., Das, S.: AODV RFC3561 experimental edition (2003)
5. Jain, M., Chand, S.: Issues and challenges in node connectivity in mobile ad hoc networks: a holistic review. Wirel. Eng. Technol. 7, 24–35 (2016)
6. Cheng, Y.C., Robertazzi, T.G.: Critical connectivity phenomena in multihop radio models. IEEE Trans- Actions Commun. 37, 770–777 (1989)
7. Philips, T.K., Panwar, S.S., Tantawi, A.N.: Connectivity properties of a packet radio network model. IEEE Trans. Inf. Theory 35, 1044–1047 (1989)
8. Piret, P.: On the connectivity of radio networks. IEEE Trans. Inf. Theory 37, 1490–1492 (1991)
9. Chen, Y.T., Horng, M.F., Lo, C.C., Chu, S.C., Pan, J.S., Liao, B.Y.: A transmission power optimization with a minimum node degree for energy-efficient wireless sensor networks with full-reachability. Sensors 13, 3951–3974 (2013). ISSN 1424-8220
10. MATLAB® & Simulink® Release (2010). Commercial software package http://in.mathworks.com/products/matlab/
11. MATLAB and Fuzzy Logic Toolbox Release (2010). The MathWorks, Inc., Natick
12. Jain, M., Chand, S.: On Connectivity of Ad Hoc Network Using Fuzzy Logic. In: Mathematical Methods in Engineering and Economics, pp. 159–165
13. Khairnar, V.D., Kotecha, K.: Simulation-based performance evaluation of routing protocols in vehicular ad-hoc network. Int. J. Sci. Res. Publ. 3(10), 1–14 (2013)
14. Qualnet Simulator Software. http://web.scalable-networks.com/content/qualnet

Improved Election of Cluster Head Using CH-PSO for Different Scenarios in VANET

Bhairo Singh Rajawat[1($\boxtimes$)], Ranjeet Singh Tomar[1],
Mayank Satya Prakash Sharma[2], and Brijesh Kumar Chaurasia[1]

[1] ITM University Gwalior, Gwalior, MP, India
brajawat301@gmail.com, er.ranjeetsingh@gmail.com,
bkchaurasia.itm@gmail.com
[2] RJIT BSF, Takenpur, Gwalior, MP, India
mayanksintal@gmail.com

Abstract. VANET is one of such network which has received parcel of enthusiasm for most recent few years. VANET intends at providing recent inventive services identifying with different methods of transport and traffic organization to enable an assortment of clients to be most prominent educated and to make utilization of transport arranges all the more safely and additionally capably. Intelligent transport framework join propelled data technology, media transmission technology, sensor innovation, control innovation and PC innovation to an indispensable transportation management framework, which is based on a larger scale. Clustering is one of the efficient technique for exploiting the life span and scalability of VANET. Various cluster-primarily based routing procedures were projected inside the literature. However, in specifically proposed protocols, the conversation amongst an automobile and its cluster head (CH) is thought in more than a few communications. In this paper, a framework proposed for the decision of CH chosen using Particle Swarm Optimization (CH-PSO) algorithm.

Keywords: VANETs · Clustering · CH · Cluster node · Routing protocol
PSO · ITS

1 Introduction

VANET is one of such framework which has gotten parcel of energy for most recent couple of years. VANET unexpectedly transformed into a dynamic area of progress in context of its enormous potential to help entire new extent of structures which will sustain purpose to relieve drivers and voyagers [1] (Fig. 1).

Vehicles (moving nodes) and road side fixed equipments both of them can be either personal (owing to public service vehicles) or community transport means (like public service vehicles) supplier of facilities. In this system each taking part vehicle fills in as single node or remote switch, permitting autos which are 100 to 300 m from each other to associate and make a framework with a huge range. As vehicles leave the scope extend and get disengaged from the system, different vehicles can unite, linking vehicles to each another making a mobile internet [2].

© Springer Nature Singapore Pte Ltd. 2019
S. Verma et al. (Eds.): CNC 2018, CCIS 839, pp. 110–120, 2019.
https://doi.org/10.1007/978-981-13-2372-0_10

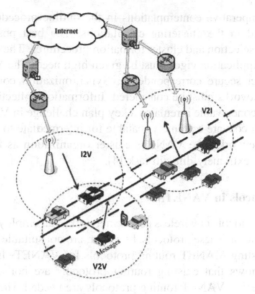

Fig. 1. VANET architecture

1.1 Clustering

During the time spent Clustering nodes like mobile devices, sensors, vehicles and so forth are grouped together in their geographical region as indicated by a few principles [3]. Usually each CN has a chance to become a CH but depending on the preposition used in the algorithms one become CH. For instance network availability, the sorts of nodes; (cluster relay) is utilized for CH choice. The size of the cluster varies from one cluster to another relying upon the transmission scope of the remote specialized gadget that a node uses.

An ideal cluster is spoken to as a hover with CH in the inside and CN around. Any CN can discuss straightforwardly with its CH and can speak with other CN either specifically or through their CH (either in 1- hop or n- hop) [3] (Fig. 2).

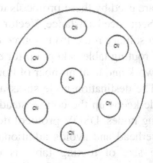

Fig. 2. Cluster with CH and cluster node

There are sure imperative contemplations in the outline procedure of cluster that ought to be followed in the clustering calculations. The best possible clusters are generated by the CH selection and cluster formation procedures. The message overhead should be reduced. Application vigor must be given high need. The VANET clustering plan needs to protect secure correspondence. Synchronization components and the adequacy of these networks must be considered. Information collection process makes energy optimization conceivable it remains a key plan challenge in VANET these days. These clustering protocols are extremely scalable for intermediate to big size networks. However in active networks like VANETs cluster organization as far as deferral and overhead included is extremely difficult task [4].

1.2   Routing Protocols in VANETS

Traditional routing protocols in wireless ad-hoc networks can employ into several types based on different criteria. These protocols, however, are not suitable for VANETs. The suitability of the existing MANET routing protocols for VANETs has been evaluated in [5]. The work shows that existing routing protocols are not able to satisfy the requirements and specific VANET routing protocols are needed. However, the routing protocols for wireless ad hoc networks can be broadly categorized into four types based on criteria as routing information update mechanism, use of temporal information for routing, routing topology and utilization of specific resources. In context of routing data or routing update mechanism are generally arranged as proactive or table-driven routing protocols, reactive or on-demand routing protocols and hybrid routing protocols.

1.2.1   Proactive Routing Protocol

This protocol is known as table-driven protocols which empower each structure node to keep up a routing table for securing the course data to every single distinctive node [5]. Each next hop node is kept up in the table passage that comes in the way towards the goal from the starting place. The routing table of each node gets refreshed at whatever point an adjustment in network topology happens because of which all the more overhead cost is incurred. These protocols offer genuine data to the network ease of use. There are various algorithms for finding shortest path which is shortest path algorithms. These algorithms are used by these protocols to discover which path has to be preferred. In Destination Sequenced Distance Vector (DSDV) Routing Protocol, routing protocol understands a solitary route from source to objective which has been kept up in the routing table. A routing table is kept up for each node containing data of each available node in the network and total number of bounces anticipated that would succeed those center points. The destination node starts a movement number to each section in the table. Each node keeps up the course steadfastness by conveying their routing table to the neighboring nodes. DSDV protocol does not permit cyclic routes, decreases control message overhead and avoids additional movement caused by frequent update. The aggregate size of routing table is decreased as DSDV keeps exclusively the most ideal way to every node rather than multi ways. DSDV can't control the networks congestion that reductions the routing efficiency [6].

1.2.2 Reactive Routing Protocol

This protocol is designed to overcome wastage of resources in maintaining the unwanted routes. These protocols used for the most part moved toward demand routing. They are called so in light of the way that on essential of a course that does not survive from source node to destination node, the course invention begins. These reductions the passage of the network and extras bandwidth flooding of the network assists in course revelation component by sending a route request for message. Any node existing on the course towards the destination on reception of the request message sends back a course reaction message to the starting place node using unicast correspondence. These routing protocols have high course discovering dormancy and are reasonable for vast estimated mobile ad-hoc networks which are very mobile and have much of the time evolving topology [4]. Other protocols of this types are Dynamic Source Routing (DSR), Temporarily Ordered Routing Algorithm (TORA), Ad-hoc On-demand Distance Vector (AODV), Associatively Based Routing (ABR) and Light-weight Mobile Routing (LMR) etc.

1.2.3 Hybrid Routing Protocol

It is the combination of the best features of the above two categories. For routing within certain distance or specific geographical zone, a table-driven approach is used. However, for nodes that are located beyond this zone, an on-demand approach is used.

1.3 Intelligent Transportation Systems

ITS join impelled data development, media transmission innovation, sensor innovation, control development and PC innovation to a crucial transportation administration structure, which depends on a greater scale. Intelligent VANET goes for giving present day creative services identifying with various procedures for transport and traffic organization, to draw in assorted clients to be greatest knowledgeable and to build employ of transport organizes more carefully and more productively [7]. The probable of Intelligent VANET is to assist acknowledge more extensive transport policy objectives lies in their wide assortment of utilizations in the diverse methods of transport for the two travelers and freight.

With the emotional increment in the populace and the development of urban areas' scales, the biggest urban communities are confronting genuine movement issues. These issues, for example, clog, contamination and mischance are getting to be a standout amongst the most huge bottlenecks that limit the advancement of these urban areas. The high caliber of life, making places availability and uniting individuals and products are the indications of a phenomenal clever framework.

Conventional activity arrangements, for example, assembling the city freeway framework, upgrading the thickness of the street, metro developments, which have produced some periodical results, demonstrate their confinements when managing the quandary urban communities defy today. Undertakings like GPPQ which targets European mainland is buckling down in creating applications and solutions for lessen the fuel utilization and blockage control as the oil assets will turn out to be rare in future. Other outstanding task, for example, ITIF which has completed significant works moved and raised the requirement for applications in Intelligent Transportation

Systems. Wise VANET is all the more generally connected to address the movement issues and give a more secure, more proficient and more monetary transportation framework, adding to make a superior city.

1.4 Particle Swarm Optimization

PSO is a heuristic optimization algorithm accredited by Kennedy and Eberhart in [8]. It was expected to deal with non- linear persistent optimization issues. It is a stochastic optimization technique based on the swarm movement and intelligence. PSO motivated from the sociological conduct of bird flocking can acquire optimal results. In this algorithm every particle moves to scan for the optimum solutions and subsequently has a speed. It regards every molecule as a point in N-dimensional space which appropriately modifies its "flying" in view of its encounters and every molecule has a memory to store its past best arrangements. ACO and PSO both are the promising varieties of swarm intelligence.

The PSO algorithm can be outlined in the going with propels

```
1. Randomly instate a swarm with levelheaded
   earth discrete position vectors.
2. Randomly consign a sensible speed vector to
   each particle.
3. Record the fitness of the entire people.
4. Determine the best molecule execution among
   the social affair.
5. Update velocity and position vectors as
   appeared by (6) and (7) for every particle.
6. Discrete the position vector.
7. If any iota flies outside the possible
   arrangement space, restore the molecule to
   its best ahead of time accomplished feasible
   solution.
8. Repeat stages 1 - 7 until the moment that the
   minute that most unmistakable number of
   cycles is come to [8].
```

The rest of the paper is organized as follows. Section 2 presents the related work; Proposed work is presented in Sect. 3. Results and analysis are discussed in Sect. 4; Sect. 5 concludes the work.

2 Related Work

In the [9] scheme, an effective new approach coordinating transmitter- oriented repetitions, ESD bitmap, message sequence number, and modulo based waiting mini-slot is given to conquer conceivable simultaneous clock due among close nodes and conceivable message impacts in the traditional separation based clock for determination of multi-bounce forwarders. The new logical models represent the effect of the Nakagami fading channel with distance dependent way loss and vehicle mobility on the reliability and execution. Extensive simulations are led to check the accuracy of our proposed plan and models under realistic network parameter settings [9]. Another proposed protocol plays out the message dispersal among MVs in two level organizations i.e. TI and T2 which diminishes the network overhead by allocating it amongst the two levels is presented in [10]. The break down the endeavored transmission likelihood of every road segment and the most extreme energy of dynamic transmitters, including their hypothetical regards [11]. In [12], assesses the execution of the HWMP in the VANET in context of Manhattan and Freeway mobility model. In [13], to expand stability, they utilized Zone Based Routing (ZBR). To locate the short route in brief period, they utilized Bacterial Foraging Optimization (BFO). To deal with questionable states of VANET, they utilized fuzzy logic. Simulation carried on FBFOZBR protocol and course execution comes about contrasted and condition of-c art routing protocol PFQAODV. In the first case, they fixed the node velocity and route performance studied at the different transmission rate. In the second case, they fixed the transmission rate and route performance studied at different node velocity. In this work, they bring forward a composite network of VANET and cellular network. The benefits of this composite network consist of firstly the high speed of transmission of V ANET and secondly the large scale cellular system. Also, this network overcomes the drawbacks of the cellular and ad-hoc network. For maintaining several features of ITS (Intelligent Transportation System) applications routing in the heterogeneous network has become a significant area of research in VANET. Without any extra network price, they are advancing a routing method for hybrid networks. The results demonstrate that the said routing algorithm has minimized the transmission time and request block rate is in [14]. In [15], proposes parallel impedance cancelation (PIC) for link activation in VANETs. Link activation (LA) remains for initiating an arrangement of correspondence links which can transmit at the same time without transmission impacts. They demonstrate the obstruction cancelation as a mixed integer programming (MIP) optimization issue where wireless link conditions are analyzed. The proposed parallel obstruction cancelation strategy can be utilized for planning of transmissions and resource sharing inside the constructed clusters. Simulations were performed for different scenarios to show the performance of the improved LA.

3 Proposed Work

In the existing technique, every node broadcasts its neighbor table details at regular intervals thru hello packets. Consequently, by investigative the neighbor table of its adjacent node, a node is capable to obtain detail approximately the nodes placed at most two-hops far from itself and save such information in two-hop topology database. Mobility of nodes and time duration utilized for choosing the CH.

In this paper, a novel strategy proposed for the choice of CH which is Cluster Head chosen using Particle Swarm Optimization (CH-PSO) algorithm. The whole process of the proposed work is explained below in the form of proposed algorithm (Fig. 3):

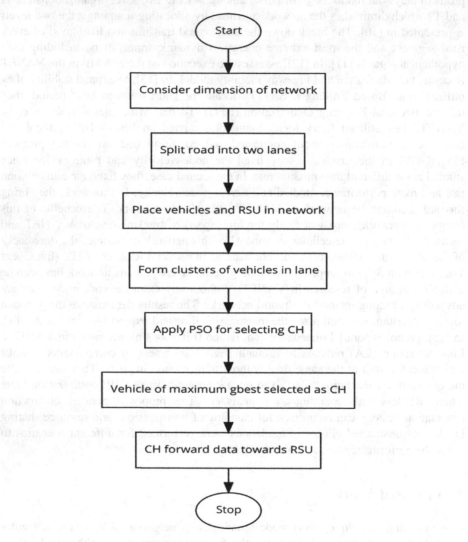

Fig. 3. Working of proposed method

Proposed Algorithm:

```
Step:1      Start
Step:2      Consider some dimension of the network
Step:3      Split the road into two lanes
Step:4      Place vehicles and RSU in the network
Step:5      Form the clusters of the vehicles in
            the lane
Step:6      Apply Particle Swarm Optimization for
            selecting Cluster head
        a.      Initialize vehicle
        b.      for each vehicle
        c.      Compute fitness of each vehicle
        d.      if present fitness value superior
                than (pbest) then
          i.  pbest = present fitness
         ii.  gbest to the greatest between all
              pbest
        e.      for each vehicle
        f.      update velocity
        g.      update position

Step:7      Vehicle of maximum gbest selected as
            Cluster Head
Step:8      Cluster Head forward the data towards
            the RSU
Step:9      Stop
```

4 Result and Analysis

In the result analysis, NS2 used for the simulation and it performed the communication among the vehicles. Different speed of vehicles is considered for the demonstration of the proposed technique in the given scenario. Network Animator is an activity tool which depends on for execution of real world packet traces and network simulation follows. It demonstrates the progression of the packets through the system. It bolsters topology network, packet level simulation, and different data examination tools (Figs. 4, 5, 6, 7 and Table 1).

Table. 1. Simulation table

Parameters	Values
Simulation used	NS2
Network size	1218 m × 632 m
Number of nodes	30
Simulation time	20 s
Antenna used	Omni directional antenna
MAC protocol	IEEE 802.11
Vehicle speed	10, 20, 30, 40 m/s

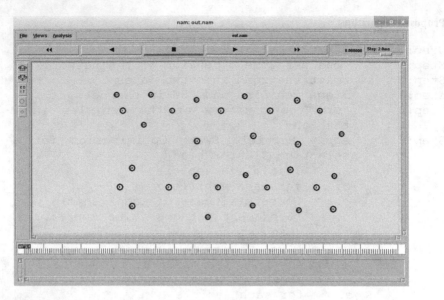

Fig. 4. Initialization of network

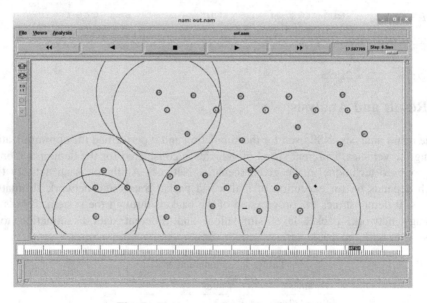

Fig. 5. Data communication performed

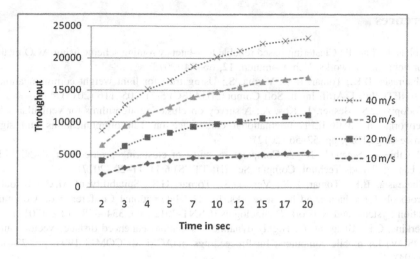

Fig. 6. Throughput graph

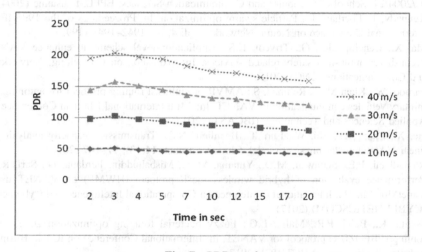

Fig. 7. PDR graph

5   Conclusion

Vehicles and road side settled equipment's them two can be either private (having a place with open service vehicles) or open methods for transport (like public service vehicles) service providers. The VANET clustering plan needs to protect secure correspondence. PSO motivated from the sociological conduct of bird flocking can acquire optimal results. In this algorithm every particle moves to scan for the optimum solutions and subsequently has a speed. In the existing technique, every node broadcasts its neighbor table details at regular intervals thru hello packets. Mobility of nodes and time duration utilized for choosing the CH. The proposed method is used to overcome the existing problems and enhancing the performance of the network.

References

1. Abbas, F., Fan, P.: Clustering-based reliable low-latency routing scheme using ACO method for vehicular networks. Veh. Commun. **12**, 66–74 (2018)
2. Chaurasia, B.K., Tomar, R.S., Verma, S.: Using trust for light weight communication in VANETs. Int. J. Artif. Intell. Soft Comput. (IJAISC) **5**(2), 105–116 (2015)
3. Vodopivec, S., Besiter, J., Kos, A.: A survey on clustering algorithms for vehicular adhoc networks. In: 35th IEEE International conference on Telecommunications and signal Processing (TSP), pp. 52–56 (2012)
4. Malathi, A., Sreenath, N.: A Comparative study of clustering protocols in VANET. Int. J. Emerg. Trends Technol. Comput. Sci. (IJETTCS) **6**(1), 11–20 (2017)
5. Chaurasia, B.K., Tomar, R.S., Verma, S., Tomar, G.S.: Suitability of MANET routing protocols for vehicular ad hoc networks. In: The International Conference on Communication Systems and Network Technologies (CSNT-2012), pp. 334–338. IEEE (2012)
6. Perkins, C.E., Bhagwat, P.: Highly dynamic destination-sequenced distance-vector routing (DSDV) for mobile computers. In: Proceedings of ACM SIGCOMM 1994, pp. 234–244 (1994)
7. Luo, J., Hubaux, J.P.: A survey of inter-vehicle communication. Technical report IC/2004/24, School of Computer and Communication Sciences. EPFL, Lausanne (2004)
8. Kennedy, J., Eberhart, R.: Particle swarm optimization. In: Proceedings of the 1995 IEEE International Conference on Neural Networks, vol. 4, pp. 1942–1948 (1995)
9. Ma, X., Kanelopoulos, G., Trivedi, K.S.: Application-level scheme to enhance VANET event-driven multi-hop safety-related services. In: Workshop on Computing, Networking and Communications (CNC) (2017)
10. Farooq, W., Khan M.A., Rehman, S.: AMVR: a multicast routing protocol for autonomous military vehicles communication in VANET. In: 14t h International Bhurban Conference on Applied Sciences and Technology (IBCAST) (2017)
11. He, X., Zhang, H., Shi, W., Luo, T., Beaulieu, N.C.: Transmission capacity analysis for linear VANET under physical model. China Commun. **14**(13), 97–107 (2017)
12. Ramadhani, P.E., Setiawan, M.D., Yutama, M.A., Misbahuddin, Perdana, D., Sari, R.F.: Performance evaluation of hybrid wireless mesh protocol (HWMP) on VANET using VanetMobiSim. In: International Conference on Computational Intelligence and Cybernetics (CYBERNETICSCOM) (2017)
13. Mehta, K., Bajaj, P.R., Malik, L.G.: Fuzzy bacterial foraging optimization zone based routing (FBFOZBR) protocol for VANET. In: International Conference on ICT in Business Industry & Government (ICTBIG) (2017)
14. Shukla, R.S., Maurya, D., Maurya, B.: Data dissemination under load distribution in hybrid network for VANET. In: Proceedings of the SMART-2016, Fifth International Conference on System Modeling & Advancement in Research Trends (2016)
15. Azizian, M., Cherkaoui, S., Hafid, A.S.: Link activation with parallel interference cancellation in multi-hop VANET. In: 84th Vehicular Technology Conference (VTC-Fall) (2017)

Utilizing Clustering Techniques for Improving the Boxplots

Kalpak Patil[1]([⊠]), Naresh Kumar Nagwani[2], and Sarsij Tripathi[2]

[1] Department of IT, NIT Raipur, Raipur, India
kapatil.mtech2016.it@nitrr.ac.in
[2] Department of CS & E, NIT Raipur, Raipur, India
{nknagwani.cs, stripathi.cs}@nitrr.ac.in

Abstract. The Boxplot is one of exploratory tools of data mining. It was originated by Tukey in 1970 [1]. The Boxplot uses five-points to display information which includes the median, the quartiles and the first and the last points. To improve on the information conveyed by existing Boxplots it is proposed to add the clustering methods during the computation of Boxplots. The clustering methods used are K-Means and DBSCAN. The results are plotted using all the above three techniques of constructing the Boxplots. The results obtained from the proposed methods of construction of Boxplots show that they are different from the original Boxplots. The results are compared with the traditional technique of generating boxplots and it is demonstrated that cluster driven boxplot generation is more effective for data analysis in real life scenario.

Keywords: Boxplot · Clustering · Density-based clustering
Data visualization · Group comparison

1 Introduction

The use of statistical techniques to find hidden patterns of data is known as exploratory data analysis. Boxplot is one of such techniques which can visualize as well as compare the groups of data. The Boxplot uses the five-point summary of data [2]. The five-points include the median, the upper and lower quartiles and lowest and highest points of data. The outliers or noisy points can be easily identified with the use of Boxplots. The Boxplots can be used to replace complex tables, so the information conveyed is more than that of those tables.

The Boxplots are being used in many applications and fields currently some of which are mentioned here. To show the variation of NO_2 concentrations across different locations and sensors in the study of using multiparameter to calibrate low cost sensors in the urban environment [3]. To visualize and compare the statistical properties of seepage data from dams in the study of transient seepage through embarkment dams [4]. To visualize the behavior of each accessor and to behold the influence of each standard used, Boxplots are used to show data for 10% and 50% dilution in the study of training of a panel to evaluate the rancid defects in soyabean oil [5]. Boxplots present the average message delays and the variations in those delays in study of latency sensitive traffic in comparison of multipath to single path transport [6]. To efficiently

© Springer Nature Singapore Pte Ltd. 2019
S. Verma et al. (Eds.): CNC 2018, CCIS 839, pp. 121–132, 2019.
https://doi.org/10.1007/978-981-13-2372-0_11

represent the imperical distribution of results of hybrid artificial bee colony algorithm solved using differential equations [7]. To compare the runtimes of various topologies the Boxplots are used in study of ensuring deadlock-freedom in low-diameter Infini-Band networks [8]. To conveniently display the obtained thresholds of software metrics to predict fault on open source software's [9]. The Boxplots are also used in advanced topics like augmented reality to compare four trackers to find corners under normal and suboptimal illumination [10]. As it is observed that the Boxplot is being used to display various information's about the data it is planned to improve the existing Boxplots so that some more information can be displayed by the same.

To improve on the information displayed by the existing Boxplots it is planned to use clustering techniques on the data before plotting the Boxplots. Clustering is one of the major data analysis methods. Clustering is distributing data into clusters which are disjoint such that the data in same clusters are similar while those in different clusters is dissimilar [11]. The dissimilarities are often based on the attribute measures and are generally the distances between two data points [12]. Clustering is a data mining tool and is also used in various fields such as biology, web security, web search etc. Clustering does not have predefined classes and hence falls into category of unsupervised learning. Clustering is further divided into types such as: Model based clustering, partition-based clustering, density-based clustering, hierarchical clustering and grid-based clustering. Partition based clustering and density-based clustering are being used here.

The partition clustering is the most popular clustering method. The partition clustering divides the data into k partitions where k must be provided by the user. This method divides the in such a way that each data falls into exactly one cluster. Most of the partition-based clustering algorithms are distance based. These methods generally require many computations. The clusters formed are spherical shaped as distance is considered to form the clusters. It is not possible to form clusters of complex shapes. K-Means and K-Medoids are the popular partition-based clustering algorithms and K-Means clustering algorithm is used [13].

The density-based clustering algorithms are based on the notion of density. A cluster is grown until the density of data points in the neighborhood is greater than some threshold. This clustering method can find arbitrary shaped clusters. The regions of high density of data points separated by the regions of low density data points form the separate clusters [14]. All the points are not necessarily grouped into clusters and can remain as outliers. These outliers can generally be considered as noise points. DBSCAN, DENCLUE and OPTICS are the popular density-based clustering algorithms and the DBSCAN clustering algorithm is used [13, 15].

The improved Boxplots are shown in the Fig. 1. The figure explains the procedure of how it is planned to implement the improved Boxplots. The five-points which are used to construct standard Boxplot named *Min, Q_1, Median, Q_3, Max* and the points to improve the Boxplot with K-Means clustering are named as C_1 to C_5. The points in the case of improving the clusters with DBSCAN clustering are named as D_1 to D_n as the number of clusters formed in the DBSCAN clustering are not fixed. The above-mentioned points are calculated for same data and mapped as shown in the diagram which is as follows. *Min* to C_1, Q_1 to C_2, *Median* to C_3, Q_3 to C_4 and *Max* to C_5 for the case of K-Means clustering. While in the case of DBSCAN clustering it is mapped as

Min to D_1, *Max* to D_n and the rest of the points are filled as per the number of clusters formed during DBSCAN clustering.

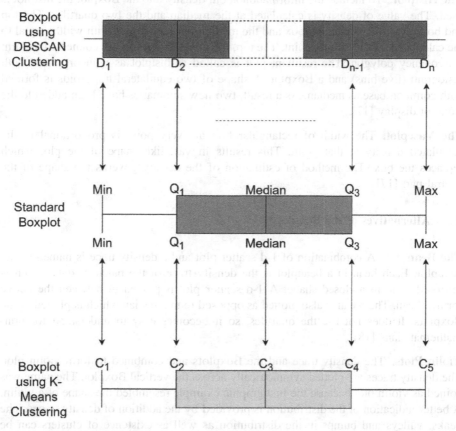

Fig. 1. Constructing Boxplots using K-Means and DBSAN clustering.

2   Related Work

The Boxplot was originated by Tukey in 1970 [1]. He called it the schematic plot. The plot was also later called as the Box-and-Whiskers plot and later it became a common practice to refer the plot as the Boxplot. There have been various variations and alternatives to the Boxplots over the years some of which are discussed below.

2.1   Variations of the Boxplot

Notched Boxplot. A confidence interval of the median of the data whose regular Boxplot is plotted is shown by removing a pair of wedges from the side of the box. The construction of these confidence intervals is such that the medians of different Boxplots are significantly different if their two notches do not overlap [16].

The Histplot. To include the information about density into the Boxplot the histplot is used. The value of density is calculated at the median and the two quartiles. The top and bottom of the rectangular box and the median lines are drawn with widths equal to the calculated density at that point. The top, median and bottoms are connected to form a frequency polygon. The resultant plot is called as histplot as it incorporates both histogram (five bins) and a Boxplot. A shape of two equilateral trapezoids is formed with common base as median. As a result, two new summaries have been added to the Boxplot display [17].

The Vaseplot. The width of rectangular box at every point is proportional to the calculated density at that point. This results in vase-like shape of the plot which replaces the box. The method of estimation of the density governs the shape of the central part [17].

2.2   Alternatives of the Boxplot

The Beanplot. A combination of 1-d scatter plot and a density trace is named as the beanplot. Each bean in a beanplot is the density trace of the batch of data which is mirrored to form a closed shape. A 1-d scatter plot is plotted in between the above formed bean. The mean is also plotted as opposed to the median which is plotted in the Boxplots. It does not use the quartiles, so it becomes easy to understand for non-mathematicians [18].

Violin Plots. The density trace and the Boxplots and combined to form violin plot. The density traces are plotted symmetrically across the vertical Boxplot. The name was coined as violin plot because the first graphic example resembled the shape of a violin. A better indication of the distribution is provided by the addition of density traces. The peaks, valleys and bumps in the distribution as well as existence of clusters can be showed with the help of the violin plots [19].

3   Methodology

This section gives the description of the methodology used to implement the techniques of improving the Boxplots.

3.1   Boxplot

A single batch of data which is univariate in nature [17, 18] is displayed easily with the help of the Boxplot. The aim of a Boxplot is to display the main features of data by summarizing the data. The Boxplot falls into exploratory data analysis which is one of the statistical technique. The Boxplot can be quickly learned and applied easily as well.

The interpretation of data can be improved by using Boxplots. The Boxplot is a tool which can improve our reasoning about quantitative information present in the data. Hidden patterns of data in a dataset can be identified with the help of Boxplots [2].

The name Boxplot is given to the plot as it contains a rectangular box which denotes the middle half of the batch of the data [17]. The top edge and the bottom edge of the rectangle are upper quartile or Q_3 and lower quartile or Q_1 of the data. A line is drawn across the rectangular box which shows the central or the median value of the data. The above features are all denoted by solid lines to attract the attention of the viewer. The summaries of univariate data focus mainly on the location and spread and hence those are shown in solid lines. The interquartile range $(Q_3–Q_1)$ multiplied by 1.5 defines the step. A vertical line is drawn from the middle of the top of the box up to the largest observation which lies within a step. Similarly, a line is drawn from the middle of the bottom of the box up to the smallest observation which lies within a step. Data points which lie away from the box and do not lie in the step range are plotted individually. These points attract attention and are potential outliers [20].

The five-points required for the construction of Boxplots are as follows:

1. The median.
   Given a set of numbers S, the median is the middle number of S when S is sorted for the case when the total number of S is odd, and the median is the average of the middle two values of S when S is sorted for the case when total number of S is even.
2. The upper quartile Q_3
   It is the 75th percentile. Given a set of numbers S, the 75th percentile is the value of 75th number if there are 100 numbers in S and they are sorted in ascending order or the value $\frac{75}{100}$ of the way in S where S is sorted in ascending order.
3. The lower quartile Q_1
   It is the 25th percentile. Given a set of numbers S, the 25th percentile is the value of 25th number if there are 100 numbers in S and they are sorted in ascending order or the value $\frac{25}{100}$ of the way in S where S is sorted in ascending order.
4. Minimum
   The minimum value denoted is calculated as follows

$$Q1 - (1.5 \times (Q3 - Q1))$$

5. Maximum
   The maximum value denoted is calculated as follows

$$Q3 + (1.5 \times (Q3 - Q1))$$

The Boxplot generally conveys a lot of information which can be summarized as follows:

1. The Boxplot graphically presents the five summaries of data which give the following information about the data.
   - A cut line in the rectangular box denotes the median which gives the location of the data.

- The distance between whiskers and the length of the box gives the spread of the data.
- Skewness of the data is shown by the deviation of the median from the center of the length of the box as well as by the difference in the lengths of the upper and lower whiskers and the number of outliers on either side of the whiskers.
- The distance between the whiskers and the edges of the rectangular box shows the longtailedness of the data.

2. Observations at the end of the data is displayed by the Boxplot along with its details.
3. Side by Side display of many Boxplots can be used to directly compare the detailed information in different batches of data.
4. Computation and plotting of the Boxplot is easy.
5. Statisticians can easily understand the meaning of Boxplot [17].

Algorithm 1 explains the procedure of construction of boxplot.

Algorithm 1: Construction of Boxplot.

    Input   : A batch of data whose Boxplot is to be constructed
    Output: Boxplot
(1) **begin**
(2) | Calculate the Median
(3) | Calculate the Upper Quartile $Q3$
(4) | Calculate the Lower Quartile $Q1$
(5) | Calculte the upper step limit or maximum value
(6) | Calculate the lower step limit or minimum value
(7) | Construct the Boxplot using the above calculated 5 points
(8) **end**

3.2 Boxplot Generation Using K-Means Clustering

K-Means is the most popular partitional clustering method. It is unsupervised, non-deterministic, iterative method [21]. It works in two different phases. In K-Means the value of k is selected in advance, it denotes the number of clusters wished to be created. The first phase selects k centers randomly. Next phase calculates the distance between each data point and the cluster center selected above. The distance used here is Euclidian distance [21]. To calculate Euclidian distance $d(x, y)$ between two data points $x = (x_1, x_2, \dots x_n)$ and $y = (y_1, y_2, \dots y_n)$ the following equation is used

$$d(x, y) = \sqrt{\sum_{i=1}^{n} (x_i - y_i)^2}$$

All the data points are grouped into clusters based on the minimum distance from the selected centers. The centers are then recalculated by taking the average of all the data points in that cluster. This process is repeated iteratively until the cluster centers do not change.

The K-Means clustering divides the data points into k clusters such that the intercluster similarity is low and the intracluster similarity is high. Thus, our data is divided into clusters which all contain similar data points [13].

To use the K-Means clustering to improve a Boxplot the cluster centers obtained are used. As it is known that the Boxplot plots the data based on the five-point summary of the data, the number of centers or the value of k is set to 5 in our K-Means algorithm. 5 cluster centers are obtained as output from the application of K-Means algorithm to the data. Further the cluster centers are sorted into ascending order and then they are mapped to the five-points based on which the Boxplot is constructed as follows

- 1st center point to the Lower step point
- 2nd center point to the Lower Quartile
- 3rd center point to the Median
- 4th center point to the Upper Quartile
- 5th center point to the Upper step point.

Using the above five-points the improved Boxplot using K-Means clustering algorithm is constructed and algorithm 2 explains the same procedure.

Algorithm 2: Construction of Boxplot using K-Means Clustering.

    Input : A batch of data whose Boxplot is to be constructed
    Output: Boxplot using K-Means Clustering
(1) **begin**
(2)   Set $k = 5$
(3)   Apply K-Means algorithm on the data
(4)   Get the 5 cluster centers of the 5 clusters
(5)   Sort the 5 points in ascending order
(6)   Map the 5 points to the 5 points required to construct the Boxplot
(7)   Construct the Boxplot using the above calculated 5 points
(8) **end**

3.3 Boxplot Generation Using DBSCAN Clustering

DBSCAN is a density-based clustering algorithm. Clusters of arbitrary shapes and sizes can be formed using this algorithm even in the presence of noisy data points [22]. Each object of a cluster formed by DBSCAN must contain a minimum number of data points *MinPts* about a given radius *Eps* to be considered a core point. The DBSCAN algorithm checks for the *Eps* neighborhood of each data point. If the neighborhood contains more than *MinPts* then a new cluster is created with the data point as the core object. The data points which are reachable within the *Eps* distance of a core data point are added to the formed cluster [23]. This process is followed iteratively till no new data point can be added to any cluster. Some points which do not get added into any clusters are then said to be as noise points. The number of clusters are not required as input to the DBSCAN clustering, hence the clusters formed by DBSCAN are the clusters which exist in the dataset [14].

To use DBSCAN clustering to improve on the Boxplot the obtained cluster labels of all the data points which are available as the output of the DBSCAN algorithm are used. Mean of the data points is calculated of those data points which belong to the same cluster. Thus n of cluster center points are obtained where the n is equal to the number of clusters generated by the DBSCAN algorithm. As the number of clusters generated by the DBSCAN depends on the data, the five-point summary cannot be applied here as it was applied in the previous two methods. The obtained cluster centers are sorted in ascending order and proceed by forming only boxes with borders as the center points of the clusters. Thus, the Boxplot generated using DBSCAN clustering is formed. Algorithm 3 describes the same process.

Algorithm 3: Construction of Boxplot using DBSCAN Clustering.

    Input   : A batch of data whose Boxplot is to be constructed
    Output: Boxplot using DBSCAN Clustering

(1) **begin**
(2)   Set appropriate *Eps* and *MinPts* values
(3)   Apply DBSCAN algorithm on the data
(4)   Get the cluster labels of the datapoints
(5)   Calculate mean of datapoints belonging to same cluster labels
(6)   Sort the means in ascending order
(7)   Construct the Boxplot using the above calculated means.
(8) **end**

---

4 Experiments, Results and Discussions

Boxplots are created for different randomly generated datasets of integers using the three different techniques namely the standard Boxplot, Boxplots using K-Means clustering technique and Boxplot formation using Density-based clustering technique. The two datasets are called *data x* and *data y*. The generated Boxplots for the two different datasets using these three techniques are presented. The different Boxplots for *data x* are shown in the Fig. 2 and the different Boxplots for *data y* are shown in the Fig. 3.

5 Comparison Explanation

The side to side comparison of the Boxplots of both the *data x* and *data y* is shown in the Fig. 4. It is observed that the Boxplots are almost similar with slight variations in the median and the quartiles. As the data is randomly generated in the same range and has same number of data points it is observed that the median fails to differentiate between the two sets of data and as a result similar Boxplots are generated.

The side to side comparison of the Boxplots generated using K-Means clustering of both the *data x* and *data y* is shown in the Fig. 5. The difference between the plots for *data x* and *data y* is clearly visible. The center point of the Boxplot is similar, but the

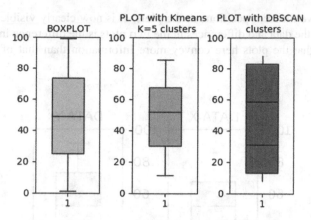

Fig. 2. Generated Boxplots for *data x*.

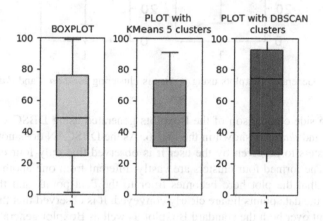

Fig. 3. Generated Boxplots for *data y*.

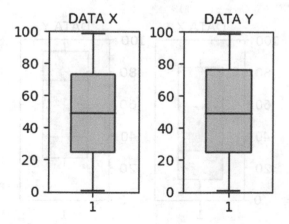

Fig. 4. Generated standard Boxplots for *data x* and *data y*.

other points have different positions in the plots. It is now clearly visible that the plot remains true to the data and differences in the two plots is the difference in the datasets. It is observed that the plots here convey more information than that of the standard Boxplots.

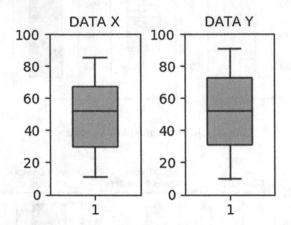

Fig. 5. Generated Boxplots using K-Means clustering for *data x* and *data y*.

The side to side comparison of the Boxplots generated using DBSCAN clustering of both *data x* and *data y* is shown in the Fig. 6. As the DBSCAN does not require the number of clusters to be given by the user it is observed that only four clusters have been formed. The formed four clusters are vastly different from one another. It is now clearly visible that the plot here becomes truer to the data points and the positions where most of the data points lie are clearly conveyed. It is observed that these plotsare an improvement over both the standard Boxplot as well as Boxplot generated using K-Means clustering.

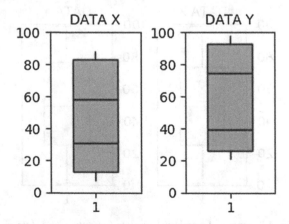

Fig. 6. Generated Boxplots using DBSCAN clustering for *data x* and *data y*.

6 Impact of the Presented Techniques

The results of the Boxplots plotted with K-Means clustering as well as with DBSCAN clustering show that the results become truer to the nature of the data. The use of clustering techniques uncovers patterns hidden in the data that were otherwise not visible. These patterns are also graphically represented. The plot uses the same space as that of normal Boxplot and conveys more information than that of the Boxplot, this would result in the benefit of authors and researchers who use these plots as their results would convey more information.

7 Conclusion and Future Directions

The Boxplot and its construction is studied. The Boxplot used median and quartiles to represent the data. To improve on this, it is proposed to use clustering techniques while construction of Boxplots. The clustering techniques used were K-Means clustering and DBSCAN clustering. The plots with K-Means and DBSCAN clustering are plotted. The Boxplot generated using K-Means clustering showed some improvement over the traditional Boxplot while the Boxplot generated with DBSCAN clustering showed improvements over the Boxplot generated using K-Means clustering as well as the traditional Boxplot. The Boxplots with both clustering represents true nature of data and can be practically more suitable for data analysis. It is suggested to keep on experimenting with the K-Means and DBSCAN algorithms and keep on changing their parameters in future to improve on the results and try to include some more meaningful information in these Boxplots.

References

1. Tukey, J.: Exploratory Data Analysis, Limited Preliminary edn. Addison-Wesley, Reading (1970)
2. Williamson, D.F., Parker, R.A., Kendrick, J.S.: The box plot: a simple visual method to interpret data. Ann. Intern. Med. 110(11), 916–921 (1989)
3. Fang, X., Bate, I.: Using multi-parameters for calibration of low-cost sensors in urban environment. Networks 7, 33 (2017)
4. Calamak, M., Yanmaz, A.M.: Uncertainty quantification of transient unsaturated seepage through embankment dams. Int. J. Geomech. 17(6), 04016125 (2016)
5. Marques, C., dos Reis, A., da Silva, L., Carpes, S., Mitterer-Daltoé, M.: Selecting and training a panel to evaluate the rancid defect in soybean oil and fish hamburgers. Grasas Aceites 68(3), 203 (2017)
6. Yedugundla, K., et al.: Is multi-path transport suitable for latency sensitive traffic? Comput. Netw. 105, 1–21 (2016)
7. Jadon, S.S., Tiwari, R., Sharma, H., Bansal, J.C.: Hybrid artificial bee colony algorithm with differential evolution. Appl. Soft Comput. 58, 11–24 (2017)
8. Schneider, T., Bibartiu, O., Hoefler, T.: Ensuring deadlock-freedom in low-diameter infiniBand networks. In: 2016 IEEE 24th Annual Symposium on High-Performance Interconnects (HOTI), pp. 1–8. IEEE (2016)

9. Arar, O.F., Ayan, K.: Deriving thresholds of software metrics to predict faults on open source software: replicated case studies. Expert Syst. Appl. **61**, 106–121 (2016)
10. Zheng, Z., et al.: Aristo: an augmented reality platform for immersion and interactivity (2017)
11. Na, S., Xumin, L., Yong, G.: Research on k-means clustering algorithm: an improved k-means clustering algorithm. In: 2010 Third International Symposium on Intelligent Information Technology and Security Informatics (IITSI), pp. 63–67. IEEE (2010)
12. Jain, A.K., Murty, M.N., Flynn, P.J.: Data clustering: a review. ACM Comput. Surv. (CSUR) **31**(3), 264–323 (1999)
13. Han, J., Pei, J., Kamber, M.: Data Mining: Concepts and Techniques. Elsevier, New York (2011)
14. Khan, K., Rehman, S.U., Aziz, K., Fong, S., Sarasvady, S.: DBSCAN: past, present and future. In: 2014 Fifth International Conference on the Applications of Digital Information and Web Technologies (ICADIWT), pp. 232–238. IEEE (2014)
15. Redkar, A.K., Todmal, S.: Extended DBSCAN algorithm to detect cluster with varied density for outlier detection
16. McGill, R., Tukey, J.W., Larsen, W.A.: Variations of box plots. Am. Stat. **32**(1), 12–16 (1978)
17. Benjamini, Y.: Opening the box of a boxplot. Am. Stat. **42**(4), 257–262 (1988)
18. Kampstra, P., et al.: Beanplot: a boxplot alternative for visual comparison of distributions (2008)
19. Hintze, J.L., Nelson, R.D.: Violin plots: a box plot-density trace synergism. Am. Stat. **52**(2), 181–184 (1998)
20. Frigge, M., Hoaglin, D.C., Iglewicz, B.: Some implementations of the boxplot. Am. Stat. **43**(1), 50–54 (1989)
21. Yadav, J., Sharma, M.: A review of k-mean algorithm. Int. J. Eng. Trends Technol. (IJETT) **4**(7), 2972–2975 (2013)
22. Shah, G.H.: An improved DBSCAN, a density based clustering algorithm with parameter selection for high dimensional data sets. In: 2012 Nirma University International Conference on Engineering (NUiCONE), pp. 1–6. IEEE (2012)
23. Kriegel, H.P., Pfeifle, M.: Density-based clustering of uncertain data. In: Proceedings of the Eleventh ACM SIGKDD International Conference on Knowledge Discovery in Data Mining, pp. 672–677. ACM (2005)

Mathematical Model for Sink Mobility (MMSM) in Wireless Sensor Networks to Improve Network Lifetime

Mohit Kumar[1][(✉)], Dinesh Kumar[2], and Md. Amir Khusru Akhtar[1]

[1] Cambridge Institute of Technology, Tatisilwai, Ranchi, Jharkhand, India
mohit.cse@citranchi.ac.in, akru2008@gmail.com
[2] Jaipur National University, Jaipur, Rajasthan 302017, India

Abstract. Sink node mobility is to uniformly distribute the load of the sink neighbors in order to balance the energy level and to delegate sink's neighbor responsibility between the sensor nodes. In this paper, we present a mathematical model that works with existing routing protocol. Sink mobility is decided on the basis of definite-stay-value $(D = \Delta * (1 - P(S|Pos)))$, where $P(S|Pos)$ is defined as closeness of sink node and sink site. Closeness means surrounding density or an area where density of sensors is very high. This model performs the SINK_TEST for the determination of sink site. We have formulated this problem with the help of prior probability and continuous Bayes' theorem. This mathematical model is verified by experiments and gives adequate accuracy for the improvement of network lifetime in independent environment.

Keywords: Wireless sensor network · Sink mobility · Mathematical model
Bayes theorem · Network lifetime

1 Introduction

Wireless sensor network (WSN) is a network of sensor nodes organized in an ad-hoc manner to accomplish some predefined goal. Sensor nodes have limitations in terms of memory, computational complexity and battery lifetime. Since, replacement of exhausted batteries becomes practically impossible due to the harsh environmental conditions, thus battery lifetime [1, 2] appears as the main constraint for a WSN. Hence, it is necessary to use the energy very cautiously in both node and network level. In the literature various models have been proposed for the improvement of network lifetime. Sink mobility is one of the most useful solutions in the literature for improving the network lifetime [1–3]. Sink node mobility is to uniformly distribute the load of the sink neighbors in order to balance the energy level and to delegate sink's neighbor responsibility between the sensor nodes. Sink node mobility can be classified as uncontrolled or controlled [4, 5]. In this paper, we focus on the controlled sink node mobility because controlled mobility has lower data latency. In this work sink node/base station is mobile and sensor nodes are stationary. All sensor nodes have

© Springer Nature Singapore Pte Ltd. 2019
S. Verma et al. (Eds.): CNC 2018, CCIS 839, pp. 133–141, 2019.
https://doi.org/10.1007/978-981-13-2372-0_12

same configuration and limited energy. Each node has the same starting energy and they are generating equal traffic in the network.

The proposed mathematical model works with existing routing protocol and Sink mobility is decided on the basis of definite-stay-value. This model performs the SINK_TEST for the determination of sink site. We have formulated this problem with the help of prior probability and continuous Bayes' theorem. Our proposed MMSM scheme moves the sink node on the basis of definite-stay-value rather than stay-value. It is a better choice to move the sink node because it uses closeness of node in addition to stay-value. Closeness means surrounding density or an area where density of sensors is very high. In this area sensors have recorded large amount of meaningful data. The communication time to connect the sink node and the sensors is to be minimized. Otherwise, we have high delivery delays or data loss due limited buffers in sensors. In SMSLRE [10], if stay-value is same for some sink site it decides in a random basis which is not an optimum solution from the current location. Even if the next location having a different closeness. We have shown the comparison of SMSLRE and MMSM in terms of active sensor nodes per round. The result shows that our proposed method is better than SMSLRE in terms of number of active sensor nodes and network life.

This mathematical model is verified by experiments and gives adequate accuracy for the improvement of network lifetime in independent environment. Experimental results show the efficiency of the proposed model. The rest of the paper is organized as follows. The related work is presented in Sect. 2. Section 3 describes the proposed mathematical model. Experimental results are shown in Sect. 4. Finally, Sect. 5 concludes the paper.

2 Related Work

Sensor nodes have limitations in terms of memory, computational complexity and battery lifetime. Since, replacement of exhausted batteries becomes practically impossible due to the harsh environmental conditions, thus battery lifetime appears as the main constraint for a WSN. Hence, it is necessary to use the energy very cautiously in both node and network level. In the literature various models have been proposed for the improvement of network lifetime. Sink mobility is one of the most useful solutions in the literature for improving the network lifetime. Sink node mobility is to uniformly distribute the load of the sink neighbors in order to balance the energy level and to delegate sink's neighbor responsibility between the sensor nodes. Sink node mobility can be classified as uncontrolled or controlled. In uncontrolled mobility movement of sink node is random and MULEs (Mobile Ubiquitous LAN Extensions) move according to their requirements and exchange data if it is required [6, 7]. The main limitation of uncontrolled mobility is that it needs large size buffers and with high data latency. In this paper, we focus on the controlled sink node mobility because controlled mobility has lower data latency.

Prakash et al. [2] proposed sink mobility in a fixed trajectory to maximize network lifetime of wireless sensor network. In this work the sink mobility is decided on the basis of closeness of subsink and sink node. In general subsink provides data to the sink node if it is in nearest proximity of that subsink. In this work authors have proposed method to find the correct subsink node from a given set of subsinks using location-aided routing on global positioning system (GPS)-enabled sensors and sink node.

Koç and Korpeoglu [8] proposed traffic-and energy-load-based sink mobility algorithms for wireless sensor networks. The proposed packet-load based sink movement algorithm uses a specified number of packets for each node at each sink position. This algorithm also considers distance of the packets and presented an integer programming formulation to compute the optimal results. This work provides a solution to the sink mobility in wireless sensor networks using node-load parameters.

Jong and Horng [9] proposed a novel queen honey bee migration algorithm for sink repositioning in WSN. In this work, the sink visit several places to find best place on the basis of highest remaining energy. The proposed method balances the energy utilization among nodes and extends the network lifetime.

Tan et al. [10] proposed sink moving scheme based on local residual energy of nodes in wireless sensor networks (SMSLRE). In the method, the sink node periodically moves to a new location on the basis of average residual energy and the number of neighbors called stay-value. Thus, this scheme balances energy consumption around sink node from draining and enhances network lifetime.

In this paper the sink mobility is decided on the basis of remaining energy level of sink's neighbors as similar to Tan et al. scheme [10] with SINK_TEST. We have formulated this problem with the help of prior probability and continuous Bayes' theorem.

3 Proposed Mathematical Model

In this section, we present a mathematical model that works with existing routing protocol. This work involves a set of nodes or sensors deployed manually into the target area. There are two types of nodes in the network, sensor nodes and sink node. Sensor nodes are responsible for sensing local data and send it to sink node. The sink node receives the data from sensor nodes for further processing. This work assumes sensor nodes are stationary while the sink node is mobile after deployment. The setting of the proposed architecture is shown in Fig. 1. Figure 1 shows a Scenario in which sink node is initially at the center of the sensing field and the proposed model chooses any of the sink sites on the basis of define-stay-value. The sink site is determined using SINK_TEST.

In this work Sink mobility is decided on the basis of definite-stay-value. This model performs the SINK_TEST for the determination of sink site. We have formulated this problem with the help of prior probability and continuous Bayes' theorem [11]. The position for the sink node is decided using definite-stay-value. Sink site determination is performed using SINK_TEST. The incidence of SINK_TEST is defined as follows:

Here Δ denotes the stay-value of a sink site calculated on the basis of average residual energy and the number of neighbors as discussed in [10]. The SINK_TEST is performed using Eq. (1).

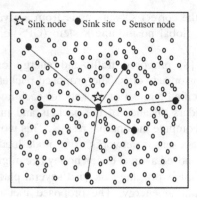

Fig. 1. Scenario 1

$$D = \Delta * (1 - P(S|Pos)) \qquad (1)$$

Where, D denotes the definite-stay-value of the sink site. A larger D indicates a better location for sink node. $P(S|Pos)$ is defined as closeness of sink node and sink site. Closeness means surrounding density or an area where density of sensors is very high. In this area sensors have recorded large amount of meaningful data. The communication time to connect the sink node and the sensors is to be minimized. Otherwise, we have high delivery delays or data loss due limited buffers in sensors [12].

Let S be the event that a sink site is closer to sink node, and S be the event that the sink site is not closer to sink node, Pos be the event that the sink site test is positive or closer to the sink note, and Neg be the event that the sink site test is negative or not a better choice for the closeness from the sink node. Closeness can be calculated using $P(S|Pos)$.

Using Bayes' theorem [11], we find that

$$P(S|Pos) = \frac{P(S)\ P(Pos|S)}{P(S)\ P(Pos|S) + P(\overline{S})\ P(Pos|\overline{S})} \qquad (2)$$

If the outcome of Eq. (2) is larger than 0.5 [11], we can conclude that the sink site is more likely than not to have closeness from the sink node. We can evaluate the same using the ratio given in Eq. (2)

$$S = \frac{P(S)\ P(Pos|S)}{P(\overline{S})\ P(Pos|\overline{S})} \qquad (3)$$

If the ratio given in Eq. (3) is larger than 1, we over conclude that the sink site is more likely than not to be closer to sink node. Later than computing the ratio N, we can derive the probability that a sink site has the closeness if Eq. (4) gives a positive result:

$$P(S|Pos) = \frac{S}{1+S} \tag{4}$$

Thus, it agrees with Eq. (2).

If $P(N|Pos)$ or $P(S)$ argues with the condition $P(S|Pos) < P(\overline{S}|Pos)$, a probable ending would be that the sink sites did not have the closeness although the test were positive. A different interpretation would be that an error in the SINK_TEST is more likely possible than the closeness of sink site itself. Because $P(S)$ is very small for lots of test, giving a subsequent test a standard procedure whenever a positive result occurs.

Now this problem can be formulated with the help of prior probability and continuous Bayes' theorem as,

Let N be the event that a sink site is closer to the sink node, $\overline{N}$ be the event that the node is not closer or farther from the sink node, and $P(x|N)$ defines the normal density. The prior probabilities are defines as P(N) and P($\overline{N}$)

$$P(x|N) = \frac{1}{\sigma_N \sqrt{2\prod}} e^{-1/2\left(\frac{x-\mu_N}{\sigma_N}\right)^2} \tag{5}$$

and

$$P(x|\overline{N}) = \frac{1}{\sigma_{\overline{N}} \sqrt{2\prod}} e^{-1/2\left(\frac{x-\mu_{\overline{N}}}{\sigma_{\overline{N}}}\right)^2} \tag{6}$$

By continuous version of Bayes' Theorem

$$P(N|x) = \frac{P(N)P(x|N)}{P(N)P(x|N) + P(\overline{N})P(x|\overline{N})} \tag{7}$$

So the sink site is slightly less likely to be closer than not to be farther. Furthermore, the ratio given in Eq. (8) can be used to find the same

$$N = \frac{P(N|x)}{P(\overline{N}|x)} \tag{8}$$

If the ratio given in Eq. (8) i.e., N < 1, the node is more likely not to be closer than to be farther. By using the ratio $\frac{N}{1+N}$, we can have the same opinion with (7).

Thus, this model classified the closeness of sink sites in terms of surrounding density. Figure 2 shows the densities of the sink sites.

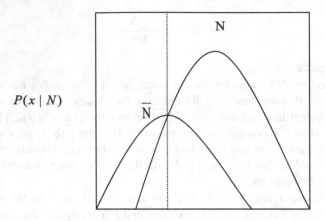

Fig. 2. Probability density function for sink site determination

4   Sink Site Determination Experiments

Sink site determination is performed by moving the sink node into a correct site location. Let S1 and S2 are the sink sites and sink node is at the center. Arrow indicates movement path of sink node. Any Point between points S1 and S2 is chosen as sink sites on the basis of definite-stay-value as shown in Fig. 3.

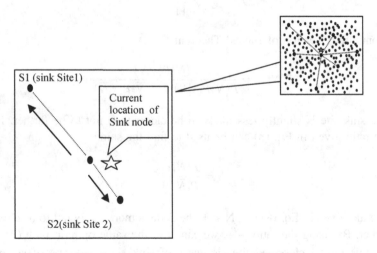

Fig. 3. Sink site determination (SINK_TEST)

In order to determine the movement of the sink node we can use Eq. (1). If the ratio given in Eq. (2) is larger than 0.5, we can conclude that the sink site (S1) is more likely not to be closer to sink node and we choose Point S2 as a sink site.

In addition to that, if $P(N|Pos)$ or $P(S)$ argues with the condition $P(S|Pos) < P(\overline{S}|Pos)$, a probable ending would be that the sink sites did not have the closeness although the test were positive. A different interpretation would be that an error in the SINK_TEST is more likely possible than the closeness of sink site itself. Because $P(S)$ is very small for lots of test, giving a subsequent test a standard procedure whenever a positive result occurs.

We have conducted rigorous simulations in our native tool developed in C programming language. Our scheme performs better than SMSLRE [10] in terms stay-value. Table 1 shows the stay-value of SMSLRE and MMSM obtained from Scenario 1.

Table 1. Stay-value comparison between SMSLRE and MMSM

Stay value (SMSLRE)	P(S|Pos)	Definite-stay-value (MMSM)
110	0.2	88
102	0.5	51
109	0.6	43.6
110	0.1	99
100	0.3	70
110	0.9	11

Our proposed MMSM scheme moves the sink node on the basis of definite-stay-value rather than stay-value which is a better choice to move the sink node. In SMSLRE, if stay-value is same but the site is farther than others then it is not an optimum one from the current location. Even if the next location having a different closeness. Figure 4 shows the Comparison of SMSLRE and MMSM in terms of active sensor nodes per round. The result shows that our proposed method is better than SMSLRE in terms of number of active sensor nodes, and network life.

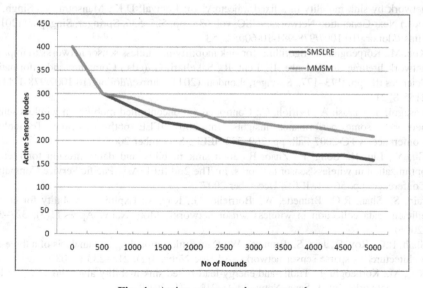

Fig. 4. Active sensor nodes per round

The result shows that our proposed method is better than SMSLRE in terms of number of active sensor nodes, and network life.

5 Conclusion

In WSNs, sensor nodes which are nearer to sink node have to forward the data, which depletes their energy rapidly. Sink node mobility is a solution to uniformly distribute the load of the sink neighbors in order to balance the energy level and to delegate sink's neighbor responsibility between the sensor nodes. This paper presents a mathematical model that works with existing routing protocol. Sink mobility is decided on the basis of definite-stay-value. This model performs the SINK_TEST for the determination of sink site. Our proposed MMSM scheme moves the sink node on the basis of definite-stay-value rather than stay-value which is a better choice to move the sink node. We have compared our scheme with SMSLRE. In SMSLRE, if stay-value is same but the site is farther than others then it is not an optimum choice from the current location. Even if the next location having a different closeness. The comparison shows the efficiency of SMSLRE and MMSM in terms of active sensor nodes per round. The result shows that our proposed method is better than SMSLRE in terms of number of active sensor nodes, and network life.

References

1. Yetgin, H., Cheung, K.T.K., El-Hajjar, M., Hanzo, L.H.: A survey of network lifetime maximization techniques in wireless sensor networks. IEEE Commun. Surv. Tutor. **19**(2), 828–854 (2017)
2. Prakash, J., Kumar, R., Gautam, R.K., Saini, J.P.: Maximizing lifetime of wireless sensor network by sink mobility in a fixed trajectory. In: Lobiyal, D.K., Mansotra, V., Singh, U. (eds.) Next-Generation Networks. AISC, vol. 638, pp. 525–536. Springer, Singapore (2018). https://doi.org/10.1007/978-981-10-6005-2_53
3. Koç, M., Körpeoglu, I.: Algorithms for sink mobility in wireless sensor networks to improve network lifetime. In: Gelenbe, E., Lent, R., Sakellari, G. (eds.) Computer and Information Sciences II, pp. 173–177. Springer, London (2011). https://doi.org/10.1007/978-1-4471-2155-8_21
4. Basagni, S., Carosi, A., Petrioli, C.: Controlled vs. uncontrolled mobility in wireless sensor networks: some performance insights. In: 2007 IEEE 66th Vehicular Technology Conference, VTC-2007 Fall, pp. 269–273. IEEE, September 2007
5. Gu, Y., Liu, H., Song, F., Zhao, B.: Joint sink mobility and data diffusion for lifetime optimization in wireless sensor networks. In: The 2nd IEEE Asia-Pacific Service Computing Conference, pp. 56–61. IEEE, December 2007
6. Jain, S., Shah, R.C., Brunette, W., Borriello, G., Roy, S.: Exploiting mobility for energy efficient data collection in wireless sensor networks. Mob. Netw. Appl. **11**(3), 327–339 (2006)
7. Shah, R.C., Roy, S., Jain, S., Brunette, W.: Data mules: modeling and analysis of a three-tier architecture for sparse sensor networks. Ad Hoc Netw. **1**(2), 215–233 (2003)
8. Koç, M., Korpeoglu, I.: Traffic-and energy-load-based sink mobility algorithms for wireless sensor networks. Int. J. Sens. Netw. **23**(4), 211–221 (2017)

9. Jong, G.J., Horng, G.J.: A novel queen honey bee migration (QHBM) algorithm for sink repositioning in wireless sensor network. Wirel. Pers. Commun. **95**(3), 3209–3232 (2017)
10. Tan, C., Xu, K., Wang, J., Chen, S.: A sink moving scheme based on local residual energy of nodes in wireless sensor networks. J. Cent. S. Univ. Technol. **16**, 265–268 (2009). https://doi.org/10.1007/s11771-009-0045-z
11. Gose, E., Johnsonbaugh, R., Jost, S.: Pattern Recognition and Image Analysis. Prentice Hall of India Private Ltd., New Delhi (2006)
12. Kinalis, A., Nikoletseas, S., Patroumpa, D., Rolim, J.: Biased sink mobility with adaptive stop times for low latency data collection in sensor networks. Inf. Fusion **15**, 56–63 (2014)

Detection of High Transmission Power Based Wormhole Attack Using Received Signal Strength Indicator (RSSI)

Prachi Sharma$^{(\boxtimes)}$ and Rajendra Kumar Dwivedi

Department of Computer Science and Engineering, Madan Mohan Malaviya
University of Technology, Gorakhpur, India
sharmapl528@gmail.com, rkdcs@mmmut.ac.in

Abstract. Wireless sensor network (WSN) is a group of various sensors which is used to sense data from the surrounding and sends it to the base station. This emerging technology has some remarkable applications for making human life better. WSN has some issues too such as power efficiency and security. Due to its open nature, it also attracts attackers toward itself which in result hampers the security of the network. Wormhole attack is one of the severe attack at network layer. It has different modes of attack and one of them is high transmission power mode. This paper proposes a model for detection of wormhole attack using received signal strength indicator (RSSI) and with the help of this model malicious node having high transmission power is detected.

Keywords: Malicious node · Wormhole attack · RSSI
High transmission power

1 Introduction

The sensor nodes are deployed randomly in WSN to collect the data from the sur-roundings [1, 10]. Sensor node is a hardware device which is a collection of electronic essentials like micro controller, sensor, battery, and transducer (Fig. 1).

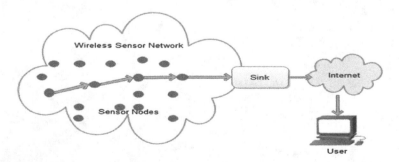

Fig. 1. A WSN environment

© Springer Nature Singapore Pte Ltd. 2019
S. Verma et al. (Eds.): CNC 2018, CCIS 839, pp. 142–152, 2019.
https://doi.org/10.1007/978-981-13-2372-0_13

WSN has many applications for hostile environment. Some of the applications are weather monitoring, underground monitoring, traffic monitoring, under water monitoring, air monitoring and moisture balance it is also widely used in military applications and medical applications [10] (Fig. 2).

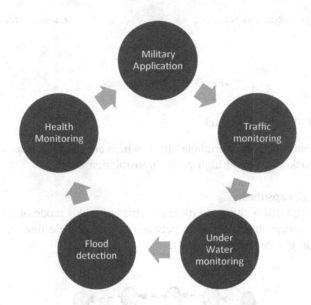

Fig. 2. Applications of wireless sensor network

The numbers of applications attract the researchers as well as attackers towards this area. There are various issues such as power efficiency, responsiveness, scalability, security etc. There are several attacks which takes place at each layer of internet model. Wormhole attack is one of the attacks at network layer of internet model [2].

The rest of the paper is organized as follows. Section 2 briefly focuses on wormhole attack and different modes of this attack. Section 3 describes RSSI. A model is proposed for detection of wormhole attack in Sect. 4. The simulation results of the proposed model are show in Section Finally, Sect. 6 concludes the work and provides conclusion and future directions.

2 Wormhole Attack

In wormhole attack a tunnel is formed between two malicious nodes. This tunnel is responsible for the shortest route between malicious nodes and it misguides the other legitimate nodes to follow the route which in result either drop the packet or it is broadcasted locally so that it cannot follow its actual route. As wormhole does not make any changes in the packet information thus cryptography cannot be used for the prevention from this attack [6, 7] (Fig. 3).

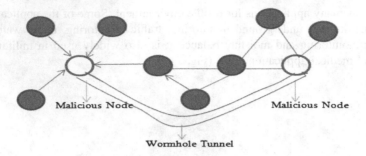

Fig. 3. Wormhole attack

2.1 Modes of Wormhole Attack

There are different modes of wormhole attack which are packet encapsulation, out of band channel, packet relay and high power transmission attack.

2.1.1 Packet Encapsulation
The Packet is misguided with wrong route information in this mode of attack. Thus the malicious node encapsulates the node between source and destination and shortest route information is received [3] (Fig. 4).

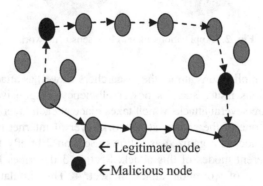

Fig. 4. Packet encapsulation

2.1.2 Out of Band Channel
In this mode, a high bandwidth tunnel is generated which is used to launch the attack. The tunnel can be established through wireless link rather than a long wired link [10]. Though the attack sounds easier but factually needs a very specialized and efficient hardware system which makes it difficult to initiate as compared to the other modes.

2.1.3 Packet Relay

In Packet Relay, the malicious node creates an illusion of being neighbor. The malicious node (M) relays the packet between the far apart nodes and creates the attack. This mode can be implemented by a single vindictive node [4] (Fig. 5).

Fig. 5. Packet relay

2.1.4 High Transmission Power

In wormhole attack with high transmission power only a single malicious node is responsible to form a shortest route between source node to destination node, generally it is implemented in homogeneous network. As a single malicious node is easy in implementation process but it is difficult to detect. This attack does not make any changes in the header format or in the routing table which makes it legitimate node and it require a different strategy for detection and prevention. As we know that in homogeneous network all the nodes have same specification thus any special hardware capability of node may attract the other nodes which increase the chances of better communication.

In high transmission power based attack nodes can be attached internally or externally. In wireless communication antenna height and transmission power has an important role as by increasing the transmission range results in expanding its communication limit. As per WSN standard destination node is not in the range of source node thus it takes help of immediate nodes to make its route [5].

In wormhole attack with high transmission power the attacker not only need to increase the transmission power but also antenna height for its wide range. Initially attacker places a malicious nodes, as its range is between source and destination or source node should be in its range. This gives a shortest route from source to destination when source generate RREQ message packet. This data packet is transmitted quickly to its destination thus shortest route is established and malicious node will be noted as a next hop in routing table.

In Fig. 6 malicious node has high transmission power and thus due to its wide range it becomes the shortest route between sender and destination node. After having a route establishment when a data packet is sent from sender then the malicious node drops the packet in between thus this attack causes loss of data packet.

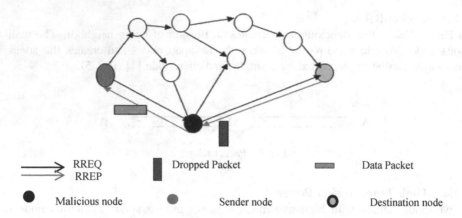

Fig. 6. High transmission power mode of wormhole

3 Received Signal Strength Indicator (RSSI) Model

Localization is one of the basic technology of WSN. Though, it is hard to detect the position of specific nodes as they are deployed randomly. As positioning from GPS (global positioning system) is energy consuming and costly, thus there are two basic algorithms used for localization which are range based and range free algorithms. Range based algorithms are far more accurate than range free algorithm.

Range base localization algorithm use distance estimation or received signal strength by some sort of measuring techniques. Just as the use of RSSI ranging need less communication overhead, lower implementation complexity, and lower cost, so it is very suitable for the nodes in wireless sensor network which have limited power [9]. RSSI circuitry is placed inside transceivers chip set in the sensor. It needs light computation for the measurement of signal strength which does not overload the sensor processing power. Therefore, it is a cost effective technology.

The connection between RSSI values and distance has the basic and the significant role in wireless sensor network for ranging and positioning technologies. There are different models of RSSI such as, HADTA model, log-distance path loss model, log-normal shadowing model (LNSM) and two-ray ground reflection model [8]. The models for signal propagation can describe the better relationship between the RSSI values and distance.

The receive signal strength of transmitter and receiver is negative as the ideal RSSI ranges at every end between −40 dBm and −50 dBm to get the appropriate data sets [11] (Table 1).

Table 1. RSSI signal values [11]

Desired RSSI	−40 to−50 dBm
Usable RSSI	−35 to−70 dBm
Strong signal	Above−35 dBm
Weak signal	Below−70 dBm

4 Proposed Model

A model is proposed for the detection of wormhole attack having high transmission power using RSSI. Wormhole attack using high power transmission is difficult to detect as it has aim for dropping of packet rather than making any changes in the data packet which makes it prone to cryptographic techniques. It can only be detected if each node can check its received signal strength. Therefore, by using RSSI, the transmission power between the receiver node and transmitted node is checked and the malicious node is detected on basis of the relation of this transmission power and distance between transmitter and receiver. Now this malicious node could be discarded.

4.1 Attack Scenario

In Fig. 7 an attack scenario is shown where the nodes are static and they are deployed in homogeneous environment; but when a node comes in the network with high transmission power then the data packets sent from sender to receiver is dropped in between.

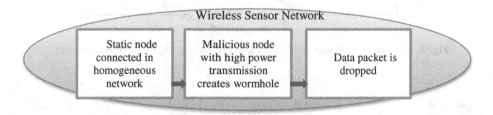

Fig. 7. WSN attack scenario

4.2 Proposed Methodology

The proposed methodology is shown in the flowchart of Fig. 8 given below. Relation between P_R, P_T, n and d is given in Eq. 1. Here P_R is the received power of the signal, P_T is the transmitted power of the signal, d is the distance between the transmitting node and the receiving node and n is the transmission factor which is dependent on a propagation environment. The value of n is between 2–3. As in this scenario, the nodes are static and deployed in a homogeneous environment. The value of n will not change. The values of P_T and P_R is obtained with the help of RSSI. Now, the distance (d) can be calculated by taking antilog of Eq. 2:

$$\log P_R = \log P_T - n \log d \qquad (1)$$

$$n \log d = \log P_R - \log P_T$$

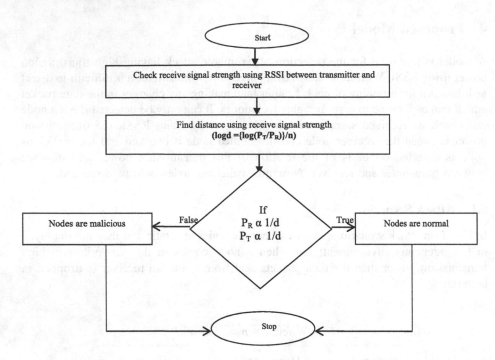

Fig. 8. Detecting malicious node from network having high transmission power

$$\log d = \{\log(P_T/P_R)\}/n \tag{2}$$

On the basis of the sensor reading, the received signal strength (P_R) and the transmitted signal strength (P_T) is taken which are shown in Table 2.

Table 2. P_R and P_T signal values

Node ID	N1	N2	N3	N4	N5
P_R	−70	−65	−55	−45	−40
P_T	−60	−50	−40	−30	−25

Now, with the help of Eq. 2 the d is calculated and is given in Table 3.

Table 3. Relation of P_R and P_T signal values with distance d

Node ID	N1	N2	N3	N4	N5
P_R	−70	−65	−55	−45	−40
P_T	−60	−50	−40	−30	−25
d	0.95	0.91	0.89	0.87	0.85

As per the data obtained in Table 3, it can be concluded that the value of d is increasing when the values of P_T and P_R are decreasing and vice versa. It indicates an inverse relation of P_T and P_R with d as shown in the Eqs. 4 and 5.

$$P_T \propto 1/d \tag{4}$$

$$P_R \propto 1/d \tag{5}$$

When we get this relationship, the nodes will be normal otherwise there would be possibility of malicious node which needs to be detected. Here, the readings of Table 3 show that the nodes are normal because we get an inversely proportional relationship of P_R and P_T with d.

If a malicious node with high transmission power is present in the network then it will show some varying effect. Table 4 shows the presence of a malicious node in the homogeneous network because the readings written with **bold** violates the rule of Eqs. 4 and 5. In other words it can be said that as per the Eqs. 4 and 5, all the normal nodes follow a relation that P_R and P_T start increasing, with the decrease of d; but the malicious nodes does not follows this relation. Thus it can be said that node N6 would be the malicious node with high transmission power in the homogenous network.

Table 4. Readings in homogeneous network indicating the malicious node (N6)

Node ID	N1	N2	N3	N4	N5	N6
P_R	−70	−65	−55	−45	−40	**−25**
P_T	−60	−50	−40	−30	−25	**−20**
d	0.95	0.91	0.89	0.87	0.85	**0.92**

5   Simulation and Results

The proposed work is implemented using Castalia simulator and the results are shown in Subsects. 5.1 and 5.2. The proposed model calculates the distance (d) and detects the malicious node with help of the relation of d with P_T and P_R.

5.1   Presence of Only Normal Nodes in Homogeneous Network

Figure 9 shows a graph between P_R and d which describes that P_R is inversely proportional to d.

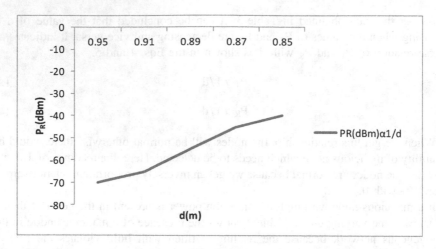

Fig. 9. Relation between P_R and d ($P_R \propto 1/d$)

Figure 10 represents a graph between P_T and d which shows that P_T is inversely proportional to d.

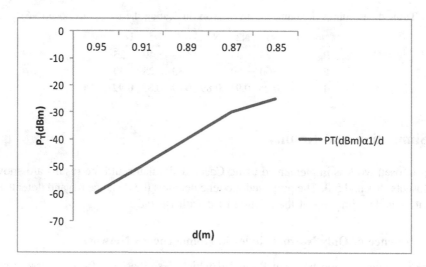

Fig. 10. Relation between P_T and d ($P_T \propto 1/d$)

5.2 Presence of Malicious Node in Homogeneous Network

Figures 11 and 12 shows the results for the presence of malicious nodes in the homogeneous network. Figure 11 shows a graph between P_R and d and Fig. 12 shows the graph between P_T and d. The results describe that here the inverse relationship is not followed. The point at which this violation of inverse relationship is obtained represents the malicious node.

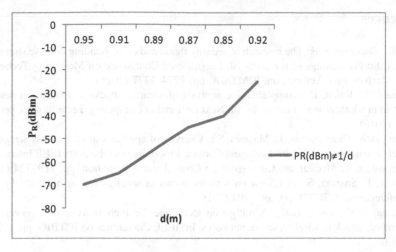

Fig. 11. Relation between P_R and d (with malicious node)

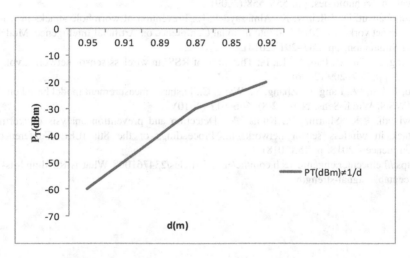

Fig. 12. Relation between P_T and d (with malicious node)

The kink in the graph of Figs. 11 and 12 represents the malicious node. Thus malicious node with high transmission power is detected.

6 Conclusion and Future Directions

In this paper high transmission power based wormhole attack is detected with the help of received signal strength. As this attack leads to data loss so by detecting the malicious node the security of the homogeneous network can be upgraded. In future, this work can be extended to optimize power efficiency too.

References

1. Yi, L., Zhongyong, F.: The research of security threat and corresponding defense strategy for WSN. In: Proceedings of the 2015 7th International Conference on Measuring Technology and Mechatronics Automation, ICMTMA, pp. 1274–1277 (2015)
2. Shanthi, S., Rajan, E.: Comprehensive analysis of security attacks and intrusion detection system in wireless sensor networks. In: Next Generation Computing Technologies, pp. 426–431 (2016)
3. Arampatzis, Th., Lygeros, J., Manesis, S.: A survey of applications of wireless sensors and wireless sensor networks. In: Intelligent Control, Proceedings of the 2005 IEEE International Symposium on Mediterrean Conference on Control and Automation, pp. 719–724 (2005)
4. Grover, J., Sharma, S.: A review on security issues in wireless sensor network. In: IEEE Conference on ICRITO, pp. 397–404 (2016)
5. Sharma, M.K., Joshi, B.K.: A mitigation technique for high transmission power based wormhole attack in wireless sensor networks. In: IEEE Conference on ICTBIG, pp. 123–130 (2016)
6. Jain, M., Kandwa, H.: A survey on complex wormhole attack in wireless ad hoc networks. In: ACT - International Conference on Advances in Computing, Control, and Telecommunication Technologies, pp. 555–558 (2009)
7. Aldhobaiban, D., Elleithy, K., Almazaydeh, L.: Prevention of wormhole attacks in wireless sensor networks. In: 2014 2nd International Conference on Artificial Intelligence, Modelling and Simulation, pp. 287–291 (2014)
8. Zheng, J., Liu, Y., Fan, X., Li, F.: The study of RSSI in wireless sensor networks, vol. 133, no. 2, pp. 207–209 (2016)
9. Xu, J., Liu, W., Lang, F., Zhang, Y., Wang, C.: Distance measurement model based on RSSI in WSN. Wirel. Sens. Netw. **2**(8), 606–611 (2010)
10. Dwivedi, R.K., Sharma, P., Kumar, R.: Detection and prevention analysis of wormhole attack in wireless sensor network. In: Proceedings of the 8th IEEE Conference on Confluence - 2018, p. 35 (2018)
11. https://helpcenter.engeniustech.com/hc/en-us/articles/234761008-What-is-RSSI-and-its-acceptable-signal-strength

Effective Data Storage Security with Efficient Computing in Cloud

Manoj Tyagi[1]([⊠]), Manish Manoria[2], and Bharat Mishra[1]

[1] Mahatma Gandhi Chitrakoot Gramodya Vishwavidyalaya, Chitrakoot, India
manojtyagi80.bhopal@gmail.com, bharat.mgcgv@gmail.com
[2] Sagar Institute Research Technology and Science, Bhopal, India
manishmanoria@gmail.com

Abstract. Cloud Computing is well-known resource sharing model uses internet to offer several computing and data storage services. Due to distributed resources and their availability for numerous users, the level of complexity for the resource allocation and security accessing, increases. The paper mainly focuses on meta-heuristic approach for resource allocation and data security using data classification approach. In the proposed framework multi-factor verification is applied to verify the user's credentials prior to data accessing. Encryption at user side not only ensures the integrity but also confidentiality of data. Here MCS (Modified Cuckoo Search), PSEC (Provably Secure Elliptic Curve) encryption and AES (Advanced Encryption Standard) is used for resource scheduling, user side encryption, and cloud side encryption respectively for attaining integrity, confidentiality and also efficient computation ability.

Keywords: Cloud computing · MCS · Authentication · AES
PSEC encryption · Confidentiality · Integrity · Resource allocation
Efficient computation

1 Introduction

Cloud Computing (CC) is basically used for resources sharing. It delivers various services like Platform (PaaS), Infrastructure (IaaS), and Software (SaaS) to its clients over the web. Clients remotely access cloud for obtaining these cost effective services as per their demand. These services became as much essential to the society as other useful services like, cooking gas, electricity power, water supply and telephony. Because of scalability, ease of utilization and flexibility, cloud computing is widely adopted and became popular as essential utility in almost all type of community and for business purpose too [1]. Well-organized resource allocation and data storage; both are the challenges in cloud, because of virtualization. Therefore, various solutions are needed for efficient computation and effective security, as both are essential component for growth of cloud computing [2]. Resource scheduling is the approach which allocates the accurate task among various resources like storage, network and CPU in well-organized manner, in this way cloud improves its resource utilization and performance in various available service like PaaS, IaaS and SaaS [3].

© Springer Nature Singapore Pte Ltd. 2019
S. Verma et al. (Eds.): CNC 2018, CCIS 839, pp. 153–164, 2019.
https://doi.org/10.1007/978-981-13-2372-0_14

Through various scheduling approaches, cloud computing performs the optimal resource allocation among the given jobs and complete the job in optimal time. Meta-heuristic scheduling approaches like ACO (Ant Colony Optimization), PSO (Particle swarm Optimization), BA (Bat Algorithm) and GA (Genetic algorithm) are generally slower than other techniques but it gives the outstanding results, so it is the vital research topic that how to improve these approaches to get quality result in minimum time [4]. In last few years, consumers adopted the cloud rapidly because of its key features like, security, portability, availability of services, elasticity and interoperability. But cloud is also facing many challenges to establish its acceptability at larger level. Security is the key factor, which is required for increasing the users of cloud computing. For maintaining the trust on the cloud it is essential to find out the solution of current security attacks like Dos attack, Side-channel attack, insiders' attacks, phishing attacks, and attacks on shared memory [5]. Reputation of cloud depends upon trust between cloud provider and its users. Trust can only be achieved when cloud provider gives guaranteed security to its user's access and confidentiality of their data [6]. Proposed work focuses on the computational efficiency and security in the cloud. PSEC cryptography is applied to obtain the integrity and confidentiality. MCS algorithm is applied to accomplish the computational efficiency.

2   Motivation

The Cloud framework provides lot off benefits such as achieving reduced implementation cost of any organization, availability of resources on demand, easy access, secured and trustworthy data storage, and variety of services. Because of multi-tenancy, virtualization and shared resource pool, many security threats exist in the proper functioning of clouds. Many users access the same cloud for their organizational requirement, so there is fair possibility of unauthorized access, malicious access and attacker's access; this causes data leakage, data theft and various security breaches. The traditional security systems were not suitable for applications and data in cloud. Lack of security of data deployed in cloud, storage efficiency and scalability are the major challenges for cloud network that creates major problems while rendering services to cloud clients. Now-a-days many individual clients and organizations are dependent completely on cloud for their computing and data storage requirement, therefore, it is necessary to develop a cloud framework that is more secure and error prone with increased reliability. These security requirement forces the researchers to deal with this current issue by providing various security features in existing cloud system. This research work addresses these problems through proposing an effective framework that provides data security using suitable encryption scheme and a way for achieving efficient computation in cloud.

3 Resource Scheduling

Resource scheduling allocates the resources for given task on some basis in order to employ the resources and complete all task in efficient manner. Efficient scheduling improves the task performance through load balancing of resources. Resource scheduling is categorized in following six classes [3] given in Fig. 1.

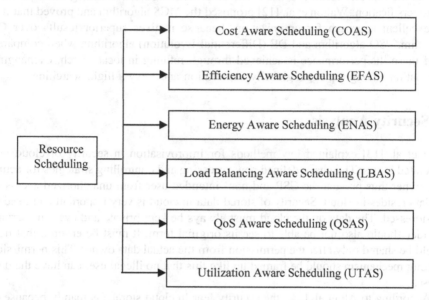

Fig. 1. Categorization of scheduling

Makhloufi et al. [7] found that meta-heuristic approaches like CS (Cuckoo Search), FP (Flower Pollination) and FA (Firefly algorithm) gives accurate solution when these are utilized to optimize the power flow. Through comparison among them, it is proved that CS performed better than FP and FA on parameters like accuracy and computation time. Raghavan et al. [8] applied BA with the approach of BBA (Binary bat algorithm) for allocating the resources for requested task with minimal cost in cloud. BA utilizes randomization for searching the optimal result and also shows the supremacy in resource sharing. Kaur et al. [9], proposed ADF (Adaptive firefly approach) algorithm for allotment of virtual machines in data centers and on the basis of experimental result, it was proved that this approach is better than ACO approach for load balancing. On the request of users for resources, cloud provider provides the resources dynamically in "on-demand" manner. Efficient load balancing is essential for optimal resource utilization for attaining maximize throughput with minimum processing time.

For improving the performance of load balancing, FP algorithm was combined with various different optimization strategies such as Quantum Theory, Tabu Search, Chaotic Theory and CSA (Clonal Selection Algorithm). Nabil [10] proposed the MFP (Modified flower pollination) approach which is the result of combining FP algorithm and CSA. Investigational findings shows that MFP algorithm give more accurate finding than other approach like SA (Simulated Annealing), GA algorithm, FP algorithm, BA algorithm and FA algorithm.

Abdel-Basset et al. [11] compared CS algorithm with FP algorithm and find that FP algorithm is superior to CS algorithm in speed while CS algorithm is superior to FP algorithm in finding optimal result. So when accuracy is required CS algorithm is preferred and when speed is required FP algorithm is much better. Meta-heuristic ensures high quality result if it has balanced search through combining intensification and diversification. Walton et al. [12] proposed the MCS algorithm and proved that it is the excellent approach for optimization, because it gives superior results over CS algorithm, PSO algorithm and DE (Differential Evolution) algorithm, when compared all of these. Its performance is achieved through refining in local search, exchanging information among top eggs, globally exploration and Levy's flight searching.

4 Security Analysis

Rong et al. [13] explained few methods for improvisation in security of cloud and associated issues. They have defined new accessing and controlling strategies for actual data owner thus prevent the CSP and non- intended user from unauthorized access of the data resides in cloud. Security of stored data in cloud is very important and need to be addressed. The data on the cloud must always be kept private and even the service provider should also not be able to see its original form. It must be ensured that data should be shared only after the permission from the actual data owner. This permission granting mechanism should be framed up like this that no illegal user can have the data access.

According to Ali et al. [14], the security fear in cloud storage is mainly because of virtualization of resources, allowing multiple users to access the cloud also known as multi-tenancy and sharing of available resources. It is obvious that the available resources are accessed through the user in sharing mode in cloud, because of that authentication of users is highly required before accessing the resources. All these resources are heterogeneous in nature and accessed in dynamic manner, this makes it difficult to control their accessing. The basic thought behind cloud services is to handle multiple users simultaneously, that is to maintain the multi-tenancy. This ability also brings critical security challenges for opposite functioning of cloud based system and proved itself as big challenge for the researchers and company professionals to provide its solutions. Virtualization is also an essential requirement for cloud implementation, as resources are not physically available to the user. As all the accessing and all the operations are virtual, it is necessary to employ some security mechanism for authorized accessing.

[15] Yahya et al. proposed security of stored data, depending on its type, according to him the sensitive data should be given more secured treatment over the non-sensitive data. Two-Stage-Encryption should be applied for Sensitive data while only one stage encryption is sufficient over non-sensitive data (Table 1).

[16] Hingwe et al. has discussed their findings that user's data should be categorized according to their security requirements, like protected data, sensitive data and highly sensitive data. Therefore different security levels of cryptography should be

Table 1. Protection levels in cloud storage [15]

Security levels	Authentication	Authorization	Encryption
Protected	Single-Factor	- Administrator	- SSL
			- AES 256 bit
Sensitive	Multi-Factor	- Administrator	- SSL
		- Safe Access Sharing	- AES 256 bit
Top secret	Multi-Factor	- Super admin	- SSL
		- Safe Access Sharing	- AES 256 bit
			- RSA
			- File Name Encryption

applied as per the nature of the data. More powerful security techniques should be applicable for highly sensitive data, and also sensitive data compared to protected data. Classifying the data make it doable to provide it appropriate security and develop an efficient system for secured data storage and its effective management.

According to Younis et al. [17] apart from the various exciting features, cloud computing also have some challenges like, security of data, misuse of services, inside attackers, and various cyber related attacks. Control over accessing the cloud is the vital need among all of these security challenges, which ensures the preventions of malicious users. In this work importance is given mainly on controlling the cloud access, which is not considered in traditional approaches. Strategy capable of protecting a resource sharing as well as diverse permissions to the same user for accessing various services is suggested.

Moghaddam et al. [18] suggested the authentication process based on client side authentication, this reduces the complexity at server side. In this model a background programming code is installed at client side machine along with client browser known as agent. The request for agent requires the registration of the machine at server side. As a result, the server generates the unique access code for this registered machine which is sent to the client either directly, or encrypted by the password provided by the client, using AES-192 or AES-256, which will be decrypted only by the requesting client. Now the agent will check the identity at client side itself thus protect against the Man in Middle Attack (MIMA).

Sood et al. [19] proposed a scheme for storing the data by the owner and accessing by the various clients. The overall security of data and its storage is based on data's taxonomy as per their security requirement. Some data requires confidentiality, some requires integrity, and some requires availability. According to the author, each client who wants data access has to request the owner to provide the digital signature, for accessing the data. Prior to accepting the request, owner verifies the clients. On successful verification, the owner sends digital signature consisting necessary detail to the requesting client. Now the client access the cloud for accessing data by using the detail provided by the owner (Fig. 2).

Meslhy et al. [20] suggested various suitable approaches for applying data's security, authentication of user, integrity of stored data by identifying various states of data like, data at rest, data in transfer state and data at processing state. According to

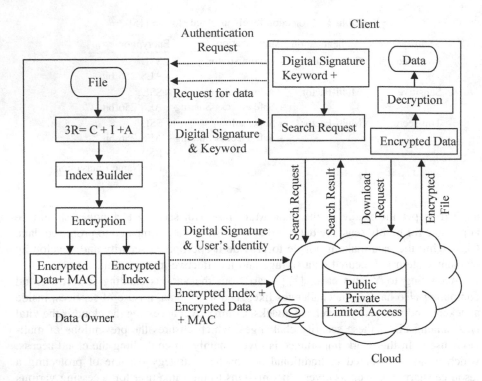

Fig. 2. Structure for accessing the data

them different security treatment should be given to data. If data is in processing state then asymmetric encryption like RSA should be applied, if it is in transit state more security is required that can be attained through security protocols like HTTPS, SSL etc., and if the data is at rest, it should be secured through symmetric encryption approach AES. They found in their work that OTP is a strongest tool for verify the user's identity based on two-fold authentication scheme.

5 Proposed Work

Cloud computing (CC) is widely used in business and in variety of community on personnel basis. It has gained wide popularity in last few years, due to its flexibility, scalability and cost effectiveness. As the CC is dependent on resource sharing, which creates various security issues; the security is an important research area in cloud computing. In the proposed work, first the diverse security approaches were analyzed and on the basis of findings for enhancing the security, a framework for storing and retrieving the data securely in cloud, is proposed. Here data is categorized according to their security requirement and protection is proposed on the class of data that is highly sensitive, sensitive, and protected. For authentication, a unique access code that installed on the user's side browser works as an authentication agent to reduce the server's overhead. A cloud-centric, secure two-fold authentication protocol for cloud storage data is proposed. This twofold process consists of identifying the cloud user and afterwards validating the identity of cloud user through mutual authentication without a verification table. Specifically, this approach does not depend on any trusted third party for secure communication and protect from MIMA attack and ACCA (Adaptive Chosen Cipher text Attack). PSEC cryptography is applied to attain the security as well as integrity in this work. On loss of the main file, the data is recovered from the remote server which provides the backup and recovery to data. This framework gives rich authentication, confidentiality, data integrity and efficient data backup and recovery for cloud storage data (Fig. 3).

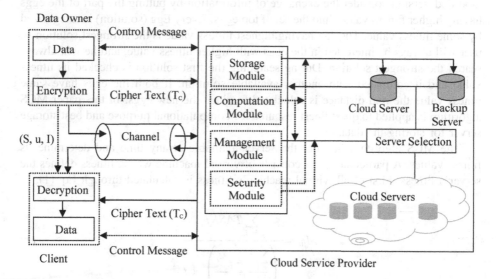

Fig. 3. Proposed framework

5.1 System Model

Data Owner (DO). It is the authority or user like any individual, company persons and any organization who is the owner of data. First it encrypt the data at own side and also calculate the tag value for integration purpose. After that the data is stored on cloud in encrypted form and sends the necessary credential which are helpful for client to access the data from cloud.

Client (C_l). It is any person or user who wants to access the encrypted data which are stored in cloud by data owner. This user decrypts this data and also checks its integrity on its own side using the credential provided by data owner.

Cloud- Service-Provider (CSP). CSP is controlling authority which handles many servers in cloud where Data Owner reside their data. It provides the data to clients after authentication when clients request for it.

5.2 Modified Cuckoo Search

CS algorithm adopts reproduction behavior of cuckoo bird for their searching process. It uses some other birdies nest to place their eggs. If the birds failed to identify that egg then cuckoo's egg is safe and after some time birth of new cuckoo takes place. The main task in this process is to find out the safe nest using lavy's flight. The MCS algorithm [12] use the lavy's flight approach with an updated lavy's flight walk size (β). At every generation the value of β get decreased in reply to make more local search in this way the user become more nearer to the solution. In conventional cuckoo search, there was no any provision for exchanging the information between two eggs, the modified version consider the exchange of information by putting the part of the eggs having higher fitness values into the set of top eggs. Every Egg (solution) is categorized by some fitness value. The egg having highest fitness value is the strongest solution so user will always be interested in the eggs with higher fitness value, and he will always search the strongest solution. During searching the first solution is checked its fitness value and it compared with another available solution. If both the eggs have same fitness value the mid distance is calculated to place the new eggs. In this paper MCS algorithm is applied to quest finest resource for computational purpose and best storage server for storing the data.

The MCS algorithm find out the server available at any time and determine its fitness values. A particular server consists of virtual machine whose fitness defines the server's fitness. First of all, virtual machine's fitness is calculated through Eq. (1).

$$
M_{fit} = \frac{\sum\limits_{j=1}^{S} TASKj}{\left(\dfrac{\sum\limits_{j=1}^{S} C_j \sum\limits_{j=1}^{S} M_j}{U} \right) \times t}
\tag{1}
$$

Where total count of Virtual Machine and Memory unit are represented by Symbol S and U respectively. Computing power and the memory utilization are denoted by Cj and M_j respectively. $TASK_J$ are number of task running in the Virtual Machine and M_{fit} is the fitness of virtual machine.

5.3 Data Storage Security

For data security, several cryptographic techniques, included in various protocol can be suited. However, few symmetric encryption techniques like DES, RC4 should be avoided in present scenario because these are not able to secure the data from new threats. New symmetric technique AES instead of these algorithm can be preferred instead of the above mentioned algorithms, because of its efficient encryption.

Asymmetric algorithm like RSA-768, RSA-1024 are breakable should be replaced by RSA-3072. But RSA 3072 takes more time in encryption so ECC is preferred, which gives same security level with small key size. Following table describes about various key sizes of ECC, AES and RSA for achieving same security level. For integrity, generally SHA-256 is preferred over MD5 in present time, for authentication ECDSA-256 or ECDSA-384 is preferred generally and ECDH-256 or ECDH- 384 should be applied in key exchange (Table 2).

Table 2. Key size recommendation of NIST 2007

Symmetric key size	Soundness	Modulus size of RSA	Key size of elliptic curve
80	Upto 2010	1024	160
112	Upto 2030	2048	224
128	Beyond 2030	3072	256
192	–	7680	384
256	–	15360	512

Data owner and Client applied PSEC [21] and cloud applied AES on their own side. Generate the symmetric key E_1 and E_2 using Diffie-Hellman, where E_1 is applied for encryption of data while E_2 is used for verification of cipher text. Here KDF is key derivation process, ENC is the encryption function utilizing symmetric-key and MAC is the message authentication code. PSEC cryptography defends the data from ACCA attacks.

For finite field F_b, an elliptic curve T is considered. In this field, consider point F of prime order b on elliptic curve. Notation used in Domain parameters are (b, F_R, T, g, h, F, K, m), Where c and d are coefficient which define the elliptic curve equation, T is randomly created elliptic curve and F_R is field representation, K stands for order of point F and m represents cofactor.

Given Equation describe an elliptic curve T over F_b.

$$y^2 = cx + d + x^3 \tag{2}$$

Where d, c $\in F_b$ satisfy $27d^2 + 4c^3 \neq 0$ (mod b).

Key Pairs. The Process of Key generation is responsible to generate secret key and public key.

Key Generation for PSEC [21]

1. Select Secret Key $K_s \in_R [1, K - 1]$.
2. Compute Public Key $K_P = K_s F$
3. Return (K_s, K_P).

Encryption. Data Owner converts its data into cipher text (T_C) at its own side after applying encryption and also calculates tag value I of cipher text.

Encryption using PSEC [21]

1. Select $p \in_R \{0, 1\}^n$, where n is bit-length of K.
2. $(E', E_1, E_2) \leftarrow$ KDF (p), where E' has bit-length n +128.
3. Compute E = E' mod K.
4. Compute S = EF and W = EK_P.
5. Compute $u = p \oplus$ KDF (S, W).
6. Compute $T_C = ENC_{E1} (T_P)$ and I = $MAC_{E2} (T_C)$.
7. Return(S, T_C, u, I).

Decryption. Clients receives data from cloud and verify the signature or tag value of cipher text, If it is matched then convert encrypted data in plain text at own side using decryption Process otherwise not received the data.

Decryption using PSEC [21]

1. Compute W = K_SS.

2. Compute $p = u \oplus$ KDF (S, W).

3. $(E', E_1, E_2) \leftarrow$ KDF (p), where E' has bit-length n +128.
4. Compute E = E' mod K.
5. Compute S' = EF.
6. If S' $\neq$ S then return ("Reject the ciphertext").
7. Compute I' = MAC_{E2} (T_C). If I' $\neq$ I then return ("Reject the ciphertext").
8. Compute $T_P = DEC_{E1}(T_C)$.
9. Return (T_P).

---

6 Conclusion

Cloud computing is one of the most popular and widely used technology in computation field, since its inception. This area has attracted large number of individual customers, organizations and research professional towards it for their various computational requirements. This paper described the existing optimization approaches for resource scheduling, and proposed MCS algorithm for efficient allotment of computing resources. Along with effective resource handling, the paper also dealt with security concern related to authentication, which is solved by using unique access code installed over data owner and client side. This eliminates the effect of Man-in-Middle attack. To maintain the confidentiality and integrity PSEC approach is used at client side, which also protects from ACCA attack. The work also considered the classification of user's data as per its security needs and provide the solution accordingly. The recovery of data is also maintained by providing the backup at the remote server. Overall the proposed work improved security provisions and increased resource performance in cloud.

References

1. Buyyaa, R., Yeoa, C.S., Venugopala, S., Broberg, J., Brandic, I.: Cloud computing and emerging IT platforms: vision, hype, and reality for delivering computing as the 5th utility. Futur. Gener. Comput. Syst. **25**, 599–616 (2009)
2. Wei, L., et al.: Security and privacy for storage and computation in cloud computing. Inf. Sci. **258**, 371–386 (2014)
3. Madni, S.H.H., Latiff, M.S.A., Coulibaly, Y., Abdulhamid, S.M.: Resource scheduling for infrastructure as a service (IaaS) in cloud computing: challenges and opportunities. J. Netw. Comput. Appl. **68**, 173–200 (2016)
4. Kalra, M., Singh, S.: A review of metaheuristic scheduling techniques in cloud computing. Egypt. Inform. J. **16**, 275–295 (2015)
5. Khorshed, M.T., Ali, A.B.M.S., Wasimi, S.A.: A survey on gaps, threat remediation challenges and some thoughts for proactive attack detection in cloud computing. Futur. Gener. Comput. Syst. **28**, 833–851 (2012)
6. Huang, J., Nicol, D.M.: Trust mechanisms for cloud computing. J. Cloud Comput.: Adv. Syst. Appl. **2**, 9 (2013)
7. Makhloufi, S., Mekhaldi, A., Teguar, M.: Three powerful nature-inspired algorithms to optimize power flow in Algeria's Adrar power system. Energy **116**, 1117–1130 (2016)
8. Raghavan, S., Marimuthu, C., Sarwesh, P., Chandrasekaran, K.: Bat algorithm for scheduling workflow applications in cloud. In: Electronic Design, Computer Networks and Automated Verification. IEEE (2015)
9. Kaur, G., Kaur, K.: An adaptive firefly algorithm for load balancing in cloud computing. In: Deep, K., et al. (eds.) Proceedings of Sixth International Conference on Soft Computing for Problem Solving. AISC, vol. 546, pp. 63–72. Springer, Singapore (2017). https://doi.org/10.1007/978-981-10-3322-3_7
10. Nabil, E.: A modified flower pollination algorithm for global optimization. Expert Syst. Appl. **57**, 192–203 (2016)
11. Abdel-Basset, M., Shawky, L.A., Sangaiah, A.K.: A comparative study of cuckoo search and flower pollination algorithm on solving global optimization problems. Libr. Hi Tech **35** (4), 595–608 (2017)
12. Walton, S., Hassan, O., Morgan, K., Brown, M.R.: Modified cuckoo search: a new gradient free optimization algorithm. Chaos, Solitons Fractals **44**, 710–718 (2011)
13. Rong, C., Nguyen, S.T., Jaatun, M.G.: Beyond lightning: a survey on security challenges in cloud computing. Comput. Electr. Eng. **39**(1), 47–54 (2013)
14. Ali, M., Khan, S.U., Vasilakos, A.V.: Security in cloud computing: opportunities and challenges. Inf. Sci. **305**, 357–383 (2015)
15. Yahya, F., Walters, R.J., Wills, G.B.: Protecting data in personal cloud storage with security classifications. In: Science and Information Conference. IEEE (2015)
16. Hingwe, K.K., Bhanu, S.M.S.: Two layered protection for sensitive data in cloud. In: Advances in Computing, Communications and Informatics. IEEE (2014)
17. Younis, Y.A., Kifayat, K., Merabti, M.: An access control model for cloud computing. J. Inf. Secur. Appl. **19**(1), 45–60 (2014)
18. Moghaddam, F.F., Moghaddam, S.G., Rouzbeh, S., Araghi, S.K., Alibeigi, N.M., Varnosfaderani, S.D.: A scalable and efficient user authentication scheme for cloud computing environments. In: Region 10 Symposium. IEEE (2014)
19. Sood, S.K.: A combined approach to ensure data security in cloud computing. J. Netw. Comput. Appl. **35**, 1831–1838 (2012)

20. Meslhy, E., Abdelkader, H., El-Etriby, S.: Data security model for cloud computing. J. Commun. Comput. **10**, 1047–1062 (2013)
21. Hankerson, D., Menezes, A., Vanstone, S.: Guide to Elliptic Curve Cryptography. Springer, New York (2004). https://doi.org/10.1007/b97644

Privacy Preserving Multi Keyword Ranked Search with Context Sensitive Synonyms over the Encrypted Cloud Data

Anu Khurana[1]([⊠]), Rama Krishna Challa[2], and Navdeep Kaur[3]

[1] I.K. Gujral PTU, Kapurthala, Punjab, India
annu_khurana@yahoo.com
[2] Department of Computer Science and Engineering, NITTTR,
Chandigarh, India
rkc_97@yahoo.com
[3] Department of Computer Science and Engineering,
Sri Guru Granth Sahib World University, Fatehgarh Sahib, Punjab, India
drnavdeep.iitr@gmail.com

Abstract. The increase in the number of people and organizations relying on cloud for storing their data has led to significant increase in the volume of data on cloud. Wherever the Cloud Service Provider (CSP) allows encryption of documents and metadata, keyword search becomes necessary for quick, easy and effective retrieval of outsourced encrypted cloud data. As the cloud users, over the period of time may tend to forget the exact keywords for issuing a search query, the keyword search therefore should support synonyms. But the synonym discovery is always context sensitive, as not all synonyms can simply replace a word in all occurrences of a query. It is therefore, important to keep the connotation of the word under consideration. As some synonyms can infuse a different meaning, than the one user actually intends for and can cause drift to user's search. In this paper, we propose a scheme Context sensitive Multi keyword Ranked Search (CSMRS) to this issue by analyzing the encrypted query click logs. The results achieved show that the synonyms selected with CSMRS are more appropriate and as per the context as intended by the user.

Keywords: Multi-keyword · Synonyms · Context sensitive
Privacy preserving · Cloud · Encrypted query click logs

1 Introduction

With cloud computing, computing now sees no border. A number of users are getting hooked up with cloud because of the enormous benefits it provides, with a good percentage, using storage as a service [1]. Since the volumes of data stored on the cloud may contain user's sensitive information as well, therefore the data is stored in encrypted format on the cloud. However, at the time of locating and retrieval of the desired documents, a user would prefer a search mechanism for easy and quick retrieval of the needed documents. Encryption though required, makes the operations like searching difficult. The notion of searchable encryption (SE) without the loss of data

S. Verma et al. (Eds.): CNC 2018, CCIS 839, pp. 165–180, 2019.
https://doi.org/10.1007/978-981-13-2372-0_15

confidentiality has been introduced for the first time by Song et al. [2]. Thereafter many researchers, have worked towards increasing efficiency and improving ways of searching over the encrypted data [3–9]. But, these searchable encryption schemes do not directly fit into the cloud environment as they lack the effective mechanism to ensure file retrieval accuracy.

Many researchers [10–19] gave keyword search schemes for searching over encrypted cloud data. Later, for enhancing the search capability, some researchers [20–22] worked in the domain of keyword ranked search allowing queries that support synonyms.

Fu et al. in [20] used searchable index tree with the document index vectors for searching related documents. They built a common synonym thesaurus on the foundation of the New American Roget's College Thesaurus. They extend the extracted keywords for building index with common synonyms in order to allow synonym based search.

Mittal et al. in [21] created a customized synonym dictionary that is updated as new keywords from the files to be outsourced are added. On finding a new keyword, synonyms for every relevant keyword are added to the synonym dictionary. They later expand their query with synonyms from this synonym dictionary and perform search for locating relevant documents.

Saini et al. in [22] builds a synonym dictionary during setup phase. For the query issued, the cloud instead of replacing the query keywords with synonym suggests some synonyms for the user. If the user selects the synonym then the query returns ranked search results for the same.

As per the literature survey the existing schemes of search over encrypted cloud data supporting synonyms either keep waiting for user input or use a fixed set of synonyms. But the synonyms are context sensitive. Synonym for a word simply cannot replace all occurrences of a word in all the queries. For e.g. the words "powerful" and "muscular" are synonyms for the word "strong" but when we use "strong coffee" we do not equally say "powerful coffee" or "muscular coffee". This means the word "powerful" is not used as a synonym for the word "strong" over here. However, in the search query "powerful man" synonym "strong" or "muscular" may replace the keyword "powerful" and we can use "strong man" or "muscular man" as parallel queries in order to get more relevant results as per user's intent.

In this paper, we propose a scheme Context Sensitive Multi keyword Ranked Search (CSMRS) that supports privacy preserving multi keyword ranked search over encrypted cloud data supporting context sensitive synonyms. CSMRS uses encrypted query click logs for locating the relevant synonyms as per the context. CSMRS limits the synonym replacement in the multi keyword queries according to relevance as per the co-occurring words in the query. The encrypted query click logs are recorded whenever a data user downloads any document against the issued search query.

2 Problem Formulation

2.1 Problem

To find the context sensitive synonyms, we need to extract the context sensitive synonyms from the full set of synonyms picked from SD for a word. Neighbouring words in a search query can help to understand the context for a word, hence the need for query click logs. However, for multi keyword ranked search with context sensitive synonyms over the encrypted cloud data we need to take care that it should be privacy preserving. It means that the search query and the search results returned to the user should be hidden from the public cloud server, despite it performing the search operation.

2.2 System Model

CSMRS considers the cloud data hosting service to involve four different entities namely the data owner, the data user, public cloud server and a trusted third party wherein the private cloud server is considered as the trusted third party. The details of the responsibilities of these entities is given in Sect. 5. The architecture of the proposed CSMRS is shown in Fig. 1.

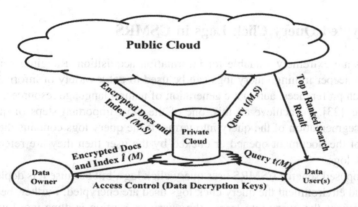

Fig. 1. Architecture of CSMRS (Context Sensitive Multi Keyword Ranked Search)

2.3 Threat Model

In this paper, we consider public cloud server to be "honest-but-curious". It is assumed that it carries out the assigned duties honestly, but is curious to examine data for additional insight. Regarding private cloud we consider it as a trusted third party.

2.4   Notations and Preliminaries

Notations

- $\hat{I}(M)$: Document Index encrypted with key M
- $\hat{I}(M, S)$: Document Index encrypted with key M further encrypted with key S
- $t(M)$: Query unique words encrypted with key M
- $t(M, S)$: Query unique words encrypted with key M further encrypted with key S
- $\cancel{WV}$: Table containing all ciphers of the word vectors
- $S\cancel{D}$: Synonym Dictionary
- $C\cancel{D}$: Collocation Dictionary
- $\bar{Q}$: Master Encrypted Query Click Log.

Preliminaries

Paillier Encryption

It is a probabilistic public key algorithm with additive homomorphic properties. This means that given $E\,(a1)$ and $E\,(a2)$ one can get $E\,(a1 + a2)$. It can also be used to find $E(a1) * a3$, where $a3$ is not encrypted. We use the ability of the Paillier encryption to increment the count (number of times a query has been issued against which documents are downloaded) in the encrypted query click logs. We also use Paillier encryption for encrypting the term frequency of the keywords and their squares in the Index.

3   Encrypted Query Click Logs in CSMRS

Query logs are extremely valuable for information acquisition. Ranging from simple statistics to deeper mining, query logs can be used to get a variety of information like user's search preferences, automatic generation of natural language resources, semantic analysis etc. [23]. To achieve all this, one of the most important steps of query processing is segmentation of the query into terms. If the query logs contains the URL or reference of the document opened or clicked by the user then they are referred to as query click logs.

The proposed scheme CSMRS uses query click logs, but because it is deployed in a public cloud environment the query click logs used are encrypted. Further, because we need to segment the query into terms, the query encryption is done word-wise/term-wise. The encrypted query click logs are maintained on the public cloud server, which can cause a threat in spite of encryption of the query terms. Also, encryption of the query term-wise can allow statistical attacks reveal the pattern of search. Even the most commonly and frequently issued queries by an organization/user may be guessed. Therefore, simply encrypting them with a deterministic encryption algorithm could result in failure in preserving the privacy of the search terms in a cloud environment. Also, if we use non-deterministic encryption algorithms, we would not be able to align the queries against each other. So, we need a mechanism which allows aligning the query terms without actually making the pattern reveal the plaintext. To overcome, the problem of retrieving the plain text through crypto attacks, CSMRS introduces and uses word vectors. It further encrypts the obtained word vectors with ciphers from the table ~~WV~~ by lookup method. The word vectors obtained for every word is different even if they have the same set of alphabets as shown in the Sect. 4.1. This uniqueness provided in the formation of word vectors makes the guessing of the plain text very difficult, as it will be needed to be done for every word. CSMRS makes the encryption of plain text even stronger as after obtaining the word vectors they are further encrypted with corresponding cipher from table ~~WV~~. CSMRS provides protection against guessing of plaintext by infusing dummy words [24] in the query and in the index.

4 Important Notion

4.1 Word Vectors

Word vector is a bit string build up with key M. The key M has the random English alphabets. It is ensured that the key has the complete alphabet set, the alphabets are repeated many times and the alphabets like 'i', 'e', 'a' and others which are more in use in the formation of English words have the repetition number higher than rest of the alphabets.

If we consider, English alphabets to have letters 'a to f' with 'a' being used in most of the English words constructed over the set {'a', 'f'} then a snippet of column matrix could be as shown in Fig. 2.

d, a, b, c, c, f, e, d, a, d, f, e, a, b........

Fig. 2. Snippet of the *1D* matrix (key *M*) on which the word vectors are built

Example: Over the set {'a', 'f'} with key M as in Fig. 2, for getting the word vector for the word "bed" check the *1D* matrix (key M), pick first character of the word "bed" i.e. 'b' and compare with *1D* matrix since first character is 'd' in *1D* matrix set it to 0, next is 'a' set it to 0, next is 'b' set it to 1. Once the bit is set 1, pick next character from the given word i.e. 'e' here. From the point last left, start checking the *1D* matrix. Keep setting all bits to 0 till a match is found so after setting three bits to 0, next bit is set to 1 for character 'e'. Now the bit is set to 1, so pick next character i.e. 'd' from the given word and start checking from the point last left. Next character is 'd' in *1D* matrix set it to 1. Since the bit has been set to 1, so pick next character from the word. We do not have any more characters left, so set remaining all bits from the point last left to 0. Hence the obtained word vector for the word "bed" is 00100011000000.

Similarly the word vectors for the words "bad", "dad", "bed", and "bead" based on the snippet of this matrix will be

$$\text{bad} = 00100000110000, \quad \text{dad} = 11000001000000,$$
$$\text{bed} = 00100011000000, \quad \text{bead} = 00100010110000$$

Obtained word vectors are further treated to ensure cryptographic strength by shifting it around by a shift factor Š. In CSMRS, mid-point is taken as the shift factor. So, the word vector 00100011000000 for the word "bed" after shifting becomes 10000000010001.

4.2 ₩₩V Table

During setup phase (offline phase) we build a ₩₩V table, wherein, we record prebuilt word vectors (of words and dummy words) and their equivalent ciphers with a non-deterministic cipher (AES in our case) with a random key S. We limit the use of non-deterministic cipher in a manner, that we encrypt it and record only one of the random cipher obtained for a word vector in the ₩₩V table. The entire table is built during the setup phase and uploaded on the private cloud server. The presence of key M and ₩₩V table at different locations provides security to the final cipher obtained and its link to the plain text. Therefore, having the key M alone does not reveal the final cipher being uploaded on the public cloud.

4.3 Encrypted Query Click Logs

Query logs are widely used in web search. As Wei et al. in [25] refers that search with synonyms is a challenging task in web as it could lead to intent drift to user's search. Wei et al. in [25] gives a solution to this issue in web search by the analysis of co-clicked queries and further alignment of these queries against each other, where the co-clicked queries are the queries leading to clicking the same documents. So, with a different methodology but similar idea, we have used encrypted query click logs. These encrypted query click logs need to be aligned word by word against each other. Therefore, their encryption as discussed, need to be word-wise or term-wise. To align the queries while preserving the privacy of the search terms, CSMRS uses word vectors for every unique word of index file $\hat{I}(M)$ and queries $t(M)$. These word vectors are created at the user's end with the help of a unique key M shared with him by the data owner. Once generated $\hat{I}(M)$ is sent to the private cloud where they are further encrypted by key S to form $\hat{I}(M, S)$. The key M gives a unique fingerprint to each word. The queries are also encrypted by keys M and S to generate $t(M, S)$.

We store this information, without feeling a threat because otherwise also, a cloud server is capable of having a history of all the search process and collect this information. To break the direct linkage, between the issued query and its recorded entry in $\bar{Q}$ in the public cloud server, the log for a file download is recorded in the private cloud server. At a suitable periodic interval i.e. depending on the number of queries being issued, these logs are written to the public cloud server.

5 Proposed CSMRS Overview

CSMRS architecture comprises of four entities data owner, data user, trusted third party (Private cloud in this case) and public cloud.

- **Data Owner**: Data owner is responsible for outsourcing a collection of documents $D = (D1, D2, D3,...)$ in an encrypted form $C = (C1, C2, C3,....)$ to the cloud server. He encrypts the document collection D with a symmetric key encryption AES with key K. In order to perform multi-keyword ranked search over the outsourced encrypted data, the data owner builds searchable index $\hat{I}(M)$. $\hat{I}(M)$ is then sent to the private cloud where all word vectors $\hat{I}(M)$ are replaced with ciphers from WV to form $\hat{I}(M, S)$ by lookup method. This is done for every document to be uploaded.

- **Data User**: Data users are authorized users who can securely search the document collection for keyword(s). They use the secret key which is shared with them by the data owner and can issue a search request. The search query $t(M)$ issued by the data user is encrypted with the same key M with which index keywords were encrypted.

- **Private Cloud**: The private cloud server on receiving the search query $t(M)$ assigns weight of 2 to the query keywords. It further checks the synonym dictionary SD and add all synonyms of the query keywords with weight 1. Then it extends the encrypted query with dummy keywords with weight 0 and further encrypts it with the key S to get $t(M, S)$. The dummy keywords are randomly added to the query to protect against statistical attacks of guessing the more frequently used terms. It then sends the search $t(M, S)$ to the public cloud server.

- **Public Cloud**: Public cloud in the offline stage constructs the collocation dictionary CD by calling the AlignQuery() procedure that works on the master encrypted query click log $\bar{Q}$. In online stage the public cloud server on receiving the search query $t(M, S)$, refines the synonyms of $t(M, S)$ with procedure SynSelection(), find the cosine similarity and returns a ranked list of top n encrypted documents to the data user. The data user can download the files of his intent and then decrypt it with the key K secretly shared with him by the data owner.

6 Proposed CSMRS Framework

This section gives a detailed description of CSMRS with integrated security and privacy mechanisms.

6.1 Build_Index()

Key_Gen(m)
With the size parameter m, generate the secret key M where M is $1D$ matrix of size m, $M \in \{a, z\}$. M contains many non-uniform occurrences of the characters 'a–z' and it is not in a collating sequence but a random order.

Algorithm 1: Build Word Vector.

Procedure Build_Word_Vector(M, WD).

Initialization: Extract the distinct words from the file, file name and the file descriptor (these are the words that acts as tag for the document, and are entered by the data owner while uploading the document) as WD.

```
for each WD as wd
    w=splitword(wd)
    for each w as wi
        if first occurrence
        set wi =1
        else
        set 0
        end if
    endfor
    Î(M) = Î(M) + Paillier Encrypted(Term Frequency, square (Term Frequency))
endfor
return Î(M)
end procedure
```

Algorithm 2: Build_Vec(Î(M),₩V).

Procedure: Build_Vec(Î(M), ₩V).

Initialization: extract the distinct word vectors from $\hat{I}(M)$ as *EW*

```
for each EW as ew
    f= Paillier Encrypted(Term Frequency, square (Term Frequency))
    Lookup ₩V
    Find corresponding cipher CR
    Î(M,S) =CR , f
endfor
Randomly add into Î(M,S) dummy keywords with Paillier encrypted (term frequency
0)
return Î(M,S)
end procedure
```

6.2   Dictionaries

Synonym Dictionary (SD)

SD is built during offline stage and kept on the private cloud. It contains commonly used synonyms for a word in all grammatical usages of a word. We used Moby Thesaurus [26] for picking the synonyms. All entries in SD are encrypted with key *M* and *S*.

Collocation Dictionary (₵Đ)

₵Đ is an M, S keys encrypted dictionary having the aligned words and the words co-occurring with these aligned words (neighbour words). AlignQuery() procedure is used to align the queries available in the co-clicked query clusters. The detailed process is as explained below:

Master Query Click Log $\bar{Q}$

Every time a user download a document for a particular query it is recorded in a log on the private cloud. All these logs from private cloud server are appended into the master query click log $\bar{Q}$ after a periodic interval. The appropriate period for update of $\bar{Q}$ depends upon the usage of the system. However, regular updating of $\bar{Q}$ gives an efficient execution of the scheme. $\bar{Q}$ contains the encrypted query $t(M, S)$ issued by the user, doc id of the document that was downloaded and the count n (number of times the same document was downloaded for the given query). n is encrypted with Paillier encryption that is additively homomorphic so that n is not revealed to the cloud server however n could be incremented on appending more entries to $\bar{Q}$.

Co-clicked Query Clustering

Co-clicked query clusters are greedily formed by first reserving all the doc-ids that are linked to a particular query and then putting into cluster all the queries that were issued with which these doc ids are linked.

Query Pair Alignment

CSMRS aligns the query pairs in a manner similar to [25]. It selects the co-clicked query pairs with similar length i.e. same number of terms. These pairs have same terms at all positions except one in order to extract the words that are replacement for each other. These extracted words become the aligned words that are recorded in the collocation dictionary along with the neighbouring keywords.

Algorithm 3: FormCluster($\bar{Q}$).

Procedure: FormCluster($\bar{Q}$).

c=1
A:
for each docid in $\bar{Q}$ *as d*
   Store into cluster c,($t(M,S)$, *docid*) for *d*
   for each t(M,S)in c extract docid
    goto A
   endfor
endfor
increment c
end procedure

Algorithm 4: AlignQuery().

Procedure: AlignQuery().

call cluster()
for each c
    pick *t(M,S)with equal number of keywords as c*
    n=count (t)
    for *i = 1 to n*
      for j = (i+1) to n
        if weight not 0 and only one keyword is different in corresponding t
          add into €Đ, differing keywords as main_word and aligned_word
          add the similar words of t as neighbor words.
        end if
      endfor
    endfor
endfor
return €Đ
end procedure

// *€Đ composition= (main_word, aligned_word, neigbour words)*

Algorithm 5: SynSelection(t(M,S), €Đ).

Procedure: SynSelection(t(M,S), €Đ).

Initialization: extract the distinct word with weight 2 as *MW and weight 1 as SW*
for each M*W* as *mw*
    Lookup €Đ
    Store into aw aligned words for mw
endfor
for each S*W* as *sw*
    if sw in aw then
    keep sw in t(M,S)
    else
    drop sw
endfor
return *t(M,S)*
end procedure

6.3 Search

$W̵V$ and $S̵D$ in the private cloud requires one time build up during the setup phase of CSMRS. Figure 6 shows the total time required to build cipher dictionary and synonym dictionary.

$C̵D$ requires time to time update to acquire more suitable synonyms. During experiments it was seen that if collocation dictionary is not updated it resulted in less number of matched synonyms. The only periodic computation cost incurred by CSMRS is aligning of queries and updating of collocation dictionary.

The search process requires users' encrypted query $t(M, S)$ to be sent to the public cloud server. Here it looks the collocation dictionary and matches the aligned words using procedure SynSelection().This process filters out all the excess synonyms added in the query. The filtered out synonym terms are those which actually were never used in the users' query simply because the use of those words together is inappropriate. Now finally we are left with the main keywords, shortlisted synonyms and dummy keywords in the $t(M, S)$. We calculate the cosine similarity using Eq. 1, and find the relevant documents. In Eq. 1, Q refers to the final query $t(M, S)$ after synonym selection phase and D refers to the stored documents. The top n relevant documents returned are ranked as per their similarity scores and returned to the user. The presence of dummy words in the query and in the index file does not affect the final scores as their term frequency was set to 0 in index file. In the entire search process only the final score are known to the cloud server. CSMRS preserves the privacy of entire data and process from the cloud server.

$$similarity = \cos(\theta) = \frac{D \cdot Q}{||D||_2 \cdot ||Q||_2} = \frac{\sum_{i=1}^{n} D_i Q_i}{\sqrt{\sum_{i=1}^{n} D_i^2} \cdot \sqrt{\sum_{i=1}^{n} Q_i^2}} \tag{1}$$

7 Experimental Results

The experiments are done in python on a Linux machine with Intel i7 processor with 8 GB RAM. For alignment of encrypted query click logs the encrypted queries were built for the search queries in accordance with selected queries from AOL-user-ct-collection [27] a corpus of query logs. We ran the word alignment algorithm on both the selected queries in plain and then on the encrypted queries of the same queries to check the similarity in the aligned words returned by them. We found that the words aligned are almost similar with both. Though with encrypted queries we only had some extra dummy keywords almost everywhere in order to conceal the actual data. The dataset of documents was specially built to make the documents suitable to run and use the queries corpus from AOL-user-ct-collection.

8   Functionality and Efficiency

8.1   Index Generation

Index generation step in CSMRS is one time computation comprising of two main steps i.e. forming $\hat{I}(M)$ and its further encryption to $\hat{I}(M,S)$. In CMSRS we include word vectors of the unique words from the document to be uploaded, unique keywords of its filename and file descriptors (these acts as document tags and are entered by the data owner while uploading the file/document). We include the term frequency of these words and their squares and encrypt them with Paillier encryption.

For constructing $\hat{I}(M)$ key M is built with English alphabets randomly placed, they are repeated many times and the frequency of most appearing alphabets in formation of words in English language is more than other alphabets. The length for M used in our scheme is 167. The randomness and repetition of alphabets is good enough to construct many English words. We experimented creating word vectors and careful examination of 10,000 English words picked from the /usr/share/ dict/british-english of Ubuntu 14.04.

Figure 3 shows the index construction time. It shows the word vector creation time and time taken for final encryption of the index by lookup method into the ~~HV~~ table. It shows that the time taken for final encryption of the word vector in private cloud is almost negligible with respect to the total time taken for index construction. The generation time of the index is increasing linearly with respect to the number of keywords.

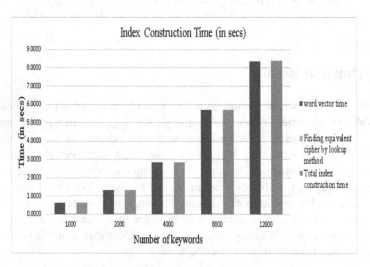

Fig. 3. Index construction *time (in secs.)*

The total index construction time in Fig. 3 includes time taken for extracting the unique keywords for the relevant document along with its term frequency and its square, word vector creation time and time taken for encryption by lookup method in ~~WV~~ table.

9 Search over Encrypted Data

9.1 Search Efficiency

The public cloud server computes the similarity scores with Eq. 1, and return the top *n* ranked list of the relevant documents during the search process. Figure 4 shows the time taken by CSMRS for searching the relevant files. It clearly shows assuming that having fixed number of keywords in the query, the search time is dependent on the number of documents in the dataset.

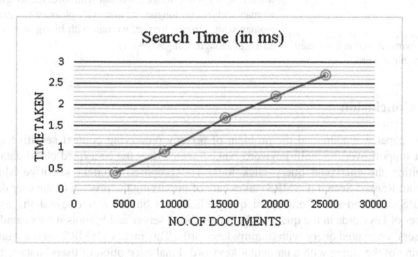

Fig. 4. Search *time (in ms)*

9.2 Synonym Quality

We experimented with some selected search queries and saw that our scheme did not give weight to "powerful" as synonym when it was listed with the word "coffee". Similarly we tried another query "ship goods to Bombay" over here the word "boat" was not given weight as synonym for the word "ship". One detailed example of the query pair alignment and reduction of synonyms from the full list of synonyms is shown in the Table 1.

Table 1. Example of reducing synonym terms by CSMRS with given queries to be aligned for the word sharp

Query	Woman with sharp tongue
Example word	Sharp
Complete synonym list	Able, acerbic, acidic, acidulous, acrid, adept, adroit, agile, annoying, artful, astringent, biting, brainy, brilliant, capable, caustic, clever, consummate, cool, cultivated, cutting, deft, dexterous, experienced, expert, effectual, effective, efficient, facile, galling, gifted, harsh, hateful, hurtful, ingenious, intelligent, keen, learned, masterful, masterly, nasty, practiced, piquant, polished, powerful, prepared, proficient, pungent, qualified, responsible, rough, sharp, savvy, skilled, skillful, smart, spiky, talented, tart, accomplished
Aligned queries in master query click log	Woman with loose tongue, woman with red tongue, woman with cut tongue, woman with pierced tongue, woman with cursing tongue, woman with sarcastic tongue, woman with rough tongue, woman with pleasant tongue, woman with pungent tongue, woman with biting tongue
Synonyms filtered and selected for example word	Sarcastic, rough, pungent, biting

10 Conclusion

In this paper, we addressed the problem of privacy preserving context sensitive synonym support over the multi-keyword ranked search over the encrypted cloud data by exploiting the encrypted query click logs. The proposed Context sensitive Multi-keyword Ranked Search (CSMRS) takes care of preserving the privacy of the user data. CSMRS uses and stores encrypted query click logs but does not reveal the exact number of keywords in the query to the public cloud server and befools it by extending the users' encrypted query with dummy keywords. This makes CSMRS secure against mapping of the cipher with a particular keyword. Final encryption of users' data (either index keywords or query keywords) is possible with cipher table in private cloud server after getting word vectors from the data user. This prevents unauthorized users to make search requests. Also the word vector design of each word provides a strong safety feature against crypto attacks. Though encrypted query click logs gives some sense of presence of similar keywords but it leaks nothing more than that, as the cloud server cannot reach to the exact plain keywords from it. Also the cloud servers are curious enough to analyze user's queries and can even get the history so our query click logs stores nothing beyond the capability of the public cloud server. Rather we are using it for our benefit. We also take care that these query click logs are first stored on the private cloud server and later it updates the public cloud server master query click logs. It does so to hide the exact relevance of the encrypted queries issued with its encrypted query click log entry. CSMRS shows improvement in the quality of the synonym selection for the expansion of search query and hence the ranked search results contains relevant documents. The search time taken by CSMRS is similar to the existing schemes.

References

1. Rightscale 2016 State of the Cloud Report - Hybrid Cloud Adoption Ramps as Cloud Users and Cloud Providers Mature (2016). http://assets.rightscale.com/uploads/pdfs/RightScale-2016-State-of-the-Cloud-Report.Pdf
2. Song, D.X., Wagner, D., Perrig, A.: Practical techniques for searches on encrypted data. In: IEEE Symposium on Security and Privacy (2000)
3. Goh, E.-J.: Secure Indexes*. Cryptology ePrint Archive: Report 2003/216 (2004)
4. Chang, Y.-C., Mitzenmacher, M.: Privacy preserving keyword searches on remote encrypted data. In: Ioannidis, J., Keromytis, A., Yung, M. (eds.) ACNS 2005. LNCS, vol. 3531, pp. 442–455. Springer, Heidelberg (2005). https://doi.org/10.1007/11496137_30
5. Boneh, D., Di Crescenzo, G., Ostrovsky, R., Persiano, G.: Public key encryption with keyword search. In: Cachin, C., Camenisch, J.L. (eds.) EUROCRYPT 2004. LNCS, vol. 3027, pp. 506–522. Springer, Heidelberg (2004). https://doi.org/10.1007/978-3-540-24676-3_30
6. Bellare, M., Boldyreva, A., Desai, A., Pointcheval, D.: Key-privacy in public-key encryption. In: Boyd, C. (ed.) ASIACRYPT 2001. LNCS, vol. 2248, pp. 566–582. Springer, Heidelberg (2001). https://doi.org/10.1007/3-540-45682-1_33
7. Boneh, D., Franklin, M.: Identity-based encryption from the weil pairing. SIAM J. Comput. 32(3), 586–615 (2003)
8. Curtmola, R., Garay, J., Kamara, S., Ostrovsky, R.: Searchable symmetric encryption: improved definitions and efficient constructions. In: ACM CC 2006 (2006)
9. Brinkman, R: Searching in encrypted data. Ph.D. thesis. University of Twente (2007)
10. Wang, C., Cao, N., Li, J., Ren, K., Lou, W.: Secure ranked keyword search over encrypted cloud data. In: Proceedings of ICDCS 2010 (2010)
11. Cao, N., Wang, C., Li, M., Ren, K., Lou, W.: Privacy-preserving multi-keyword ranked search over encrypted cloud data. In: Proceedings of IEEE INFOCOM, pp. 829–837 (2011)
12. Ahsan, M.M., Chowdhury, F.Z., Sabilah, M., Wahab, A.W.B.A., Idris, M.Y.I.B.: An efficient fuzzy keyword matching technique for searching through encrypted cloud data. In: International Conference on Research and Innovation in Information Systems (ICRIIS) (2017)
13. Yang, C., Zhang, W., Xu, J., Xu, J., Yu, N.: A fast privacy-preserving multi-keyword search scheme on cloud data. In: International Conference on Computing & Processing (Hardware/Software), pp. 104–110 (2012)
14. Xu, Z., Kang, W., Li, R., Yow, K., Xu, C.Z.: Efficient multi-keyword ranked query on encrypted data in the cloud. In: ICPADS 2012, pp. 244–251 (2012)
15. Xu, J., Zhang, W., Yang, C., Xu, J., Yu, N.: Two-step-ranking secure multi-keyword search over encrypted cloud data. In: International Conference on Computing & Processing (Hardware/Software), pp. 124–130 (2012)
16. Yang, C., Zhang, W., Xu, J., Xu, J., Yu, N.: A fast privacy-preserving multi-keyword search scheme on cloud data. In: International Conference on Computing & Processing (Hardware/Software), pp. 104–110 (2012)

17. Handa, R., Challa, R.K.: A cluster based multi-keyword search on outsourced encrypted cloud data. In: 2nd IEEE International Conference on Computing for Sustainable Global Development, pp. 115–120 (2015)
18. Krishna, C.R., Handa, R.: Dynamic cluster based privacy-preserving multi-keyword search over encrypted cloud data. In: 6th IEEE International Conference on Cloud System and Big Data Engineering, pp. 146–151 (2016)
19. Khan, N.S., Krishna, C.R., Khurana, A.: Secure ranked fuzzy multi-keyword search over outsourced encrypted cloud data. In: 5th IEEE International Conference on Computer and Communication Technology, pp. 241–249 (2014)
20. Fu, Z., Sun, X., Linge, N., Zhou, L.: Achieving effective cloud search services: multi-keyword ranked search over encrypted cloud data supporting synonym query. IEEE Trans. Consum. Electron. **60**(1), 164–172 (2014)
21. Krishna, C.R., Mittal, S.A.: Privacy preserving synonym based fuzzy multi-keyword ranked search over encrypted cloud data. In: International Conference on Computing, Communication and Automation (ICCCA2016), pp. 1187–1194 (2016)
22. Saini, V., Challa, R.K., Khan, N.S.: An efficient multi-keyword synonym-based fuzzy ranked search over outsourced encrypted cloud data. In: Choudhary, R.K., Mandal, J.K., Auluck, N., Nagarajaram, H.A. (eds.) Advanced Computing and Communication Technologies. AISC, vol. 452, pp. 433–441. Springer, Singapore (2016). https://doi.org/10.1007/978-981-10-1023-1_43
23. Medelyan, O.: Why not use query logs as corpora? In: Ninth ESSLLI Student Session, pp. 1–10 (2004)
24. Liu, C., Zhu, L., Wang, M., Tan, Y.: Search pattern leakage in searchable encryption: attacks and new construction. J. Inf. Sci.: Int. J. **265**, 176–188 (2014)
25. Wei, X., Peng, F., Tseng, H., Lu, Y., Wang, X., Dumoulin, B.: Search with synonyms: problems and solutions. In: Coling 2010, Poster Volume, Beijing, pp. 1318–1326 (2010)
26. (2017). http://moby-thesaurus.org/
27. (2017). http://www.cim.mcgill.ca/~dudek/206/Logs/AOL-user-ct-collection

An Optimized High Gain Microstrip Patch Array Antenna for Sensor Networks

Chandra Shekhar[✉]

Indian Institute of Technology Kanpur, Kanpur, India
gchandra@iitk.ac.in

Abstract. Wake-up receivers exhibit a wake-up range of few meters while the sensor nodes present a communication range of hundred meters. This gap between wake-up range and communication range limits the use of wake-up receivers with sensor nodes. In this paper, a high gain and compact size microstrip patch array antenna is presented for wake-up receiver in order to increase the wake-up range. The antenna is designed at operating frequency of 2.45 GHz for low loss RT/Duroid 4003C substrate. The fabricated antenna exhibits a gain of 8 dBi while occupies an area of just 64x81 mm^2. The measurement results are closely matching with the simulation results.

Keywords: Microstrip antenna · Array antennas
Antenna feed network · Sensor networks

1 Introduction

An antenna is a transducer that converts RF fields into alternating current or vice-versa. A microstrip patch antenna (MPA) consist of a metal patch (copper or gold) of any shape (circular, rectangular, elliptical, etc.) on the surface of a printed circuit board (PCB) and a ground plane on the back side of the PCB [1]. The radiation from the MPA is primarily due to the fringing field between metal patch and ground plane. By choosing a thicker PCB of a low dielectric constant, the gain and bandwidth of the MPA can be improved but size of MPA increases [2–4]. An array arrangement of MPAs increases the gain and directivity as well as reduces the overall area [5–7].

Wake-up receiver (WUR) is used with sensor node to minimize its energy consumption resulting in longevity of the network [8,9]. The WUR normally consumes very low power (sometimes zero power) and exhibits a wake-up range (WR) of few meters as compared to sensor nodes [9]. In this paper, a high gain & compact size microstrip patch array antenna (MPAA) is designed and fabricated to raise the WR of WURs (which operates in 2.4 GHz ISM band). The rest of paper is organized as follows. Section 2 describes the design procedure of an antenna. Design of 2x2 MPAA is given in Sect. 3. Section 4 presents EM simulation results. Fabrication of high gain antenna followed by measurement results are discussed in Sect. 5. Finally, Sect. 6 provides the conclusion and future scope of work.

© Springer Nature Singapore Pte Ltd. 2019
S. Verma et al. (Eds.): CNC 2018, CCIS 839, pp. 181–190, 2019.
https://doi.org/10.1007/978-981-13-2372-0_16

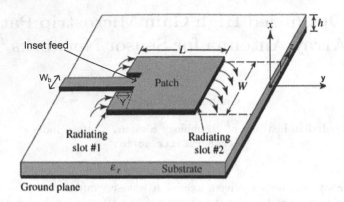

Fig. 1. Basic structure of MPA [12]

2   Design Procedure

There are many methods to analyze the microstrip patch antenna (MPA) and one of the simplest methods is transmission line model (TLM) [1,10,11]. In the TLM, the MPA consists of a transmission line of length L that separates two slots of width W and height h as shown in Fig. 1. The Rogers RT/Duroid 4003C LoProTM laminate (Dielectric constant $(\epsilon_r) = 3.38$, Substrate height (h) = 1.524 mm and Metal thickness (t) = 35 μm) is chosen due to its smoother copper surface lower insertion loss as compared to FR4 substrate [13]. The TLM as discussed in [10] is used to compute the physical dimensions/parameters of MPA. The design equations and calculation of physical dimensions of an antenna is discussed in [7]. The calculated physical parameters are: W = 40.9, L = 32.6 (for $\epsilon_r = 3.38$, h = 1.524 mm and tanδ = 0.002).

Table 1. Optimized dimensions of patch antenna

Parameter	Value
Patch width (W_P)	24 mm
Patch length (L_P)	33.7 mm
Feed offset (Y)	12.75 mm
Feed width (W_b)	0.86 mm
Patch gap (W_g)	1.87 mm
Antenna gain	4.1 dBi

By using these parameters values, the patch antenna was designed using IE3D simulation software which is a full-wave electromagnetic (EM) simulator [14]. Since the objective of our work was to attain the maximum gain with minimum size, we optimized the patch antenna size. The inset-feed is cut at

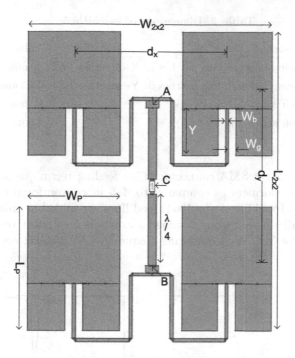

Fig. 2. Proposed structure of inset-fed 2x2 MPAA

$y = Y$ to achieve $100\,\Omega$ antenna impedance (this is explained in next section). The optimized dimensions as a result of iterative simulations are listed in Table 1 and are used for the designing of array antenna explained in the next section.

3   A 2x2 Microstrip Patch Array Antenna

The proposed inset-fed MPAA consists of 4 single patches and a feeding network as shown in Fig. 2. The spacing between patches is very important parameter for array antenna because it decides the overall antenna gain. The patch array gives maximum gain when the patches are separated by 2λ but it increases the array size significantly [6]. The standard value of spacing d normally lies between 0.6 to 0.9λ [15]. A special care is needed to avoid spurious radiations of the feed which otherwise increase side lobe levels and cross polarization (results in low antenna gain). Our objective is to make an antenna for WUR which should have smaller size and high gain. In the proposed design, the impedance of single patch antenna is chosen to $100\,\Omega$ (in place of $50\,\Omega$) because two $100\,\Omega$ feed lines joined at point A (same for point B) will result in a total of $50\,\Omega$. Further, these two points (A and B) are to be connected with point C which should have $50\,\Omega$ impedance. So, two quarter wave transformers (one for point A and another for point B)are used to transform the $50\,\Omega$ impedance into $100\,\Omega$. These two $100\,\Omega$ feed lines meet at point C and gives resultant $50\,\Omega$ impedance. Then a co-axial

Table 2. Dimensions of 2x2 MPAA

Parameter	Value
Spacing between two patches in X-direction (d_x)	40 mm
Spacing between two patches in Y-direction (d_y)	47.5 mm
Patch array width (W_{2x2})	64 mm
Patch array length (L_{2x2})	81 mm

feed is used to connect SMA connector. This feeding technique needs only two quarter wave transformers as compared to 4–5 in conventional corporate feed networks [10,16]. In addition, the 100 Ω feed lines are folded in order to fit larger lengths into smaller area. So our designed antenna is area effective. The physical parameters of the MPAA at operating frequency of 2.45 GHz are tabulated in Table 2.

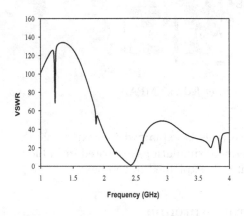

Fig. 3. VSWR of 2x2 MPAA

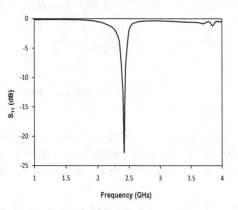

Fig. 4. S_{11} of 2x2 MPAA

4   EM Simulation Results

The proposed MPAA is designed and simulated using IE3D software. The voltage standing wave ratio (VSWR) and input reflection coefficient (S_{11}) of the designed antenna are plotted in Figs. 3 and 4, respectively. The designed MPAA presents the S_{11} of −23 dB at 2.45 GHz and 1.13 VSWR at 2.45 GHz. This low value of VSWR indicates that impedance matching between transmitter (or receiver) and antenna is proper. Figure 5 shows the 2-D radiation (elevation) pattern of directivity of E-total in $phi = 0°$ and $90°$. It is clear from Fig. 5 that the radiation pattern at operating frequency of 2.45 GHz is normal to the surface.

The gain is one of important parameters for the antenna. The variation of antenna gain with respect to frequency is plotted in Fig. 6, where the maximum

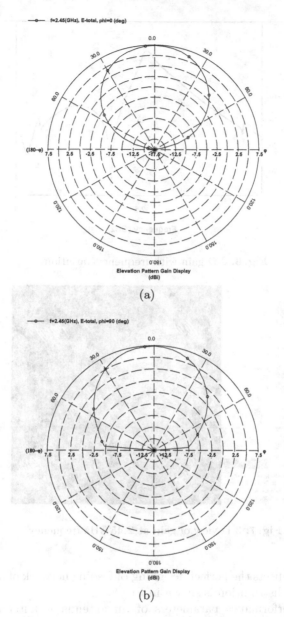

Fig. 5. 2-D radiation pattern (a) E-total at phi = 0° (b) E-total at phi = 90°

gain is 8.4 dBi at 2.45 GHz. Further the 3D view of antenna radiation pattern (gain) is given in Fig. 7, where the radiation pattern of array antenna is perpendicular to the surface and provides a narrow beam-width. It is also clear from gain pattern that there are no side-lobes (spurious radiations) at operating

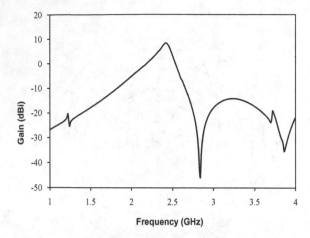

Fig. 6. 2-D gain with frequency variation

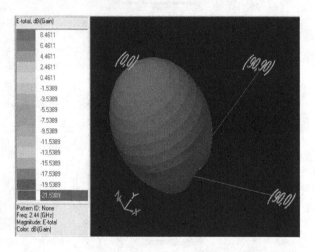

Fig. 7. 3-D view of gain at 2.45 GHz frequency

frequency. This reflects the perfect designing of feeding network of array antenna. The 2-D current distribution is shown in Fig. 8.

The other performance parameters of an antenna is antenna efficiency[1]. Figure 9 shows the dependency of antenna efficiency on frequency. The maximum antenna efficiency comes to 80.5 % at 2.45 GHz.

---

[1] Antenna efficiency (also known as radiation efficiency or simply efficiency) is a measure of the radiated power (as electromagnetic waves) through antenna to the power fed to antenna terminals.

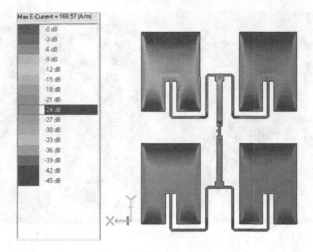

Fig. 8. 2-D current distribution at 2.45 GHz frequency

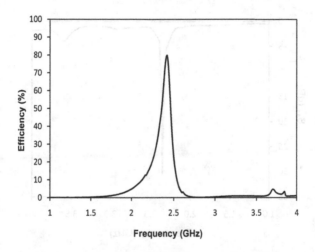

Fig. 9. Antenna efficiency with frequency variation

5   Measurement Results

The MPAA is fabricated on Rogers 4003C LoPro-TM laminate which has smoother copper surface and presents much lower insertion loss [13]. The LoPro technology also yields a copper clad panel with slightly lower dielectric constant than the standard RO4003C laminate. The fabricated antenna is shown in Fig. 10. An Agilent ENA-5071A vector network analyzer (VNA) recorded the s-parameters and SWR of an antenna. The VNA was calibrated in the 1 to 4 GHz frequency range. The frequency response of the fabricated antenna in terms of S_{11} is plotted in Fig. 11. The simulation result gives S_{11} of -23 dB

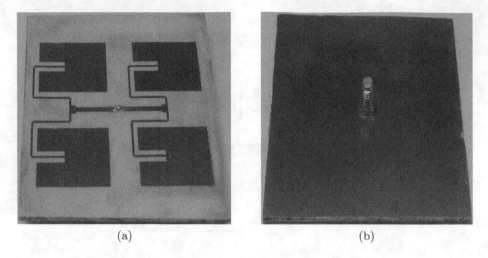

(a)   (b)

Fig. 10. Fabricated 2x2 MPAA (a) Top view (b) Bottom view

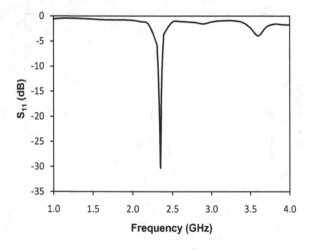

Fig. 11. Measured S_{11} of MPAA

at operating frequency of 2.45 GHz while the measurement result gives S_{11} of −31 dB at 2.45 GHz.

To measure the antenna gain, we have used two TelosB sensor nodes. First we measured the range by using standard antennas. Then we replaced these standard antennas with 2 sets of our designed antenna and measured the range. After putting these values in Friss equation, we can estimate the gain of our designed antenna. The summary of measurement results is tabulated in Table 3.

Table 3. Summary of measurement results

Parameter	Value
S_{11}	-31 dB
Resonance frequency	2.4 GHz
VSWR	1.12
Gain	8 dBi
Impedance	50 Ω

6 Conclusion

In this paper, a high gain and compact size MPAA is designed and fabricated in order to overcome the gap between WR and communication range. The designed MPAA exhibits a gain of 8 dBi for 2.45 GHz operating frequency and occupies just 64x81 mm^2 area. A co-axial feed is used to connect the antenna with the WUR and sensor node. The advantage of co-axial feed is that an antenna parks itself on the WUR and sensor node. Thus keeps the overall form factor of the assembly low. The WUR [8] presents a WR of 6 m. After incorporating designed high gain antenna, the WR turns out to be 13 m (increases $\approx$ by a factor of 2). Future work includes the use of 2D defected ground structures with the MPAA for improving the performance and reducing the area. Other substrates will also be evaluated.

Acknowledgment. Author would like to thank Rogers Corporation, US for providing free high frequency Duroid laminates.

References

1. Zurcher, J.-F., Gardiol, F.E.: Broadband Patch Antennas. Artech House, Norwood (1995)
2. Kumar, G., Gupta, K.C.: Nonradiating edges and four edges gap-coupled multiple resonator broad-band microstrip antennas. IEEE Trans. Antennas Propag. **34**, 173–178 (1985)
3. Song, Q., Zhang, X.X.: A study on wideband gap-coupled microstrip antenna arrays. IEEE Trans. Antennas Propag. **43**, 313–317 (1995)
4. Agrawal, S., Gupta, R.D., Parihar, M.S., Kondekar, P.N.: A wideband high gain dielectric resonator antenna for RF energy harvesting application. AEU-Int. J. Electron. Commun. **78**, 24–31 (2017)
5. Honarbakhsh, B.: High-gain low-cost microstrip antennas and arrays based on FR4 epoxy. AEU-Int. J. Electron. Commun. **75**, 1–7 (2017)
6. Khraisat, Y.S.H.: Design of 4 elements rectangular microstrip patch antenna with high gain for 2.4 GHz applications. Mod. Appl. Sci. **6**, 68–74 (2012)
7. Ninan, C., Shekhar, C., Radhakrishna, M.: Design and optimization of a 2x2 directional microstrip patch antenna. In: Gaur, M.S., Zwolinski, M., Laxmi, V., Boolchandani, D., Sing, V., Sing, A.D. (eds.) VDAT 2013. CCIS, vol. 382, pp. 353–360. Springer, Heidelberg (2013). https://doi.org/10.1007/978-3-642-42024-5_42

8. Philippe, L.H., Sebastien, R.: Low power wake-up radio for wireless sensor networks. Mob. Netw. Appl. J. **15**, 226–236 (2010)
9. Shekhar C., Varma S., Radhakrishna M.: A 2.4 GHz passive wake-up circuit for power minimization in wireless sensor nodes. In: 2015 IEEE Region 10 Conference (TENCON), pp. 1–6 (2015)
10. Balanis, C.A.: Antenna Theory: Analysis and Design. Wiley, Hoboken (2012)
11. Guo, Y.X., Mak, C.L., Luk, K.M., Lee, K.F.: Analysis and design of L probe proximity fed patch antennas. IEEE Trans. Antennas Propag. **49**, 145–149 (2001)
12. Roo-Ons, M.J., Shynu, S.V., Seredynski, M., Ammann, M.J., McCormack, S.J., Norton, B.: Influence of solar heating on the performance of integrated solar cell microstrip patch antennas. Sol. Energy **84**, 1619–1627 (2010)
13. Rogers Corporation: Data sheet RT/Duroid 4003 laminates. http://www.rogerscorp.com
14. IE3D 15. Mentor Graphics Inc., Fremont, CA
15. Pozar, D.M.: Input impedance and mutual coupling of rectangular microstrip antennas. IEEE Trans. Antennas Propag. **30**, 1191–1196 (1982)
16. Alam, M.M., Sonchoy, M.M.R., Goni, M.O.: Design and performance analysis of microstrip array antenna. In: Progress in Electromagnetic Research Symposium Proceedings, pp. 18–21 (2009)

An Efficient Data Aggregation Algorithm with Gossiping for Smart Transportation System

Sudhakar Pandey, Ruchi Jain[✉], and Sanjay Kumar

Department of Information Technology, National Institute of Technology,
Raipur, India
spandey96@gmail.com, ruchijain630@gmail.com,
skumar.it@nitrr.ac.in

Abstract. As there is a continuous increase in number of vehicles in urban as well as rural areas, the congestion of vehicles is becoming a very big problem. Smart transportation systems are used to collect information about existing traffic on roads. Wireless sensor networks offer better performance and reduced cost when used in the smart transportation system. Data aggregation algorithms can be used to reduce sensor network congestion. This paper discusses the use of wireless sensor networks for smart transportation system and data aggregation algorithm to reduce the network traffic. In this paper, we used hybrid data aggregation algorithm with gossiping incorporating mobility of nodes. We evaluated the performance of proposed scheme with the existing hybrid aggregation algorithm. The result analysis shows that proposed scheme is efficient and scalable.

Keywords: Smart transportation system · Data aggregation
Wireless sensor network · Gossiping

1 Introduction

Congestion on roads became a very big problem nowadays. Smart Transportation System provides a way to collect traffic data from roads and uses this data for providing useful information to peoples. Smart transportation system aims to provide a better way to manage traffic. It enables various users to be more informed, and more secure. The smart transportation system is an integration of several elements like people, vehicles, roads which in turn provides an informative and efficient traffic management service. There are various areas where smart transportation system can be used such as Arterial and Freeway Management Systems, Freight Management Systems, Transit Management Systems (TMS), Incident Management Systems, Emergency Management Systems, Regional Multimodal and Traveler Information Systems/Information Management (IM) etc. [1].

Traditional Smart Transportation Systems use wired sensors for data gathering, such as inductive loops, video cameras and ultrasonic sensors. Due to many drawbacks, these sensors can affect the efficiency of the entire system. Therefore, wireless sensor

© Springer Nature Singapore Pte Ltd. 2019
S. Verma et al. (Eds.): CNC 2018, CCIS 839, pp. 191–200, 2019.
https://doi.org/10.1007/978-981-13-2372-0_17

network provides a better alternative. Wireless sensor network (WSN) technology is emerging as the most exciting and promising area for research [2]. The Wireless Sensor Network (WSN) can be defined as a group of devices forming a wireless network, which are used to collect information from the environment using sensors. Small sensor devices can provide reliable data without creating any obstruction to the user. With the use of sensors, various information from the roads can be collected such as weather conditions in a particular area, air pollution status, and also a count of vehicles in a particular are at a certain time interval. The main challenge in Wireless Sensor Network is energy efficiency. Since the devices in Wireless Sensor Network are low powered, their energy should be used in an efficient way. But in the proposed model, the sensor nodes are powered by a continuous power supply. Since they are deployed either on vehicles or on lampposts, where power can be easily supplied. Therefore, there is no issue regarding energy consumption.

Transportation information collection and communication plays a key role in all intelligent transport application [3]. To efficiently collect this information data aggregation algorithms are used. With the help of data aggregation techniques network traffic can be reduced and the network lifetime can be enhanced [4]. There is a number of factors which decide the efficiency of a sensor network such as network architecture, routing algorithm and the data aggregation algorithm used. In this paper, we incorporated mobility of nodes, data aggregation and gossiping routing algorithm (Fig. 1).

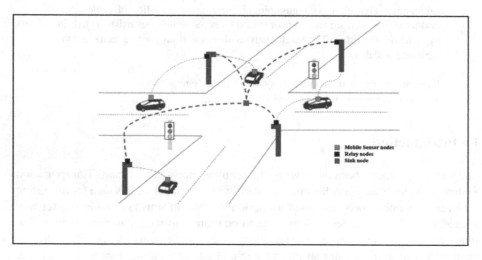

Fig. 1. A smart transportation system scenario.

The rest of the paper is organized as follows. Section 2 provides an overview of related works. Section 3 discusses the assumptions regarding network and main network topology and design. Section 4 presents the proposed algorithm. In Sect. 5 the simulation results are discussed. Finally, in Sect. 6, the conclusion is given.

2 Related Work

The area of Smart transportation system for research has been extensively explored, however, use of WSN along with data aggregation in the smart transportation is yet not much explored. The work done in [3] suggests the use of WSN in the intelligent transportation system (ITS) and proposes a system architecture in which mobile nodes can query a largely deployed WSN in ITS scenario. In [5], an approach for reliable detection of vehicles in the parking area is proposed using WSNs. They conducted an elaborate car counting experiment for one-day duration to show the efficiency of their proposed approach. The work done in [6] also suggests use of WSN in the smart transportation system. It uses the sensors to sense the speed of vehicles and also to classify them according to the length of vehicles. In [15] a novel wireless sensor is proposed for traffic monitoring. Detection and classification of vehicles, their speed and length estimation can be done using this smart sensor. There are various methods for data aggregation. Data aggregation algorithms can lessen the number of packets transmitted to base station [4]. Data aggregation based on entropy of sensors is proposed in [13]. They also proposed an efficient method for clustering. A WSN protocol framework is proposed in [7]. They also proposed a spatial correlation data hybrid aggregation (HA) algorithm. It uses two parameters similarity and similarity constraint to perform aggregation. For WSN based ITSs a dynamic data aggregation algorithm is proposed to reduce the energy consumption [8]. It uses a hybrid network structure and evidential reasoning for data aggregation. A WSN based traffic data collection algorithm to forward urgency data efficiently is proposed in [10].

3 Preliminaries

3.1 Assumptions

The following assumptions are taken for the proposed approach with respect to the network.

- The nodes are deployed randomly.
- All the sensor nodes are aware of their positions.
- Sensor nodes can be of heterogeneous nature with respect to memory, and computational capacity.
- The nodes in the network are supposed with uninterrupted power supply.

3.2 Network Topology

The infrastructure of a transportation system in urban areas consists of numerous components including traffic lights, vehicles, lamp posts, electronic boards. These all components can be used to deploy sensors for monitoring and analyzing the environment and traffic conditions.

The topology of this model is hierarchical in which nodes can be categorized into three types: sensor nodes (static and mobile), relay nodes (static), and a sink node. Sensor nodes are used to gather data from the surroundings. They can be deployed on vehicles and lamp posts. Sensor nodes directly communicate to relay nodes using single hop communication. Single hop communication as compared to multi-hop communication saves a significant amount of power and the total number of packets transferred in the network.

The collected data from sensors is transferred to relay nodes. Relay nodes act as the link between sensor nodes and sink nodes. These nodes receive data from sensor nodes, aggregate it and then transfer it to sink node. Sink node act as a base station which receives data from relay nodes and then processes it to make decisions.

For mobility of sensor nodes deployed on vehicles, Random Waypoint Model is used. Random Waypoint Model is the most common model used for mobility in networks. It provides a way to model the movement of mobile nodes, their velocity and location [9]. The destination of nodes is chosen randomly and independently. Each node selects a random destination within the simulation area and a random speed within a specified interval. Before moving to next destination each node waits for a fixed time interval. Figure 2 shows the flow of data in the network.

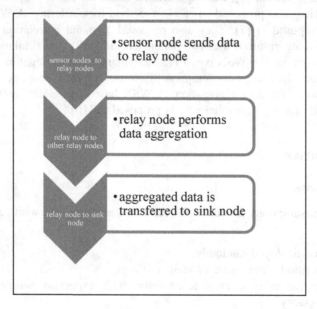

Fig. 2. Flow of data in network.

4   Routing in Smart Transportation System

There are various routing algorithms for WSN. But the routing algorithm should be according to the application where it will be used. It should not consume many resources since sensors nodes in WSNs have limited resources. In the proposed system, sensor nodes directly transmit the data to nearby relay nodes and then routing is performed by relay nodes. The traffic information in Smart Transportation System can be classified into two types: periodic traffic information and non-periodic traffic information [10]. Routing of later type is simpler since the data is in small quantities. But the data with large quantity should be exchanged efficiently. For this purpose, data aggregation algorithms are used.

4.1 Data Aggregation

The sensed data from multiple sensors is transmitted to the base station. Since the data from nearby sensor nodes are generally highly redundant and correlated, and the sensor nodes are resource constrained. It will be very inefficient to transmit this data directly to the base station. Hence, we need to aggregate this data and then it can be transferred to the base station. Data aggregation is an in-network processing technique for the computation of smaller representation of a number of messages. This representation should be equivalent to the original individual messages. If there are two messages, then an aggregation function will compute a new message such as

$$<E> = f(<Z_1, Z_2>).$$ (1)

Here Z_1 and Z_2 are the two messages, E is the aggregated message, and f is the aggregation function. The simplest aggregation function can be mean [16], since it should not increase complexity of the system. Data aggregation in WSN is a very efficient technique to reduce the total number of packets transferred in the network, as well as to eliminate redundant transmission [4] (Fig. 3).

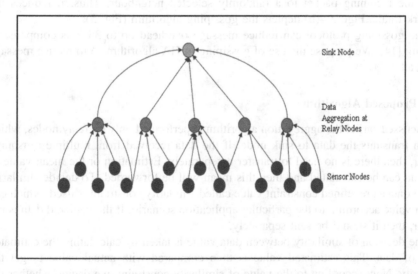

Fig. 3. *Data aggregation.*

4.2 Routing of Aggregated Data

Flooding is a very common routing algorithm used in WSNs. It is simple and does not require costly maintenance. Flooding uses a reactive approach whereby each node receiving a data or control packet sends the packet to all its neighbours [10]. Figure 4 (a) illustrates the concept of flooding in a network. Despite the simplicity of flooding algorithm, it has some major drawbacks such as traffic implosion and resource blindness.

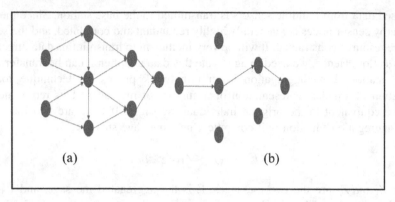

(a)   (b)

Fig. 4. (a) Flooding in WSN. (b) Gossiping in WSN.

To address these shortcomings another similar approach gossiping can be used. Unlike flooding, gossiping does no broadcast a data packet. In gossiping, each node sends the incoming packet to a randomly selected neighbour. Thus, it reduces the network traffic. Figure 4(b) depicts the gossiping algorithm (Fig. 5).

The gossiping protocol can reduce message overhead up to 35% as compared to flooding [14]. We propose the use of gossiping in HA algorithm so to reduce message overhead.

4.3   Proposed Algorithm

As discussed earlier the aggregation algorithm is performed only by relay nodes, which in turn transmits the data to sink node. If the data received from multiple sensors is similar, then there is no need to transfer it separately. Estimation or the mean value of this data can be calculated and then this mean will be forwarded. To decide similarity among data a predefined constraint value called similarity constraint is used, which can have a value according to the particular application scenario. If the gathered data is not similar, then it should be sent separately.

The decision of similarity between data value is taken by calculating the estimated value of data. This estimated value is then compared with actual value to get the similarity. Now according to the value of similarity constraint, we decide whether the data should be aggregated or not.

BEGIN
//calculate the estimated value E
//m is the number of sensor nodes
//Z_i is the data from sensor node i
//e is the similarity constraint

$$E = \frac{1}{m}\sum_{i=1}^{m} Z_i$$

FOR each sensor node i
//calculate the similarity value S_i

$$S_i = \frac{|E - Z_i|}{Z_i}$$

IFS_i>e
Forward Z_i to all adjacent relay nodes using gossiping
Discard Z_i
END IF
END FOR
//Data Aggregation
//calculate estimated value E' for remaining data
//$m'$is the number of remaining sensor nodes
//Z_i' is the remaining data

$$E' = \frac{1}{m'}\sum_{i=1}^{m'} Z_i'$$

Forward E' to all adjacent relay nodes using gossiping
END

Fig. 5. Routing algorithm.

5   Simulation Results

This section discusses the simulation results. The simulation is performed on MATLAB R2016a. To evaluate the results a simulation area of 1000×1000 m is taken with number of sensor nodes varying from 100 to 500 and the number of relay nodes kept fixed as 50. The nodes are randomly deployed over the simulation area.

We assume each node of the network to be aware of its position. In order to evaluate the proposed work, we compared it with flooding, hybrid aggregation (HA) algorithm with flooding in a mobile environment, and the proposed HA algorithm with gossiping. Table 1 shows a list of simulation parameters used in the simulation. These parameters were decided according to the previous similar work done in [7–10].

Table 1. Simulation parameters.

S.no.	Parameter	Value
1.	Number of nodes	75–550
2.	Simulation area	1 km × 1 km
3.	Packet size	1024 Bytes
4.	MAC protocol	IEEE 802.11 g
5.	Mobility model	Random waypoint
6.	Node speed	10–50 km/h

The main problem with the gossiping algorithm is that the message may die out very early without reaching to its destination. The main reason for this is a low gossiping probability. By choosing a proper value for gossiping probability this problem can be avoided [14]. In the simulations, we have found that for probability above 0.6, the premature death of messages can be avoided. The results are evaluated based on two parameters which are relayed packets, average latency (Fig. 6).

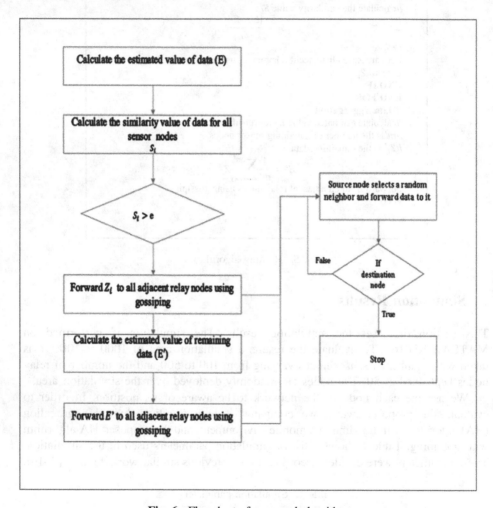

Fig. 6. Flowchart of proposed algorithm.

5.1   Relayed Packets

Figure 7 shows graph for total number of relayed packets versus total number of nodes. It is observed that flooding generates a larger number of packets as the sensor nodes increase. HA algorithm with gossiping produces the least number of packets as compared to flooding and HA algorithm, and it is much steady with increasing sensor number. Since flooding algorithm broadcasts the data the number of packets transferred in the network using it is maximum. But when the gossiping algorithm is used this number is reduced significantly since does not broadcast packets.

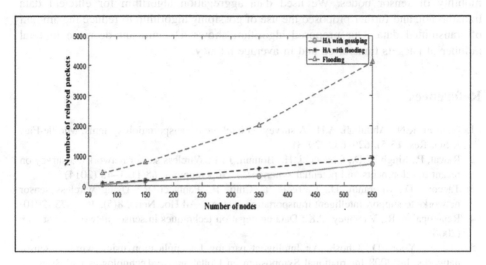

Fig. 7. Total number of relayed packets versus number of sensor nodes.

5.2 Average Latency

Figure 8 shows average latencies for both the algorithms, HA and the proposed one. The latency defines how long it takes for an entire message to completely arrive at the destination from the time the first bit is sent out from the source [11]. It is observed that the latencies for both the algorithm are comparable.

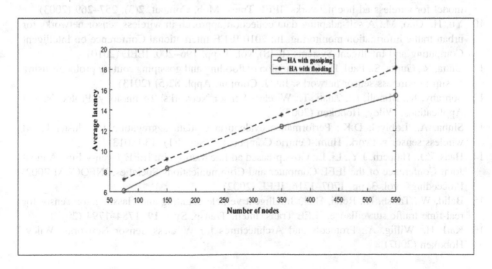

Fig. 8. Average latency versus number of sensor nodes.

6 Conclusion

We have presented a WSN based smart transportation system, which incorporates mobility of sensor nodes. We used data aggregation algorithm for efficient data transmission and further proposed the use of gossiping algorithm to reduce the amount of transmitted data. Our proposed algorithm shows a significant decrease in total number of packets transferred and in average latency.

References

1. Qureshi, K.N., Abdullah, A.H.: A survey on intelligent transportation systems. Middle-East J. Sci. Res. 15(5), 629–642 (2013)
2. Rawat, P., Singh, K.D., Chaouchi, H., Bonnin, J.M.: Wireless sensor networks: a survey on recent developments and potential synergies. J. Supercomput. 68(1), 1–48 (2014)
3. Tacconi, D., Miorandi, D., Carreras, I., Chiti, F., Fantacci, R.: Using wireless sensor networks to support intelligent transportation systems. Ad Hoc Netw. 8(5), 462–473 (2010)
4. Rajagopalan, R., Varshney, P.K.: Data aggregation techniques in sensor networks: a survey (2006)
5. Lee, S., Yoon, D., Ghosh, A.: Intelligent parking lot application using wireless sensor networks. In: 2008 International Symposium on Collaborative Technologies and Systems, CTS 2008. IEEE, pp. 48–57 (2008)
6. Tubaishat, M., Zhuang, P., Qi, Q., Shang, Y.: Wireless sensor networks in intelligent transportation systems. Wirel. Commun. Mob. Comput. 9(3), 287–302 (2009)
7. Hu, X., Yang, L., Xiong, W.: A novel wireless sensor network frame for urban transportation. IEEE Internet Things J. 2(6), 586–595 (2015)
8. You, Z., Chen, S., Wang, Y.: An efficient traffic data aggregation scheme for WSN based intelligent transportation systems. J. Inf. Hiding Multimed. Signal Process. 6(6), 1117–1129 (2015)
9. Bettstetter, C., Resta, G., Santi, P.: The node distribution of the random waypoint mobility model for wireless ad hoc networks. IEEE Trans. Mob. Comput. 2(3), 257–269 (2003)
10. Yu, H., Guo, M.: A self-adapting data collection approach in wireless sensor networks for urban traffic information monitoring. In: 2010 IEEE International Conference on Intelligent Computing and Intelligent Systems (ICIS), vol. 1, pp. 196–200. IEEE (2010)
11. Dutta, R., Gupta, S., Paul, D.: Comparision of flooding and gossiping routing protocols using tossim in wireless sensor networks. Int. J. Comput. Appl. 82(5) (2013)
12. Sohraby, K., Minoli, D., Znati, T.: Wireless Sensor Networks: Technology, Protocols, and Applications. Wiley, Hoboken (2007)
13. Sinha, A., Lobiyal, D.K.: Performance evaluation of data aggregation for cluster based wireless sensor network. Hum.-Centric Comput. Inf. Sci. 3(1), 13 (2013)
14. Haas, Z.J., Halpern, J.Y., Li, L.: Gossip-based ad hoc routing. In: IEEE Twenty-First Annual Joint Conference of the IEEE Computer and Communications Societies, INFOCOM 2002, Proceedings, vol. 3, pp. 1707–1716. IEEE (2002)
15. Balid, W., Tafish, H., Refai, H.H.: Intelligent vehicle counting and classification sensor for real-time traffic surveillance. IEEE Trans. Intell. Transp. Syst. 19, 1784–1794 (2017)
16. Karl, H., Willig, A.: Protocols and Architectures for Wireless Sensor Networks. Wiley, Hoboken (2007)

Lane Change in Roundabout for Reduced Trip Time

Hitender Vats[✉] and Ranjeet Singh Tomar

ITM University, Gwalior, India
HVATS@HOTMAIL.com, er.ranjeetsingh@gmail.com

Abstract. The Increasing the capacity of intersection of traffic flow at Roundabout without compromising safety is challenge we face. Better Algorithm/Protocol is needed which suits cooperative vehicular control in ITMS utilising VANET that is efficient and ensures reliability/safety. The time taken by a vehicle to cross the Roundabout has to be reduced for increasing the throughput of intersection. This paper presents a new approach of cooperative traffic management utilising VANET, by use of Lane with Lane change mechanism without compromising the safety of vehicles. This Intersection Side Unit (ISU) based system will increase the efficiency of roundabout by means of shorter average trip time. The ride for passenger will also be smoothened by reducing sudden jerks since this method utilises Lane instead of cells utilised by researchers till now. The modular use of Lane with lane change in control strategy will greatly enhance the capacity utilisation of Roundabout as analysed by Simulation. A new Simulator 'RoundSim' was also developed Exclusively for simulation in Roundabout.

Keywords: ITMS · ITS · VANET · Cooperative driving · Multi agent system

1 Introduction

With rapid urbanisation and lack of proper mass transportation system, maximum people spend a consideration amount of time on roads in developing country like India. Since road are common resource which is shared by vehicle with different dimensions and dynamic characteristic being driven by drivers with different level of perception and driving style, a traffic jam is the most common phenomenon affecting millions of people around globe. Analytically it can be easily inferred that traffic jams are caused whenever two flow of traffic movement Intersect each other. These intersection would take place at Lane merging, Crossings (with or without Traffic Light), Roundabouts and T-junctions.

Intersection is theoretically modelled as an obstacle to flow. Among the various solutions to alleviate traffic congestion, traffic-light or signal control is one of the most effective and common method. Depending on type of signalling such 'obstacle' may appear or disappear. Traffic lights are modelled by varying queue discharge capacity. A lot of work has already been done in making adaptive Red Light control system, which changes the Green light timing period as well change the Light Phase sequence for better optimisation. All these method uses 'Passive' method of finding the queue/no.

© Springer Nature Singapore Pte Ltd. 2019
S. Verma et al. (Eds.): CNC 2018, CCIS 839, pp. 201–212, 2019.
https://doi.org/10.1007/978-981-13-2372-0_18

of vehicle at Red-light, these is a new technology evolving which makes a vehicle **Intelligent**. These vehicles has sensor on-board and 'actively' tell their position, parameters and intended future movement on road. Intelligent Traffic Management System (**ITMS**) is a breakthrough in the intersection control paradigm, which may eliminate the necessity of stopping of vehicles and increase the capacity of intersections (number of vehicles crossing per unit time) is highly possible using V2V (Vehicle to Vehicle) communication. This has been proved that the **CACC** (Cooperative Adaptive Cruise Control) systems can safely drive vehicles with very short headway by forming platoons to improve traffic-flow capacity of a road. The concept of following a vehicle with a short gap in CACC can be extended to offer a new intersection control paradigm, in which nearly conflicting vehicles from different approaches can cross the intersection keeping marginal gaps without using any traffic signal thereby eliminating stop delay, reducing travel time, and increasing the capacity of an intersection.

Since weather and obstruction limits a driver's ability to take well informed decision, cooperative driving utilising VANET can effectively contribute in providing smooth traffic interaction at intersections. Safety can be enhanced and Pollution can be minimised by reducing the time a vehicle has to stop at intersection by using VANET based distributed control system. This can be achieved by two ways: firstly with use of a central controller at ISU (Inter Section control Unit) which is installed at intersection. All vehicle which has to transverse the intersection send message about its position, speed, vehicular parameter and intention to use lane number before & after crossing the intersection. The control algorithm will decide and transmit about who will have the right of way and which vehicle will have to decelerate to avoid any potential conflict in track. Second way is that an algorithm utilising distributed control algorithm running on all vehicle will decide about course of action. Here all vehicle will transmit the Message set to all vehicle in its vicinity and will calculate their future tracks. In case of a impending crash all vehicle will cooperatively decide about who will decelerate or even can accelerate also, to avoid any conflict.

Since both lateral and longitudinal vehicle control are necessary on the merging, Lane change decisions and speed controls needs to be coordinated and optimized to reduce the overall braking and achieve greater traffic throughput. These models are evaluated for travel times, fuel consumption, number of lane changes and the overall braking globally for all vehicles on the considered road segment. To optimise the interaction of vehicles at crossing, following Lane merging sequence are involved: (i) determining the *Merge Sequence (MS)* i.e., order in which vehicles cross the intersection region (ii) ensuring safety at intersection region and (iii) achieving an optimization goal such as minimizing the maximum *(DTTI)*, time taken by a vehicle to reach the intersection region.

It is necessary to secure the sufficient headway in order to cross the intersection smoothly without crash. The way drivers in manually driven vehicles resolve the conflict at intersection region in practice. The drivers who are closest to the merge region on each road decide among themselves the order in which they will pass through the region (based on some criteria, say *First Come First Serve*). For a reliable and efficient communication in VANET for ITMS, there is a need for a better control strategy using a new algorithm specifically tailored for Crossing and Roundabout traffic management. The goal of optimization will be to achieve minimum average DTTI or maximum throughput.

2 Roundabout Traffic Control Management System

Roundabouts are another form of Traffic Intersection than that of Crossing/Red-lights. They are actually used as "Traffic Smoothers" as it intends to streamline the traffic flow in a easy to manage 'One way traffic'. In this process of streamlining the average speed of vehicles reduces which is variable of Traffic density as well as Roundabout's Geometry. Due to slow speed, smaller gaps are acceptable between vehicles which increases the traffic volume and it can be summarised that roundabout outperform crossing regards to throughput and capacity.

Roundabout Traffic management can also be achieved through **collaboration of vehicles** having VANET capability and acting as independent intelligent agents without need of a centralised control infrastructure like ISU. The problem with RSU is that they can act a Single Point of Failure thereby compromising Safety on crossings.

It was Yang et al. [1] who have proposed A New method of traffic signal control for modern Roundabout using signal phasing with different signal timing. They have proposed TSLT (Two Stop Lines for Left Turn) control wherein that left turn vehicle will stop at 2 Red Lights to avoid weaving (First at Entry lane and Second Stoplight on circulatory lane). Tan, Wang et al. [2] have presented a concept of Optimal Number of Vehicles within the Roundabout (ONVR) and find that the Roundabout can get a higher real-time capacity if the Current Number of Vehicles within the Roundabout is kept on the ONVR level. Zhang et al. [3] have utilised Artificial Intelligence which employs Fuzzy Logic with two fuzzy layers for controller of signalised roundabout. The outer layer is utilised for selecting the most urgent phase subset. The inner layer was used for calculation of extension time of current phase.

Azimi et al. [4] presented a Non Signalised/Non-RSU algorithm CDAR (Collision Detection Algorithm for Roundabout) using CC-IP (Concurrent Crossing Intersection Protocol) & MP-IP (Maximum Progression Intersection Protocol). The algorithm determines if there is any common cell along the trajectory which might result is a collision. This cell which might lead to conflict is defined as TIC (Trajectory Intersecting Cell). The CCIP is designed to increase the throughput at roundabout while avoiding collision. This is ensured by allowing only vehicle without any conflicting trajectory i.e. TIC in a roundabout. Here low priority vehicle with conflicting trajectory i.e. even a single TIC will wait and stop before entering the roundabout. While the MPIP utilises the updated CROSS message and allows a vehicle enters the roundabout evenif it has knowledge of a TIC but will stop before that TIC & wait for that cell to be free before continuing its trajectory thereby increasing the throughput considerably.

Bento et al. [5] described an ITMS with operation mode in Time-Space Reservation Algorithm. The space used by a vehicle is allocated in a 3-D matrix where each layer represents the map divided in cells for a determined time instance 't'. The 3-Matrix composed by a group of layer with each layer corresponding to consecutive sampling time. The information sent by the vehicle with its position and destined lane is used for trajectory generation by the Reservation process. If the vehicle is trying to reserve a space in a layer already reserved/occupied, the algorithm instruct the vehicle to slow down before it reaches the occupied zone. Sun et al. [6] conducted a comparative study on Capacity of a signalized Roundabout, Signalised Intersection & Un-Signalised

Roundabout. They developed a shockwave-based model to capture impact of signal at circulatory lanes on queuing and clearance time of left turning vehicles. A generalised model for timing and capacity were also developed. A sensitivity analysis elaborated to test how temporal and spatial parameters affect capacity of roundabout.

In our opinion the presence of Red Light at the Roundabouts (as envisaged by many researchers) defeats the very purpose of Roundabout itself. In moderate to heavy traffic density it will result in considerable time at Stopping which is nothing but Red Lights itself. So Roundabout Traffic Management System is required which utilise VANET communication to intelligently manoeuvre the lanes of roundabout.

3   Algorithm for Lane Change in Roundabout

The basic of our proposed algorithm is that any traffic scenario can be modelled with help of basic building block of Lane. Two lanes, inner left and outer Right lane, will constitute 'Segment' (we have used a Right hand drive system). For analysis purpose, a number of segment can be interconnected to model complete traffic system. We have studied the case of intersection in form of Roundabouts, which is also modelled with help of Segments. Each Roundabout is divided into 4 equal segment which is one quarter of a circle. Each segment is further divided into to 2 lane which are curved thus each roundabout has 8 Lane. Lane change is allowed only within segment i.e. between two adjacent lanes in each segment. Once a vehicle transverses one Lane it contest with other vehicle who want to utilise this particular intended lane. Lane change is performed only after 50 m in each lane. This modular concept of Lane with lane change algorithm is morphed giving rise to requirement and suitability of OOPS (Object Oriented Programming Software) concept. This was the very reason that Python was zeroed on for Simulation purpose which is very widely used and Open source OOPS language.

As seen in Fig. 1, the Roundabout is having two lanes with 4 Cloves (N, E, W, S) each at right angle. Vehicle which have to go Left and Straight will use outer lane while which have to go Right turn and U-Turn will use Inner lane. The vehicle starting from leftmost point (West-in lane) and willing to go in south will transverse through Wi going into WN segment of Roundabout followed by NE. It will transverse through ES segment for exiting Roundabout followed by South out segment of clove.

Therefore a **RSL** (Route Segment List) is prepared which determine all the road Segment a vehicle will transverse from incoming segment to outgoing segment. All the possible scenarios are tabulated in Table 1.

3.1   Collision Avoidance at Roundabout Algorithm-CARA

Here the ISU is an agent which runs the simulation, checks for any impending collision, receives and transmit messages to all other vehicle agents in its jurisdiction area for efficient and safe traffic movement. When a vehicle enter Area of Control (which can be painted on road with Yellow or any other prominent colour), no vehicle is allowed to take its own decision, but will strictly follow command from ISU. At ISU

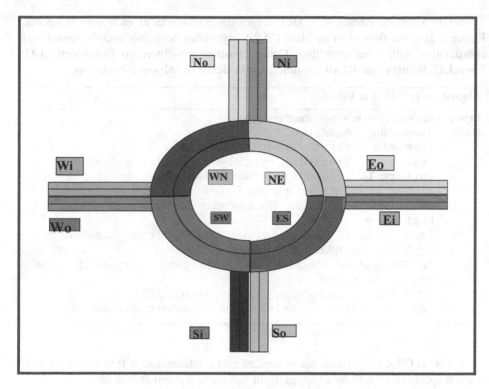

Fig. 1. Shows a typical 2 lane roundabout

Table 1. RSL (Route segment list)

Coming from	Exiting ➡			
	North	East	South	West
North	Ni-NE-ES-SW-WN-No	Ni-NE-Eo	Ni-NE-ES-So	Ni-NE-ES-SW-Wo
East	Ei-ES-SW-WN-No	Ei-ES-SW-WN-NE-Eo	Ei-ES—So	Ei-ES-SW-Wo
South	Si-SW-WN-No	Si-SW-WN-NE-Eo	Si-SW-WN-NE-ES-So	Si-SW-Wo
West	Wi-WN-No	Wi-WN-NE-Eo	Wi-WN-NE-ES-So	Wi-WN-NE-ES-SW-Wo

the main algorithm CARA is working which control the overall function and also control all the sub-algorithms working, each for

1. Lane Insert for mitigating conflict at entry point of roundabout.
2. Lane Exit for safely exiting the Roundabout.
3. Force Lane Change algorithm.
4. Elective Lane change algorithm LC working for each lane/within each Lane.

While a vehicle edition of CARA algorithm also works at each vehicle agents. Figure 2 give the flow chart of Main CARA algorithm depicting overall control and coordination with other algorithm. Detail of other sub-algorithm like **ElectiveLC**, **ForceLC**, **REntry** and **RExit** are described in detail in subsequent sections.

Algorithm 1: CARA at Vehicle

Input: Received Vehicle's movement message
Output: Transmitting Vehicle's state

```
1. Transmit Present  Speed, Position
2. Follow the preceding vehicle in Cruise Control
3. Perform LC if Required( when self-cruise velocity is
   higher than preceding Vehicle)
4. If within reach of Roundabout : Transmit Intended
   Exit Lane
5. Decelerate if DECL received (ISU Performs Lane Entry)
   or Enter Roundabout Segment
6. In Roundabout Segment Perform Lane change if lane
   Change Received
7.  Decelerate and Join back on Abort LC Signal
8.  Exit at Intended ExitLane & Transmit Exited Signal
```

Below is CARA algorithm that is applied and implemented at ISU which controls the full spectrum of activities happening in the traffic system at Roundabout.

Algorithm2 : CARA At ISU

Input: Received Vehicle's state
Output: Transmit Vehicle's movement order

```
1. If Entered AoC(Area of Control =500 Mtrs before the
   roundabout) then
2. Determine Lane based on Location
3. Check Intended Exit Segment
4. Calculate List of Segments that this vehicle need to
   transverse(Prepare RSL).
5. If takingRight or U-Turn:     Move on to Lane 2 ( if
   not in Lane 2)--
6. If taking Left Turn or Going Straight: Move on to
   Lane 1( if not in Lane 2)- :   Perform Force LC in
   both cases
7. Enter roundel in Designated lane: Perform Roundabout
   Entry
8. Explore for ElectiveLC
9. End of current segment: Enter next segment
10.     At 100 Mtrs before Exit Segment perform
    RoundaboutExit (CompulsoryLC) to Left Lane
11.     Broadcast Clear message
```

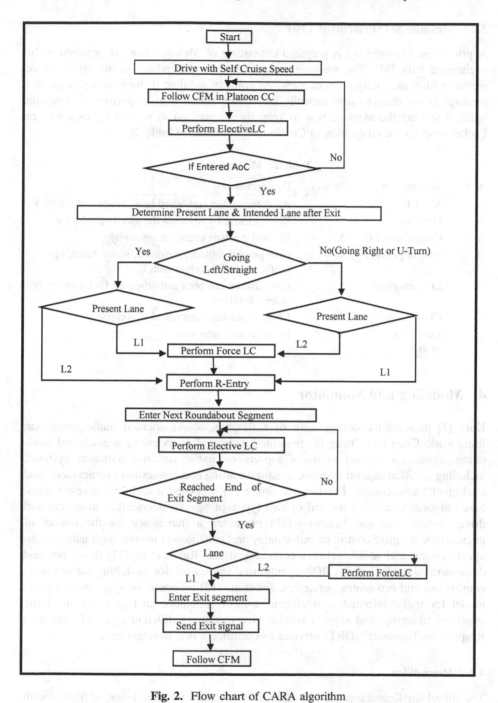

Fig. 2. Flow chart of CARA algorithm

3.2   Message Set (Prioritised List)

A prioritised Message list is prepared consisting of Message that are required to be exchanged with ISU. The message were prioritised depending on the criticality of message from the safety point of view. At point of anytime if the intended/ expected message is not received automatically Decelerate action is to be performed. The aim while designing the message was to keep them short, so as to avoid packet loss or Packet drop due to congestion in Communication traffic (Table 2).

Table 2. Message set

S.N.	Message Set	Priority	Description
a.	Abort LC	1.	Abort the earlier authorised lane change and fall back
b.	DeAccel	2.	De-accelerate by reducing the speed of vehicle
c.	Compulsory LC	3.	Perform the lane change mandatorily
d.	Present position	4.	Give present latitude, longitude, speed, breaking coefficient, total weight with load
e.	LC authorised	5.	Lane change has been authorised by ISU with safety criteria fulfilled
f.	Clear	6.	Roundabout has been exited by vehicle
g.	Lane after of exit	7.	Intended lane after exit

4   Modeling and Simulator

Kurz [7] presents the development of a flexible, object oriented traffic simulation framework. Chen and Cheng [8] presented a general overview of agent based modelling techniques applied to many aspects of traffic and transportation systems, including decision support systems, dynamic routing and congestion management, and intelligent traffic control. Dresner and Stone [9] proposed a multi-agent reservation-based algorithm which consisted of two types of agents: intersection managers and driver agents. Zou and Levinson [10] presented a framework for the impact of microscopic adaptive control on traffic delay and collisions at intersections using multi-agent systems and ad-hoc network communications. Rakha et al. [11] developed and demonstrated the INTEGRATION agent-based framework for modelling various user-equilibrium and eco-routing strategies. Jin et al. [12] proposed an agent based hybrid model for traffic information intelligent control simulation that performs the basic interface, planning, and support services for managing different types of "Demand Responsive Transport" (DRT) services to optimize traffic management.

4.1   RoundSim

The Simulator RoundSim has been designed specially for Simulation of Traffic with different driving model but can be customised for all other traffic scenario including Red Light Crossings. This Simulator can give output in form of Text output, Graph of Video output for better understanding and comprehending the controller protocol (Fig. 3).

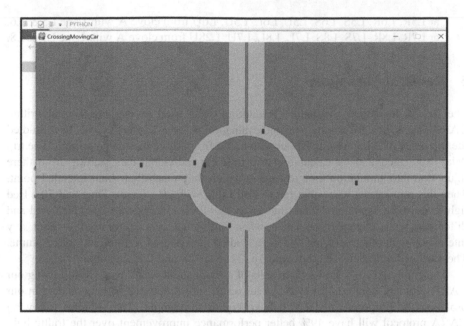

Fig. 3. Snapshots of RoundSim

The ISU controller was the main agent interacting with all other vehicle agents in its AoR. The lateral interaction among vehicle was restricted to cruise control only. The cars were injected into system with random variables/ parameters in term of velocity, position, route i.e. intended direction after exiting the Roundabout and braking co-efficient.

The following assumption have been made to facilitate comparative study–

1. No skidding at turn.
2. No slowing down at Turn.
3. We neglect driver behaviour.
4. Dimension/size of all vehicles is taken same
5. No delay. All vehicle immediately follow the ISU instruction.
6. All the vehicles were taken to be of same size.

4.2   Experimental Setup for RoundSim

Test setup consist of a Two Lane Roundabout having mean radius of 200 m. with 4 Cloves each at right angle with each other with Lane 1 & 2. Each clove is 2 Km. in length. There will be Four cars/vehicle Originating at each of cloves in each lane with a random time interval between them. One vehicle out of these four will go Straight (S) while one will take U-Turn (Car U). The other two will take Left Turn (L) and Right turn (R) each. So we can have total of 32 car Route named as follows:-

Car L1R, L2R, L1S, L2S, L1L, L2L, L1U, L2U from clove A with Lane L1 & L2.
Car L3R, L4R, L3S, L4S, L3L, L4L, L3U, L4U from clove A with Lane L3 & L4.

Car L5R, L6R, L5S, L6S, L5L, L6L, L5U, L6U from clove A with Lane L5 & L6.
Car L7R, L8R, L7S, L8S, L7L, L8L, L7U, L28U from clove A with Lane L7 & L8.

5   Result and Analysis

The newly developed Simulator 'RoundSim' was used to evaluate our algorithm CARA. The matric for comparison and evaluation was the Trip Delay. We have studied the trip delay of 2-Lane Roundabout with traffic from four direction entering it. The trip delay was calculated by calculating trip time for individual cars starting from there injunction into simulation time to time at which they reach their final intended point. Then this roundabout was subjected to Red Light with 30 s Green Time and 30 s Red light cycle. The average of total time taken by all cars in system were calculated and difference with average time taken when individual cars were used without any interaction with other vehicles. We have studied the system for different traffic volume. The various traffic density used were 16, 32, 64, 128 and 256 cars/min.

The graph in Fig. 4 shows the results of a roundabout where cars are following our CARA protocol with control at ISU. Our result shows that due to lane change in our protocol, the proposed model will have higher throughput. The vehicles following CARA protocol will have 49% better performance improvement over the traffic light model with a 30 s green light time. The result proves that our proposed protocol will perform significantly better than the traffic light model. There is a 60% improvement if vehicles are allowed elective lane change in roundabout. It can be seen from results that the effect of our proposed protocol CARA will reduce with increase in traffic density. The reason is that there is no space (gap between vehicles) left for lane change and

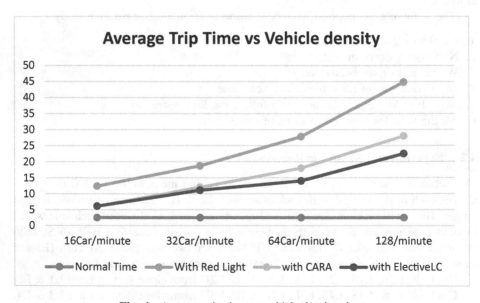

Fig. 4. Average trip time vs vehicle density chart

hence as expected the betterment in performance will decreases. Since there was safety criteria put in place forcing cars to slow down and in some cases even come to complete halt, there were no accidents reported and verified from video graphic simulation result.

6 Conclusion and Future Work

To improve the efficiency of traffic system bottlenecks in form of Intersection will have to be better managed. There is a urgent need to eliminate the traffic disrupting Redlights at crossing which are both irritating to drivers and also Pollution creator due to over consumption of fuel. So to maximise the capacity of crossing area simultaneous movement of non-conflicting trajectory is a must. To further enhance the capacity Lane change in crossing area definitely deserve a consideration.

This paper has presented a new protocol for management of traffic in a Roundabout to maximise the throughput and to reduce the trip delays. A new Simulator based on multi-agent framework was developed in Python Language which also give graphical output in form of Video which help in better appreciation of the protocol being developed. Since the only safety criteria considered in this paper is ' distance of car length plus 5 m between two adjacent vehicles' in future the speed/acceleration differential or other criteria can be studied. Here we have studied effect of our proposed protocol on safety involving the 2-Lane traffic which further need to be studied for 3-Lane traffic system.

In future authors propose to develop a new communication protocol which will be customised for our protocols managing traffic at Roundabout under ITMS. The main goal of the envisaged protocol will be to reduce the message delivery latency of such information while ensuring the correct reception of warning messages in the vehicle's neighbourhood as soon as a dangerous situation occurs. Also the effect of packet loss due to congestion in bandwidth is to be studied for further strengthening the security robustness.

References

1. Yang, X., Li, X.: A new method of traffic signal control for modern roundabout. In: 2003 IEEE Intelligent Transportation Systems, Proceedings, vol. 2, pp. 1094–1100 (2003)
2. Tan, G., Wang, Y., Wang, Y., Ge, H.: A new traffic-signal control for large multi-branch roundabouts, pp. 7–11 (2011)
3. Gong, Y., Zhang, J.: Real-time traffic signal control for roundabouts by using a PSO-based fuzzy controller. In: 2012 IEEE Congress on Evolutionary Computation, pp. 1–8 (2012)
4. Azimi, R., Bhatia, G., Rajkumar, R., Mudalige, P.: V2V-intersection management at roundabouts. SAE Int. J. Passeng. Cars-Mech. Syst. 6(2013-01-0722), 681–690 (2013)
5. Bento, L.C., Parafita, R., Nunes, U.: Intelligent traffic management at intersections supported by V2V and V2I communications, pp. 1495–1502 (2012)
6. Ma, W., Sun, X., Huang, W.: Comparative study on the capacity of a signalised roundabout. IET Intell. Transp. Syst. 10(3), 175–185 (2016)

7. Kurz, A.Y.: Agent-based modeling and simulation of cooperative driving (2014). http://digitalcommons.uri.edu/theses/470
8. Chen, B., Cheng, H.H.: A Review of the applications of agent technology in traffic and transportation systems. IEEE Trans. Intell. Transp. Syst. **11**(2), 485–497 (2010)
9. Dresner, K., Stone, P.: A multiagent approach to autonomous intersection management. J. Artif. Intell. Res. **31**, 591–656 (2008)
10. Zou, X., Levinson, D.M.: Vehicle-based intersection management with intelligent agents. In: ITS America Annual Meeting Proceedings (2003)
11. Rakha, H., Zohdy, I., Du, J., Park, B.B., Lee, J., El-Metwally, M.: Traffic signal control enhancements under vehicle infrastructure integration systems. Mid-Atlantic Universities Transportation Center (2011)
12. Jin, X., Itmi, M., et al.: A cooperative multi-agent system simulation model for urban traffic intelligent control. In: Proceedings of the 2007 Summer Computer Simulation Conference, Society for Computer Simulation International, San Diego, CA, pp. 953–958 (2007)

High Dimensional Data Representation and Processing

Fundamental Survey of Map Reduce in Bigdata with Hadoop Environment

Maulik Dhamecha[1]([⊠]) and Tejas Patalia[2]

[1] Computer Engineering, Gujarat Technological University, Ahmedabad,
Gujarat, India
mvdhamecha@gmail.com
[2] Computer Engineering Department, VVP Engineering College,
Gujarat Technological University, Rajkot, Gujarat, India
pataliatejas@rediffmail.com

Abstract. The terminology "Big Data" was initiated for variety of industry processes, methods and technology to explore new field. Big organizations like Amazon, flip cart and also many government subsidiaries like ISRO, NASA and BISAG are considering Big Data to fulfill their analytical objectives with mapping technique and reducing technique. We can consider Big Data as key factor related large or small-sized data repositories and consortium which have been identifies the possible (which is random manner extensively) to make capital out of. And for that hadoop is very effective platform to shows the efficiency of map reduce technique.

Keywords: Mapreduce · Mapping technique · Reducing technique
Hadoop

1 Introduction

Into the computational market the term "big data" is very usually used term. In a data world, Big Data means every one's data. It is the Knowledge or relevant fact considered by particular organization, gathered and deal with recent methods or procedure to generate best result in precise manner.

As we start the learning about Big Data, data analytics will elaborate the subject precisely likely to talking about "The three V's" - "volume, velocity and variety," this points which identifies the challenge of data analytics word. In brief, it is big amount of attribute processing in fast and various manner. User's executable processing records, databases of production for organization, influx of web log files, live video file, current media's user conversations and many more could be involved. Mark van Rijmenam told about main 3 V's that "Why the 3 V's Are Not Sufficient to Describe Big Data," also says that "veracity, variability, visualization, and value" to the definition. Rijmenam also says that "90% of all data ever created, was created in the past two years. From now on, the amount of data in the world will double every two years" [1, 4].

A software framework for distributed processing of large data sets on compute clusters of commodity hardware is known as Hadoop MapReduce (Hadoop Map/Reduce)" [2]. It is a partial part of the Apache Hadoop. Organizing endeavor,

© Springer Nature Singapore Pte Ltd. 2019
S. Verma et al. (Eds.): CNC 2018, CCIS 839, pp. 215–222, 2019.
https://doi.org/10.1007/978-981-13-2372-0_19

surveil them and re-surveil any crashed tasks ware taking care about the framework. "According to The Apache Software Foundation, the primary objective of Map/Reduce is to split the input data set into independent chunks that are processed in a completely parallel manner" [1, 15]. The framework of Hadoop MapReduce can organize the output data for mapping class, which output becomes input of reduce class. So, all incoming data and the outgoing data relevant of tasks are saved in a resulted file system.

2 Hadoop Features and Characteristics

Apache Hadoop is the most powerful and very precise big data tool. "Hadoop provides the most reliable storage layer – HDFS, a batch processing engine – MapReduce and a Resource Management Layer – YARN" [4]. There are some important Hadoop Features which are stated as below-

Open source: Apache Hadoop is known as open source project. So, we can modified code according to business requirements.

Distributed processing: data is processed in parallel way on a cluster of different nodes because can be saved in a distributed manner in Haoop Distributed File System across that cluster of nodes [7].

Fault Tolerance: There are 3 replicas of each block was stored across that cluster in Hadoop in default manner and it can also be modified also as per the given requirement. So if any node will become down, data can be recovered from any other nodes in easy manner. [2, 11] By the framework, automatically data can be recovered if failures of nodes or tasks are occurred. This is how we can says this is one of the important feature of Hadoop.

Reliability: Data is satisfactory stored on the different nodes of cluster in a case machine failures due to replication. [15] If your machine will going to fail for work then also your data will be stored satisfactory.

High Availability: Due to number of copies of data is large, data can be available and ready to despite of hardware failure. If any hardware crashes of machine will happen, then data will be accumulate from another pathway also [15].

Scalability: whenever any new hardware can be easily accommodate to the given nodes we can say that hadoop is highly scalable. When any extra nodes can be accommodate on the urgent way without any downtime, we can says that it also provides horizontal scalability [7, 15].

Economy: As we apply it of commonly connected hardware, we can says that Apache Hadoop is not very expensive. Cluster have no need any specialized node for it. Hadoop gives us huge cost cutting and also as it is very simple to accumulate more machines on that cluster over here. [9] So whenever any requirement will increases in time manner, you can also put up the machines and also without any alteration and without so much pre-planning for that.

Data Locality: "move computation to data instead of data to computation" -
Hadoop is working on this fundamental principle of data locality. [8] Whenever any
user will submits the MapReduce process, this process will moved to data in that
cluster in place of transferring data to that place where the process is submitted.

3 Functionality of Map-Reduce

We can say that Apache Hadoop, Mapreduce is the heart. It will behave like the
programming structure which permit for extendibility into the big number of clusters of
a Server. We can say that MapReduce paradigm is comparatively easy to catch for the
known users about the scaling processing of cluster.

Understanding for new users can be difficult about this topic, because it is not
generalize concept for people to have been expand as n former times. If you are new for
the Hadoop MapReduce tasks, don't be hesitate, we will try to get knowledge in it that
you will pick up it quickly.

"This term MapReduce is refers two different and distinct tasks that Hadoop programs platform. [9]"As shown in Fig. 1, Map job is initial task, which gets a cluster of
attributes and transfer it into different cluster of attributes, into that every attributes are
tumbledown into attributes like key pairs or value pairs. Outgoing data going to the
reduce job through a map function as incoming and segregate particular data attributes
like key pairs or value pairs into a small chunks of attributes. Name of MapReduce
itself says that, every time reduce job is occurred only after the completion of the map
job.

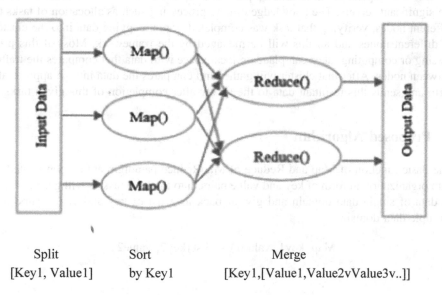

Split	Sort	Merge
[Key1, Value1]	by Key1	[Key1,[Value1,Value2vValue3v..]]

Fig. 1. Basics of Map-reduce

The fundamental of Hadoop says that "The MapReduce framework works mainly on <key, value> pairs, that is, the framework views the input to the task as a pair of <key, value> set and produces a pair of <key, value> sets as the output of the task, producing of different types [15]".

The key classes and value classes have been put in sequentially by the Hadoop framework and that's for that reason necessity to implant the Writable interface. In Addition, the set of key values will implant the accessible pathway to ordering by the framework.

Here is the Input & Output of a MapReduce job:

"(input) <key1, value1> -> map -> <key2, value2> -> combine -> <key2, value2> -> reduce -> <key3, value3> (output)" [4].

Commonly the MapReduce concept is concern about the data sending to the node at which place the result is placed. MapReduce processed in three ways, first is mapping, shuffling and reducing.

Mapping Stage: The input data process is known as map or mapper's task. Data which are file or directory typed which are stored in the Hadoop distributive file system (HDFS) as input. The input data of file is going through the mapper function interpretably. This data would be processed by the mapper stage and creates into many small parts of this data.

Reducing Stage: "This stage is the combination of the two stage: the Shuffle stage and the Reducing stage" [9]. The main task of Reducer's is to get the data from mapper stage and process that data. After completion of this process, it produces a new group of output, which will saved in the Hadoop distributive file system HDFS.

Into the MapReduce task, Hadoop pass the Map and Reduce tasks into the cluster to the significant servers. The knowledge of data-processing such as allocation of tasks to different nodes, verifying that task was completed or not, copying data into the cluster of different nodes and all this will be managed by the framework. Most of this processing or computing takes can place on local space with data that compares the traffic between nodes. After that cluster will gather and compares the data into an appropriate form and sends this resultant data to the server after completion of this given tasks.

4   Proposed Algorithm

The basic function of Map and Reduce of MapReduce paradigm are known related to data organization in form of key and value pairs. Into the Map task, it will get single set of data of single data domain and give it back as a list of key and value pairs in a multiple data domain:

$$\text{Map}\,(\text{key1, value1}) \rightarrow \text{list}\,(\text{key2, value2})$$

This mapper function is applicable in a serialized way to each key1 and value pair into the input datasets. This will generates a series of key2 and value pairs for every of the call. Completion of this process, this framework gathers all data pairs with the original key2 from the all list, make groups of those data and generate single group for every key.

After then applied the Reduce function in serialized way to every group, which produces the values in collective manner the common domain:

$$\text{Reduce (key2, list(value2))} \rightarrow \text{list(value3)}$$

Though one massage will permit to giving back multiple value of data, every single Reduce massage generate either the value v3 or a none return. This returns of that all massages are gathered as the expected result of the list.

The proposed algorithm is as below.

```
function map (String name, String document):
  // name: document or file name
  // document: document or file contents
  for each word w in document or file:
    emit (w, 1)


function reduce(String word, Iterator partial counts):
  // word: a word
  // partial Counts: a list of aggregated partial counts
  sum = 0
  for each pc in partial Counts:
    sum += pc
  emit (word, sum)
```

4.1   Example

Here we can try to understand this topic with an example. Suppose user contain four files of data and particular file have two columns data ("a key and a value in Hadoop terms") that shows the value as name of city and relevant temperature of particular city for the different days. As we are taking this data just as an example so it is simple to understand. We can understand that any real time application is not so simple because we are talking about big data as it was containing record numbers of rows and may be it was not be preprocessed this data. Here no matter that what amount of data we are analyzing, the unique principles we are highlighting here is remain as it is. And for this example, "we had taken city is the key and temperature is the value.

Ahmedabad, 21
Vadodara, 26
Rajkot, 23
Surat, 33

Here, we have to find highest temperature of every city from every collection from all the data we have collected. We can cut down this in 5 major mapping tasks, at there every single map task works on 1 out of 5 given files, also map task going into the data and gives back with the maximum temperature value for every particular city using the MapReduce framework. The final value is look like as below:

(Ahmedabad, 21)(Vadodara, 26)(Rajkot, 23)(Surat, 33)

Think that given four other mapper tasks generate the below interim results:

(Ahmedabad, 18) (Vadodara, 27)
(Rajkot, 32) (Surat, 37)
(Ahmedabad, 32) (Vadodara, 20)
(Rajkot, 33) (Surat, 38)
(Ahmedabad, 22) (Vadodara, 19)
(Rajkot, 20) (Surat, 31)
(Ahmedabad, 31) (Vadodara, 22)
(Rajkot, 19) (Surat, 30)

Into the reduce tasks, feed all output stream of these files which added the results of all input data and single value of output data of particular every city, produced the executable output set as below:

(Ahmedabad, 32)(Vadodara, 27)(Rajkot, 33)(Surat, 38)

Similarly, you may also find an example of "census was conducted in Roman where the census bureau would dispatch its people to each city in the empire for map and reduce tasks. Work is like each census taker in each city would be tasked to count the number of people in that city and return the results to the capital city."

"Thus, the results from each city will be reduced to a single count (sum of all cities) to calculate the overall population of the empire. This mapping of people of cities, in parallel way and then combining the results is more efficient than sending an alone person to count every person in the empire in a serial" [16].

Here in Table 1, some basic commands are given for implementation of this basic map-reduce functionality.

Table 1. Hadoop basic commands [8]

Options	Description
"namenode –format"	"Formats the DFS filesystem"
"secondarynamenode"	"Runs the DFS secondary namenode"
"namenode"	"Runs the DFS namenode"
"datanode"	"Runs a DFS datanode"
"dfsadmin"	"Runs a DFS admin client"
"mradmin"	"Runs a Map-Reduce admin client"
"fsck"	"Runs a DFS filesystem checking utility"
"fs"	"Runs a generic filesystem user client"
"balancer"	"Runs a cluster balancing utility"
"oiv"	"Applies the offline fsimage viewer to an fsimage"
"fetchdt"	"Fetches a delegation token from the NameNode"
"jobtracker"	"Runs the MapReduce job Tracker node"
"pipes"	"Runs a Pipes job"
"tasktracker"	"Runs a MapReduce task Tracker node"
"historyserver"	"Runs job history servers as a standalone daemon"
"job"	"Manipulates the MapReduce jobs"
"queue"	"Gets information regarding JobQueues"
"version"	"Prints the version"
"jar < jar>"	"Runs a jar file"
"distcp < srcurl > < desturl>"	"Copies file or directories recursively"
"distcp2 < srcurl > < desturl>"	"DistCp version 2"
"archive -archiveName NAME –p"	"Creates a hadoop archive"
"classpath"	"Prints the class path needed to get the Hadoop jar and the required libraries"
"daemonlog"	"Get/Set the log level for each daemon"

5   Conclusion

When we are talking about the processing of large amount of data sets, Hadoop MapReduce paradigm accessible for the scheduling such large amount of data in a protective and efficient way. Hadoop is a highly scalable platform and behind scalability, the main reason is to save and distribute huge amount of data in different servers. While every addition of data servers it can increase more processing throughput.

Acknowledgement. First of all I would like to thank the VVP Engineering College, Rajkot, Gujarat, India for providing me suitable working environment and because of this I am able to find the scope of my research work. With the use of the practical laboratory environment of VVP Engineering College, Rajkot, Gujarat I was able to get the results of my research work.

I am also very great full to Dr. Tejas Patalia to guide me throaty in my research. He is guiding me time to time for improvement in my research work and motivate me to work deep in this keen area of research. Without his kind support it's not possible for me to continue my research journey. In last, I am thankful to all my colleague for supporting me and encourage me in my research.

References

1. Godhani, G., Dhamecha, M.: A study on movie recommendation system using parallel MapReduce technology. IJEDR **5**, 7683–7692 (2017)
2. Song, G., Meng, Z., Huet, F., Magoules, F., Yu, L., Lin, X.: A hadoop MapReduce performance prediction method. In: IEEE (2013)
3. Shvachko, K., Kuang, H., Radia, S., Chansler, R.: The hadoop distributed file system. IEEE (2010)
4. Subramaniyaswamy, V., Vijayakumar, V., Logesh, R., Indragandhi, V.: Unstructured data analysis on big data using map reduce. Science direct (2015)
5. Dean, J., Sanjay, G.: MapReduce: simplied data processing on large clusters. In: OSID (2004)
6. Dhamecha, M., Ganatra, A., Bhensadadiya, C.K.: Comprehensive study of hierarchical clustering algorithm and comparison with different clustering algorithms. In: CiiT (2011)
7. Cuzzocrea, A., Song, Y., Davis, K.C.: Analytics over large-scale multidimensional data: the big data revolution!. In: ACM (2011)
8. Tungkasthan, A., Premchaiswadi, W.: A parallel processing framework using MapReduce for content-based image retrieval. In: IEEE (2013)
9. Xu, W., Luo, W.: Analysis and optimization of data import with hadoop. In: IEEE (2012)
10. Chandarana, D., Dhamecha, M.: A survey for different approaches of outlier detection in data mining. In: IEEE (2015)
11. Maitrey, S., Jha, C.K.: Handling big data efficiently by using map reduce technique. In: IEEE (2015)
12. Agarwal, P., Shroff, G., Malhotra, P.: Approximate incremental big-data harmonization. In: IEEE (2013)
13. Wang, G., Salles, M.V.: Behavioral simulations in MapReduce. In: IEEE (2010)
14. Dean, J., Ghemawat, S.: MapReduce: simplified data processing on large clusters. In: Proceedings of the 6th Symposium on Operating Systems Design and Implementation, San Francisco CA (2004)
15. Shvachko, K.V.: HDFS scalability: the limits to growth. In: IEEE (2010)
16. Acharya, S., Chellappan, S.: Big Data and Analytics. Wiley, Hoboken (2015)
17. https://en.wikipedia.org/wiki/Big_data
18. www.bigdatahadoop.info

Improve Tampered Image Using Watermarking Apply the Distance Matrix

Nisha Chauhan$^{(\boxtimes)}$ and Arun Agarwal

Department of Computer Science and Engineering, ITM Group of Institution,
Gwalior, MP, India
chauhannisha716@gmail.com, arun.agarwal@itmgoi.in

Abstract. In the part of tamper detection and recuperation, there are a few of procedures to embed the element data in have picture for recuperation. Right when the host picture has been tampered, the part information can be utilized to reestablish the preeminent picture. In any case, it doesn't have the ability to verbs the duty regarding copyright. In this article, a photograph watermarking plan with alter affirmation and recuperation is proposed. The basic target is to see and recover the tampered zone totally. This paper proposed a digital watermarking and tampering, Due to utilization of this method in our proposed image tamper detection method. First, the select cover image from the set of images or folder. Then, secondly select the watermarked image from the folder. Apply defocusing on the cover image. Apply defocusing on the Watermark image. Then embed the two images. On the embedded image, apply tempering. The quality is calculated by the Minoswki TP Rate and Bhattacharya TP Rate and Chi-Square TP Rate but in the proposed scheme get better result as compared to base.

Keywords: Image tampering · Digital watermarking · Minoswki
Bhattacharya · Chi-Square distance matrix

1 Introduction

With the headway in information technology and image processing software the control of the pictures has expanded considerably from past few years. Retouching of the pictures has been prevalent that these days one can barely trust their authenticity. Retouching may be done for enhancement purpose by keeping the contents of the image in place or for making manufactured images by intentionally modifying the contents.

(Image manipulation is done usually for some specific purpose). It may be done to hide some content from the image or to alter the contents by combining it with other images [1].

With the progress of exceedingly refined advanced photograph altering programming, it has now turned out to be anything but difficult to control computerized pictures in a way that a human thinks that it's hard to perceive the progressions in stripped eyes. The far reaching utilization of web based systems administration enables a man to share and transfer any kind of pictures to the Internet. In the event that the picture is manufactured, and it is proliferated by the web-based social networking, the print media, or

© Springer Nature Singapore Pte Ltd. 2019
S. Verma et al. (Eds.): CNC 2018, CCIS 839, pp. 223–234, 2019.
https://doi.org/10.1007/978-981-13-2372-0_20

the electronic media, the loss may have disgrace, disapproval, and injury. Along these lines, it is fundamental to check the legitimacy of the photo. There are a couple of works in the writing about picture fraud discovery. They are apportioned into two portions, one is dynamic and another is inactive.

In the dynamic approach, it is typical that the photo has watermark embedded, and the approach removes the watermark and check it against the first watermark. If the evacuated watermark matches with the first watermark, by then the acceptability of the photo is affirmed. In the uninvolved approach, it is normal that we have no past information about the watermark, regardless of whether it is installed into the picture or not. In this approach, the hints of falsification are being extricated from the picture; if a couple of takes after are found, at that point the picture is thought to be manufactured. Right now we are focusing on aloof ways to deal with image forgery detection [2].

In this paper, we propose an enhanced watermark inserting and alter recuperation arrange for which is better than various strategies. The sensitive watermark includes one correspondence section and two copies of modifying zone. In alter location stage; the identification calculation utilizes most of the three watermark territories with the end goal that the false recognition likelihood can be diminished. In recuperation stage, two duplicates of reclamation segment give double opportunity to square recovery [3].

We have discussed related techniques in light based tampering detection and watermarking and utilizing method literature survey in Sects. 1, 2 and 3. The proposed technique is clarified in Sect. 4. Section 5 elaborates the details of interest of various situations of tampering considered and the results obtained. At last, conclusion and future work are indicated in Sect. 6.

1.1 Image Tampering

Instantly, we need to totally consider image tampering operation itself, to perceive image tampering. In, the digital forgery operation is isolated into six unmistakable arrangements: compositing, changing, re-touching, redesigning, PC producing and painting. In reality, all best in class altering revelation technique goes for compositing operation. With the assistance of effective image tampering instrument (e.g. Photoshop, picasa or picsart), compositing tampered images is fundamentally more straightforward and can realize significantly more practical images. Image tampering incorporates the choice, change, synthesis of the photo segments and the altering of the last picture. Here, we have to feature that an altered picture infers some bit of the substance of a bona fide picture is changed. This thought excludes those completely coordinated picture, e.g. pictures completely rendered by PC outline or by surface union. By the day's end, a picture is altered proposes that it joins into two segments: the legitimate part and the altered part. Every one of the calculations showed later concentrate on the altered pictures delineated here.

Digital Watermarking Technology

Advanced watermarking covers the copyright information into the electronic data through certain estimation. The secret information to be embedded can be some substance, maker's serial number, association logo, pictures with some uncommon significance. This mystery information is introduced to the computerized information (pictures, sound, and video) to ensure the security, data approval, ID of proprietor and copyright confirmation and copyright security. The watermark can be masked in the electronic information either clearly or impalpably. For a strong watermark introducing, an awesome watermarking method is ought to have been associated. Watermark can be embedded either in spatial or repeat zone. Both the domains are different and have their own pros and cons and are used in different scenario.

1.2 Using Distance Matrix

1. *Bhattacharyya*
   The Bhattacharyya disconnect measures the identicalness of two discrete or industrious probability allotments. It is almost connected with the Bhattacharyya coefficient which is a measure of the measure of cover between two factual examples or populaces.
   The coefficient can be used take the relative closeness of the two cases being considered. It is used to evaluate the reparability of classes all together and it is acknowledged to be more strong than the Mahalanobis discrete, when the standard deviations of the two classes are an indistinguishable then from the Mahalanobis remove is a particular instance of the Bhattacharyya separate.
2. Chi-square
   The chi-squared division is a nonlinear metric and is normally used to think about histograms
3. Minkowski
   The Minkowski remove is a metric in a normed vector space which is the Euclidean detachment and the Manhattan separate both can be considered as a Generalization.

2 Literature Survey

[5] Reis et al. present that Sound validation is an essential undertaking in mixed media legal sciences unpleasant solid strategies to hit upon and distinguish altered sound chronicles. In this content, a fresh out of the box new strategy to distinguish defilements in sound chronicles is proposed by abusing odd versions inside the Electrical Network Frequency (ENF) flag at long last inserted in an addressed sound account. These unordinary versions are because of sudden fragment discontinuities in light of additions and concealments of sound bites amid the altering errand. Initially, we suggest an ESPRIT-Hilbert ENF estimator nearby an exception finder based at the example kurtosis of the expected ENF. Next, we use the figured kurtosis as entering for a Support Vector Machine (SVM) classifier to propose the nearness of altering. The proposed plot, wherein extraordinary as SPHINS, radically beats related past altering location strategies inside the performed appraisals. We favor our things the use of the Carioca 1 corpus with a hundred unedited affirmed sound accounts of phone calls.

[6] Hosseini et al. present that In this paper another methodology for identification of camera altering is proposed. There is couple of cases of camera altering are: shaking the camera, camera development, intrusion, and pivot of camera. The tampering may

be think or sudden. In the proposed calculation, notwithstanding identification of the correct idea of tampering, the correct measure of tampering in like way can be perceived. (i.e. the sum and bearing of development). This will help administrator in lingual authority making for administration in observation framework. The proposed calculation recognize the shaking using present and past edges, and furthermore by building up a total establishment in light of all casings and building an impermanent foundation in view of last 10 outlines. The proposed strategy uses the SURF incorporate locator to find intrigue focuses in both of two foundations and analyze and facilitate them using MSAC calculation. The change network can be procured to distinguish the camera development; camera picture zoom and camera turn. Finally, using the system sobel edge ID the camera obstruction and defocus can be perceived. The procedure likewise identify the sudden close downs in camera or pictures misfortune. Another component of the calculation is giving the information concerning the camera tampering.

[7] Alhussein et al. present that this paper proposed a fresh out of the box new IT identification method construct absolutely with respect to neighborhood surface descriptor and extreme learning machine (ELM). The IT fuses both joining and CMF To begin with, the photograph changed into shading channels (one luminance and two Chroma), and each channel was disconnected into non-covering pieces. Nearby surfaces in the condition of local binary pattern (LBP) had been disconnected from each square. The histograms of the examples of the greater part of the squares had been linked to frame a component vector. The trademark vector turned out to be at that point sustained to an ELM for class. The ELM is an extraordinary and speedy characterization approach. The trials were performed using two straightforwardly open databases. The trial comes about demonstrated that the proposed system achieved high identification precision in both the databases.

[8] Bhatkar et al. present that this paper presents a unmarried segment virtual power meter primarily based on a microcontroller. This virtual meter does now not have any rotating elements and the electricity consumption can be without difficulty study from a digital shows additionally at far flung region it's far easily possible to check energy intake and TD with the aid of the usage of GSM generation. When deliver wills cut-off, the meter will restart with the stored value. Today power robbery is a global hassle that contributes heavily to sales losses. Consumers have been determined manipulating their electric powered meters; try and cause them to stop, or maybe bypassing the meter, successfully the utilization of energy without buying it. This strength meter can come across tampering in a strength meter by means of the use of microcontroller and provide there information at remote location.

[9] Pun et al. In this paper, we gift a singular TD version that may create an exact, thing level altering limitation quit final product. Initial, a versatile picture division method is proposed to stage the photo into shut locales in view of solid edges. By then, the shading and capacity highlights of the shut regions are expelled as a criminological hash. Moreover, a geometrical invariant altering restriction rendition named Image Alignment based Multi-Region Matching (IAMRM) is proposed to build up the area correspondence among the acquired and scientific pictures by abusing their inherent shape insights. The model gauges the parameters of geometric enhancements through a hearty picture arrangement approach fundamentally in view of triangle closeness;

furthermore, it fits various locales simultaneously through using complex rating in light of stand-out chart frameworks and capacities. Trial outcomes show that the proposed IAMRM is a promising technique for question organize TD contrasted and ultra-present day procedures.

[10] Warbhe et al. present that, It turned out to be simple to capture and create DI. It's no greater a more expensive affair, as a maximum of the hand held digital devices along with mobile telephones are prepared with digital cameras. Today, there is ample PC and cellular apps available which might be evolved to manipulate captured pictures. One can easily take a picture, manipulate it with the installed app and make it viral through the internet. Hence, these DI should not be interpreted as they speak. DIs is the good proof of events and places. Hence, this DIs can be presented as evidence before a court of law. It turns into very crucial in such instances then, to show the DI in question to be authentic. DI forensics plays an essential role in such situations. DI legal sciences are a branch of advanced legal sciences which offers with breaking down the DIs for their validity and validness. In this paper, we gift a DI forensic technique that could hit upon considered one of such IT. As photographs can be tampered in some of methods, on this paper, we cope with a not unusual case known as copy-paste tampering. Our proposed strategy is strong to relative transform; particularly to rotation and scaling.

3 Proposed Work

Another thought is introduced to incorporate the image watermarking and image tamper detection and recovery. The algorithm is portrayed in the following. Figure 1 demonstrates a square outline of the proposed picture tamper detection strategy and to plot histogram for check their brilliance. First, the select cover image from the set of images or folder. Then, secondly select the watermarked image from the folder. Apply defocusing on the cover image. Apply defocusing on the Watermark image. Then embed the two images and embedding also plot histogram for check brightness. On the embedded image, apply tempering. The quality is calculated by the Minoswki TP Rate and Bhattacharya TP Rate and Chi-Square TP Rate but in the proposed scheme get better result as compared to base.

Propose algorithm

(1) First we have to select the cover image from the set of images or folder.
(2) Then we will select the watermarked image from the folder.
(3) Apply defocusing on the cover picture.
(4) Apply defocusing on the watermark image.
(5) At that point embed the two images (watermarked & cover).
(6) On the embedded image, apply tempering.
(7) Inserting and tampering also plot histogram for check brightness.
(8) Then extract the cover and watermark image.
(9) Result evaluation performance.
(10) The calculate the Minoswki TP Rate, Bhattacharya TP Rate and Chi-Square TP Rate.

Flow chart-

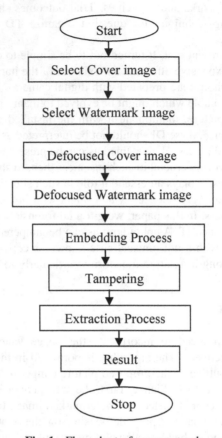

Fig. 1. Flow chart of propose work

4 Result Analysis

Analyses recreation of image watermarking scheme, and tamper detection and recovery plan. Comparison with other research works is recorded too. The simulation results are given to show the effectiveness of the proposed technique (Figs. 2, 3, 4, 5, 6, 7, 8, 9, 10, 11, 12, 13, 14 and 15 and Tables 1, 2 and 3).

Fig. 2. Image dataset

Fig. 3. First run the source code.

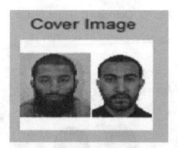

Fig. 4. Select the cover image for hiding secret image.

Fig. 5. Select watermark image.

Fig. 6. Defocused cover image.

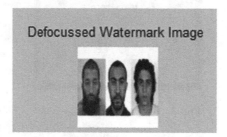

Fig. 7. Defocused secret image.

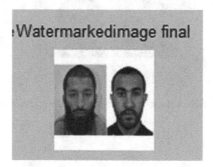

Fig. 8. Hide the secret image into cover image.

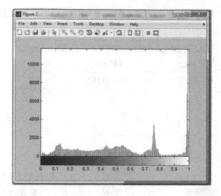

Fig. 9. Plot histogram to check the brightness or embedded image.

Fig. 10. Tampers the embedded image

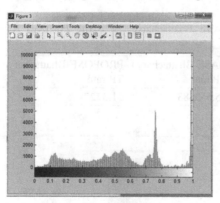

Fig. 11. Plot histogram to check the brightness of tampered image

Fig. 12. Extract the image from tampered image.

Table 1. Comparison BASE Minoswki TP (True Positive) Rate and PROPOSE Minoswki TP Rate

BASE Minoswki TP rate	PROPOSE Minoswki TP rate
53.8858	76.2015

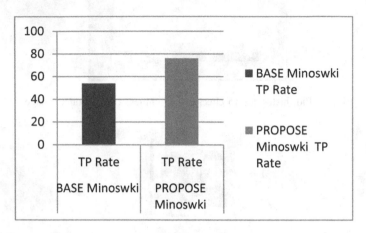

Fig. 13. Graph 1. Comparison BASE Minoswki TP (True Positive) Rate and PROPOSE Minoswki TP (True Positive) Rate

Table 2. Comparison BASE Bhattacharya TP (True Positive) Rate and PROPOSE Bhattacharya TP Rate

BASE Bhattacharya TP rate	PROPOSE Bhattacharya TP rate
45.650883	51.372747

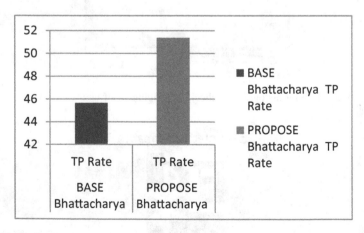

Fig. 14. Graph 2. Comparison BASE Bhattacharya TP (True Positive) Rate and PROPOSE Bhattacharya TP Rate

Table 3. Comparison BASE Chi-Square TP (True Positive) Rate and PROPOSE Chi-Square TP (True Positive) Rate

BASE chi-square TP rate	PROPOSE chi-square TP rate
58.3796	85.3457

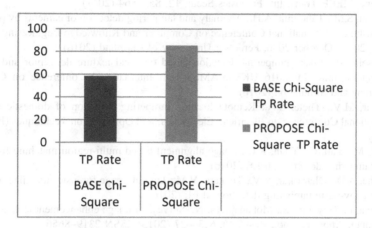

Fig. 15. Graph 3 Comparison between BASE Chi-Square TP (True Positive) Rate and PROPOSE Chi-Square TP Rate

5   Conclusion

In this paper showed a successful methodology for detection of tampering using watermarking. Digital Watermarking is very useful technique for detection of tampering, localization and recovery of image. The quality is calculated by the Minoswki TP Rate and Bhattacharya TP Rate and Chi-Square TP Rate but in the proposed scheme get better result as compared to base. Experimental results shows that proposed strategy work efficiently and identify tampered areas effectively. There is an exploratory outcomes demonstrates a high trait image tampering esteems.

References

1. Gupta, S.: Highlighting image tampering by feature extraction based on image quality deterioration. In: 2016 International Conference on Computing for Sustainable Global Development (INDIACom) (2016)
2. Alhussein, M.: Image tampering detection based on local texture descriptor and extreme learning machine. In: 2016 UKSim-AMSS 18th International Conference on Computer Modelling and Simulation. 978-1-5090-0888-9/16 $31.00©. IEEE (2016). https://doi.org/10.1109/UKSIM.2016.39

3. Wu, C.-M., Shih, Y.-S.: A simple image tamper detection and recovery based on fragile watermark with one parity section and two restoration sections. Opt. Photonics J. **3**, 103–107 (2013)

4. Wang, W., Dong, J., Tan, T.: A survey of passive image tampering detection: In: Ho, A.T.S., Shi, Y.Q., Kim, H.J., Barni, M. (eds.) IWDW 2009. LNCS, vol. 5703, pp. 308–322. Springer, Heidelberg (2009). https://doi.org/10.1007/978-3-642-03688-0_27

5. Reis, P.M.G.I., da Costa, J.P.C.L., Miranda, R.K., Del Galdo, G.: ESPRIT-Hilbert based audio tampering detection with SVM classifier for forensic analysis via electrical network frequency. IEEE Trans. Inf. Forensics Secur. 12, 853–864 (2017)

6. Hosseini, S.M., Taherinia, A.H.: Anomaly and tampering detection of cameras by providing details. In: 6th International Conference on Computer and Knowledge Engineering (ICCKE 2016), 20–21 October 2016, Ferdowsi University of Mashhad (2016)

7. Alhussein, M.: Image tampering detection based on local texture descriptor and extreme learning machine. In: 2016 UKSim-AMSS 18th International Conference on Computer Modelling and Simulation (2016)

8. Bhatkar, M.V., Thete, S.A.: Remote location tampering detection of domestic load. In: International Conference on Electrical, Electronics, and Optimization Techniques (ICEEOT) (2016)

9. Pun, C.M., Yan, C., Yuan, X.C.: Image alignment based multi-region matching for object-level tampering detection. IEEE (2016)

10. Warbhe, A.D., Dharaskar, R.V., Thakare, V.M.: Digital image forensics an affine transform robust copy-paste tampering detection. IEEE (2016)

11. Suganya, P., Gayathri, S., Mohanapriya, N.: Survey on image enhancement techniques. Int. J. Comput. Appl. Technol. Res. **2**(5), 623–627 (2013). ISSN 2319–8656

A Novel Approach for Image Fusion with Guided Filter Based on Feature Transform

Krishnavijay Tripathi and Ashutosh Sharma[✉]

Department of ECE, GEC, Bhopal, Madhya Pradesh, India
krishnavijay.tripathi@gmail.com,
ashu_vidisha@yahoo.co.in

Abstract. A quick and successful multi-center picture combination strategy is proposed for making a very educational intertwined picture through consolidating at least two pictures. The proposed technique depends on a two-scale decay of a picture into a base layer containing extensive scale varieties in force, and a detail layer catching little scale points of interest. A proposed GFF-FT (Guided-Filtering Fusion with Feature Transform) based weighted normal strategy is proposed to make full utilization of spatial consistency for combination of the base and detail layers. We propose depicting input pictures by SIFT descriptors. Filter descriptors are removed from the first pictures on premise of surface, shading and shape. The weighted normal method is execute based on SIFT include descriptors. Test comes about show that the proposed strategy can acquire best in class execution for combination of multi-center pictures.

Keywords: Guided filter · Scale-Invariant Feature Transform
Multi-focus image fusion · Spatial consistency · Two-scale decomposition

1 Introduction

Picture combination is a vital strategy for different picture preparing and PC vision applications, for example, highlight extraction and target acknowledgment. Through picture combination, diverse pictures of a similar scene can be consolidated into a solitary melded picture [1]. The intertwined picture can give more complete data about the scene which is more valuable for human and machine discernment. For example, the execution of highlight extraction calculations can be enhanced by melding multi-ghastly remote detecting pictures [2]. The combination of multi-presentation pictures can be utilized for computerized photography [3]. In these applications, a great picture combination technique has the accompanying properties. To start with, it can protect the vast majority of the valuable data of various pictures. Second, it doesn't create relics. Third, it is hearty to defective conditions, for example, mis-enrollment and clamor.

© Springer Nature Singapore Pte Ltd. 2019
S. Verma et al. (Eds.): CNC 2018, CCIS 839, pp. 235–247, 2019.
https://doi.org/10.1007/978-981-13-2372-0_21

Multi-center picture combination is testing errand in the zone of computerized picture handling and therefore has "holding nothing back concentration" picture that coordinate correlative and excess data from various pictures. Critical utilizations of picture combination incorporate therapeutic imaging, remote detecting, PC vision, and mechanical technology. Likewise, picture combination is of specific significance in present day microscopy where the determination is traded off by the constrained profundity of core interest. Picture combination is the way toward joining data of at least two pictures of a scene into an exceedingly enlightening picture that contains more data than some other unique picture. That picture contains all noteworthy data from multi-center pictures that are aftereffect of good sensors or diverse profundity of center a similar sensor. The genuine combination process can be performed at various levels of data portrayal [2]. A typical classification is to recognize:

(1) pixel level, (2) feature level, (3) symbol level.

Picture combination at pixel level means combination at the most minimal preparing level alluding to the converging of estimated physical parameters. This combination technique is otherwise called nonlinear combination strategy. Combination at include level requires highlight extraction earlier, to recognize qualities, for example, estimate, shape, difference and surface. The combination is accordingly in view of those extricated includes and empowers the discovery of valuable highlights with higher certainty. Combination at image level enables the data to be successfully joined at the most abnormal amount of deliberation. The decision of the suitable level relies upon various factors, for example, information sources, application and accessible devices.

1.1   Image Feature Descriptor

Low-level picture include portrayal is one of the key parts for highlight choice frameworks. Three kinds of visual highlights were utilized as a part of this work, including shading, shape and surface.

A. Shading Feature

We can utilize one of the accompanying strategies for discovering shading highlight vector of picture.

- Color Histogram
- Color Coherence Vector
- Color Moments

Shading Histogram strategy is moderately coldhearted to position and introduction changes and they are adequately exact. Be that as it may, they don't catch spatial relationship of shading locale. So they are constrained to segregating power. Shading Coherence Vector technique is superior to shading histogram strategy. This strategy consolidates the extraordinary relationship of shading districts and also the worldwide dispersion of neighborhood uncommon connection of hues. In any case, there is one detriment of this technique it requires exceptionally costly calculations. So in our undertaking we have utilized shading minute technique for shading highlight extraction. This strategy is more vigorous and runs quicker than histogram based techniques.

B. Surface Feature

Surface is another well known component utilized as a part of picture combination. We utilized surface highlights in light of wavelet change. The Discrete Wavelet Transformation (DWT) was first connected to pictures with a Daubechies-4 wavelet channel. 3-levels of wavelet disintegration is utilized to acquire ten sub-pictures in various scales and introductions. One of the sub-pictures is a sub-examined normal picture of the first one and was disposed of in light of the fact that it contains less valuable data. At that point entropies of the other nine sub-pictures are utilized surface component of a picture. Real normal for surface is the reiteration of an example or examples over a district in a picture. The components of example are called as textons. The contrast between two surfaces can be because of level of variety of the textons. It can likewise be because of spatial appropriation of the textons in the picture.

C. Shape Feature

Edge highlights have been appeared to be compelling in picture combination since it gives data about states of various items. Watchful edge recognition is utilized to get the histogram for edge heading. At that point, the edge course histogram was quantized into 18 receptacles of every one of 20°. So there are 18 distinctive shape highlights are utilized to remove shape include from a picture. Shape can generally be characterized as the depiction of a question less its position, introduction and size. Consequently, shape highlights ought to be invariant to interpretation, revolution, and scale, for a viable picture combination, when the course of action of items in the picture isn't known ahead of time. To utilize shape as a picture highlight, it is fundamental to section the picture to identify question or district limits; and this is a test. Systems for shape portrayal can be isolated into two classes. The main class is limit based, utilizing the external form of the state of a protest and the second classification is locale based, utilizing the entire shape district of the question. The most unmistakable delegates of these two classifications are Fourier descriptors and minute invariants. The principle thought behind the Fourier descriptors is to utilize the Fourier-changed limits of the articles as the shape highlights, while the thought behind minute invariants is to utilize area based geometric minutes that are invariant to interpretation and pivot.

1.2 Problem Identification

An expansive number of picture combination strategies [4, 7] have been proposed in writing. Among these techniques, multi-scale picture combination [5] and information driven picture combination [6] are extremely effective strategies. They center on various information portrayals, e.g., multi-scale coefficients [8, 9], or information driven disintegration coefficients [6, 10] and diverse picture combination guidelines to manage the combination of coefficients. The real preferred standpoint of these techniques is that they can well protect the points of interest of various source pictures. Be that as it may, these sorts of techniques may deliver brilliance and shading bends since spatial consistency isn't very much considered in the combination procedure. To make full utilization of spatial setting, streamlining based picture combination approaches, e.g., summed up arbitrary strolls [3], and Markov irregular fields [11] based strategies have been proposed. These techniques center on assessing spatially smooth and edge-adjusted weights by illuminating a vitality capacity and after that melding the source pictures by weighted normal of pixel esteems. Be that as it may, streamlining based techniques have a typical confinement, i.e., wastefulness, since they require different emphases to locate the worldwide ideal arrangement. In addition, another disadvantage is that worldwide improvement based strategies may over-smooth the subsequent weights, which isn't useful for combination. To tackle the issues specified over, a novel picture combination technique with guided separating utilizing SIFT is proposed in this work. Exploratory outcomes demonstrate that the proposed technique gives an execution practically identical with best in class combination approaches. A few points of interest of the proposed picture combination approach are featured in the accompanying.

(1) Traditional multi-scale picture combination techniques require more than two scales to get acceptable combination comes about. The key commitment of this paper is to show a quick two-scale combination strategy which does not depend intensely on a particular picture deterioration technique. A basic normal channel is fit the bill for the proposed combination system.

(2) A novel weight development technique is proposed to join pixel saliency and spatial setting for picture combination. Rather than utilizing improvement based techniques, guided sifting is embraced as a nearby separating strategy for picture combination.

(3) A vital perception of this paper is that the parts of two measures, i.e., pixel saliency and spatial consistency are very unique while combining distinctive layers. In this paper, the parts of pixel saliency and spatial consistency are controlled through changing the parameters of the guided channel.

2 Previous Work

In this segment talk about the survey of picture combination in view of guided sifting and diverse combination strategies. The picture combination procedures including different techniques, for example, observational mode decay, non-subsampled counterlet change, reciprocal inclination based sharpness foundation and so on.

A basic yet viable auxiliary fix disintegration (SPD) approach for multi-presentation picture combination (MEF) that is powerful to ghosting impact. We decay a picture fix into three adroitly autonomous parts: flag quality, flag structure, and mean force. After intertwining these three parts independently, we recreate a coveted fix and place it once more into the combined picture. This novel fix decay approach benefits MEF in numerous perspectives [1].

Picture combination is an essential method for different picture handling and PC vision applications, for example, highlight extraction and target acknowledgment. Through picture combination, diverse pictures of a similar scene can be consolidated into a solitary intertwined picture. The melded picture can give more thorough data about the scene which is more helpful for human and machine discernment. For example, the execution of highlight extraction calculations can be enhanced by combining multi-ghastly remote detecting pictures [2].

To stifle the Pseudo-Gibbs marvels caused by the Contourlet, the Non-subsampled Pyramids Filter Banks and the Non-subsampled Directional Filter Banks are consolidated to build the non-subsampled contourlet change (NSCT). Subsequently, The NSCT not just has the fundamental highlights of multi-scale, multi-directional and time-recurrence limitation, yet additionally offers the property of the move invariant which is indispensable to picture preparing. Right off the bat, multi-scale deterioration is performed on source pictures utilizing NSCT to get high-recurrence and low-recurrence pictures. Besides, the Novel Sum-Modified-Laplacian and Local Neighbor Sum of Laplacian are separately used to choose the low pass coefficient and high pass coefficients to join melded picture. At long last, the opposite non-subsampled contourlet change is connected to acquire combined picture. Test result demonstrates the proposed approach out plays out the customary discrete wavelet change based and the contourlet-based picture combination techniques (Geng, Gao and Hu 2013).

Picture combination is ending up exceptionally well known in advanced picture handling, so various multi-center picture combination calculations have been proposed lately. There are numerous applications that as results have better or more awful "holding nothing back concentration" picture today. A picture combination technique in view of division locale utilizing DWT is proposed by creators. Multi-center picture combination conspire based around wavelet parcel change (WPT) that sums up the discrete wavelet change and gives a more adaptable apparatus to the time-scale investigation of information is proposed. Likewise, there are calculations that utilization spatial recurrence and hereditary calculation and they joins picture combination at pixel and highlight level [3].

A novel picture combination calculation in view of the non sub-tested contourlet change (NSCT) and a picture disintegration display (IDM) is proposed, going for taking care of the combination issue of multi-center pictures. To choose the coefficients of the intertwined picture legitimately, the determination standards for various sub groups are examined, individually. For picking the low recurrence sub band coefficients, most extreme nearby vitality is utilized as the concentration measure to combine the low recurrence sub band. While picking the high recurrence sub-band coefficients, the most extreme outright esteem is utilized as the action level estimation to choose coefficients from the high recurrence sub pictures (Wang, Qi and Han 2012).

The multimodal restorative picture combination is a vital application in numerous therapeutic applications. This is utilized for the recovery of correlative data from medicinal pictures. The MRI and CT picture gives high determination pictures auxiliary and anatomical data. The CT picture is utilized as a part of tumor and anatomical recognition and MRI is utilized to get data among tissues. In this paper, we have proposed another approach of multimodal medicinal picture combination on Daubechies wavelet change coefficients. The combination procedure begins with examination of square savvy standard deviation estimations of the coefficients. Here the standard deviation can be utilized to portray the neighborhood varieties inside the piece. The execution of proposed picture combination strategy is contrasted and existing calculations and assessed with common data amongst info and yield pictures, entropy, standard deviation, combination factor measurements (Swathi and Bindu 2013).

3 Methodology

The Algorithm of proposed technique is clarified underneath:

[fused_image] = GFF-FT (image1, image2)

/image1 and image2 are two multi-center grayscale picture in particular determination, GFF-FT is a capacity/for execute the guided separating based combination with scale invariant element change on image1 and/image2.

Stage 1: Consider the two multi-center source pictures in grayscale shape with same determination.

Stage 2: Now we discover the SIFT descriptors of each source picture of cell cluster for pictures of picture dataset. Filter strategy play out the accompanying succession of ventures for discover the keypoint descriptors for surface element.

Scale-Space Extreme Detection: The underlying advance of assessment discovers add up to all scale-space and distinctive picture zone in picture dataset hubs [4]. It is totally apply viably by utilizing a Difference-of-Gaussian (DoG) mapping to speaks to potential intrigue keypoints of highlight descriptors which are scale invariant and introduction in picture dataset hubs.

Keypoints Localization: All hopeful territory of picture in chose ROI (Region of Interest), a nitty gritty model is fit to examine keypoints region and its scale-space. Keypoints of picture zone in picture ROI are picks premise on figure of existing dependability.

Introduction Assignment: at least one introductions errand are connected to each keypoints zone in view of neighborhood picture information hubs slope course. Every single future picture activities are actualized on picture keypoint dataset which has been changed in respect to the connected introduction, scale, and area for each element descriptor, consequently giving invariance to these changes in picture information hubs.

Keypoints Descriptor: The nearby picture slopes esteem are estimated at the pick scale-space in the Region of Interest (ROI) around all keypoints in picture dataset focuses. These are changed into an introduction that grants for critical levels of nearby shape, area and introduction and changes in enlightenment of picture dataset focuses.

Stage 3: Above advance are perform in rehashed frame, at that point all the descriptor of pictures are store, Now apply Guided Filtering technique for acquiring intertwined picture.

Stage 4: In Guided Filtering, apply two-scale picture disintegration utilizing normal channel for discover base and detail layer of each source picture from picture database.

Stage 5: Now apply weight delineate strategy, acquire saliency outline source pictures and think about saliency guide and highlight descriptor of relating pictures at that point discover weight guide of base and detail layer of each source picture from picture database.

Stage 6: Now picture remaking has been perform based on base layer and detail layer of each source picture. Consequently, the recreated picture is taken as combined picture.

We take any two pictures with same size in grayscale mode. From that point forward, apply SIFT method for get keypoint descriptors. According to following figure, ascertain DoG (Difference of Gaussian) and recognize keypoint descriptor of all scales per octave. After every introduction task produce highlight descriptor. When one octave has been prepared then next octave of down inspected picture is considered. This procedure is proceeds until the point when all octaves of a picture is experienced. At long last, recover the element descriptor of source pictures image1 and image2.

4 Experimental Works

Examinations are performed on multi-center picture databases, i.e., the Petrovic' database which contains 56 sets of multi-center pictures including ethereal pictures, open air pictures and indoor pictures (with various concentration focuses and introduction settings. The testing pictures are numbered from 1 to 56. Each combine of pictures has same size and perspective proportion. Each even or odd numbered multi-center picture have diverse configuration. We have setup MATLAB R2013b adaptation for execute the proposed strategy specifically as GFF-FT.

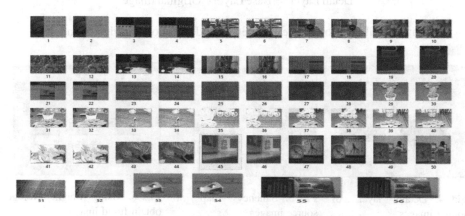

Fig. 1. Multi-focus image dataset

The multi-center picture dataset is as per the following (Fig. 1).

At starting, we take two source pictures with same size and organization. For this reason, imread() use for read the source picture from required way (Fig. 2).

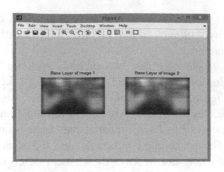

Fig. 2. Load multi-focus source images   **Fig. 3.** Base layer of source images

Above figure demonstrate that the how recover the source pictures from required way. After discover the source picture, apply normal channel through fspecial() and imfilter(). Rather than normal channel, we utilize the middle and in addition Gaussian channel. At the point when normal channel is connected to source picture at that point get base layer of source picture, this layer mirror the fundamental surface of picture. Detail layer of a picture can be found based on base layer and unique source picture. The essential recipe for acquiring point of interest layer is as per the following.

$$\text{Detail Layer} = \text{Base Layer} - \text{Original Image}$$

Base and detail layer of source pictures is said in following Figs. 3 and 4.

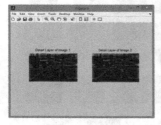
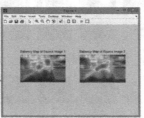

Fig. 4. Detail   layer   of   **Fig. 5.** Saliency   map   of   **Fig. 6.** Using weight average
source images   source images   obtain fused image

Both base and detail layer is identified with each other. Detail layer of picture mirror the foundation surface element. The above Fig. 5 demonstrates the saliency measure guide of picture, saliency outline get from unique picture (source picture). Saliency guide of picture mirrors the brightening level central profundity with multi-color determination (Fig. 6).

5 Result and Analysis

The analysis of the existing work (SPD-MEF) and the proposed work (GFF-FT) on the basis of different quality parameters are given in Table 1.

Table 1. Analysis of comparison the value of MSE, PSNR, NCC, AD, SC in between of SPD-MFF and GFF-FT with different sizes (From 1 to 28 source images).

FI	SI	Size	SPD-MEF [1]					GFF-FT				
			MSE	PSNR	NCC	AD	SC	MSE	PSNR	NCC	AD	SC
1	1	178 × 134	268.8	12.49	0.56	57.32	2.92	152.27	26.3	1.0	0.18	0.97
	2		396.8	12.64	0.56	55.04	2.89	85.52	23.57	0.99	2.1	0.96
2	3	225 × 162	263.9	14.98	0.53	36.05	3.16	131.41	26.94	0.98	0.68	0.99
	4		309.7	14.83	0.52	36.09	3.32	186.59	25.42	0.94	0.73	1.05
3	5	261 × 177	471.2	11.62	0.56	62.37	2.78	390.92	22.20	0.95	3.33	1.05
	6		883.2	12.62	0.62	51.66	2.28	816.33	19.01	1.02	-7.38	0.86
4	7	264 × 177	383.2	11.5	0.49	64.55	3.69	312.3	23.19	0.92	3.64	1.1
	8		377.4	12.47	0.55	57.2	2.99	306.7	23.26	1.02	-3.71	0.89
5	9	254 × 167	688.7	11.51	0.42	62.76	4.3	541.17	20.8	0.88	1.84	1.06
	10		700.9	11.47	0.42	62.89	4.45	553.33	20.7	0.86	1.97	1.09
6	11	267 × 171	555.1	11.54	0.39	63.14	5.13	457.94	21.52	0.85	2.01	1.13
	12		369.1	11.89	0.41	61.73	4.74	302.91	23.32	0.92	0.6	1.04
7	13	258 × 177	721.1	14.2	0.6	37.45	2.26	554.46	20.69	0.95	-0.51	0.97
	14		517.7	14.37	0.6	38.86	2.29	308.57	23.24	0.97	0.88	0.98
8	15	263 × 165	1546	10.41	0.42	67.5	3.99	1191.7	17.37	0.78	8.06	1.2
	16		808.1	11.62	0.49	61.04	3.43	546.13	20.75	0.92	1.6	1.03
9	17	265 × 168	113.7	12.72	0.38	55.32	6.25	66.44	29.9	0.96	0.33	1.03
	18		163.9	12.68	0.38	55.3	6.3	90.03	28.58	0.95	0.3	1.04
10	19	210 × 270	401.1	12.93	0.2	53.19	9.78	220.22	24.7	0.72	1.7	1.25
	20		261.7	13.28	0.23	51.93	8.34	146.08	26.48	0.85	0.44	1.06
11	21	267 × 175	142.7	12.61	0.52	56.39	3.48	87.47	28.7	0.99	0.1	0.99
	22		238.1	12.53	0.51	56.1	3.56	180.78	25.56	0.97	-0.18	1.01
12	23	268 × 175	94.9	11.83	0.39	64.29	6.14	88.14	28.68	0.94	1.27	1.06
	24		301.5	11.62	0.38	64.61	6.44	199.88	25.12	0.89	1.6	1.12
13	25	267 × 177	144.8	11.9	0.36	63.44	7.03	84.52	28.86	0.94	0.77	1.08
	26		105.6	11.98	0.37	63.1	6.96	77.25	29.25	0.94	0.43	1.06
14	27	267 × 177	104.8	12.15	0.07	62.03	7.09	84.97	28.7	0.44	1.27	2.6
	28		75.7	12.2	0.08	61.89	4.24	60.76	30.29	0.62	1.13	1.67

Here the comparisons result tested on the basis of different image size and measure the various result parameters shown in the comparisons tables. The fused image indexes from 1 to 14 are compares in between of SPD-MEF and GFF-FT (in Table 1). The value of MSE (for GFF-FT) is less than value of MSE (for SPD-MEF). The value of PSNR (for GFF-FT) is more than value of PSNR (for SPD-MEF). The value of NCC (for GFF-FT) is more than value of NCC (for SPD-MEF). The value of AD (for GFF-FT) is less than value of AD (for SPD-MEF). The value of SC (for GFF-FT) is less than value of SC (for SPD-MEF). Hence the performance of the proposed work is better as compared to the existing technique (Figs. 7, 8, 9, 10 and 11).

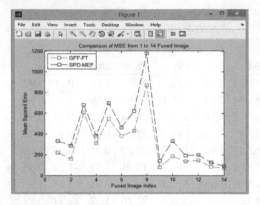

Fig. 7. Compare of MSE   **Fig. 8.** Compare of PSNR

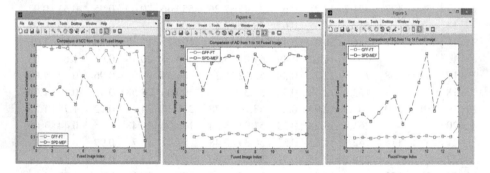

Fig. 9. Compare of NCC   **Fig. 10.** Compare of AD   **Fig. 11.** Compare of SC

6   Conclusion

In this exploration work, a consolidated multi-center picture combination strategy was proposed by considering the correlative property of the two unique techniques, for example, GFF (Guided Filtering based Fusion) and SIFT (Scale-Invariant Feature Transform). In our calculation, right off the bat, every one of the enrolled pictures is deteriorated into two parts (base and detail layer) by utilizing a normal channel. The exploratory outcomes on a few sets of multi-center picture demonstrated that the proposed strategy has preferable execution over the guided separating based combination calculation. The significant accomplishment of proposed strategies is least ancient rarities and greatest edge conservation. The claim is very much supported from the outcomes where ground truth was made accessible. This unmistakably shows the proposed strategies acquaints least ancient rarities contrasted and existing systems and this is a noteworthy accomplishment, as antiquities may prompt wrong translations which can be disastrous. Particularly in applications like observation and medicinal pictures, this can be essential as curios can come about into false cautions. Furthermore, the proposed techniques additionally yield phenomenal sharpness, clearness and edge conservation alongside increment in data, common data, data symmetry and high relationship. The creators are likewise taking a shot at combination of infrared and unmistakable band observation pictures keeping in mind the end goal to check the nature of execution. We have displayed a novel picture combination technique in light of guided sifting. The proposed strategy uses the normal channel to get the two-scale portrayals, which is basic and successful. All the more significantly, the guided channel is utilized as a part of a novel method to make full utilization of the solid relationships between's neighborhood pixels for weight enhancement. Examinations demonstrate that the proposed strategy can well save the first and integral data of various info pictures.

The execution of the calculations can be enhanced by presenting the directional situated multi-determination changes, for example, steerable pyramids, contourlets and so on and move invariant changes, for example, un-demolished wavelet changes and complex wavelet changes in the multi-determination decay organize. We can utilize SURF (Speeded Up Robust Feature), CHoG (Compressed Histogram of Gradient) for discover the component descriptor of picture surface.

References

1. Ma, K., Li, H., Yong, H., Wang, Z., Meng, D., Zhang, L.: Robust multi-exposure image fusion: a structural patch decomposition approach. IEEE Trans. Image Process. **26**(5), 2519–2532 (2017)
2. Li, S., Kang, X., Hu, J.: Image fusion with guided filtering. IEEE Trans. Image Process. **22**(7), 2864–2875 (2013)
3. Savić, S., Babić, Z.: Multifocus image fusion based on empirical mode decomposition. In: 19th IEEE International Conference on Systems, Signals and Image Processing (IWSSIP) (2012)
4. Socolinsky, D.A., Wolff, L.B.: Multispectral image visualization through first-order fusion. IEEE Trans. Image Process. **11**(8), 923–931 (2013)
5. Shen, R., Cheng, I., Shi, J., Basu, A.: Generalized random walks for fusion of multi-exposure images. IEEE Trans. Image Process. **20**(12), 3634–3646 (2012)
6. Li, S., Kwok, J., Tsang, I., Wang, Y.: Fusing images with different focuses using support vector machines. IEEE Trans. Neural Netw. **15**(6), 1555–1561 (2004)
7. Pajares, G., de la Cruz, J.M.: A wavelet-based image fusion tutorial. Pattern Recognit. **37**(9), 1855–1872 (2004)
8. Looney, D., Mandic, D.P.: Multimodel image fusion using complex extensions of EMD. IEEE Trans. Sig. Process. **57**(4), 1626–1630 (2013)

9. Kumar, M., Dass, S.: A total variation-based algorithm for pixel-level image fusion. IEEE Trans. Image Process. **18**(9), 2137–2143 (2009)
10. Burt, P., Adelson, E.: The Laplacian pyramid as a compact image code. IEEE Trans. Commun. **31**(4), 532–540 (1983)
11. Rockinger, O.: Image sequence fusion using a shift-invariant wavelet transform. In: Proceedings of International Conference on Image Process, Washington, DC, USA, vol. 3, October 1997
12. Liang, J., He, Y., Liu, D., Zeng, X.: Image fusion using higher order singular value decomposition. IEEE Trans. Image Process. **21**(5), 2898–2909 (2012)
13. Xu, M., Chen, H., Varshney, P.: An image fusion approach based on markov random fields. IEEE Trans. Geosci. Remote Sens. **49**(12), 5116–5127 (2011)
14. He, K., Sun, J., Tang, X.: Guided image filtering. In: Daniilidis, K., Maragos, P., Paragios, N. (eds.) ECCV 2010. LNCS, vol. 6311, pp. 1–14. Springer, Heidelberg (2010). https://doi.org/10.1007/978-3-642-15549-9_1
15. Farbman, Z., Fattal, R., Lischinski, D., Szeliski, R.: Edge-preserving decompositions for multi-scale tone and detail manipulation. ACM Trans. Graph. **27**(3), 67-1–67-10 (2008)
16. Durand, F., Dorsey, J.: Fast bilateral filtering for the display of high-dynamic-range images. ACM Trans. Graph. **21**(3), 257–266 (2002)
17. Draper, N., Smith, H.: Applied Regression Analysis. Wiley, New York (1981)
18. Petrović, V.: Subjective tests for image fusion evaluation and objective metric validation. Inf. Fusion **8**(2), 208–216 (2007)
19. Piella, G.: Image fusion for enhanced visualization: a variational approach. Int. J. Comput. Vis. **83**, 1–11 (2009)
20. Li, S., Kang, X., Hu, J., Yang, B.: Image matting for fusion of multi-focus images in dynamic scenes. Inf. Fusion **14**(2), 147–162 (2013)
21. Tessens, L., Ledda, A., Pizurica, A., Philips, W.: Extending the depth of field in microscopy through curvelet-based frequency-adaptive image fusion. In: Proceedings of IEEE International Conference on Acoustics, Speech and Signal Processing, vol. 1, April 2007
22. Zhang, Q., Guo, B.: Multifocus image fusion using the nonsubsampled contourlet transform. Sig. Process. **89**(7), 1334–1346 (2009)
23. Tian, J., Chen, L.: Adaptive multi-focus image fusion using a wavelet-based statistical sharpness measure. Sig. Process. **92**(9), 2137–2146 (2012)
24. Hossny, M., Nahavandi, S., Creighton, D.: Comments on information measure for performance of image fusion. Electron. Lett. **44**(18), 1066–1067 (2008)
25. Yang, C., Zhang, J., Wang, X., Liu, X.: A novel similarity based quality metric for image fusion. Inf. Fusion **9**(2), 156–160 (2008)
26. Cvejic, N., Loza, A., Bull, D., Canagarajah, N.: A similarity metric for assessment of image fusion algorithms. Int. J. Sig. Process. **2**(3), 178–182 (2005)
27. Xydeas, C., Petrović, V.: Objective image fusion performance measure. Electron. Lett. **36**(4), 308–309 (2000)
28. Zhao, J., Laganiere, R., Liu, Z.: Performance assessment of combinative pixel-level image fusion based on an absolute feature measurement. Int. J. Innov. Comput. Inf. Control **3**(6), 1433–1447 (2007)
29. Liu, Z., Blasch, E., Xue, Z., Zhao, J., Laganiere, R., Wu, W.: Objective assessment of multiresolution image fusion algorithms for context enhancement in night vision: a comparative study. IEEE Trans. Pattern Anal. Mach. Intell. **34**(1), 94–109 (2012)
30. Qu, G., Zhang, D., Yan, P.: Information measure for performance of image fusion. Electron. Lett. **38**(7), 313–315 (2002)
31. Wang, Z., Bovik, A., Sheikh, H., Simoncelli, E.: Image quality assessment: from error visibility to structural similarity. IEEE Trans. Image Process. **13**(4), 600–612 (2004)

32. Wang, Z., Bovik, A.: A universal image quality index. IEEE Sig. Process. Lett. **9**(3), 81–84 (2002)
33. Crow, F.C.: Summed-area tables for texture mapping. In: Proceedings of SIGGRAPH 1984, 11th Annual Conference on Computer Graphics and Interactive Techniques, vol. 18, no. 3, pp. 207–212, January 1984
34. www.matlab.com
35. www.Plagiarismchecker.com

Networks and Information Security

Man in the Middle Attack on NTRU Key Exchange

Vijay Kumar Yadav, S. Venkatesan[(⊠)], and Shekhar Verma[(⊠)]

Department of IT, Indian Institute of Information Technology, Allahabad,
Allahabad 211012, U.P., India
{Pcl2014002,venkat.ta,sverma}@iiita.ac.in

Abstract. A cryptographic scheme is as strong as its underlying key exchange algorithm. In this paper we explored NTRU key exchange and found that it is exposed to Man In The Middle (MITM) attack. Similar vulnerability has been found in original Diffie-Hellman key exchange and prevented using Zero Knowledge Proof (ZKP). We applied ZKP scheme to solve the lattice based NTRU key exchange MITM and found that even with ZKP, NTRU scheme is still vulnerable to MITM attacks. Implementation results confirm this vulnerability of MITM attack in NTRU key exchange algorithm with ZKP.

Keywords: NTRU key exchange · Diffie-Hellman · Man in the middle attack
Zero Knowledge Proof

1 Introduction

1.1 Lattices

Let $B = \{v_1, v_2, \ldots v_n\}$, be n linearly independent vectors $\in R^m$ where, $m \geq n$. The set of all vectors $\mathcal{L}(B) = a_1 v_1 + a_2 v_2 + \ldots + a_n v_n$. where $a_i \in Z$ called integer lattice [1] and n is called the dimension of the lattice. If $m = n$ then it is called full rank lattice.

1.2 Fundamental Domain

Let $b_1, b_2, \ldots b_n$ a basis for lattice $\mathcal{L}$ and let $\mathcal{L}$ be a lattice of dimension n. The fundamental parallelepiped (or fundamental domain) for lattice corresponding to the basis is the set.

$$\mathcal{F}(b_1, b_2, \ldots, b_n) = a_1 b_1 + a_2 b_2 + \ldots + a_n b_n : 0 \leq a_i < 1.$$

The shaded area in Fig. 1 shows fundamental domain of two dimension.

S. Verma et al. (Eds.): CNC 2018, CCIS 839, pp. 251–261, 2019.
https://doi.org/10.1007/978-981-13-2372-0_22

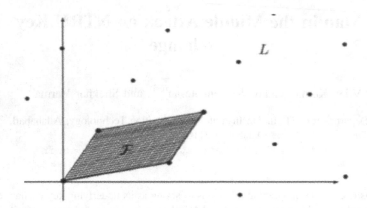

Fig. 1. A lattice $\mathcal{L}$ and fundamental domain $\mathcal{F}$

1.3 Problems with Lattices

Shortest Vector Problem (SVP): In a lattice $\mathcal{L}$ finding the shortest non-zero vector v whose Euclidian norm is minimum is difficult [3].

Closest Vector Problem (CVP): In a lattice $\mathcal{L}$, suppose a non-zero vector v such that $v \in \mathcal{L}$ and let m be a non-zero vector $\notin \mathcal{L}$. Finding the vector v which is very closed to m is difficult [3].

For computation of SVP and CVP are very difficult as the dimension grows SVP are *NP* hard under certain randomized reduction and CVP are known to be *NP* hard. In implementation it is found that CVP is examine to be a little bit harder than SVP, since CVP can often be reduced to SVP in a slightly higher dimension. For the proof see [11] that SVP is no harder than CVP. The complexity of different types of lattice problem [12].

In this paper we discovered MITM attack which is vulnerability in the lattice based in NTRU key exchange. This type of vulnerability can be removed by ZKP but NTRU scheme with ZKP is still vulnerable to MITM attacks.

In Sect. 2, we explored the basis of key exchange algorithms and their working followed by Sect. 3 containing basic notation, definition and mathematical background that have been used in NTRU key exchange. In Sect. 4 we explain how NTRU encryption, decryption schemes work. Section 6 explains existing NTRU-KE, formalize the underlying hard problem, and analyze the lattice attacks. MITM attack on NTRU key exchange is explained in Sect. 7. We describe ZKP technique of MITM prevention in Diffie-Hellman in Sect. 8.1. Section 8.2 describes MITM attack on NTRU key exchange with ZKP. Finally, we concluded the findings of this work in Sect. 9.

2   Related Work

2.1   Diffie-Hellman Key Exchange

The Diffie-Hellman key exchange protocol [8] allows two party to share secret information over insecure channel. Two parties Alice and Bob choose a large prime number p and a non-zero integer g (primitive root) and make both p and g public. The key exchange algorithm proceeds as follows:

Step 1: Alice takes a private number $x \in Z_p^*$ computes $R_1 = g^x \bmod p$ and sends this R_1 to Bob. Similarly, Bob takes a private number $y \in Z_p^* \psi$ computes $R_2 = g^y \bmod p \psi$ and sends this R_2 to Alice.
Step 2: After Alice received the value of R_2, she computes $Key_{Alice} = R_2^x \bmod p = g^{xy} \bmod p$. Similarly Bob computes $Key_{Bob} = R_1^y \bmod p = g^{xy} \bmod p$. This makes $Key_{Alice} = Key_{Bob}$ as the common key. The Diffie-Hellman key exchange is based on the hardness of CDH problem.

2.2   Elliptic Curve Diffie-Hellman Key Exchange

Alice and Bob agree on an elliptic curve $E(F_p)$ and point $P \in E(F_p)$. The key exchange steps are as under

Step 1: Alice takes a secret integer m_a, calculates $Q_a = m_a P$ and sends this Q_a to the Bob. Similarly Bob calculates $Q_b = m_b P$ and sends to this to Alice.
Step 2: Alice prepares $Key_{Alice} = m_a Q_b = m_a m_b P$, and Bob creates $Key_{Bob} = m_b Q_a = m_b m_a P = Key_{Alice}$ [7] to obtain the shared key.

2.3   Ring-LWE Based Diffie-Hellman Key Exchange

In ring-LWE based Diffie-Hellman-like key exchange algorithm [2], two users exchange a single ring-LWE "sample" or public key each to arrive at approximate or "noisy" agreement on the ring element. In this protocol, both Alice and Bob agree on a public "big" a in $R_q = Z[x]/(x^n + 1)$ where R_q is a polynomial ring. The key exchange steps are as under

Step 1: Alice takes random "*small*" $s, e \in R_q$ computes $b = a.s + e (mod q)$ and sends this b to Bob. Similarly, Bob takes $s', e' \in R_q$ computes $b' = as' + e'$ and sends this b' to Alice.
Step 2: After Alice receives the value of b', she computes the shared secret $Key_{Alice} = s.b' = s(a.s' + e') = s.a.s'$, similarly Bob calculates $Key_{Bob} = s'.b = s'(a.s + e) = s.a.s'$. This makes $Key_{Alice} = Key_{Bob}$.

3 Mathematical Background

The ring R of convolution polynomials [10] is the quotient ring whose degree is less than N (fix integer) $R = Z[x]/(x^N - 1)$ similarly, $R_q = (Z/qZ)[x]/(x^N - 1)$ is a truncated polynomial whose degree less than N and coefficient $\in R_q$. Suppose two polynomial of the form $a(x) = (a_0 + a_1 x + \ldots + a_{N-1} x^{N-1}) \in R$, $b(x) = (b_0 + b_1 x + \ldots + b_{N-1} x^{N-1}) \in R$ the multiplication of two polynomial is denoted by $*$ which is also called convolution product. $a(x) * b(x) = p(x)$ with

$$p_k = \sum_{i+j \equiv k(modN)} a_i b_{k-1}$$

where the summation defining p_k, $\forall i, j$ between $0 \leq k \leq N - 1$ Multiplication of two polynomial $a(x) * b(x) \in R_q$ is same with only difference being the modulus over q.

4 NTRU Encryption

In NTRU-Encryption algorithm [4], set of public parameter are used as $\{N, p, q, d\}$, where, N is a prime number, q is an integer, p is an integer which is smaller than q, $\gcd(N, p) = \gcd(p, q) = 1, q > (6d + 1)p$ and set of four $N - 1$ degree polynomial $\mathcal{L}_f, \mathcal{L}_g, \mathcal{L}_m, \mathcal{L}_r$ All the four polynomials have small either binary $\{0, 1\}$ or ternary $\{-1, 0, 1\}$ coefficient. We are using ternary coefficient polynomial because it resists lattice reduction and hybrid MITM attack. We further define the notation

$$T(d_1, d_2) = a(x) \in R : \begin{cases} a(x) \text{ has } d_1 \text{ coefficients equal to 1} \\ a(x) \text{ has } d_2 \text{ coefficients equal to } - 1 \\ \textit{otherwise } 0 \end{cases}$$

Polynomials in $T(d_1, d_2)$ are called ternary polynomials. We choose random polynomials of the form:

$\mathcal{L}_f \in T(d_1 + 1, d_2)$ is a small set of polynomials selected as private key.
$\mathcal{L}_g \in T(d_1, d_2)$ Similar small set of polynomials selected as another private key.
$\mathcal{L}_m \in T(d_1, d_2)$ Polynomials used as message space.
$\mathcal{L}_r \in T(d_1, d_2)$ Taken as random polynomial.

4.1 Key Generation

In order to generate NTRU (private and public) key pair, first we choose two random polynomials $f \in \mathcal{L}_f$ and $g \in \mathcal{L}_g$. The polynomial f requires that its inverse $f_p \in R_p$ and also its inverse $f_q \in R_q$ satisfy the condition $f * f_q \equiv 1 (mod\, q)$ and $f * f_p \equiv 1 (mod\, p)$. The polynomial $h = f_q * g (mod\, q)$ is the public key and polynomial f, f_p, are the private keys.

4.2 Encryption

To encrypt a message $m \in \mathcal{L}_m$, we take a random polynomial $r \in \mathcal{L}_r$, and compute cipher text as $e = pr * h + m(mod\ q)$.

4.3 Decryption

To decrypt m from cipher text e, we first compute $a = e * f(mod\ q)$ using one of the private keys f then center lift $a \in R$ and $m = f_p * a(mod\ q)$ is computed using another private key f_p.

5 Our Contribution

In this paper, we discovered MITM vulnerability in NTRU key exchange. Diffie Hellman with ZKP was proposed to prevent MITM attack on the key exchange [6]. We have used same technique to prevent MITM attack in NTRU key exchange. We found that even with ZKP, NTRU scheme is still vulnerable to MITM attack.

6 NTRU Key Exchange

In this section, NTRU-Key exchange process [5] in lattice based public key cryptography is explained. Figure 2 shows the working model of NTRU key exchange. The key exchange between Alice and Bob is given below.

Alice	Bob
STEP: 1	
$f_i \leftarrow \mathcal{L}_f, g_i \leftarrow \mathcal{L}_g$ $h_i \equiv f_i^{-1} \star g_i\ (mod\ q)$	$f_j \leftarrow \mathcal{L}_f, g_j \leftarrow \mathcal{L}_g$ $h_j \equiv f_j^{-1} \star g_j\ (mod\ q)$
$\xrightarrow{\quad h_i \quad}$	
	$\xleftarrow{\quad h_j \quad}$
STEP: 2	
$r_i \leftarrow \mathcal{L}_r$ $e_i = pr_i \star h_j + f_i\ (mod\ q)$	$r_j \leftarrow \mathcal{L}_r$ $e_j = pr_j \star h_i + f_j\ (mod\ q)$
$\xrightarrow{\quad e_i \quad}$	
	$\xleftarrow{\quad e_j \quad}$
STEP: 3	
$a_i = f_i \star e_j\ (mod\ q)$ $K_i = a_i\ (mod\ p)$ $K_i = f_i \star f_j\ (mod\ p)$ $K_i = K_j$	$a_j = f_j \star e_i\ (mod\ q)$ $K_j = a_j\ (mod\ p)$ $K_j = f_j \star f_i\ (mod\ p)$ $K_j = K_i$

Fig. 2. NTRU-KE

Step 1: Both Alice and Bob choose random polynomial $f_i \in \mathcal{L}_f, g_i \in \mathcal{L}_g$ and $f_j \in \mathcal{L}_f, g_j \in \mathcal{L}_g$ respectively. Alice computes $h_i = f_i^{-1} \star g_i \; (mod \; q)$ and sends this h_i to Bob. Similarly, Bob computes $h_j = f_j^{-1} \star g_j \; (mod \; q)$ and sends this h_j to Alice.

Step 2: Alice generates random polynomial $r_i \leftarrow \mathcal{L}_r$, computes $e_i = pr_i \star h_j + f_i$ $(mod \; q)$ and sends this e_i to Bob. Similarly Bob generates $r_j \in \mathcal{L}_r$, computes and sends $e_j = pr_j \star h_i + f_j \; (mod \; q)$ to Alice.

Step 3: After Alice receives e_j, she computes $a_i = f_i \star e_j \; (mod \; q)$ and $K_i = a_i \; (mod \; p) = f_i \star f_j \; (mod \; p)$. Similarly Bob computes $a_j = f_j \star e_i \; (mod \; q)$, $K_j = a_j \; (mod \; p) = f_j \star f_i \; (mod \; p)$. This makes $K_j = K_i$.

7 MITM Attack on NTRU-KE

Figure 3 shows how MITM attack works on NTRU-KE. Global parameter selection in NTRU-KE is same as the NTRU-Encrypt Algorithm. MITM attack on NTRU-KE is as under:

Step 1: Alice takes a random polynomial of the form $f_i \leftarrow \mathcal{L}_f$ such that its inverse exists in R_q and a random polynomial $g_i \leftarrow \mathcal{L}_g$. She computes $h_i \equiv f_i^{-1} \star g_i \; (mod \; q)$ and sends this to the Bob.

Similarly, Bob takes a random polynomial of the form $f_k \leftarrow \mathcal{L}_f$ such that its inverse exists in R_q, and another random polynomial of the form $g_k \leftarrow \mathcal{L}_g$. He computes $h_k \equiv f_k^{-1} \star g_k \; (mod \; q)$ and sends this to the Alice.

Here, MITM attacker also chooses same parameters which are defined globally in the above NTRU-Encrypt algorithm. He selects a random polynomial of the form $f_j \leftarrow \mathcal{L}_f$ such that its inverse exists in R_q, and another random polynomial of the form $g_j \leftarrow \mathcal{L}_g$. He, then, computes $h_j \equiv f_j^{-1} \star g_j \; (mod \; q)$ and sends this to both Alice and Bob and also captures both h_i, h_k sent by Alice and Bob respectively.

Step 2: Alice expecting h_k from Bob receives h_j sent by MITM as Attacker intercept the messages and keeps h_k to self. Now, Alice generates a random polynomial $r_i \leftarrow \mathcal{L}_r$ computes $e_i = pr_i \star h_j + f_i (mod \; q)$, and sends this to Bob. Similarly, Bob also receives h_j in place of h_i thinking it is from Alice. Bob generates a random polynomial $r_k \leftarrow \mathcal{L}_r$, computes $e_k = pr_k \star h_j + f_k \; (mod \; q)$, and sends this to Alice. Attacker in the middle intercepts the messages and captures e_i, e_k. He generates his own random polynomial $r_j \leftarrow \mathcal{L}_r$, computes $e_{j,i} = pr_j \star h_i + f_j \; (mod \; q)$ and $e_{j,k} = pr_j \star h_k + f_j$ $(mod \; q)$, and sends these values to Alice and Bob respectively.

Step 3: Alice receives the value $e_{j,i}$ computes $a_i = f_i \star e_{j,i} \; (mod \; q)$ and $K_i = a_i \; (mod \; p)$. Similarly, Bob computes $a_k = f_k \star e_{j,k} \; (mod \; q)$ and $K_k = a_k \; (mod \; p)$ using $e_{j,k}$. Attacker again captures e_i and e_k sent by Alice and Bob respectively. He computes $a_{j,i} = f_j \star e_i \; (mod \; q)$, $a_{j,k} = f_j \star e_k \; (mod \; q)$, $K_{j,i} = a_{j,i} \; (mod \; p)$ and $K_{j,k} = a_{j,k} \; (mod \; p)$. This makes $K_i = K_{j,i}$ and $K_k = K_{j,k}$ i.e. key between Alice and Attacker and Key between Bob and Attacker both are equal.

Alice	Attacker	Bob
Step 1:		
$f_i \leftarrow \mathcal{L}_f,\ g_i \leftarrow \mathcal{L}_g$ $h_i \equiv f_i^{-1} \star g_i\ (mod\ q)$ $\xrightarrow{\quad h_i \quad}$	$f_j \leftarrow \mathcal{L}_f,\ g_j \leftarrow \mathcal{L}_g$ $h_j \equiv f_j^{-1} \star g_j\ (mod\ q)$ $\xleftarrow{\quad h_j \quad}$ $\xrightarrow{\qquad\qquad}$	$f_k \leftarrow \mathcal{L}_f,\ g_k \leftarrow \mathcal{L}_g$ $h_k \equiv f_k^{-1} \star g_k\ (mod\ q)$ $\xleftarrow{\qquad\qquad}$
Step 2:		
$r_i \leftarrow \mathcal{L}_r$ $e_i = \mathrm{pr}_i \star h_j + f_i\ (mod\ q)$ $\xrightarrow{\quad e_i \quad}$	$r_j \leftarrow \mathcal{L}_r$ $e_{j,i} = \mathrm{pr}_j \star h_i + f_j\ (mod\ q)$ $e_{j,k} = \mathrm{pr}_j \star h_k + f_j\ (mod\ q)$ $\xleftarrow{\quad e_{j,i} \quad}$ $\xrightarrow{\quad e_{j,k} \quad}$	$r_k \leftarrow \mathcal{L}_r$ $e_k = \mathrm{pr}_k \star h_j + f_k\ (mod\ q)$ $\xleftarrow{\quad e_k \quad}$
Step 3:		
$a_i = f_i \star e_{j,i}\ (mod\ q)$ $K_i = a_i\ (mod\ p)$ $K_i = f_i \star f_j\ (mod\ p)$ $K_i = K_{j,i}\ (mod\ q)$	$a_{j,i} = f_j \star e_i\ (mod\ q)$ $K_{j,i} = a_{j,i}\ (mod\ p)$ $K_{j,i} = f_j \star f_i\ (mod\ p)$ $K_{j,i} = K_i\ (mod\ q)$ $a_{j,k} = f_j \star e_k\ (mod\ q)$ $K_{j,k} = a_{j,k}\ (mod\ p)$ $K_{j,k} = f_j \star f_k\ (mod\ p)$ $K_{j,k} = K_k\ (mod\ q)$	 $a_k = f_k \star e_{j,k}\ (mod\ q)$ $K_k = a_k\ (mod\ p)$ $K_k = f_k \star f_j\ (mod\ p)$ $K_k = K_{j,k}\ (mod\ q)$

Fig. 3. MITM attack in NTRU-KE

8 Zero Knowledge Proof and Man in the Middle Attack

The original Diffie-Hellman key exchange algorithm was also vulnerable to MITM attack and to secure it, ZKP has been proposed [6]. However, we found that even with ZKP, NTRU key exchange in our experiment was exposed to MITM attack.

8.1 Diffie-Hellman Key Exchange Using Zero Knowledge Proof

Figure 4 describes Diffie-Hellman key exchange using ZKP. Here, ZKP provides authentication without revealing the secret information [9]. Alice and Bob want to communicate over unprotected channel and both agree on global value g (primitive root) and p (large prime number). The key exchange proceeds as under:

Step 1: Alice takes a private number x, computes $R_1 = g^x\ mod\ p$ and sends this to Bob.

Step 2: After receiving the value of R_1, Bob computes $R_2 = g^y\ mod\ p$ and $K_{Bob} = R_1^y\ mod\ p = g^{yx}\ mod\ p$. He encrypts the value R_2 using key K_{Bob} i.e. $C_1 = E(R_2, K_{Bob})$ and sends this C_1, R_2 to Alice.

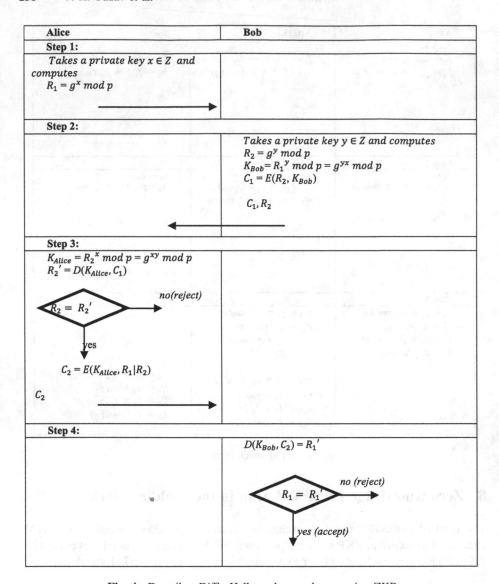

Fig. 4. Describes Diffie-Hellman key exchange using ZKP

Step 3: After Alice receives C_1, R_2 she computes $K_{Alice} = R_2^x \bmod p = g^{xy} \bmod p$.
She decrypts the cipher text C_1 i.e. $R_2' = D(K_{Alice}, C_1)$ and compares the values of R_2
and R_2'. If $R_2 = R_2'$ she thinks it is not Bob and terminates the connection.
Otherwise she, encrypts $C_2 = E(K_{Alice}, R_1|R_2)$ and sends this value to Bob.
Step 4: Bob Decrypts the value C_2 sent by Alice i.e. $R_1' = D(K_{Bob}, C_2)$ and compares
R_1 and R_1'. Here Alice is prover and Bob is verifier. If $R_1 = R_1'$ then, he assumes that
message came from Alice and accepts (verified) otherwise it is a dishonest prover
(rejected).

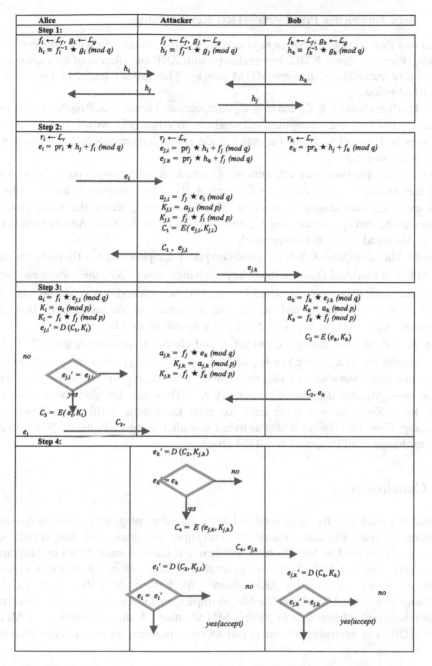

Fig. 5. Man in the middle attack on modified NTRU key exchange

8.2   Zero Knowledge Proof with NTRU Key Exchange

Alice and Bob want to exchange keys over unsecured channel with an Attacker in the middle. Figure 5 shows NTRU key exchange with ZKP and success of the exploitation of security vulnerability through MITM attacks. The various stages of the attack is described below.

Step 1: Alice choses $f_i \in \mathcal{L}_f$ and $g_i \in \mathcal{L}_g$ computes and sends h_i to Bob. Similarly, Bob selects $f_k \in \mathcal{L}_f, g_k \in \mathcal{L}_g$ computes and sends h_k to Alice. The Attacker in the middle captures both h_i and h_k, he also selects $f_j \in \mathcal{L}_f, g_j \in \mathcal{L}_g$, computes h_j and sends this to both Alice and Bob.

Step 2: Alice and Bob receive h_j thinking it came from other trusted party. Now, Alice and Bob selects $r_i \leftarrow \mathcal{L}_r$ and $r_k \leftarrow \mathcal{L}_r$ respectively. Both compute e_i and e_k using h_j and exchange this among themselves. The Attacker replicates the same process, computes $e_{j,i}$ and $e_{j,k}$, creates key $K_{j,i}$ and encrypts $e_{j,i}$ to form C_1. Attacker sends C_1, $e_{j,i}$ to Alice and $e_{j,k}$ to Bob respectively.

Step 3: Alice computes K_i using $e_{j,i}$ and decrypts the cipher text C_1. By using the base algorithm of modified Diffie Hellman key exchange using ZKP, she compare $e'_{j,i}$ with $e_{j,i}$. Since both data were calculated by attacker, hence condition results as true. So, Alice creates C_3 using e_i and key K_i and transmits. At the same time, Bob also calculates K_k to encrypt e_k giving C_2. C_2 is transmitted to Alice.

Step 4: The Attacker decrypts C_2 to get e'_k and checks its equality e_k using ZKP. He, then, creates cipher C_4 using key $K_{j,k}$ that is $C_4 = E(e_{j,k}, C_4)$ and sends $e_{j,k}, C_4$ to Bob for verification. Bob after receiving the values $e_{j,k}, C_4$ decrypts C_4 using key K_k. At the same time, Attacker decrypts C_3 using key $K_{j,i}$. Thus, attacker gains both Alice and Bob keys. Since he sent these keys for zero knowledge verification. Hence, the equating. Condition always results as true. Even after using ZKP, the modified NTRU key exchange is still exposed to MITM attack.

9   Conclusion

NTRU key exchange has been used in Lattice based cryptography given its quantum resistant computation and security. In this paper we discovered that NTRU key exchange is exposed to MITM attack and hence it leaves Lattice based cryptography vulnerable. Original Diffie-Hellman key exchange also suffered from same vulnerability which was solved using ZKP scheme. We further added ZKP in NTRU key exchange to make it MITM immune but, in implementation we uncovered the fact that even this hybrid scheme fails to prevent MITM attack. A suitable solution for MITM over NTRU key exchange scheme is still an open problem for research community.

References

1. Chi, D.P., Choi, J.W., San Kim, J., Kim, T.: Lattice based cryptography for beginners (2015)
2. Bos, J.W., Costello, C., Naehrig, M., Stebila, D.: Post-quantum key exchange for the TLS protocol from the ring learning with errors problem (2015)
3. Hoffstein, J., Howgrave-Graham, N., Pipher, J., Whyte, W.: Practical lattice-based cryptography: NTRUEncrypt and NTRUSign. In: Nguyen, P., Vallée, B. (eds.) The LLL Algorithm Information Security and Cryptography. Springer, Heidelberg (2009). https://doi.org/10.1007/978-3-642-02295-1_11
4. Hoffstein, J., Pipher, J., Silverman, J.H.: An Introduction to Mathematical Cryptography. Springer, New York (2008). https://doi.org/10.1007/978-0-387-77993-5
5. Lei, X., Liao, X.: NTRU-KE: a lattice-based public key exchange protocol
6. Ibrahem, M.K.: Modification of Diffie-Hellman key exchange algorithm for zero knowledge proof. In: 2012 International Conference on Future Communication Networks, Baghdad, pp. 147–152 (2012). https://doi.org/10.1109/ICFCN.2012.6206859
7. Bos, J.W., Halderman, J.A., Heninger, N., Moore, J., Naehrig, M., Wustrow, E.: Elliptic curve cryptography in practice. In: Christin, N., Safavi-Naini, R. (eds.) FC 2014. LNCS, vol. 8437, pp. 157–175. Springer, Heidelberg (2014). https://doi.org/10.1007/978-3-662-45472-5_11
8. Ahmed, M., Sanjabi, B., Aldiaz, D., Rezaei, A., Omotunde, H.: Diffie-Hellman and its application in security protocols. Int. J. Eng. Sci. Innov. Technol. (IJESIT) 1, 69–73 (2012)
9. Maurer, U.: Unifying zero-knowledge proofs of knowledge. In: Preneel, B. (ed.) AFRICACRYPT 2009. LNCS, vol. 5580, pp. 272–286. Springer, Heidelberg (2009). https://doi.org/10.1007/978-3-642-02384-2_17
10. Hoffstein, J., Howgrave-Graham, N., Pipher, J., Whyte, W.: An Introduction to Mathematical Cryptography, pp. 387–392. Springer, New York (2008). https://doi.org/10.1007/978-0-387-77993-5
11. Goldreich, O., Micciancio, D., Safra, S., Seifert, J.-P.: Approximating shortest lattice vectors is not harder than approximating closest lattice vectors. Inf. Process. Lett. 71(2), 5561 (1999)
12. Micciancio, D., Goldwasser, S.: Complexity of Lattice Problems: A Cryptographic Perspective. The Kluwer International Series in Engineering and Computer Science, vol. 671. Kluwer Academic Publishers, Boston (2002)

Information Theoretic Analysis of Privacy in a Multiple Query-Response Based Differentially Private Framework

Bodhi Chakraborty[1]([⊠]), Debanjan Sadhya[2], Shekhar Verma[1],
and Krishna Pratap Singh[1]

[1] Indian Institute of Information Technology, Allahabad, India
{rsl66,sverma,kpsingh}@iiita.ac.in
[2] Indian Institute of Technology, Roorkee, India
debanjan.sadhya@gmail.com

Abstract. Data privacy or safeguarding data from potential threats has become a critical issue in our data-centric world. Among the developed mechanisms catering to the objective of privacy preservation, differential privacy has emerged as a popular and effective technique which provides the required level of user privacy. In our work, we have information theoretically analyzed differential privacy in a multiple query-response based environment. We have evaluated our model on a real-world database and subsequently evaluated the effects of externally added noise on the resulting privacy. The simulated results confirm the notion that the privacy risk is inversely proportional to the amount of noise added in the system (defined by ε).

Keywords: Differential privacy · Information theory · Laplace noise
Micro-database

1 Introduction

Micro-databases are specific datasets which contain person specific information about the participating respondents. Micro-databases are generally published by independent organizations and sometimes government agencies for research related purposes. Typical examples of such micro-databases include census data and hospital medical records. Preserving the privacy of these micro-databases has been a major area of research recently. Since these databases are made available in the public domain, there is a high probability that an adversary might retrieve some sensitive information from any micro-database about any targeted individual. These privacy threats further increase when the intruder has some independent auxiliary side information. In this regard, privacy preservation relates to the rigorous guarantee that any personal or private information of the respondents cannot be extracted from the released micro-databases.

Based upon the nature of the data which they represent, the micro-database attributes can be categorized into three categories namely Identifiers, Key attributes (or quasi-identifiers) and confidential (sensitive) attributes [8]. Identifiers are those

© Springer Nature Singapore Pte Ltd. 2019
S. Verma et al. (Eds.): CNC 2018, CCIS 839, pp. 262–272, 2019.
https://doi.org/10.1007/978-981-13-2372-0_23

attributes which unambiguously identify the respondents. Typical examples of these in micro-databases include *SSN number* and *passport number*. These attributes are either removed or encrypted prior to distribution due to the high privacy risks associated with them. Key attributes are those properties which can be linked or combined with external sources or databases to re-identify a respondent. Typical examples of such attributes include *age, gender* and *address*. Sensitive attributes contain the most critical data of the users; maintaining their confidentiality is the primary objective of any database security scheme. Disclosure of information about these properties is considered as a direct breach of privacy for the users. Examples of these important attributes include *medical diagnosis, political affiliation* and *salary*.

In a multiple-query based environment, an adversary gradually gains information by issuing a systematic collection of queries on the micro-database. The responses to these queries gradually combine and converge towards the true value of the sensitive attribute. Our work in this paper concentrates on information theoretically quantifying the achievable guarantees of differential privacy under such constraints. For achieving such objectives, we have initially constructed a generic query-response based framework and subsequently embedded the notion of differential privacy in it. The rest of the sections are organized as follows. Section 2 notifies about the multiple background works related with the problem statement; we require contribution from all these works to formally tackle this multi-description query-response based privacy preservation problem. Section 3 is the core of our work wherein the inter-dependencies of several parameters associated with our proposed model are investigated. Section 4 deals with the simulation results with their analysis and finally Sect. 5 concludes this study.

2 Background Prerequisites

In this section, we provide some basic ideas and notions which have facilitated in our work. We specifically chalk out a series of studies which have directly motivated the construction of our framework.

2.1 Information Theoretic Basis of Privacy

The notion of privacy was rigorously analyzed in [8], wherein an information theoretic framework was provided to it. For achieving privacy *t*-closeness [6] mechanism is the primary framework used. The authors introduced two metrics related to measuring the overall distortion induced in the database (after enforcing a sanitization mechanism) and the associated privacy risk. These are defined as –

Definition 1 (Distortion $(\mathcal{D})$ [8]). For a dataset X and its perturbed form X', the Distortion $(\mathcal{D})$ is:

$$\mathcal{D} = \mathbb{E}[d(X, X')]$$

where $d(.,.)$ is an error measure.

Mean square error (MSE) or $d(x, x') = \|x - x'\|^2$ is the error function normally measured. Thus, $\mathcal{D}$ is the amount by which the perturbed data deviates from the original data. The associated privacy risk is subsequently defined as –

Definition 2 (Privacy Risk ($\mathcal{R}$) [8]). Let X denote a random variable representing the key values of a dataset, X' be another random variable which denotes the perturbed key values and W be a third random variable which represenst the sensitive values in the dataset. The associated Privacy Risk ($\mathcal{R}$) is:

$$\mathcal{R} = KL(p_{w|x'} \| p_w) = \mathbb{E}\left[\log \frac{p(W|X')}{p(W)}\right] = I(W; X') = H(W) = H(W|X')$$

Herein, p_w is the prior distribution of the sensitive attribute and $p_{w|x'}$ is the posterior distribution of the same when the adversary observes the perturbed key attributes. Moreover, $KL(.\|.)$ is the Kullback-Leibler divergence between two distributions, the mutual information between two random variables is $I(.;.)$, the entropy of a random variable is $H(.)$ and $H(.|.)$ is the conditional entropy among two r.v's.

2.2   Differential Privacy

Dwork [3] first conceptualized the idea of differential privacy in a query-response framework. In a query-response scenario, a query is fired on the database and an appropriate response is obtained from it. The collection of these responses is collaboratively utilized for subsequent analysis purposes (e.g. data and pattern mining). However, the privacy of a particular individual becomes very much jeopardized if an attacker finds out some critical information about the individual after analysis of the released results. Dwork presented the concept of differential privacy to provide privacy in such situations. The instinct behind this thought was that the participants would feel safe to present their information on the off chance that they realized that the response to any query fired on the database would be same irrespective of whether they submitted their sensitive information in any case. Then again, it can be expressed that an individual would appreciate differential privacy if the risk related with the individual does not change whether the user took part or not in the survey.

Definition 3 (ε differential privacy [3]). A randomized function K gives ε-differential privacy if for all data sets D_1 and D_2 differing on at most one element, and all $S \subseteq Range(K)$,

$$Pr(K(D_1) \in S) \le e^{\varepsilon} \times Pr(K(D_2) \in S)$$

where, Pr represents the randomized function's probability distribution.

Differential privacy is attained by introducing random noise in the responses acquired from the database. The noise magnitude relies on the largest change that a participant can impact on the responses. This is termed as Global sensitivity (Δf) or $L1$ sensitivity.

Definition 4 (Global sensitivity (Δf) **[3]).** For any function $f : D \rightarrow R^d$, the L1-sensitivity of f is

$$\Delta f = max_{D_1, D_2} \|f(D_1) - f(D_2)\|$$

for all D_1, D_2 varying in at most one element.

Differential privacy is generally implemented by adding noise which is suitably adjusted with respect to the output of the queries. The noise is considered to have a Laplace distribution. The probability density function of the laplace noise is-

$$Laplace(x, \lambda) = \frac{1}{2\lambda} e^{-|x|/\lambda}$$

where λ is determined by both Δf and desired privacy controlling parameter ε.

Theorem 1 (Laplace Noise mechanism [4]). For any function $f : D \rightarrow R^d$, the mechanism

$$Laplace(D, f, \varepsilon) = f(D) + [L_1(\lambda), L_2(\lambda), \ldots, L_d(\lambda)]$$

gives ε-differential privacy if $\lambda = \Delta f / \varepsilon$ and $L_i(\lambda)$ are i.i.d. Laplace random variables.

An important notion associated with differential privacy is that of composability. Composability means the guarantee that the privacy essentials remain satisfied even when several responses are considered together and subjected to joint examination. Let M be a mechanism for providing ε-differential privacy to a random variable X via the Laplace noise addition method.

Theorem 2 (Sequential Composition [7]). Let each M_i provide ε_i-differential privacy. Then the sequence of $M_i(X)$ provides $\sum_i \varepsilon_i$-differential privacy.

In-spite of all the positive prospects, differential privacy lags in preventing the attacker from concluding about individuals from the aggregate results over the population. This limitation gets exposed when multiple query is fired by the attacker. Greater the number of query fired, closer the attacker gets to his goal thus decreasing differential privacy level.

3   Development of Proposed Frameworks

This section is dedicated in detailing the construction process of the proposed framework. We initiate our framework development process by discussing about the generic system, query and adversarial models associated with it.

3.1   System Model

The core of our system comprises of a micro-database DB containing x number of key attributes $K = \{K_1, K_2, \ldots, K_x\}$ and one sensitive attribute S (thus totaling to $x + 1$

attributes). Privacy is breached on the disclosure of any value of S corresponding to an entity. Moreover, the total number of records in the database is assumed to be y. The complete database is not disclosed to the adversary as our framework is being developed in a query-response based model. The details of the employed sanitization mechanism are stated in Sect. 3.4.

3.2   Adversarial Model

The adversary is considered to be a polynomial time attacker who is having a restricted memory and computational power (i.e. the adversary cannot issue an infinite number of queries). The adversary wants to disclose the value of S corresponding to a targetted individual of the DB. Consequently, our objective is the prevention of the revelation of the exact value S. The adversary fires n queries $Q = \{Q_1, Q_2, \ldots, Q_n\}$ on DB, each operating on K or S. It is noticeable that without the applying any privacy preservation technique, the adversary can easily compute the exact value of S (for a particular individual) after firing n queries.

3.3   Query Model

We have assumed a few general rules for the nature of the queries issued by an adversary. Enforcing these rules is the obligation of the entity which manages the flow and nature of the submitted queries.

1. The queries should not be fired simultaneously but sequentially.
2. In the sequence Q each query should be unique i.e. there should be no repeatation of query in the sequence. Any duplicate query in the sequence is not entertained. The adversary can use multiple operations so as to average out and subsequently cancel noise thereby revealing the value of S. To restrict the adversary from doing this the following constraint is imposed.
3. The queries directly seeking the information about the sensitive attribute S will remain unanswered. This is so because our main objective is to conceal the actual values of S. But queries relating to any aggregate information about S can be answered.

3.4   Main Framework

The working model for implementation of differential privacy in DB is shown in Fig. 1.

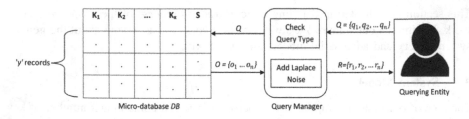

Fig. 1. The query response based framework.

As discussed previously, the adversary initially fires a series of n queries on DB represented by $Q = \{Q_1, Q_2, \ldots, Q_n\}$. After checking the validity of the queries, the query manager forwards these queries on DB. The true responses obtained from DB corresponding to Q are represented by $O = \{O_1, O_2, \ldots, O_n\}$. However, these responses are perturbed by the addition of appropriate Laplace noise. The generated noise should be carefully calibrated for enforcing the notion of differential privacy. More specifically, the noise N should be generated via the Laplace noise mechanism (Theorem 1) having the following specific parameters - $Mean(\mu) = 0$, Scale parameter $(\sigma) = \frac{\Delta f}{\varepsilon}$ and $Variance = 2\sigma^2$. Herein, Δf is the corresponding global sensitivity as described in Definition 4. The term ε is the parameter for controlling the privacy which is adjusted according to the requirements of the application.

Theorem 3. The framework proposed in Sect. 3.4 is $\left(\sum_n \varepsilon_n\right)$-differentially private.

Proof. In total, there are n query-responses in the proposed model. Every response is perturbed according to Theorem 1 for satisfying the notion of ε-differential privacy. Hence in accordance with Theorem 2 (Sequential Composition), our proposed framework satisfies $\left(\sum_n \varepsilon_n\right)$-differential privacy. This concludes the proof.

As argued in [9], the adversary's knowledge about the sensitive information S is directly proportional to the total number of fired queries. Consequently, the adversary's knowledge gain becomes so large after just a few number of queries that the further addition of Laplace noise fails to provide privacy. As a countermeasure to this problem, we can alter the variance of the added noise with the number of queries. As our model mainly consists of simple difference and sum queries, the variance is decreased with respect to the queries. The variance of the nth query is fixed to $2\sigma^2$ the original value, and then we move up the query sequence its value is linearly increased by a constant factor of k we reach Q_1 (the first query). This hierarchy is shown in Table 1.

Table 1. Calibration of noise according to the queries.

Query number $(Q_i), 1 \leq i \leq n$	Variance of noise
1	$2\sigma^2 + (n \times k)$
2	$2\sigma^2 + ((n-1) \times k)$
...	...
n	$2\sigma^2$

After adding noise N to the outputs O, the results are delivered to the intruder as the responses to Q, the query set. Let these responses be represented by $R = \{R_1, R_2, R_3, \ldots, R_n\}$. Let's assume that O and R are denoted by the probability distributions $p(O) = p(O_1, O_2, \ldots, O_n)$ and $p(R) = p(R_1, R_2, \ldots, R_n)$ respectively. Subsequently, we can represent O and R by the random variables X_O and X_R which follow the aforementioned distribution functions. Finally, the estimated value of the sensitive attribute S is computed from R and is then represented as R'.

3.5   Information Theoretic Establishment of Privacy

In this section we present and analyze the information theoretic outlooks of differential privacy (implemented in the proposed framework). Essentially, we broaden the information theoretic concepts in [8] to differential privacy providing our multiple query-response framework. Privacy Risk ($\mathcal{R}$) and Distortion ($\mathcal{D}$) are the two parameters that we focus on. As discussed previously in Definition 1, the deviation of responses from the original values after addition of noise is represented by $\mathcal{D}$. This is nothing but the MSE (Mean Square Error) between the noise added responses R and the unmodified outputs O. So for n queries,

$$\mathcal{D} = \frac{1}{n}\sum_{i=1}^{n}(R_i - O_i)^2 \tag{1}$$

Evidently, $\mathcal{D}$ relies on how much noise is added in the framework which is dependent on ε. Greater the value of ε lesser is the addition of noise and lower is the value of $\mathcal{D}$.

Lemma 1. The value of $\mathcal{D}$ lies in $[0, \infty]$.

Proof. There is no defined upper bound on $\mathcal{D}$ since we can keep adding any amount of external noise by decreasing ε. Hence,

$$\mathcal{D}_{max} = \infty \tag{2}$$

Conversely, the minimum value of $\mathcal{D}$ occurs when we do not alter the original responses by adding any noise. For such a case, $\mathcal{D}_{min} = 0$ since $R_i = O_i \, \forall \, 1 \leq i \leq n$. Hence,

$$\mathcal{D}_{min} = \frac{1}{n}\sum_{i=1}^{n}(R_i - R_i)^2 = 0 \tag{3}$$

Combining Eqs. 2 and 3, we obtain the range of $\mathcal{D}$ as $[0, \infty]$. This concludes the proof.

The second parameter which we consider is Privacy Risk ($\mathcal{R}$). As stated in Definition 2, $\mathcal{R}$ is the mutual information between two discrete random variables (X_R and X_O in our case). Formally treating,

$$\begin{aligned}
\mathcal{R} &= I(X_R; X_O) \\
&= \sum_{R,O} p(O,R) \times \log\frac{p(O,R)}{p(O)p(R)} = H(X_R) - H(X_R|X_O) = H(X_O) - H(X_O|X_R)
\end{aligned} \tag{4}$$

In Eq. 4, $H(X_R)$ and $H(X_O)$ denote the entropy of R and O respectively.

Lemma 2. The value of $\mathcal{R}$ lies in $[0, H(X_O)]$.

Proof. The maximum value of $\mathcal{R}$ occurs when the perturbed responses complete fail to masquerade the true responses (i.e. addition of noise has no effect). Consequently, the adversary gains maximum knowledge about the true responses of his/her queries. For such a case, $H(X_O|X_R) = 0$. Thus,

$$\mathcal{R}_{max} = H(X_O) - 0 = H(X_O) \tag{5}$$

Alternatively, the minimum value of $\mathcal{R}$ occurs when the perturbed responses reveal no knowledge of the true responses. Consequently, the adversary gains no knowledge about the true responses of his/her queries. This can also be alternatively stated by the statement that the X_O and X_R are independent of each other.

For such a case, $I(X_R; X_O) = 0$. Hence,

$$\mathcal{R}_{min} = 0 \tag{6}$$

Combining Eqs. 5 and 6, we obtain the range of $\mathcal{R}$ as $[0, H(X_O)]$. This concludes the proof.

4 Results and Discussions

This section provides the results computed by simulating the proposed frameworks and thereafter evaluating its parameters. As we have conducted our tests on real life data, we first formally present the data set that has been used for testing.

4.1 Database

The CASC project's EIA dataset is being used for the purpose of our work. The project details can be found in [5]. The complete EIA dataset can be obtained from the U.S. Energy Information Authority, as described in [1, 2]. This data-set consists of 4092 records corresponding to 15 attributes (13 numeric and 2 character). In this regard, the following points are noted -

1. For simplicity we have deleted the 'YEAR', 'UTILNAME' and 'STATE' attributes from the dataset as they are of no use for our analysis. Rather, we maintain a different file which has the mapping between 'UTILITYID' and 'UTILNAME' is preserved.
2. As 'UTILITYID' is the attribute which identifies each entity separately so we considered it to be the primary key. 'TOTSALES' is considered to be the sensitive attribute as we can treat the company sales revenue as a confidential information. As all other attributes can be combined uniquely so as to identify each tuple so they are treated as key attributes. As such, the disclosure of the estimation of 'TOTSALES' which corresponds to a 'UTILITYID' is treated as a breach in privacy. Alternatively, the goal of the adversary is to find out the value of total revenue sales (i.e. 'TOTSALES') of a targeted company.

3. *DB* is the database which is obtained after modification of the EIA dataset. As mentioned previously, The entire *DB* is not published, but we restrict it to only a sequence of queries which are allowed to be fired in it.

4.2 Query Set Structure

For the testing our framework, we suppose that for company with 'UTILITYID' = 213 the intruder wants to its 'TOTSALES'. *Q* a sequence of queries on *DB* is fired by the adversary for achieving the objective. The exact query sequence which we have simulated is presented as follows -

> Q_1 = **SELECT SUM**(DB.TOTSALES)
> **FROM** database DB
> **WHERE** DB.UTILITYID = 213 **AND** DB.UTILITYID = 599;

> Q_2 = **SELECT SUM**(DB.TOTSALES)
> **FROM** database DB
> **WHERE** DB.UTILITYID = 213 **AND** DB.UTILITYID = 3522;

> Q_3 = **SELECT SUM**(DB.TOTSALES)
> **FROM** database DB
> **WHERE** DB.UTILITYID = 213 **AND** DB.UTILITYID = 6129;

> Q_4 = **SELECT SUM**(DB.TOTSALES)
> **FROM** database DB
> **WHERE** DB.UTILITYID = 213 **AND** DB.UTILITYID = 7353;

> Q_5 = **SELECT SUM**(DB.TOTSALES)
> **FROM** database DB
> **WHERE** DB.UTILITYID = 3522 **AND** DB.UTILITYID = 6129 **AND**
> DB.UTILITYID = 7353 **AND** DB.UTILITYID = 599;

4.3 Framework Analysis

The adversary can accurately estimate the required sensitive information (R') by evaluating Eq. 7 -

$$R' = \frac{(Q_1 + Q_2 + Q_3 + Q_4) - Q_5}{4} \tag{7}$$

However, the value of calculated R' differs from that of the original value (S) because of the implementation of the differential privacy mechanism based in Laplace noise. In our simulation we have considered the value of Global Sensitivity (Δ) to 1 as we are using difference and sum and queries as demonstrated in the example in [9].

The results obtained from the simulation are illustrated in Fig. 2. It vindicates the general notion that Privacy Risk and Distortion are contrasting quantities. As evident in Fig. 2, a value of $\mathcal{D}$ higher than 15 corresponds to $\mathcal{R}$ less than 0.4 (i.e. there is low risk of privacy breach). Alternatively, a distortion level of about 2 translates to a higher value of $\mathcal{R}$ (about 1.4). In such a case, an adversary can accurately estimate the exact value of the critical information which is sensitive in nature.

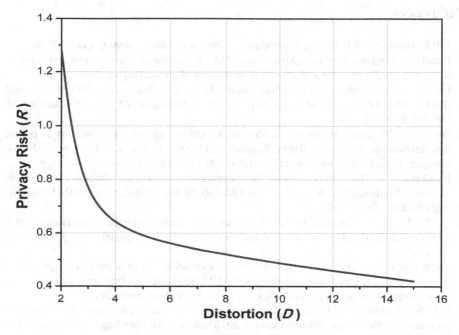

Fig. 2. Variation of $\mathcal{D}$ with $\mathcal{R}$.

An important feature in Fig. 2 is related to the nature of the resulting curve. In this case, the dependent parameter changes non-linearly with the independent parameter. The reason for this observation can be attributed to the addition of external noise which is nonlinear. More specifically, the noise was generated based on the Laplace distribution which is a double exponential distribution.

5   Conclusion and Future Works

In present technological age security and data privacy is a primary area of concern. In this paper, we have attempted this area by information theoretically analyzing the privacy guarantees of differential privacy in a multiple query-response based environment. Essentially, we have theorized two metrics termed as Privacy Risk ($\mathcal{R}$) and Distortion ($\mathcal{D}$), and subsequently analyzed their dependencies in such an environment.

In this work, we have modeled the design of the framework and the associated simulations considering only one sensitive attribute. However, we did not consider the scenario in which that there may be multiple critical attributes present in a micro-data table (which is more practical). Moreover, we have also not considered the database utility after subjecting it to a sanitization mechanism. The trade-off between data utility and data perturbation is a very crucial aspect and thus, the framework should be optimized so as to strike the correct balance between the two.

References

1. U.E.I. Authority: EIA data set. http://www.eia.doe.gov/cneaf/electricity/page/eia826.html
2. Brand, R., Domingo-Ferrer, J., Mateo-Sanz, J.M.: Reference data sets to test and compare SDC methods for protection of numerical micro-data. Technical report, April 2002
3. Dwork, C.: Differential privacy. In: Bugliesi, M., Preneel, B., Sassone, V., Wegener, I. (eds.) ICALP 2006. LNCS, vol. 4052, pp. 1–12. Springer, Heidelberg (2006). https://doi.org/10.1007/11787006_1
4. Dwork, C., McSherry, F., Nissim, K., Smith, A.: Calibrating noise to sensitivity in private data analysis. In: Halevi, S., Rabin, T. (eds.) TCC 2006. LNCS, vol. 3876, pp. 265–284. Springer, Heidelberg (2006). https://doi.org/10.1007/11681878_14
5. Hundepool, A.: The CASC project. In: Domingo-Ferrer, J. (ed.) Inference Control in Statistical Databases. LNCS, vol. 2316, pp. 172–180. Springer, Heidelberg (2002). https://doi.org/10.1007/3-540-47804-3_14
6. Li, N., Li, T., Venkatasubramanian, S.: t-Closeness: privacy beyond k-anonymity and l-diversity. In: 2007 IEEE 23rd International Conference on Data Engineering, pp. 106–115, April 2007
7. McSherry, F.D.: Privacy integrated queries: an extensible platform for privacy-preserving data analysis. In: Proceedings of the 2009 ACM SIGMOD International Conference on Management of Data, SIGMOD 2009, pp. 19–30. ACM, New York (2009)
8. Rebollo-Monedero, D., Forne, J., Domingo-Ferrer, J.: From t-Closeness-Like privacy to postrandomization via information theory. IEEE Trans. Knowl. Data Eng. 22(11), 1623–1636 (2010)
9. Sarathy, R., Muralidhar, K.: Evaluating laplace noise addition to satisfy differential privacy for numeric data. Trans. Data Privacy 4(1), 1–17 (2011)

Security in MQTT and CoAP Protocols of IOT's Application Layer

Anup Burange, Harshal Misalkar[✉], and Umesh Nikam[✉]

Amravati, India
{awburange, hdmisalkar, uvnikam}@mitra.ac.in

Abstract. The Internet of Things (IoT) is a framework of interconnected computing devices mechanical and digital machines, internationally identifiable physical objects (or things) or people that are have unique identity and the ability to transfer data over a network without human-to-human or human-to-computer interaction., their combination with the Internet, and their representation in the digital world. The accessibility and availability of cheap components of IoT devices enables a extensive range of applications and provide smart environments. These devices perform actuating and sensing tasks and identified through unique addresses. The IoT devices are connected to the Internet and expected to use the Constrained Application Protocol (CoAP) at the application layer as a main web transfer protocol. Message Queuing Telemetry Transport (MQTT) does not enforce the use of a particular security approach for its applications, but instead leaves that to the application designer. Therefore, IoT solutions can be based on application context and specific security requirements. MQTT is a Client Server publish/subscribe messaging transport protocol. It is lightweight, open, uncomplicated, and designed to make implementation more easier. These characteristics of MQTT make it perfect for use in most of the situations, including communication in Machine to Machine (M2M) and Internet of Things (IoT). In IOT there is major use of Wireless Sensor Networks (WSN) which connects virtual world to physical world. In this paper focus is given to application layer of IOT. In application layer two important protocols are MQTT and CoAP. Security mechanism is proposed in the paper for these protocols.

Keywords: MQTT · CoAP · IOT

1 Introduction

The IoT is built on three main pillars related to the capability of objects which must have communication capability, computational capability and may have interaction capability:

(i) Communication capability: Objects in IoT must have a minimal set of communication capability. What we mean by this is not only a communication channel, but also everything related to it, in order to make an efficient communication, such as, an address, identifier, and name. The objects may have all these features or some of them [8].

© Springer Nature Singapore Pte Ltd. 2019
S. Verma et al. (Eds.): CNC 2018, CCIS 839, pp. 273–285, 2019.
https://doi.org/10.1007/978-981-13-2372-0_24

(ii) Computational capability: Objects must have some basic or complex computational capability, in order to process data and networks configurations. For instance, receive commands over the communications channel, manage network tasks, save the status from a sensor, activate an effector.

(iii) Interaction capability: The IoT technology may have an interaction capability in terms of sensing and actuating. This can be done either by, sensors and/or actuators. Sensors are things which sense or detecting the real world environment (e.g., light, humidity, temperature, movement, voice, etc.). Effectors are things that change or effect the real world such as, switches that allow you to trigger or to turn on/off anything that can change the real word such as motors, beepers, cameras, etc [1].

Table 1. IoT stack with standaridized security solutions.

IoT layer	IoT protocol	Security protocol
Application	CoAP	User-defined
Transport	UDP	DTLS
Network	IPv6, RPL	IPsec, RPL security
6LoWPAN	6LoWPAN	None
Data-link	IEEE 802.15.4	802.15.4 security

2 IOT Architecture

Many architecture models have been proposed from different organizations and researchers. Figure 1 provides the main and general model which consists of three-layer architecture perception layer, network layer, and application layer. The definitions of these layers are defined below:

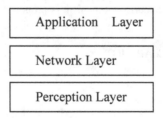

Fig. 1. IOT architecture

1. Perception layer: The perception layer can also be called physical layer. This layer consists of physical objects or devices such as sensors, RFID system, meters, GPS system. This layer basically collect identification or information depends on the type of the sensor or the physical device.

2. Network layer: The network layer is also known as transmission layer. This layer is responsible for interconnection and communication functions. The transmission can

be done through wired or wireless communication technologies such as Wi-Fi, Bluetooth, 3G, ZigBee. Many transmission and security protocols can be deployed in this layer such as: IPV4, IPV6, DTLS, IPsec. This layer should securely transfer the data from the physical layer to application layer.

3. Application layer: The application layer provides and manages application services for users needs. Many application protocols can be deployed in this layer such as CoAP, and HTTP depends on the type of application and the IoT devices [7].

The recent challenge in consideration with security of IOT devices is to fix security bugs & its security updation. In addition to new protocols that are designed specifically for the Internet of Things such as Message Queuing Telemetry Transport (MQTT) and Constrained Application Protocol (CoAP), security mechanisms should need to be developed or upgrade [2].

3 MQTT (Message Queueing and Transport Protocol)

For IoT devices and applications, MQTT is the most recognized messaging protocol and it is the base of many active groups or industries in the IoT field. Lightweight, easy-to-use message protocols are being provided by MQTT as IOT solutions. MQTT involves some safety mechanisms in addition to common implementations such as SSL/TLS for transport protection [5]. For applications MQTT does not implement the use of a specific security approach, but in its place handover that task to the application designer, because of this IoT solutions are based on application structure and definite security necessities. MQTT uses transport layer security (TLS), for most of the deployments where data is encrypted and its reliability is validated. To control admittance most implementations of MQTT also use permission features in the MQTT server.

3.1 Architecture

Every sensor in a client/server model of MQTT is known as client that connects to a broker, that broker act as a server. Connection is established using TCP/IP. As MQTT is message oriented protocol, each message is having discrete amount of data, transparent to the broker. The broker is a server which can be installed on any machine. MQTT runs on TCP/IP layer therefore it is connection oriented protocol, every client must establish connection with the broker before starting communication. Every message is available to an address, identified as a topic. Clients may subscribe to several topics. Clients can subscribe to various topics. Each client subscribed to a topic gets every message published to the topic. Consider a simple network with three nodes that release TCP connections with the broker. Nodes Y and Z are subscribe to the topic humidity (Fig. 2).

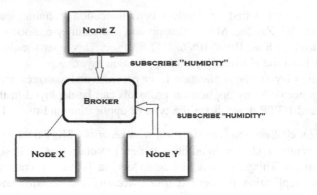

Fig. 2. Architecture of MQTT

Afterward Node X displays a value of 30% for topic humidity, then the broker transmits the message to all the subscribed notes.

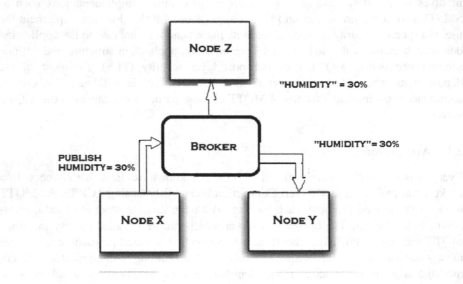

Fig. 3. Architecture of MQTT

The publisher-subscriber model on which MQTT works allows MQTT clients to communicate one-to-one, one-to-many and many-to-one.

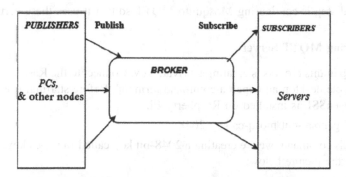

Fig. 4. Publisher-subscriber model of MQTT

3.2   MQTT Vulnerabilities

The MQTT protocol carries a number of potential vulnerabilities. For example, open ports can be used to launch denial-of-service (DoS) attacks as well as buffer overflow attacks across networks and devices [6]. Depending on the number of IoT devices connected and use cases supported, the complexity of "topic" structure can grow significantly and cause scalability issues. MQTT message payloads are encoded in binary, and corresponding application/device types must be able to interoperate. Another problem area is with MQTT message usernames and passwords, which are sent in clear text. Transport encryption with SSL and TLS can protect data when implemented correctly. To protect against threats, sensitive data including user IDs, passwords, and any other types of credentials should always be encrypted. To secure MQTT protocol we should consider the security of client, broker, operating system.

3.3   MQTT Security

By its nature, MQTT is a plain protocol. All the information exchanged is in plain-text format. In other words, anyone could access to this message and read the payload. There are several use cases where we want to keep information private and guarantee that it cannot be read or modified during the transmitting process. In this case, there are several approaches we can use to face the MQTT security problem:

1. Create a VPN between the clients and the server.
2. Use MQTT over SSL/TSL to encrypt and secure the information between the MQTT clients and MQTT broker.

Our attention is, on how to create an **MQTT over SSL**. To make MQTT a secure protocol, we have to follow these steps:

- Create a private key (CA Key).
- Generate a certificate using the private key (CA cert).
- Create a certificate for Mosquitto MQTT server with the key.

The final step is configuring Mosquitto MQTT so that it uses these certificates.

3.4 Securing MQTT Server

The first step in this process is creating a private key. Connect to the Raspberry Pi using ssh or a remote desktop and open a command terminal. Before starting, it is important to ensure OpenSSL is installed on Raspberry Pi.

[openssl genrsa -out mosq-ca.key 2048]

Using this command, we are creating a 2048-bit key called mosq-ca.key. The result is shown in the picture below:

The next step is creating an X509 certificate that uses the private key generated in the previous step. Open the terminal again and, in the same directory in which private key is stored, write:

[openssl req -new -x509 -days365 -key mosq-ca.key -out mosq-ca.crt]

In this step, we need to provide different information before creating the certificate.

- Country Name
- State or Provenance Name
- Locality Name
- Organization Name
- Organizational Unit Name
- Common Name
- Email Address.

3.5 Creating the MQTT Server Certificate

Once the private key and the certificate are ready, we can create the MQTT server certificate and private key:

$$[openssl\,genrsa\ -out\,mosq\text{-}serv.key\,2048] \qquad (1)$$

During this step, we need to create a CSR (Certificate Signing Request). This certificate should be sent to the Certification authority that, after verifying the author identity, returns a certificate. We will use a self-signed certificate:

$$[openssl\,req\ -new\ -key\,mosq\text{-}serv.key\ -out\,mosq\text{-}serv.csr] \qquad (2)$$

we have used the private key generated in the step before. Finally, we can create the certificate to use in our MQTT Mosquitto Server:

$$[openssl\,x509\ -req\ -in\,mosq\text{-}serv.csr\ -CA\,mosq\text{-}ca.crt\ -CAkey\,mosq\text{-}ca.key\ -$$

$$CAcreateserial - out\,mosq\text{-}serv.crt\ -days\,365\ -sha256] \qquad (3)$$

All done! We have completed the steps necessary to secure our MQTT server.

$$[openssl\,x509\ -in\,mosq\text{-}serv.crt\ -noout\ -text\,javascript{:}void(0)] \qquad (4)$$

4 CoAP (Constrained Application Protocol)

CoAP runs over UDP, not TCP. Clients and servers communicate through connectionless datagrams. Retries and reordering are implemented in the application stack. Removing the need for TCP may allow full IP networking in small microcontrollers. CoAP allows UDP broadcast and multicast to be used for addressing. CoAP follows a client/server model. Clients make requests to servers, servers send back responses. Clients may GET, PUT, POST and DELETE resources. CoAP employs a client-server model and request/response message pattern, where client devices send information requests directly to server devices, which then respond. Support for an observer message pattern enables clients to receive an update whenever a requested state changes, for example a valve opening or closing, while confirmed message delivery provides some level of assurance under the connectionless UDP transport.

The Constrained Application Protocol (CoAP) is a web transfer protocol at the application layer intended to be used with constrained devices The Internet Engineering Task Force (IETF) working group has designed this protocol to be used for M2M applications, IoT objects and suitable for constrained devices that have limited amount of ROM and RAM [9]. One design goal of CoAP is limiting the need for fragmentation by using small message overhead. Moreover, this protocol suitable for constrained networks such as 6LoWPAN which supports the fragmentation of IPv6 packets into small frames. CoAP provides an interaction model similar to the client/server of HTTP.

0			1	2	3

```
 0                   1                   2                   3
 0 1 2 3 4 5 6 7 8 9 0 1 2 3 4 5 6 7 8 9 0 1 2 3 4 5 6 7 8 9 0 1
┌─┬─┬───┬───────────┬───────────────────────────────────────────┐
│V│T│TKL│   Code    │              Message ID                     │
├─┴─┴───┴───────────┴───────────────────────────────────────────┤
│              Token (if any, TKL bytes) ...                      │
├────────────────────────────────────────────────────────────────┤
│              Options (if any) ...                               │
├─────────────────┬──────────────────────────────────────────────┤
│ 1 1 1 1 1 1 1 1 │          Payload (if any) ...                 │
└─────────────────┴──────────────────────────────────────────────┘
```

Fig. 5. CoAP message format

CoAP Architecture as shown it extends normal HTTP clients to clients having resource constraints. These clients are known as CoAP clients. Proxy device bridges gap between constrained environment and typical internet environment based on HTTP protocols. Same server takes care of both HTTP and CoAP protocol messages [4].

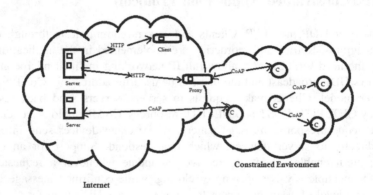

Fig. 6. CoAP architecture

4.1 DTLS for CoAP Security

DTLS is used more than CoAP to provide continuous security. Just as TLS being used for securing HTTP over TCP, Datagram TLS (DTLS) is used for securing CoAP over UDP. DTLS is implemented between transport layer and application layer as in Fig. 7. As DTLS operated on top of the UDP protocol, the complexity of its implementation increased which requires mechanisms to provide reliability. To design a DTLS version that can be used in constrained environments, it is important to minimize the code size, and the number of messages exchanged to get an optimized handshake protocol.

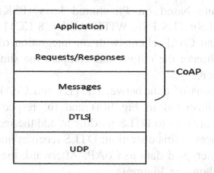

Fig. 7. Abstract Layering of DTLS-Secured CoAP

Figure 8 shows how the DTLS handshake works using CoAP, providing communication reliability by CON and ACK messages using CoAP block-wise transfer which contain DTLS handshake messages as a payload. When the DTLS handshake session has finished, the client can initiate the first CoAP request.

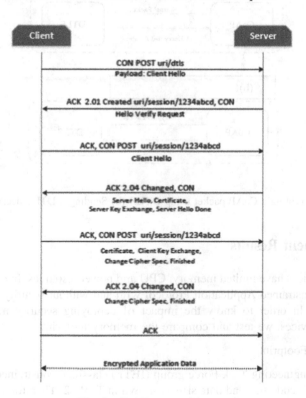

Fig. 8. CoAP protocol layers

4.2 DTLS over CoAP (CoAPs)

DTLS protocol can be integrated with CoAP to provide end-to-end security. In this implementation, we used the open source TinyDTLS and CoAP libraries. Tiny DTLS supports the cipher suite based on Pre-shared keys (PSK) with the Advanced Encryption Standard (AES): TLS PSK WITH AES 128 CCM 8. We implement two nodes a CoAP server and CoAP client, with an integration of Tiny DTLS for both server and client. We observe the output and compare the simulation result with the previous CoAP simulation.

The general interactions of data between DTLS and CoAP in both forward and reverse directions are illustrated in Fig. 9(a) and (b) respectively. In the forward direction, CoAP packets are sent to DTLS module to add the security functionality [3].

There are two interfaces in this operation: DTLS receives normal data packets from CoAP and then sends encrypted data to CoAP. Afterward, the encrypted packets are sent across to UDP as shown in Figure (a).

In the reverse direction, the secured packets received from UDP are sent across to DTLS for decryption then sending it back to CoAP as shown in Figure (b).

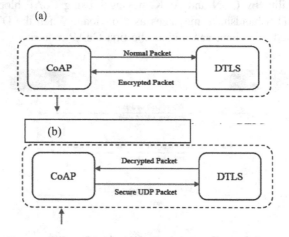

Fig. 9. (a) Encrypting a CoAP packet using DTLS (b) Sending a DTLS decrypted to CoAP

5 Experiment Results

IoT sensor devices have limited memory, CPU and power resources. In our experiment, we test the Constrained Application Protocol with and without security in constrained sensor nodes. In order to know the impact of deploying security mechanisms on constrained devices, we test and compare the memory footprint:

(a) Memory Footprint

The Internet Engineering Task Force group (IETF) classified constrained devices with consideration of code size and data size as shown in Table 2. Therefore, it is important to know the code size and the data size for an application to measure the memory usage. The difficulty of providing a secure communication increase with limited resources. The classification of constrained devices is shown below:

Class 0 devices are very constrained nodes. They have limited memory and processing capabilities and may not have enough resources to communicate securely and directly to the Internet. Thus, they need a help of larger devices such as a proxy or gateway to participate in Internet communications.

Class 1 devices are quite constrained nodes. They cannot easily use full protocol stack such as HTTP or TLS. However, they are capable to use protocols that designed for constrained nodes such as CoAP over UDP. In our implementation, we use Wismote node which has 16 KB of RAM and 128 KB ROM and considered as a class 1 device.

Class 2 devices can support most protocols used in Internet communication.

Table 2. Classes of constrained devices

Name	Data size (e.g., RAM)	Code size (e.g., Flash)
Class 0	$\ll$ 10 KB	$\ll$ 100 KB
Class 1	$\sim$ 10 KB	$\sim$ 100 KB
Class 2	$\sim$ 50 KB	$\sim$ 250 KB

The memory footprint is provided by the MSP430-GCC compiler. We obtained the RAM and ROM by utilizing the MSP430-GCC size command of the firmware files. Table 3 shows the require memory size for both server and client with and without security implementation for Wismote sensor. Figures 10 and 11 show the impact of deploying security for CoAP. The difference of the RAM size between the two codes is about 30%. Whereas, the flash memory or ROM has increased by approximately 59%.

Table 3. Memory footprint

Node type	RAM [bytes]	ROM [bytes]
CoAP Client	8210	44831
CoAP Server	8200	50224
CoAPs Client	11396	86583
CoAPs Server	11274	89737

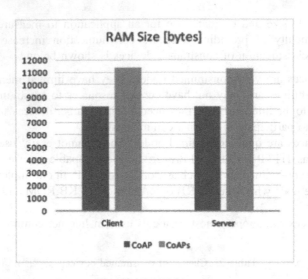

Fig. 10. RAM footprint

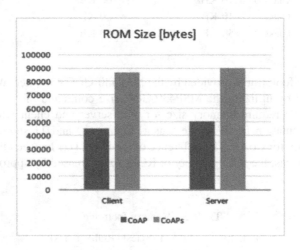

Fig. 11. ROM footprint

6 Conclusion

The Internet of Things is considered as one of the largest improvement to the existing technology nowadays. It is extremely important to have a secure IoT system in order to develop and improve this technology to be used in a large scale. In this paper, we address the fundamentals of the Internet of things and the key features and requirements. Followed by the the Constrained Application Protocol (CoAP) as it will be a significant part of IoT. We present an overview of the Datagram Transport Layer Protocol (DTLS) which is one way of providing an end-to-end security for IoT applications. We also addressed security techniques for securing MQTT protocol, which is also one of the important protocol of IOT.

References

1. Asim, M.: A survey on application layer protocols for Internet of Things (IoT). Int. J. Adv. Res. Comput. Sci. **8**(3), 996–1000 (2017). ISSN 0976-5697
2. Kraijak, S., Tuwanut, P.: A survey on IoT architectures, protocols, applications, security, privacy, real-world implementation and future trends. In: 11th International Conference on Wireless Communications, Networking and Mobile Computing (WiCOM 2015), pp. 1–6, September 2015. https://doi.org/10.1049/cp.2015.0714
3. Rahman, R.A., Shah, B.: Security analysis of IoT protocols: a focus in CoAP. In: 2016 3rd MEC International Conference on Big Data and Smart City (ICBDSC), pp. 1–7. IEEE (2016)
4. Ugrenovic, D., Gardasevic, G.: CoAP protocol for web-based monitoringin IoT healthcare applications. In: 2015 23rd Telecommunications Forum Telfor(TELFOR), pp. 79–82, November 2015
5. Thangavel, D., Ma, X., Valera, A., Tan, H.-X., Tan, C.K.-Y.: Performance evaluation of MQTT and CoAP via a common middleware. In: IEEE Ninth International Conference on Intelligent Sensors, Sensor Networks and Information Processing 2014, Singapore (2014). ISSNIP.2014.6827678
6. Chen, M., Wan, J., Gonzalez, S., Liao, X., Leung, V.C.M.: A survey of recent developments in home M2M networks. IEEE Commun. Surv. Tutor. **16**(1), 98–114 (2014). First Quarter
7. Wang, M., Zhang, G., Zhang, C., Zhang, J., Li, C.: An IoT-based appliance control system for smart homes. In: 2013 Fourth International Conference on Intelligent Control and Information Processing (ICICIP), pp. 744–747, 9–11 June 2013
8. Miorandi, D., Sicari, S., De Pellegrini, F., Chlamtac, I.: Internet of Things: vision, applications and research challenges. Ad Hoc Netw. **10**(7), 1497–1516 (2012)
9. Ishaq, I., Hoebeke, J., Moerman, I., Demeester, P.: Experimental evaluation of unicast and multicast CoAP group communication. Sensors **16**(7), 1–8 (2016). NCBI

Forensic Analysis of a Virtual Android Phone

Aman Sharma[1], Animesh Kumar Agrawal[2(✉)], Bhupendra Kumar[3],
and Pallavi Khatri[2]

[1] GFSU, Gandhinagar, India
amansharma1894@gmail.com
[2] Department of CSE, ITM University, Gwalior, India
akag9906@gmail.com,
pallavi.khatri.cse@itmuniversity.ac.in
[3] Raipur, India

Abstract. With the world moving towards digital era and India's special thrust in making the country a cashless economy, the use of digital device is increasing phenomenally and with it, the number of digital frauds. However, with increasing security features and new mobile versions being released on a near daily basis, getting an analysis tool which can extract data from most of the mobiles is a herculean task. To overcome this challenge, there is a need to carry out research on forensics analysis of smart phones. Since Android OS has a near monopoly in the smartphone market, the mobile forensics has to be focused more towards Android phones. This work tries to present a novel method of forensic analysis of Android phones in a virtualized environment using an emulator called Genymotion.

Keywords: Mobile forensics · Virtual device · Genymotion · Root
Android

1 Introduction

With the increased awareness and proliferation of mobile devices to the rural population, the digital transactions have more than quadrupled in the recent years. And with it the cases of digital crimes and financial frauds have also increased drastically. In order to prevent such cases from boomeranging, it is very important that digital forensics is given adequate importance. Since, people are migrating to smart phones for all their personal and official work, the importance of mobile forensics needs no additional emphasis. Android based smartphones have more than 80% of market share and hence this research is also based on forensic analysis of android phones.

In order to extract data from an android phone, there is a need to get hold of a physical phone. However, with so many android versions in the market, getting hold of devices with different android versions would not be practically feasible to carry out a study. To overcome this difficulty, an android emulator called Genymotion was used. Trial version of the emulator called "Genymotion for Personal Use" [1] was used for this research. Version 2.11.0 of Genymotion for Windows base OS was downloaded and installed in a virtual box environment. Genymotion is available for other platforms such as Linux and Mac, too. There are a number of android emulators as brought out in Fig. 1 like the one supplied by android developers themselves as part of Android Studio, Bluestacks, Genymotion, YouWave etc. However, the user friendly interface and ease of use makes Genymotion a better choice for the research.

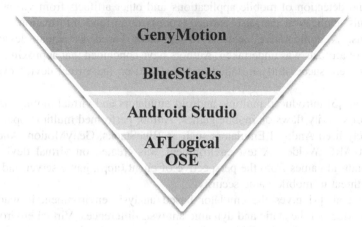

Fig. 1. Different types of android emulators both commercial as well as free.

Android emulators have traditionally been used for testing apps and games before deployment, because they provide an exact replica of the actual environment of physical android phone. Since the behavior and interface of a virtually created device is exactly the same as experienced in a real android device, it was used to carry out the present research. Non-availability of actual android devices was also a motivation to work on an emulator.

Using an emulator has multiple advantages. Being a virtual interface, it can be used any number of times without any issue of damage of operating system or loss of data. Malware behavior can also be easily analyzed in an emulator as there is no problem of infection during testing. Also, extracting data becomes easier since problems of enabling usb debugging, stay awake, RSA key fingerprint, etc. is not there in a virtual device. Another major plus point of using a virtual device is that a desired test environment can be created which may not be feasible in a real phone thus providing a better platform for testing. The challenge of rooting the phone to access the file system and deleted data is also overcome in a virtual device.

The paper is organized as follows: In Sect. 2 work done by other authors along with their proposed techniques has been discussed. Section 3 brings out the essential steps to create the virtual device on the emulator. Section 4 elucidates the simulation results. Section 5 concludes by summarizing the work.

2 Literature Survey

Alzaylaee et al. [2] discussed about the basic mobile forensic procedure consisting of static and dynamic analysis. The research was carried out on android emulator (android SDK) due to wide range of features and easy accessibility. The analysis was done on real as well as virtual environment. Authors proposed a tool named Bouncer, for analysis and detection of mobile applications and other artifacts from virtual android device. This application can also extract process dump and information of running applications. A comparative analysis of emulator based vs actual device based extraction of artifacts was undertaken. Authors have concluded that approximately 24% more apps were successfully installed and analyzed on the virtual device over actual phone.

Lee et al. [3] introduced multiple android emulators and virtual mobile devices for detection of security flaws on mobile games. Author performed multiple operations on some widely used Android Emulators such as BlueStacks, GenyMotion, Andy, You-Wave and ARC Welder. A test environment was created on virtual device to test multiple android games from the perspective of client (app), game server and network to reduce threat to mobile game security.

Singh et al. [4] gives the emulator based analysis environment instead of real devices to bring out the static and dynamic analysis differences. Virtual environment is created for analysis of an intelligent apk that can extract the details of the device like IEMI number, GPS locations, call details etc. As it is in an emulator and all the operations are performed on virtual device instead of real device, thereafter it can act benignly and pass the test undetected and keep the environment anonymous.

Shavers et al. [5] discuss virtual machine concepts and forensic analysis of any virtual environment hosted on an emulator. Authors have described the basic architecture of a virtual device, its configuration and the way to enhance the performance of any virtual machine. Restoring virtual machines with respect to forensic procedures and analysis is also discussed by the authors. The paper also discusses the procedure of taking the 'dd' image, dump of system ram (nvram), virtual disks (vmdk), vmx files, vss (snapshots), etc. Booting process of any forensic image (dd) on virtual machine is also discussed.

Sylve et al. [6] talks about acquiring physical memory of an android device and its analysis. The authors said that that there is no direct method available to acquire physical memory of a phone. A rooted HTC EVO 4G with different versions of kernel was used to gather the test results. Extensive use of built in emulator of Android SDK has been done to perform repeated tests. Plugins have been developed for Volatility software for carrying out the memory acquisition.

Grispos et al. [7] has tried to present the comparison of the different methods by which information can be extracted from a Windows mobile phone. The HTC Touch Pro2 running Windows version 6.1 Professional OS was used for testing the results. The paper mainly focuses on use of Cellebrite UFED as an acquisition tool.

Numerous studies have been done by researchers on virtual device and android emulators that provides an exact platform as the actual device. Some of the novel researches and approaches are discussed above which illustrate with mobile forensic.

Emulator is being increasingly used to carry out research on android platform because of ease of use and similarity with actual device.

3   Experimental Setup

The experimental setup was created using four virtual Android devices having four different Android versions. To create virtual phones Genymotion trial version is used and TAMER4 (a Linux based android forensic VM) is used to connect the physical phone with systems for analysis.

In order to carry out the various experiments, the following hardware and software were utilized:-

- Genymotion trial version software
- Tamer4 VM
- Virtual box software
- wxHexEditor
- adb commands
- MOBILEdit Forensic Tool
- Test Data consisting of two different file types i.e. pdf and jpeg.

To create a virtual Android phone a series of steps is followed which are as described below:-

3.1   Step 1

After installing Genymotion go to the virtual device creation wizard and then select the device model along with the Android version as shown in Fig. 2. The phone models whose image is provided in the emulator are visible to the user. However, an account has to be created in Genymotion and logged in to get access to these virtual images.

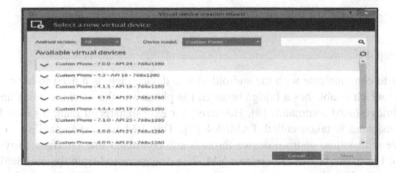

Fig. 2. List of custom phone images with respect to their specific android versions.

3.2 Step 2

A dialogue box appears asking for the confirmation for creating and deploying the virtual device as shown in Fig. 3.

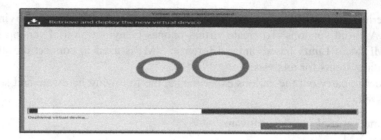

Fig. 3. New virtual phone being created.

3.3 Step 3

After the successful creation of the virtual device a screen will appear as shown in the Fig. 4 given below.

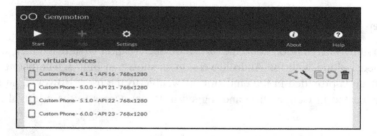

Fig. 4. Different virtual phone with their android version.

3.4 Step 4

In order to communicate with the android virtual device there is a need to have a base machine which establishes a bridge between the phone and the machine using android debug bridge (adb) commands [8]. However, for easy transfer of data, a Linux based virtual machine is taken called TAMER4 [9]. This VM has the capability to communicate with virtual android device through adb command line interface. Any other flavor of Linux can be used to create a VM. The data extracted from the mobile device is stored in this VM and subsequently analyzed using a free Hex editor like wxHexEditor [10]. The data dumped from the mobile device is in a raw format which cannot be read in a text editor. In the absence of memory map of an android device, interpretation of the hex dump is a puzzle which needs to be solved. For this, use of header and footer concept has been used as described in [12] which is unique to each file type (Fig. 5).

Fig. 5. Android virtual phone (Ver 6.0) created in Genymotion

4 Simulation Results and Discussion

In order to check the efficacy of our proposed work, experiment was done on different android versions as brought out in Table 1.

Table 1. Depicts different virtual devices which were created in Genymotion along with their Android versions.

Virtual devices	Versions	Name
Device 1	4.1	Jelly Bean
Device 2	4.4	Kitkat
Device 3	5.0	Lollypop
Device 4	6.0	Marshmallow

All the devices given in Table 1 were created on custom phones using Genymotion as a virtual platform. Virtual phones having different android versions as shown in Table 1 have been illustrated in Fig. 6.

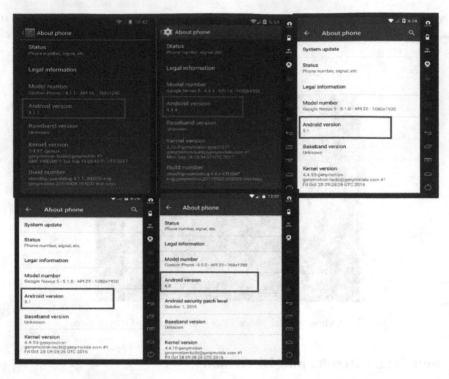

Fig. 6. Virtual android devices having different android versions.

After storing the test data on each of the device, the same was manually extracted from each of the created virtual device. In order to check whether the data extracted was the actual data, the hex dump in the form of dd image was fed to universally accepted and used, licensed commercial mobile forensic tool called MOBILedit [11] and the experiment was repeated. The files extracted were compared by comparing their hash values. The complete set of experiment was repeated by deleting the test data and then trying the recover the deleted files. The result of the experiments is tabulated in the result section.

4.1   Experiment I

In this experiment test data containing two different file types (pdf and jpeg) i.e. one sample of each file type was pushed into the virtual device's "sdcard". As these virtual emulator based custom android devices are already rooted, so all the four virtual devices were connected one by one to the Android Tamer using "adb connect". Raw image was then extracted from/data partition using "dd" command. The table given below illustrates the data extracted from one virtual phone. The image made through dd command was given as input to MOBILedit for each of the 04 android virtual phones and the test data was extracted (Table 2).

Table 2. Depicts the successful extraction of non-deleted test data from manual method as well as from commercial tools.

File types	Data extracted from virtual phone version 5.1	
	Manual	Tool 1
JPEG(1)	✓	✓
PDF(1)	✓	✓

Similarly, the process was repeated for rest of the Android versions i.e. 4.1, 4.4 and 6.0 respectively.

4.2 Experiment II

This experiment demonstrates the extraction of the deleted data using the method described in Experiment I. For this the sample data that was pushed into the device was deleted intentionally. Before deleting, names of the files were noted down for further comparison. After deleting, dd image of all the four devices were made and data was extracted. Similarly, experiment II was also repeated for rest the Android versions. The raw dump was then searched for the deleted files using headers and footers [12] as the data that was deleted was of known file types. As it was described earlier two different file formats i.e. jpeg and pdf were taken for the experiment (Figs. 7 and 8).

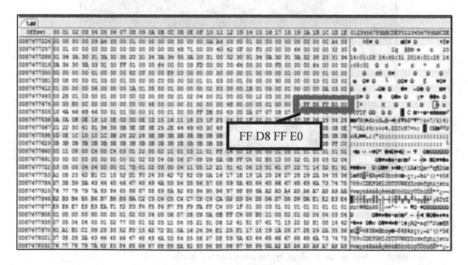

Fig. 7. Shows the header of the jpeg file.

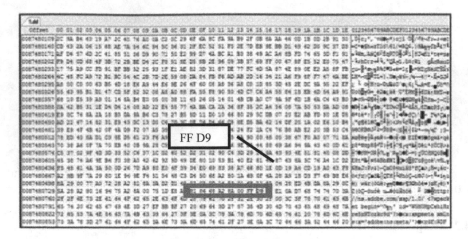

Fig. 8. Shows the footer of a jpeg file

The bytes between this header and footer were selected and were saved as .jpeg file. The output was a complete recovered .jpeg image file as shown below in Fig. 9. Similarly the process was repeated for the pdf file format and both the files were successfully extracted using this method. Table 3 given below shows the results.

Fig. 9. Shows the recovered deleted image (.jpeg).

Table 3. Depicts the successful extraction of deleted test data from manual method as well as from commercial tool.

File Types	Data extracted from virtual phone version 5.1	
	Manual	Tool 1
PDF(1)	✓	✓
JPEG(1)	✓	✓

Successfully extracted test data in Table 3 illustrates that apart from these two file formats that have been used in this paper many other types of files can be recovered using this method. Maintaining integrity is one of the best practices in the forensics process. So the hash of the test data before and after extraction was verified to make the results more relevant.

Hash of the test data was taken before and after the experiments was carried out. If the values matched, then it proved that the evidence was not tampered during the forensic process. Given below is the hash of the .jpeg file in Figs. 10 and 11 which was calculated before and after the experiment.

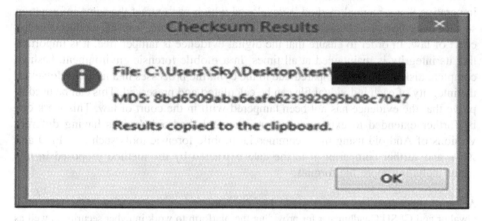

Fig. 10. Shows the MD5 hash value of the original file (.jpeg).

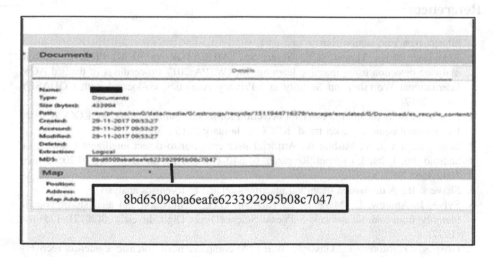

Fig. 11. Shows the MD5 hash value of the deleted file (.jpeg) after recovery

The data got successfully extracted through the method proposed in this paper which proves that data can also be taken out from the Android devices in the absence of commercially available mobile forensic tools.

5   Conclusion and Future Work

The work brings out a novel method of extracting data from an android device using manual method without the use of expensive commercial mobile forensic tools. In any academic institution, small scale industry or medium enterprise, creating a cyber-forensic setup is an expensive proposition. In the absence of commercial tools, it is imperative that a manual method is developed which can extract the same information so that the culprit can be brought to books and the evidence can be produced in the court of law. In order to ensure that the digital evidence is tamper free, it is important that its integrity is maintained at all times. In a mobile forensic environment, hash of complete disk cannot be compared due to the dynamic processes in a mobile. However, the integrity of each individual file can be calculated and preserved. This can be used to prove that the evidence has not been tampered with in the court of law. This work can be further extended to extract data from physical Android devices having different versions of Android using more commercial mobile forensic tools such as UFED and XRY and further comparing it to the data extracted by the method proposed in this paper including more file formats.

Acknowledgments. The authors would like to express sincere gratitude to ITM University Gwalior and GFSU Gandhinagar for providing the platform to work in cyber security as well as mobile forensics.

References

1. https://www.genymotion.com
2. Alzaylaee, M.K., Yerima, S.Y., Sezer, S.: EMULATOR vs REAL PHONE: android malware detection using machine learning. In: IWSPA 2017 Proceedings of the 3rd ACM International Workshop on Security and Privacy Analytics, co-located with CODASPY 2017 (2017)
3. Lee, S.: A study on android emulator detection for mobile game security. In: KOCCA, 2014 International content market trend, KOCCA, January 2015
4. Singh, S., Singh, S., Mishra, B.: Artificial user emulator to detect intelligent malware on android. Int. J. Intell. Comput. Research. **6**, 640–646 (2015). https://doi.org/10.20533/ijicr. 2042.4655.2015.0079
5. Shavers, B.: A discussion of virtual machines related to forensics analysis
6. Sylve, J., Andrew, C., Marziale, L., Richard, G.G.: Acquisition and analysis of volatile memory from android devices. SciVerse ScienceDirect Digit. Investig. **8**(2012), 175–184 (1997)
7. Grispos, G., Storer, T., Glission, W.B.: A comparison of forensic evidence recovery techniques for a windows mobile smart phone. Digit. Investig.: Int. J. Digit. Forensics Incid. Response. **8**(1), 23–36 (2011)

8. https://developer.android.com/studio/command-line/adb.html
9. https://androidtamer.com/tamer4-release
10. http://www.wxhexeditor.org/download.php
11. http://www.mobiledit.com/
12. https://www.garykessler.net/library/file_sigs.html

Implementation of Security Algorithm and Achieving Energy Efficiency for Increasing Lifetime of Wireless Sensor Network

Harshal Misalkar, Umesh Nikam[✉], and Anup Burange[✉]

Amravati, India
{hdmisalkar, uvnikam, awburange}@mitra.ac.in

Abstract. The wireless sensor network is mainly needed for smart network functions or for emergency solutions where human interface is not possible. It is made of large number sensors for monitoring the physical and environmental situations e.g. Temperature, sound and motion etc. Main limitation of WSN is low power and minimum processing as well as they have to self organized as per the requirements of user. If WSN are installed in remote location, it become to much difficult to recharge the battery. In order to increase Lifetime of WSN sustainable consumption of power is required. This paper presents an approach for the cluster Head selection using basic information of node and objective functions. The proposed work minimizes the length of the packet by processing the data at the node. Moreover we emphasize on Node state switching mechanism which helps to increase the lifetime of WSN. With these things, the confidentiality, integrity and authentication of the communicated information becomes vital. In this article, we have focused on a lightweight encryption technique which encompasses faster encryption thereby, bringing down the computing time which increases the duration i.e. lifespan of wireless sensor network. The introduction of both symmetric and asymmetric cryptography in the two phase hybrid encryption algorithm, check marks the main aim of cryptography, i.e., Confidentiality, Integrity and Authenticity. Moreover hybrid encryption attempts to exploit the advantages of both symmetric and asymmetric encryption.

Keywords: Sensor nodes · Cluster heads · WSNs · Lifetime · Encryption
Decryption

1 Introduction

Wireless sensor network is a field which contains large number of applications such as distributed system processing, embedded systems, wireless communications and have contributed a large revolution in Sensor Network (WSN) [7]. Wireless Sensor Network are a collection of small devices of low power, low cost, light weight sensor nodes working together to capture/monitor a particular event like temperature, pressure, movement etc [8]. Each sensor node sense the event, process it and communicate it with the other nodes present in same network [12]. Wireless sensor network are used in different application areas which includes home automation, healthcare, traffic control, industrial monitoring and many more [1]. A sensor node consists of power unit,

© Springer Nature Singapore Pte Ltd. 2019
S. Verma et al. (Eds.): CNC 2018, CCIS 839, pp. 298–307, 2019.
https://doi.org/10.1007/978-981-13-2372-0_26

communication unit, processing unit and sensing unit [9] as shown in below fig (Fig. 1).

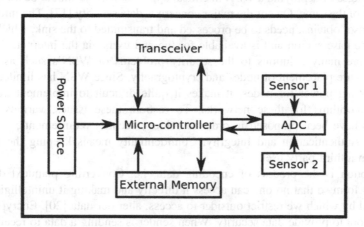

Fig. 1. Sensor node architecture

1.1 The Characteristics of Wireless Sensor Network

- Capability to ensure strict environmental conditions.
- Wireless sensor network are simple to use [15].
- It has capacity to handle with node failures.
- Cross Layer Design.
- Limited power consumption to save the battery [10].
- Wireless sensor network are scalable in nature.

1.2 Important Ways to Save the Energy/Power of WSN

- Deployment of the sensor nodes in Wire Sensor Network [6].
- Power Efficient Clustering Strategy is used [5].
  Power Effective Scheduling approach is used.
- It support power Efficient routing technique is used.
- Fix time interval is used by sensor node to switch from Active to Idle and Idle to Active in order to save energy [2].
- Coding methodologies to minimize the quantity of data.
- It ensure an optimal transaction between connectivity and energy consumption [3].
- Data Aggregation.

2 Security

The advantages of deploying a WSN in critical applications, one should be aware of the limitations of the same. One of the major concern is data security [17]. The information that the sensor obtains, needs to be processed and transmitted to the sink, which is then given to the base station and is available for the end users via the internet.

There are many solutions to the security problems of WSN's such as, routing security, secure placement of nodes and cryptography. Since WSN has limited energy and processing power for nodes, it makes it quite difficult to implement traditional security algorithms for these networks. To restrain these issues, various security algorithms have been proposed in order to achieve security requirements, i.e. Confidentiality, Authentication and Integrity. Confidentiality means keeping the message secret from a third party user.

Encryption is the process of encoding data, i.e. Converting plaintext data into cipher text form so that no one can access it directly and making it unintelligible. It is the method by which we restrict outsider to access, alter our data [20]. Encryption is a powerful tool to provide data security. When sender is sending a data to receiver, it is important to maintain data integrity so that receiver will receive in-order data. Such cryptographic services protect confidential data such as credit card number by converting plaintext data into unreadable cipher text (Fig. 2).

There are two types of cryptography algorithm

(1) Symmetric key algorithm
(2) Asymmetric key algorithm.

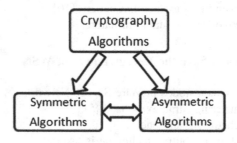

Fig. 2. Cryptography algorithms

3 Proposed Mechanism

Many researchers have point out different procedures for minimizing power consumption and increase wireless sensor network lifespan during data communication (Fig. 3).

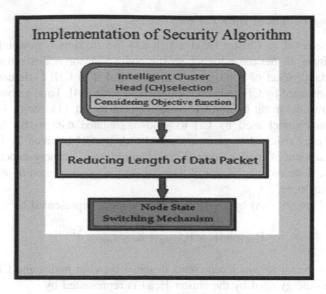

Fig. 3. Proposed mechanism

3.1 Cluster Head Selection

In wireless sensor network, all nodes sense the data from their respective environment and send it to the most powerful (which has maximum energy/power) node of Wireless Sensor Network called Cluster Head [19]. Well defined desired procedure is required to select particular node as Head of WSN. Election procedure among all the nodes on the basis of auction data which made-up of Local battery power, external battery support and overall topology power [4].

The maximum duration of the node within network, is represented by

$$T_{Emax} = \text{TEAE}_m + \text{Eo} \tag{1}$$

Where Eo = is the value of External battery backup [1].

3.2 Objective Function

We are considering objective function to increase the working duration of the network which will be based on external battery support and local available strengths

$$\text{Max } \beta 0 = (\Delta_m) + \text{Bj}^* \Delta m \tag{2}$$

$\beta 0$ is represent value of sum of total duration (Life).

$$\text{Where Bj} = 1 \tag{3}$$

Hence to determine lifetime of WSN we are analyzing local energy and external energy from all adjacent nodes in the network [1].

3.3 Reducing Length of Data Packet

The node is selected as Cluster Head which has the maximum power [16]. It will receive data from all desired adjacent sensor nodes. Sensor nodes sense the event, generate the data packet of appropriate size and send it to CH. Different amount of energy will consumed by CH and non Cluster Head node [14]. Total amount of energy required to sense the event by non CH node is given by Eq. (1). Single or Multi hop communication channel used by CH to send aggregated data to the base station. Amount of energy required to perform desired task by CH is given by Eq. (2). It is analyzed that amount of energy required for communication purpose depend on length of data packet. If we reduce the size of data packet then energy used to send that data packet is also reduces.

Amount of energy used by non cluster head node is represented by

$$E_{NCH} = K \times E_{elecsig} + K \times \varepsilon_{mp} \times d^4 \tag{4}$$

Where d is the value which represents distance between nodes and Cluster Head. Amount of energy used by the cluster Head is represented by

$$E_{CH} = K \times (E_{elecsig} + E_{DTAgg}) + K \times \varepsilon_{mp} \times d^4 \tag{5}$$

$E_{TotErg} = E_{NCH} + E_{CH}$

E_{DtAgg} is the total amount of energy required for data aggregation purpose by the Cluster Head [1].

Further Delta modulation technique is being used to reduce energy consumption.

Amount of energy used by the Cluster Head near to the Base Station with Delta Modulation technique is represented by

$$E = k \times E_{elecsig} \{N + (n+1)\} + n \times k \times \varepsilon_{mp} \times d^4 CH, BS \tag{6}$$

N is the total number of nodes within a cluster. And n is the total number of data packet to be transmitted.

Amount of energy used by the nodes without Delta Modulation technique

$$E = (2n-1) \times K \times E_{elecsig} + n \times K \times \varepsilon_{mp} \times d^4 \tag{7}$$

Amount of energy used by the nodes with Delta Modulation technique is represented by

$$E_{DM} = (2n-1) \times k \times E_{elecsig} + n \times k \times \varepsilon_{mp} \times d^4 \tag{8}$$

n is the total number of data packets transmitted in the cluster.

k represents value of data packet length. (k < K) Hence the huge energy is saved [1].

3.4   Node State Switching Mechanism

In this paper we used node state (active and idle) switching technique which helps to increase the life of the wireless sensor network.

Suppose A and B are two nodes of Wireless Sensor Network. Nodes either in active mode or idle mode. Two types of communications are taken in consideration i.e. Node to node and node to base station. If node A is self sufficient to control overall network then node B will enter in idle mode, after fix time interval node B will enter in active state to know whether the network is still under control with A or not. To do this B will send a data packet to A and it will wait for acknowledgement (Fig. 4).

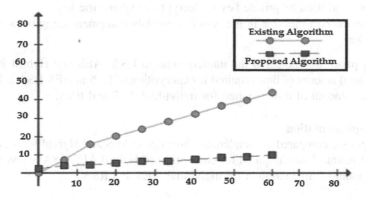

Fig. 4. Graphical result shows energy consumption

3.5   Implementation of Security Algorithm

In proposed algorithm our goal is to combine two algorithm called RSA and AES to form Hybrid AES and RSA (Fig. 5).

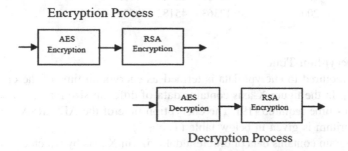

Fig. 5. Block diagram of hybrid AES and RSA

To encrypt a message in a hybrid system, Sender performs the following:

- First Receiver public key is required.
- Data encapsulation technique is being used for which new symmetric key is generated.
- Newly generated symmetric key is used to encrypt the message.
- Receiver's public key will be used to encrypt the symmetric key under the key encapsulation technique.
- Send both of these encryptions to Receiver.

To decrypt this hybrid cipher text, Receiver performs the following

- Receiver will used its private key to decrypt the symmetric key
- Receiver decrypt message in the data encapsulation segment using the same symmetric key.

In this paper we compared the implementation RSA, AES and Hybrid RSA and AES. The total amount of time required for encryption of Hybrid AES-RSA is less than that of total amount of time required for individual AES and RSA.

3.5.1   Implementation

In this paper we compared the implementation RSA, AES and Hybrid RSA and AES. The total amount of time required for encryption of Hybrid AES-RSA is less than that of total amount of time required for individual AES and RSA.

Table 1. Encryption time for each algorithm

Data size (bytes)	AES	RSA	Hybrid AES and RSA
100	128033	5855	5358
500	126531	21903	12292
1000	126039	29907	21220
1500	126018	38347	31103
2000	123639	45182	40522

3.5.2   Encryption Time

Total time required to encrypt data is termed as encryption time of the cryptographic system [17]. In the figure X-axis contains data of different size for experiments and Y axis contains time required [19]. The encryption time of the AES, RSA and proposed hybrid algorithm is given in below table (Table 1):

The diagram contains data of different data size in X axis by which experiments are conducted. Similarly Y axis contains amount of time in microseconds. The results show proposed algorithm consumes less time as compared to AES and RSA algorithm. According to mean performance proposed Hybrid algorithm consumes less amount of time with respect to AES and RSA algorithm (Fig. 6).

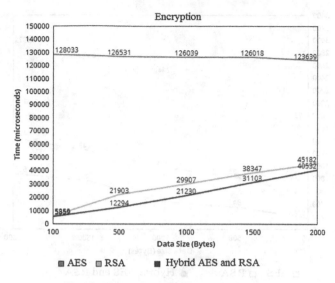

Fig. 6. Encryption time for each algorithm

The time to recover original data from cipher is known as decryption time [17]. Figure shows comparative performance of AES, RSA [18] and proposed Hybrid algorithm. In this figure X-axis contains data of different size for experiments and Y axis contains time required. The total amount of time required for decryption in the proposed algorithm is efficient as compared to individual AES and RSA algorithm (Table 2).

Table 2. Decryption time for each algorithm

Data size (bytes)	AES	RSA	Hybrid AES and RSA
100	533	1720	174
500	824	2146	345
1000	976	2442	432
1500	1243	2672	763
2000	1426	2922	863

The results as defined in figure shows, the proposed technique is efficient as compared to AES and RSA algorithm. The results shows proposed Hybrid algorithm provides advantage over AES and RSA algorithm. Thus proposed technique reduces the time consumption as compared to both AES and RSA algorithm (Fig. 7).

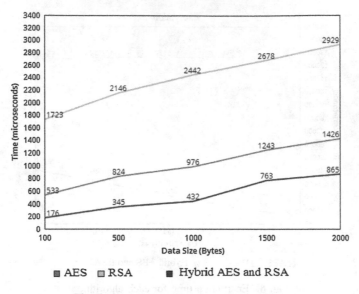

Fig. 7. Decryption time for each algorithm

4 Conclusion

In This paper we are proposing a different technique in order to improve the efficiency and Lifetime of Wireless sensor network. It considers the objective function effectively to select a Cluster Head. We have discussed mainly four approaches: First regarding selection of Cluster Head considering objective function. Second approach is a method to reduce length of data packet. Third approach is for node state switching mechanism to maximize lifetime of network. Final approach is to protect intended data from hacking by using Hybrid cryptography.

In fourth approach we discussed about cryptography AES and RSA and our proposed hybrid algorithm using AES and RSA algorithms. Cryptographic algorithms play a very important role in Network security. The hybrid algorithm is better than AES and RSA in terms of encryption time and decryption time and security. This four mechanism effectively work for reducing energy consumption. With the reduction in energy consumption, the life of sensor network can be increased.

References

1. Misalkar, H.D., Burange, A.W., Nikam, U.V.: Increasing lifespan and achieving energy efficiency of wireless sensor network. In: International Conference on Information Communication and Embedded System (ICICES 2016) (2016)
2. Akshay, N., Kumar, M., Harish, B., Dhanorkar, S.: An efficient approach for sensor deployments in wireless sensor network. In: 2010 International Conference on Emerging Trends in Robotics and Communication Technologies (INTERACT), pp. 350–355 (2010)

3. Chamam, A., Pierre, S.: On the planning of wireless sensor networks: energy-efficient clustering under the joint routing and coverage constraint. IEEE Trans. Mob. Comput. **8**(8), 1077–1086 (2009)

4. Xin, G., HuaYang, W., DeGang, B.: EEHCA: an energy-efficient hierarchical clustering algorithm for wireless sensor networks. Inf. Technol. J. **7**(2), 245–252 (2008)

5. Cui, S., Ferens, K.: Energy efficient clustering algorithms for wireless sensor networks. In: Proceedings of ICWN, pp. 18–21 (2011)

6. Heinzelman, W.B., Chandrakasan, A.P., Balakrishnan, H.: An application-specific protocol architecture for wireless microsensor networks. IEEE Trans. Wirel. Commun. **1**(4), 660–670 (2002)

7. Ruperee, A., Nema, S., Pawar, S.: Achieving energy efficiency and increasing network life in wireless sensor network. In: 2014 IEEE (2014)

8. Huang, C.F., Tseng, Y.C.: The coverage problem in a wireless sensor Network. In: ACM International Workshop on Wireless Sensor Networks and Applications (WSNA) (2010)

9. Huang, C.F., Tseng, Y.C.: The coverage problem in a wireless sensor network. In: ACM Mobile Networks and Applications (MONET) special issue on Wireless Sensor Networks (2008, to appear)

10. Slijepcevic, S., Potkonjak, M.: Power efficient organization of wireless sensor networks. In: ICC 2011, Helsinki, Finland, June 2011

11. Ruperee, A., Nema, S., Pawar, S.: Achieving energy efficiency and increasing network life in wireless sensor network. In: 2014 IEEE International on Advance Computing Conference (IACC), pp. 171–175 (2014)

12. Cardei, M., Thai, M., Li, Y., Wu, W.: Energy-efficient target coverage in wireless sensor networks. In: IEEE INFOCOM 2005, March 2005

13. Nagarajan, M., Karthikeyan, S.: A new approach to increase the life time and efficiency of wireless sensor network. In: 2012 IEEE (2012)

14. Abidoye, A.P., Azeez, N.A., Adesina, A.O., Agbele, K.K.: ANCAEE: a novel clustering algorithm for energy efficiency in wireless sensor networks. Wirel. Sens. Netw. **3**(9), 307–312 (2011)

15. Kapoor, V., Yadav, R.: A hybrid cryptography technique for improving network security. Int. J. Comput. Appl. (0975–8887) **141**(11), 25–30 (2016)

16. Li, Y., Thai, M., Wu, W.: Wireless Sensor Networks and Applications. Springer, Boston (2008). https://doi.org/10.1007/978-0-387-49592-7

17. Li, C., Ye, M., Chen, G., Wu, J.: An energy-efficient unequal clustering mechanism for wireless sensor networks. In: 2005 IEEE International Conference on Mobile Adhoc and Sensor Systems Conference, vol. 8, p. 604 (2005)

18. Elminaam, D.S.A., Abdual Kader, H.M., Hadhoud, M.M.: Evaluating the performance of symmetric encryption algorithms. Int. J. Netw. Secur. **10**(3), 213–219 (2010)

19. Vimal Kumar, D., Divya Jose, J.: Over view of cryptographic algorithms for information security. Int. J. Adv. Res. Comput. Comm. Eng. **5**(5), 18–20 (2016)

20. Singh, L., Bharti, R.K.: Comparative performance analysis of cryptographic algorithms. Int. J. Adv. Res. Comput. Sci. Softw. Eng. **3**(11), 563–568 (2013)

Secure Portable Storage Drive: Secure Information Storage

Ashish Dhiman[1], Vishal Gupta[2], and Damanbir Singh[3]($\boxtimes$)

[1] BITS Pilani, Pilani 333031, Rajasthan, India
ashishdhiman.delhi@gmail.com
[2] Jangoo Technology, Vasant Kunj, New Delhi 110070, India
vishal258120i@gmail.com
[3] Software Data India Ltd, Noida 201301, India
damanbirs@gmail.com

Abstract. The aim of this paper is to propose a design for a prototype device, which can further be developed and used to replace existing commercial USB storage media with a secure data access mechanism that is intended to be used in a confidential environment, such as defense establishments. The prototype construction involved configuration of target microcontroller board as a Full Speed USB 2.0 Mass Storage Class Device and MicroSD Card as storage media with read/write speeds of 9 Mbps/7 Mbps respectively. Realization of two independent, non-overlapping critical/non critical storage areas has been explained. Password based Login procedure to enable critical storage area using Keypad has been showed. Password Management using 256-bit SHA-2 HASH function has been explained. Functionality to erase data from critical storage area in emergency conditions through a hardware erasure switch has been explained. As a proof of concept, encryption using stream cipher RC4 generated key stream has been presently implemented to ensure confidentiality of data being stored. Choice of best suited encryption algorithm for the given purpose is an independent research on its own, hence, integration of custom encryption algorithm for enhanced security would be considered for future improvement. Thus, this in-house designed and developed hardware authentication based encrypted storage device can be used to manage critical data securely and safely in confidential work environments.

Keywords: Embedded system · Encrypted drive · Hardware erasure switch
Encryption · FAT filesystem · Microcontroller · MicroSD · Multiple LUNs
RC4 · Secure portable media · SHA2 · STM32 · USB
Information security and cryptography

1 Introduction

We typically rely on Commercial-Off-the-Shelf (COTS) products such as USB Portable Pen Drives, USB External Hard Disks and other Mass storage devices to perform tasks of data transfer and temporary storage of data. Portable Storage media available from various manufacturers cannot be trusted in a confidential work environment to have the correct authentication techniques implemented or an assurance of absence of back door

© Springer Nature Singapore Pte Ltd. 2019
S. Verma et al. (Eds.): CNC 2018, CCIS 839, pp. 308–316, 2019.
https://doi.org/10.1007/978-981-13-2372-0_27

or some pre-installed Trojans, etc. The relevance of an in-house developed Secure Storage Drive is that there exists no such indigenously developed trusted product that can meet the current requirements of a security overlay of authentication and confidentiality. The objective of the project is to design and develop a device which can act as a replacement of currently used COTS portable storage media. The end product is aimed at serving as a portable secure storage media which can essentially incorporate features like Access by Authentication, storage separation of critical viz-a-viz non-critical data, encryption of stored data, one-touch erasure of critical data in emergency situations, and finally, efficiency in terms of data transfer speed.

2 Related Work

With the advent of computers and information technology, came the problem of sharing data. USB storage drives are one of the most used and preferred storage mediums. USB storage drives are designed for the same purpose as floppy disks and optical disks i.e. for storage, data back-up and transfer of data. They merit against counter-parts as they are smaller, faster, and more durable and reliable. Floppy disk drives have been abandoned due to their lower capacity compared to USB flash drives. In 2010, Sony stopped the production of Floppy Disk. USB mass storage standard is supported in almost all modern OS natively. First USB drives were sold by Trek Technology under the brand name Thumb Drive and IBM's "DiskOnKey" manufactured by M-Systems [1].

As the popularity increased the threats also increased. As of 2011, according to the ESET's [2] Global Threat Report of 2011, 9 out of 10 of the top ten computer threats embedded in software files in world spreads through removable storage media such as USB storage drives.

Also, there have been increased reports of Trojans, virus and spy programs embedded in hardware., More recent times have seen the emergence of what has been dubbed by some as the "Silicon Trojan", these Trojans are embedded at the hardware level and can be designed directly into chips and devices.

During the early 80s, there was a big focus on secure operating system (OS). Large investments were made in adapting UNIX to mil-grade security models. The most famous of the assurance criteria used was the Orange Book. A US Army's effort to evaluate a version of UNIX cost rose from an extra US$640 per line of code (loc) has risen to $1000 per loc. This rising cost and cheap microchips and COTs products from economies like China makes risk of inclusion of untrusted risky components in the current infrastructure high. The threat becomes more tangible if the resource of a nation state which manufactures vast numbers of the products is applied to the task for espionage purposes. The report recommended efforts to counter Trojans developed in the design process, and inserted during the manufacture process. This resulted in both a "Trusted Foundry Program" used for security critical ICs, and a DARPA program to examine trust in ICs created by untrusted processes. Currently, there is no such program in our country. Also, a distributed denial of service kind of attack will be targeted upon low cost, trailing edge general purpose circuits integrated into a wide range of systems and peripherals. Physical layer chips like Ethernet PHY chips, USB transceivers used in NIC cards, USB storage devices etc. These facts were discussed in details by Anderson, North and Yiu [3].

One case of silicon embedded backdoor inserted into the Actel/Microsemi ProA-SIC3 chips which was discovered by differential power analysis (D P A) techniques is studied by Skorobogatov and Woods [2]. Also many other articles over web discussed and raised this incident [4–6].

These research and findings motivates us to use trusted components with indigenous designs and discourages the use of COTs products wherever viable in confidential environment.

Even FIPS 140-2 Level 2 Certified encrypted USB Memory Stick tends to be unreliable since there is no assurance of implementation of correct access authentication techniques. One such case happened in early 2010 when SySS security experts found a flaw in authorization procedure of password entry mechanism and almost all encrypted drives at that time used the same technique. For a successful authentication event, a fixed string was passed irrespective of password entered on to the encrypted drive which initiates the process of decrypting the data on disk as requested by OS. So, Syss security experts wrote a small tool which modified active password entry program's RAM which always made sure that the appropriate string was sent to the drive. The following drives were said to be effected:- Kingston Data Traveler Black Box, the SanDisk Cruzer Enterprise FIPS Edition and the Verbatim Corporate Secure FIPS Edition. This incidence was discussed in many web security articles [7–9].

A whitepaper published by SanDisk suggests that attacks like Brute force attacks, Cold boot attack, Malicious code, Dependence on OS security are more efficiently tackled in using Hardware Based Encryption and keeping the Access by Authentication procedure on Storage Drive only [10].

So, this motivated us to design an in-house designed, developed and authorization techniques implemented in a proper manner secure portable storage device which allows hardware encryption.

3 Materials and Methods/Our Approach

3.1 Basic Working

As represented in Fig. 1, STM32F407ZG is the heart of the system, and communicates to the host PC by getting detected as a USB device in mass storage class. On detection for the first time, since the user is not authenticated, only the non-critical storage area is mounted. As soon as the user authenticates itself by punching the correct password, the LOCK/UNLOCK LED glows and the critical storage area is made available. Multiple Logical Storage Units (LUNs) has been implemented over the SD Card which has enabled realization of two independent, non-overlapping storage devices (critical/non-critical storage space). The data residing in critical and non-critical region is inherently encrypted by a crypto engine configured in the controller itself. Currently, as a Proof of Concept, stream cipher RC4 [11, 12] encryption algorithm has been used for encryption/decryption. Study on choice of stream/block cipher and the appropriate cipher itself is beyond the scope of this project and shall be taken up as a future scope of work.

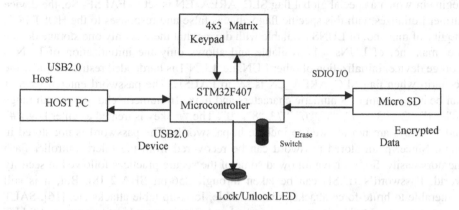

Fig. 1. Architecture block diagram

An ERASE SWITCH has been provided, which can be used in emergency situations to erase all data in a single touch. The device is required to be powered up by connecting to a PC and the user can initiate the emergency erasure by pressing the emergency erasure switch post authentication.

3.2 Development Environment

An appropriate microcontroller ST Microelectronics STM32F407ZG was chosen to accomplish the above said goals. Features of the microcontroller [13] are as follows:-

- clock speed up to 130 MHz
- 1 MB of Flash memory
- 192 + 4 KB of RAM
- USB 2.0 high-speed/full-speed device/host/OTG controller with dedicated DMA having on-chip full-speed as well as support for external ULPI chip for high speed USB 2.0 operation mode and many more features

The development board chosen for this purpose was Olimex's STM32H407 [14]. It is based on the same microcontroller STM32F407ZG. The board has a slot for Micro SD CARD which is being used as a storage memory, a full speed USB2.0 OTG connector, lots of exposed GPIOs etc. The debugger used was Olimex's ARM-USB-Tiny-H [15] along with OPEN OCD as the debugger control software.

The OS for development was UBUNTU 12.04. CODE SOURCERY TOOL-CHAIN for ARM. The development IDE was Eclipse Luna.

3.3   Secure Authentication Protocol Password Management

Here, when being connected to host PC, initialization routine of USB device library begins in which a special global flag SEC_AREA_EN is set to FALSE. So, the device further initializes with this specific flag value as false and responses to the HOST PC's inquiry of max. no. of LUNS available with device that there is only one storage device (i.e. max. no. of LUNs = 1) available and allows only the initialization of LUN 0 storage device. Initialization of other LUN, i.e. LUN 1 is hardcoded restricted under the scenario when flag SEC_AREA_EN is set to FALSE. The password entered by user can be a minimum of 8 numeric characters and max. 16 numeric characters with range "0", "1", "2", "3", "4", "5", "6", "7", "8", "9". The "#" key is treated as enter key. "#" and "*" keys are not allowed to include in passwords. The password is not stored in plain. Since, plain stored password can be recovered from the microcontroller flash memory easily. So, we have followed some of the secure practices followed in security world. Password's HASH can be taken through 256-bit SHA-2 [8]. But, it is still vulnerable to brute-force attacks, rainbow table, look-up table attacks etc. [16]. SALT is added before HASH of password is calculated. There are at least two types of SALT that needs to be added to the password before HASH could be stored as suggested by Manber [16]. There are two types of salt added:-

Fixed Salt: - 256 bytes of fixed salt is concatenated before the password. This fixed salt is hardcoded in the firmware.

Random Salt: - 256 bytes of random salt is generated by on-board hardware RNG every time the password is changed. This random salt is concatenated before Fixed Salt. Then, the HASH is calculated:-

$$\text{HASHVALUE (256byte)} = \text{HASH ([RANDOM SALT]} \\ \text{[FIXED SALT][PASSWORD])} \tag{1}$$

The controller's programmable Flash area is written by the random stream generated through on-board hardware RNG. Then at a pre-defined memory location the previously generated HASH VALUE is written. Then, at another pre-defined memory location the Random Salt is written.

When the user enters the password, the Fixed Salt is concatenated before password and Random Salt is picked up from the pre-defined location to be concatenated before Fixed Salt. Then, HASH is calculated and compared to the HASH VALUE stored at the predefined location. If a match is found out the user has entered the CORRECT PASSWORD, otherwise the password entry is considered as WRONG PASSWORD.

Upon user's entry of password, a routine check password is initiated:-

(1) *CORRECT PASSWORD:* Upon entry of correct password starts a special re-initialization routine of USB device library which in turn sets up the special global flag SEC_AREA_EN to TRUE. So, the device re-initializes with this specific flag value as TRUE and responses to the HOST PC's inquiry of max. no. of LUNS available with device that there is two storage devices (i.e. max. no. of LUNs 2) available and allows the initialization of LUN 0 storage device and LUN 1 storage device.

(2) *WRONG PASSWORD:* Upon entry of correct password, the device discards the password entered and waits for re-entry of password by user. It also maintains a consecutive wrong password counter, which keeps a tab of consecutively wrong password entered and upon 5 consecutive wrong entries, de-initializes the USB device library and requires a power cycle to the device to continue working.

This is required to avoid attacks when attacker tries to make an automated brute-force attack by somehow gaining access to the keypad lines for entering password. Initially, the user is provided with a default password of "012345678" and is required to change it as soon as possible.

3.4 Separation of Critical and Non-critical Data Area

To create two separate and independent data areas over the same memory device, concept of multiple LUN was used. For multiple LUNs, in the definition of Disk operation functions shown in table, the return value of function STOR-AGE_GetMaxLun () is kept as N (No. of LUN,2 in our case). Apart from this, since both the diff LUNs in our case refers to the diff. storage areas of the same storage device, we need to modify the default definition of few functions in table.

As soon as the device gets enumerated in the host in Mass Storage Class, the host through diff callbacks tries to know max. No. of LUNs (i.e. no. of diff. Logical storage devices), then we ask for the storage medium capacity? We calculate the max. No. of blocks present on the medium and returns half the max. No. of blocks denoted by block_num for both LUN = 0 and LUN = 1.

In the STORAGE_Read_HS and STORAGE_Write_HS,

Conditional response has been applied based on the LUN value in the argument. if argument is LUN = 0, the function call is treated for the non-critical area and being the first LUN write address will range from 0 to block_num ((max. no. of blocks)/2). Now, for LUN = 1, it will be treated as critical area and to avoid overlap of non-critical area, an Increment of block_num ((max. no. of blocks)/2) in the write address. So, the first half gets dedicated to non-critical area and second half gets dedicated to critical area. Same is performed in STORAGE_Read_HS for LUN = 0 and LUN = 1 values. The host treats them both as separate STORAGE devices and sends the write or read addresses ranging from 0 to block_num ((max. no. of blocks)/2) but due to the hard coding area definition in microcontroller code never gets overlapped and are completely independent.

3.5 Encryption over SD Card

For added security, encryption at the SD Card access layer is implemented by modifying the BSP Layer API to fit in the encryption in read and write cycles.

A randomly pre-generated 128-bit key from the microcontroller's in-built RNG is hardcoded in the firmware. This key is given as an input to the RC4's key scheduling algorithm, which generates an 256-byte state. This state is given to the function responsible for the key stream generation. Starting 4096 bytes are discarded since there is a known weakness in the first 256-byte of key stream generated as suggested by

Mironov [17]. Since the standard sector/block size in our case is 512 bytes, 512 bytes are taken after discarding initial 4096 bytes and are saved in a temp. variable for encryption or decryption by XOR-ING the temp. variable with the data to be enc/dec.

Now, decryption is implemented just after read from the SD Card.

Decrypted Data = Data Read from SD Card (Encrypted Data) xor RC4 key stream.

Encryption is implemented just before write on the SD Card.

Encrypted Data = Data to be written over SD Card (Plain Data) xor RC4 key stream.

3.6   Design and Implementation of One Touch Erasure Mechanism

There are situations where we require erasing data due to an emergency situation and we do not have enough time to log on to a machine and do a quick format by HOST PC software. So, we have provided a hardware controlled mechanism to quickly erase the data by just connecting the device to any powered up machine, punching in the password, authenticate by entering the correct password and an erase sequence. The user needs to press the erasure switch for 2 s. The user LED will blip two times once the erasure is completed.

If an erase sequence is initiated without authentication, the LED will not blimp and the erasure request will be discarded. There are two types of hardware controlled erasures:-

(3) *Soft Erasure:-* Here, we do an internal quick format by just erasing the MBR (first 512 bytes) and re-writing it with a fat32 partition table entry. The erase sequence is "*", "1", "*", "#".

(4) *Hard Erasure:-*Here, we do an internal full erasure by erasing and re-writing every sector by a random 512-byte generated by on-board RNG. The erase sequence is "*", "2", "*", "#".

Hardware erasure switch is used to generate an interrupt, which is detected by the microcontroller when pressed for 3 s. Upon detection, the interrupt generated in microcontroller makes program start a routine. This routine checks the authentication of user and initiates the erasing procedure as requested. i.e. either a SOFT ERASURE or a HARD ERASURE.

3.7   Results

The identified target microcontroller is configured as a USB Mass Storage Class Device and use MicroSD Card as storage media. So, STM32F407ZG variant 144 pin was identified as a suitable 32-bit target microcontroller. SDIO interface is configured to read/write on MicroSD Card. Multiple Logical Storage Units (LUNs) are implemented over the SD Card which acts as two independent, non-overlapping storage devices. FatFs Open Source library was configured and integrated to provide microcontroller the ability to manage/erase storage areas over the storage medium. Keypad and LED is integrated to accept/change password and know the result and initiate the erase sequence. Password based Login procedure to enable/disable critical/non-critical storage area using Keypad and LED is incorporated. Password Management using recommended practices was implemented using trusted public domain hash algorithm 256-bit SHA-2. Functionality to erase all data from critical storage area in emergency conditions through a hardware emergency erasure switch is incorporated. Encryption using stream cipher RC4 generated key stream is implemented at SD Card Level to demonstrate a custom encryption implementation in future.

The printing area is 122 mm × 193 mm. The text should be justified to occupy the full line width, so that the right margin is not ragged, with words hyphenated as appropriate. Please fill pages so that the length of the text is no less than 180 mm, if possible.

Use 10-point type for the name(s) of the author(s) and 9-point type for the address (es) and the abstract. For the main text, please use 10-point type and single-line spacing. We recommend the use of Computer Modern Roman or Times. Italic type may be used to emphasize words in running text. Bold type and underlining should be avoided.

Papers not complying with the LNCS style will be reformatted. This can lead to an increase in the overall number of pages. We would therefore urge you not to squash your paper.

4 Conclusions and Future Work

The final aim of designing and developing a microcontroller based Secure Portable Storage Drive with the following features was achieved:-SD Card based secure storage having hardware-based encryption.

- Separation of critical and non-critical storage space
- Emergency erasure of data in critical storage area
- Keypad base authentication to access critical storage space is implemented on device itself without any requirement of any software

The device works in USB 2.0 Full SPEED mode. After testing practically it provided read throughputs of 9mbps with RC4 implementation of encryption and write throughputs of 7mbps with 10Mbytes of single file.

Currently at the prototyping level, device is working in Full Speed mode, but our microcontroller and the USB Device library supports USB 2.0 High Speed Mode operation using a ULPI [10] Transceiver.

So, with current speeds, the targeted use of operation is for general office environment use, where the majority of usage involves transferring files of small sizes like presentations & documentation.

There are following points for future work:-

- Since, this is the work done at the prototyping level. The production level can have a ULPI transceiver to enable microcontroller work in USB HIGH SPEED MODE.
- The production version will be targeted to feature the microcontroller from the same family but with the encryption standard like AES-256 as ASIC implemented onboard. So, on top of the Standard encryption, a layer of custom encryption could be

carried out. The current version is a proof of concept for implementation of light weight custom encryption.

- Implementation of dynamically monitoring and policing of storage of files with allowed file extension by reading their extension signatures.
- Include a battery for RTC support and implementing emergency erasure without requiring connecting to a HOST PC

References

1. USB flash drive. http://en.wikipedia.org/wiki/USB_flash_drive
2. Global threat report, December 2011. http://www.eset.com/us/resources/threat-trends/Global_Threat_Trends_December_2011.pdf
3. Anderson, M.S., North, C.J.G., Yiu, K.K.: Towards Countering the Rise of the Silicon Trojan, vol. 11, pp. 2–5. Australian Government DoD-DSTO (2008)
4. Backdoor Found (Maybe) in Chinese-Made Military Silicon Chips. https://www.schneier.com/blog/archives/2012/05/backdoor_found.html
5. Backdoors Embedded in DoD Microchips From China. http://www.scribd.com/doc/95282643/Backdoors-Embedded-in-DoD-Microchips-From-China
6. Proof That Military Chips From China Are Infected? http://defensetech.org/2012/05/30/smoking-gun-proof-that-military-chips-from-china-are-infected/#ixzz3IZntQYTYDefense.org
7. FIPS 140-2 Level 2 Certified USB Memory Stick Cracked. https://www.schneier.com/blog/archives/2010/01/fips_140-2_leve.html
8. Flash drive manufacturers warn: Hackers can decrypt 'secure' USBsticks. https://nakedsecurity.sophos.com/2010/01/05/flash-drive-manufacturers-warn-hackers-decrypt-secure-usb-sticks/
9. Decrypting USB flash drives is easy. http://blog.erratasec.com/2010/01/decrypting-usb-flash-drives-is-easy.html#.VF9qfVdYsvK
10. SanDisk: Assessing the Security of Hardware-Based vs. Software-Based Encryption on USB Flash Drives (2008)
11. RC4. http://en.wikipedia.org/wiki/RC4
12. Stallings, W.: The RC4 Stream Encryption Algorithm (2005). http://www.st.com/web/en/resource/technical/document/datasheet/DM00037051.pdf
13. STM32-H407 development board USER'S MANUAL. https://www.olimex.com/Products/ARM/ST/STM32-H407/resources/STM32-H407.pdf
14. ARM-USB-TINY-H ARM JTAG DEBUGGER USER S MANUAL. https://www.olimex.com/Products/ARM/JTAG/_resources/ARM-USB-TINY_and_TINY_H_manual.pdf
15. Patel, P., Patel, J., Virparia, P.: A cryptography application using salt hash technique. Int. J. Appl. Innov. Eng. Manag. (IJAIEM) 2(6), 1 (2013)
16. Manber, U.: A simple scheme to make passwords based on one-way functions much harder to crack. Comput. Secur. 15, 4 (1996)
17. Mironov, I.: (Not so) random shuffles of RC4. In: Yung, M. (ed.) CRYPTO 2002. LNCS, vol. 2442, pp. 304–319. Springer, Heidelberg (2002). https://doi.org/10.1007/3-540-45708-9_20

Performance Evaluation of Facenet on Low Resolution Face Images

Monika Rani Golla[✉] and Poonam Sharma

Department of Computer Science and Engineering,
Visvesvaraya National Institute of Technology, Nagpur, Maharashtra, India
gmonikarani@gmail.com, dr.poonamasharma@gmail.com

Abstract. In recent years, deep learning has become a very prevalent technology in face recognition. Google came up with a deep convolution neural network called Facenet which performs face recognition using only 128 bytes per face. As claimed by Google, Facenet attained nearly 100-percent accuracy on the widely used Labeled Faces in the Wild (LFW) dataset. But in the case of low resolution face images it's the other way round. This low resolution challenge occurs in many existing face recognition algorithms, due to which satisfactory performance has become hard to be achieved. The goal of this paper is to present the obtained results after evaluating the performance of Facenet on low resolution face images compared to high resolution face images.

Keywords: Deep learning · Face recognition
Deep convolution neural network · Facenet · Low resolution

1 Introduction

Face recognition is one of the most successful applications in the past decade. The process of matching two faces by finding the similarities between their extracted external features is defined as face recognition [1]. Face recognition may not be the most reliable and efficient biometric but it has several advantages over the other biometrics like fingerprint, iris, and speech recognition. One of the major advantages is that it can uniquely distinguish one person from a crowd of people. Face recognition is already being used around the world to examine, investigate, and monitor. Usually, a face representation process and a face matching process together contribute to a face recognition system. Face image descriptor-based methods [2] and deep learning-based methods [12] are the two prominent categories of face representation methods that dominate recent research.

A face recognition system is not only applicable for identifying a person but also helpful in verifying a person from a digital image. Generally, this is achieved by comparing selected discriminated features of face from the test image with that of a face dataset. For an instance, the system may examine the position, dimension and shape of the facial features like eyes, eyebrows, jaw lines and so on. Some challenges [18] have to be faced while recognizing faces. These include *Orientation Problem*: Rotation of image may be different with respect to optical axis of camera, *Expression of face*: Face expression can affect the appearance of face, *Problem of pose*: there may be side view

© Springer Nature Singapore Pte Ltd. 2019
S. Verma et al. (Eds.): CNC 2018, CCIS 839, pp. 317–325, 2019.
https://doi.org/10.1007/978-981-13-2372-0_28

or front view, *Occlusion:* Due to presence of beards and glasses and *Resolution:* Difference in the size of images that are used for training and testing purpose.

Generally, in face recognition applications, it is possible that from classification perspective the HR gallery images have to be matched with the LR probe images. Hence this results in the dimensional mismatch issue between training and test images. There are methods such as upscaling, inter-resolution Space and downscaling which can be considered to solve this issue. In the first method, most of the super-resolution techniques output super-resolved images from low resolution input faces and later go for recognizing faces. The next method constructs integrated feature space with optimal mapping methodologies, or resolution-robust feature extraction methodologies where they perform directly on the native LR images. And the final method, down-scaling is a bad choice for resolving the LR issue in performance perspective.

In this paper the reason why the performance evaluation of face recognition system had to be done is stated in the following literature survey section. Then the effects of deep learning, the emerging Artificial Intelligence technology, in improving the recognition rate is discussed in Sect. 3 which is followed by the introduction of Google's Facenet which uses deep leaning for face recognition purpose. And finally, in Sect. 5 the results after evaluating the performance of Facenet on low resolution face images of LFW dataset are presented.

2 Literature Survey

It has been observed that the recognition rate of face recognition in constrained environments is higher compared to that in real-life applications where the subjects are far from cameras, or the used face patches are prone to be very small. The performance degradation of face recognition systems is still remained as an unsolved problem, partially due to low-resolution (LR) image quality [31]. If the LR problem has been considered from recognition perspective rather than vision purpose then even variations in illumination comes under LR problem. This is the main reason for the failure of most of the existing methods [7].

The extraction of human facial features from a LR image is a more difficult task for humans and machines too. This happens due to less variations in the features of LR face image. Some of the major factors of face recognition performance degradation on low resolution images are inaccurate alignment of input face patches, noise due to variation of pose, size and expression of the individuals. So, the effective descriptors like Gabor [32] and Dual Cross Patterns [2] need to be modified for low resolution. And one more factor is the difference in dimension of images that are used for training and testing purpose in conventional subspace learning methods.

In contrast to a LR images, a High Resolution (HR) face images contain clear features that are crucial for recognizing faces. In other words, the capacity to discriminate useful features can be determined by image resolution too. It has been observed that it is easier to recognize faces that are distinguished by overall features even if those faces are in lower resolutions [33] where the image batches from low to high resolutions are represented by pyramidal data structure with factors that are enlarged from 1 to 64, in steps of 2, and the results have overwhelmed everyone that the best performance has been not achieved in the case of classifying the highest resolution images.

In the upscaling approaches, reconstruction technique has a dominant recognition rate over the interpolation. In the reconstruction technique [19], the piece-division has been applied for each image of LR and the corresponding HR image, where each piece contributes to a single model, resulting in diminishing the model and increasing the reconstruction speed, while the better prediction is achieved by test images. For the given images that are of low resolution, the results achieved by interpolation are 20% to 30%, while the accuracy of reconstruction based algorithm are 55% to 62%. However, the expected recognition rate, around 80% to 90%, has not been acquired.

Shi et al. [20] proposed the coupled mappings to enhance the recognition rate of low-resolution (LR) face images, which projects the LR test images and HR training images into inter-resolution space that plays a vital role in measuring the similarity of the images that differ in size. A global structure that contributes to mappings has been built in the training phase by preserving the discriminative features information of the face images while ensuring the consistency between the LR test set and HR gallery set. This method evades the matrix singularity issue and thus outputs consistent results. The Principal Component Analysis [29] module has to be executed in order to clear out noises in the inputted LR or HR face images, which results in enhancement of performance in recognizing LR faces. To be considered, it also increases the computational cost.

Besides this, the down-scaling used in [21] is helpful for reducing the differences caused by varying facial expression and poses between images of a same face. The image outputted after down-scaling contains large-scale and LR details of the input image whereas the difference image contains the same inputted image details. That is why the output image looks more precise than the difference image. But, performance wise this approach is not a good choice.

The issues regarding low-resolution face recognition are addressed in [22]. In this paper the support vector data description based learning technique has been discussed. The results depicted that the images obtained using this technique were as same as HR images, hence it made easy to recognize LR face images. Good results are obtained in recognizing the images that are used in the gallery set. But, the performance was degraded when recognizing the images that are not part of the gallery set.

Detecting faces correctly from low resolution image plays vital role before recognizing those faces. The problem in face detecting while considering critical background is stated in [23, 24]. The authors, Garcia et al. [25] and Wu et al. [26] have done feature extraction from all separated face images in an single image. In [27], the image color details are utilized in the detection of the faces in an image. The drawbacks of this model is that it cannot detect faces that are of gray scale image and far from the camera, since in the filtering process they are treated as noise. A new concept called face structural similarity which is similar to the structure information was proposed in [16]. In this approach the structure information has been obtained first, and then the discriminative information while changing from LR to HR. the conventional face detectors such as AdaBoost [34], could also fail in LR scenario. Hence, inventing an efficient and effective face detector is much required for solving the LR challenges, mostly in the security perspective areas.

The straightforward way to solve low resolution challenge is super-resolution (SR) [7], which first takes several LR faces to reconstruct super-resolved faces and then performs recognition with the obtained faces. In recent years other promising methods like multi-modal tensor super-resolution (MTSR) [8], RQCr color features for degraded images [9], multi-dimensional scaling (MDS) [10], and coupled kernel embedding (CKE) [11] have been proposed. However, all of these are limited to some or the other conditions and do not help in fully solving the problem. More and in-depth research is very much needed in order to reach the goal of resolution-robust face recognition.

3   The Role of Deep Learning in Face Recognition

In the recent years, deep learning [5] based face recognition approaches have been dominating the image processing field. In which Deep Convolutional Neural Networks (CNN) are high-capacity classifiers with very wide range of parameters that must be learned from millions of training examples. The deep architecture of CNN acts as its vital strength, which allows for a set of discriminating features extraction at multiple levels of abstraction. Currently, the focus of the researchers is on more powerful model architectures and better learning techniques in order to improve deep CNNs.

CNNs were developed by Facebook's Artificial Intelligence team. It is concluded that the renowned social media site, Facebook is making use of a Convolutional Neural Network for its face recognition system. In 2015, after a continuous inventions in the field of AI by the top organizations, a human had lost the competition to a machine at an object recognition event which was never happened before. This was treated as trivial success, since the CNNs helped in reducing the rate of error in detecting images. A deep CNN has multiple layers that progressively compute features from input images. It contains three basic components: convolutional, pooling and fully-connected layers. Out of which, the main component of CNN is the convolutional layer that detects local features at all locations of the input image by learning a filter bank. Each filter prolongates through the complete input volume depth, but it is tiny as per the width and height dimensions. The convolutional layer discovers the most relevant features that the net has to consider which is then ensured by the pooling layer. Hence, this results in limited storage and computing requirements in order to execute a CNN. A fully-connected layer is a layer in which every input neuron is connected to every output neuron. Each neuron's activation can hence be calculated using matrix multiplication and bias offset. In order to provide training signals (class labels), the last layer of CNNs is normally associated with some loss, and the training for CNNs can be done by doing gradient descent on the parameters with respect to the loss.

Modern deep models like ImageNet [13], GoogleNet [14], DeepID [15] and so on have reported perfect accomplishment on the famous, long-established standard: Labeled Faces in the Wild (LFW) [4], which because of its complication, regarded as the de facto benchmark for evaluating face recognition systems.

4 Face Recognition Using Facenet

Facenet [3], designed by Google, has been trained to solve the face recognition problem with efficiency at scale, and also used for solving the face verification and clustering problems. It uses a deep convolution network which learns a mapping from face patches to a dense euclidean space in which the face similarity is measured by distance. This learning in training phase results in optimizing the embeddings, where as other deep learning approaches focus on an in-between bottleneck layers.

Once the euclidean space has been obtained then the face recognition problem can be easily solved using the standard approaches since the major face recognition problem will be broken down to k-NN classification problem [17]. For training purpose the triplets of approximately aligned similar/dissimilar face images have been used in Facenet. The triplets consists of two face thumbnails, tight face crops performed on an image, of same person and a different person. These thumbnails are obtained by scaling and translation. As already stated Facenet directly gives a compact 128-Dimension embedding as an output after the training phase by using a triplet-based loss method, whose goal is to break apart the similar pair from the dissimilar pair by a distance measure. Figures 1 and 2 shows the structure of the Facenet and Triplet Loss performed at the end of the model respectively.

Fig. 1. Facenet Model Structure: The model contains a batch input layer and a architecture of deep CNN which is then followed by L^2 normalization that outputs the embedding of face. During training the triplet loss has been induced at the end.

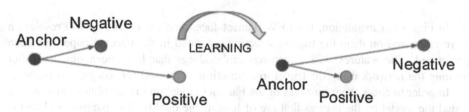

Fig. 2. The triplet loss reduces the distance between the face pairs if they are of the same person, and increases it if the pairs are of different persons.

In Facenet, the Convolution Neural Network (CNN) used is of Zeiler and Fergus [30] model that contains 22 deep layers and Inception [14] model. The both types of networks differ in respect to the computer performance measures like the number of parameters and FLOPS. These models used rectified linear units as the non-linear activation function. From the second model, the 5×5 convolutions have been removed as there was not much impact of them on the results. The triplets used for training purpose have to be carefully selected since they effect the speed of the CNN convergence. It has been stated that if less amount of triplets in mini-batches are used then that results in convergence improvement.

Facenet has given optimized performance of embedding face recognition where for each face it used 128-bytes only. And upon evaluated on LFW, it achieved 99.63% accuracy, whereas 95.12% on Youtube Faces DB.

5   Facenet Performance Evaluation on Low Resolution Images of LFW Dataset

Face recognition becomes a very challenging task if the given set of images are of low resolution. Because, while taking pictures the subjects might be far away from the camera. Other challenge is in finding a model that works fine within a range of unfavorable conditions. The techniques like Super Resolution [7] and Image hallucination [16] have been developed to enhance the image resolution, but the outcomes of these are not up to the mark in improving the quality of the super-resolved images.

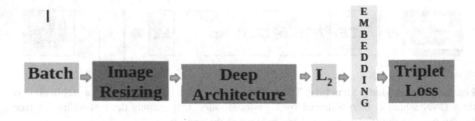

Fig. 3. The proposed model for testing facenet on low resolution images

In Fig. 3 our evaluation, the LFW dataset faces that are of 160×160 resolution were taken and on them the triplets selection as stated in the Facenet paper has been performed. The features, 128 dimension embeddings that have been obtained after training the network using the triplet loss function were used for recognition purpose.

In order to check the robustness of the Facenet model on low resolution images, we tested the model on the images that are of low image quality. The parameters like the positive to negative triplet distance margin, the number of images per person, the number of people per batch, the number of images to process in a batch and the number of batches per epoch have remained unchanged since they don't effect the accuracy. The prominent change was made in the size of the images used for evaluation. At first, the images were resized to 10×10, 20×20, 40×40, 60×60, 80×80 and 100×100 respectively using nearest neighbor interpolation. All the images are of .png type. Totally, ten input splits that contain few positive pairs and 300 negative pairs of faces per split were considered for training purpose. And then these low resolution images were trained with eight input splits that contain both positive and negative pairs of the identities and tested with remaining two splits on Facenet. The results obtained alarmed the need for the invention of more robust face recognition systems.

5.1 Experiment Results

The results after evaluating Facenet on LFW dataset are shown in Table 1. This dataset is a collection of more than 13,000 images of faces collected from the Internet. As the name suggests each face image in LFW has been labeled with the pictured person's name. 1680 of the labeled persons have more than one variant poses in the dataset. All the face images in the dataset have been detected using Viola-Jones face detector [6]. The default size of the images in LFW is 250×250 whereas in our evaluation, the dataset has been aligned using MTCNN [28] in order to reduce the image resolution. For the given image size 160×160, the accuracy obtained is 99.2% and the validation rate is 97.1%. It has been observed that as the input size has been decreased the accuracy has also been gradually decreased.

Table 1. The results after evaluating the performance of facenet on low resolution images

Input image size	Accuracy (in percentage)	Validation rate
160×160	99.2	97.1
100×100	99.2	97.1
80×80	99.2	96.4
60×60	98.9	94.7
40×40	98.5	88.5
20×20	64.3	01.9
10×10	58.2	01.6

6   Conclusion

In real-world face recognition applications, one often has to recognize face images from a very far distance. Since such images are with low resolution the recognition task is very challenging. In this paper the results after evaluating Facenet on low resolution face images have been depicted. The goal of this paper is to bring forth the necessity of developing resolution-robust face recognition systems that give accurate results.

References

1. Zhao, W., Chellappa, R.: Face recognition, a literature survey. ACM Comput. Surv. (CSUR) **35**(4), 399–458 (2003). National Institute of Standards and Technology
2. Ding, C., Choi, J., Tao, D., Davis, L.S.: Multi-directional multi-level dual-cross patterns for robust face recognition. In: IEEE Transactions on Pattern Analysis and Machine Intelligence, vol. 38, no. 3, pp. 518–531 (2016)

3. Schroff, F., Kalenichenko, D., Philbin, J.: FaceNet: a unified embedding for face recognition and clustering. In: 2015 IEEE Conference on Computer Vision and Pattern Recognition (CVPR), Boston, MA, pp. 815–823 (2015)
4. Learned-Miller, E., Huang, G.B., RoyChowdhury, A., Li, H., Hua, G.: Labeled faces in the wild: a survey. In: Kawulok, M., Celebi, M., Smolka, B. (eds.) Advances in Face Detection and Facial Image Analysis, pp. 189–248. Springer, Cham (2016). https://doi.org/10.1007/978-3-319-25958-1_8
5. Lu, Z., Jiang, X., Kot, A.: Enhance deep learning performance in face recognition. In: 2017 2nd International Conference on Image, Vision and Computing (ICIVC), Chengdu, pp. 244–248 (2017)
6. Viola, P., Jones, M.: Rapid object detection using a boosted cascade of simple features. In: Proceedings of the 2001 IEEE Computer Society Conference on Computer Vision and Pattern Recognition, CVPR 2001, vol. 1, pp. I-511–I-518 (2005)
7. Raghavendra, R., Raja, K.B., Yang, B., Busch, C.: Comparative evaluation of super-resolution techniques for multi-face recognition using light-field camera. In: 2013 18th International Conference on Digital Signal Processing (DSP), Fira, pp. 1–6 (2013)
8. Jia, K., Gong, S.G.: Multi-modal tensor face for simultaneous super-resolution and recognition. In: Proceedings of IEEE 10th International Conference on Computer Vision (ICCV), October 2005, Beijing, China, vol. 2, pp. 1683–1690 (2005)
9. Choi, J.Y., Ro, Y.M., Plataniotis, K.N.: Color face recognition for degraded face images. IEEE Trans. Syst. Man Cybern. Part B Cybern. 39(5), 1217–1230 (2009)
10. Biswas, S., Bowyer, K.W., Flynn, P.J.: Multidimensional scaling for matching low-resolution face images. IEEE Trans. Pattern Anal. Mach. Intell. 34(10), 2019–2030 (2012)
11. Ren, C.X., Dai, D.Q., Yan, H.: Coupled kernel embedding for low-resolution face recognition. IEEE Trans. Image Process. 21(8), 3770–3783 (2012)
12. Ghazi, M.M., Ekenel, H.K.: A comprehensive analysis of deep learning based representation for face recognition. In: 2016 IEEE Conference on Computer Vision and Pattern Recognition Workshops (CVPRW), Las Vegas, NV, pp. 102–109 (2016)
13. Krizhevsky, A., Sutskeyer, I.: ImageNet classification with deep convolutional neural networks. In: Proceedings of the 25th International Conference on Neural Information Processing Systems, NIPS 2012, vol. 1, pp. 1097–1105 (2012)
14. Szegedy, C., et al.: Going deeper with convolutions. In: 2015 IEEE Conference on Computer Vision and Pattern Recognition (CVPR), Boston, MA, pp. 1–9 (2015). https://doi.org/10.1109/CVPR.7298594
15. Ouyang, W., et al.: DeepID-Net: deformable deep convolutional neural networks for object detection. In: 2015 IEEE Conference on Computer Vision and Pattern Recognition (CVPR), Boston, MA, pp. 2403–2412 (2015)
16. Wang, X.G., Tang, X.O.: Hallucinating face by eigen transformation. IEEE Trans. Syst. Man Cybern. Part C Appl. Rev. 35(3), 425–434 (2005)
17. Laaksonen, J., Oja, E.: Classification with learning k-nearest neighbors. In: 1996 IEEE International Conference on Neural Networks, Washington, DC, vol. 3, pp. 1480–1483 (2002)
18. Kurmi, U.S., Agrawal, D., Baghel, R.K.: Study of different face recognition algorithms and challenges. Int. J. Eng. Res. 3, 112–115 (2014). https://doi.org/10.17950/ijer/v3s2/216
19. Li, Z., Hou, Y., Liu, H., Li, X.: Very low resolution face reconstruction based on multi-output regression. In: 2014 IEEE Workshop on Electronics, Computer and Applications, Ottawa, ON, pp. 74–77 (2014)
20. Shi, J., Qi, C.: From local geometry to global structure: learning latent subspace for low-resolution face image recognition. IEEE Signal Process. Lett. 22(5), 554–558 (2015)

21. Xu, Y., Jin, Z.: Down-sampling face images and low-resolution face recognition. In: 3rd International Conference on Innovative Computing Information and Control, Dalian, Liaoning, p. 392 (2008)
22. Lee, S.-W., Park, J., Lee, S.-W.: Low resolution face recognition based on support vector data description. Pattern Recognit. **39**(9), 1809–1812 (2006). ISSN 0031-3203
23. Dai, Y., Nakanom Y.: Extraction for facial images from complex background using color information and SGLD matrices. In: 1st International Workshop on Automatic Face and Gesture Recognition, pp. 238–242 (1995)
24. Yang, G., Huang, T.S.: Human face detection in a complex background. Pattern Recognit. **27**, 53–63 (1994)
25. Garcia, C., Tziritas, G.: Face detection using quantized skin color regions merging and wavelet packet analysis. IEEE Trans. Multimed. **1**, 264–277 (1999)
26. Wu, H., Yokoyama, T., Pramadihanto, D., Yachida, M.: Face and facial feature extraction from color image. In: 2nd International Conference on Automatic Face and Gesture Recognition, pp. 345–350 (1996)
27. Sarkar, R., Bakshi, S., Sa, P.K.: A real-time model for multiple human face tracking from low-resolution surveillance videos. Procedia Technol. **6**, 1004–1010 (2012). ISSN 2212-0173
28. Zhang, K., Zhang, Z., Li, Z., Qiao, Y.: Joint face detection and alignment using multitask cascaded convolutional networks. IEEE Signal Process. Lett. **23**(10), 1499–1503 (2016)
29. Kaur, R., Himanshi, E.: Face recognition using principal component analysis. In: IEEE International Advance Computing Conference (IACC), Banglore, pp. 585–589 (2015)
30. Zeiler, M.D., Fergus, R.: Visualizing and understanding convolutional networks. In: Fleet, D., Pajdla, T., Schiele, B., Tuytelaars, T. (eds.) ECCV 2014. LNCS, vol. 8689, pp. 818–833. Springer, Cham (2014). https://doi.org/10.1007/978-3-319-10590-1_53
31. Pnevmatikakis, A., Polymenakos, L.: Far-field, multi-camera, video-to-video face recognition. In: Delac, K., Grgic, M. (eds.) Face Recognition, pp. 467–486 (2007)
32. Nazari, S., Moin, M.S.: Face recognition using global and local Gabor features. In: 2013 21st Iranian Conference on Electrical Engineering (ICEE), Mashhad, pp. 1–4 (2013)
33. Kurita, T., Otsu, N., Sato, T.: A face recognition method using higher order local autocorrelation and multivariate analysis. In: Proceedings of IEEE 11th International Conference on Pattern Recognition (ICPR), The Hague, The Netherlands, vol. B, pp. 213–216 (1992)
34. Xingjing, D., Dongmei, Z., Hongyun, Z.: Study of fast Adaboost face detection algorithm. In: International Conference on Computer Application and System Modeling (ICCASM 2010), Taiyuan, pp. V6-136–V6-139 (2010)

Computing Techniques for Efficient Networks Design

Grading and Defect Detection in Potatoes Using Deep Learning

Nikhil Pandey(✉), Suraj Kumar, and Raksha Pandey

School of Studies in Engineering and Technology,
Guru Ghasidas Vishwavidyalaya, Bilaspur, India

Abstract. Deep learning has been employed in a number of tasks. Taking inspiration from detection of tumors in medical tiff images, we had an idea of doing the same with other objects such as vegetables and plants which get affected by disease very often and still there are not many feasible approach of its detection. In this paper we present a practical approach to grade potato and classify the defects that might be present. We have used U-Net for segmentation of image containing on an average 50–60 potatoes. A physical object (marker) of known length is present along the potatoes for length reference. The U-net segmented result is then processed by computer vision algorithms (Distance transformation and watershed) to get the actual skin of the object of interest. After that we have used transfer learning to classify the skin for a number of defects such as greening, mechanical defect, rotting, sprouting etc.

Keywords: Deep CNN · Grading · U-Net · Potato

1 Introduction

Agriculture in India provides employment to millions and it is also the third highest contributor to the GDP of India. This sector underwent significant changes in the early eighties and the nineties by the government's green revolution. The changes that led to an increase in the crop yield per hectare, were area under cultivation and use of high yielding variety seeds.

But these improvements does not reflect in the income of farmers. One of the major causes for this is the losses incurred due to various diseases affecting the crops which result in a decrease in crop yield and also increases the amount of money spent on pest and disease control by farmers.

The use of disease specific pesticides is still not prevalent in Indian agriculture sector as the farmers have no means of accurately identifying the disease affecting their crop. A significant amount of damage to crops can be averted if the disease affecting them can be identified and treated in their initial phase.

We have worked on developing an algorithm which can accurately and efficiently identify the disease affecting the crop using only an image showing the infected crop. The image need not be of very high quality as the algorithm should work on images clicked by middle range smartphones.

S. Verma et al. (Eds.): CNC 2018, CCIS 839, pp. 329–339, 2019.
https://doi.org/10.1007/978-981-13-2372-0_29

We chose potato as our reference model considering its high share in the cold storage and the economic impact of diseases affecting potatoes. The abundance of good quality images was another reason for choosing potatoes.

Researches in the field of computer science have tried and used various advanced techniques from computer vision and machine learning to classify the diseases affecting crops.

2 Literature Review

We have done an extensive literature research on the work that has been done on developing modern techniques of defect classification of plants and flora. One of the main techniques that we encounter was Curvelet transform to analyze the defects crops. The data extracted from curvelet transform is thoroughly analyzed by techniques of statistics. Khoje et al. [1] have used this technique to identify defects in guava and lemon.

Another approach is use of the unsupervised learning algorithm K-Means clustering presented by Dubey et al. [2] for detection of infected fruit part. They have used a two part process in which first they've applied K-Means clustering on image pixels based on color next they combined the pixels to a fixed number of regions which is dependent on the image.

The removal of background from images so as to obtain only the components which are necessary for detection by a machine learning algorithm like SVM is demonstrated by Razamjooy et al. [3]. They have used mathematical binarization to sort the objects and then a color based classifier to perform segmentation.

A Machine learning model of an object detector which can count the number of Apples of different variety in an image and thereby estimating the yield of an orchard is demonstrated by Bargoti et al. [4]. The object detector uses a three layer Multi-layer perceptron architecture. Another Machine learning algorithm called Random Forest had been applied to classify images of Apples, Oranges and Strawberries by Zawba et al. [5]. Before providing the images as input to the classifier they have used Scale Invariant Feature Transform (SIFT).

The IMAGENET challenge has provided a humongous dataset containing over 14 million images across 22 thousand categories. The winners of this competition have used deep convolutional neural network to classify the images to its category. Deep CNN has outperformed every other machine learning algorithm in this competition. AlexNet [6] and GoogleNet [7] are two of the mostly preferred choice of neural network architecture.

3 Segmentation

The segmentation process is our first step of processing the image. Technically segmentation means partitioning an image into different regions based on some intrinsic property. For our purpose we need to get the exact surface of a potato from an image. The image in RGB color space undergoes segmentation to get an binary image in which positive pixel corresponds to the presence of a potato, a bit like classification of pixel and then separately get the touching object using watershed algorithm.

3.1   Binarization Using U-Net

We tried many elementary techniques of computer vision for binarization of region of interest. Best of these was HSV masking within a set of particular RGB values to get an binary image where the white represents the surface (skin) of a potato. While in absence of noises such as dirt, pebbles etc. the approach was somewhat good however it proved to be extremely prone to noises. As we have made it clear that our plan was to develop the algorithm so that it can process in bulk, noises were inevitable part. Thus we needed a strong supervised learning algorithm that can tackle with noises. In our research we came across U-Net architecture by Olaf Ronneberger et al. [9]. We used JSS segmentation for segmentation and trained the U-Net on a training set containing over 10000 potatoes, healthy as well as defected (Fig. 1).

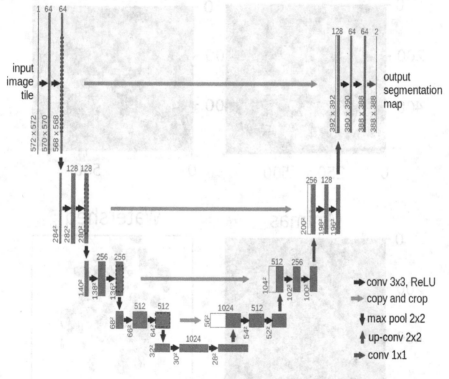

Fig. 1. Architecture of U-Net

The binary prediction obtained performed better than our expectation with a training dice-score of 98.4 and validation dice-score of 97.61.

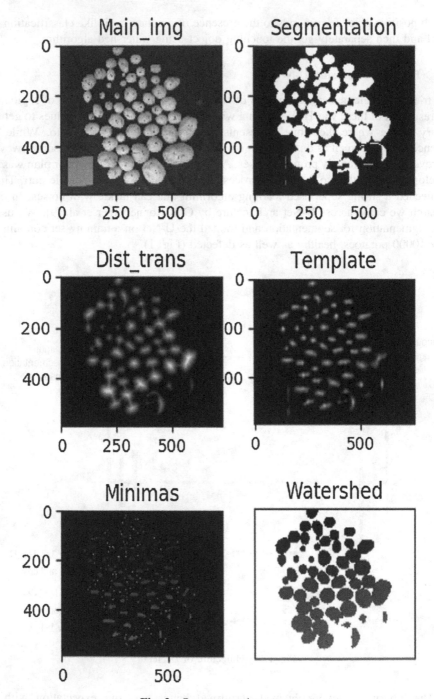

Fig. 2. Output at various stages

3.2 Distance Transformation and Watershed

Since we have got a nearly perfect binary image, the next step was to clearly distinguish all the tuber that represented an individual potato. One of the best ways of separating touching objects in binary images is to utilize the distance transform and the watershed method. A border is formed as far as possible from the center of the overlapping objects. Object with curvature like a potato (round) can be separated by this method. First we did template matching of ellipse as 2D projection of potato is generally elliptical. This further removed false positives if present. After that the resulting image undergo distance transformation to get the minimas that will be further utilized in water shedding. These minimas are filled with water. We continue the work of filling water and building barriers until all the peaks are submerged. The barriers resulting gives segmentation hence separate potatoes.

3.3 Contouring and Measurement

The output of previous process is then processed for getting contours. We store them in a dictionary and iterate over them. The contours are passed to cv2.approxPolyDP() which is an implementation of Douglas-Peucker algorithm. After applying this, we get several point of inflection along the curve of contour. The longest possible distance among these points (Θ) comes as the length of the contours. Since we have an object of known length in the original image we can get a relationship between the length of objects and pixels required to represent this length in the image (μ).

The marker as can be seen in Fig. 3 is a red square. We calculate the two diagonals of the marker in terms of pixels that would require to draw them and get relationship between as:

$$\mu^2 = \frac{d^2}{L * R_{\text{cm/px}}}$$

Where
d = diagonal of the marker in cm
L = longest distance in pixel
R = second longest distance
Length of the contour (L) = theta * μ cm.

4 Final Grading

As we are able to separate individual contours, we are also able to get the maximum possible length of the contours. That gives us the length of the potato itself. We then measure the maximum length perpendicular to length of contour and thus we get the width (Fig. 2).

The image shown in Fig. 3 contains bounding boxes around individual potatoes. Sometimes it is hard to differentiate two or more overlapping potatoes. The image shown is our worst case scenario prediction and still we were able to predict the size

Fig. 3. Bounding boxes around potatoes (Color figure online)

distribution with an accuracy of 97.2% in this particular image. On an average we had a variance of 4 to 6% in our data.

The curve shown in Fig. 4 shows the size distribution in the sample image. We analyze such curves to give grade to the product.

5 Defect Classification

On an average the defects contribute to only 2.5% of a ton in a typical Indian cold storage. We talked to few cold storage owners and they told us how they tackled the diseased potatoes. They manually sort such potatoes and throw it away if a customer ask for a higher standard of potatoes, otherwise they just let them be with the healthy potatoes. As the temperature of a cold storage is typically 4 °C, the disease usually

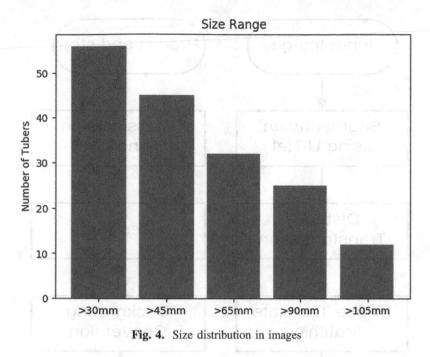

Fig. 4. Size distribution in images

don't spread but the ability to predict which disease is affecting the produce and up to what extent can be extremely helpful. As we try to sample the entire produce by randomly selecting 10% of the produce, we can map the observation of the sample onto the produce. In our method, let's say if we were to grade 1 ton of potato of a store, we would randomly pick 100 kg worth of bags containing potatoes and process it through our algorithm.

As we were able to separate the contours, we paste them onto a blue background and this data was ready for classification. The choice of a blue background was quite peculiar as there is no defect that we came across that had color blue in it. We had 6 categories of defects that a single counters was to be classified into. These were: Wet Rot, Dry Rot, Mechanical Damage, Sprouting, Insect Damage and Normal. You can see these categories in Fig. 6.

But there was a major problem that limited our capability to classify the defects and it was the skewness of the training data. The "Normal" class which was meant to represent healthy potato had more than 5000 training objects as opposed to the "Mechanical Damage" which had less than 250 training objects. This would have been a good enough dataset if we were to make one-vs-all classifier but that was not the solution we needed (Fig. 5).

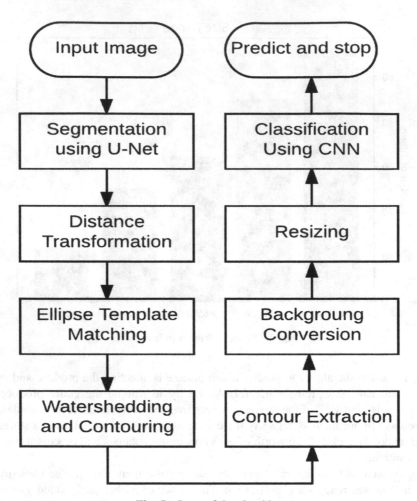

Fig. 5. Steps of the algorithm

6 CNN Defect Classifier

We decided to make a multi class CNN classifier with 1200 training example of each. Those classes which didn't had 1200 training objects, we made artificial training objects by augmenting images.

The input to the network was a Numpy array consisting images that were reshaped to [150×150] array and were coupled by a class label. The CNN architecture we used had 6 Convolution layer followed by respective pooling layers and two fully connected layer with RELU as activation layer and finally a regression layer with Adam optimizer. After 35 epochs we attained training accuracy of 87.9% however our validation accuracy was just 72.37%. This was an issue of over-fitting.

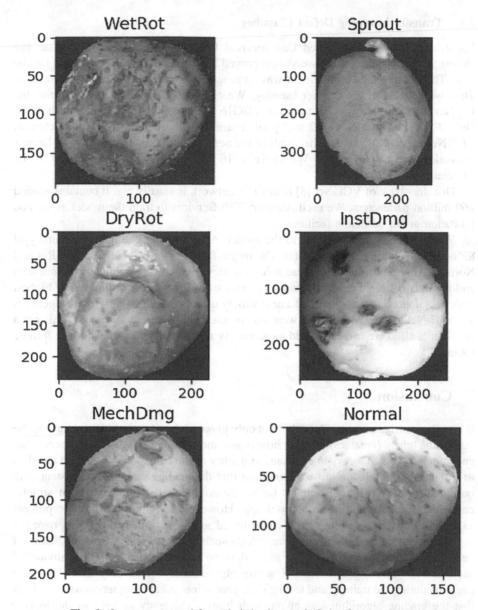

Fig. 6. Images separated from their background (Color figure online)

We optimized the parameter such as using loss function SGD with activation Sigmoid etc. but not much was achieved. The skewness of data also resulted in a biased for healthy potatoes.

As training a new network was a non-practical solution for us, we decided to use transfer learning for classification.

6.1   Transfer Learning Defect Classifier

For a brief time we considered Unsupervised Learning to classify the diseases but almost all the techniques that we visited proved not prudent enough to be used for the task. The training data requirement was enormous as compared to the available data. Thus we decided to use transfer learning. We chose VGGNet16 model to use as the ImgNet data that was used to train the VGG16 is quite similar to the potato images. Only 3×3 convolution and 2×2 pooling are used throughout the whole network. VGGNet [8] also shows that the depth of the network plays an important role. Deeper networks give better results. We chose a 16 layered network that proved to be sufficient.

One drawback of VGGNet [8] is that this network is usually big. It contains around 160 million parameters. We used Amazon Web Services to train the model as we had limitation at our academic facilities.

We added 6 more categories to the model. After training, we had an accuracy of 89% on validation set (unseen data). The major fault was in two classes: Wet Rot and Normal. After a bit tuning we were able to achieve satisfactory results as the our data and the data collected manually had a variance of as little as 2% at times. The highest error was noticed when we passed a new variety of potato (Kufri Jyoti) to the algorithm as the U-Net [9] and VGG16 [8] were trained on Santana variety of potato. This not a problem at all as we can easily add more variety to our database and can make it more robust.

7   Conclusion

It is clear now that after the algorithm not only gives us the necessary data regarding the size of the tubers (potatoes) but also how many and what kind of diseased tubers it has encountered. Thus it's easy to estimate the quality of the entire stock based on this data as in our cross validation test we found out that the grading remained consistent with our prediction. We initially aimed for an algorithm that could have been simpler enough to implemented as an android app. However this algorithm is quite process expensive yet we can utilize via a cloud based app. We further aim to improve the segmentation quality as there are more defects such as Greening and Bruising that as of yet we are unable to teach the U-Net as the data we have contained very little amount of such defects. Training a machine learning algorithm is not an easy task. We were cautious during the training and testing data generation. After completion we found out that the grading algorithm was at par with human efficiency as long as the marker detection was flawless. Thus we have confidence that this algorithm if applied on large scale would be a great help to farmers as they often cannot negotiate the price and would be the most adversely affected by wrong grading. We hope that with the advent of smartphone, we'd be able to develop an application that farmers could directly use to grade their produce.

References

1. Khoje, S.A., Bodhe, S.K., Adsul, A.: Automated skin defect identification system for fruit grading based on discrete curvelet transform. Int. J. Eng. Technol. (IJET) 0975–4024
2. Dubey, S.R., Dixit, P., Singh, N., Gupta, J.P.: Infected fruit part detection using K-means clustering segmentation technique. Int. J. Artif. Intell. Interact. Multimed. 2(2). https://doi.org/10.9781/ijimai.2013.229
3. Razmjooy, N., Mousavi, B.S., Soleymani, F.: A real-time mathematical computer method for potato inspection using machine vision. Comput. Math. Appl. 63, 268–279 (2012)
4. Bargoti, S., Underwood, J.P.: Image Segmentation for Fruit Detection and Yield Estimation in Apple Orchards. arXiv: 1610.08120v1 [cs.RO]
5. Zawbaa, H.M., Hazman, M., Abbass, M., Hassanien, A.E.: Automatic fruit classification using random forest algorithm. In: 2014 International Conference on Hybrid Intelligent Systems (HIS). IEEE (2014). 978-1-4799-7633-1/14/31.00
6. Krizhevsky, A., Sutskever, I., Hinton, G.E.: ImageNet Classification with Deep Convolutional Neural Networks, pp. 1097–1105. Curran Associates, Inc. (2012)
7. GoogLeNet presentation. http://image-net.org/challenges/LSVRC/2014/slides/GoogLeNet.pptx
8. Simonyan, K., Zisserman, A.: Very Deep Convolutional Networks for Large-Scale Image Recognition. CoRR/abs/1409.1556. http://arxiv.org/abs/1409.1556
9. Ronneberger, O., Fischer, P., Brox, T.: U-Net: Convolutional Networks for Biomedical Image Segmentation. CoRR/abs/1505.04597. http://arxiv.org/abs/1505.04597

Rough Fuzzy Technique for Giant Cell Tumor Detection

Krupali Mistry[1](✉), Sweta Dargad[2], and Avneet Saluja[1]

[1] Department of Computer Science and Engineering,
ITM Universe, Vadodara, Gujarat, India
`krupalimistry1993@gmail.com, aveefriend@gmail.com`
[2] Department of Computer Engineering, U.V. Patel College of Engineering,
Ganpat University, Mehsana, India
`swetamaheshwari02@gmail.com`

Abstract. The bone tumors are masses of tissue which are formed within the bone cells. Giant cell tumor of bone (GCT) is a one of a kind of benign (noncancerous) bone tumor. It is an osteolytic lesion which leads to progressive bone destruction, fracture and disability. For imaging the human body a medical technique called Magnetic Resonance technique (MRI) is used. MRI gives superlative imaging modality for medical research work because of its superior contrast resolution and multiplanar imaging capabilities. In this paper, we have used Rough Fuzzy C-Means Technique, an image processing clustering technique for detection of Giant Cell Tumor. We were able to reach the accuracy of 86.16% and with lesser computational time using this technique of Rough Fuzzy C-Means for detection of Giant Cell Tumor.

Keywords: Medical imaging · Clustering technique · Rough fuzzy
Bone tumor detection

1 Introduction

Image processing in medical science is an emerging and important field of research. Here we want to detect the Giant Cell tumor. In this research we are mainly concerned about the interactions of the tissue cells in human body. Irregular growth of human body tissues creates abnormal mass of tissue Tumors can be identified by simply doing proper examination of the region of the human body where there is swelling of tissue [1]. Bone tumors are formed in bones of human body. In tumor the healthy tissues are replaced by irregularly growing cells. Bone tumors develop when cells within a bone divide themselves uncontrollably, also forming a lump or mass of abnormal tissue [1]. Various types of bone tumor are there having several types of features. Noncancerous (Benign) and Cancerous (Malignant) [2] are mainly two types of bone tumors. Non cancererous tumor that is the benign tumor inclines to be growing slower, does not occupy nearby tissue also it is not easily expand to other parts of the body as the Malignant tumor does [11]. The Cancerous tumor that is the Malignant tumor is very hazardous because its cells can expand irrepressibly in a disorganized manner and produces immortal daughter cells. The cells nucleus is different from normal cell

© Springer Nature Singapore Pte Ltd. 2019
S. Verma et al. (Eds.): CNC 2018, CCIS 839, pp. 340–350, 2019.
https://doi.org/10.1007/978-981-13-2372-0_30

nucleus. It has a large nucleus and also reoccur after they are removed [3, 7]. The cancerous tumor weakens the human bone as well also harm the healthy tissue.

Giant cell tumors (GCTs) of bone, also known as osteoclastomas. Osteoclastomas that is Giant cell tumor of bone (GCT) is not spreadable because it is Benign i.e. Non Cancerous and locally aggressive tumor. The way the Giant cell tumors appear in the microscope its named as Giant cell tumor. By combination of several individual cells in a one, larger complex cells. Although Giant cell tumor is benign tumor but still it can regrow once it is removed just like malignant tumor. When they regrow they become more aggressive and transform to a cancerous tumor. It is more likely to occur between the ages of 20–45, the one who has reached skeletal maturity. Giant cell tor mainly happens at skin bone, end points of thigh bone as well as in the lower arm bone. Giant cell tumors too can produce in the pelvis, spine, ribs, skull and sacrum. The most common location is around the knee where 50% of giant cell tumor grows [1].

Different medical test are used by doctors to identify and diagnose medical problems like CT scans, Magnetic resonance Imaging and X rays. Magnetic Resonance imaging is used by physicians to diagnose medical conditions like tumor. The higher resolution that is provided by MRI imaging technique is the best. To produce a very clear image of the affected area the Magnetic resonance imaging (MRI) scan uses high magnetic fields and radio waves. MRI scan does not harm any part of the human body. This scan can study any human body part therefore this scan is most widespread among doctors to identify the tumor in the body. Dominant magnet is contained in an MRI scanner that is a huge tube. A non-invasive medical system Magnetic resonance imaging (MRI) is used to display 2D images of the human body [3]. MRI images gives data which is most appropriate and it assist in early discovery of tumorsa and also of tumor boundaries exact estimation [10].

To provide different information of tumors various Magnetic resonance sequences T1 weighted, diffusion weighted, T2 weighted, flow sensitive and 'miscellaneous' weighted scans. On T2W they appear intermediate to high intense (gray to white) [10]. T2W MRI Series Giant Cell Tumor has intensity and bright range. This strong reason has abided us on selecting T2W MRI series. Researching many online sources of T2W series of Giant Cell Tumor we were able to find a very precise case of thigh and knee bone from sources like radiologyanalyst.nl and radiopedia.org.

The paper Rough Fuzzy Technique for Giant cell tumor is prepared as under. In second section, we have explained the concept of Rough Fuzzy C-Means which is a clustering technique which we have used for segmentation. In section three we have presented the proposed work flow using a flowchart for bone tumors detection. In section four we have shown the calculation using procedures like accuracy, sensitivity and specificity and also the performance calculation. In the last sections we have added the conclusion of this research and future work which we will try to focus in our next research.

2 Rough Fuzzy Technique

In early 1980s Zdzisław Pawlak introduced Rough Set Theory. It was further advanced and in last 25years it has provided an approach which can be used for granular computing [4]. This research focuses on a basic idea that is to determine on what level a certain collection of objects (example, image pixel windows) estimates another collection of objects of concern. So taking in to consideration these description of objects and comparing them. So Rough set theory is an new approach to achieve any uncertainty of data dependencies, importance of features, patterns in the sample data, feature space dimensionality reduction and also the classification of objects. Rough set theory can help us to find the set of elements which totally belong to a individual an equivalence relation R, when defined in it can lead towards a partition cluster and also to the collection of elements that belongs partially or probably to that cluster [4].

Rough set theory depends upon two main concepts lower and upper approximations. We have assumed $U \neq \emptyset$, an equivalence relation R is defined which leads to a partition of U, we denote $U/R = \{X1, X2, ..., Xn\}$, here subset Xc is called a category. Xc represents an equivalence class of R [5]. We have used the concept of approximations to represent the roughness. The R-upper and R-lower approximations of the subset X are defined as,

$$\begin{cases} \overline{RX} = \cup \{Y \in U/R | Y \cap X \neq \emptyset\} \\ \underline{RX} = \cup \{Y \in U/R | Y \subseteq X\} \end{cases} \tag{1}$$

Here the symbol X certainly contains all the subsets that is contained in the lower approximation and the upper approximation holds all subsets that are possibly included in X. R-positive, R-negative and R-boundary regions of X are based on the lower and upper approximation. So the boundary regions of X can be justified by the following formula [5]:

$$\begin{cases} POS_R(X) = \underline{RX} \\ NEG_R(X) = U - \overline{RX} \\ BN_R = \overline{RX} - \underline{RX} \end{cases} \tag{2}$$

3 Proposed Methodology

The proposed system detects the Giant Cell Tumor (GCT) from the MRI series of T2W images. The proposed methodology is divided into four stages. Initially we are performing preprocessing stage that is meant for de-noising the image, further stage is segmenting the denoised image in which Rough Fuzzy C-Means techniques is used, after that the further stage consist of identification of tumor using the mean pixel intensity and finally the tumor is detected. The overall workflow is shown in Fig. 1.

3.1 Preprocessing

Initially we are performing the preprocessing stage so that the image is denoised and quality of an image is improved. So the image is de-noised. The image which is captured using MRI imaging is of poor quality. In order to remove noise, improve the

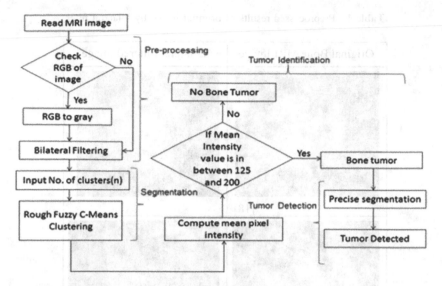

Fig. 1. Proposed work flow

quality, conserving and sharpening edges we use filters [10]. The algorithm initially converts RGB images to grayscale images and are filtered by performing nonlinear bilateral filter [10]. The bilateral filter is similar to Gaussian convolution and is defined as a weighted average intensities of neighboring pixels and to preserve edges it takes the difference in value of adjacent pixels [6]. The bilateral filter main task is that for a pixel to effect another pixel, it should occupy a nearby location and also have a similar value [6] (Table 1).

3.2 Image Segmentation (Clustering Technique)

After de-noising the original MRI T2W images, they are given as an input to RFCM clustering image segmentation technique. Initially the filtered and denoised image are given as an input to Fuzzy C-Means and the formation of clusters is done according to Fuzzy C- Means by giving the number of clusters as an input number [10]. After that the clustered image is given as an input to RFCM, where fuzziness is applied to the image using rough set theories. The objective is to minimized the objective function, but here as its objective is rough set theory which contains the concept of upper and lower approximation we will consider here upper approximation and accordingly our objective function formed is [4]:

$$J_m(U, V) = \sum_{j=1}^{n} \sum_{i=1, x_j \in upper(w_i)}^{k} \mu_{ij}^{m} d_{ij}^{2} \tag{3}$$

Table 1. Preprocessed results of original image by bilateral filter

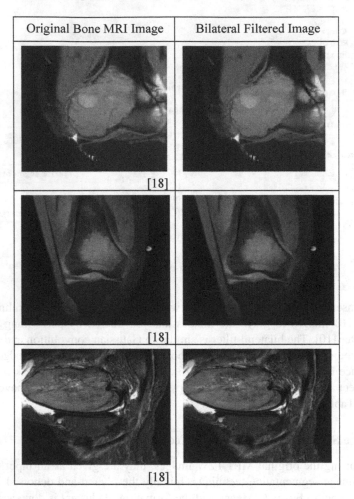

Constraint conditions are [4]

$$\mu_{ij} \in [0,1], 0 \leq \sum_{j=1}^{n} \mu_{ij} \leq N, \sum_{i=1, x_j \in upper(w_i)}^{k} \mu_{ij} = 1 \ and \ d_{ij} = \|x_j - v_i\| \qquad (4)$$

The membership function of Rough Fuzzy C-Means is given below [4].

$$\mu_{ij} = \frac{1}{\sum_{l=1, x_j \in upper(w_i)}^{k} \left(\frac{d_{ij}^2}{d_{ij}^2}\right)^{\frac{1}{m-1}}} \qquad (5)$$

Calculation of the centroid is done as follows [4].

$$v_i = \frac{\sum_{j=1}^{n} \mu_{ij}^m x_j}{\sum_{j=1}^{n} \mu_{ij}^m} \tag{6}$$

u_{ij} is the degree of membership of x_i in the cluster j, m is the real number (m = 2), x_j is the jth of d-dimensional centre of the cluster, v_i is the d-dimensional centre of the cluster and cluster as input we have taken as k = 5. As the concept of rough set theory the upper approximation limit here we have taken is $pper(w_i) = 40$, $\varepsilon > 0$ and s = 0. First calculate the centers using Eq. (6) $v_i^{(s)}$. After the centres are been calculated check the condition $x_j \notin upper(w_i)$, then $u_{ij} = 0$ otherwise according to formula update $u_{ij}^{(s)}$. The closing condition of iteration is [9].

$$\left\| \mu_{ij}^{(s)} - \mu_{ij}^{(s+1)} \right\| < \varepsilon \tag{7}$$

Here $\varepsilon > 0$ if this condition is not satisfied then s = s + 1, again calculate the centres. u_{ij} is the membership of x_j belonged to w_i, whose calculation is only related with the concept of rough set theory the upper approximation contained x_j, and if x_j is not contained in the upper approximation set of a certain class w_k, then with this the membership of x_j to this class has no contribution.

3.3 Tumor Identification

The identification of tumor is done by calculation of the MPI (mean pixel intensity) of the clustered image. The sum of pixel intensities for the clustered extracted tumor part is S and the number of pixels is N [8, 10]. So the MPI (Mean Pixel Intensity) is given as follows:

$$\text{Mean Pixel Intensity} = \frac{\text{Sum of the pixel intensities for the extracted tumor part (S)}}{\text{No. of pixels for the extracted tumor part (N)}} \tag{8}$$

The calculated Mean Pixel Intensity follows in the range from 125 to 200, then it is considered as a detected tumor otherwise the image is classified as a non-tumor image.

3.4 Detection of Tumor Using MATLAB Function

When we successfully identify the tumor from the clustered segmented tumor image, the image contains some artefacts. This artefacts can be removed by using the Matlab tool which contains the function for all connected small portion components [10]. This Matlabfunction calculates the area of the entire segmented regions, but only the region with maximum area is considered and other regions are discarded. The above mentioned Matlab function calculates the area of the clustered segmented region of tumor and considers the region with maximum area while the other small detected areas are rejected (Tables 2 and 3).

Table 2. Segmented image

Clustered Image	RFCM Segmented Image

Table 3. Results of precise segmentation of giant cell tumor

Actual Segmented Image	Calculated MPI (Mean Pixel Intensity)
	190.8155
	130.6155
	125.5230

4 Performance Evaluation Using Measure Analysis

We performed analysis on 44 different MRI images of knee bone. For analyzing these images we used some performance evaluation parameters like accuracy, sensitivity and specificity. For evaluating performance we require some alarms or measure analysis mechanisms, that are TP, TN, FP, FN as shown in below table. Here ROI is Region of Interest means the part that is detected (Table 4).

Table 4. Measure analysis parameters [7]

TP - True positive	The correctly segmented number of pixels that are in ROI region
TN - True Negative	The correctly segmented number of pixels that are in non-ROI region
FP - False positive	The incorrectly segmented number of pixels that are in ROI region
FP - False positive	The incorrectly segmented number of pixels that are in non-ROI region

The performance evaluation based on the Measures Analysis TP, TN, FP and FN is given as:

The measures of the degree of closeness between the segmented image and the ground truth images, known as Accuray is given by following formula.

$$\text{Accuracy} = \frac{TP + TN}{TP + TN + FP + FN} \tag{9}$$

The measure of the proportion of correct pixels of Region of Interest is Sensitivity given by following formula.

$$\text{Sensitivity} = \frac{TP}{TP + FN} \tag{10}$$

The measures of the proportion of correct pixel of non-ROI region is Specificity given by following formula.

$$\text{Specificity} = \frac{TN}{TN + FP} \tag{11}$$

Table 5. Measures of giant cell tumor

Performance evaluation based on measure analysis			
Images	Accuracy	Sensitivity	Specificity
T1	75.73	21.58	88.45
T2	84.47	15.76	87.52
T3	89.97	37.96	89.06
T4	86.90	42.71	77.61
T5	86.17	36.11	84.33
T6	88.18	40.39	85.84
T7	70.68	46.12	85.23
T8	87.25	49.59	86.31
T9	87.18	50.90	87.73
T10	83.41	43.04	83.12
.	.	.	.
Average	**86.16**	**41.84**	**90.59**

We achieved overall Accuracy 86.16%, Sensitivity of 41.84% and Specificity of 90.59% by finding the average for 44 images with this mechanism of Rough Fuzzy C-Means technique of Giant Cell Tumor on MRI images (Table 5). The processing time taken by fuzzy c-means and rough fuzzy c-means are shown below in the table (Table 6):

Table 6. Time taken for detection of giant cell tumor

Images	Computational time taken to detect giant cell tumor	
	FCM	RFCM
T1	48.4732	14.4846
T2	30.0675	12.3642
T3	39.9977	10.3604
T4	65.7485	20.3659
T5	116.4141	87.5236
T6	51.6685	20.3659
T7	42.5119	5.4256
T8	122.6466	90.2365

5 Future Enhancement and Conclusion

In this paper Rough fuzzy technique for Giant cell tumor we tried on 44 images of Giant cell tumor Magnetic resonance imaging (MRI) and after testing we got the Accuracy of 86.16%, Sensitivity 41.84% and Specificity 90.59%. And we can conclude that Rough fuzzy C-means method gives the precise segmentation as compared to other methods like Fuzzy C-Means (FCM). The method we used that is the Rough fuzzy C-Means approach takes lesser computational time also it provides higher accuracy and the time required to processed is also less as compared to other methods. The sensitivity measure that we achieved by using our method that was 41.84% can be further improved and also in the future features like area, shape can also be detected.

References

1. American Academy of Orthopaedic Surgeons: ÖrthoInfo. www.orthoinfo.aaos.org/bonetumors
2. Abdel-Maksoud, E., Elmogy, M., Al-Awadi, R.: Brain tumor segmentation based on a hybrid clustering technique. Egypt. Inform. J. **16**(1), 71–81 (2015)
3. Grünberg, K., Rehnitz, C., Weber, M.-A.: Benign and malignant bone tumors: radiological diagnosis and imaging features clinical orthopedic imaging (2013)
4. Bhattacharya, A., Patnaik, K.S.: Modified rough fuzzy C means algorithm for MR image segmentation. In: 2013 International Conference on Machine Intelligence and Research Advancement (ICMIRA), pp. 407–411. IEEE (2013)
5. Ji, Z., Sun, Q., Xia, Y., Chen, Q., Xia, D., Feng, D.: Generalized rough fuzzy c-means algorithm for brain MR image segmentation. Comput. Methods Programs Biomed. **108**(2), 644–655 (2012)
6. Tomasi, C., Manduchi, R.: Bilateral filtering for gray and color images. In: 1998 Sixth International Conference on Computer Vision, pp. 839–846. IEEE (1998)
7. Machado, D., Giraldi, G., Novotny, A., Marques, R., Conci, A.: Topological derivative applied to automatic segmentation of frontal breast thermograms. In: Workshop de Visao Computacional, Rio de Janeiro (2013)

8. Afshan, N., Qureshi, S., Hussain, S.M.: Comparative study of tumor detection algorithms. In: 2014 International Conference on Medical Imaging, m-Health and Emerging Communication Systems (MedCom), pp. 251–256. IEEE (2014)

9. Hooda, H., Verma, O.P., Singhal, T.: Brain tumor segmentation: a performance analysis using K-means, fuzzy C-means and region growing algorithm. In: 2014 International Conference on Advanced Communication Control and Computing Technologies (ICACCCT), pp. 1621–1626. IEEE (2014)

10. Mistry, K.D., Talati, B.J.: Integrated approach for bone tumor detection from MRI scan imagery. In: International Conference on Signal and Information Processing (IConSIP), pp. 1–5. IEEE (2016)

11. Benign Tumor: Types, Causes and Treatment. https://www.webmd.boots.com/cancer/benign-tumours

Face Recognition in Surveillance Video for Criminal Investigations: A Review

Napa Lakshmi[1(✉)] and Megha P. Arakeri[2]

[1] Nitte Meenakshi Institute of Technology, Bengaluru, India
napa.lakshmi@nmit.ac.in
[2] Ramaiah Institute of Technology, Bengaluru, India
meghalakshman@gmail.com

Abstract. Face recognition from surveillance video in a forensic scenario is a very challenging task. Much of the existing work focuses on face recognition in a video where the video frames are of high-resolution, containing faces in frontal pose and in optimal lighting conditions. However, new challenges are encountered as applications of face recognition advance from cooperative and constrained scenarios to uncooperative subjects in unconstrained scenarios such as video surveillance. These challenges are due to low image resolution, variant expressions, face orientations, partial occlusion, complex background and the differences in surrounding illumination. In criminal investigations, the aim is to identify a culprit by collecting the information from the various face input media that includes video tracks, still face images, 3D model of a face, and verbal descriptions of the person presented by eyewitness. Face sketch may be generated from these verbal descriptions which can be matched against mug shot database. This paper reviews various methods and techniques used to identify a person of interest in an unconstrained environment with the above-mentioned challenges.

Keywords: Video surveillance · Face recognition · Partial occlusion
Forensic sketch · Pose · Expression · 3D face model · Datasets

1 Introduction

Face recognition technology is the most significant tool for identifying individuals and solving crimes. It has the potential to assist law enforcement in watch list surveillance or criminal investigations by identifying the suspect from the evidence available from a crime scene like a video or images. Generally, Forensic examiners manually inspect the facial images or videos to match a trace with an image of a suspect face or with a large database of mug-shots which takes lot of time. When comparing facial images manually, the differences may be unseen because of under-exposure, over-exposure, low resolution, out of focus, distortions in the imaging process. Automatic face recognition overcomes the narrow vision of human eye in recognizing extensive number of human faces [32].

Figure 1. shows the key steps in automated facial recognition. They are (1) face detection in video frames, (2) record detected faces, (3) compare recorded faces with

© Springer Nature Singapore Pte Ltd. 2019
S. Verma et al. (Eds.): CNC 2018, CCIS 839, pp. 351–364, 2019.
https://doi.org/10.1007/978-981-13-2372-0_31

the gallery set and (4) automatic process to find the closest match to send alerts when a positive match occurs [33].The different approaches that are used for detecting a face in the effective video frames are feature based approaches such as Random Labeled Graph Matching [45], Template Matching techniques like Active Appearance Model [46], Appearance based methods include Example based Learning [47], Haar features with AdaBoost algorithm [42], Part-based methods such as Generative models [48], Component-based with SVM [49] etc.

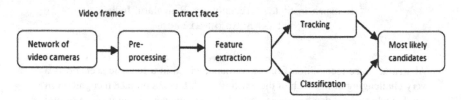

Fig. 1. General automated face recognition system

There are various concerns to be addressed with automatic face recognition system specific to the forensic domain. Firstly, the existing face recognition techniques are not robust to the pose variations, lighting conditions, facial expressions [22]. Secondly, the quality of available images is normally low in the forensic scenario. Thirdly, the investigators must make use of all the handy information to assist in subject recognition. Typically, the face images of a suspect are obtained from surveillance cameras, mobile cameras (video tracks), images from social media sites forensic sketches and demographic information (age, gender, and race). Automatic face recognition system is not intended to replace forensic expert, but helps in minimizing the time taken to search for suspect in large sized video surveillance data.

2   Literature Review

There are many review papers existing on general face recognition [22, 35] but very few papers discussed on face recognition in video surveillance for forensic investigations [3, 6]. This paper outlines the various techniques developed so far in forensic face recognition in an unconstrained environment along with the various challenges that still exists, performance measures and the available datasets for the research.

2.1   Forensic Sketch Recognition

In most of the criminal cases, a sketch is used to identify the suspect if his photo is not available. The sketches that are accessed in criminal investigations are either created by computer software (composite sketches) or drawn by forensic artists (forensic sketches) with the verbal information provided by a bystander or the victim. Sketch based face recognition has been improved with the idea of converting sketches and photos into same modality so that sketch to sketch or photo to photo recognition can be carried out easily with the aid of the available face recognition algorithms.

Three approaches can be used for cross modality conversion such as synthesis-based, feature based and subspace projection based approaches. Synthesis-based approaches focus on conversion of a photo to a sketch and vice-versa. Projection based approaches maps photo and sketch into a common subspace that can be directly comparable. Feature based approaches find invariant features for each modality but unlike to each person.

Tang and Wang [1] used a photo-to-sketch transformation method to obtain pseudo-sketch which is compared with the real sketch using the Eigen-face method. The limitations are: the data which may be helpful for the recognition phase is lost with the photo to sketch conversion and the effects of illumination variation can result in imprecise face sketches. Li et al. [2] projected a technique in which a hybrid space method is used to synthesize a real face image from the composite sketch. Klare et al. [3] used feature SIFT descriptors that were constant between the photo and sketch modalities for sketch and photo encoding however inefficient in finding global differences and the extracted features from photos and sketches may have large inter-modality variations [4]. Zhang et al. [5] used a feature based approach called coupled information-theoretic encoding to quantize the local structures of face photos and sketches into discrete codes. The codes of photo and sketch of the same subject are highly correlated thus reducing inter-modality gap.

The composite sketches can be generated by using one the facial composite software systems such as FACES [8], IdentiKit [9], and Photo-Fit [10] that are accessible to forensic agencies. Han et al. [11] discussed matching of composite sketches with the photos using component based approach in which facial landmarks in face photos and composite sketches are detected using active shape model (ASM). Each facial component features are calculated using multi-scale local binary patterns (MLBPs). But, this paper doesn't address the age variation of a formerly captured mugshot and the present suspect's face. Klum et al. [12] presented a FaceSketchID System which considered surveillancecomposites along with software generated composites and hand-drawn composites to match with mug-shots. They also combined holistic as well as component based algorithms to boost matching performance. Galea [54] discussed 3-D morphable model to create new images by varying facial features which helps deep convolutional neural network to learn the relationships between photos and sketches. After converting photos and sketches into the same modality, techniques like PCA, Bayesianface, Fisherface, null-space LDA, dual-space LDA and Random sampling LDA can be applied for homogeneous face recognition [3].

Matching strategies of a sketch and mugshot are multi-class classifiers such as Nearest Neighbour (NN) and model based verification strategies. NN classifier makes use of different distance metrics such as chi-square or cosine distance. The merit of NN approach is that they do not explicitly require the training dataset and they are used to verify a face in a pre-defined set of people. Model- based verification strategies are applied to check whether a face matches with someone in the watch-list (Table 1).

Table 1. Summary of sketch based face recognition techniques

Approach	Technique	Advantages and drawbacks	Recognition strategy
Synthesis-based	Eigen sketch transformation [1]	New sketch is constructed using a linear combination of training sketch samples. The drawback is synthesized sketches lack the details which has negative impact on final matching accuracy	Karhunen-Loeve Transform (KLT)
	Markov Random Fields(MRF) [50]	Synthesizes local face components at multiple scales. The drawback is it cannot handle well non-facial components like hair style, glasses etc.	Random sampling LDA (RS_LDA)
	Embedded Hidden Markov Model(E-HMM) [51]	Converts photo to sketch instead of generating photo from sketch	PCA, Fisherface, Bayesianface
	Local Linear Embedding (LLE) [52]	A sketch is created from a photousing image patches instead of holistic photos	
	Multiple representations based Face Sketch Synthesis (MrFSPS) [60]	Image patch is represented by combining multiple representations using Markov networks-based framework and learns the weights of multiple representations adaptively and selects candidate patches for the target patch	Fisherface, RS-LDA
Feature-based	Scale invariant feature transform (SIFT) [3]	Represents image patch as a vector of magnitude, spatial distribution of image gradients and orientation	NN with Euclidean distance
	Self-Similarity [53]	Extracts features from local regions of photos and sketches independently	NN
	Coupled Information-Theoretic Encoding (CITE) [5]	Distinctive local facial components can be captured	PCA + LDA
	Gabor shape [55]	Captures significant visual features such asorientation sensitivity, spatial localization and spatial frequency	NN, Chi-square

(continued)

Table 1. (*continued*)

Approach	Technique	Advantages and drawbacks	Recognition strategy
	Extended Uniform Circular Local Binary Pattern (EUCLBP) [56]	Facial patterns are created by high frequency information in face images. After computing EUCLBP descriptors, the optimal weights are found using Genetic algorithm based weight optimization technique for every facial patch	Weighted Chi-square
	Histogram of Averaged Oriented Gradient (HAOG) [57]	Extracts features from stronger gradients like eyes, eyebrows, ears, mouth, nose etc.	NN, Chi-square
	Local Randon Binary Pattern (LRBP) [58]	Face images are mapped into Randon space and these face images are determined by Local Binary Pattern (LBP). Then histograms of local LBPs are concatenated to compute LRBP	NN, PMK (pyramid match kernel), Chi-square
	Geometric features [59]	The aspect ratio of facial structures such as eyebrows, eyes, nose, and lips are encoded as feature vectors	K-NN
	Visual saliency and attribute feedback [61]	Composite sketches are matched with digital photos by combining facial features along with attributes such gender, ethnicity and age. HOG features are extracted	Chi-square distance
Projection-based	Common Discriminant Feature Extraction (CDFE) [3]	Projects photo and sketch into common feature space that performs matching effectively	NN
	Partial Least Squares (PLS) [3]	Linearly maps images of different modalities into a common subspace where mutual covariance is maximized	NN
	Kernel-based Nonlinear Discriminant Analysis (KNDA) [52]	The pseudo-sketch is generated by preserving the geometry between the photo and a sketch	LDA

2.2 Restoring Partially Occluded Face

An obstacle in the way of viewing an object is known as occlusion. It can be natural or synthetic. Natural occlusion is when some object hinders the view of the face. Synthetic occlusion is hiding the face intentionally by covering it with objects like scarf, hair, sunglasses or other accessories. The methods developed so far to detect and restore occluded regions are divided into the following three categories.

Part-Based Methods: The overlapping and non-overlapping parts of the face image are identified that are used for recognition. Sharif et al. described various part based methods such as Principal Component Analysis (PCA), Independent Component Analysis (ICA), Linear Discriminate Analysis (LDA), Non-negative Matrix Factorization (NMF), Local Non -negative Matrix Factorization (LNMF) [13]. However, these techniques results in a large computation cost in training and testing the data.

Feature-Based Methods: Wang et al. [14] explained AdaBoost, SVM and Local Gaussian Summation techniques that deals with the occlusion by considering only the individual attributes such as region around eyes, nose and mouth and overlook other characteristics that can be unique with different individuals.

Appearance-Based Methods: Texture information is used to discover and repairimages of face occluded regions. Image reconstruction can be done with PCA, principal component scores of each division of input image are calculated and used this information to reconstruct the entire input image. PCA reconstructs occluded regions by using only effective pixels. Tomoki et al. proposed Fast Weighted Principal Component Analysis (FW-PCA) [15] that calculates PCA with only effective pixels. This method is computationally heavy.

Image inpainting is the way of rebuilding missing, corrupted or occluded parts in an image with the help of neighboring visual pixels while restoring its unity. The techniques used are Partial Differential Equation (PDE) based image inpainting, Texture synthesis based image inpainting, Exemplar based image inpainting [18] and Hybrid inpainting. The limitation with these methods is that they produce blurring artifacts and not well suited for the reproduction of large texture regions [11]. Texture synthesis based algorithms use the idea of synthesizing artificial texture by filling the unfilled regions using other similarly damaged neighbor pixels [17], but fails to reproduce structured/regular textures. Pixel based (nonparametric) texture synthesis techniques fail to grow large structured textures.

Mahroosh et al. [19] explained Exemplar-based in painting methods that are faster than PDE pixel based approaches. The patches of the known part of the image are used to create entire patches by these techniques. Omkar et al. [20] introduced a new method in which exemplar based method with a super-resolution technique can be used. These algorithms cannot handle curved structures properly and generate staircase effect in the image. Hybrid based image inpainting approaches combine both PDE based inpainting and texture synthesis for filling the hole [7]. It divides the image into two parts, structure and texture regions. Edge propagating algorithms and texture synthesis techniques are used to fill the large missing regions of decomposed regions and also preserve both structure and texture in a visually possible manner [16]. It needs more computational time for large holes.

2.3 Pose and Expression

Pose specifies how the subject is placed relative to the camera. Pose variation becomes a major concern when the face is to be recognized from a surveillance video because the subject may not be cooperative with the camera and the face appears in arbitrary poses in the frames to be recognized. Hu et al. [23] presented a novel method known as the multi-oriented two- dimensional principal component analyses (PCA) to generate more training images in various degrees. Considering the fact that face structure is axis-symmetrical, Xu et al. [24] used the mirror image method that overcomes some misalignment problems and also eliminates the pose and the illumination variation and makes it more robust. These methods have better performance but encounter some challenges when they were applied in video monitoring where video faces were captured in low-resolution, illumination variation and uncontrolled poses.

The pose-invariant 2D face recognition methods are divided into three categories, such as real view-based matching [28], pose transformation in image space [34], and in feature space [20]. These methods are required to gather a great number of gallery images per subject covering various poses. Large pose variations result in image discontinuities in the 2D image space. Under such situations, 3D methods usually perform better than 2D techniques. Face recognition methods are categorized into three categories with an aid of 3D face models, i.e., (1) generic shape based approaches, (2) image-based 3D reconstructions, and (3) feature-based 3D reconstructions. Xiao et al. [25] developed a 3D face model from a high-resolution 2D anterior face and it is used to produce several virtual faces with different poses. Both original frontal face image and virtual face images were put into a gallery set. But, the generation of a 3D model is a complex process.

Zheng et al. [26] discussed an appearance-based approach that is used to handle pose variations with the frontal as well as side faces. Ghinea et al. [27] proposed an approach that makes of image gradient information which are invariant to pose and illumination differences. Lin [29] presented a method to build an accurate 3D face model by acquiring five images from a fixed camera by rotating the object 450 apart. Asthana et al. [30] discussed a method in which front view of each face image is synthesized by normalizing pose of each gallery and query image. Then, 2D locations of landmark points in face images are located using Active Appearance Model (AAM) and handles a continuous range of poses. The drawback of this technique is that large occluded regions are formed in more extreme poses after rotation to frontal [31].

To mitigate the pose variations either of the following two methods is used. One is to use large number of images with different poses and the other way is to normalize the images with various poses to single frontal image. Alternative to these methods, Masi et al. [63] have proposed Pose-Aware Models (PAM) in which deep convolutional neural network (CNN) [65] is used process face image where a very few images are available for training. Using CNN it's tough to localize facial landmarks and to classify the gender under extreme poses.

Yin and Liu [64] proposed multi-task learning (MTL) to detect face as well as recognize with extreme poses using CNN framework. Ranjan et al. [68] developed HyperFace which combines CNN and MTL to detect face, to localize facial landmarks, classifies the gender and assesses the head pose. Peng et al. [67] generates various non-frontal faces from a single frontal face and extracts pose invariant features using deep neural network.

2.4 Performance Evaluation Techniques

Performance of the various face recognition techniques can be evaluated using the following techniques [44].

- **ROC curve** (Receiver Operating Characteristic curve) are used for verification that are drawn with false accept rate versus verification rate
- **CMC** (cumulative match curve) curves are used for identification which provides recognition accuracy for each rank.
- **Confusion matrix for face recognition**

Ground truth	Identified (Positive)	Not identified (Negative)
Face images present in the dataset	True positive (TP)	False negative (FN)
Face images not present in the dataset	False positive (FP)	True negative (TN)

True positive specifies the number of face images that are identified correctly. False positive indicates the number of face images which are not matching but identified as one of the face in the database. True negative specifies the face images that are not matching with the gallery set are correctly not identified. False negative indicates the number of faces that are of the database.

- **Precision** is the "fraction of the correctly detected faces to the total number of all detected faces".
  Precision = TP/(TP + TN)
- **Recall** is the fraction of the relevant images that were correctly detected
  Recall = TP/(TP + FN)
- **Fallout** is the proportion of non-relevant images that were detected as positive.
  Fallout = TN/(TN + FP)
- **F-measure** gives the average of precision(P) and recall(R) and gives the summary of PR curve
  F-measure = (2*P*R)/(P + R)
- **Accuracy** gives the fraction of number of correct classification to the total number of samples.
  Accuracy = (TP + TN)/(TP + TN + FP + FN)
- **FAR** (False Accept Rate) is "the probability that the system incorrectly matches the input face image to a non-matching face image in the gallery".
  FAR = FP/(FP + FN)
- **FRR** (False Reject Rate) is the "probability that the system fails to detect a match between the input face image and a matching face image in the gallery.
  FRR = FN/(TP + FN)

3   Existing Datasets

The different datasets for different tasks (pose, expression, occlusion, and sketch) in face recognition in unconstrained environment is mentioned in the Table 2.

Table 2. Datasets for unconstrained face recognition

Dataset	Size	Purpose
SCface - surveillance Cameras Face database [36]	4160 static images of 130 subjects in visible and infrared spectrum	Used for pose variation and 3D face recognition
YouTube Faces database [37]	3,425 videos of 1,595 different subjects	To study the issue of face recognition in unconstrained videos
Labeled Faces in the Wild [38]	13,000 face images of 1680 subjects collected from the web	To test the face verification scenario under unconstrained conditions
AR face database [39]	4,000 color images of 126 subjects (70 men and 56 women)	Variations in facial expressions, illumination conditions, and occlusions (sun glasses and scarf)
IIIT-Delhi Semi-forensic Sketch database [40]	140 semi forensic sketches with corresponding photos and 190 forensic sketches	Useful for sketch face recognition
The pattern recognition and Image Processing Hand-Drawn Composite (PRIP-HDC) database [12]	265 hand drawn and composite sketches along with the corresponding mug-shots. These are drawn based on verbal description by eyewitness or victim	Useful for forensic sketch recognition
CUHK Face Sketch FERET dataset (CUFSF) [43]	1194 subjects, a sketch and a photo is provided for each subject	Used to benchmark Sketch based face recognition
CMU Pose, Illumination, and Expression (PIE) database [41]	41368 images of 68 subjects	Image of each person with 13 different poses, 43 various illumination conditions, and with 4 distinct expressions
EFIT-V [62]	600 composite sketches of 300 subjects	Helps in more robust evaluation of composite face sketch recognition
IJB-A (IARPA Janus Benchmark A) dataset [66]	Consists of 5712 images and 2085 videos of 500 subjects	Benchmark dataset to evaluate unconstrained face detection and recognition algorithms with full pose and occlusion

4 Challenges

Face recognition in an uncontrolled environment is not an easy task. Most facial recognition algorithms outstand in matching one image of a secluded face with another such as a driver's license or a passport in which pose, illumination, and expression are firmly controlled. This section emphasizes the challenges in applying face-recognition technique to forensics domain and also gives an outline of future research work that can be carried out in this field.

- *Recognition of suspect's face in a crowd under varied illumination and low resolution*: The reasons for the poor quality of images captured in CCTV cameras include large distance between the subject and the camera, reduced spatial resolution of the camera, the speed at which the subject is moving, changes in the illumination at the monitored location.
- *Face recognition under partial occlusion:* As the subject is not anticipated to be cooperative, it may be blocked by other moving objects or the subject may cover his face from the camera deliberately not to reveal his identity.
- Another challenge is to generate a 3D face model from manifold still images or video frames to nullify pose variance.
- Face mark or scar based matching and retrieval also serves as valuable evidence in legal testimony. However, the challenge is to build an automated system for modeling the face at given target age effectively and synthesize a facial image with the aging effects.
- Facial aging process affects the face shape and its texture which deteriorates the performance of the automated face system. Thus, matching composite sketches with age variant face images is a significant research area.
- Exploring the effects of plastic surgery in thermal-infrared imagery will be the notable future research directions. Face recognition algorithms present degraded performance when matching face images before and after plastic surgery.
- Many issues in Low Resolution Face Recognition are yet unresolved, such as super-resolution (SR) for face recognition, unified feature spaces, resolution-robust features [6] and face detection at a distance, although many approaches have been developed for it.

5 Conclusion

Even though sufficient research and effort are placed into enhancing performance of the contemporary face recognition systems, very less effort is put in incorporating face recognition technology to criminal investigations. In this paper, various methods and techniques to identify a person of interest in an unconstrained scenario such as video surveillance are discussed. Major challenges in forensic face recognition such as matching a forensic sketch to mug shot database, identifying the suspect image in a video of low resolution, in different lighting conditions, under different poses, and with partial occlusion are presented. These challenges lead to less system accuracy. Thus, many forensic organizations have yet to embrace this technology in full. This paper also presented available standard databases and performance evaluation techniques.

References

1. Tang, X., Wang, X.: Face sketch recognition. IEEE Trans. Circuits Syst. Video Technol. **14**(1), 50–57 (2004). https://doi.org/10.1109/tcsvt.2003.818353
2. Li, Y.-H., Savvides, M., Bhagavatula, V.: Illumination tolerant face recognition using a novel face from sketch synthesis approach and advanced correlation Filters. IEEE (2006). ISBN 1-4244-0469-X, ICASSP
3. Ouyang, S., et al: A survey on heterogeneous face recognition: sketch, infra-red, 3D and low-resolution. Image Vis. Comput. (2016). http://dx.doi.org/10.1016/.imavis
4. Klare, B., Li, Z., Jain, A.: Matching forensic sketches to mug shot photos. IEEE Trans. Pattern Anal. Mach. Intell. **33**(3), 639–646 (2011)
5. Zhang, W., Wang, X., Tan, X.: Coupled information theoretic encoding for face photo-sketch recognition. In: Proceedings of IEEE CVPR (2011)
6. Wang, Z., Miao, Z., Wu, Q.J., Wan, Y., Tang, Z.: Low resolution face recognition: a review. Vis. Comput. **30**(4), 359–386 (2014)
7. Mahajan, K.S., Vaidya, M.B.: Image inpainting techniques: a survey. IOSR J. Comput. Eng. **5**(4), 45–49 (2012)
8. FACES 4.0, IQ Biometrix 2011 (2011). http://www.iqbiometrix.com
9. Identi-Kit, Identi-Kit Solutions 2011. http://www.identikit.net/
10. Wells, G., Hasel, L.: Facial composite production by eyewitnesses. Curr. Dir. Psychol. Sci. **16**(1), 6–10 (2007)
11. Suthar, R., Patel, K.R.: A survey on various image inpainting techniques to restore image. Int. J. Eng. Res. Appl. **4**(2), 85–88 (2014). ISSN 2248-9622
12. Klum, S.J., Han, H., Klare, B.F., Jain, A.K.: The FaceSketchID system: matching facial composites to mugshots. IEEE Trans. Inf. Forensics Secur. **9**(12), 2248–2263 (2014)
13. Sharif, M., Adeel, K., Mudassar, R., Sajjad, M.: Face recognition using gabor filters. J. Appl. Comput. Sci. Math. **5**(11), 53–57 (2011)
14. Wang, X., Han, T.X., Yan, S.: An HOG-LBP human detector with partial occlusion handling. In: 12th IEEE International Conference on Computer Vision (ICCV) (2009). ISBN 978-1-4244-4419-9
15. Hosoi, T., Koichi Ito, S.: Restoration of occluded regions using FW-PCA for face recognition. IEEE (2012). ISBN 978-1-4673-1612-5/12
16. Criminisi, A., Perez, P., Toyama, K.: Region filling and object removal by exemplar-based image inpainting. IEEE Trans. Image Process. **13**(9), 1200–1212 (2004)
17. Pandya, N., Limbasiya, B.: A survey on image inpainting techniques. Int. J. Curr. Eng. Technol. **3**(5), 1828–1831 (2013)
18. Guillemot, C., Le Meur, O.: Image inpainting. IEEE Signal Process. Mag. January 2014. 1053-5888/14
19. Banday, M., Sharma, R.: Image inpainting – an inclusive review of the underlying algorithm and comparative study of the associated techniques. Int. J. Comput. Appl. **98**(17), 0975–8887 (2014)
20. Shewale, O.: Restoration of image using SR based image inpainting techniques. IJISET – Int. J. Innov. Sci. Eng. Technol. **2**(4) (2015). ISSN 2348–7968

21. Huang, J., Yuen, P.C., Chen, W.S., Lai, J.H.: Choosing parameters of kernel subspace LDA for recognition of face images under pose and illumination variations. IEEE Trans. Syst. Man Cybern. 37(4), 847–862 (2007). https://doi.org/10.1109/tsmcb.2007.895328

22. Akhtar, Z., Rattani, A.: A face in any form: new challenges and opportunities for face recognition technology, pp. 0018–9162. IEEE (2017)

23. Hu, X., Yu, W., Yao, J.: Multi-oriented 2DPCA for face recognition with one training face image per person. J. Comput. Inf. Syst. 6(5), 1563–1570 (2010)

24. Xu, Y., Li, X., Yang, J., Zhang, D.: Integrate the original face image and its mirror image for face recognition. Neurocomputing 131, 191–199 (2014)

25. Hu, X., Liao, Q., Peng, S.: Video surveillance face recognition by more virtual training samples based on 3D modeling. In: 11th International Conference on Natural Computation (ICNC). IEEE (2015). ISBN 978-1-4673-7679-2

26. Zhang, X., Gao, Y., Leung, M.K.H.: Recognizing rotated faces from frontal and side views: an approach toward effective use of mugshot databases. IEEE Trans. Inf. Forensics Secur. 3 (4), 684–697 (2008)

27. Ghinea, G., Kannan, R., Kannaiyan, S.: Gradient-orientation-based PCA subspace for novel face recognition. IEEE Access (2014). https://doi.org/10.1109/access.2014.2348018

28. Ding, C., Tao, D.: A comprehensive survey on pose-invariant face recognition. ACM Trans. Intell. Syst. Technol. arXiv:1502.04383v3 (2016)

29. Lin, Y., Medioni, G., Choi, J.: Accurate 3D face reconstruction from weakly calibrated wide baseline images with profile contours. In: Proceedings of CVPR (2010)

30. Asthana, A., Marks, T.K., Jones, M.J., Tieu, K.H., Rohith, M.: Fully automatic pose-invariant face recognition via 3D pose normalization. In: Proceedings of ICCV (2011)

31. Matthews, I., Baker, S.: Active appearance models revisited. Int. J. Comput. Vis. 60, 135–164 (2004)

32. Devi, N.S., Hemachandran, K.: Automatic face recognition system using pattern recognition techniques: a survey. Int. J. Comput. Appl. 83(5), 0975–8887 (2013)

33. Akhtar, Z., Rattani, A.: A face in any form: new challenges and opportunities for face recognition technology. IEEE Computer Society (2017). ISSN 0018-9162

34. Jiménez, D.G., Alba-Castro, J.L.: Toward pose-invariant 2-D face recognition through point distribution models and facial symmetry. IEEE Trans. Inf. Forensics Secur. 2(3–1), 413–429 (2007)

35. Arya, S., Pratap, N., Bhatia, K.: Future of face recognition: a review. In: Second International Symposium on Computer Vision and the Internet (VisionNet 2015) (2015). https://doi.org/10.1016/j.procs.2015.08.076

36. Grgic, M., Delac, K., Grgic, S.: SCface - surveillance cameras face database. Multimed. Tools Appl. J. 51(3), 863–879 (2011)

37. Wolf, L., Hassner, T., Maoz, I.: Face recognition in unconstrained videos with matched background similarity. In: IEEE Conference on Computer Vision and Pattern Recognition (2011)

38. Learned-Miller, E., Huang, G.B., RoyChowdhury, A., Li, H., Hua, G.: Labeled faces in the wild: a survey. In: Kawulok, M., Celebi, M.E., Smolka, B. (eds.) Advances in Face Detection and Facial Image Analysis, pp. 189–248. Springer, Cham (2016). https://doi.org/10.1007/978-3-319-25958-1_8

39. http://www2.ece.ohio-state.edu/~aleix/ARdatabase.html

40. http://www.iab-rubric.org/resources/sketchDatabase.html

41. Sim, T., Baker, S., Bsat, M.: Technical report, CMU-RI-TR-01-02, Robotics Institute, Carnegie Mellon University, January 2001

42. Patil, S., Shubhangi, D.C.: Forensic sketch based face recognition using geometrical face model. In: I2CT (2017). ISBN 978-1-5090-4307-1

43. Zhang, W., Wang, X., Tang, X.: Coupled information-theoretic encoding for face photo-sketch recognition. In: Proceedings of IEEE Conference on Computer Vision and Pattern Recognition (CVPR) (2011)
44. Sundaram, M., Mani, A.: Face recognition: demystification of multifarious aspect in evaluation metrics. In: Ramakrishnan, S. (ed.) Face Recognition - Semisupervised Classification, Subspace Projection and Evaluation Methods. InTech (2016) https://doi.org/10.5772/62825
45. Leung, T.K., Burl, M.C., Perona, P.: Finding faces in cluttered scenes using random labeled graph matching. In: Proceedings of Fifth IEEE International Conference on Computer Vision, pp. 637–644 (1995)
46. Cootes, T.F., Edwards, G.J., Taylor, C.J.: Active appearance models. In: Burkhardt, H., Neumann, B. (eds.) ECCV 1998. LNCS, vol. 1407, pp. 484–498. Springer, Heidelberg (1998). https://doi.org/10.1007/BFb0054760
47. Sung, K.K., Poggio, T.: Example-based learning for view-based human face detection. IEEE Trans. Pattern Anal. Mach. Intell. **20**(1), 39–51 (1998)
48. Fergus, R., Perona, P., Zisserman, A.: Object class recognition by unsupervised scale-invariant learning. In: IEEE Conference on Computer Vision and Pattern Recognition, vol. 2, pp. 264–271 (2003)
49. Heisele, B., Serre, T., Pontil, M., Poggio, T.: Component-based face detection. In: IEEE Conference Computer Vision and Pattern Recognition, pp. 657–662 (2001)
50. Wang, X., Tang, X.: Face photo-sketch synthesis and recognition. TPAMI **31**, 1955–1967 (2009)
51. Zhong, J., Gao, X., Tian, C.: Face sketch synthesis using E-HMM and selective ensemble. In: ICASSP, pp. 485–488 (2007)
52. Liu, Q., Tang, X., Jin, H., Lu, H., Ma, S.: A nonlinear approach for face sketch synthesis and recognition. In: CPVR, pp. 1005–1010 (2005)
53. Khan, Z., Hu, Y., Mian, A.: Facial self similarity for sketch to photo matching. In: DICTA, pp. 1–7 (2012)
54. Galea, C., Farrugia, R.: Forensic face photo-sketch recognition using a deep learning based architecture. IEEE Signal Process. Lett. **24**(11), 1586–1590 (2017)
55. Galoogahi, H., Sim, T.: Face photo retrieval by sketch example. ACM, pp. 1–4 (2012)
56. Bhatt, H., Bharadwaj, S., Singh, R., Vatsa, M.: On matching sketches with digital face images. In: BTAS, pp. 1–7 (2010)
57. Galoogahi, H., Sim, T.: Inter-modality face sketch recognition. In: ICME, pp. 224–229 (2012)
58. Galoogahi, H., Sim, T.: Face sketch recognition by local randon binary pattern: LRBP. In: ICIP, pp. 1837–1840 (2012)
59. Pramanik, S., Bhattacharjee, D.: Geometric feature based face-sketch recognition. In: PRIME, pp. 409–415 (2012)
60. Peng, C., Gao, X., Wang, N., Tao, D.: Multiple representations-based face sketch photo synthesis. IEEE Trans. Neural Netw. Learn. Syst. **27**(11), 2201–2215 (2016)
61. Mittal, P., Jain, A., Goswami, G., Vatsa, M., Singh, R.: Composite sketch recognition using saliency and attribute feedback. Inf. Fusion **33**, 86–99 (2017)
62. Galea, C., Farrugia, R.: A large-scale software-generated face composite sketch database. In: Proceedings of International Conference Biometrics Special Interest Group, pp. 1–5 (2016)
63. Masi, I., et al.: Learning pose-aware models for pose-invariant face recognition in the wild (2017). https://doi.org/10.1109/tpami.2018.2792452
64. Yin, X., Liu, X.: Multi-task convolutional neural network for pose-invariant face recognition, vol. 27, no. 2 (2018). https://doi.org/10.1109/tip.2017.2765830

65. Masi, I., Rawls, S., Medioni, G., Natarajan, P.: Pose-aware face recognition in the wild. In: Proceedings of Conference Computer Vision Pattern Recognition (2016)
66. Klare, B.F., et al.: Pushing the frontiers of unconstrained face detection and recognition: IARPA janus benchmark a. In: CPVR, pp. 1931–1939 (2015)
67. Peng, X., Yu, X., Sohn, K., Metaxas, D.N., Chandraker, M.: Reconstruction-based disentanglement for pose-invariant face recognition. In: Proceedings of ICCV, pp. 1–10 (2017)
68. Ranjan, R., Patel, V.M., Chellappa, R.: HyperFace: a deep multi-task learning framework for face detection, landmark localization, pose estimation, and gender recognition (2017). https://doi.org/10.1109/tpami.2017.2781233

Prototype to Control a Robot by Android System Remote Controller

Tanvir Rahman[✉], Fazal Mahmud Hassan, Shamma Binte Zakir,
Md. Ashraful Alam, Bir Ballav Roy, and Hasib Ahmed

BRAC University, 66 Mohakhali, Dhaka 1212, Bangladesh
tanvirpritom@gmail.com, fazal.mahmud.hasan@gmail.com,
sbzl430102@gmail.com, farhan.hazari@gmail.com,
roybirballav@gmail.com, ahmedhasib6@gmail.com

Abstract. Since its dawn modern science has been trying to minimize the workload of humans, and one weapon to do so is robot. Moreover, Android is the most popular operating system there is these days - it is easy to apply and comprehend. Thus, we are proposing a model to control a machine with an android system remote controller. Essentially our goal is to control all the machines with remote controller and for that we will use android. Therefore, we are going to propose a model and its implementation by hardware design of a prototype how to control a machine by android system remote controller.

Keywords: Robot · Arduino · Android · Control · Bluetooth
Remote controller

1 Introduction

Nowadays, smart phones, especially the apps are getting more popular day by day. Robotics, on the other hand, always has been our ultimate goal to replace human workforce. Robots that can be controlled using Bluetooth [1], or apps to be exact, thus, have come to modern day life to stay. Smart phones have become more powerful than ever because of the advancement of processor, multiple functions and availability. Bluetooth is a wireless technology standard for exchanging data over short distances (using short-wavelength UHF radio waves in the ISM band from 2.4 to 2.485 GHz) from fixed and mobile devices and building personal area networks (PANs). Invented by telecom vendor Ericsson in 1994, it was originally conceived as a wireless alternative to RS-232 data cables. It can connect several devices, overcoming problems of synchronization. Our main goal here, for this project, is to use robots to perform functions that are too dangerous for humans to perform. For that we need robots that can move towards multi directions, not only that, it receives the data we send to it and acts accordingly [2].

2 Proposed Model

2.1 Model

Our model of robotic vehicle includes an Arduino Uno integrated in it with a Bluetooth chip to receive command from the Android operated cell phone or other devices.

S. Verma et al. (Eds.): CNC 2018, CCIS 839, pp. 365–372, 2019.
https://doi.org/10.1007/978-981-13-2372-0_32

Android operated devices use a special application to send out instructions via the device's Bluetooth module. The other Bluetooth device located on the vehicle receives that signal and sends it to the Arduino Uno and upon receiving the signal Arduino Uno decodes it and acts accordingly.

Our model was designed keeping in mind the fact that, accessing some routes may turn out to be impossible for human directly and can also be proven dangerous. In scenarios such as this, we intend to send in our vehicle which can be controlled easily by a smartphone running any version of android. This makes our model very easy to deploy in complex situations and it uses very less resources. The application which is used in the Android device has a very user-friendly GUI which helps to train the operator very easily. The operator can guide the vehicle any way he needs and as the vehicle is small in size it can reach places which are not possible for human. However, the same method of control can be used for larger vehicles as well [6].

2.2 Components Used

At the heart of the device, lies an Arduino Uno, containing ATmega328P microcontroller. Communication was done on the receiving device, the vehicle by using HC-06 Bluetooth module. To drive the motors which powered the wheels we used a L298N motor driver. Two regular DC motors were used with the driver. The whole electronic setup was powered by two 3.7-V 18650 lithium ion batteries. The vehicle was constructed by using prebuilt acrylic chassis containing two rubber wheels and a cluster. Necessary whole were drilled to route the wires from one component to another [3, 4].

2.2.1 Android Device

Communication between the HC-06 Bluetooth device (contained in the vehicle) and Android operated device was made by using a special Android Application. Both devices use Socket connection protocol to establish connection. The Application which we used to operate the vehicle is an open source one and was downloaded from Google Play store. However, we needed to modify the application in a few place to send out some customized instruction to the receiving device. Our Android device was an ASUS Zenfone 6, which ran Android version 5.0, which is also known by its codename, Android Lollipop [7] (Fig. 1).

Fig. 1. Android device (cell phone) [Source: https://www.asus.com/phone/zenfone-products/]

2.2.2 Arduino Uno

Arduino is an open source electronic platform which is very easy to use and has a very user friendly hardware design and software programming interface. There are a number of variants of Arduino boards. In our model we used the Arduino Uno. The main reason for going with an Arduino Uno variant is that it is cheap and less complicated to work with. Also maintains a very small form factor and lite weight which gives our vehicle physical advantages. Moreover, the Arduino IDE is very easy to code with and also has vast resources- such as libraries and sample codes- which make coding the microcontroller much easier [8]. The specification for the Arduino board which we used in particular is as follows (Fig. 2):

- Based on ATmega328P microcontroller
- Has input voltage ranging from 7 V to 12 V
- Has an operating voltage of V
- Contains 14 digital I/O pins, among them 6 are able to generate PWM
- Contains 6 analog input pins
- Has a flash memory of 32 KB
- Has a SRAM of 2 KB
- Has a clock speed of 16 MHz
- Has a maximum of 20 mA Direct Current per I/O pin.

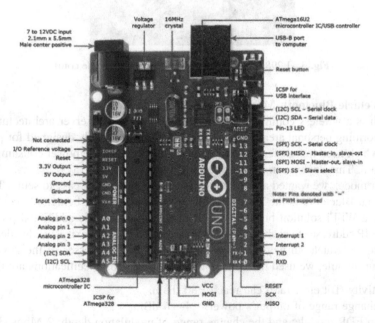

Fig. 2. Arduino Uno [Source: www.google.com]

2.2.3   L298N DC Motor Driver

As mentioned in the introduction, the main improvement that we brought into our model is that we made our vehicle multi-directional. Multi-directional means a model which has the ability to move 360° on a surface. In order to achieve this, it was essential to use a motor driver. Motor driver can reverse the polarity of each motor according to instruction received from the Arduino Uno which results in multi-directional movement of our vehicle. In our model, we opted for the very popular L298N motor driver to drive our 2 DC motors. L298N has the following specifications (Fig. 3):

- Is able to control 2 motors (combination of both DC and stepper) at the same time.
- Has bidirectional drive current of maximum 1A
- Has maximum power drive of 75 W at 75 °C
- Has a wide range of operating voltage from 4.5 V to 36 V maximum.

Fig. 3. L298N motor driver [Source: www.google.com]

2.2.4   Vehicle Bluetooth Module

Bluetooth is a wireless communications protocol with client-server architecture, suitable for forming personal area networks. This device is specially designed for portable devices which need to transfer data wirelessly while keeping the power consumption to a minimum. This device can operate flawlessly on low power [5].

In our model, we wanted a communication solution which is easy to setup. To meet this criteria, Bluetooth is the only possible option for the time being. We could have opted for a Wi-Fi solution but then we would need to face the additional process of assigning IP addresses to each device [8]. So to omit this complexity, we decided to opt for Bluetooth. Bluetooth works depending on the MAC addresses of the device [10, 11]. In our module, we used the Bluetooth module HC-06. Specifications are (Fig. 4):

- Sensitivity (Bit error rate) can reach −80 dBm.
- The change range of output's power: −4−+6 dBm.
- Has an EDR module; and the change range of modulation depth: 2 Mbps–3 Mbps.
- Has a build-in 2.4 GHz antenna.
- Can work at the low voltage (3.1 V–4.2 V).
- The current in pairing is as low as in the range of 30–40 mA.
- The current in communication is 8 mA.

- Has a working voltage of 5 V.
- Small (27 mm × 13 mm × 2 mm) & Peripherals circuit is simple.
- It's at the Bluetooth class 2 power level.
- Storage temperature range: −40 °C–85 °C.
- Working temperature range: −25 °C–+75 °C.

Fig. 4. HC06 bluetooth device [Source: www.google.com]

2.3 Software and Hardware Setup

We began the built process by attaching the Arduino Uno, motor driver, DC motors, Bluetooth, batteries module on the robotic chassis. After the physical build was done we moved on to the software part. The software part consisted two main segments. One of them was coding the Arduino Uno so that it can receive signals from the Bluetooth device and operate the motor driver accordingly and the other part was to customize the Android application for our convenience. We used the IDE that is designed for the Arduino platform to code the microcontroller. When the coding was done the microcontroller was ready to receive signals via Bluetooth from the Android application. When some specific buttons are pressed on the GUI of the Android application some predetermined characters are sent to the vehicle via Bluetooth. The microcontroller receives this characters and determines what instruction is associated with that particular input and operates the motor driver accordingly.

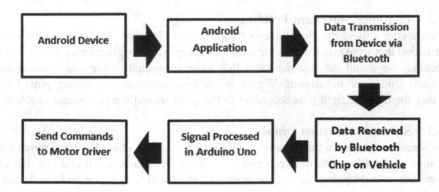

2.4 Program Code

Here is a portion of our code that was used to program the microcontroller. Here, we are just showing the part of the code which does the initial setup of the microcontroller such as initializing variables and declaring the state of the microcontroller pins.

```
int cmd; //Int to store app cmd state.
int Speed = 204; // 0 - 255. it wqas 204 previously
int Speedsec;
int buttonState = 0;
int lastButtonState = 0;
int Turnradius = 180; //Set the radius of a turn, 0 - 255
Note:the robot will malfunction if this is higher than
int Speed.it was 0 i made 180
int brakeTime = 45;
int brkonoff = 0; //1 for the electronic braking system,
0 for normal.
void setup() {
  pinMode(in1, OUTPUT);
  pinMode(in2, OUTPUT);
  pinMode(in3, OUTPUT);
  pinMode(in4, OUTPUT);
  pinMode(LED, OUTPUT); //Set the LED pin.
  Serial.begin(9600);    //Set the baud rate to your
Bluetooth module.
}
```

2.5 Trial and Error, and Debugging

2.5.1 Bluetooth TX RX Pin Problem

The very first problem which was faced was wrong pin configuration. The Bluetooth chip uses the TX and RX chip to transmit and receive data. However, the Arduino also uses these pins to communicate with the computer for coding. As our model was connected with the computer, the pins were preoccupied and Bluetooth chip was not able to communicate with the microcontroller. Our problem was solved by freeing those pins from one task when another task was ongoing.

2.5.2 Improper Movement Problem

After having solved the first issue our model ran. However, it did not follow the instruction that were sent through the android device. The movement was wrong. Upon checking, we found out that the wires that were connected to the motor driver and Arduino Uno were misaligned. Wrong wires were connected to wrong pins. Connecting them to the right pins according to the code solved the movement problem.

2.5.3 Sudden Connection Drops

The connection between the Android device and the Arduino Uno Dropped sometimes because of the Bluetooth device. Upon examining the cause, we found out that the connection was dropping because the wiring of the Bluetooth device and the Arduino

Uno was not perfect. We replaced the Jumper cables and the problem was solved. However, connection drop due to interference from other wireless devices could not be solved completely. We tried to omit this by not using other wireless devices such as - Wi-Fi routers - while operating the model.

2.5.4   Uneven DC Motor RPM Problem

Due to how the DC motors are made, the motors did not have the same RPM on the both wheels on the same voltage and current. As a result, our model was not able to go on a straight line. This issue was solved by manually adjusting the PIDs in the motor.

3   Conclusion

Wireless technology is one of the most harmless activities to save human efforts to do dangerous jobs like coal mining and dive deep into the seas. Unfortunately, due to some demerits we are not utilizing it to its full. Normally robots that are this cheap cannot perform multi-directional moves, nor can they receive the data we sent them. Moreover, android apps are very cheap and available. For future implementation, we are willing to add a camera and see through it. Besides, our ultimate goal is to add AI in its software to make it ongoing by itself. As we target to replace human efforts from dangerous jobs (i.e. coal mining, deep sea diving, rescue from fire incidents), we present it as a prototype of a big ambitious model to give back to human kind. Bluetooth here is being used to send the command (Fetch), then the command is sent to Arduino Uno, and performed by motor driver (Decode & execute).

Acknowledgement. We completed our project not only by the combined endeavor of all the teammates but also by the help and guidance of our coordinator, Assistant Professor Dr. Jia Uddin, thanks to him for motivating us to finish the project and his guidance and help in making this project a reality. We are grateful to achieve this opportunity to work with him as we got to learn a lot from him and all the possible ways that helped us overcome our difficulties to make this project a successful one. Also, thanks to our lab Lecturers, Rubayat Ahmed Khan and Sharmin Afrose who helped us to give a better knowledge about hardware codes and simulation like in Arduino and helped us improvise on our project ideas to make it what it is now, we can never thank them enough for their encouragements towards us. Moreover, thanks to BRAC University and the Respective departments for creating such a course that helps Undergraduate Students to accomplish successful events and projects. This course encourages the students to work with hardware, which a very important field of Computer & amp; Software Engineering. Therefore, we get to learn the functionalities of different kinds of components and practically use them and that makes us efficient in this field besides the software field.

References

1. Arduino official website – Arduino and Genuino products
2. Sandler, B.-Z.: Introduction: brief historical review and main definitions. In: Robotics, 2nd edn, pp. 1–36. Academic Press, San Diego (1999). ISBN 9780126185201

3. eLab Peers Electronic Components product specifications. http://www.elabpeers.com/bc417-bluetooth-to-serial-arduino.html
4. Forum for Electronics – Arduino HC06 vs. HC05. http://www.edaboard.com/thread329083.html
5. Jannet, K., Mamun, T., Sharif, M., Hossain, H.: Migrating Responsive Bin (2014). http://dspace.bracu.ac.bd/xmlui/bitstream/handle/10361/4073/Mr%20BIN%20Thesis%20Final.pdf
6. Jokitulppo, M.: Arduino-controlled robot. JAMK University of Applied Sciences (2015)
7. Pahuja, R., Kumar, N.: Android mobile phone controlled bluetooth robot using 8051 microcontroller. Int. J. Sci. Eng. Res. (IJSER) 2(7). www.ijser.in/archives/v2i7/SjIwMTMzMjQ%3D.pdf
8. Micropik Store Components - Ultrasonic Ranging Module HC-SR04. www.micropik.com/PDF/HCSR04.pdf
9. Nocks, L.: The Robot: The Life Story of a Technology. Greenwood Publishing Group, Westport (2007)
10. Parmar, D., Tripathi, D., Sahni, A., Singh, P.: Bluetooth operated robot vehicle using mobile android app. Int. J. Res. Eng. Adv. Technol. (IJREAT) 3(2) (2015). www.ijreat.org/Papers%202015/Issue14/IJREATV3I2010.pdf
11. SparkFun Electronics L298 motor driver datasheet. https://www.sparkfun.com/datasheets/Robotics/L298_H_Bridge.pdf

Plane-Wise Encryption Based Progressive Visual Cryptography for Gray Image

Suresh Prasad Kannojia[(⊠)] and Jasvant Kumar[(⊠)]

ICT Research Laboratory, Department of Computer Science,
University of Lucknow, Lucknow 226007, India
spkannojia@gmail.com, er.jaswantsingh786@gmail.com

Abstract. Visual secret sharing is a powerful technique, which allows to diffuse and disguise a secret image into two or more shares. To reconstruct the secret image these shares are stacked and viewed by the human visual system. Unluckily, Visual cryptography is not in primary use because of the degradation process entails severe problems in reconstructed image quality. Degradation reflects in terms of pixel expansion and loss in contrast, which makes visual cryptography unsuitable to handle visual information (image, video etc.) for the purpose of sharing and protection. The visual secret sharing techniques performed computation in order to absolve reconstructed secret image from pixel expansion and loss in contrast. Progressive visual cryptography (PVC) inherits all the advantageous features of traditional visual cryptography except the decryption process. In PVC, contrast of the reconstructed secret image increases gradually as the number of stacked shares increase but quality of reconstructed secret images still an issue for the researchers. To resolve the issue, this paper proposes a plane-wise encryption based progressive visual cryptography scheme for gray image. The effectiveness of the proposed scheme are carried out by experimental results and compared with state of the art approaches. Experimental results show that proposed scheme is well suited for applications where quality of secret image is a major issue.

Keywords: Image sharing · Visual cryptography · Visual secret sharing
Progressive visual cryptography · Plane-wise encryption

1 Introduction

Advances in computation and communication technologies facilitate fast and easy transmission of visual information over the internet, social media, this leads to insecurity of visual information. Thus security of the digital images a major issue for the researchers. To secure the digital information various techniques such as cryptography, steganography, biometrics and watermarking etc. are developed. One of them is visual cryptography [1], a visual secret sharing technique. It takes digital secret image as input and processes it using codebooks to make n share images as output. These n share images are assigned to n members of a group of participants. Any less than k members from a group of participant have no clue about input secret image. Now any k, $2 \leq k \leq n$ members of the group can reveal the secret image by stacking their share

© Springer Nature Singapore Pte Ltd. 2019
S. Verma et al. (Eds.): CNC 2018, CCIS 839, pp. 373–384, 2019.
https://doi.org/10.1007/978-981-13-2372-0_33

images printed on transparencies. Such type of visual secret sharing is called as threshold visual cryptography. Major drawbacks of threshold visual cryptography schemes are that if any one of the required shares is missing, then all other shares are useless and secret information cannot be revealed except this, proper alignment [2] of shares is necessary to reveal the secret image. The basic principle of visual cryptography has been illustrated through Fig. 1. Each pixel 1 (*black*) or 0 (*white*) of binary secret image encoded into n_1 black and n_2 white sub-pixels, in each share where m is pixel expansion and defined as $m = n_1 + n_2$, $0 \leq n_1 \leq m$ and $0 \leq n_2 \leq m$. In the Fig. 1, $m = 2$ and $n_1 = n_2 = 1$. Using bits of shares basis matrices are created. For example, matrix M_0 generated by row-wise arrangement of bits of the shares corresponding to row R_1 and matrix M_0 corresponding to row R_2 is column-permutation of M_0 corresponding to row R_1. Thus, for m pixel expansion, $m!$ are the total available options to encode black or white pixels of the secret image. Matrices M_0 and M_1 are codebooks to encrypt white and black pixels respectively. To show the working of Visual Secret Sharing consider a case where $k = 2$ and $n = 2$ or 2-out-of-2 shown in Fig. 2. It is a special case of (k, n)-visual cryptography scheme. Figure 2a is secret image and Fig. 2b and c are shares while Fig. 2d is reconstructed secret image. The reconstructed image is poorer than the original secret image due to appearance of noisy pixels. This degradation in image quality is termed as loss in *contrast*. The size of secret image (89×93) pixels shares (89×186) pixels and revealed image (89×186) pixels respectively. It is obvious that size of shares and reconstructed secret image increases two times than the original image in width, which leads to the *pixel expansion*.

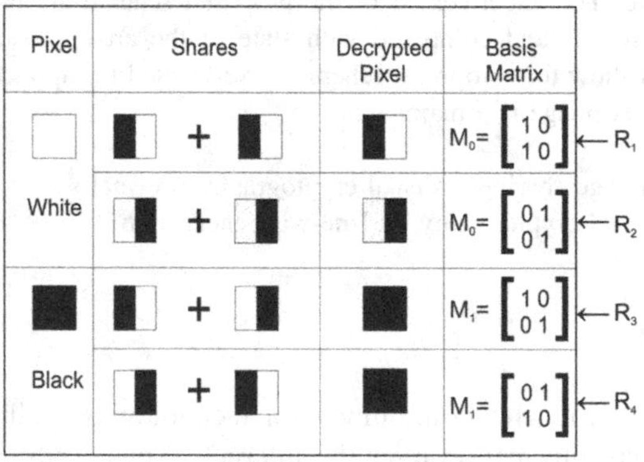

Fig. 1. Basic 2-out-of-2-visual cryptography scheme with m = 2

Due to beauty of perfect secrecy of visual cryptography, its associated problem of secret sharing and physical properties such as pixel expansion, contrast and color of secret image was taken into interest extensively by various researchers worldwide. In literature, visual cryptography for general access structure proposed by Ateniese et al. [3]. General access structure is composed of qualified set and forbidden set. Any subset of qualified set can reveal the secret information while subset of forbidden set cannot reveal the same. Beside this other application areas of visual cryptography includes: information hiding [4], watermarking [5], copyright protection [6], authentication and identification [7], print and scan application [8], and transmitting passwords [9] etc.

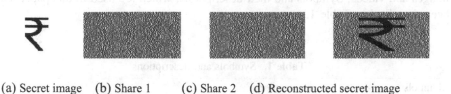

(a) Secret image   (b) Share 1   (c) Share 2   (d) Reconstructed secret image

Fig. 2. Example of 2-out-of-2 OR-based visual cryptography scheme (*a*) secret image (*b*) share1 (c) share2 (d) reconstructed secret image

To extend the application of visual cryptography to gray-scale, color images and to improve the contrast of the reconstructed image halftone visual cryptography (HVC) proposed [10, 11]. Halftone technique converts the gray level image into binary then uses basic visual cryptography techniques to secure the secret image. In case of color images, color models are used along with halftone techniques to achieve the objective. The shares produced by schemes [1, 3, 10, 11] are meaningless due to which it is very difficult for the users to manage a pile of such meaningless shares. To overcome this problem Ateniese et al. [12] proposed extended visual cryptography scheme (EVCS). In EVCS general constructions are defined which are further used to produce meaningful shares, unlike the traditional visual cryptography schemes while Loss in resolution and contrast still retains in this scheme. To resolve the problem of pixel expansion, probabilistic visual cryptography [13–15] and random grid visual cryptography [17–19] are elegantly proposed. Further visual cryptography technique Proposed by Yang et al. [14], generalized by Cimato et al. [16]. The model proposed by Cimato et al. tolerates between deterministic visual cryptography and probabilistic visual cryptography. General constructions are defined based on pixel expansion *m* when *m* = 1, model behaves like probabilistic visual cryptography and when *m* > 1 it behaves like deterministic visual cryptography. In probability based visual cryptography schemes resolution is maintained at the cost of sacrifice of construction of black and white pixels because there is no guarantee to reconstruct the pixels correctly.

Although the concept of random grids proposed by Kafri et al. [17] in 1987. Further, work on random grid extended by Shyu et al. [18, 19]. The major advantages of these schemes are that they do not need implicit or explicit codebooks to encrypt the secret image. The quality of the reconstructed secret images still an issue to be handled. This paper proposes a plane-wise encryption based progressive visual cryptography scheme for gray image.

The proposed scheme enables to obtain reconstructed secret image in original. It also resolves the problem of alignment of shares, loss of resolution and loss of contrast. Even, secret image with reduced visual quality can be obtained in case of any missing share This feature of proposed scheme makes it suitable for sharing and protection of images and videos. Symbols and their descriptions, which are used in this paper, have been described in Table 1.

Table 1. Symbols and descriptions

Symbols	Descriptions
$C_n, n = 2$	Matrix for codebook generation
C_n^0	Codebook to encrypt white pixels
C_n^1	Codebook to encrypt black pixels
SI	Secret image
$^kSI, 1 \leq k \leq 8$	k^{th} plane of the secret image
$^{kn}S, 1 \leq k \leq 8,$ $0 \leq n \leq 1,$	Complimentary shares for k^{th} plane of the secret image
^kR	k^{th} plane after performing XOR operation between complementary shares of kth plane
^kSI	Reconstructed secret image

In the remaining sections: Sect. 2 describes progressive visual cryptography. Proposed work presented in Sect. 3. Experimental results and comparisons with state of the art approaches are given in Sect. 4, followed by conclusion in Sect. 5.

2 Progressive Visual Cryptography

To reconstruct the secret image three types of the decryption process enable the recovery of secret image with varying quality. First one is stacked of physical transparencies (shares printed on transparencies). Second one is improved stacking technique; in this technique result of the decryption process is halftone image. Third one employs progressive stacking of shares to enable the schemes reconstruct secret with gradually increasing contrast.

Progressive visual cryptography differs from traditional visual cryptography due to the decryption process. Progressive visual cryptography employs stacking of shares progressively. Using the progressive mechanism of decryption many state-of-the-art schemes are proposed. Fang et al. [20] proposes progressive visual cryptography for monochrome images. In 2005, progressive color visual cryptography proposed by Jin et al. [21]. To improve quality of reconstructed image, traditional OR operation substituted with XOR operation and new encryption scheme based on 3×3 micro blocks and corresponding look-up table developed. Jin et al. proposes a series of schemes which are flexible to decode the secret image with varying quality. Schemes, proposed by Fang and Lin suffer from some security issues which are handled by Hou et al. [22]. In literature, number of research [23–25] proposed a user-friendly progressive visual cryptography. All the user-friendly progressive visual cryptography schemes produce meaningful shares to ease the share management. Verifiable progressive visual cryptography proposed by Shivani et al. [26] to ensure that genuine shares are presented by the participants at the time of decryption. This scheme also suffers from pixel expansion as well as loss in contrast.

3 Progressive Visual Cryptography Scheme for Gray Image

The State-of-the-art progressive visual cryptography schemes suffers from the loss of contrast in the decrypted secret image and also not suitable for gray and color images. Hence, to reconstruct secret image perfectly along with the benefits of traditional visual cryptography schemes this paper proposes a scheme which extracts the bit planes of the secret image after that encodes them using codebooks. Required codebooks obtained by using Algorithm 1 and Algorithm 2.

3.1 Codebook Generation

To generate required codebooks a matrix of order $2^n \times n$, $n = 2$, is needed. This matrix holds the binary equivalent of the decimal numbers from 0 to $2^n - 1$. This matrix is divided into two matrices C_n^0 and C_n^1 using Algorithm 2. Matrices C_n^0 and C_n^1 are used as codebooks to encrypt white and black pixels respectively. Execution result of Algorithm 1 for $n = 2$ is denoted by C_n. Now divide matrix C_n into two $2^{n-1} \times n$ sub-matrices C_n^0 and C_n^1 by using Algorithm 2.

Algorithm 1: Matrix for Codebook Generation

Input: Parameter n.

Output: A $2^n \times$ n matrix C_n

1: **for** i= 1 to 2^n **do**

2:   C(i,1 to n) = de2bi(i− 1, n) . \\Convert decimal number i− 1 to n bit binary number

3: **end for**

4: **for** for j= 1 to n **do**

5:   C_n(1 to 2^n, j) = C(1 to 2^n, n − j + 1) . \\Reverse the entire row vectors of matrix C.

6: **end for**

7: **return** C_n

Algorithm 2: Algorithm to divide C_n into C_n^0 and C_n^1

Input: A $2^n \times n$ matrix C_n generated by algorithm 1.
Output: The matrices C_n^0 and C_n^1.
1: $counter_1 \leftarrow 1$
2: $counter_2 \leftarrow 1$
3: **for** $i = 1$ to 2^n **do**
4:     **for** $j = 1$ to n **do**
5: $w \leftarrow w_h(i, 1 \ to \ j)$. \\Hamming weight of vector i having j columns
6:     **if** w is an even number **then**
7:         $C_n^0(counter_1, 1 \ to \ j) = C_n(i, 1 \ to \ j)$
8:         $counter_1 = counter_1 + 1$
9:     **else**
10:        $C_n^1(counter_2, 1 \ to \ j) = C_n(i, 1 \ to \ j)$
11:        $counter_2 = counter_2 + 1$
12:     **end if**
13:     **end for**
14: **end for**
15: **return** C_n^0, C_n^1

$$C_n = \begin{bmatrix} 0\,0 \\ 0\,1 \\ 1\,0 \\ 1\,1 \end{bmatrix}_{4\times2} , \quad C_n^0 = \begin{bmatrix} 0\,0 \\ 1\,1 \end{bmatrix}_{2\times2}, \quad C_n^1 = \begin{bmatrix} 0\,1 \\ 1\,0 \end{bmatrix}_{2\times2}$$

3.2   Bit-Planes for Gray Image

Let SI be an 8 bit gray-scale image. It means the gray image is composed of 8 bit planes. Each bit of every pixel corresponding to the respective plane of the image. It means each pixel of the image contributes to the quality of the image. To get the bit-planes of image, Algorithm 3 is used, where bitget(.) and logical(.) are MATLAB functions. For example, a standard image Leena (image) is used as secret image, which is shown in Fig. 3(a). All extracted bit-planes are shown in Fig. 3(b) to (i) corresponding to bits 1 to 8 of pixels from least significant bit (LSB) to most significant bit (MSB).

Algorithm 3: Bit-plane Extraction

Input: Secret image SI.

Output: Bit-planes ^{k}SI, $1 \leq k \leq 8$. \\. Bit-plane corresponding to k^{th}bit of every pixel in SI

1: **for** i= 1 to k **do**

2: ^{i}SI=bitget(SI, i)

3: ^{i}SI=logical(^{i}SI, i)

4: **end for**

5: **return** ^{k}SI, $1 \leq k \leq 8$.

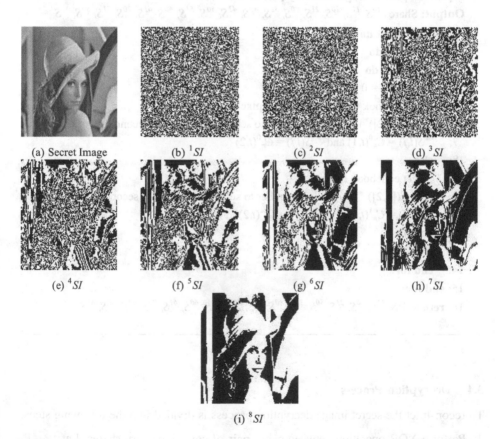

(a) Secret Image   (b) ^1SI (c) ^2SI (d) ^3SI

(e) ^4SI (f) ^5SI (g) ^6SI (h) ^7SI

(i) ^8SI

Fig. 3. (*a*) Secret image (*b*) to (*i*) are bit-planes corresponding to bits 1 to 8 of pixels from LSB to MSB

3.3 Proposed Scheme

To share the gray-scale secret image between the participants in such a way that decryption will be achieved in progressive order. First of all, bit-planes of secret image extracted using Algorithm 3. To obtain the complementary shares, extracted bit-planes are fed as input to the Algorithm 4. For every $^k SI(i, j)$, $1 \leq k \leq 8$, $1 \leq i \leq r$, $1 \leq j \leq c$, pixel of each bit-plane Algorithm 4 generates two complementary shares ^{k0}S and $^k S$ with the help of codebooks C_n^0 and C_n^1. To do so depending upon the pixel value of the bit-plane codebooks are chosen. After that to select the row of selected codebook a random number t, $t = 1$, generated. Next step is to assign share values for that pixel to the complementary shares. Steps of the encryption algorithm for proposed scheme are given below.

Algorithm 4: Encryption Algorithm

Input: Bit-planes $^k SI$, generated by algorithm 3.
Output: Shares ^{10}S, ^{11}S, ^{20}S, ^{21}S, ^{30}S, ^{31}S, ^{40}S, ^{41}S, ^{50}S, ^{51}S, ^{60}S, ^{61}S, ^{70}S, ^{71}S, ^{80}S, ^{81}S

  1: **for** $m = 1$ to k **do**
  2: **for** $i = 1$ to r **do**   \\ r rows in SI
  3: **for** $j = 1$ to c **do**   \\ c column in SI
  4:   **if** $^m SI(i,j) == 0$ **then**
  5: Select codebook C_n^0 \\ $(i,j)^{th}$ pixel of mth bit-plane
  6: $t = randi([1,2])$ \\ t random number to select either first or second row of C_n^0
  7:   $^{m0}S(i,j) = C_n^0(t,1)$ and $^{m1}S(i,j) = C_n^0(t,2)$
  8:   **else**
  9:   Select codebook C_n^1
10: $t = randi([1,2])$ \\ t random number to select either first or second row of C_n^1
11:   $^{m0}S(i,j) = C_n^1(t,1)$ and $^{m1}S(i,j) = C_n^1(t,2)$
12:   **end if**
13:   **end for**
14:   **end for**
15: **end for**
16: **return** ^{10}S, ^{11}S, ^{20}S, ^{21}S, ^{30}S, ^{31}S, ^{40}S, ^{41}S, ^{50}S, ^{51}S, ^{60}S, ^{61}S, ^{70}S, ^{71}S, ^{80}S, ^{81}S

3.4 Decryption Process

To reconstruct the secret image decryption process is divided into the following steps.

1. Perform XOR-operation between every pair of complementary shares. Let $^1 R$, $^2 R$, $^3 R$, $^4 R$, $^5 R$, $^6 R$, $^7 R$ and $^8 R$ be the results of XOR-operation.

2. Ignore complementary share of the missing share and assume $^k R$ value null for that pair.
3. Then reconstruct the secret image using the formula given in Eq. 1

$$^r SI = \bigoplus_{i=0}^{7} (2^i \times^{i+1} R) \tag{1}$$

where, $^r SI$ reconstructed secret image and $\oplus$ is OR-operator.

4 Experimental Results

Proposed scheme as discussed in Sect. 3 is implemented using MATLAB. Figures 3 and 4 shows the experimental results on the standard image leena. Figure 3, shows all the bit-planes ^1SI, ^2SI, ^3SI, ^4SI, ^5SI, ^6SI, ^7SI and ^8SI for input secret image. Shares corresponding to these bit-planes are given in Fig. 4(a) and (b) are shares for ^1SI, (c) and (d) for ^2SI, (e) and (f) for ^3SI, (g) and (h) for ^4SI, (i) and (j) for ^5SI, (k) and (l) for ^6SI, (m) and (n) for ^7SI, (o) and (p) for ^8SI and (q) is reconstructed image. From the experimental results, it is found that no one can get any clue by merely seeing the shares and reconstructed secret image perfectly, when all the shares are available.

4.1 Comparison with State-of-the-Art Approaches

Experimental results of the proposed scheme are compared with state of the art approaches using following parameters such as format of secret image, share type (meaningful or meaningless), contrast loss, pixel expansion and quality of reconstructed image are taken into consideration. Experimental results of proposed scheme and state of the art approaches based on above mentioned parameters are listed in Table 2. It is found that most of the state of the art approaches works on the half-toned images and reconstructs halftone images while proposed scheme takes gray image as input and reconstructs secret image perfectly.

Table 2. Comparison with state-of-the-art approaches

Schemes	Secret image	Meaningful share	Contrast loss	Pixel expansion	Reconstructed image quality
Fang et al. [20]	Binary	No	Yes	Yes	Reduced
Jin et al. [21]	Halftone	No	Yes	No	Varying
Hou et al. [22]	Halftone	No	Yes	No	Halftone
Fang et al. [23]	Halftone	Yes	Yes	Yes	Halftone
Lin et al. [24]	Binary, gray	Yes	Yes	No	Reduced
Shivani et al. [25]	Binary	Yes	Yes	No	Reduced
Shivani et al. [26]	Binary	Yes	Yes	No	Reduced
Proposed	**Gray**	**No**	**No**	**No**	**Original**

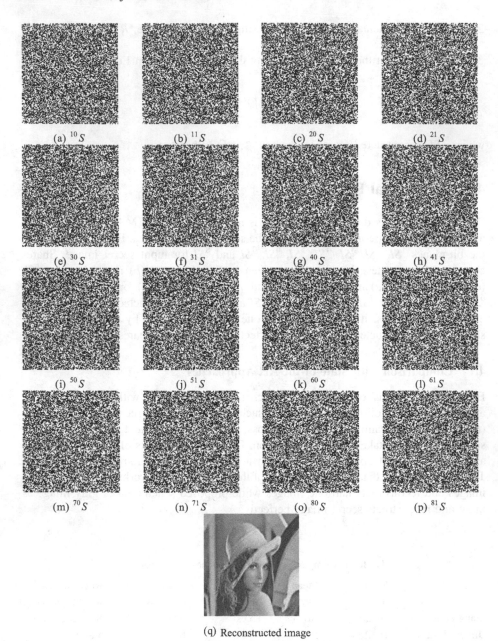

(a) ^{10}S (b) ^{11}S (c) ^{20}S (d) ^{21}S

(e) ^{30}S (f) ^{31}S (g) ^{40}S (h) ^{41}S

(i) ^{50}S (j) ^{51}S (k) ^{60}S (l) ^{61}S

(m) ^{70}S (n) ^{71}S (o) ^{80}S (p) ^{81}S

(q) Reconstructed image

Fig. 4. Experimental results: (*a*) and (*b*) are shares for ^{1}SI, (*c*) and (*d*) for ^{2}SI, (*e*) and (*f*) for ^{3}SI, (*g*) and (*h*) for ^{4}SI, (*i*) and (*j*) for ^{5}SI, (*k*) and (*l*) for ^{6}SI, (*m*) and (*n*) for ^{7}SI, (*o*) and (*p*) for ^{8}SI and (*q*) is reconstructed image

5 Conclusion

This paper proposes plane-wise encryption based progressive visual secret sharing scheme for gray-scale images. Experimental results show that reconstructed image is same as the original secret image when all the shares are available. The proposed scheme tolerates to the quality of the reconstructed image if any share is missing and reconstructs partial secret image. The quality of proposed scheme is better than the state-of-the-art approaches.

Acknowledgment. Author thanks to Prof. Kirti Sinha, Head, Department of Computer Science, University of Lucknow, Lucknow, for providing infrastructure facilities. Second author thankful to University Grant Commission, India for providing RGNSRF to sustain his research (RGNF award No: F1-17.1/201415/RGNF-2014-15-SC-UTT-87345/(SA-III/Website)).

References

1. Naor, M., Shamir, A.: Visual cryptography. In: De Santis, A. (ed.) EUROCRYPT 1994. LNCS, vol. 950, pp. 1–12. Springer, Heidelberg (1995). https://doi.org/10.1007/BFb0053419
2. Liu, F., Wu, C.K., Lin, X.J.: The alignment problem of visual cryptography schemes. Des. Codes Cryptogr. **50**(2), 215–227 (2009)
3. Ateniese, G., Blundo, C., De Santis, A., Stinson, D.R.: Visual cryptography for general access structures. Inf. Comput. **129**(2), 86–106 (1996)
4. Yan, X., et al.: New approaches for efficient information hiding-based secret image sharing schemes. SIViP **9**(3), 499–510 (2015)
5. Chen, T.-H., Tsai, D.-S.: Owner? Customer right protection mechanism using a watermarking scheme and a watermarking protocol. Pattern Recognit. **39**(8), 1530–1541 (2006)
6. Chang, C.-C., Wu, H.C.: A copyright protection scheme of images based on visual cryptography. Imaging Sci. J. **49**(3), 141–150 (2001)
7. Naor, M., Pinkas, B.: Visual authentication and identification. In: Kaliski, B.S. (ed.) CRYPTO 1997. LNCS, vol. 1294, pp. 322–336. Springer, Heidelberg (1997). https://doi.org/10.1007/BFb0052245
8. Yan, W.-Q., Jin, D., Kankanhalli, M.S.: Visual cryptography for print and scan applications. In: Proceedings of the 2004 International Symposium on Circuits and Systems, ISCAS 2004, vol. 5. IEEE (2004)
9. Tuyls, P., Kevenaar, T., Schrijen, G.-J., Staring, T., van Dijk, M.: Visual crypto displays enabling secure communications. In: Hutter, D., Müller, G., Stephan, W., Ullmann, M. (eds.) Security in Pervasive Computing. LNCS, vol. 2802, pp. 271–284. Springer, Heidelberg (2004). https://doi.org/10.1007/978-3-540-39881-3_23
10. Zhou, Z., Arce, G.R., Di Crescenzo, G.: Halftone visual cryptography. IEEE Trans. Image Process. **15**(8), 2441–2453 (2006)
11. Wang, Z., Arce, G.R., Di Crescenzo, G.: Halftone visual cryptography via error diffusion. IEEE Trans. Inf. Forensics Secur. **4**(3), 383–396 (2009)
12. Ateniese, G., Blundo, C., De Santis, A., Stinson, D.R.: Extended capabilities for visual cryptography. Theor. Comput. Sci. **250**(1), 143–161 (2001)

13. Ito, R., Kuwakado, H., Tanaka, H.: Image size invariant visual cryptography. IEICE Trans. Fundam. Electron. Commun. Comput. Sci. **82**(10), 2172–2177 (1999)
14. Yang, C.N.: New visual secret sharing schemes using probabilistic method. Pattern Recognit. Lett. **25**(4), 481–494 (2004)
15. Yang, C.N., Chen, T.S.: Size-adjustable visual secret sharing schemes. IEICE Trans. Fundam. Electron. Commun. Comput. Sci. **88**(9), 2471–2474 (2005)
16. Cimato, S., De Prisco, R., De Santis, A.: Probabilistic visual cryptography schemes. Comput. J. **49**(1), 97–107 (2005)
17. Kafri, O., Keren, E.: Encryption of pictures and shapes by random grids. Opt. Lett. **12**(6), 377–379 (1987)
18. Shyu, S.J.: Image encryption by random grids. Pattern Recognit. **40**(3), 1014–1031 (2007)
19. Shyu, S.J.: Image encryption by multiple random grids. Pattern Recognit. **42**(7), 1582–1596 (2009)
20. Fang, W.P., Lin, J.C.: Progressive viewing and sharing of sensitive images. Pattern Recognit. Image Anal. **16**(4), 632–636 (2006)
21. Jin, D., Yan, W.Q., Kankanhalli, M.S.: Progressive color visual cryptography. J. Electron. Imaging **14**(3), 033019 (2005)
22. Hou, Y.C., Quan, Z.Y.: Progressive visual cryptography with unexpanded shares. IEEE Trans. Circuits Syst. Video Technol. **21**(11), 1760–1764 (2011)
23. Fang, W.P.: Friendly progressive visual secret sharing. Pattern Recognit. **41**(4), 1410–1414 (2008)
24. Lin, C.H., Lee, Y.S., Chen, T.H.: Friendly progressive random-grid-based visual secret sharing with adaptive contrast. J. Vis. Commun. Image Represent. **33**, 31–41 (2015)
25. Shivani, S., Agarwal, S.: Progressive visual cryptography with unexpanded meaningful shares. ACM Trans. Multimed. Comput. Commun. Appl. (TOMM) **12**(4), 50 (2016)
26. Shivani, S., Agarwal, S.: VPVC: verifiable progressive visual cryptography. Pattern Anal. Appl. **21**(1), 1–28 (2016)

An Advanced Throttled (ATH) Algorithm and Its Performance Analysis with Different Variants of Cloud Computing Load Balancing Algorithm

Saurabh Gupta[✉], Nitin Dixit, and Pradeep Yadav

Department of Computer Science, ITM GOI, Gwalior, India
saurabh256837@gmail.com

Abstract. Cloud computing is an vast area in which computing resources, network access and accessing vast distributed over the network. To coordinate and distribute the task is complicated in cloud computing, in order to avoid overload and resource management and utilization are some challenging task. Load balancing is the main feature for the operations in cloud computing. It is a method to distribute the workload across the network, to minimize the processing time and response time it plays an important role. The load balancing is required to maximize the throughput and increase the performance of the cloud services. Here we discussed some of the algorithms which are as follows Throttled, round robin and advanced throttled algorithm. For evaluation we used the cloud analyst tool.

Keywords: Throttled algorithm
Round robin algorithm and advanced throttled · Cloud analyst

1 Introduction

The cloud computing is a new technological advancement in which resources [1] like memory, processors and other storage are provided as a wide-ranging utilities. The resources can be sublet and released by users through the Internet in an on-demand basis. The appearance of 'Cloud Computing' has made an massive impact on IT industry over the past few years. The business companies try to find to reshape and improve their business models to gain benefit from Cloud Computing services. Large companies such as Google, Amazon and Microsoft strive to provide more powerful, reliable and cost-efficient cloud platforms [2].

The architecture of a cloud computing consist of four layers shown in Fig. 1.

(1) The hardware layer: This layer shows that in the data centre the thousands of computers are interconnected through router and switches. So obviously many issues will rise in this layer related to the hardware configuration, fault tolerance, cooling and performance of the devices.

© Springer Nature Singapore Pte Ltd. 2019
S. Verma et al. (Eds.): CNC 2018, CCIS 839, pp. 385–399, 2019.
https://doi.org/10.1007/978-981-13-2372-0_34

(2) The infrastructure layer: Sometime this layer is also known as the virtualization layer. By using virtualization technologies such as Xen [3], KVM [4] and VMware we can create a group of storage and computing resources by dividing the physical resources.

(3) The platform layer: On the top of the above layer there is platform layer which consist of the operating system. It work as a bridge between both the application and operating system. The work of this layer is to minimize the burden.

(4) The application layer: It is some time also known as the cloud. It is the top most layer which work as a cloud for the applications. It provides the better facilities to overcome the difficulties; it provides the better performance and lower operating cost. Cloud computing has been widely adopted in the IT industry [5, 6].

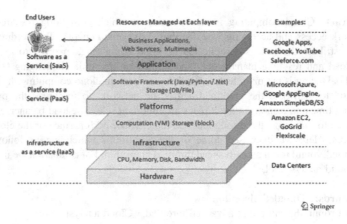

Fig. 1. Cloud computing architecture [1]

2 Load Balancing Algorithms

Generally the load balancing is divided into two different types of Static Load Balancing and Dynamic Load Balancing.

Static means fixed, as in this each node is fixed and balancing decisions are made at compile time [7], these are non defensive so that if once the load is due to the node it cannot be transferred to the other node.

In round robin all task assign in FCFS manner periodically because in this algorithm we have time quantum. All work tasks should be assigned to the computing nodes on round robin fashion. After calculating the last node first node will compute. All nodes maintain local load i.e. independent from remote node [8].

The datacenter controller sends the request to the VMs randomly from the group and then it assigns the request in a circular manner. After VM is allotted it is shifted to the end of the list. Round robin is the simplest algorithm to give out the load between the nodes.

The best informative load balancing decision is made by dynamic load balancing while run time state information execute. In it load is distributed between the processor at running time. It monitor the changes and redistribute the work if load occurs.

In dynamic load balancing algorithm we have throttled load balancer, it maintains table for all the VMs and whenever a new request appears in the table it is parsed by the load balancer, VM id is returned to data controller if suitable VM is not found then −1 is returned.

It is similar to throttle algorithm with a little change in VM index table. According to this algorithm an index table is maintained by load balancer that contain all the currently allocated request of VM. As the new request arrived VM with the least load balance is chosen by the load balancer.

Load balancer deallocates the VM after completion of the task (Figs. 2 and 3).

The proposed algorithm is named as Advanced Throttled (ATH) Algorithm, it is an improvement over Throttled algorithm and it distributes work load evenly among virtual machines [8]. This modified version works as follows:

1. It maintains index table of VMs
2. In it data-centre queries the ATH VM load balancer for next allocation.
3. For the next queries the ATH VM Load Balancer parses the allocation table after the recently allocated VM till the table is completely parsed [9].
4. If VM is available then it returns VM id.
5. Data centre controller sends the notice to the new ATH VM load balancer.
6. It update the allocation table.

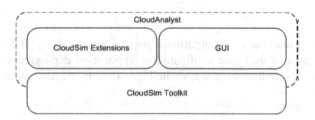

Fig. 2. CloudAnalyst architecture

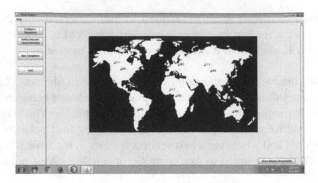

Fig. 3. CloudAnalyst GUI

3 Parameters

Region: Cloud analyst divides the world into six regions. There are two more entities on user basis and data centers are also belong to these region.

Users: In order to generate the traffic for simulation, User Base models a group of users (may be hundreds or thousands) which will be measured as a single unit in the simulation.

Data center controller: A single Data Center Controller is mapped to a single cloudsim. The data center object managed all activities such as VM creation and destruction, routing of user requests received from User Bases through the Internet to the VMs.

VM load balancer: During the simulation the VM load balancer allocate the load on various datacenter according to the request.

4 Results

For simulation of load balancing algorithms using CloudAnalyst, [10] the parameters are set on the basis of user base configuration, application deployment configuration, and data center configuration as shown in Figs. 4, 5, 6. As shown in Fig. 4 in six

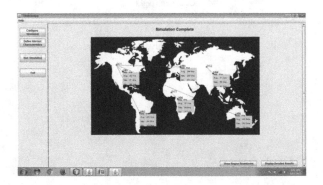

Fig. 4. Result screen of simulation RR with 6UBs

different regions of the world the location of user bases has been defined. The request of three different user are handled by three data centers. DC1 located in region 0, DC2 in region 1 and DC3 in region 2. Here we have taken 6 user bases. 50 VM are allocated in each Data Center. The simulation duration is set as 60 h [11].

Fig. 5. Result screen of simulation TH with 6UBs

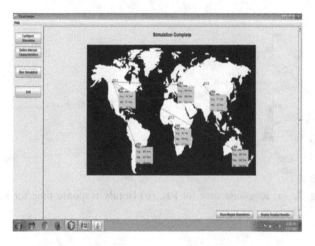

Fig. 6. Result screen of simulation ATH with 6UBs

4.1 Response Time

For RR, TH and ATH the overall response time and user Base hourly response time are as shown in Figs. 7, 8 and 9 respectively.

Overall Response Time Summary

	Avg (ms)	Min (ms)	Max (ms)
Overall response time:	141.45	37.66	366.27
Data Center processing time:	0.84	0.03	2.01

Response Time by Region

Userbase	Avg (ms)	Min (ms)	Max (ms)
UB1	50.74	38.13	61.38
UB2	199.92	154.64	241.64
UB3	299.49	233.14	366.27
UB4	51.33	40.26	60.76
UB5	50.15	37.66	59.41
UB6	200.57	155.64	242.64

(a)

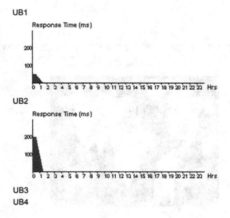

Fig. 7. (a) Response time for RR. (b) Hourly response time for RR

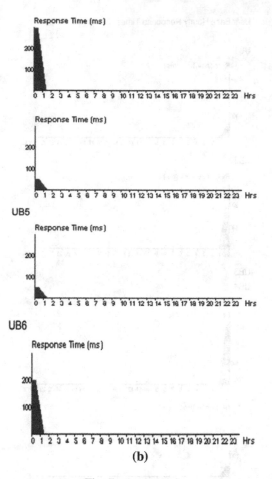

Fig. 7. (*continued*)

Overall Response Time Summary

	Avg (ms)	Min (ms)	Max (ms)
Overall response time:	141.47	37.66	366.27
Data Center processing time:	0.84	0.03	2.01

Response Time by Region

Userbase	Avg (ms)	Min (ms)	Max (ms)
UB1	50.70	38.13	61.38
UB2	199.95	154.64	241.64
UB3	299.51	233.14	366.27
UB4	51.32	40.26	60.76
UB5	50.15	37.66	59.41
UB6	200.71	155.64	242.64

(a)

Fig. 8. (a) Response time for TH. (b) Hourly response time for throttled

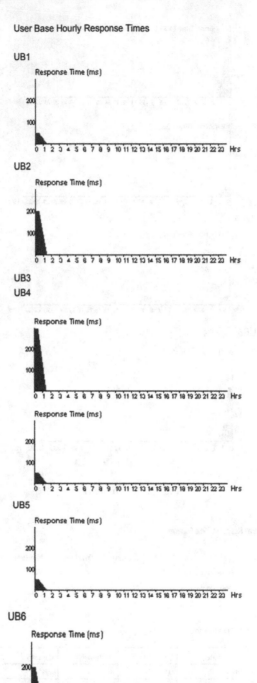

Fig. 8. (*continued*)

Overall Response Time Summary

	Avg (ms)	Min (ms)	Max (ms)
Overall response time:	141.50	37.66	366.27
Data Center processing time:	0.84	0.03	2.01

Response Time by Region

Userbase	Avg (ms)	Min (ms)	Max (ms)
UB1	50.69	38.13	61.38
UB2	199.98	154.64	241.64
UB3	299.70	233.14	366.27
UB4	51.33	40.26	62.01
UB5	50.12	37.66	59.41
UB6	200.70	155.64	242.64

(a)

User Base Hourly Response Times

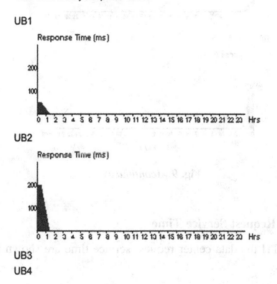

Fig. 9. (a) Response time for ATH. (b) Hourly response time for ATH

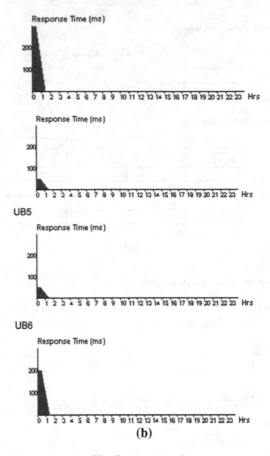

Fig. 9. (*continued*)

4.2 Data Center Request Service Time

For RR, TH and ATH the data center request service time are shown in Figs. 10, 11 and 12 respectively.

Data Center Request Servicing Times

Data Center	Avg (ms)	Min (ms)	Max (ms)
DC1	0.75	0.07	1.38
DC2	1.57	0.13	2.01
DC3	0.50	0.03	0.90

Fig. 10. Data center request service time for RR

Data Center Request Servicing Times

Data Center	Avg (ms)	Min (ms)	Max (ms)
DC1	0.75	0.07	1.38
DC2	1.58	0.13	2.01
DC3	0.50	0.03	0.90

Fig. 11. Data center request service time for TH

Data Center Request Servicing Times

Data Center	Avg (ms)	Min (ms)	Max (ms)
DC1	0.75	0.07	1.38
DC2	1.58	0.13	2.01
DC3	0.50	0.03	0.90

Fig. 12. Data center request service time for ATH

4.3   Processing Cost

For RR, TH and ATH the processing cost are shown in Figs. 13, 14, 15, 16, 17 and 18 respectively.

Cost

Total Virtual Machine Cost ($):	10.54
Total Data Transfer Cost ($):	0.38
Grand Total: ($)	10.92

Data Center	VM Cost $	Data Transfer Cost $	Total $
DC2	5.02	0.06	5.08
DC1	5.02	0.26	5.27
DC3	0.50	0.07	0.57

Fig. 13. Processing cost for RR

Cost

Total Virtual Machine Cost ($):	10.54
Total Data Transfer Cost ($):	0.38
Grand Total: ($)	10.92

Data Center	VM Cost $	Data Transfer Cost $	Total $
DC2	5.02	0.06	5.08
DC1	5.02	0.26	5.27
DC3	0.50	0.07	0.57

Fig. 14. Processing cost for TH

Cost

Total Virtual Machine Cost ($):	10.54
Total Data Transfer Cost ($):	0.38
Grand Total: ($)	10.92

Data Center	VM Cost $	Data Transfer Cost $	Total $
DC2	5.02	0.06	5.08
DC1	5.02	0.26	5.27
DC3	0.50	0.07	0.57

Fig. 15. Processing cost for ATH

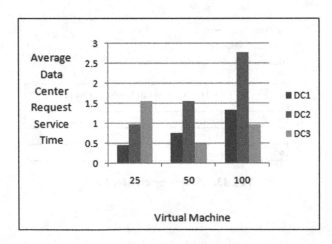

Fig. 16. The results of simulation using RR of 3 data centers with 25, 50, 100 VMs.

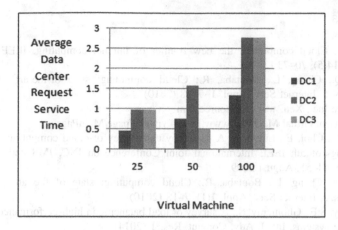

Fig. 17. The results of simulation using TH of 3 data centers with 25, 50, 100 VMs

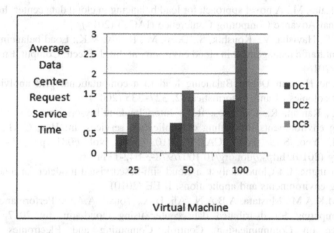

Fig. 18. The results of simulation using ATH of 3 data centers with 25, 50, 100 VMs

5 Conclusion

In cloud environment for executing the user request, we have simulated three existing load balancing algorithms i.e. Round Robin (RR), Throttled (TH) Algorithm. Also we have simulated our proposed algorithm Advanced Throttled Algorithm (ATH) for comparing the results. From the graphs it is proved that our proposed algorithm Advanced Throttled (ATH) Algorithm is more efficient as compared to the existing static and dynamic load balancing algorithms.

These results can still be improved by using some advanced algorithms that can handle Big Data in heterogeneous environment. So further in future we can develop an algorithm that can reduce the overall cost of processing and fulfill user requests in lesser time.

References

1. Pallis, G.: Cloud computing: the new frontier of internet computing. IEEE J. Internet Comput. **14**(5), 70–73 (2010)
2. Zhang, Q., Cheng, L., Boutaba, R.: Cloud computing: state of-the-art and research challenges. J. Internet Serv. Appl. **1**, 7–18 (2010)
3. XenSource Inc., Xen. www.xensource.com
4. Kernal Based Virtual Machine. www.linux-kvm.org/page/MainPage
5. Rima, B.P., Choi, E., Lumb, I.: A taxanomy and survey of cloud computing systems. In: Proceedings of 5th IEEE International Joint Conference on INC, IMS and IDC, Seoul, Korea, pp. 44–51, August 2009
6. Zhang, Q., Cheng, L., Boutaba, R.: Cloud computing: state of the art and research challenges. J. Internet Serv. Appl. **1**(1), 7–18 (2010)
7. El-Zoghdy, S.F., Ghoniemy, S.: A survey of load balancing in high-performance distributed computing systems. Int. J. Adv. Comput. Res. **1** (2014)
8. Singh, A., Goyal, P., Batra, S.: An optimized round robin scheduling algorithm for CPU scheduling. Int. J. Comput. Electr. Eng. (IJCEE) **2**(7), 2383–2385 (2010)
9. Soni, G., Kalra, M.: A novel approach for load balancing in cloud data center. In: 2014 IEEE International Advance Computing Conference (IACC) (2014)
10. Sasidhar, T., Havisha, V., Koushik, S., Deep, M., Reddy, V.K.: Load balancing techniques for efficient traffic management in cloud environment. Int. J. Electr. Comput. Eng. (IJECE) **6**, 963–973 (2016)
11. Mohsen and Hossein Delda: Balancing load in a computational grid applying adaptive, intelligent colonies of ants. Informatica **32**, 327–335 (2008)
12. Buyya, R., Ranjan, R., Calheiros, R.N.: InterCloud: utility-oriented federation of cloud computing environments for scaling of application services. In: Hsu, C.-H., Yang, L.T., Park, J.H., Yeo, S.-S. (eds.) ICA3PP 2010. LNCS, vol. 6081, pp. 13–31. Springer, Heidelberg (2010). https://doi.org/10.1007/978-3-642-13119-6_2
13. Wickremasinghe, B.: Cloud analyst: a cloud sim-based visual modeler for analyzing cloud computing environments and applications. IEEE (2010)
14. Alnazir, M.K.A.M., Mustafa, A.B.A.N., Ali, H.A., Yousif, A.A.O.: Performance analysis of cloud computing for distributed data center using cloud-sim. In: 2017 International Conference on Communication, Control, Computing and Electronics Engineering (ICCCEE), pp. 1–6 (2017). https://doi.org/10.1109/iccccee.2017.7867662
15. Pavithra, B., Ranjana, R.: A comparative study on performance of energy efficient load balancing techniques in cloud. In: 2016 International Conference on Wireless Communications, Signal Processing and Networking (WiSPNET) (2016)
16. Ragmani, A., El Omri, A., Abghour, N., Moussaid, K., Rida, M.: A global performance analysis methodology: case of cloud computing and logistics. In: 2016 3rd International Conference on Logistics Operations Management (GOL) (2016)
17. Kaneria, O., Banyal, R.K.: Analysis and improvement of load balancing in cloud computing. In: 2016 International Conference on ICT in Business Industry & Government (ICTBIG) (2016)
18. Joshi, S., Kumari, U.: Load balancing in cloud computing: challenges & issues. In: 2016 2nd International Conference on Contemporary Computing and Informatics (IC3I) (2016)

19. Mesbahi, M.R., Hashemi, M., Rahmani, A.M.: Performance evaluation and analysis of load balancing algorithms in cloud computing environments. In: 2016 Second International Conference on Web Research (ICWR), pp. 145–151 (2016). https://doi.org/10.1109/icwr.2016.7498459
20. Ghosh, S., Banerjee, C.: Priority based modified throttled algorithm in cloud computing. In: 2016 International Conference on Inventive Computation Technologies (ICICT), vol. 3 (2016)

Role of Cache Replacement Policies in High Performance Computing Systems: A Survey

Purnendu Das[✉]

Department of Computer Science, Assam University Silchar,
Silchar, Assam, India
purnen1982@gmail.com

Abstract. Cache replacement policies play important roles in efficiently processing the current big data applications. The performance of any high performance computing system is highly depending on the performance of its cache memory. A better replacement policy allows the important blocks to be placed nearer to the core. Hence reduces the overall execution latency and gives better computational efficiency. There are different replacement policies exits. The main difference among these policies is how to select the victim block from the cache such that it can be replaced with another newly fetched block. Non-optimal replacement policy may remove important blocks from the cache when some less important (dead) blocks also present in the cache. Proposing better replacement policy for cache memory is a major research area from last three decades. The most widely used replacement policies used for classical cache memories are Least Recently Used Policy (LRU), Random Replacement Policy or Pseudo-LRU. As the technology advances the technology of cache memory is also changing. For efficient processing of big data based applications today's computer having high performance computing ability requires larger cache memory. Such larger cache memory makes the task of replacement policies more challenging. In this paper we have done a survey about the innovations done in cache replacement policies to support the efficient processing of big data based applications.

Keywords: Cache memory · Multicore-system · Efficient data processing
Replacement policies

1 Introduction

Replacement Policies plays an important role in cache memory systems [1]. The current demand of big data applications makes it more important to use a better replacement policy for cache memories [1–3]. Since all the data needs to be fetched to the processor for any computation, using efficient replacement policy will allow the heavily used blocks to be kept in cache memory. To support better big data processing and high performance computing, larger cache size (especially for Last Level Cache) is required. This large sized cache has high capacity which helps the big data applications. Though the larger cache reduces the number of misses but it has some other complexities like access latency [4, 5], dead blocks [6, 7] etc. Implementing efficient

© Springer Nature Singapore Pte Ltd. 2019
S. Verma et al. (Eds.): CNC 2018, CCIS 839, pp. 400–410, 2019.
https://doi.org/10.1007/978-981-13-2372-0_35

replacement policy for such cache is also challenging as the associativity of such cache are high [8].

All set-associative and fully associative cache memory need Replacement policy. A set-associative cache is like a two-dimensional array where each row is called a set and each column is called a way. For example a 4-way set associative cache has 4-columns. The number of sets in a cache depends on the size of the cache. Each cache entry (considering an element in 2D array) stores a cache block that is fetched from lower level of memory. Each block has a separate address and the block is placed into the cache based on its address. In case of set-associative cache some address bits decides the set-index and the block always maps to a fixed set. The block can be placed in any of the ways available in the set. But if no free way is available then an existing block has to be replaced from the set to place the new block. The purpose of replacement policy in cache memory is to select the **victim block** that can be replaced from the cache. The fully associative cache has only one set and many numbers of ways. The purpose of replacement policy in fully-associative cache is same as in set-associative cache. In set-associative cache each set has its own replacement policy.

Efficient selection of victim block is important for the performance of the cache. The replacement policy should take the maximum advantage of the temporal locality1: a recently accessed block will be very likely accessed again in near future. If a replacement policy selects a recently used block as victim and evicts it from the cache then the cache will face a miss in its next access. Hence selecting a better replacement policy is very important for every cache memory systems. In this paper we have done a survey on the different replacement policies starting from the basic policies to the most recent policies [2, 3, 8, 9]. We have discussed the policies proposed for current larger sized cache memories which are required for the computers designed for high performance computing. The current challenges and the possible research directions are also discussed in this paper. The paper will be helpful for those researchers who want to start research in this area.

The organization of this paper is as follows. The next section discuss about the basic concept of cache organization as it is important to understand cache memory before understanding the replacement policies. Section 3 explains the details about how replacement policy works. The traditional replacement policies are also discussed in this section. Advancement of replacement policies are discussed in Sect. 4. The current issues and possible research opportunities are discussed in Sect. 5. The procedures for experimental analysis of cache memory as well as replacement policies are discussed in Sect. 6. Finally Sect. 7 concludes the paper.

2 Cache Organization

To discuss about replacement policies it is important to first discuss about the cache architecture. As mentioned earlier a cache can be either fully associative or set-associative. In today's multiprocessors where multiple cores are placed in a single chip each core has some private level of caches and all the cores shared a large size Last Level Cache called **LLC**. For example in case of Intel-i7 processor there are four cores, each has its own L1 and L2 cache and all the cores share a common L3 cache as LLC.

Figure 1 shows an example of such cache organization. In the figure there are four cores, each core has its own L1 Data and L1 Instruction cache. All the cores are sharing a common large size LLC. The cores and LLC here are connected with an on-chip interconnect. The interconnect can be either bus or network-on-chip [1, 10]. The LLC is also divided into multiple parts called banks; the detail description about banks is outside the scope of this paper [4, 11].

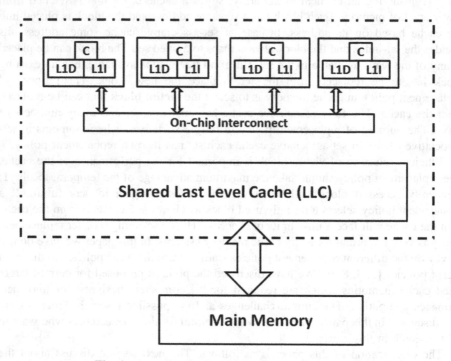

Fig. 1. An example of multi-level cache organization

Most of the caches used by today's processors are set-associative cache. Figure 2 shows an example of set-associative cache. Each cache, irrespective of its level, uses some replacement policy. In this paper from now onwards we will assume L2 as LLC. When a core requests for a block it first searched in its local L1 cache. If the block is found in local L1 cache then it is a hit and the data will be sent to the core. In case the block is not in L1 then it is a cache miss and the request will be forwarded to the LLC (L2). If the block is also not found in L2 then the main memory will be contacted and the block will be first fetched from main memory to L2. To place a newly incoming block, an existing block from cache has to be selected as victim block. The replacement policy is used for this purpose.

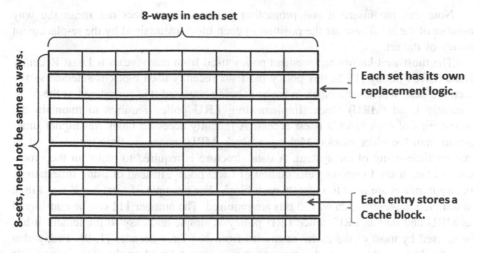

Fig. 2. Example of set-associative cache.

3   The Basic Concept of Replacement Policies

As mentioned in Sect. 2, in case of set-associative cache each set has its own replacement policy. To maintain this policy some additional data structure has to be used. Such hardware components consume additional storage, power and chip area. Also complex replacement policy can increase the cache access time. Hence a better and efficient replacement policy is always required. As the technology changes the replacement policies are also changing to meet the current demands.

3.1   Traditional Replacement Policies

The best replacement policy is a theoretical replacement policy proposed by Belady in 1966 [12]; it is called as Belady's Optimal Replacement Policy (OPT). The policy said that every time the victim should be the block which will be used in farthest future among all the existing blocks. It is not possible to implement in real hardware because knowing future is not possible. All the real replacement policies has a huge performance gap with Belady's OPT [8]. Though the Belady's OPT is not implementable in real hardware but it is possible to simulate it to compare with other policies. To do this the simulator will first run the application and record all the block requests as traces. These traces are then can be analyzed to simulate Belady. The details of this process are given in [8].

The three main tasks of any replacement policies are [1]:

1. **Victim Selection:** Select a victim block to be replaced by another.
2. **Block Insertion:** Where to insert a newly incoming block. Traditional rule is to insert the new incoming block at MRU position.
3. **Block Promotion:** Where to promote a block after an access of the block. Traditional rule is to promote the block as MRU.

Note that the insertion and promotion position above does not mean the way number of the set. These are the position of each block maintained by the re-placement policy of the set.

The most well-known replacement policy used from many years is Least Recently Used (LRU) policy [1]. In this policy the least recently used block is selected as the victim block. Whenever a block in cache is being accessed it is considered as the Most Recently Used (MRU) block. Implementing LRU policy requires to maintain the timestamps of each block's latest access. A recently accessed block has higher time-stamp than the older blocks. Making a block MRU means its timestamps is set as current time-stamp of the system. A data structure is required to maintain the timestamps of each set. In real implementation of LRU policy, instead of using timestamps, binary numbers are used to separate each block. For example, if a set has 8-ways then to uniquely represent each way, 3 bits are required. The number 111 can be considered as MRU and 000 as LRU. Since LRU policy is simple and easy to implement it has been used by most of the cache memories from last three decades [1, 9]. Today also most of the recently proposed replacement policies are based on the aging concept of LRU [3, 8]. Other well-known replacement policies are Random replacement and MRU replacement [13]. Random policy selects a random block as victim and MRU works just as the opposite of LRU.

3.2   Issues with Traditional Replacement Policies

The major issue of LRU policy is the presence of dead blocks [6]. There are many blocks which are requested by the cores to use only once. Such blocks when fetched are placed in MRU position (according to LRU policy) but since it will never request again by the core the block is dead. Since LRU only selects the least recently used block (*lru block*) as victim, it will take time to become a dead block as *lru block* and being evicted from the cache. There is no technique possible to detect dead blocks in cache as it requires to see the future but a dead block can be predicted with high accuracy [8]. Section 4 discusses about the innovative improvements of LRU policy to handle dead blocks. The issue of dead block is more in LLC than the upper level of caches. It has been found that the most of the benefits of temporal locality is consumed by the upper level of caches and hence the chances of being a block dead in LLC are very high [1, 8]. The random replacement policy can evict the important block early hence it is not practical to use [13].

As discussed above the traditional replacement policies (LRU and random) has performance issues. The situation has become more critical as the size of the LLC becomes larger. There are many innovative techniques has been proposed to improve the performance of LRU based policies [14–22]. A better LRU policy means more number of hits, less hardware overhead and less number of dead blocks. In this paper we will discuss about them.

4 Improved Replacement Policies

To understand these techniques we can assume that the replacement policy is maintaining a list with LRU block in one end and MRU in another end. The blocks change the position after every access. As mentioned above there are blocks exists which require only once by the core. In [23, 24] the author proposed a technique to place the incoming block at lru position i.e. the block insertion policy places the block at *lru* position. The victim selection and block promotion techniques are remain same as traditional LRU policy. These designs reduce the dead blocks in the cache. In Bimodel Insertion Policy (BIP) a block is inserted in MRU with some probability. Finally they proposed Dynamic Insertion Policy (DIP) where both BIP and LRU are used based on some statistics.

To reduce the gap between implementable replacement policies and Belady's OPT algorithm, a distance prediction based replacement policy is proposed in [19]. In this policy the reuse distance of a block in future is predicted. The concept is a combination of reuse distance and LRU policy. The policy tries to select the block having the highest reuse distance as victim block. In case a block has no predicted reuse distance then LRU policy is used to select victim. Some other LRU based replacement policies are Shepherd Cache [20], Extra Light-weight Shepherd Cache [21], Re-Reference Interval Prediction [17] and Pseudo-LIFO [25]. In [26] the authors have proposed a memory-level-parallelism based replacement policy.

Most of the modifications and experience with replacement policies are per- formed with lower level caches especially LLC. As the L1 cache is directly associated with the core, all the processors use simple LRU policy for L1. In LLC the associativity may vary from 4 to 32. Better dead-block detection technology can improve the replacement policies. In [13] the author proposed a Random LRU where LRU policy is only applied to the half of the ways. Other ways use random replacement policy. The victim is always selected from the LRU position. After evicting the victim block a random block will be moved to LRU section and the newly incoming block is placed in random section. This removes the dead blocks early from the cache. Care has been taken not to evict important blocks because of random selection. A randomly selected block is moved to the LRU to provide some more chances to be in the cache.

As mentioned earlier that the detection of dead block is not possible but it can be predicted. Some researchers use machine learning based techniques in LLC to predict the dead blocks [2, 6, 7, 9]. Such deadlock prediction techniques have high accuracy but have some hardware overhead. Due to such overheads these policies cannot be implemented for higher level of caches. Reused counter based policy and cost based polices are also used as alternative of traditional LRU policy. In reused counter based policies a counter is maintained for each block in the set. The counter is incremented after every access (hit) of the block. During the eviction, a block having least value in reuse counter is selected as victim. The assumption behind this technique is that a highly accessed block will be accessed again in future with high probability. The disadvantage of such policy is that a new important block may also have low reuse value which will be used in future. Some additional mechanisms are required to select victim in these policies. Cost based policies tries to reduce some cost by selecting the victim block. The cost can be either latency, number of misses, energy consumption, number of instruction executed during miss etc. [29].

4.1 Adaptive Replacement Policies

The adaptive replacement policy changes behavior or victim selection techniques based on the dynamic behavior of the systems. It is mostly required for the hybrid last level caches [27, 28]. Today's large size LLC are designed with combination of SRAM and other technologies like PCM [27], STT-RAM [27] etc. Both PCM and STT-RAM are expensive in terms of writes. Using an adaptive replacement policy in upper level of cache, the number of writes in LLC can be dynamically controlled. Some of the exiting works in this area are [2, 3, 9, 29].

4.2 Cache Partitioning

Replacement policy can also serve some additional purpose to improve the cache performance. Normally in multi-core systems different core execute different ap- plication simultaneously. Most of the high performance computing systems has multiple cores and the core runs different applications [1]. Such simultaneous execution may create contention in LLC as it is shared by all the cores. A heavily used application may forcefully remove all the blocks of another application from LLC. Such issues can be handled by cache partitioning. Replacement policy has a major role to implement any cache partitioning technique [30–32].

As mentioned above, based on the requirement of the application, the cache should be partitioned its ways, to all the cores. Such partitioning is possible by changing the insertion and victim selection process of LRU based policies. A block from low demanding application can be inserted into middle position and the blocks from highly demanding applications can be inserted at *mru* position. Such policy will allow more blocks from heavy applications to reside in the cache as the blocks from light applications will be evicted faster. The above technique is implemented in [31]. To select the proper load requirement of each application an Utility Based Monitor has been used. The main issue with this technique is that the partition is static. For example, consider a two-core system where both the cores are executing different applications. Assume that out of 8-ways, 3 ways are given to first core (C1) and 5 ways to second core (C2). After some time if the load requirement of C2 decreases and the same for C1 increases then the policy cannot change its partition dynamically. Another policy for handing such dynamic partitioning is proposed in [33]. An improved version of this technique is proposed in [34].

4.3 Global Replacement Policies

The replacement policies used by each set of set-associative cache separately are called local replacement policy. They called as local because each set has its own replacement policy. These local policies may not select the best victim block every time. For example, the victim block selected by the LRU policy of *set-0* may not be the oldest block in the cache. There may be older blocks present in other sets. Such issues are not required to handle if the cache is traditional set-associative cache. There are some other cache architectures like V-Way [35], Z-Cache [36] and T-DNUCA [37] where global replacement policy is required. In V-way the tag and data array of the cache are completely separated and any tag location can map to any data location. The tag array is same as set-associative but the data cache is fully-associative. Such type of cache architectures is required for better utilization of cache sets [38, 39]. More detail explanation about uniform cache utilization is out of scope for this paper. V-way uses a global replacement policy for its data array. To reduce the complexity and latency of such replacement policy the author proposed a low cost global replacement policy.

5 Current Issues with Replacement Policies

The LLC size is increasing in the era of big data. The replacement policy must handle such highly associative caches efficiently. Most of the existing replacement polices are proposed to reduce number of misses in cache. Other parameters like chip temperature, power consumption and hit rate are also important for the large size LLCs. The machine learning based techniques used for predicting dead block are complex and not possible to implement for upper level of caches as it will increase the access latency as well as the hardware overhead. Designing less complex dead block detector of upper level of caches is a challenging task. As the technology changes the current system with high computing power are using DRAM based cache as LLC [27]. These DRAM caches are placing in both 2D and 3D chips. Due to its larger size and associativity the traditional replacement policy may degrade the performance of the system. As per our knowledge very less work has been done to propose hardware efficient replacement policies for DRAM caches.

6 Procedure for Experimental Analysis

For experimental analysis designing the physical hardware component is ex- pensive and may not be possible for research oriented works. Hence most of the researchers working in computer architecture use different simulation tools to simulate the hardware systems. There are different types of simulator exits: full-system simulator [40, 41], NoC based simulator [42], Cache modeler [43], Power/Energy Simulator etc. Implementing replacement policies in simulators is very simple. It can be done with almost all full system simulators. A simulator is called full-system simulator if it has capability to simulate the entire system. The simulated environment is act as an virtual machine within a real machine. Some of the full system simulators are: GEMS [41], Simics [44], and Gem5 [40] etc. Some standalone application can also be developed for experimenting re- placement policies [8].

7 Conclusion

Replacement Policies plays an important role in cache memory systems [1]. The current demand of big data applications makes it more important to use a better replacement policy for cache memories [1–3]. Since all the data needs to be fetched to the processor for any computation, using efficient replacement policy will allow the heavily used blocks to be kept in cache memory. The most widely used replacement policies used for classical cache memories are Least Recently Used Policy (LRU), Random Replacement Policy or Pseudo-LRU. As the technology advances the technology of cache memory is also changing. For efficient processing of big data based applications the larger cache memory has to be used. Such larger cache memory makes the task of replacement policies more challenging. In this paper we have done a survey about the innovations in cache replacement policies in last 15 years to support the efficient processing of big data based applications.

References

1. Balasubramonian, R., Jouppi, N.P., Muralimanohar, N.: Multi-Core Cache Hirarchies. Morgan and Claypool, California (2011)
2. Chen, Z., Xiao, N., Lu, Y., Liu, F.: Me-CLOCK: a memory-efficient framework to implement replacement policies for large caches. IEEE Trans. Comput. 65(8), 2665–2671 (2016)
3. Kharbutli, M., Sheikh, R.: LACS: a locality-aware cost-sensitive cache replacement algorithm. IEEE Trans. Comput. 63(8), 1975–1987 (2014)
4. Kim, C., Burger, D., Keckler, S.W.: An adaptive, non-uniform cache structure for wire-delay dominated on-chip caches. SIGOPS Oper. Syst. Rev. 36, 211–222 (2002)
5. Chishti, Z., Powell, M.D., Vijaykumar, T.N.: Distance associativity for high-performance energy-efficient non-uniform cache architectures. In: Proceedings of the 36th Annual IEEE/ACM International Symposium on Microarchitecture (MICRO), pp. 55–66 (2003)
6. Liu, H., Ferdman, M.,. Huh, J, Burger, D.: Cache bursts: a new approach for eliminating dead blocks and increasing cache efficiency. In: 2008 41st IEEE/ACM International Symposium on Microarchitecture, pp. 222–233, November 2008
7. Khan, S.M., Jim'enez, D.A., Burger, D., Falsafi, B.: Using dead blocks as a virtual victim cache. In Proceedings of the 19th International Conference on Parallel Architectures and Compilation Techniques. PACT 2010, pp. 489–500 (2010)
8. Das, S., Kapoor, H.K.: Latency aware block replacement for L1 caches in chip multiprocessor. In: 2017 IEEE Computer Society Annual Symposium on VLSI (ISVLSI), pp. 182–187, July 2017
9. Kharbutli, M., Solihin, Y.: Counter-based cache replacement and bypassing algorithms. IEEE Trans. Comput. 57(4), 433–447 (2008)
10. Wang,Y., Zhang, L., Han, Y., Li, H., Li, X.: Address remapping for static NUCA in NoC-based degradable chip-multiprocessors. In: Proceedings of the IEEE 16th Pacific Rim International Symposium on Dependable Computing (PRDC), pp. 70–76, December 2010
11. Huh, J., Kim, C., Shafi, H., Zhang, L., Burger, D., Keckler, S.W.: A NUCA substrate for flexible CMP cache sharing. In: Proceedings of the 19th Annual International Conference on Supercomputing. ICS 2005, pp. 31–40 (2005)

12. Belady, L.A.: A study of replacement algorithms for a virtual-storage computer. IBM Syst. J. **5**(2), 78–101 (1966)
13. Das, S., Polavarapu, N., Halwe, P.D., Kapoor, H.K.: Random-LRU: a replacement policy for chip multiprocessors. In: Gaur, M.S., Zwolinski, M., Laxmi, V., Boolchandani, D., Sing, V., Sing, A.D. (eds.) VDAT 2013. CCIS, vol. 382, pp. 204–213. Springer, Heidelberg (2013). https://doi.org/10.1007/978-3-642-42024-5_25
14. Jeong, J., Dubois, M.: Optimal replacements in caches with two miss costs. In: Proceedings of the Eleventh Annual ACM Symposium on Parallel Algorithms and Architectures. SPAA 1999, pp. 155–164 (1999)
15. Jeong, J., Dubois, M.: Cost-sensitive cache replacement algorithms. In: Proceedings of the 9th International Symposium on High-Performance Computer Architecture. HPCA 2003, pp. 327–337 (2003)
16. Wong, W.A., Baer, J.L.: Modified LRU policies for improving second-level cache behavior. In: Proceedings Sixth International Symposium on High-Performance Computer Architecture. HPCA-6 (Cat. No. PR00550), pp. 49–60 (2000)
17. Jaleel, A., Theobald, K.B., Steely, Jr., S.C., Emer, J.: High performance cache replacement using re-reference interval prediction (RRIP). In: Proceedings of the 37th Annual International Symposium on Computer Architecture. ISCA 2010, pp. 60–71 (2010)
18. Ju, R.D.-C., Lebeck, A.R., Wilkerson, C.: Locality vs. criticality. In: Srinivasan, S.T. (ed.) Proceedings of the 28th Annual International Symposium on Computer Architecture. ISCA 2001, pp. 132–143 (2001)
19. Keramidas, G., Petoumenos, P., Kaxiras, S.: Cache replacement based on reuse-distance prediction. In: 2007 25th International Conference on Computer Design, pp. 245–250, October 2007
20. Rajan, K., Ramaswamy, G.: Emulating optimal replacement with a shepherd cache. In: 40th Annual IEEE/ACM International Symposium on Microarchitecture (MICRO 2007), pp. 445–454, December 2007
21. Zebchuk, J., Makineni, S., Newell, D.: Re-examining cache replacement policies. In: 2008 IEEE International Conference on Computer Design, pp. 671–678, October 2008
22. Lee, D., et al.: LRFU: a spectrum of policies that subsumes the least recently used and least frequently used policies. IEEE Trans. Comput. **50**(12), 1352–1361 (2001)
23. Qureshi, M.K., Jaleel, A., Patt, Y.N., Steely, S.C., Emer, J.: Adaptive insertion policies for high performance caching. In: Proceedings of the 34th Annual International Symposium on Computer Architecture. ISCA 2007, pp. 381–391 (2007)
24. Jaleel, A., Hasenplaugh, W., Qureshi, M., Sebot, J., Steely, Jr., S., Emer, J.: Adaptive insertion policies for managing shared caches. In: Proceedings of the 17th International Conference on Parallel Architectures and Compilation Techniques, PACT 2008, pp. 208–219 (2008)
25. Chaudhuri, M.: Pseudo-LIFO: the foundation of a new family of replacement policies for last-level caches. In: 2009 42nd Annual IEEE/ACM International Symposium on Microarchitecture (MICRO), pp. 401–412, December 2009
26. Qureshi, M.K., Lynch, D.N., Mutlu, O., Patt, Y.N.: A case for MLP-aware cache replacement. SIGARCH Comput. Archit. News **34**(2), 167–178 (2006)
27. Mittal, S., Vetter, J.S., Li, D.: A survey of architectural approaches for managing embedded dram and non-volatile on-chip caches. IEEE Trans. Parallel Distrib. Syst. **26**(6), 1524–1537 (2015)
28. He, J., Callenes-Sloan, J.: A novel architecture of large hybrid cache with reduced energy. IEEE Trans. Circuits Syst. I Regul. Pap. **64**(12), 3092–3102 (2017)

29. Sheikh, R., Kharbutli, M.: Improving cache performance by combining cost-sensitivity and locality principles in cache replacement algorithms. In: 2010 IEEE International Conference on Computer Design (ICCD), pp. 76–83, October 2010

30. Suh, G.E., Rudolph, L., Devadas, S.: Dynamic partitioning of shared cache memory. J. Supercomput. **28**(1), 7–26 (2004)

31. Qureshi, M.K., Patt, Y.N.: Utility-based cache partitioning: a low-overhead, high-performance, runtime mechanism to partition shared caches. In: 2006 39th Annual IEEE/ACM International Symposium on Microarchitecture (MICRO 2006), pp. 423–432, December 2006

32. Sundararajan, K., Porpodas, V., Jones, T., Topham, N., Franke, B.: Cooperative partitioning: energy-efficient cache partitioning for high-performance CMPs. In: 2012 IEEE 18th International Symposium on High Performance Computer Architecture (HPCA), pp. 1–12 (2012)

33. Xie, Y., Loh, G.H.: PIPP: promotion/insertion pseudo-partitioning of multi-core shared caches. SIGARCH Comput. Archit. News **37**(3), 174–183 (2009)

34. Halwe, P.D., Das, S., Kapoor, H.K.: Towards a better cache utilization using controlled cache partitioning. In: 2013 IEEE 11th International Conference on Dependable, Autonomic and Secure Computing, pp. 179–186, December 2013

35. Qureshi, M.K., Thompson, D., Patt, Y.N.: The V-Way cache: demand based associativity via global replacement. ACM SIGARCH Comput. Architect. News **33**(2), 544–555 (2005)

36. Sanchez, D., Kozyrakis, C.: The ZCache: decoupling ways and associativity. In: Proceedings of the 43rd Annual IEEE/ACM International Symposium on Microarchitecture (MICRO), pp. 187–198 (2010)

37. Das, S., Kapoor, H.K.: Exploration of migration and replacement policies for dynamic NUCA over tiled CMPs. In: Proceedings of the 28th International Conference on VLSI Design (VLSID) (2015)

38. Das, S., Kapoor, H.K.: Victim retention for reducing cache misses in tiled chip multiprocessors. Microprocess. Microsyst. **38**(4), 263–275 (2014)

39. Das, S., Kapoor, H.K.: Dynamic associativity management using fellow sets. In: Proceedings of the 2013 International Symposium on Electronic System Design (ISED), pp. 133–137 (2013)

40. Binkert, N., et al.: The Gem5 simulator. ACM SIGARCH Comput. Archit. News **39**(2), 1–7 (2011)

41. Martin, M.M.K., et al.: Multifacet's general execution-driven multiprocessor simulator (GEMS) toolset. SIGARCH Comput. Archit. News **33**(4), 92–99 (2005). http://www.cs.wisc.edu/gems/

42. Agarwal, N., Krishna, T., Peh, L.-S., Jha, N.: GARNET: a detailed on-chip network model inside a full-system simulator. In: IEEE International Symposium on Performance Analysis of Systems and Software. ISPASS 2009, pp. 33–42, April 2009

43. Muralimanohar, N., Balasubramonian, R., Jouppi, N.: Optimizing NUCA organizations and wiring alternatives for large caches with CACTI 6.0. In: Proceedings of the 40th Annual IEEE/ACM International Symposium on Microarchitecture. MICRO 40, pp. 3–14 (2007)

44. Magnusson, P.S., et al.: Simics: a full system simulation platform. Computer **35**(2), 50–58 (2002). \http://www.simics.net

Edge Detection Techniques in Dental Radiographs (Sobel, T1FLS & IT2FLS)

Aayushi Agrawal(✉) and Rosepreet Kaur Bhogal

Lovely Professional University, Phagwara, India
aayushiagrawal20495@gmail.com,
rosepreetkaur12@gmail.com

Abstract. Dental image processing plays a vital role in case of human identification. Proceeding a pace ahead in the area where image processing of dental radiographs for effective detection and diagnosis of dental diseases required. Edge detection plays an important role on dental radiographs as it contains the information of object discontinuity in an image. In this research, three edge detection techniques are implemented they are Sobel, Type 1 Fuzzy Logic System (T1FLS) and Interval Type 2 Fuzzy logic System (IT2FLS) on dental radiographs of different patients. If the image information of healthy and effected teeth are available in the form of pixels, the diseases can easily be identified by edge detection technique for further better diagnosis. The main aim of this research is to provide fast and best edge detection technique applied on the dental radiographs. Comparison among mentioned techniques are on the bases of total edge detected pixels, time taken by algorithm and ability to detect the dental diseases clearly. By considering all those parameters, IT2FLS gives better results shown in this paper.

Keywords: Dental diseases · Sobel operator · T1FLS · IT2FLS
Edge detection

1 Introduction

In dental x-ray imaging, edge detection acts a very helpful function in detecting and diagnosis of the dental diseases. Since, brightness of x-ray image are not good enough because of sequins occurs due to the presence of water on teeth. The biggest difference between the digital dental x-ray of other important x-ray development mechanisms is that the digital dental x-rays are usually recorded by the dentist by the use of x-ray equipment in several orientations although with other significant x-ray mechanisms, the x-ray device is also static or goes in a solidly aligned path. Dental radiograms are poor and complicate in some of the diseases extraction such as tooth decay, cavities [2], tooth abscess [3], impact tooth, chipped tooth, diastema, crooked teeth etc.

Edge detection is the procedure of placing and positioning lack of continuity, differences and divergent orientations in an image. Edges plays a vital role in image processing applications. It can be specified by the group of immediate pixel location where a sudden changes in intensity information occurs. Edges be the outline of objects and background. An edge detector can be applied for feature extraction, image segmentation and object identifications [1].

© Springer Nature Singapore Pte Ltd. 2019
S. Verma et al. (Eds.): CNC 2018, CCIS 839, pp. 411–421, 2019.
https://doi.org/10.1007/978-981-13-2372-0_36

Conventional edge detectors Sobel, Perwitt and Roberts [4] are centered on derivatives of an image concentration purpose. They have high performance speed and are widely implemented. However, they fail to detect edges in complex medical images and those with acquisition artifacts. Therefore, it necessitates a comprehensive modification to enhance their performance. The algorithm of Multiple Morphological Gradient (mMG) is applied in [5] for clearly visibility of boundaries of object in panoramic radiograms. Furthermore, mMG algorithm should be applied for the detection of more number of dental diseases.

To overcome the problems of conventional edge detectors. Fuzzy Logic technique came into existence. Fuzzy logic is soft computation procedure designed for modeling partial information or ambiguous information. The usage of type-1 fuzzy logic in actual computer structures is wide, especially in user productions and operating applications. Fuzzy logic is field of soft computation which alters a computer organization to argue with uncertainness. A fuzzy inference system (FIS) comprises a set of rules determined above fuzzy sets. Fuzzy sets simplify the theory of a conventional set by granting the degree of membership to be several value with in 0 and 1 [6].

Nowadays, the effectiveness of type-2 fuzzy logic is what it accept one further pace towards the destination of 'Computing with Words' or the purpose of computers to act human sensing. This study focused on the impression of a fuzzy set whereas the membership degree of a fuzzy sets are evaluated with linguistic relations such as small, medium and large. [7, 8] at this phase, the explore was of extremely numerical, theoretic nature and actually was around constructing more or less of the foundations to more recent work.

The section of this research is prepared as follows; the description of sobel edge detector and the way of edge detection process used by gradient method is demonstrated in Sect. 2. The detection of edges using T1FLS with all the inputs applied at the time of process is described in Sect. 3 same as in Sect. 4, edge detection with IT2FLS along with input and output membership function are described and fuzzy inference rules which is applied in both T1FLS and T2FLS to evaluate the input and output variables. In Sect. 5, results and discursion takes place by taking different types of dental radiographs of different patients. Finally, in Sect. 6, conclusion and future scope according to the results takes place on the basis of parameters found in previous sections.

2 Sobel Edge Detection

Sobel edge detector applied on the digital image having gray scale values, that computes gradients of an intensity of the light of every pixels, affording the way of larger potential gain of dark to light [9]. Sobel operator comprises of the matrix of 3×3 masks for convolution over an input image. As shown in Eq. (1) where the $Sobel_x$ and $Sobel_y$ are sobel operators across horizontal and vertical direction respectively used for detection of edges in an image in respective directions. For the result, this mask moves throughout over an image [9].

$$\text{Sobel}_x = \begin{bmatrix} -1 & 0 & 1 \\ -2 & 0 & 2 \\ -1 & 0 & 1 \end{bmatrix} \quad \text{Sobel}_y = \begin{bmatrix} 1 & 2 & 1 \\ 0 & 0 & 0 \\ -1 & -2 & 1 \end{bmatrix} \tag{1}$$

$$G_x = \text{Sobel}_x * I \tag{2}$$

$$G_y = \text{Sobel}_y * I \tag{3}$$

$$g = \sqrt{gx^2 + gy^2} \tag{4}$$

Equations (2) and (3) defines '*' defines the convolution operator, 'I' as input image (dental radiographs), 'Gx', 'Gy' shows that images of every level comprises of horizontal, vertical derivative estimation and in Eq. (4) magnitude is determined that is given by 'g'.

3   Edge Detection with Type-1 Fuzzy Logic System (T1FLS)

Especially, in biomedical images, where there the images are less contrasted, there edges are advantageous to detect. Because, the wrong choice of edges might contribute to improper treatment to the diseases. After concerning all those problems edge detection using T1FLS is introduced to detect edges, which considers image be a fuzzy. And extract some parameters of images for creating fuzzification using membership functions. In majority of images where edges aren't distinctly determined, that is to say edges are discontinued, unclear, or blurred and in that situation edge detection gets more hard. For this purpose, different steps to be followed by fuzzy logic system that are fuzzification, applying rule base, decision making unit and defuzzification process to get desired output [10].

3.1   Input to T1FLS

In the T1FLS method, primarily four inputs be required, out of them two are based on the gradients computed called as variable GH and GV respectively which are mentioned in Eqs. (2) and (3) of previous section and another two inputs are the filters that are high pass filter (HPF) and low pass filter (LPF) shown in Eqs. (5) and (6). First two inputs calculated the edges in different direction of images and next two that are HPF and LPF are used to calculate the high frequency (edges) and blurring of image. For these function, two mask of HPF and LPF are used that are shown in Eqs. (5) and (6)

$$\text{HPF} = \begin{bmatrix} -1/16 & -1/8 & -1/16 \\ -1/8 & 3/4 & -1/8 \\ -1/16 & -1/8 & -1/16 \end{bmatrix} \tag{5}$$

$$LPF = (1/25) \times \begin{bmatrix} 1 & 1 & 1 & 1 & 1 \\ 1 & 1 & 1 & 1 & 1 \\ 1 & 1 & 1 & 1 & 1 \\ 1 & 1 & 1 & 1 & 1 \\ 1 & 1 & 1 & 1 & 1 \end{bmatrix} \qquad (6)$$

Therefore, the inputs to T1FLS are GH, GV, HP = HPF * I and D = LPF * I where 'I' denotes the input image (dental radiograph) and '*' denotes the convolution operator.

3.2   Input and Output Membership Functions

Membership function comprises of linguistic variables say low, medium and high. Basically, MFs are used at the time of fuzzification process in fuzzy logic system. Different types of MFs are available, but in this research gaussian MFs are used because of always continuity provides by this type of curve. Here, three linguistic variables are applied they are low, medium and high represented by blue, red and yellow color curve in following figures. The four parameters of images extracted in previous section are shown in the form of membership functions used as the input and output of fuzzy variables that are GH, GV, HP, D and EDGES in T1FLS (Figs. 1, 2, 3, 4 and 5).

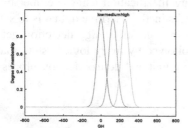

Fig. 1. Input variable GH (Color figure online)

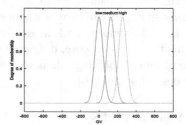

Fig. 2. Input variable GV (Color figure online)

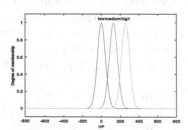

Fig. 3. Input variable HP (Color figure online)

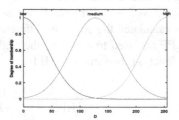

Fig. 4. Input variable D (Color figure online)

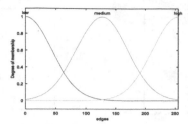

Fig. 5. Output variable edges (Color figure online)

4 Edge Detection with Interval Type-2 Fuzzy Logic System (IT2FLS)

Similarly, for IT2FLS all process of fetching the desired output is same as T1FLS but the difference is that in IT2FLS input and output membership functions has been fuzzy type-2 sets. And for conversion of type 2 sets to type 1 sets, one additional unit is required in the process called type reduction. Benefits of using IT2FLS are, it is much helpful in conditions where it's hard to defines appropriate membership functions towards the fuzzy sets [11].

Edge detection with IT2FLS follows the same process that in T1FLS but only difference is in applied membership function and results outcomes after the comparison. It consists of upper and lower MFs with the broad of the footprint of uncertainty (FOU) [12] which is the union of all primary MFs. FOU is the bounded region between upper and lower MFs.

4.1 Input and Output Membership Functions

The major difference between T1FLS and IT2FLS is difference in membership function used. Here, membership function itself in fuzzy set. The MFs used to define the input and output variables of IT2FLS are also Gaussian type curve. Following are the membership functions defined for the fuzzy variable as an input and output that are GH, GV, HP, D and EDGES for IT2FLS. As all these variables are shows in previous section of this research (Figs. 6, 7, 8, 9 and 10).

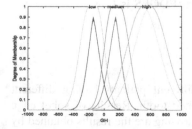

Fig. 6. Input variable GH

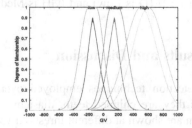

Fig. 7. Input variable GV

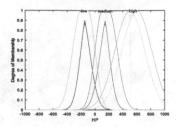

Fig. 8. Input variable HP

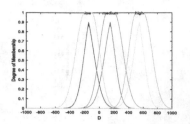

Fig. 9. Input variable D

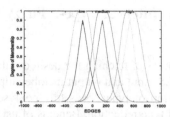

Fig. 10. Output variable edges

4.2 Fuzzy Inference Rules

The main principle of fuzzy inference is to map given input in an output by the use of fuzzy logic. The process of this mapping comprises one essential unit that is 'rule base'. Rule base consist of if-then statements depending upon application. For aggregation of these rules conjunctive operator is applied which calculates the minimum of both antecedents used in the rules. Following are the inference rules [13] which is used for evaluation of the input and output variables for both T1FLS and IT2FLS.

> **Rule 1 :** If (GH is Low) and (GV is Low) then (EDGES is Low).
> **Rule 2 :** If (GH is Medium) and (GV is Medium) then (EDGES is High).
> **Rule 3 :** If (GH is High) and (GV is High) then (EDGES is High) .
> **Rule 4 :** If (GH is Medium) and (HP is Low) then (EDGES is High).
> **Rule 5 :** If (GV is Medium) and (HP is Low) then (EDGES is High).
> **Rule 6 :** If (D is Low) and (GV is Medium) then (EDGES is Low).
> **Rule 7 :** If (D is Low) and (GH is Medium) then (EDGES is Low).

5 Results and Discussion

Edge detection techniques employed over three different patients having different diseases they are chipped teeth, diastema and crooked tooth. Results of sobel edge detection are shown at different threshold values. Following are the results obtained by applying implemented algorithms (Sobel, T1FLS and IT2FLS) (Figs. 11, 12 and 13).

From figure results of applied techniques it is clearly visible that edge detection using IT2FLS gives better results because edge detected pixels of patient 1 are 125406 which are comparatively larger than the other techniques applied in this research. In sobel edge detection, four threshold values are taken, through which at threshold 210 more number of edge detected pixels are detected say for patient 1 total 5072 pixels present in the output image. In the above images, red boxes indicates the area of concern, used by doctor in the process of diagnosis.

Table 1 shows the total number of edges obtained from sobel, T1FLS and IT2FLS for all the three images. Thus, IT2FLS is improved than T1FLS. It can be seen from the table that IT2FLS provide more edge pixel than T1FLS of same image and edge pixels have good appearance in IT2FLS than T1FLS. Table 2 shows comparison is based on total time taken by the algorithm to detect edges from the image, which shows that less time is taken by IT2FLS.

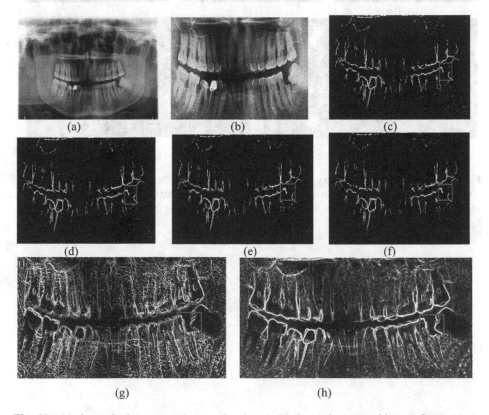

Fig. 11. (a) shows the input x-ray image of patient 1, (b) shows the cropped image, figure (c) to (f) shows the results of sobel operator at various thresholds that are 210, 220, 230 and 240 respectively, figure (g) shows the results of T1FLS and (h) shows the results of IT2FLS. (Color figure online)

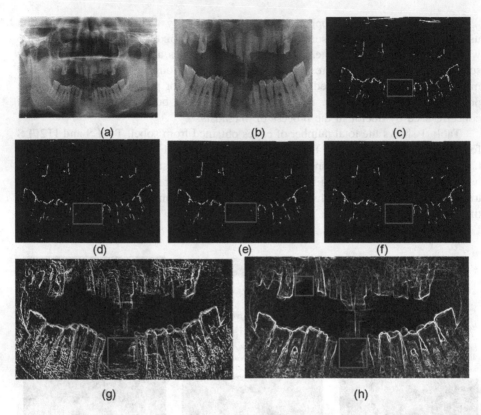

Fig. 12. (a) shows the input x-ray image of patient 2, (b) shows the cropped image, figure (c) to (f) shows the results of sobel operator at various thresholds that are 210, 220, 230 and 240 respectively, figure (g) shows the results of T1FLS and (h) shows the results of IT2FLS. (Color figure online)

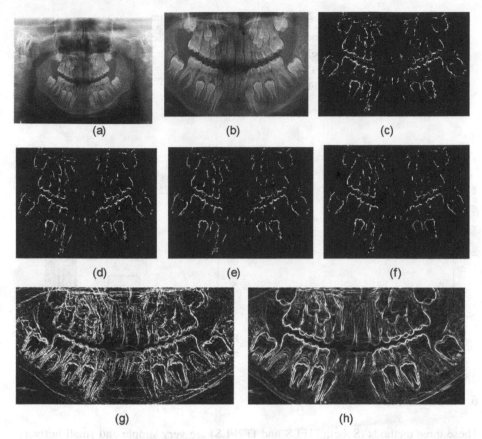

Fig. 13. (a) shows the input x-ray image of patient 3, (b) shows the cropped image, figure (c) to (f) shows the results of sobel operator at various thresholds that are 210, 220, 230 and 240 respectively, figure (g) shows the results of T1FLS and (h) shows the results of IT2FLS.

Table 1. Total edge detected pixel and dental diseases detected

Input images of patients	Algorithms						Diseases (trying to detect)
	Sobel edge detector				T1FLS	IT2FLS	
	T = 210	T = 220	T = 230	T = 240			
P1	5072	4565	4118	3769	25120	**125406**	Chipped teeth
P2	2030	1749	1530	4133	16017	**125385**	Diastema
P3	4125	3623	3192	1344	20552	**125113**	Crooked tooth

Table 2. Total time taken by algorithm

S. No.	Name of algorithm	Time taken in seconds
1	Sobel	100.838 s
2	T1FLS	109.303 s
3	IT2FLS	**97.841 s**

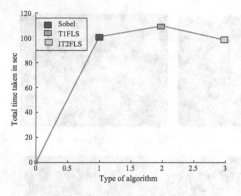

Fig. 14. Total time taken by algorithms

Fig. 15. Total edge detected pixels by algorithms

6   Conclusion

These three methods (Sobel, T1FLS and IT2FLS) are very simple and small but very efficient algorithms to shorten the concepts of artificial intelligence and digital image processing. The parameters, total edge detected pixels and total time taken by algorithm are helpful for the conclusion of this research, that a large number of edge pixels are detected by IT2FLS can be easily analyzes by the following graphs. And less time is taken by IT2FLS for the process of edge detection method. Since, IT2FLS is useful to handle and deals with real world uncertainties. Thus the results of three algorithms, shows to the doctor and that results are very helpful for them, for the identification and better diagnosis of dental diseases from edge detected x-ray image. Following are the graphs based on total time taken and total edge detected pixels from image by all three algorithm shows in Figs. 14 and 15 respectively.

Time shown in Fig. 14 is in second and for sobel edge detector average time taken for all threshold value executions. In Fig. 15 graph shows between type of algorithm and total edge pixels detected.

In Future Research, look forward to get more precise and improved results by applying general type-2 fuzzy logic system (GT2FLS) [14, 15] for detection of edges application because it deals with real time application by taking consideration all possible parameters. Additionally, helpful in detecting several types of dental diseases from the edge detected image.

Acknowledgments. The authors would like to special thanks to Mr. Puneet Gupta [16] who helps in providing database of dental radiograph.

References

1. Canny, J.: A computational approach to edge detection. IEEE Trans. Pattern Anal. Mach. Intell., 679–698
2. Kaushik, A., Mathpal, P.C., Sharma, V.: Edge detection and level set active contour model for the segmentation of cavity present in dental X-ray images. Int. J. Comput. Appl. **96**, 24–29 (2014). ISSN 0975-8887
3. Mahant, P.M., Desai, N.P., Jain, K.R., Mahant, M.G.: Optimal edge detection method for diagnosis of abscess in dental radiograph. IJRSI (2015)
4. Ansingkar, N.P., Dhopeshwarkar, M.G.: Study and analysis of edge detection techniques for segmentation using dental radiograph. Int. J. Eng. Comput. Sci. **3**, 8362–8366 (2014)
5. Naam, J., Harlan, J., Madenda, S., Wibowo, E.P.: The algorithm of image edge detection on panoramic dental X-ray using multiple morphological gradient (mMG) method. Int. J. Adv. Sci. Eng. Sci. Technol. **6**, 1012–1018 (2016)
6. Sivanandam, S.N., Sumathi, S., Deepa, S.N.: Introduction to Fuzzy Logic using MATLAB. Springer, Berlin (2007). https://doi.org/10.1007/978-3-540-35781-0
7. John, R., Simon, C.: Type-2 fuzzy logic: a historical view. In: IEEE, Centre for Computational Finance and Economic Agents (CCFEA). University of Essex, Leicester (2007)
8. Zadeh, L.A.: The concept of a linguistic variable and its application to approximate reasoning. Inf. Sci. **8**, 199–249 (1975)
9. Senthilkumaran, N., Rajesh, R.: Edge detection techniques for image segmentation and a survey of soft computing approaches. Int. J. Recent Trends Eng. **1**, 250–254 (2009)
10. Mendoza, O., Melin, P., Licea, G.: A new method for edge detection in image processing using interval type-2 fuzzy logic. IEEE Transactions (2007)
11. Melin, P., Mendoza, O., Castillo, O.: An improved method for edge detection based on interval type-2 fuzzy logic. Expert Syst. Appl. **37**, 8527–8535 (2010)
12. Wu, J., Yin, Z., Xiong, Y.: The fast multilevel fuzzy edge detection of blurry images. IEEE Signal Process. Lett. **14**, 344 (2007)
13. Chen, S., Chang, Y., Pan, J.: Fuzzy rules interpolation for sparse fuzzy rule-based systems based on interval type-2 Gaussian fuzzy sets and genetic algorithms, 412–425
14. Gonzalez, C.I., Melin, P., Castro, J.R.: An improved sobel edge detection method based on generalized type-2 fuzzy logic. Soft. Comput. **20**, 773–784 (2016)
15. Melin, P., Gonzalez, C.I., Castro, J.R., Mendoza, O., Castillo, O.: Edge detection method for image processing based on generalized type-2 fuzzy logic. IEEE Trans. Fuzzy Syst. **22**, 1515–1525 (2013)
16. Bishen, K.A., Chhabra, K.G., Sagari, S., Gupta, P.: Nationwide survey on barriers for dental research in India. J. Pharm. Bioallied Sci. **7**, 201–206 (2015)

Review of Deep Learning Techniques for Object Detection and Classification

Mohd Ali Ansari$^{(\boxtimes)}$ and Dushyant Kumar Singh

Motilal Nehru National Institute of Technology Allahabad, Allahabad, India
mohdaliucer@gmail.com, dushyant@mnnit.ac.in

Abstract. Object detection and classification is a very important integrant of computer nature vision domain. It has its role in various sectors of life as security, safety, fun, heath & comfort etc. Under safety and security, surveillance is one critical application area where, Object detection has gained the growing importance. Object in such case could be human being and other suspicious and sensitive objects. Correct detection and classification on accuracy measures is always a challenge in these problems. Now days, deep learning techniques are getting utilized as an effective and efficient tool for different classification problems. Looking over these facts, a review of available deep learning architectures has been presented in this paper, for the problem of object detection and classification. The classification models considered for review are AlexNet, VGG Net, GoogLeNet, ResNet. The dataset used for experimentation is Caltech-101 dataset and the standard performance measures utilized for evaluation are True Positive Rate (TPR), False Positive Rate (FPR) and Accuracy.

Keywords: Object detection · Classification · Deep learning
Convolutional Neural Network (CNN) · AlexNet · VGG net · ResNet

1 Introduction

Computer vision provides the ability to the machine to see and gather information from the environment. This field contains methods for acquiring, processing and analyzing the images, to be able to extract important information from them. Recently in computer vision, a lot of research has been seen for classification and recognition of objects in images and videos. Many applications are using object classification and recognition technique to solve the real world problem.

Frame-differencing and Background Subtraction are the two major techniques for object detection in an image or video. Noises are the biggest reason due to which the efficiency of these approaches is affected most. Due to the noise and motion, in frame differencing it creates a lot of data; there is an added difficulty in differencing images, as the noise has similar properties in different images or videos. In case of Background subtraction, due to motion in the background, it's become difficult to identify which part of an image is background, which makes the efficiency lower. Other approaches work on object features and a classifier. In this approach firstly extract some feature from the object after that using some classifier technique to classify the objects on the basis of extracted feature [10].

© Springer Nature Singapore Pte Ltd. 2019
S. Verma et al. (Eds.): CNC 2018, CCIS 839, pp. 422–431, 2019.
https://doi.org/10.1007/978-981-13-2372-0_37

In object detection technique the toughest part is to detect and identify the features in the raw input data and on the basis of that feature it detects objects. While in deep learning there is no manual step for finding the feature of an object. In deep learning, at the time of training, it discovers the most useful. In deep learning, there is no need to select any special feature to classify and for the detection of the object. In comparison to other classification and detection technique, deep learning has better accuracy if using sufficient amount of depth in the classification model.

2 Related Work

There are several approaches proposed by the researcher using different techniques of classification and recognition.

Krizhevsky et al. [1] proposed the technique for object classification. They perform classification task on 1.28 million images that belong to 1000 classes. In this technique, they use CNN for object classification. They use 5 convolutional layers and 3 fully-connected layers. They use different filter size at different convolutional layer with the different stride. AlexNet obtains 57.0% accuracy for top-1 while for top-5 it obtains 80.3% accuracy. Simonyan and Zisserman [2] perform classification task on 1.3 million images that belong to 1000 classes. In this technique, they use CNN for object classification. They make the network that contains 19 layers out of which 16 are the convolutional layer and 3 are the fullyconnected layer. They use very small filter size to all convolutional layer with one stride. VGG obtains 70.5% accuracy for top-1 while for top-5 it obtains 90.0% accuracy.

Szegedy et al. [3] proposed the technique for object classification. In this technique, they use inception module for object classification. They make the network that contains 22 layers. They use 1×1, 3×3, 5×5 filters to convolutional layer. GoogLeNet obtains 68.7% accuracy for top-1 while for top-5 it obtains 88.9% accuracy He et al. [4] make deeper neural network for more accurate object classification. They present a residual network to training that are substantially deeper than those used previously ResNet can get more accuracy as we increase depth. ResNet trained on imagenet dataset that contain approx 1.2 million images with approximately 2000 classes. Resnet-152 obtains 80.62% accuracy for top-1 while for top-5 it obtains 95.51% accuracy.

3 Deep Learning Models

CNN is composed of multiple layers; each layer has specific work to do. To extract useful information pass the input through the layers [7]. CNN contains multiple layers each layer have some parameters that are trained on the data set, CNN automatically extracts most useful information or feature. CNN is better to work with images.

3.1   AlexNet

This model is trained on a subset of the ImageNet database [1], which is used in ImageNet Large-Scale Visual Recognition Challenge (ILSVRC). The model is trained on more than a million images and can classify images into 1000 object categories. As the winner of ILSVRC 2012, the AlexNet architecture has about 650 thousand neurons and 60 million parameters. AlexNet includes five convolutional layers, two normalization layers, three maxpooling layers, three fullyconnected layers, and a linear layer with softmax activation function in the output. Moreover, it uses the dropout regularization method to reduce overfitting in the fullyconnected layers and applies Rectified Linear Units (ReLUs) for the activation of those and the convolutional layers (Fig. 1).

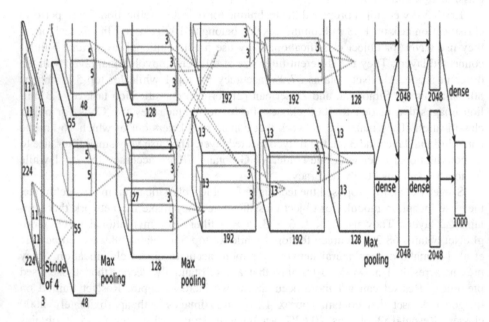

Fig. 1. AlexNet CNN architecture [1].

3.2   GoogLeNet

The GoogLeNet architecture was first introduced by Szegedy et al. in their 2014 [3]. GoogLeNet is an inception architecture that enables one to increase the width and depth of the network for an improved generalization capacity per a constant computational complexity. GoogLeNet architecture involves 6.8 million parameters with nine inception modules, two convolutional layers, one convolutional layer for dimension reduction, two normalization layers, four max-pooling layers, one average pooling, one fullyconnected layer, and a linear layer with softmax activation function in the output. Each inception module in turn contains two convolutional layers, four convolutional layers for dimension reduction, and one maxpooling layer. GoogLeNet also uses dropout regularization in the fullyconnected layer and applies the ReLU activation function in all of the convolutional layers (Fig. 2).

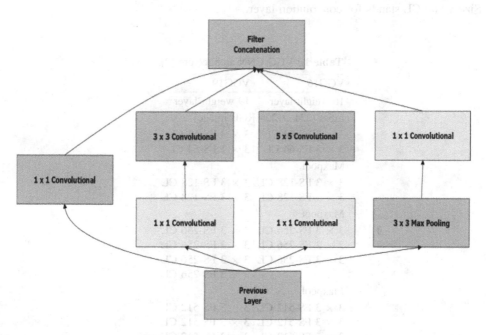

Fig. 2. GoogLeNet inception model [3].

3.3 VGG

The VGG network architecture was introduced by Simonyan and Zisserman [2]. The largest VGGNet architecture involves 144 million parameters from 16 convolutional layers with very small filter size of 3 × 3, five max-pooling layers of size 2 × 2, three fullyconnected layers, and a linear layer with Softmax activation function in the output. This model also uses dropout regularization in the fullyconnected layer and applies ReLU activation to all the convolutional layers. In Table 1 FS stands for Filter Size while CL stands for convolution layer.

3.4   ResNet

The ResNet architecture was first introduced by He et al. in their 2015 [5]. ResNet is a classification model that is totally different from our previous models. In ResNet author use very deep network to train model. When they use very deep neural network then they expected high accuracy but in reality the training error increased. To overcome the training error problem author uses the residual model. In Table 2 FS stands for Filter Size while CL stands for convolution layer.

Table 1. VGG CNN architecture [2].

VGG16	VGG19
16 weight layer	19 weight layer
Input (224 × 224 RGB image)	
3 × 3 FS-64 CL	3 × 3 FS-64 CL
3 × 3 FS-64 CL	3 × 3 FS-64 CL
Maxpool	
3 × 3 FS-128 CL	3 × 3 FS-128 CL
3 × 3 FS-128 CL	3 × 3 FS-128 CL
Maxpool	
3 × 3 FS-256 CL	3 × 3 FS-256 CL
3 × 3 FS-256 CL	3 × 3 FS-256 CL
3 × 3 FS-256 CL	3 × 3 FS-256 CL
	3 × 3 FS-256 CL
Maxpool	
3 × 3 FS-512 CL	3 × 3 FS-512 CL
3 × 3 FS-512 CL	3 × 3 FS-512 CL
3 × 3 FS-512 CL	3 × 3 FS-512 CL
	3 × 3 FS-512 CL
Maxpool	
3 × 3 FS-512 CL	3 × 3 FS-512 CL
3 × 3 FS-512 CL	3 × 3 FS-512 CL
3 × 3 FS-512 CL	3 × 3 FS-512 CL
	3 × 3 FS-512 CL
Maxpool	
FC(4096)	
FC(4096)	
FC(1000)	
Softmax	

Table 2. First column a plain network with 34 parameter layers. Second column is a residual network with 34 parameter layers. The blue color shortcuts increase dimensions.

34 Layer Plain	34 Layer Residual
Input image	
7 x 7 FS-64 CL,/2	7 x 7 FS-64 CL,/2
3 x3 FS-64 CL	3 x3 FS-64 CL
3 x3 FS-64 CL	3 x3 FS-64 CL
3 x3 FS-64 CL	3 x3 FS-64 CL
3 x3 FS-64 CL	3 x3 FS-64 CL
3 x3 FS-64 CL	3 x3 FS-64 CL
3 x3 FS-64 CL	3 x3 FS-64 CL
3 x3 FS-128 CL,/2	3 x3 FS-128 CL,/2
3 x3 FS-128 CL	3 x3 FS-128 CL
3 x3 FS-128 CL	3 x3 FS-128 CL
3 x3 FS-128 CL	3 x3 FS-128 CL
3 x3 FS-128 CL	3 x3 FS-128 CL
3 x3 FS-128 CL	3 x3 FS-128 CL
3 x3 FS-128 CL	3 x3 FS-128
3 x3 FS-256 CL,/2	3 x3 FS-256 CL,/2
3 x3 FS-256 CL	3 x3 FS-256 CL
3 x3 FS-256 CL	3 x3 FS-256 CL
3 x3 FS-256 CL	3 x3 FS-256 CL
3 x3 FS-256 CL	3 x3 FS-256 CL
3 x3 FS-256 CL	3 x3 FS-256 CL
3 x3 FS-256 CL	3 x3 FS-256 CL
3 x3 FS-256 CL	3 x3 FS-256 CL
3 x3 FS-256 CL	3 x3 FS-256 CL
3 x3 FS-256 CL	3 x3 FS-256 CL
3 x3 FS-256 CL	3 x3 FS-256 CL
3 x3 FS-512 CL,/2	3 x3 FS-512 CL,/2
3 x3 FS- 512 CL	3 x3 FS- 512 CL
3 x3 FS- 512 CL	3 x3 FS- 512 CL
3 x3 FS- 512 CL	3 x3 FS- 512 CL
3 x3 FS- 512 CL	3 x3 FS- 512 CL
3 x3 FS- 512 CL	3 x3 FS- 512 CL
Avg Pooling	
FC 1000	

4 Experimental Results

There are four classification model AlexNet, VGG-16, ResNet-50 and Inception-v3 [8, 9] used in this paper. To check the performance of above mentioned models on other datasets. In this paper we used Caltech-101 dataset, which contains 101 classes and approximately 10k images. This dataset contains large number of images, so we reduced the number of images down to 1400. Then we apply testing on this reduced dataset to all four classification models. To check the performance of classification models, we have used True Positive Rate (TPR), False Positive Rate (FPR), Precision and Accuracy [5, 6], which are described below (Tables 3, 4, 5 and 6).

Table 3. Confusion matrix for AlexNet model.

Total input (1420)	Ant	Beaver	Cougar	Electric guitar	Flamingo	Grand piano	Other
Ant	8	0	0	0	0	0	12
Beaver	0	8	0	0	0	0	12
Cougar	0	0	24	0	0	0	16
Electric guitar	0	0	0	8	0	0	12
Flamingo	0	0	0	0	17	0	23
Grand piano	0	0	0	0	0	14	6
Other	1	2	4	2	0	0	771

Table 4. Confusion matrix for VGG model.

Total input (1420)	Ant	Beaver	Cougar	Electric guitar	Flamingo	Grand piano	Other
Ant	14	0	0	0	0	0	6
Beaver	0	11	0	0	0	0	9
Cougar	0	0	33	0	0	0	7
Electric guitar	0	0	0	13	0	0	7
Flamingo	0	0	0	0	21	0	19
Grand piano	0	0	0	0	0	15	5
Other	2	1	1	2	0	0	873

Table 5. Confusion matrix for ResNet model.

Total input (1420)	Ant	Beaver	Cougar	Electric guitar	Flamingo	Grand piano	Other
Ant	15	0	0	0	0	0	5
Beaver	0	15	0	0	0	0	5
Cougar	0	0	36	0	0	0	4
Electric guitar	0	0	0	17	0	0	3
Flamingo	0	0	0	0	24	0	16
Grand piano	0	0	0	0	0	16	4
Other	0	2	0	1	0	0	965

Table 6. Confusion matrix for inception model.

Total input (1420)	Ant	Beaver	Cougar	Electric guitar	Flamingo	Grand piano	Other
Ant	14	0	0	0	0	0	6
Beaver	0	14	0	0	0	0	6
Cougar	0	0	37	0	0	0	3
Electric guitar	0	0	0	19	0	0	1
Flamingo	0	0	0	0	30	0	10
Grand piano	0	0	0	0	0	19	1
Other	1	1	4	1	0	0	1027

True Positive Rate (TPR): It is ratio of correctly classified elements [5, 6].

$$\text{TPR} = \frac{TP}{TP + FN} \tag{1}$$

Precision: It is ratio of correctly classified elements with total correct classification.

$$\text{Precision} = \frac{TP}{TP + FP} \tag{2}$$

False Positive Rate (FPR): It is ratio of incorrect elements that classified correct.

$$\text{FPR} = 1 - \text{TNR} \tag{3}$$

Accuracy: It is ratio of correctly classified element with total number of prediction.

$$\text{Accuracy} = \frac{TP + TN}{TP + TN + FP + FN} \tag{4}$$

Table 7. TPR, precision, FPR, and accuracy.

	Inception	ResNet	VGG	AlexNet
TPR	0.815	0.765	0.693	0.612
Precision	0.974	0.963	0.943	0.905
FPR	0.169	0.231	0.331	0.506
Accuracy	0.817	0.766	0.69	0.598

Figure 3 shows the accuracy of AlexNet is minimum among all, Precision is approx same in all model and FPR is maximum is AlexNet and minimum in Inception model. Table 7 shows that inception model having the best accuracy among these models. It also shows that inception model is best in precision among them.

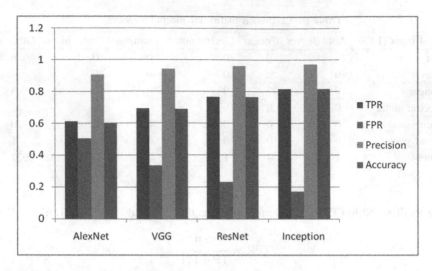

Fig. 3. TPR, FPR, precision and accuracy graph.

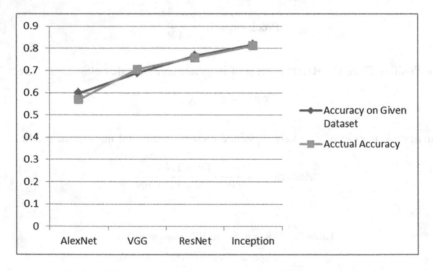

Fig. 4. FPR, precision and accuracy graph. (Color figure online)

In Fig. 4 there are two lines, red line represents the accuracy on given dataset Caltech-101 and the blue one represent the accuracy according to claimed accuracy [1–4]. Figure 8 shows, there is no difference between accuracies. In above graph accuracy is calculated on the basis of classification of objects correctly. But if we calculate the probability of the object in top-5 predicted objects by models then we get following accuracy improvement AlexNet obtains 57.0% accuracy for top-1 while for top-5 it obtains 80.3% accuracy, VGG obtains 70.5% accuracy for top-1 while for top-5 it obtains 90.0% accuracy, Resnet-152 obtains 75.8% accuracy for top-1 while for top-5 it obtains 92.9% accuracy while Inception obtains 81.2% accuracy for top-1 while for top-5 it obtains 95.8% accuracy.

5   Conclusion

There are four different classification and recognition approaches is presented in this paper and performed comparison on these classification models. For comparison of classification algorithm we used four parameters true positive rate, precession, false positive rate and accuracy. These derivatives shows which comparison model is better with comparison to other. Inception classification model having the highest accuracy and lowest false positive rate among all, while AlexNet classification model have the lowest accuracy and highest false positive rate among all.

References

1. Krizhevsky, A., Sutskever, I., Hinton, G.E.: Imagenet classification with deep convolutional neural networks. In: Advances in Neural Information Processing Systems, pp. 1097–1105 (2012)
2. Simonyan, K., Zisserman, A.: Very deep convolutional networks for large-scale image recognition. arXiv preprint arXiv:1409.1556 (2014)
3. Szegedy, C., et al.: Going deeper with convolutions. In: Proceedings of the IEEE Conference on Computer Vision and Pattern Recognition, pp. 1–9 (2015)
4. He, K., Zhang, X., Ren, S., Sun, J.: Deep residual learning for image recognition. In: Proceedings of the IEEE Conference on Computer Vision and Pattern Recognition, pp. 770–778 (2016)
5. Agarwal, A., Gupta, S., Singh, D.K.: Review of optical flow technique for moving object detection. In: 2016 2nd International Conference on Contemporary Computing and Informatics (IC3I), pp. 409–413. IEEE, December 2016
6. https://en.wikipedia.org/wiki/Confusion_matrix
7. https://www.analyticsvidhya.com/blog/2017/06/architecture-of-convolutional-neural-networks-simplified-demystified/
8. Shin, H.C., et al.: Deep convolutional neural networks for computer-aided detection: CNN architectures, dataset characteristics and transfer learning. IEEE Trans. Med. Imaging 35(5), 1285–1298 (2016)
9. Xia, X., Xu, C., Nan, B.: Inception-v3 for flower classification. In: 2017 2nd International Conference on Image, Vision and Computing (ICIVC), pp. 783–787. IEEE, June 2017
10. Singh, D.K.: Gaussian elliptical fitting based skin color modeling for human detection. In: 2017 IEEE 8th Control and System Graduate Research Colloquium (ICSGRC), pp. 197–201. IEEE, August 2017

Improved Symmetric Key Technique Using Randomization

Anshu Chaturvedi[1] and Hirendra Singh Sengar[2]([✉])

[1] Department of Master of Computer Applications,
M.I.T.S., Gwalior 474005, India
anshu_chaturvedi@yahoo.co.in
[2] SOS in Computer Science & Applications, Jiwaji University,
Gwalior 474011, India
hirendra.sengar@gmail.com

Abstract. Cryptography is the process of turning something readable into something unreadable. Nowadays, internet is being used by the people for exchanging information electronically. The rapid growth of internet increased the number of electronic transactions made by internet users. The information traveled over the internet is very much confidential which need to be secured from unauthorized access, resulted the need of cryptography. In this paper, an innovative technique has been proposed where the three symmetric keys were generated through a randomization process and used for encryption and decryption. Combination of three random keys was used in the encryption process which makes this technique unbreakable and secured against brute force attack and other similar attacks. This technique generates different-different ciphertext each time for the same message which also ensures the protection against various cryptanalytic attacks. This technique can be used to encrypt and decrypt the alphanumeric data in milliseconds which makes the technique more efficient.

Keywords: Symmetric key cryptography · Encryption · Decryption
Cryptanalysis

1 Introduction

The symmetric key cryptography is also known as secret key cryptography where same keys are used for both encryption and decryption.

Cryptanalysis is a technique used to find out the weaknesses in the system for breaking the code used in the encryption process without knowing the secret keys. Cryptanalysis is the study of knowing how the system works and finding a private key. Cryptanalysis is also known as the technique for cracking the code or breaking the code. The cryptanalyst can use one or more attacks' model to break the cipher, depending on what information is available and what type of cipher is being analyzed.

In network security and cryptography domain, some major cryptanalytic attacks are as follows-

- Ciphertext only attack (Brute force attack)

S. Verma et al. (Eds.): CNC 2018, CCIS 839, pp. 432–442, 2019.
https://doi.org/10.1007/978-981-13-2372-0_38

- Known plaintext attack
- Chosen plaintext attack
- Chosen ciphertext attack

2 Literature Review

Johari et al. [1] used three keys for encryption and decryption. Three prime numbers served as the keys. Some mathematical operations like addition, subtraction and multiplication were performed on keys to create different cipher texts. They also performed binary operations like shift operations on binary values of the ASCII characters to enhance the security level.

Kamalakannan et al. [2] presents the FPGA implementation of elliptic curve cryptography. The ASCII value of each character of text message mapped to the affine point. By using matrix mapping method these points were mapped again. For encryption and decryption they used ElGamal encryption and decryption techniques. The entire design is implemented on FPGA.

Singh et al. [3] removed the mapping of characters to affine points in elliptic curve. They paired up the ASCII values of plain text. The paired up values were taken as input. Their proposed technique removes mapping overheads and both the parties are not bothered about sharing of common lookup table. Any type of script can be encrypted or decrypted by using their proposed technique.

Paira et al. [4] developed innovative symmetric key cryptography algorithm on the basis of concepts of data structure and binary to gray code conversion techniques. They proposed the folding logic along with the circular shift operation. The proposed algorithm is secured against brute force attack and Man-In-Middle attack.

Iyer et al. [5] created a hybrid operation model using two cipher techniques AES and ECC. A QR code equivalent of the keys is generated in image form which is then used by the system to extract the key in the text form. This provides an extra level of security to the AES key. For the second level of the security, ECC public key was used to encrypt AES key. Later on, the encrypted AES key was used to encrypt the base64 encoded plain text to convert it into a corresponding cipher text. The resulting cipher text is already compressed and has undergone two levels of mixed encryption, ECC and AES. Their proposed idea and methodology provides a much better level of security than single model individually.

Shoukat et al. [6] studied about research issues of cryptographic elements and concluded that requirement of randomness in both the key and data blocking to get higher security. They analyzed that they can achieve higher security by creating random probabilities under the optimal key length. They also analyzed that hybrid encryption scheme can provide more security.

Shrivastava et al. [7] proposed an algorithm that has two rounds and both of these rounds, uses ASCII code of characters. In their proposed work, two operations addition and XOR used for encryption process and other two operations subtraction and addition used for generating two sub keys. Removing the correlation between cipher text and plain text is the objective of their algorithm. No of rounds reduced up to only two rounds makes the algorithm faster. Since they are encrypting plain text twice with a different key, thus they get a strong cipher which is difficult to break.

Raja et al. [8] developed high security encryption mechanism by performing rotation and flipping operations on matrix. Their method ensures two levels of security, first one is data encryption by generating encrypted array and performing matrix operations and second one is authentication by hash value computation.

Mathur et al. [9] proposed a technique in which Advanced Encryption Standard algorithm was used to encrypt plain text and ECC algorithm was applied to encrypt the AES key. They also used software countermeasures to prevent possible vulnerabilities posed by the timing side channel attack. They tested their system on the basis of some parameters those are: key length, no. of rounds, algorithm, maintenance of keys and attack performed. They also focused on verifying cache timing attack and investing some of the countermeasures by implementing them.

Naik et al. [10] developed the color substitution method that encrypts the text into a single image after converting each character to a color block. The sender must specify the values for RED (R), GREEN (G), and BLUE (B) channels. All the characters of text are then converted to color blocks formed by combining the values of RED (R), GREEN (G) and BLUE (B). The block size and selected channel form the key.

Patel et al. [11] developed a cryptographic technique to secure the information stored in mobile devices through cloud computing, they used a hybrid approach for secure transmisson of data by combining capabilities of ECC and blowfish algorithms. For increasing the computational complexity they used random numbers. They also randomized the number of rounds of blowfish for performance improvement. Generally, subkeys stored in EEPROM on a mobile phone can be easily hacked by attacker so they developed the enhanced blowfish technique for data protection with some modifications.

Prof. Kallam et al. [12] a block cipher technique is developed by them involves color substitution with iterative and modular arithmetic functions. They used large key of 128 bits and further it was divided into four subkeys by using subkey generation algorithm. First two keys are the input of the function selected on the basis of third key out of available functions then the output of the function gives the incremental values for color substitution and last key used for transposition of the cipher. They performed cryptanalysis and found that their technique generates a strong cipher.

Joshi et al. [13] proposed an efficient technique that increases the complexity of decryption performed by attacker by reducing the length of the encrypted message. They reduced the size of the cipher text by half so that the total size of the key and the cipher text is equal to the size of the original message. Their proposed technique is protected against brute force attack because each time a new key is generated for the message.

Bendovschi [14] analyzed the attack reported in last five years and provides a general view on cyber crime from the perspective of specialized literature, international law and historical facts and then she presented some countermeasures for ensuring security and to control the cyber crime around the globe.

Chandra et al. [15] proposed content based algorithm that performs some logical operations on binary values like circular bit shifting operation and binary addition.

Plaintext was encrypted two times to generate the secured cipher text using binary addition operation. Folding method was used for generating the secret key.

Shemin et al. [16] proposed a new method by combining three cryptographic techniques visual cryptography, quantum cryptography and steganography. In their proposed method visual cryptography hides the authentication details of the customer by generating two shares for customer and bank respectively. For ensuring the security of one time password, quantum cryptography was used and for the security of customer's share steganography was used. Their work saves customers through man in middle attack and identity theft issues.

Pozo et al. [17] used a secret key and a series of prime numbers generated through bi-directional matrix. The time taken in encryption and decryption process is very short which optimizes the battery of smart phone. The algorithm runs in quadratic polynomial complexity and because of such mathematical complexities, attacker is unable to intercept the message.

Ahmad et al. [18] proposed technique encrypts product's order and payment information by ECC algorithm and send both the things parallely over the network. At the time of decryption, recipient decrypts the message through private key and encryption algorithm. Their proposed technique overcome the failure of SET. Through their proposed work they assure the secure E-transactions.

Patil et al. [19] analyzed and compared all the popular cryptographic algorithms. The experiment has been done on different files of various sizes. Their experiment shows that time taken by the blowfish is the least among other algorithms and the time taken by the RSA algorithm is the highest, if time and memory are major factors then blowfish is the best suited algorithm, if cryptographic strength is major concern then AES is best suited algorithm and if network bandwidth is major factor then DES is best suited.

Kester et al. [20] proposed image encryption technique for the security of image data in health sector. In health sector safety, privacy and security of medical images is major concern. Unauthorized access to medical data will violate the privacy of patients. They proposed an effective security information system with a fully recoverable and reversible technique for authentication and security of medical images and all the pixel values remain same as it was before.

3 Security Analysis of Existing Proposals

Security analysis of the existing proposals over various cryptanalytic attacks has been done here.

In Johari et al. [1] method, they used three mathematical equations given below in decryption process to get the plain text back.

$$D1 = (N + K3) \bmod 26 \tag{1}$$

$$D2 = (D1 - K2) \bmod 26 \tag{2}$$

$$D = (D2 * K1^{-1}) \bmod 26 \tag{3}$$

where k1, k2 are the first two keys and third key is generated by performing the inverse modulo operation on first key k1. D1 and D2 are set of intermediate values and D is set of final calculated decimal values.

After performing the cryptanalysis, we found that values of N (N is a set of encoded values [0, 1, ..., 25] used for alphabets) can be easily determined from cipher text message by performing UNICODE to decimal conversion, right shift operation, binary to ASCII conversion and assigning encoded values to characters.

With some modifications in the mathematical formulas, by putting the guessed values in formulas and with the help of values of set N, the attacker can easily decrypt the whole plain text message.

Modified Mathematical formulas are given below

$$K1 = |D1 - N| \tag{4}$$

$$K2 = |D2 - D1| \tag{5}$$

$$K3 = \text{Inverse modulo } (D2/D) \tag{6}$$

They used "modulo by 26" operation that always generates value between 1 to 26 numbers as shown below

$$(11 + 7) \bmod 26 = 18 \tag{7}$$

$$(18 - 3) \bmod 26 = 23 \tag{8}$$

$$(15 * 21) \bmod 26 = 3 \tag{9}$$

For getting all keys, only 26 * 26 = 676 combinations of numerical values of D1 have to be guessed. By putting these guessed values in the above mentioned formulas, the first key k1 can be easily determined. Cryptanalysis is as shown below (Table 1).

As soon as values of first key in third and fourth columns are equal, that value is the final value of first key. In subsequent cryptanalysis process, the values of keys k2 and k3 can also be determined by using these modified mathematical equations. Once the values of these keys are determined, the values of set D can also be determined easily. This contains ASCII values of characters of the plain text message. By converting these values to their corresponding ASCII characters, we can easily get the plain text message back hence this method is vulnerable to the chosen ciphertext attack and brute force attack.

In Johari et al. [1] method order of letters and words of cipher text message is not changed during the message transmission. No transposition, rotation and reversal operations done on ciphertext. Each letter in the ciphertext has the same position as it had into plain text message which makes this method vulnerable to the different cryptanalysis attacks.

Table 1. Cryptanalysis of triplicative cipher technique

First guessed value	Second guessed value	K1 = |D1 − N|	K1 = |D1 − N|
1	1	10	15
1	2	10	14
.	.	.	.
.	.	.	.
18	18	7	2
18	19	7	3
18	20	7	4
18	21	7	5
18	22	7	6
18	23	7	7
.	.	.	.
.	.	.	.
26	26	15	10

4 Proposed Technique

4.1 Encryption

1. Get the plain text message and store it into an array of characters.
2. Generate three keys k1, k2 and k3 by using the random number generation procedure. The value of each key is a random number under the range of 256.
3. Convert each character value of plain text message to its equivalent UNICODE value and multiply each value with the three symmetric key values and store the resulted big integer values of characters into another array.
4. Reverse the array of big integer values of the characters.
5. Send the values of this array as ciphertext to the receiver side.

4.2 Decryption

1. Get the cipher text and store it into an array of numeric values.
2. Now reverse the array of numeric values.
3. Divide the each value of the array of the numeric values by using the three symmetric key values and convert these UNICODE values into their equivalent character values and store it into an array of characters.
4. The resulting array contains the required message (Fig. 1 and Table 2).

4.3   Simulation of Text Encryption and Decryption

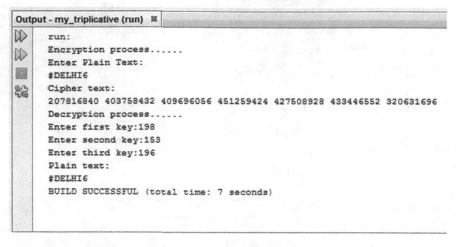

Fig. 1. Output for encryption and decryption of alphanumeric data

Table 2. Simulation environment

Operating system	Windows 7 Ultimate
Processor	Intel Core i3 2310 M
Memory	2 GB
IDE	NetBeans
IDE version	8.1
Language used	JAVA
JAVA version	1.8.0_91

5   Performance Comparison

5.1   Encryption and Decryption Time

Figure 2 shows that Triplicative cipher technique takes more time for encryption than the proposed technique. The use of various mathematical operations like shift operations, modulus operations, arithmetic operations and binary conversions makes triplicative cipher technique slower as compared to proposed technique. Triplicative cipher technique [1] also used encoding of alphabets to their positional value hence this mapping process makes encryption procedure slower (Fig. 3).

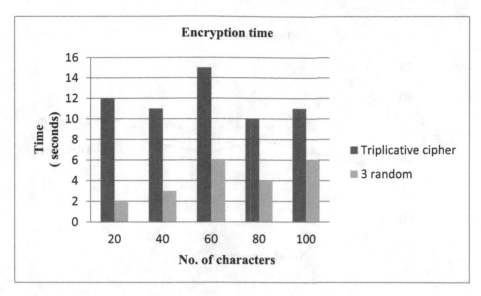

Fig. 2. Encryption time vs no. of characters for triplicative and 3 random (proposed technique)

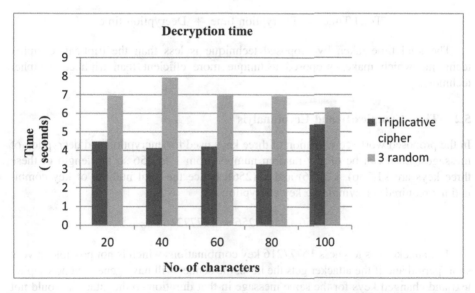

Fig. 3. Decryption time vs no. of characters for triplicative and 3 random (proposed technique)

Figure 4 shows the comparison of total time for both the algorithms, calculated by using the following equation.

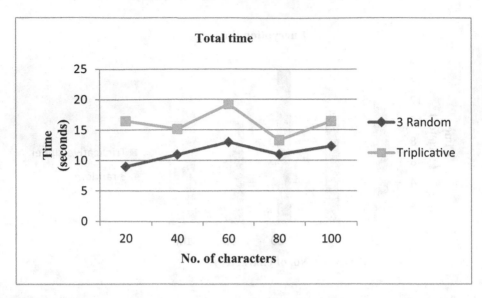

Fig. 4. Total time vs no. of characters for triplicative and 3 random (proposed technique)

$$\text{Total Time} \;=\; \text{Encryption time} \;+\; \text{Decryption time}$$

The total time taken by proposed technique is less than the triplicative cipher technique which makes proposed technique more efficient than triplicative cipher technique.

5.2   Time Complexity and Cryptanalyis

In the proposed work, combination of three keys used for encryption and decryption of messages. Each can be of any random number from 1 to 256 so the length of these three keys are k1(256), k2(256) and k3(256), hence the total number of key combinations required for symmetric key encryption is

$$256 * 256 * 256 = 16777216$$

The attacker has to guess 16777216 key combinations which is not possible in very short period and if the attacker gets the keys, the sender will have generated new cipher text and changed keys for the same message in that duration so the attacker would not be able to decrypt the cipher text hence the proposed algorithm is stronger than the triplicative cipher technique and secured against ciphertext only attack and brute force attack.

6 Conclusion

In our research work, we have implemented a innovative symmetric key algorithm through randomization where three random keys were used in encryption and decryption process. After evaluating the algorithm based on the some parameters we can say that this algorithm is secured against various cryptanalytic attacks. Total time taken in the encryption and decryption process is very less which makes the algorithm efficient for resource constraint devices.

References

1. Johari, R., Bhatia, H., Singh, S., Chauhan, M.: Triplicative cipher technique. In: International Conference on Information Security and Privacy, pp. 217–223. Elsevier, New Delhi (2015)
2. Kamalakannan, V., Tamilselvan, S.: Security enhancement of text message based on matrix approach using elliptical curve cryptosystem. In: 2nd International Conference on Nanomaterials and Technologies (CNT), pp. 489–496. ELSEVIER (2015)
3. Singh, L., Singh, K.: Implementation of text encryption using elliptic curve cryptography. In: Eleventh International Multi-Conference on Information Processing, pp. 73–82. Elsevier (2015)
4. Paira, S., Chandra, S., Safikul Alam, S., Bhattacharyya, S.: Symmetric key encryption through data structure and binary-gray conversion. In: Shetty, N.R., Prasad, N.H., Nalini, N. (eds.) Emerging Research in Computing, Information, Communication and Applications, pp. 1–10. Springer, New Delhi (2015). https://doi.org/10.1007/978-81-322-2550-8_1
5. Iyer, S., Sedamkar, R.R., Gupta, S.: A novel idea on multimedia encryption using hybrid crypto approach. In: 7th International Conference on Communication, Computing and Virtualization, pp. 293–298. Elsevier (2016)
6. Shoukat, I., Bakar, K., Iftikhar, M.: A survey about the latest trends and research issues of cryptographic elements. Int. J. Comput. Sci. Issues 8(3), 140 (2011)
7. Shrivastava, M., Jain, S., Singh, P.: Content based symmetric key algorithm. In: International Conference on Computational Modeling and Security, pp. 222–227. Elsevier (2016)
8. Raja, Y., Perumal, S.: WSES: high secured data encryption and authentication using weaving, rotation and flipping. ICTACT J. Commun. Technol. 6(4), 1200–1207 (2015)
9. Mathur, N., Bansode, R.: AES based text encryption using 12 rounds with dynamic key selection. In: 7th International Conference on Communication, Computing and virtualization, pp. 1036–1043. Elsevier (2016)
10. Naik, M., Tungare, P., Kamble, P., Sabnis, S.: Color cryptography using substitution method. Int. Res. J. Eng. Technol. 3(3), 941–944 (2016)
11. Patel, P., Patel, R., Patel, N.: Integrated ECC and blowfish for smartphone security. In: International Conference on Information Security & Privacy, pp. 210–216. Elsevier, Nagpur (2015)
12. Kallam, R., Kumar, S., Babu, A.: A modern play color cipher involving dynamic permuted key with iterative and modular arithmetic functions. Int. J. Adv. Res. Comput. Sci. 2(3), 208–213 (2011)

13. Joshi, A., Wazid, M., Goudar, R.: An efficient cryptographic scheme for text message protection against brute force attack and cryptanalytic attacks. In: International Conference on Intelligent Computing, Communication & Convergence, pp. 360–366 (2015)

14. Bendovschi, A.: Cyber-attacks – trends, patterns and security countermeasures. In: 7th International Conference on Financial Criminology, pp. 24–31. Elsevier (2015)

15. Chandra, S., Mandal, B., Alam, Sk., Bhattacharyya, S.: Content based double encryption algorithm using symmetric key cryptography. In: International Conference on Recent Trends in Computing, pp. 1228–1234. Elsevier (2015)

16. Shemin, P.A., Vipinkumar, K.S.: E–payment system using visual and quantum cryptography. In: International Conference on Emerging Trends in Engineering, Science and Technology (ICETEST), pp. 1623–1628. Elsevier (2016)

17. Pozo, I., Iturralde, M.: A encryption mechanism for instant messaging in mobile devices. In: International Workshop on Mobile Computing Security, pp. 533–538 (2015)

18. Ahmad, K., Shoaib, M.: E-commerce security through elliptic curve cryptography. In: International Conference on Information Security & Privacy (ICISP), pp. 867–873

19. Patil, P., Narayankar, P., Narayan, D.G, Meena, S.M.: A comprehensive evaluation of cryptography algortihms: DES, 3DES, AES, RSA and Blowfish. In: International Conference on Information Security & Privacy. Nagpur: ELSEVIER, pp. 617-624 (2015)

20. kester, Q., Nana, L., Pascu, A., Gire, S., Eghan, J., Quaynor, Nii.N.: A cryptographic technique for security of medical images in health information systems. In: The Second International Symposium on Computer Vision and the Internet (VisionNet): Signal Processing, Images Processing and Pattern Recognition (SIPP), pp. 538–543. Elsevier

An Interpretable SVM Based Model for Cancer Prediction in Mammograms

Abhishek Verma, Prashant Shukla(✉), Abhishek, and Shekhar Verma

Department of Information Technology, Indian Institute of Information Technology, Allahabad, Allahabad 211012, Uttar Pradesh, India
{ism2013002, rsi2016502, rsi2016006, sverma}@iiita.ac.in

Abstract. Machine learning algorithms are inherently not interpretable, and this poses a problem in risk-averse applications of machine learning. Mammographic images are widely used tool to predict breast cancer. Various machine learning algorithms like SVM, RBFNN are used to detect the mass in the mammographic images and classify for cancer, but the classification by SVMs are not intuitive. Our aim is to counter this problem by employing a novel method of using multiple SVMs to elucidate the area affected by cancer. We also color-code the patches for further clarification.

Keywords: SVM interpretability · Classification · Ridge regression
Mammograms

1 Introduction

In the purview of machine learning, interpretability means to explain or to present the artifacts in understandable terms to a human [1]. Basic decision trees, fuzzy rules and random forests are easy to understand as they use simple comparable rules for prediction but using sophisticated methods like SVM or neural networks changes the scenario. Though, SVMs and neural networks tend to increase the prediction accuracy, the user does not have any insight of these methods hence, they appear as black box where we feed in data and get output but do not know how they work. Lack of interpretation leads to model distrust as when model gives wrong prediction for known data, correctness of model becomes a big concern.

Interpretability is important in areas where human intervention is important such as medical sector. Machine learning algorithm are extensively used for detecting cancers and other ailments, but it still requires a go from the domain expert (radiologist, doctor etc.) to act upon the given diagnosis from the underlying model. The prediction backed up with an explanation by the model will help the human expert to make an informed decision rather than blindly trusting the given prediction. Thus, model interpretability is highly needed in such areas where the decisions made are crucial and lives depend on it.

Several techniques have been proposed to interpret SVMs using numerical or visual models. Hybrid models are the most used ones. In [2–4] Various Fuzzy models and decision tree models corresponding to SVMs have been proposed which generally give fuzzy rules for each support vectors.

© Springer Nature Singapore Pte Ltd. 2019
S. Verma et al. (Eds.): CNC 2018, CCIS 839, pp. 443–451, 2019.
https://doi.org/10.1007/978-981-13-2372-0_39

In [5] multiple kernel learning has been shown to be a solution for increasing the interpretability of decision function and hence, improves classifier performance. This has been a revelation which opened a new stream towards using a linear combination of kernels for learning. But, it has its problems alike. Kernel weights selection and increased parameters are the said problems. Such problems have been tackled by using an enhanced spatial pyramid match kernel that can be then solved by a projected gradient method. Weights can be included in the SVM risk minimization problem with second norm which will then promote sparsity.

In [6] a parallel nomogram visualization technique has been proposed which can model the entire setup in one page. Nomograms are not dependent on the dimensionality of the dataset, rather they are dependent on the kernel used and the properties it possesses. Nomograms provide an easily interpretable visualization of the black-box technique SVM is considered to be. Internal structure of SVM can be exposed using nomograms. To achieve this, nomograms employ logistic regression. Logistic regression is employed to obtain a probability value from the distance from the separating hyperplane that is available in SVM. Increase in dimensions does not stop nomograms from uncovering the mysteries of SVM. In case of multi-dimensionality, attributes are stacked vertically in nomograms, hence, compacting a plethora of dimensions into a single one. Nomograms can be visualized in 2D while demonstrating the effects of nonlinear and non- monotonic effect. To capture the attribute interactions, a decomposable kernel is imperative and that can be tackled by interaction analysis, model selection or making sparse and smooth kernels a preference in optimization problem, which shall alleviate the problem while combining the above goal and the actual task of learning in SVM. Nomograms can be used for model selection also in case of SVM.

In [7] SVM has been applied in the area of process modelling and interpretability is a must in case of process modelling. To do so, a system is required that reduces the complexity of the structure and in turn, increases the interpretability. For this to come to fruition, the data is first clustered using Mountain Method. Support vector learning is then employed to find centers and related data. The model is then considered to be very similar to a neuro-fuzzy network. The pre-processing aided the support vector learning algorithm and the support vector learning algorithm was able to provide more generalization ability than the previously used RBF learning algorithms.

Mammograms are specialized medical images and are readily not interpretable [8]. In case of cancer classification, as image does not segregate the cancerous area by default, domain expert identifies the affected area based on his training and hence, justifies the treatment prescribed to the patient. The process is similar in modeling a machine learning algorithm for cancer prediction in mammograms. The model is trained with expert annotated images and on test images, it tries to match features similar to what has been learnt during training. The difference, however, comes where a human expert pinpoints the cancerous region but the underlying model fails to imitate this. Hence, even if the models' prediction is correct, when it is not supported with any substantial evidence, it reduces confidence on such models.

The challenges in mammogram interpretation can also be solved by using easy to understand models such as decision trees or random forests which ultimately leads to trade-off between interpretation and accuracy. This makes the mammogram interpretation challenge even more severe as accuracy cannot be compromised. In [9], it was concluded that the computer-aided detection does not help in improving the diagnostic accuracy of the mammograms. In [10], RBFNN is used to increase the accuracy of mammograms significantly but RBFNN in itself is a black box model. [11] uses dynamic time warping as a measuring approach to classify RoI (Regions of Interest) in mammograms as cancerous or noncancerous ones but the computational complexity of the approach is very high. In [12], Ibrahim et al. have used shearlet transform and KPCA to classify breast tumours giving better understanding and high accuracy. In [13], Azar et al. have analysed the performance of various variants of SVM to classify mammograms. In [14], rule based alternative model of SVM classifiers have been used to improve the understanding of mammograms.

In this paper, we propose a novel solution to interpret both SVM and given mammogram images by giving supportive evidence for each prediction as extracted from underlying SVM which ultimately increases the models reliability. This paper has been structured in the following sections: Sect. 2 gives a brief problem description. Section 3 explains the proposed methodology that finds the most important regions in the mammogram to support the predicted decisions. Section 4 describes and discusses the obtained results followed by Sect. 5 containing the conclusion of the work.

2 Problem Description

In mammograms, the RoI do not always depict the severity of the problem and they may be erroneous due to false positive and false negative results. The errors occur because the sampling is not uniform and training data samples does not cover the whole sample space. The false negative results of the models are more risky and in such cases, we need to identify the RoI which are more prone to contain lesions even if the whole image is classified as benign. They can further be analysed by experts and the model can be retrained using such features which were missing from training set. Lack of SVM interpretation increases the severity of mammogram interpretation. Our aim is to create such SVM model which can give prediction supportive evidence to enhance reliability and trust of underlying model.

3 Proposed Methodology

In our work, we are trying to identify acute lesions in mammograms and give appropriate score to the RoI accordingly by dividing the images into n patches and then training them on respective n SVMs[1]. Each SVM_i result is then accumulated with different weight determined using cross validation. On test images, the RoI with significant weights are highlighted which defines cancer-prone region severity.

---

[1] n depends on appropriate number of patches in which a mammogram can be divided.

3.1   Pre-processing

In this step, labels are removed by finding the connected components and discarding the smaller one. In this case, we employ the following:

$$X_i = argmaxconComp(X_i) \qquad (1)$$

where X_i is the ith image. By using the above formula, the smaller connected component was discarded and hence, giving us a clean image devoid of the label that were dangerous to SVMs' decision ability. The images are divided into n patches; where n depends upon the application and domain expert. The patches containing irrelevant data beyond threshold are labeled as non-cancerous.

3.2   Training and Testing of SVMs

In this step, RBF SVM has been used to classify the patches.

$$f(x_i) = \sum_{k=1}^{N} \alpha_k y_k \ \exp\left(-\frac{|x_i - x_k|^2}{2\sigma^2}\right) \qquad (2)$$

where x_i is the ith patch of the image, α is weight and σ is a free parameter. Images in the training set are used to train the n SVMs corresponding to each of the patches. Further, to find the importance of the n SVMs, the trained SVMs are used to make predictions for additional labeled data and these predictions along with the ground truth values are used as input for ridge regression.

$$\sum_{i=1}^{n} \left(y_i - \beta_0 - \sum_{j=1}^{p} \beta_i x_{ij}\right)^2 + \lambda \sum_{j=1}^{p} \beta_j^2 \qquad (3)$$

where β_j is the jth ridge regression coefficient and λ is the tuning parameter. The output of ridge regression comes out to be:

$$C = \{c_1, c_2, \ldots, c_n\} \qquad (4)$$

where c_i is the ith ridge regression coefficient.

3.3   RoI Highlighting

The patches with top coefficients are considered as important patches given the condition that the corresponding SVM predicts cancer in that patch. For finding the RoI, rather than using standard independent component analysis [15] we will employ the following equation:

$$argmax\{C \cdot Y\} \qquad (5)$$

where C is the coefficient vector derived from ridge regression and Y is the prediction made for the particular test image. The four top coefficients are selected and the patches corresponding to them are colored. The four colors are in decreasing order of severity are red, yellow, blue and green. The methodology to interpret the mammographic images is summarized in Fig. 1. The process of interpreting the mammographic images for cancer prediction as shown in Fig. 1 includes the steps given in Algorithm 1.

4 Results and Discussion

In our experiment, the dataset used is miniMIAS [16], which is derived from MIAS [17] dataset. The latter contains images which are digitized at 50 micron pixel edge whereas former contains images which are digitized at 200 micron pixel edge. Each miniMIAS image has been clipped/padded to make all of them of same size i.e. 1024 by 1024 pixels. The uniform dimensions of the images in the dataset aid to our workflow. The dataset contains 207 cancerous scans out of 322 scans. The files are of the type.pgm (Portable Graymap Format).

Algorithm 1

1: Remove the labels occurring in the images.

2: Divide each image into n patches.

3: Train n SVMs corresponding to each patch from the training set.

4: Using the trained SVMs for predictions and the ground truth values, find the weights for each patch using ridge regression.

5: Find out the threshold for the cancer classification by obtaining prediction values using those images not included in training.

6: Find the prediction values for the test data and using threshold, predict label for test data.

7: For each test image, find the patches having the highest weights given the corresponding SVMs predicts cancer in the patches.

8: Color the top patches with colors red, yellow, blue and green, in order of decreasing weights.

The workflow consist of four steps, pre-processing, patch division, training and testing of SVMs and highlighting the significant RoI. All images were padded to be 1024×1024. This presented problems to classifier because when an image is divided in several patches, some of the patches contain the black padded regions containing no relevant information. If the image has been classified as cancerous then these patches will also carry the same ground truth values, this reduces the SVMs' discriminative power between cancerous and non-cancerous images. Labels on mammograms pose another problem as for SVMs, they appear as useful information which ultimately worsens the models accuracy. The 322 images are processed, and each image of 1024 by 1024 pixels was divided into 16 patches of 256 by 256 pixels. The decision to take 256 by 256 pixels is done based on the observation that the patch size is able to contain the largest cancer classified patch. For training, separate SVM is trained for each patch i.e. 16 SVMs for 16 patches. A collection of randomly picked 150 mammograms were used for training (Fig. 2).

To arrive at a decision function and importance factor of each SVM, we used 200 mammograms (150 from training set + 50 from test set). Initially, each patch prediction is compared to their corresponding ground truth values and then, ridge regression is

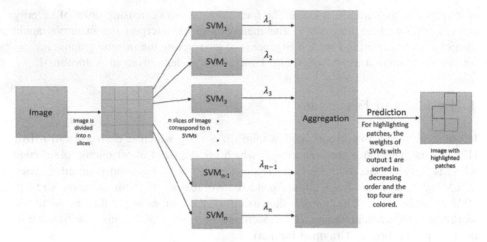

Fig. 1. Block diagram of the process of predicting cancer

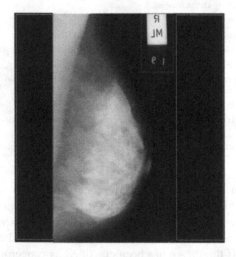

Fig. 2. A sample image from the dataset pointing out the two major issues with the data. The red box shows the labels that occur often in the data and the yellow boxes show the padding done to achieve the perfect square size (Color figure online)

applied to derive the coefficients or importance for each SVM. To generalize the result, the process is run 1000 times to remove any local discrepancies of data (Figs. 3 and 4).

After training, in order to make final decision, dot product of all 16 SVMs' output and the previously obtained 16 coefficients are calculated. Based on each SVMs' accuracy, for unseen 50 test set images, the threshold to detect patch severity was set. To highlight the RoI, four patches have been colored according to their severity i.e. the weight given to the SVM. The proposed algorithm is able to provide the interpretation of the mammograms which is demonstrated by Fig. 5. In a non-cancerous image, the algorithm does not highlight any significant patch as shown in Fig. 5(a). In Fig. 5(d), a

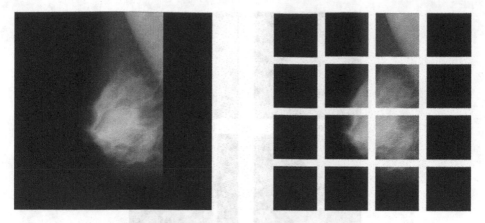

Fig. 3. A sample image and its 16 patches

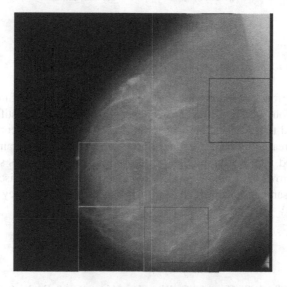

Fig. 4. An output image obtained after highlighting the patches

cancerous image is predicted as cancerous with most significant patches highlighted according to their severity. Figure 5(c) is a depiction of false positive result in which highlighted regions can be interpreted as high probability of cancer development regions. The image contains some features similar to cancerous mammograms hence, the severe areas can be re-examined for a better prescription. If it still results in false positive then features from such mammograms can be used to retrain the underlying model to further increase the accuracy. The most important concern is false negative result shown in Fig. 5(b). Though, cumulative results classifies them as non-cancerous, our algorithm highlights three regions which are predicted as cancer-prone.

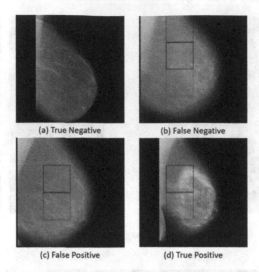

(a) True Negative   (b) False Negative

(c) False Positive   (d) True Positive

Fig. 5. Results predicted on test data

5 Conclusion

The proposed approach of identifying the most significant patches of images to classify them into cancerous and non-cancerous ones gives an intuitive justification by highlighting them and thus, makes the decisions more reliable. The accuracy of the algorithm can be increased by incorporating more such images in the training which have been misclassified. The RoI highlighted in the noncancerous images signify that there is a need to improve the training process by incorporating such misclassified images and to cover the sample space, which can further increase the accuracy of the algorithm as well.

References

1. Ribeiro, M.T., Singh, S., Guestrin, C.: Why should i trust you?: Explaining the predictions of any classifier. In: Proceedings of the 22nd ACM SIGKDD International Conference on Knowledge Discovery and Data Mining, pp. 1135–1144. ACM (2016)
2. Nguyen, D.H., Le, M.T.: Improving the interpretability of support vector machines based fuzzy rules. arXiv preprint arXiv:1408.5246 (2014)
3. Barakat, N.H., Bradley, A.P.: Rule extraction from support vector machines: a sequential covering approach. IEEE Trans. Knowl. Data Eng. **19**(6), 729–741 (2007)
4. He, J., Hu, H.J., Harrison, R., Tai, P.C., Pan, Y.: Rule generation for protein secondary structure prediction with support vector machines and decision tree. IEEE Trans. Nanobioscience **5**(1), 46–53 (2006)
5. Fu, S., ShengYang, G., Hou, Z., Liang, Z., Tan, M.: Multiple kernel learning from sets of partially matching image features. In: 19th International Conference on Pattern Recognition, 2008, ICPR 2008, pp. 1–4. IEEE (2008)

6. Jakulin, A., Možina, M., Demšar, J., Bratko, I., Zupan, B.: Nomograms for visualizing support vector machines. In: Proceedings of the Eleventh ACM SIGKDD International Conference on Knowledge Discovery in Data Mining, pp. 108–117. ACM (2005)

7. Pereira, C., Dourado, A.: On the complexity and interpretability of support vector machines for process modeling. In: Proceedings of the 2002 International Joint Conference on Neural Networks, IJCNN 2002. vol. 3, pp. 2204–2209. IEEE (2002)

8. Oliver, A., Lladó, X., Freixenet, J., Martí, J.: False positive reduction in mammographic mass detection using local binary patterns. In: Ayache, N., Ourselin, S., Maeder, A. (eds.) MICCAI 2007. LNCS, vol. 4791, pp. 286–293. Springer, Heidelberg (2007). https://doi.org/10.1007/978-3-540-75757-3_35

9. Lehman, C.D., Wellman, R.D., Buist, D.S., Kerlikowske, K., Tosteson, A.N., Miglioretti, D. L.: Diagnostic accuracy of digital screening mammography with and without computer-aided detection. JAMA Intern. Med. **175**(11), 1828–1837 (2015)

10. Pratiwi, M., Harefa, J., Nanda, S., et al.: Mammograms classification using graylevel co-occurrence matrix and radial basis function neural network. Procedia Comput. Sci. **59**, 83–91 (2015)

11. Gardezi, S.J.S., Faye, I., Bornot, J.M.S., Kamel, N., Hussain, M.: Mammogram classification using dynamic time warping. Multimed. Tools Appl. **77**, 1–22 (2017)

12. Ibrahim, A.M., Baharudin, B.: Classification of mammogram images using shearlet transform and kernel principal component analysis. In: 2016 3rd International Conference on Computer and Information Sciences (ICCOINS), pp. 340–344. IEEE (2016)

13. Azar, A.T., El-Said, S.A.: Performance analysis of support vector machines classifiers in breast cancer mammography recognition. Neural Comput. Appl. **24**(5), 1163–1177 (2014)

14. Ferreira, P., Dutra, I., Salvini, R., Burnside, E.: Interpretable models to predict breast cancer. In: 2016 IEEE International Conference on Bioinformatics and Biomedicine (BIBM), pp. 1507–1511. IEEE (2016)

15. Christoyianni, I., Koutras, A., Dermatas, E., Kokkinakis, G.: Computer aided diagnosis of breast cancer in digitized mammograms. Comput. Med. Imaging Graph. **26**(5), 309–319 (2002)

16. Suckling, J., et al.: The mammographic image analysis society digital mammogram database. In: Exerpta Medica. International Congress Series, vol. 1069, pp. 375–378 (1994)

17. Suckling, J., et al.: Mammographic image analysis society (mias) database v1. 21 (2015)

DPVO: Design Pattern Detection Using Vertex Ordering a Case Study in JHotDraw with Documentation to Improve Reusability

Arti Chaturvedi[1]($\boxtimes$), Manjari Gupta[2], and Sanjay Kumar Gupta[1]

[1] School of Studies in Computer Science and Applications, Jiwaji University,
Gwalior, M.P., India
arti.2408@gmail.com, sanjaygupta9170@gmail.com
[2] DST-CIMS, Faculty of Science, Banaras Hindu University,
Varanasi, U.P., India
manjari_gupta@rediffmail.com

Abstract. Documentation is one of the elements of reusability. A good documentation can make the software module more reliable since it makes it easier to understand [8]. Design Patterns are software modules that are proven solutions to common design problems. They improve many qualities of software like Reusability. If better reusability is required for existing software where design patterns are used, then an approach that can detect design pattern in the existing software will be useful. The result of detection approach gives occurrences of specific design pattern in existing software. In this paper we propose a tool DPVO for design pattern detection and a case study in JHotDraw (existing software) with documentation. This documentation provide location (class name) of design pattern in JHotDraw and helpful to improve reusability of this existing software.

Keywords: Reusability · Design pattern · Sub-graph isomorphism
Vertex ordering · Documentation

1 Introduction

Design pattern discovery in object oriented software will improve the reusability of existing software. It is a good solution to reduce the burden of software developers and maintainers. Design Patterns are proven solution to common recurring design problems. Knowledge of design patterns availability in existing software for reuse will improve software reusability. Design patterns are frequently used by software developer and maintainers. The availability of patterns related information, implemented in existing software is not well documented, and result of that it is not available for reuse. Therefore, a reliable design pattern discovery approach is required. Design pattern detection is one of the useful works in reverse engineering. Sufficient work has been done in this area by the researchers but still lot of possibilities exists to improve further. In this paper, we propose a design pattern detection tool "DPVO" (Design Pattern Vertex Ordering). This tool deals with vertex ordering concept and graph matching using sub-graph isomorphism conditions. "DPVO" tool has three components. First component of "DPVO" is our previous developed tool "TXGR" [5]. "TXGR"

© Springer Nature Singapore Pte Ltd. 2019
S. Verma et al. (Eds.): CNC 2018, CCIS 839, pp. 452–465, 2019.
https://doi.org/10.1007/978-981-13-2372-0_40

generates a complete UML design structure [1] of specific design pattern in graph format as well as gives structural information (such as class type and relationship among classes) about existing application domain in graph view. Second component of DPVO provides an ordered sequence of vertices for specific design pattern. However, this sequence is independent from application graph that minimizes the search space in the application graph and thus it shortens the time of overall detection process. Further, third component of DPVO is a matching algorithm which is verifies existence of design pattern structure in application software according to sub-graph isomorphism conditions. In DPVO, output of one component will be used as input of another component respectively. In this work, an open source project JHotDraw 7.0 [7] is used as domain software and consider the class structure of design patterns proposed by Gamma [1]. The process of vertex ordering and graph matching is described in our previous paper [4]. In this paper we summarized the conditions for vertex ordering of design pattern graph and conditions for graph matching between specific design patterns and existing software as propose in [4]. The main Objective of this paper is to explore the outcomes of the algorithm.

The rest of the paper is organized as follows: Methodology of algorithm is proposed in Sect. 2. Section 3 explore algorithm with an example. Section 4 proposed a case study with outcomes using existing software JHtDraw 7.0. and proposes Documentation for outcomes of algorithm as an instance of different design pattern in JHtDraw. Section 5 defines related work. Finally the conclusion is given in Sect. 6.

2   Methodology

The idea for design pattern detection is based on sub-graph isomorphism search. This search algorithm is detecting all possible occurrences of specific design pattern graph (DPg) in existing software graph (or model graph Mg) where design pattern graph is sub-graph of existing software graph. Moreover, before applying search algorithm on both graphs, we propose a vertex ordering process on design pattern graph and as outcomes we got an ordered sequence of specific design pattern graph vertices. The node to node mapping between both graphs start according to this ordered sequence. The flow of this detection process is shown in (Fig. 1).

2.1   Rules for Vertex Ordering of Design Pattern Graph

We apply a greedy algorithm Greatest Constraint First [2] to find an ordered sequence of vertices of design pattern graph [4]. Greatest Constraint First visits the design pattern graph based on a scoring function. It starts from a vertex u0 in the design pattern graph that has the maximum number of neighbors among vertices in the design pattern graph. If more than one vertex has maximum number of neighbors then we choose arbitrarily one of them. The algorithm iteratively proceeds until all vertices in the design pattern graph are inserted in ordered sequence μ. Moreover this process consider two list, first list μ include vertices that satisfied the condition of vertex ordering and second list u_m includes vertices that are candidate for vertex ordering list. The value of u_m find out using below mention three conditions..

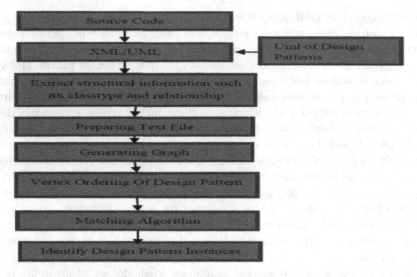

Fig. 1. Flow of design pattern detection approach

1. $V_{m,vis=}$ set of vertices in μ that are neighbors of u_m
2. $V_{m,neig}$ = set of vertices that are neighbors of u_m and connected to μ, but not in μ.
3. $V_{m,unv}$ = set of vertices that are not in μ, not even neighbors of μ but are neighbors of u_m.

2.2 Rules of Graph Matching Algorithm

After getting an ordered sequence of design pattern graph vertices, we apply a graph matching algorithm between design pattern graph and existing software graph based on sub-graph isomorphism conditions, describe in [4]. These conditions discard unnecessary vertex and edges from existing application graph and reduce the search space. These matching conditions are as follows:

1. Neither the vertex of Design Pattern graph nor vertex of existing software graph is already matched in the current path.
2. The label of vertex of Design Pattern graph is matched with label of vertex of existing software graph.
3. Number of incoming edges to vertex of Design Pattern graph is less than or equal to, number of incoming edges to vertex of existing software graph.
4. Number of outgoing edges from vertex of Design Pattern graph is less than or equal to, number of outgoing edges from vertex of existing software graph.
5. Label of edge connected to vertex of Design Pattern graph is same as the label of edge connected to vertex of existing software graph.
6. The constraints deriving from the topology (class and relationship structure) of design pattern graph up to this point in the path are met in existing software graph and edges label are also matched in this topology.

3   Example

The algorithms have been described with the help of an example. Here, we have taken an example of existing software graph (called model graph Mg) shown in Fig. 2(a) and command design pattern graph (DPg) shown in Fig. 2(b) which is detected in Model graph. In these graphs, there are three types of node (vertex) label which defines class type such as (a) Abstract class denoted by (1, 0, 0). (b) Concrete subclass denoted by (0, 1, 0) and (c) Concrete class denoted by (0, 0, 1) and edge label define four types of relationships such as (a) Dependency denoted by "1" (b) Generalization/Inheritance denoted by "2" (c) Association denoted by "3" and (d) Aggregation denoted by "4".

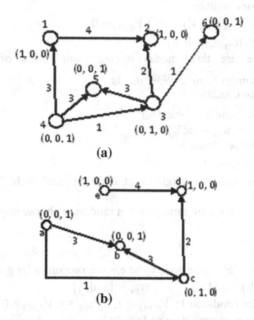

(a)

(b)

Fig. 2. (a) Model graph (Mg) corresponding to existing software design. (b) Command Design Pattern Graph (DPg).

Fig. 3. Snapshot of result of vertex ordering of command design pattern graph

3.1   Implementation of Vertex Ordering of Design Pattern Graph

First we apply vertex ordering condition describe in Sect. 2.1, on command design pattern graph shown in Fig. 2(b).

Round I:

1. Choose the vertex with maximum degree which is 'c' having degree 3 in the graph in figure 3. "c" is kept in μ while all the other nodes are now kept in u_m.

    So, $\mu = \{c\}$

    $$u_m = \{a, b, d, e\}$$

2. Checking for condition 1:

    $V_{a,vis} = 1, V_{b,vis} = 1, V_{d,vis} = 1, V_{e,vis} = 0$

    So, updated $u_m = \{a, b, d\}$

    Since there are three nodes having same value of $V_{m,vis}$, we will calculate $V_{a,neig}, V_{b,neig},$ and $V_{d,neig}$

3. Checking for condition 2:

    $V_{a,neig} = 1, V_{b,neig} = 1, V_{d,neig} = 0$

    Now, updated $u_m = \{a, b\}$

4. Checking for condition 3:

    $V_{a,unv} = 0, V_{b,unv} = 0$

    Because no vertex is neighbor of node "a" and node "b" that satisfying condition 3.

    As, both the values are same, we can randomly choose any node between "a" and "b".

Round II:

Let's choose "b" as the node to be chosen randomly for graph ordering.

So $\mu = \{c, b\}$ and $u_m = \{a, d, e\}$

Checking for condition 1: $V_{a,vis} = 2, V_{d,vis} = 1, V_{e,vis} = 0$

Thus our next candidate node is "a".

And updated $\mu = \{c, b, a\}$ and $u_m = \{d, e\}$.

Round III:

We have, $\mu = \{c, b, a\}$ and $u_m = \{d, e\}$

Now Checking for condition 1: $V_{d\ vis} = 1, V_{e,vis} = 0$

Thus next candidate node is "d".

So, updated $\mu = \{c, b, a, d\}$ and $u_m = \{e\}$

Round IV:

We have, $\mu = \{c, b, a, d\}$ and $u_m = \{e\}$

Here only node left is "e". So, adding "e" in "μ".

Finally, the vertex ordering sequence $\mu = \{c, b, a, d, e\}$.

If vertices of the command design pattern graph are matched in this order it will be fast to match/search the graph of command design pattern in the system design (existing application software) graph. Because in this vertex ordering technique, according to conditions we choose vertex at different step randomly (if required), so that more than one sequence of vertex ordering possible but all sequences are define specific design pattern structure.

3.2 Implementation of Graph Matching Algorithm

Now for simplicity, we modified graph matching rules proposed in [4] and further explore our example for command design pattern. In previous section we got an ordered sequence $\mu = \{c, b, a, d, e\}$ for command design pattern graph. Now, according to this vertex ordering sequence, we apply graph matching algorithm between command design pattern graph shown in Fig. 2(b) and Model graph (Mg) corresponding to existing software design shown in Fig. 2(a) based on sub-graph isomorphism conditions descried in Sect. 2.2 for design pattern detection as follows.

1. The first vertex (node) in the order vertices is node "c". Only node "3" is compatible to node "c" as labels of both nodes are same. Number of incoming edges of node "c" $\leq$ number of incoming edges of node "3". As well as number of outgoing edges of node "c" $\leq$ number of outgoing edges of node "3". Labels of incoming edges are 1 and labels of outgoing edges are 2 and 3 in both design pattern graph and model graph. Thus the mapping is $\{(c, 3)\}$.

2. The next vertex in the order of vertices is "b". It is compatible to three nodes in the model graph: node "4", "5", and "6". But number of incoming edges of node "b" $\leq$ number of incoming edges of node "5" and labels of these incoming edges are also same, while number of incoming edges of node "b" > number of incoming edges of node "4" and node "6", so this condition is not true for node "4" and node "6" and node "5" is only candidate for mapping. Now there is no outgoing edge from node "b" as well as from node "5". Thus node "b" can be mapped to node "5". Now we will check the condition (6) to identify whether this pair (b, 5) should be added into the mapping M or not. There is only one edge from node "c" to node "b" with label 3 and there is a single edge from node "3" to node "5" with label 3. Thus we will include this pair in the mapping and mapping till now is $\{(c, 3)\ (b, 5)\}$.

3. The next vertex in the order of vertices is "a". Label of node "a" is matched with label of node "4", "5" and "6". Node "5" is already considered so there are two nodes, "4" and "6" will be applicant for mapping. Number of incoming edges to node "a" is $\leq$ number of incoming edges to node "4" and node "6". Number of outgoing edges from "a" is $\leq$ number of outgoing edges from node "4" and labels of these edges are also same. But number of outgoing edges from "a" is > number of outgoing edges from node "6", so this condition is not true for node "6". Thus only node "4" is mapped to node "a". Now we will check the connectivity (condition 6) among node "a" and node "c" and node "b". Similarly the connectivity among node "4" and node "3" and node "5". There is one edge from node "a" to node "b" with label 3 and one edge from node "a" to node "c" with label 1. There is one edge from "4" to node "5" with label 3 and one edge from node "4" to node "3"

with label 1. Thus we will add pair (a, 4) in the mapping and mapping till now {{c, 3) (b, 5) (a, 4)}.

4. Next vertex in the order of vertices is "d". The label of node "d" is matched with labels of node "1" and node "2". Number of incoming to node "d" ≤ number of incoming edges to node "2". But number of incoming edges to "d" > number of edges to node "1", this condition is not true for node "1". Thus only candidate node for mapping is "2". Label of incoming edges on both node are also same. Number of outgoing edges neither from node "2" nor from node "d". Thus node "d" is mapped to node "2". Now it is to be checked that whether pair (d, 2) can be added in mapping M or not. Again we will do this by checking condition (6). So we will check whether all the edges from node "d" to nodes "c", "b", "a" in design pattern graph is present in edges from node "2" to nodes "3", "5", "4". There is only one edge from node "c" to "d" with label 2. There is no edge between node "b" and node "d", and between node "a" and node "d". Similarly there is only one edge from node "3" to node "2" with label 2. There is no edge between node "5" and node "2", and between node "4" and node "2". Thus this pair (d, 2) will be added in the mapping.

5. The last node in the sequence is "e", which is compatible with two nodes "1" and "2". But node "2" is already considered for mapping, thus we will check either node "e" can be mapped to node "1" or not. Number of incoming edges to node "e" ≤ number of incoming edges to node "1". Number of outgoing edges of node "e" ≤ number of outgoing edges of node "1". Edge label of these outgoing edges are same that is 4. Thus node "e" is mapped to node "1" of the model graph. Now we will check the connectivity (condition 6) among node "e" and node "c", "b", "a", and "d". Similarly the connectivity among node "1" and node "3", "5", "4", and "2". There is no edge from node "e" to node "c", node "b", and node "a". Only one edge from node "e" to node "d" with label 4. Similarly there is no edge from node "1" to node "3", node "5", and node "4". Only one edge from node "1" to node "2" with label 4. Thus this pair (e, 1) will be added in the mapping. Thus design pattern graph (DPg) is found in model graph (Mg) according to mapping {(c, 3) (b, 5) (a, 4) (d, 2) (e, 1)}.

4   Case Study

In this work, we apply design pattern detection technique on an open source project JHotDraw 7.0 as existing software domain. JHotDraw is a drawing editor that allows user to create and manipulate 2D vector figures. It was originally developed in 1998 by Gamma and Eggenschwller as a showcase for the use of design pattern [3]. Source code of this JHotDraw project is converted into graph format by our previously developed tool TXGR [5].The graph of JHotDraw project and all 23 GoF design pattern graphs are presented in our previous paper [5].

4.1   Outcomes of Vertex Ordering Algorithm

Vertex ordering algorithm generates a sequence of vertices of specific design pattern graph. This algorithm applicable for all 23 design pattern proposed by Gamma et al.

[1]. Using vertex ordering sequence of specific design pattern graph, the graph matching algorithm reduces the search space in existing software domain and speed up the process of design pattern detection. Vertex ordering sequences of participating classes for all 23 GoF [1] design patterns are shown in Table 1.

Table 1. Sequence of participating classes of design pattern after vertex ordering

Design pattern name	Sequence of participating classes of design pattern
Abstract factory	(Concrete Factory, Product, Abstract Product, Abstract Factory, Client)
Builder	(Builder, Concrete Builder, Director, Product)
Factory method	(Concrete Product, Concrete Creator, Creator, Product)
Prototype	(Prototype, Concrete Prototype, Client)
Singleton	(Singleton)
Adapter class	(Adapter, Target, Adaptee, Client)
Adapter object	(Target, Adapter, Client, Adaptee)
Bridge	(Implementer, Abstraction, redefine Abstraction, Concrete Implementer)
Composite	(Component, Leaf, Composite, Client)
Decorator	(Component, Decorator, Concrete Component, Concrete Decorator)
Facade	(Façade, Sub-system Class)
Flyweight	(Flyweight, Concrete Flyweight, Unshared Concrete Flyweight, Flyweight Factory, Client)
Proxy	(Real Subject, Subject, Proxy)
Chain of responsibility	(Handler, Concrete Handler, Client)
Command	(Concrete Command, Receiver, client, Command, Invoker)
Interpreter	(Abstract Expression, Client, Context, Terminal Expression, Non-Terminal Expression)
Iterator	(Concrete Aggregate, Concrete Iterator, Iterator, Aggregate, Client)
Mediator	(Colleague, Mediator, Concrete Colleague, Concrete Mediator)
Memento	(Memento, Originator, Caretaker)
Observer	(Concrete Subject, Concrete Observer, Observer, Subject)
State	(State, Context, Concrete State)
Strategy	(Strategy, Context, Concrete Strategy)
Template method	(Abstract Class, Concrete Class)
Visitor	(Visitor, Client, Object Structure, Element, Concrete Element, Concrete Visitor)

4.2 Outcomes of Graph Matching Algorithm

By simulating this graph matching algorithm between different GoF design patterns graphs and existing software domain (JHotDraw) graph, we found instance of 10 different type of design patterns [1]. In this section we explain result of graph matching algorithm in documented form using UML where we shows complete class structure (Topology) of design pattern in existing software JHotDraw (Fig. 4).

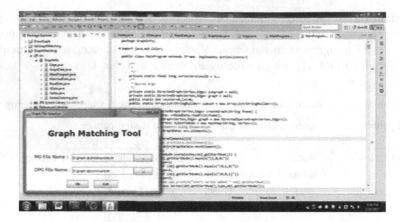

Fig. 4. Snapshot of input of JHotDraw graph and command design pattern graph.

4.2.1   Documentation for Location of Design Pattern in JHotDraw Software

I. Façade Design Pattern

Façade design pattern has two classes. One is façade class which is matched with Composite Figure class and second is sub-system class which is matched with Attributed key of JHotDraw. The relationship between JHotDraw classes makes an instance of Façade design pattern class structure (Fig. 5).

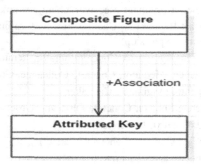

Fig. 5. Façade design pattern in JHotDraw

II. Singleton Design Pattern

In Singleton design pattern, singleton class is concrete class and makes a self-loop with association relationship. In JHotDraw, Pert Panel class is only one class that is concrete class and has self-looped with association relationship. This structure form an instance of Singleton design pattern in JHotDraw (Fig. 6).

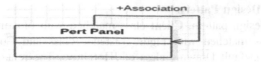

Fig. 6. Singleton design pattern in JHotDraw

III. Proxy Design Pattern

In Proxy design pattern subject class is matched with Abstract Handle class, Real Subject class is matched with Bezier node Handle class and Proxy class is matched with Bezier Figure Class of JHotDraw. The relationships between JHotDraw classes make an instance of Proxy design pattern class structure (Fig. 7).

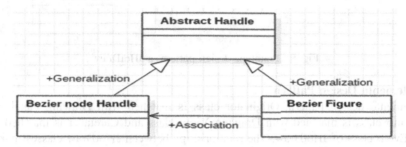

Fig. 7. Proxy design pattern in JHotDraw

IV. Builder Design Pattern

In Builder design pattern, Director Class is matched with Tool Event class; Builder class is matched with Drawing View class and Concrete Builder class matched with Default Drawing View class of JHotDraw. The relationships between JhotDraw classes make an instance of Builder design pattern class structure (Fig. 8).

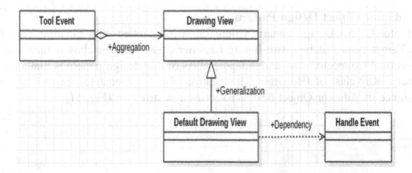

Fig. 8. Builder design pattern in JHotDraw

V. Prototype Design Pattern

In prototype design pattern, **Client** class matched with Floating Text Area class and Prototype class matched with Figure Listener class and Concrete Prototype class matched with Default Drawing class of JHotDraw. The relationships between JHot-Draw classes make an instance of prototype design pattern class structure (Fig. 9).

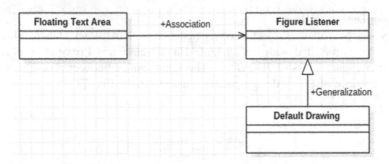

Fig. 9. Prototype design pattern in JHotDraw

VI. Memento Design Pattern

In Memento design pattern, Originator class is matched with Drawing Panel class, Memento class is matched with Drawing View class and Caretaker is matched with Tool Event class of JHotDraw. The relationships between JHotDraw classes make an instance of Memento design pattern class structure (Fig. 10).

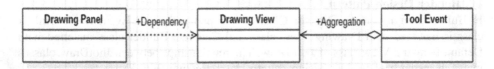

Fig. 10. Memento design pattern in JHotDraw

VII. Adaptor Object Design Pattern

In Adaptor Object Design Pattern, Client class is matched with Floating Text Field class, Target class matched with Figure Listener class, Adapter class is matched with Bidirectional Connector class and Adaptee class of this design pattern is matched with Attributed Key class of JHotDraw. The relationships between JHotDraw classes make an instance of Adaptor Object design pattern class structure (Fig. 11).

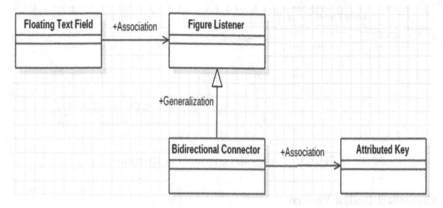

Fig. 11. Adaptor object design pattern in JHotDraw

VIII. Observer Design Pattern

In Observer design pattern, Subject class is matched with Abstract Connector class, Observer class is matched with Figure class, Concrete Observer class matched with Chop Eclipse Connector class and Concrete Subject class is matched with Chop box connector class of JHotDraw. The relationships between JHotDraw classes make an instance of Observer design pattern class structure (Fig. 12).

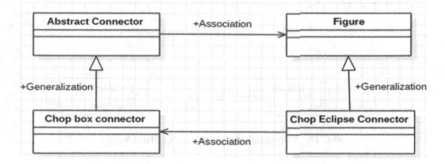

Fig. 12. Observer design pattern in JHotDraw

IX. Strategy Design Pattern

In strategy design pattern structure, Context class is matched with Drawing Panel class, Strategy class is matched with Drawing Editor and Concrete Strategy class is matched with Default Drawing Editor class of JHotDraw. The relationships between JHotDraw classes make an instance of strategy design pattern class structure. The class structure of State design pattern is same as strategy design pattern so that Fig. 13 is also shows an instance of State design pattern in JHotDraw.

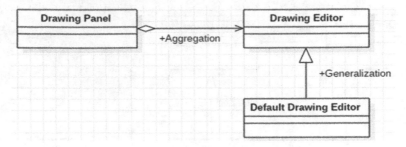

Fig. 13. Strategy design pattern in JHotDraw

X. Command Design Pattern

In Command design pattern, Client class is matched with Bezier class, Receiver class of command pattern is matched with Bezier path class, Command class is matched with Connection Figure class, Concrete Command class of command design pattern is matched with Line Connection figure class and Invoker class is matched with Abstract Figure class of JHotDraw. The relationships between JHotDraw classes make an instance of Command design pattern class structure (Fig. 14).

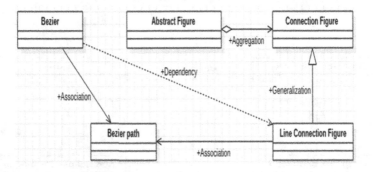

Fig. 14. Command design pattern in JHotDraw

5   Related Work

We are also proposed another approach for design pattern detection [6] where we use genetic algorithm. In this algorithm we consider two graphs, one for existing software and second for specific design pattern and applying genetic operations based on sub-graph isomorphism conditions. If any sub graph of existing software graph is isomorphic to specific design pattern graph than we found an instance of that design pattern. This algorithm is works for only those design patterns having at most three classes in the UML class diagram.

6 Conclusion

Design pattern detection is one of the approaches that improve the reusability of existing software. We developed a reverse engineering tool TXGR [5] that generates graph for all 23 design pattern proposed by Gamma et al. [1] as well as graph of existing software JHotDraw. Using resultant graphs of TXGR we proposed an algorithm based on sub-graph isomorphism concept for design pattern detection where design pattern graph is pattern graph and existing software graph is target graph (where design pattern is detected). In this paper we proposed a new concept "vertex ordering of design pattern graph" and therefore we named this tool DPVO (i.e. Design Pattern Vertex Ordering). Moreover this tool first finds out vertex ordering of pattern graph which is an ordered sequence of design pattern vertices (or node). Using this ordered sequence DPVO perform node to node mapping between design pattern graph and existing software graph and search complete class structure of specific design pattern in existing software. Vertex ordering of design pattern graph is reducing the search space in existing software and speedup the detection process. As a result of this algorithm we got complete topology (or class structure) for Façade, Singleton, Proxy, Builder, Prototype, Memento, Adapter Object, Observer, Strategy, Command design patterns. For improving reusability of existing software, we proposed outcomes in documented form where a UML class diagram shows complete class structure of specific design pattern.

References

1. Gamma, E., Helm, R., Johnson, R., Vlissides, J.: Design Patterns Elements of Reusable Object-Oriented Software. Addison-Wesley, Boston (1995)
2. Bonnici, V., Giugno, R., Pulvirenti, A., Shasha, D., Ferro, A.: A sub-graph isomorphism algorithm and its application to biochemical data. In: 9th Annual Meeting of the Italian Society of Bioinformatics (BITS) Catania, Sicily (2013)
3. Ng, J.K.Y., Gueheneuc, Y.G., Antoniol, G.: Identification of behavioural and creational design motifs through dynamic analysis. J. Softw.: Evol. Process 22(8), 597–627 (2010)
4. Chaturvedi, A., Gupta, M., Gupta, S.K.: An idea towards improving design pattern detection. Int. J. Syst. Softw. Eng. 3(2), 8–13 (2015)
5. Chaturvedi, A., Gupta, M., Gupta, S.K.: TXGR: a reverse engineering tool to convert design patterns and application software into graph. In: Dash, S.S., Das, S., Panigrahi, B.K. (eds.) International Conference on Intelligent Computing and Applications. AISC, vol. 632, pp. 215–225. Springer, Singapore (2018). https://doi.org/10.1007/978-981-10-5520-1_21
6. Chaturvedi, A., Gupta, M., Gupta, S.K.: Design pattern detection using genetic algorithm for sub-graph isomorphism to enhance software reusability. Int. J. Comput. Appl. 135(4), 33–36 (2016)
7. Randelshofer W.: JHotDraw (2011). https://sourceforge.net/projects/jhotdraw/
8. Hristov, D., Hummel, O., Huq, M., Janjic, W.: Structuring software reusability metrics for component-based software development. In: Proceedings of International Conference on Software Engineering Advances (ICSEA), vol. 226 (2012)

Intelligent Aggregation for Ensemble LSTM

Ashima Elhence, Abhishek[✉], and Shekhar Verma

Department of Information Technology, Indian Institute of Information
Technology, Allahabad, Allahabad 211012, Uttar Pradesh, India
{ism2013015,rsi2016006,sverma}@iiita.ac.in

Abstract. Analysis of time series data requires extracting hidden patterns and accurate detection of outliers and anomaly. Long Short Term Memory based neural network's ability to hold relevant information for extended time makes it suitable for such analysis. A single network increases the prediction accuracy but is limited by the group of similar patterns it can learn which results in overfitting. Ensemble of thinned networks using dropout regularization solves this problem but due to lack of efficient aggregation method, its capability gets restricted. In this paper, we explore two intelligent ensemble aggregation methods which allows to maximize the thinned networks' performance. Extensive experiments on Yahoo! benchmark dataset show that both aggregation techniques are capable of handling unwanted effects in data to improve the average performance by ≈52% as compared to single network.

Keywords: Time series prediction · LSTM · Ensemble · Weighted aggregation
Window based aggregation

1 Introduction

Successive equally spaced data instances varying against time is defined as time series data e.g. IoT [1], health care monitoring [1], financial monitoring, anomaly detection [2], scene labeling [3] etc. Time series data analysis requires behavioral study of the data by extracting the underlying pattern for accurate predictions on future values. Presence of anomaly and outliers pose major challenges in time series analysis. An accurate identification of anomaly and outliers conditions would allow underlying model to plan preventive or reactive measures accordingly. As time series data is non-stationary and frequently varying, multiple conditional behaviors can be observed [4]. It is very important to build a robust and reliable model which is able to handle different aspects of data and make accurate predictions accordingly. At the same time underlying model should not be biased to some specific behaviors.

A RNN (Recurrent Neural Network) [5] uses its internal memory to process sequence of inputs unlike feedforward neural network which makes them efficient for time series analysis. A basic RNN can be constructed using single instance of the model but it may not be capable of extracting all patterns inside the given data. Time series analysis remains delay intolerant and needs real time prediction. One network overloaded with whole analysis takes more time to process and give result which makes it inefficient. A possible solution would be create multiple instances of the

© Springer Nature Singapore Pte Ltd. 2019
S. Verma et al. (Eds.): CNC 2018, CCIS 839, pp. 466–475, 2019.
https://doi.org/10.1007/978-981-13-2372-0_41

model but since identical models will learn similar functions and would extract same patterns, this also becomes inefficient. Thus, a generalized model can be constructed by creating separate basic models optimized for different patterns and thereafter creating an ensemble of them. The predictive performance and the generalizability of the model is improved significantly with ensemble learning [6].

LSTM (Long Short Term Memory) [7] is one of the most frequently used RNN model used for time series analysis, natural language processing, sequence modelling and learning. RNN taps into the temporal and sequential aspects of the data in a fixed number of computational steps making them fast and suitable for delay intolerant applications. Along with advantages of traditional RNN, LSTMs simple model, capability to handle potentially infinite dynamic data and ability to store important information for a significantly longer duration makes it preferable model for time series analysis e.g. time series prediction [8], event forecasting [9], anomaly detection [10] etc. Multiple LSTM networks replacing single deep LSTM network [2, 5] increase the accuracy by analyzing single or a group of similar behaviors. Ensemble LSTM independently trains each of the component models such that no two models are identical.

Final prediction from ensemble LSTMs require aggregation. A basic aggregation technique can be done by averaging prediction of different networks. As different LSTM networks are trained for different functions, giving them equal importance leads to inaccurate predictions. In this paper, we propose two weighted aggregation techniques which gives appropriate importance to different LSTM networks which further increases the models accuracy. Rest of the paper is organized in following sections, Sect. 2 describes the problem faced in ensemble LSTM aggregation followed by Sect. 3 containing the proposed intelligent aggregation methods. Results obtained from extensive experiments are shown in Sect. 4. Conclusion and findings of the proposed work is described in Sect. 5.

2 Problem Description

Given time series data set $\{x_i, y_i\}_{i=1}^{t-1}$ containing labels or predictions uptil time instance $(t-1)$. Time (t) onwards, for a given data instance $\{x_t\}$, we need to predict accurate $\{y_t\}$. Ensemble LSTM network containing n differently trained LSTMs $\{L_k\}_{k=1}^{n}$ are built. The existing aggregation is done by

$$y_t = \frac{1}{n} \sum_{k=1}^{n} L_k(x_t)$$

As this aggregation gives equal weight to all networks hence, even the least accurate network is able to adversely affect the final prediction. Our aim is to develop aggregation technique to give appropriate importance to underlying LSTMs based on their individual performance. Additionally the aggregation should be able to give higher preference to recent instances in order to extract the current trend.

3   Aggregation of Ensemble Thinned LSTMs

A time series predictor harness the power of LSTM and takes advantage of ensemble networks to provide accurate next time instance prediction. Given a time series data till $(t - 1)$, the point at time step (i) is represented by $\{x_i\}$, the next predicted data point $\{x_t\}$ at time t is given by

$$x_t = f(x_1, x_2, \ldots x_{t-1} : \phi_{t-1}^*) \tag{1}$$

Here f is the function responsible for capturing the behavior of the time series and $\phi(t - 1)$ are the parameters of the trained model till $(t - 1)$. The parameters get updated with each new observation. As a data instance arrives, the loss function of the model is updated by

$$\phi_{t-1}^* = \frac{argmin}{\phi_{t-1}} \| x_{t-1} - f(x_1, x_2, \ldots x_{t-2} : \phi_{t-2}^*) \|_2^2 \tag{2}$$

3.1   Long Short Term Memory

LSTM is an advanced version of RNN which is capable of remembering the extracted information for an extended interval of time as compared to the basic RNN used for Deep Learning. LSTM has the capability to store relevant or indicative information for a sufficiently long time. It also selects important and reduces irrelevant features automatically to avoid curse of dimensionality [11].

A single LSTM unit consists of current, input, output and forget gate. A single layer of LSTM consist of multiple such units and the whole LSTM network contains several such layers.

- **Current Memory**
  It is the currently stored information present in the LSTM cell which is used to make predictions. The update that is made on the previous cell state C_{t-1} which results in the new cell state C_t

$$C_t = f_t * C_{t-1} + i_t * C_t \tag{3}$$

Output from the current time step is prediction for the immediately following step. LSTM also stores the necessary cell state and information for the future predictions thereafter. After the cell state is updated for the future time instance, the output prediction for the immediate time step is given using a Sigmoid function

$$O_t = W_0 * [h_{t-1}, x_t] + b_0 \tag{4}$$

here, with respect to output gate, W_o is its weight, b_o represents bias, and O_t is the output given by the cell at time (t).

- **Forgetting Mechanism**
  It enables the model to decide whether to remember or discard the previously acquired information. The sigmoid function is used for forget gate is as described

$$f_t = \sigma(W_f * [h_{t-1}, x_t] + b_f) \tag{5}$$

here, W_f is the forget gate's weight, b_f denotes bias, and h_{t-1} represents the output of previous time instance$(t-1)$.

- **Saving Mechanism**
  It allows the model to extract new information from just arrived data. The logic used for the function is

$$i_t = \sigma(W_i * [h_{t-1}, x_t] + b_i) \tag{6}$$

here, W_i and b_i represents weight and bias of the input gate respectively. A tanh activation function is used for updating state of the LSTM cell. The vector of new values as stored in the LSTM can be defined as

$$C_t = tanh(W_c * [h_{t-1}, x_t] + b_c) \tag{7}$$

here, W_c and b_c are the weight and bias of the current memory gate respectively.

The architecture used for prediction is an LSTM network is similar to the baseline [12] as shown in Fig. 1.

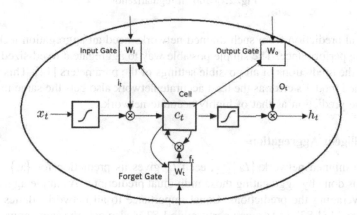

Fig. 1. LSTM representation

3.2 Ensemble LSTM

As a single network specializes in specific or group of similar patterns, they tend to become less accurate as time grows. Ensemble of weak models make more powerful model than individual deep models. As a single deep model takes more time to train and predict, latency intolerant analysis get adversely affected from this. It may also become particularly overfitted according to some peculiar trend in the data. Presence of outliers and anomaly also have a higher impact on single instance. On the other hand a collection of independent models, each differently trained are able to solve the above problems. Independent models are also capable of controlling the biasness by bringing in variance and making overall model independent of both the training data as well as the model's architecture.

In a time series prediction using LSTM neural networks, variance among the different models of the ensemble is done by using dropout regularization [13]. Dropout regularization allows neural network layers to drop units along with their connections during training as shown in Fig. 2b. These thinned networks are hence trained independently and differently from each other as different neurons are dropped from each of them. As due to different trainings, the models do not co-adapt together. Also, dropping different neurons helps avoiding function overfitting problem.

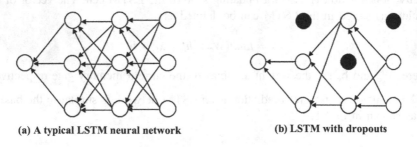

(a) A typical LSTM neural network   (b) LSTM with dropouts

Fig. 2. Dropout regularization

The final prediction from such thinned networks need an aggregation technique to improve the performance. The simple possible way to aggregate a fixed-sized model is to average the predictions of all possible settings of the parameters [14]. This increases the combined model's error as the least accurate network also gets the same importance to affect the prediction as that of highly accurate network.

3.3 Intelligent Aggregation

In multiple thinned network $\{L_k\}_{k=1}^n$, each L_k gives its prediction for $\{x_t\}$. The final prediction is done by aggregating those individual predictions. A simple aggregation is done by averaging the predictions. Equal importance to all networks defies the logic behind ensemble LSTM. As worst performing LSTM also gets the same power to affect the final result as compared to best performing network. Also, not all the functions learnt through thinned networks contains the same information gain hence, giving then equal weight does no t always increase the model's accuracy.

Weighted Aggregation. Rather than simply taking the mean of all the predictions and giving equal importance, an alternative technique is to give them weights according to their current performance and take a weighted mean of all the predictions to generate the output. The models which are performing better in terms of accuracy as measured by low $\varsigma/RMSE$ (Root Mean Square Error) should be given higher weight than those with higher ς. Hence, the importance coefficient maintains inverse proportional relationship with ς. Given labeled data $\{x_i, y_i\}_{i=1}^{t-1}$ till time $(t-1)$, it is divided in two parts for training and coefficient calculation respectively.

$$\{x_i, y_i\}_{i=1}^{t-1} = \{x_i, y_i\}_{i=1}^{t-l} \cup \{x_j, y_j\}_{j=t-l+1}^{t-1}$$

Each $L_k \in \{L_k\}_{k=1}^{n}$ is trained using $(t-l)$ labeled data $\{x_i, y_i\}_{i=1}^{t-l}$. A prediction is obtained from all thinned LSTMs using l labeled data $\{x_j, y_j\}_{j=t-l+1}^{t-1}$ as

$$\hat{y}_{kj} = L_k(x_j)$$

where $\hat{y}_{kj}$ is the label predicted by LSTM $\{L_k\}_{k=1}^{n}$ for data $\{x_j, y_j\}_{j=t-l+1}^{t-1}$, ς is calculated from

$$\varsigma_k = \sqrt{\frac{\sum_{j=t-l+1}^{t-1} \| \hat{y}_{kj} - y_j \|^2}{t-l}}$$

Weighted m Window Aggregation. In weighted aggregation, we consider the whole prediction of thinned networks but in time series analysis, recent data have more importance than previous data. By keeping the λ fixed based on previous experience may lead to erroneous prediction. The models training is done similar to previous method using $t-l$ instances. Labeled data from $t-l+1$ to $t-1$ is divided in m sized time windows. λ is calculated on a these m sized time windows and accordingly the coefficients are changed for enhancing recent trend prediction. After each m instances, the ς is calculated using

$$\varsigma_k = \sqrt{\frac{\sum_{j=t-m-1}^{t-1} \| \hat{y}_{kj} - y_j \|^2}{m}}$$

As each ς is on different scale, it needs to be normalized for both aggregation methods. The normalized & is obtained by

$$\Rightarrow \varsigma_k = \frac{\varsigma_k - \mu_\varsigma}{\sigma_\varsigma}$$

where, μ_ς is the mean of all n LSTMs and σ_ς is its standard deviation. Importance coefficient λ for each thinned network is calculated from

$$\Rightarrow \lambda_k = \frac{1}{\varsigma_k}$$

where, λ_k is coefficient of kth LSTM and $1 \leq k \leq n$. Aggregation of data instance from time instance t onwards is obtained using this λ weighted LSTMs

$$\hat{y}_t = \frac{1}{n}\sum_{k=1}^{n}\lambda_k L_k(x_t)$$

(8)

where, $\hat{y}_t$ is the final prediction of weighted aggregation (Fig. 3).

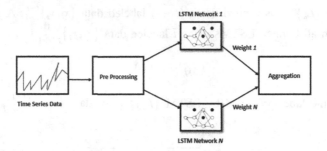

Fig. 3. Weighted aggregation of LSTM

4   Result and Analysis

The analysis was conducted on the Yahoo! Webscope [15], a time series benchmark dataset. It consist of four (A1–A4) benchmark data. In our analysis, real [1–3] and synthetic [1–3] dataset were used. Each dataset contains $\approx$1500 entries distributed among three fields (timestamp, value and is anomaly).

The Real dataset from A1 benchmark is based on real production traffic to the Yahoo! Properties while the synthetic is generated from artificial time-series with random seasonality, trend and noise. Former dataset has a periodic interval of one hour while the outliers in the later dataset are inserted at random positions. The underlying base architecture consists of three layered LSTM network [12]. A performance comparison of the proposed ensemble architectures weighted and m window with the baseline and simple mean aggregation model has been done using both real world and synthetic dataset. Various parameters taken for experiment are shown in Table 1.

Table 1.   Parameters

Parameter	Value
Total instances	1500
t − 1	500
l	100
n	3
m	7

Figure 4 shows the result obtained from different aggregation techniques on the A2-synthetic 2 dataset when mapped with the actual data. Performance of single LSTM is shown in Fig. 4a, as the graph shows that this method is not able to predict the ground values hence gives an error $\varsigma = 173:439$. Simple mean aggregation on the other hand is able to predict more accurate values as shown in Fig. 4b. The convergence with the actual values is much better than the single model. It increases accuracy by ≈45% than single LSTM. Weighted aggregation further enhances the prediction accuracy by ≈67% and gives better prediction as shown in Fig. 4c than simple mean aggregation. An m window performs even better than weighted aggregation based LSTM by about ≈65%. As can be seen in the case of real data in the given table, giving preference to recent data window does not go well since the recent trend does not follows well with the underlying actual annotation.

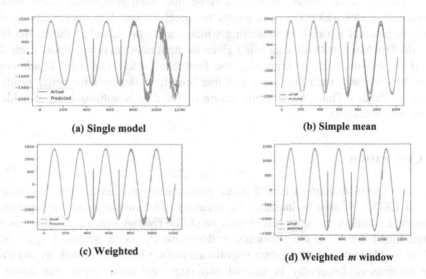

(a) Single model

(b) Simple mean

(c) Weighted

(d) Weighted m window

Fig. 4. Aggregation result of synthetic time-series

A comprehensive comparison of the results can be seen in Table 2. As evident from the result, weighted and m window clearly outperform baseline and simple mean aggregation. Among overall result, basic single model gives least performance followed by simple mean aggregation. On real dataset, weighted aggregation performs best among all as it is able to do a better approximation on inconsistent manual annotation. A window based aggregation on the other hand works best on synthetic data as extracting recent trend helps tackle random seasonality and noise.

Weighted and m window aggregation helps restrict model uncertainty, misspecification and inherent noise [16] to tolerable limits. Incorrect or ignored parameters based model leads to uncertainty. Dropout regularization helps solve uncertainty as it makes each of the models different from one another. The probability based neurons dropping in each network remains different. These thinned models makes the overall ensemble avoid wrongly trained or overfitted parameters.

Table 2. Predition error (ς)

Dataset	Base	Mean	Weighted	m Window
Real 1	0.076	0.036	0.031	0.034
Real 2	457.682	279.867	191.93	214.114
Real 3	0.28	0.123	0.113	0.117
Synthetic 1	39.514	34.062	25.467	18.788
Synthetic 2	173.439	93.867	39.596	12.662
Synthetic 3	173.521	128.994	106.737	77.616

A training dataset containing non-uniform samples that does not cover the whole sample space leads to model misspecification. Proposed methods considering the local performance of each thinned network and ne tune their importance helps build a generalized model which removes model misspecification. The uncertainty in data results in inherent noise. It is something which cannot be solved at the model level since the problem is with the data being given as input rather than the model itself. It is solved by systematically incorporating the feature of online Learning. It allows the model to learn with each prediction and fine tune its parameters for better result on upcoming dataset. Thus, the dynamic nature of the data is automatically considered during model training.

5   Conclusion

The study proves that single LSTM gives unsatisfactory predictions and ensemble of thinned LSTMs is able to increase the accuracy. The simple mean aggregation of ensemble LSTMs gives better results than single LSTM but with equal importance to all individual networks, the performance degrades. Proposed weighted aggregation method is able to define appropriate importance to each thinned network by analyzing their correctness. Especially in manual annotated real data, importance based on exhaustive past data counters the inconsistency in annotation. Weighted aggregation's performance degrades in presence of random outliers and noise. A m window based aggregation solves this problem by calculating thinned networks' importance based on last m data instances. Recent trend based importance factor is able to segregate outliers and noise accurately.

References

1. Zhao, R., Yan, R., Chen, Z., Mao, K., Wang, P., Gao, R.X.: Deep learning and its applications to machine health monitoring: a survey. arXiv preprint arXiv:1612.07640 (2016)
2. Malhotra, P., Vig, L., Shro, G., Agarwal, P.: Long short term memory networks for anomaly detection in time series. In: Proceedings, p. 89. Presses universitaires de Louvain (2015)

3. Byeon, W., Breuel, T.M., Raue, F., Liwicki, M.: Scene labeling with LSTM recurrent neural networks. In: Proceedings of the IEEE Conference on Computer Vision and Pattern Recognition, pp. 3547–3555 (2015)
4. Sundermeyer, M., Schluter, R., Ney, H.: LSTM neural networks for language modeling. In: Thirteenth Annual Conference of the International Speech Communication Association (2012)
5. Kingma, D.P., Ba, J.: Adam: a method for stochastic optimization. arXiv preprint arXiv: 1412.6980 (2014)
6. Dietterich, T.G.: Ensemble methods in machine learning. In: Kittler, J., Roli, F. (eds.) MCS 2000. LNCS, vol. 1857, pp. 1–15. Springer, Heidelberg (2000). https://doi.org/10.1007/3-540-45014-9_1
7. Gers, F.A., Schraudolph, N.N., Schmidhuber, J.: Learning precise timing with LSTM recurrent networks. J. Mach. Learn. Res. 3(Aug), 115–143 (2002)
8. Gers, F.A., Schmidhuber, J., Cummins, F.: Learning to forget: continual prediction with LSTM (1999)
9. Laptev, N., Yosinski, J., Li, L.E., Smyl, S.: Time-series extreme event forecasting with neural networks at uber
10. Malhotra, P., Ramakrishnan, A., Anand, G., Vig, L., Agarwal, P., Shro, G.: LSTM-based encoder-decoder for multi-sensor anomaly detection. arXiv preprint arXiv:1607.00148 (2016)
11. Assaad, M., Bone, R., Cardot, H.: A new boosting algorithm for improved time-series forecasting with recurrent neural networks. Inf. Fusion 9(1), 41–55 (2008)
12. Guo, T., Xu, Z., Yao, X., Chen, H., Aberer, K., Funaya, K.: Robust online time series prediction with recurrent neural networks. In: 2016 IEEE International Conference on Data Science and Advanced Analytics (DSAA), pp. 816–825. IEEE (2016)
13. Srivastava, N., Hinton, G., Krizhevsky, A., Sutskever, I., Salakhutdinov, R.: Dropout: a simple way to prevent neural networks from overfitting. J. Mach. Learn. Res. 15(1), 1929–1958 (2014)
14. Xiong, H.Y., Barash, Y., Frey, B.J.: Bayesian prediction of tissue-regulated splicing using rna sequence and cellular context. Bioinformatics 27(18), 2554–2562 (2011)
15. Laptev, N., Amizadeh, S.: Yahoo anomaly detection dataset s5
16. Zhu, L., Laptev, N.: Deep and confident prediction for time series at uber. In: 2017 IEEE International Conference on Data Mining Workshops (ICDMW), pp. 103–110. IEEE (2017)

Optimal Low Rank Tensor Factorization for Deep Learning

Antra Purohit, Abhishek, Rakesh$^{(\boxtimes)}$, and Shekhar Verma

Department of Information Technology, Indian Institute of Information
Technology, Allahabad, Allahabad 211012, Uttar Pradesh, India
{ise2016013, rsi2016006, pcl2014003, sverma}@iiita.ac.in

Abstract. Dense connectivity in latent variable models, recommender systems and deep neural networks make them resource intensive. As the data keeps on growing, the memory and processing requirements also increases. It is not always feasible to extend these physical units hence, tensor methods are used to optimize and improve their performance in a resource constrained environment. Tensors make them fast, accurate and scalable in machine learning however, this results in trade-off between accuracy and resource requirement. In this paper, we explore the feasibility to convert the dense matrices to tensor train format such that number of parameters are reduced and the expressive power of layers are preserved. Based on tensor rank effect observation, a novel decomposition method is proposed which preserves the underlying model's accuracy along with time and space optimization by tensor methods.

Keywords: Tensor decomposition · Neural networks
Time and space optimization

1 Introduction

High dimensional data generated from domains like image classification [15], speech recognition, latent variable models [3, 4] etc. are difficult to analyze due to redundant features and noise in the data. Model's discriminative power in given dimension gets diluted as most of the instances lie on its periphery. Dimensionality reduction solves this problem by preserving most relevant features such that the data changes to maximum discriminative dimension which makes analysis easy. A user defined dimension in dimensionality reduction technique may lead to information loss.

To overcome this problem of possible information loss, another solution is to feed given data to deep neural network where the model is capable of identifying most relevant features itself. The deep neural network extracts the important features at various stages (each stage identifies specific feature(s)), this natural way of extraction increases the model accuracy and avoids information loss. A Deep neural network consists of multiple layers (>3 layers). A CNN (Convolutional Neural Network) [1, 16] contains deep layers of networks and are trained using huge data instances. Each layer consists of multiple nodes which in turn are connected to every node of next layer. This fully connected graph results in dense weight matrix which requires large amount of memory space and processing capability (Fig. 1).

© Springer Nature Singapore Pte Ltd. 2019
S. Verma et al. (Eds.): CNC 2018, CCIS 839, pp. 476–484, 2019.
https://doi.org/10.1007/978-981-13-2372-0_42

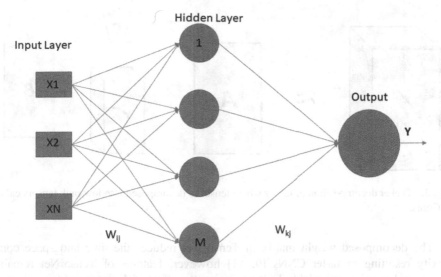

Fig. 1. A typical neural network with one hidden layer

As the data grows, the resource requirement also increases but it is not always feasible to upgrade hardware as per requirement. Data compression has been a primary method to tackle such a dense graphs. Many experiments have been performed to adjust weights of fully connected network in a more compact manner. Another way of handling this is to use weight matrix with minimal ranks. Weight matrix analysis proved that it contains redundant weights and by using minimal rank matrix, it can be optimized (Fig. 2).

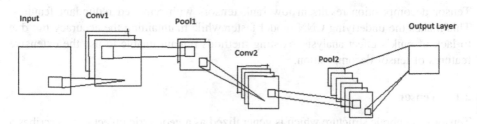

Fig. 2. Architecture of Convolutional Neural Network

Tensor methods are used to optimize the dense matrix for resource constrained environment without degrading the underlying model's performance. Tensors are used to represent the given high dimensional data into multilinear format called as Tensor-Train [7, 12, 14]. It uses only few parameters to represent CNN's dense weight matrix without compromising accuracy or impacting the layers' functionality [8, 10, 13]. The layer's built using tensor methods are called Tensor-Train-Layers and respective network is referred as TensorNet (Fig. 3).

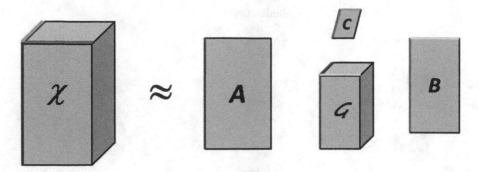

Fig. 3. Tucker decomposition of tensor where tensor is decomposed into low rank tensors called as Cores.

The decomposed weight matrix in TensorNet reduces the time and space complexity resulting in faster CNNs [9, 11] however, features of TensorNet remains unexplored as existing model lacks in analyzing the effect of decomposed tensor's rank with respect to the data class, dimension, instances and model's accuracy.

In this paper, we analyzed the effects of tensor rank and propose a novel decomposition function to unlock the features of TensorNet which further increases the underlying model's accuracy. The paper further proceeds with proposed decomposition method in Sect. 2 followed by experimental results and detailed analysis in Sect. 3. Section 4 concludes the findings of this paper.

2   Proposed Methodology

Tensor decomposition results in low rank tensors with removed redundant features. This makes the underlying CNN model faster while maintaining the accuracy but due to lack of rank's effect analysis, existing methods remain unable to use the extensive features of tensor decomposition.

2.1   Tensor

Tensor is algebraic structure which is generalized as a geometric object that describes a linear relation between vectors, scalars and other tensors. It consist of high dimensional arrays and are denoted by T. The tensor elements are represented using $A(i) = A(i_1, i_2, ..., i_d)$ where, d is the dimensionality of the tensor. The following is representation of a d-dimensional tensor elements:

$$T(l_1, ..., l_d) = K_1[l_1]K_2[l_2]...K_d[l_d]. \tag{1}$$

where $K_k[l_k]$ are matrices defined for each dimension as well as for every value in each dimension. All matrices $K_k[l_k]$ of same dimension k has to be of same size $r_{k-1} \times r_k$. [7]. The values r_0 and r_d are kept 1 so that the matrix product should of size 1×1 [7], this is referred as tensor decomposition. The sequence $r_{k-1} \times r_k$. is the tensor train ranks and the collection of matrices corresponding to same dimension are called the cores [7].

The mathematical procedures such as summation and product of tensors; and computation of global characteristic of tensor can be effectively performed with the help of decomposed tensors. The format of tensor decomposition is equivalent to a low-rank matrix.

On a large vector, a tensor is defined by $v \in \mathbb{R}^N$, where $N = \prod_{k=1}^{d} n_k$. A mapping μ between the coordinate $1 \in \{1, \ldots, N\}$ of v and d-dimensional vector-index $\mu(l) = (\mu_1(l), \ldots, \mu_d(l))$ of the corresponding tensor $\mathbf{B}$ has performed, where $\mu(l) = (\mu_1(l), \ldots, \mu_d(l))$ [6, 7]. The tensor $\mathbf{B}$ is then defined by the corresponding vector elements: $B(\mu(l)) = v_l$. A compact format of vector i.e. tensor train vector [7] is obtained. A tensor train representation of matrix is defined as $\mathbf{W} \in \mathbb{R}^{P \times Q}$, where $P = \prod_{k=1}^{d} p_k$ and $Q = \prod_{k=1}^{d} q_k$. The bijections $u(i) = (u_1(i), \ldots, u_d(i))$ and $\mu(j) = (\mu_1(j), \ldots, \mu_d(j))$ map row and column indices i and j of matrix $\mathbf{W}$ to the d dimensional vector indices whose k-th dimensions are of size $p_k q_k$ and is indexed by the tuple $(u_k(i), \mu_k(j))$ [7]. The tensor $\mathbf{W}$ is then converted into the tensor train format by

$$\begin{aligned}
\mathbf{W}(i,j) &= \mathbf{W}((u_1\{(i), \mu_1(j)), \ldots, (u_d(i), \mu_d(j)))) \\
&= K_1[u_1(i), \mu_1(j)] \ldots K_d[u_d(i), \mu_d(j)]
\end{aligned} \quad (2)$$

where, the matrices $K_k[u_k(i), \mu_k(j)]$, $k = 1, \ldots, d$ serve as the cores with tuple $(u_k(i), \mu_k(j))$ is the index. The efficiency of tensor depends on the mapping between the vector element and tensor element. Column major reshape command has been used to make d dimensional tensor from given data sample.

A deep neural network with fully connected layer consumes more time and space. As the training data set is large and computational complexity is high, tensors based neural network models are used to reduce time and space complexity with less number of hidden parameters. Tensor Layer is built by linking fully connected layer where the weight matrix for each layer is stored as tensor format. This kind of neural network is known as tensor neural network.

Linear Transformation of typical neural network can be written as:

$$y = \mathbf{W}x + b. \quad (3)$$

where, $W \in \mathbb{R}^{M \times N}$ contains the weights, $b \in \mathbb{R}^M$ represents bias and x is N-dimensional input vector and y is M-dimensional output vector. The major benefit of tensor Layer is optimization of space as compared to a normal neural network. The above linear equation when defined using tensor form gives

$$Y(i_1, \ldots, i_d) = \sum_{j_1, \ldots, j_d} K_1[i_1, j_1] \ldots K_d[i_d, j_d] K(j_1, \ldots, j_d) + B(i_1, \ldots, i_d). \quad (4)$$

The time complexity using proposed methodology in forward pass is $O(r^2 md \, maximum\{M, N\})$ which is better than $O(MN)$. The space complexity is $O(r \, maximum\{M, N\})$ which is better than $O(MN)$, where r is maximal rank, $m_1 \times \ldots \times m_d$ is shape of input tensor, $n_1 \times \ldots \times n_d$ is shape of output tensor and m is $\max_{k=1, \ldots, d} m_k$.

2.2   Neural Learning

Stochastic gradient descent algorithm is used for training neural network. The parameters' gradients are calculated from back-propagation procedure [5]. The process initiates from the last layer and sequential proceeds to next layer in reverse order. The gradients of current layer are computed using precomputed gradient of previous layer. The gradients is calculated using

$$\frac{\partial L}{\partial x} = \mathbf{W}^T \frac{\partial L}{\partial y},$$
$$\frac{\partial L}{\partial y} = \frac{\partial L}{\partial y} x^T, \tag{5}$$
$$\frac{\partial L}{\partial b} = \frac{\partial L}{\partial y}.$$

In the next step of stochastic gradient descent calculation, the derivative of loss function is calculated with respective to weight matrix which uses the above mentioned gradients. It is given by

$$\mathbf{W}_{k+1} = \mathbf{W}_k + \gamma_k \frac{\partial L}{\partial \mathbf{W}}. \tag{6}$$

Direct computation of $\frac{\partial L}{\partial W}$ requires $O(MN)$ memory which is optimized by computing these gradient directly from the cores of tensor of $\mathbf{W}$. The indices are obtained by

$$i_k^- := (i_1, \ldots, i_{k-1}), i_k^+ := (i_{k+1}, \ldots, i_d), i = (i_k^-, i_k, i_k^+)$$
$$P_k^- [i_k^-, j_k^-] := K_1[i_1, j_1] \ldots K_{k-1}[i_{k-1}, j_{k-1}], \tag{7}$$
$$P_k^+ [i_k^+, j_k^+] := K_{k+1}[i_{k+1}, j_{k+1}] \ldots K_d[i_d, j_d].$$

The tensor layer transformation for k = 2,...,d − 1 is obtained from [7]

$$Y(i) = Y(i_k^-, i, i_k^+) = \sum_{j_k^-, j, j_k^+} P_k^- [i_k^-, j_k^-] K_k[i_k, j_k] P_k^+ [i_k^+, j_k^+] X(j_k^-, j, j_k^+) + B(i). \tag{8}$$

The gradient of the loss function L with respect to the k-th core in position $[i_k, j_k]$ can be computed using the chain rule as [7]

$$\frac{\partial L}{\partial K_k[i_k, j_k]} = \sum_i \frac{\partial L}{\partial Y(i)} \frac{\partial Y(i)}{\partial K_k[i_k, j_k]}. \tag{9}$$

The gradient $\frac{\partial Y(i)}{\partial K_k[i_k j_k]}$ is computed from

$$\frac{\partial Y\left(i_k^-, i_k, i_k^+\right)}{\partial K_k[i_k, j_k]} = \sum\nolimits_{j_k^-, j_k^+} \left(P_k^-\left[i_k^-, j_k^-\right]\right)^T \left(P_k^+\left[i_k^+, j_k^+\right]\right)^T X\left(j_k^-, j, j_k^+\right). \qquad (10)$$

This partial product sum that has been calculated above is saved for future computations. We have applied dynamic programming for precomputed stored product.

The time complexity using proposed methodology in backward pass is $O(r^4 md^2 maximum\{M, N\})$ which is better than $O(MN)$. The space complexity is $O(r^3 maximum\{M, N\})$ which is better than $O(MN)$, where r is maximal rank, m_1 x... x m_d is shape of input tensor, n_1 x... x n_d is shape of output tensor and m is $max_{k=1,...,d}m_k$.

3 Discussion and Analysis

3.1 Implementation Details

All experiments have been carried out on MATLAB 2015b and MATCONVNET for CNN implementation. TensorTool box library has been used for tensor and its related operations. CNN has been trained by the forward and backward pass algorithm for neural network developed by (Alexander Novikov, 2015) [2].

3.2 Experimental Results

The main focus of this work is to analyze the properties of tensor layer. We also found different approaches for fixing parameters: Dimensions of tensors which represent the input/output of the layers and ranks of tensors. By analyzing different policies we can compress the weight matrix. We also tested various ways of reshaping the input-output tensors and try various ranks of tensor layer.

As a standard measure we consider neural network where there are two fully connected layers and one rectified linear unit for testing purpose. We resize original image 28×28 to 32×32 wherever required.

CIFAR-10 Dataset
We have performed experiment on CIFAR-10 dataset which is basically a classification dataset that consists of 10 classes with 6000 images per class. Images have been grouped for training and testing as 50000 images for training and 10000 for testing. The dataset is divided into five training batches and one test batch, each with 10000 images. The 10 classes are: air-plane, automobile, bird, cat, deer, dog, frog, horse, ship, truck.

Then we preprocess the image by subtracting the mean and performing normalization. Here as a standard measure we use the CIFAR-10 CNN, which consists of convolutional, pooling and ReLu layers [7]. There are also two fully-connected layers of sizes 1024×1024 and 64×10. The convolution part of this network is fixed but we substitute fully-connected part by $1024 \times N$ Tensor-layer followed by ReLU and by a $N \times 10$ fully connected layer. We used input mode size $4 \times 4 \times 4 \times 4 \times 12$ and second mode size $5 \times 5 \times 5 \times 5 \times 15$ with all ranks as 1. The train error that we got is

23% which is slight better than train error that (Alexander Novikov, 2015) [2] has got; that is 24.39% where they have treated input and output vectors as $4 \times 4 \times 4 \times 4 \times 4$ and $5 \times 5 \times 5 \times 5 \times 5$ tensors respectively with all ranks as 8. And the validation error that we got is 22%.

By all the other experiments that we have conducted we conclude that better accuracy can be obtained by increasing the dimensions and decreasing the rank of tensors (Fig. 4).

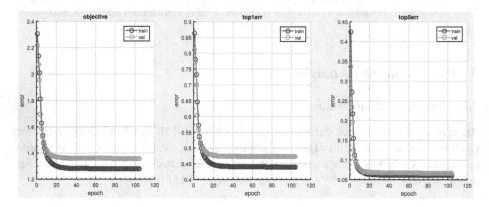

Fig. 4. Train and validation error of TensorNet after training for more than 100 epochs on CIFAR-10 dataset. The input mode size $4 \times 4 \times 4 \times 4 \times 12$ and second mode size $5 \times 5 \times 5 \times 5 \times 15$. Rank of all tensors are 1.

4   Conclusion

In deep learning, Tensor methods are proved to have better efficiency than other low rank matrix ideas. Time and space complexity can be optimized by using TensorNet with particular ranks thus instead of using matrix rank, Tensor rank provides much better accuracy and flexibility. In future, we can attempt to reduce the parameters of neural network with the help of tensors and without compromising accuracy.

References

1. Mourad, R., Sinoquet, C., Zhang, N.L., Liu, T., Leray, P.: A survey on latent tree models and applications. J. Artif. Intell. Res. **47**, 157–203 (2013)
2. Maillard, J., Clark, S., Grefenstette, E.: A type driven tensor based semantics for CCG. In: Proceedings of the EACL 2014 Workshop on Type Theory and Natural Language Semantics, pp. 46–54 (2014)
3. Lu, L., Zheng, Y., Carneiro, G., Yang, L.: Deep Learning and Convolutional Neural Networks for Medical Image Computing. Springer, Cham (2017). https://doi.org/10.1007/978-3-319-42999-1

4. Dahl, G.E.: Deep learning approaches to problems in speech recognition, computational chemistry, and natural language text processing, p. 101 (2015)
5. Sculley, D., et al.: Hidden technical debt in machine learning systems, pp. 1–9
6. Anandkumar, A., Ge, R., Hsu, D., Kakade, S.M., Telgarsky, M.: Tensor decompositions for learning latent variable models. J. Mach. Learn. Res. 15(1), 2773–2832 (2014)
7. Anandkumar, A., Hsu, D., Kakade, S.M.: A method of moments for mixture models and hidden Markov models. In: Conference on Learning Theory, pp. 33–34 (2012)
8. Ba, J., Caruana, R.: Do deep nets really need to be deep? In: Ghahramani, Z., Welling, M., Cortes, C., Lawrence, N.D., Weinberger, K.Q. (eds.) Advances in Neural Information Processing Systems, vol. 27. pp. 2654–2662. Curran Associates, Inc. (2014)
9. Krizhevsky, A., Sutskever, I., Hinton, G.E.: Imagenet classification with deep convolutional neural networks. In: Advances in neural information processing systems, pp. 1097–1105 (2012)
10. Aghdam, H.H., Heravi, E.J.: Guide to Convolutional Neural Networks: A Practical Application to Traffic-Sign Detection and Classification. Springer, Heidelberg (2017). https://doi.org/10.1007/978-3-319-57550-6
11. Denil, M., Shakibi, B., Dinh, L., Ranzato, M., de Freitas, N.: Predicting parameters in deep learning. In: Proceedings of the 26th International Conference on Neural Information Processing Systems, NIPS 2013, USA, vol. 2, pp. 2148–2156. Curran Associates Inc. (2013)
12. Gong, Y., Liu, L., Yang, M., Bourdev, L.D.: Compressing deep convolutional networks using vector quantization. CoRR abs/1412.6115 (2014)
13. Yang, Z., et al.: Deep fried convnets. CoRR abs/1412.7149 (2014)
14. Hornik, K., Stinchcombe, M., White, H.: Multilayer feedforward networks are universal approximators. Neural Netw. 2(5), 359–366 (1989)
15. Oseledets, I.V.: Tensor-train decomposition. SIAM J. Scientific Comput. 33(5), 2295–2317 (2011)
16. Zhang, Z., Yang, X., Oseledets, I.V., Karniadakis, G.E., Daniel, L.: Enabling high-dimensional hierarchical uncertainty quantification by anova and tensor-train decomposition. IEEE Trans. Comput.-Aided Des. Integr. Circuits Syst. 34(1), 63–76 (2015)
17. Novikov, A., Rodomanov, A., Osokin, A., Vetrov, D.: Putting MRFs on a tensor train. In: International Conference on Machine Learning, pp. 811–819 (2014)
18. Denil, M., Shakibi, B., Dinh, L., De Freitas, N., et al.: Predicting parameters in deep learning. In: Advances in Neural Information Processing Systems, pp. 2148–2156 (2013)
19. Sainath, T.N., Kingsbury, B., Sindhwani, V., Arisoy, E., Ramabhadran, B.: Low-rank matrix factorization for deep neural network training with high-dimensional output targets. In: 2013 IEEE International Conference on Acoustics, Speech and Signal Processing (ICASSP), pp. 6655–6659. IEEE (2013)
20. Xue, J., Li, J., Gong, Y.: Restructuring of deep neural network acoustic models with singular value decomposition. In: Interspeech, pp. 2365–2369 (2013)
21. Denton, E.L., Zaremba, W., Bruna, J., LeCun, Y., Fergus, R.: Exploiting linear structure within convolutional networks for efficient evaluation. In: Advances in Neural Information Processing Systems, pp. 1269–1277 (2014)
22. Lebedev, V., Ganin, Y., Rakhuba, M., Oseledets, I., Lempitsky, V.: Speeding-up convolutional neural networks using fine-tuned CP-decomposition. arXiv preprint arXiv: 1412.6553 (2014)
23. Chen, W., Wilson, J., Tyree, S., Weinberger, K., Chen, Y.: Compressing neural networks with the hashing trick. In: Bach, F., Blei, D. (eds.) Proceedings of the 32nd International Conference on Machine Learning. Proceedings of Machine Learning Research, PMLR, Lille, France, 07–09 July 2015, vol. 37, pp. 2285–2294 (2015)

24. Cybenko, G.: Approximation by superpositions of a sigmoidal function. Math. Control, Signals Syst. **2**(4), 303–314 (1989)
25. Dinu, G., Baroni, M.: How to make words with vectors: phrase generation in distributional semantics
26. Bayer, J., Osendorfer, C.: Learning Stochastic Recurrent Networks, pp. 1–9 (2014)
27. Oseledets, I.V., Savostyanov, D.V., Tyrtyshnikov, E.E.: Linear algebra for tensor problems. Computing **85**(3), 169–188 (2009)
28. Huang, F., Niranjan, U., Hakeem, M.U., Anandkumar, A.: Online tensor methods for learning latent variable models. J. Mach. Learn. Res. **16**(1), 2797–2835 (2015)
29. Hinton, G.: Dropout: a simple way to prevent neural networks from Overfitting. J. Mach. Learn. Res. (JMLR) **15**, 1929–1958 (2014)
30. Socher, R., Huang, E.H., Pennington, J., Ng, A.Y., Manning, C.D.: Dynamic pooling and unfolding recursive autoencoders for paraphrase detection. In: NIPS, pp. 1–9 (2011)
31. Paulus, R., Socher, R., Manning, C.D.: Global Belief Recursive Neural Networks, pp. 1–9
32. Welling, M., Teh, Y.W.: Bayesian learning via stochastic gradient Langevin dynamics. In: Proceedings of the 27th International Conference on Machine Learning (ICML) (2011)
33. Lake, B.M., Ullman, T.D., Tenenbaum, J.B., Gershman, S.J.: Building machines that learn and think like people, vol. 2, pp. 1–44 (2016)
34. Gopalan, P., Charlin, L., Blei, D.: Content-based recommendations with Poisson factorization. In: Advances in Neural Information Processing Systems (2014)
35. Rumelhart, D.E., Hinton, G.E., Williams, R.J.: Learning representations by backpropagating errors. Nature **323**(6088), 533 (1986)
36. Goller, C., Kuchler, A.: Backpropagation through structure
37. Tucker, L.R.: Some mathematical notes on three-mode factor analysis. Psychometrika **31**(3), 279–311 (1966)
38. Aridhi, H., Zaki, M.H., Tahar, S.: Fast statistical analysis of nonlinear analog circuits using model order reduction. Analog Integr. Circuits Signal Process **85**(3), 379–394 (2015)
39. Novikov, A., Podoprikhin, D., Osokin, A., Vetrov, D.P.: Tensorizing neural networks. In: Advances in Neural Information Processing Systems, pp. 442–450 (2015)
40. Winship, T., Morgan, G.: Counterfactuals and Causal Inference (2015)
41. Liang, D.: Deep collaborative Poisson factorization (2014)
42. Wainwright, M.J., Jordan, M.I.: Graphical Models, Exponential Families, and Variational Inference. Found. Trends Mach. Learn. **1**(2), 1–305 (2007)
43. Csiszár, I., Shields, P.C.: Information Theory and Statistics: A Tutorial. Now Publishers Inc., Breda (2004)
44. Hinton, G.E., Osindero, S., Teh, Y.W.: A fast learning algorithm for deep belief nets. Neural Comput. **18**, 1527–1554 (2006)
45. Anderson, J.R.: A mean field theory learning algorithm for neural networks. Complex Syst. **1**, 995–1019 (1987)
46. Krizhevsky, A., Hinton, G.: Learning multiple layers of features from tiny images (2009)
47. Russakovsky, O., et al.: Imagenet large scale visual recognition challenge. CoRR abs/1409.0575 (2014)
48. Simonyan, K., Zisserman, A.: Very deep convolutional networks for large-scale image recognition. CoRR abs/1409.1556 (2014)
49. Ellis, K.: Dimensionality reduction via program induction, pp. 1–8

Performance Analysis of Naive Bayes Computing Algorithm for Blood Donors Classification Problem

Anil Kewat[1(✉)], P. N. Srivastava[2], and Arvind Kumar Sharma[3]

[1] Jagannath University, Jaipur, India
anil.kewat2007@gmail.com
[2] Bundelkhand University, Jhansi, India
pn_shrivastava@yahoo.com
[3] Kota University, Kota, India
drarvindkumarsharma@gmail.com

Abstract. The term like intelligent systems, knowledge based systems, expert systems, and so forth., are meant to express message that it is possible to construct machines that can exhibit intelligence just like people in doing a little easy tasks. In these tasks we search for the final result of the performance of the machine for evaluation with the overall performance of a human being. We characteristic intelligence to the machine if the overall performance of the machine and human being are the identical. In the recent trends soft computing algorithms with the data mining techniques are applied in the different application domain for the prediction, knowledge extraction and performance evaluation tasks. Healthcare is one of them. In this paper a Naïve-Bayes soft computing algorithm is used with the data mining technique for investigating the performance of the blood bank and blood donors in a particular city on the idea of real-world datasets. Naive-Bayes computing algorithm has the capability of supervised learning in addition to the statistical learning. Performances of Naive-Bayes algorithm on the idea of varied parameters are evaluated and results are collected.

Keywords: Naïve Bayes · Soft computing · Blood-donors · Neural network Dataset

1 Introduction

Recently using of soft computing techniques as an excellent tool for knowledge discovery in huge amounts of data. These hybrid combinations have the potential to handle large amount of data in a very quick and effective manner. Since the data to be analyzed is having with inexact and uncertainty. Therefore traditional techniques are not adequate. Properties of the same kind are typical of soft computing. Therefore the application of soft computing techniques results in systems that have high device ratio. Recently most widely used soft computing techniques are as follows:

© Springer Nature Singapore Pte Ltd. 2019
S. Verma et al. (Eds.): CNC 2018, CCIS 839, pp. 485–496, 2019.
https://doi.org/10.1007/978-981-13-2372-0_43

1.1 Genetic Algorithm

Genetic algorithms are adaptive seek algorithms based totally on the evolutionary thoughts of natural choice and genetics. As such they constitute a sensible exploitation of a random are seeking used to resolve optimization hassle. The simple techniques of the genetic algorithm are designed to simulate manner in herbal structures vital for evolution, in particular people who examine the principles of nice survival. Genetic algorithms are higher than the tough computing algorithms in that they are more robust. In looking a large nation location a genetic algorithm may additionally offer substantial blessings over greater widespread optimization techniques. In famous, genetic set of rules starts as follows. An initial population is created which consist of randomly generated regulations. Every rule can be represented via a string of bits. Based at the belief of survival of the fittest, a ultra-modern populace is common to encompass the fittest regulations within the modern-day populace, as well as offspring of those suggestions. Normally, the fitness of a rule is classed through the usage of its class accuracy on set of education samples. Offspring are created by means of making use of genetic operators including crossover and mutation. In crossover, substrings from pairs of tips are swapped to shape new pairs of rules. In mutation, randomly selected bits in a policies string are inverted. The technique of producing new populations primarily based on in advance populations of guidelines keeps till a populace, P, evolves in which each rule in P satisfies a pre-particular health threshold. Genetic algorithms are without troubles parallelizable and had been used for class as well as extraordinary optimization troubles. In information mining, they will be used to evaluate the health of other algorithms [1].

1.2 Neural Networks

New models of computing to participate in pattern recognition tasks are influenced with the aid of the constitution and performance of our organic neural community. A set of processing models when assembled in a intently interconnected community, offers a wealthy structure exhibiting some features of the organic neural community. This kind of constitution is known as an artificial neural network. Considering ANNs are applied on computer systems, it is valued at evaluating the processing capabilities of a computer with these of the brain. Neural networks are sluggish in processing understanding, on the grounds that cycle time akin to a neural event promoted by using an outside stimulus happens in milliseconds range therefore the pc method expertise virtually one million time faster. Neural networks can participate in massively parallel operations for the reason that prompted from organic networks where mind operates with hugely parallel operations each and every of them having comparatively fewer steps. Neural networks have gigantic number of computing elements and the computing isn't restrained to within neurons. Neural networks retailer expertise within the strengths of the interconnections. In a neural community new understanding is added via adjusting the interconnections strengths, without destroying the historic information. Consequently expertise in the brain is adaptable whereas in the laptop it's strictly replaceable. Neural networks exhibit fault tolerance considering that the expertise is dispensed within the connection throughout the network. There's no significant manage for processing expertise within the brain. In a neural network each and every neuron acts established on the neurons connected to it. Accordingly there is not any specified manipulate mechanism outside to the computing undertaking [2].

1.3 Support Vector Machine

Support vector machine, a promising new approach for the category of each linear and nonlinear data. An SVM is a set of rules that works as follows. It uses a nonlinear mapping to transform the authentic training records into a higher measurement. Within this new dimension, it searches for the linear greatest keeping apart hyper aircraft. With the ideal nonlinear mapping to a sufficiently excessive measurement, information from instructions can usually be separated through a hyper plane. The SVM reveals this hyper plane using help vectors and margins. the first paper on SVM became offered in 1992 through Vladimir Vapnik and colleagues, even though the ground work for SVM has been around because the Sixties. Although the training time of even the fastest SVM may be extremely sluggish, they're noticeably correct, due to their capacity to model complex nonlinear decision obstacles. They are a lot less susceptible to over fitting than different methods. The guide vector additionally offer a compact description of the discovered version. SVMs can be used for prediction as well as class. They had been carried out to some of areas, consisting of handwritten digit popularity, object recognition, and speaker identity, in addition to benchmarks time series prediction checks.

1.4 Fuzzy Logic

The concept of fuzzy sets was first introduced by Zadeh in 1965 to represent vagueness present in human reasoning. Fuzzy sets can be considered as a generalization of the classical set theory. In a classical set an element of the universe either belongs to or does not belong to the set. Thus the belongingness of an element is crisp. In a fuzzy set the belongingness of an element can be a continuous variable. Mathematically, a fuzzy set is a mapping from the universe of discourse to [0, 1]. The higher the membership value of an input pattern to a class, the more is the belongingness of the pattern to the class [3]. The membership function is usually designed by taking into consideration the requirements and constraints of the problem. Fuzzy logic deals with reasoning with fuzzy sets and fuzzy numbers. it's far to be noted that fuzzy uncertainty isn't the same as probabilistic uncertainty. In the network outputs are interpreted as fuzzy membership values. Learning laws are derived by minimizing a fuzzy objective function in a gradient descent manner. In the concept of cross entropy was extended to incorporate fuzzy set theory. Incorporation of fuzziness in the objective functions led to better classification in many cases. In Kohonen's clustering network has been generalized to its fuzzy counterpart. The merits of this approach is that the final weight vectors do not depend on the sequence of presentation of the input vectors. The method uses a systematic approach to determine the learning rate parameter and size of the neighbourhood.

1.5 Rough Sets

In many type tasks the aim is to shape lessons of objects which might not be considerably unique. These indistinguishable objects are beneficial to construct knowledge base concerning the task. For instance if the objects are classifieds consistent with color (red, black) and shape (triangle, square and circle) then the indiscernible classes are red triangles, black squares, red circles, and so on. As a result these attributes make a partition in the set of objects. Now if red triangles with distinct regions belong to different classes, then it is not possible for anybody to classify these two red triangles primarily based on the given attributes. This form of uncertainty is known as rough uncertainty. Pawlak formulated the rough uncertainty in terms of rough sets. The rough uncertainty is absolutely prevented if we will successfully extract all of the important capabilities to represent distinct objects. But it may now not be feasible to guarantee this as our knowledge about the system generating the records is limited. It should be stated that rough uncertainty is different from fuzzy uncertainty. Using rough sets it could be feasible to lower the dimensionality of the input without dropping any statistics. A set of features is enough to categorize all of the input patterns if the rough ambiguity, for this set of capabilities is equal to 0. The use of this quantity it's far possible to pick a right set of features from the given data.

2 Literature Review

Nowadays there is a huge amount of information being collected and confine databases everywhere across the globe. There are valuable information and information "hidden" in such databases; and while not automatic ways in which for extracting this information it's much impossible to mine for them. Throughout the year's many algorithms were created to extract what is referred to as nuggets of knowledge from huge sets of information. There are several methodologies to approach this drawback.

Boonyanusith and Jittamai [4] on this studies the sample of blood donors' behaviours based on elements influencing blood donation choice is accomplished the usage of on line questionnaire. The surveyed records are used for device studying techniques of synthetic intelligence to classify the blood donor company into donors and nondonors. the accuracy finding out of the surveyed facts is achieved the usage of the synthetic neural network (ANN) and choice tree techniques on the way to are looking ahead to from a series of individual Blood conduct information whether or not or now not each character is a donor. The consequences suggest that the accuracy, precision, and do not forget values of ANN method are better than those of the choice tree method [4].

Classification is an information analysis technique to extract models describing necessary knowledge classes and predict future values. Processing uses classification techniques with machine learning, image process, language method, applied mathematics and visualization techniques to seek out and gift info in a clear format. Most of the classification algorithms in literature are memory resident, usually presumptuous a little info size. Recent processing analysis has designed on such techniques, developing ascendable and durable classification techniques capable of handling huge disk-resident knowledge. The classification has varied applications in addition to flight classification, fraud detection, target promoting, performance prediction, manufacturing, and identification. The performance of the classification techniques is measured by the metrics like accuracy, speed, robustness, quality, comprehensibility, time and interpretability. Classification technique depends on the inductive learning principle that analyzes and finds the patterns from the knowledge. If the character of an environment is dynamic, then the model ought to be adaptive i.e. it got to be able to learn and map with efficiency.

Bhardwaj et al. [5] focuses on data mining and trends associated with it. In this paper, the main purpose of the system is to increase blood donor's rate as well as to attract more blood donors to donate blood. The work has been made to classify and predict the number of blood donor's according to their age and blood group. In this work, the WEKA data mining tool and the J48 algorithm is used to classify the data and evaluation of the data. Limère et al. Presented a model for firm growth with call tree induction principle. It offers fascinating results and fits the model to economic info like growth competence and resources, growth potential and growth ambitions.

Shilton and Palaniswami printed a unified approach to support vector machines. This unified approach is developed for binary classification and after extended to one-class classification and regression. Takeda et al. projected a unified durable classification model that optimizes the prevailing classification models like SVM, minimax likelihood machine, and Fisher discriminate analysis. It provides several blessings like well-defined theoretical results, extends the prevailing techniques and clarifies relationships among existing models.

Yee and Nursingd Haykin viewed the pattern classification as an ill-posed disadvantage, it is a demand to develop a unified theoretical framework that classifies and solves the unwell expose problems. Recent literature on classification framework has reportable higher results for binary class datasets alone. For multiclass datasets, there's an absence of accuracy and lustiness. So, evolving an economical classification framework for multiclass datasets remains an open analysis downside. The evaluation of the parameters which influence the psychology of blood donors has been conducted largely because of the numerous effect of blood insufficiency at the continuance of patients [6]. The approach in discovering new styles of huge statistics units is recorded processing. It is able to be accustomed extract information from a present information set and redecorate into a character's perceivable structure for any use [7]. It utilizes techniques on the intersection of information, facts systems, gadget mastering, and computing. ANN might be a way of facts processing it really is accustomed predict or classify records inside the area of ideas or emotions and behaviors of customers efficiently [8]. It is fashioned in getting to know styles of the statistics [9]. To resolve the difficulty of category and grouping records are effective to investigate the promoting databases [10]. Multi-layer Perceptron may be a giant and useful feed-forward ANN version, which might be accustomed examine dataset to categories the focused cluster [11]. Moreover, choice Tree is one many of the useful strategies in type by way of getting to know patterns of the dataset. it will display end result diagrammatically as a tree model a good way to factor every step of concluding process from input to output [12].

Borkar and Deshmukh [13] planned using Naïve Thomas Bayes classifier for detection of swine-flu disease. The method starts with finding likelihood for every attribute of swine flu against all output. The probabilities of every attribute are then increased. Choosing the most likelihood from all the possibilities, the attributes belong to the category variable with the most worth. The promising results of the planned theme is used for investigation more the swine flu disease in patients using info technology. Patil et al. [14] worked within the direction of diagnosis whether or not a patient along with his given info relating to age, sex, pressure, blood glucose, chest pain, electrocardiogram reports etc. will have a cardiovascular disease later in life or not.

The experiments involve taking the parameters of the medical tests as inputs. The proposal is effective enough in getting used by nurses and medical students for training functions. the data mining technique used is Naive Thomas Bayes Classification for the event of decision network in cardiovascular disease Prediction System (HDPS). The performance of the proposal is additional improved employing a smoothing operation.

Kharya et al. [15] proposed detecting in patients the chances of having Breast Cancer later in life. The severity of Breast Cancer is necessary seeing it becoming the second most cause of death among women. A Graphical User Interface (GUI) is designed for entering the patient's record for the prediction. The records are mined through the data repository. Naïve Bayes classifier, being simple and efficient is chosen for the prediction. The results obtained by the Naïve Bayes classifier are accurate, have low computational effort and fast. Implementation of the proposal is done through Java and the training of data is done using from UCI machine repository [16]. Another advantage of the proposed system is that the system expands according to the dataset used.

Hickey [17] proposed using Naïve Bayes soft Classifier for public health domain. The public health data are used as an input and the purpose of the study was to analyze one or several attributes that predict a target attribute without the need for searching the input space exhaustively. The proposal achieved its goal with the increase in accuracy of classification. The target attributes were related to diagnosis or procedure codes.

Ambica et al. [18] developed an efficient decision support system for Diabetes disease by using Naïve-Bayes soft computing algorithm. The developed classification system contains two steps. The first step explains analysis of optimality of the dataset and accordingly extraction of the optimal feature set from the training dataset.

The second step create the new dataset as the optimal training dataset and the developed classification scheme is now applied on the optimal feature set. The mismatched features from the training data are ignored and the dataset attributes are used for the calculation of posterior probability. The proposed procedure, therefore, shows elimination of unavailable features and document wise filtering.

3 Proposed Methodology

The proposed methodology used to accomplish the various task is shown by following Fig. 1.

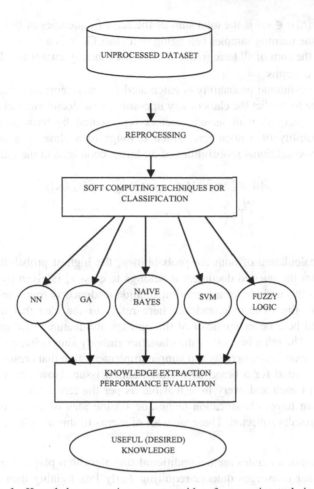

Fig. 1. Knowledge extraction process with soft computing techniques

3.1 Working Methodology of the Naive Bayes Classifier

Naïve Bayes Classification method starts with text document as an input. For measuring the relative degree of association between the class-word pairs, the classifier makes a log-linear decision rule that assigns an independent parameter to each class-word pair. The two steps of the classifier include Calculation of class conditional probability and Calculation of classification or posterior probability. For each term t and class c_j, the class conditional probability $(t_i|c_j)$ taking into consideration only one training set is represented as follows:

$$\widehat{p}(t_i/c_j) = \frac{\Sigma tf(t_i, d \in c_j) + \alpha}{\Sigma N_{d \in c_j} + \alpha.M} \qquad (1)$$

Where $\Sigma tf(t_i, d \in c_j)$ is the total sum of the term frequencies of the word from all documents in the training samples belonging to a class C_J, α, is a smoothing parameter. And $\Sigma N_{d \in c_j}$ is the sum of all term frequencies in the training dataset for class C_j, and M is the number of terms.

Once the conditional probability is calculated for each term and class, the trained classifier is able to predict the class of any upcoming new document. Let the document to be queried query is with feature vectors represented by term frequencies. The posterior probability of a document which belongs to a class c_j is the product of individual class conditional probabilities of all terms contained in the query document.

$$\widehat{p}(d\,/c_j) = \widehat{p}(t1/\,c_j) \cdot \widehat{p}(t2/\,c_j)\ldots\widehat{p}(t_m/\,c_j)$$
$$= \prod_{i=1}^{M} \widehat{p}(t_i/\,c_j)^{tf(ti,d)} \tag{2}$$

After the calculation of both the probabilities, the highest probability of class c_k which show that the queried document d belongs to class c_k is given by k = argmax$_j$.

As long as the underlying assumption of independence is true, the Naïve Bayes classifier works fine. The independence here refers to the idea that the underlying category should be a better predictor of the options, the features that are independent given the class. The other benefits of the classifier embody simplicity, quick to classify, not sensitive to extraneous options and simple implementation that create it a promising technique to be tried for a brand new classification issue. However, the underlying assumption isn't each and every time feasible as per the real world situation. Performances of naive bayes classification technique on the idea of varied parameters are evaluated and results collected. There are a lot of merits of this algorithm some of them are as follows:

1. When the input variables are unconditional this algorithm plays nicely.
2. This classifier converges quicker requiring fairly less training data than different discriminative models such as logistic regression.
3. It is less difficult to expect the class of the test dataset in this algorithm. This classifier is an excellent guess for multi-class predictions also.
4. This algorithm has offered excellent performance in numerous application areas in spite of conditional independence assumption.
5. There are different flavours of Naive Bayes algorithms such as Gaussian naïve bayes, Multinomial naïve bayes, Bernoulli naive bayes.
6. It is best suited for text classification problems. Generally it is used for spam email classification problem
7. This algorithm can also be used to train small dataset.

There are numerous areas where naive bayes algorithm are used some of them are as follows.

1. To check whether your email is junk mail or not.
2. For characterizing news articles about entertainment, politics, sports, technology etc. this algorithm is used.

3. It is used by social sites such as face book to break down announcements communicating positive or negative feelings.
4. It is also used as a document classification for indexing the document in a database.

4 Experimental Evaluation

The blood donor's information collected from the Kota blood bank having 5656 instances with 12 attributes. In principle, the usage of big data set to construct the classifier version will increase the performance while classifying new statistics due to the fact it would be less complicated to assemble an extra trendy model and subsequently finding a suitable match for our dataset. The dataset used to construct the classifier model is dependent on a variety of things which include the scale of the type of problem, the classifier algorithm used and the statistics set. The blood donor classification model was evaluated using a Naive-Byes classification technique. There are two categories of the blood donor' male and female. There are 5656 Instances of the blood donors dataset and there are seven attributes which are Bag-no, Age, Date Group, Available, Tested and Sex. The Testing mode is set at 10-fold cross-validation. The total execution time to build model is 0.02 s. The results of blood donors dataset for Naïve Bayes Classification technique is shown in the Table 1.

Table 1. Classified/unclassified instances

Truly classified instances	5515	97.5588%
Badly classified instances	138	2.44412%
Unknown instances	03	
Total instances	5526	

In the following step of the experiment we have calculated the classification accuracy in the Table 2.

Table 2. Classification accuracy

MAE	0.04890
RMSE	0.1574
RAE	102.9244%
RRSE	102.3834%

Where MAE, RMSE, RAE, RRSE are Mean absolute, Root mean squared, Relative absolute and Root relative squared errors respectively. According the male and female class accuracy is given in the following Table 3.

Table 3. Male and female class accuracy

Class	Male	Female
True positive rate	1	0
False positive rate	1	0
Precision	0.976	0
Recall	1	0
F-measure	0.988	0
ROC-area	0.634	0.63

The following graph shows the Accuracy of Male and Female class (Fig. 2).

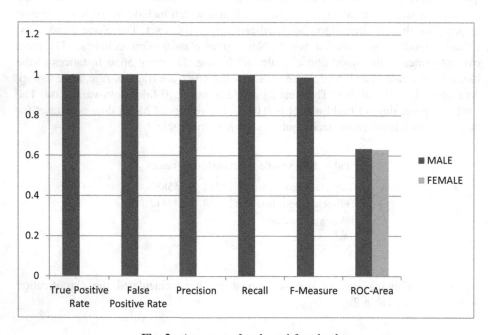

Fig. 2. Accuracy of male and female class

In the Table 4 we have shown the classified male and female blood donors according their blood groups.

Table 4. Classified male and female blood donors

Blood group	Male	Female
A+	1332	30
AB+	415	20
O+	1587	370
B+	1930	53
O−	690	1
B−	113	1
A−	581	1
AB−	20	2
Total	5524	145

The following output screen generated when we run Naive Bayes computing algorithm is shown in the following Fig. 3.

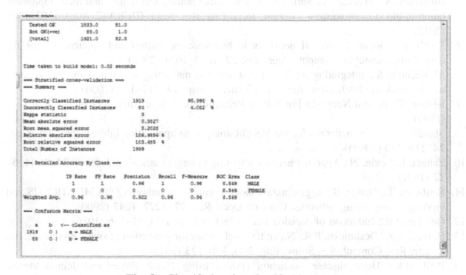

Fig. 3. Classified and unclassified instances

5 Conclusion

There are so many parameters comparing the performance and accuracy of an algorithm. The objective of this research paper is for the classification and prediction of blood donors according their sex and blood group. In this paper we have discussed that how a Naive-Bayes soft computing algorithm can be used in knowledge discovery for classification and prediction. During this work a data mining model is developed and tested for extracting knowledge of blood donor's classification which can be used to support certain kind of decisions in blood bank organization. The blood donor's dataset collected from an authentic government blood bank centre. The experimental outcomes represents that the generated classification rules carried out perfectly with accuracy rate 97.5588%. In the next paper the soft computing techniques with KDD will be implemented on the real world dataset for predicting the blood donor's conduct and mindset.

References

1. Holland, J.H.: Adaptation in Natural and Artificial Systems. University of Michigan Press, Ann Arbor (2004)
2. Mitchell, T.M.: Machine Learning. McGraw Hill International Editions, New York (1997)
3. Jang, J.S.R., Sun, C.T., Mizutani, E.: Neuro-Fuzzy and Soft Computing. Pearson Education, London (2004)
4. Boonyanusith, W., Jittamai, P.: Blood donor classification using neural network and decision tree techniques. In: Proceedings of the World Congress on Engineering and Computer Science (2012)
5. Bhardwaj, A., Sharma, A., Shrivastava, V.K.: Data mining techniques and their implementation in blood bank sector – a review. Int. J. Eng. Res. Appl. (IJERA) 2(Aug), 1303–1309 (2012)
6. Smith, K., Gupta, J.: Neural networks in business: techniques and applications for the operations researcher. Comput. Oper. Res. 27, 1023–1044 (2000)
7. McKechnie, S.: Integrating intelligent systems into marketing to support market segmentation decisions. Intell. Syst. Account. Financ. Manag. 14, 117–127 (2006)
8. Bishop, C.: Neural Networks For Pattern Recognition. Oxford University Press, New York (1999)
9. Sharda, R.: Neural networks for the MS/OR analyst: an application bibliography. Interfaces 24, 116–130 (1994)
10. Zahavi, J., Levin, N.: Applying neural computing to target marketing. J. Direct Mark. 11, 5–22 (1997)
11. Reutterer, T., Natter, B.: Segmentation-based competitive analysis with MULTICLUS and topology representing networks. Comput. Oper. Res. 27, 1227–1247 (2000)
12. Quinlan, J.R.: Induction of decision trees. Mach. Learn. 1(1), 81–106 (1986)
13. Borkar, A.R., Deshmukh, P.R.: Naïve Bayes classifier for prediction of swine flu disease. Int. J. Adv. Res. Comput. Sci. Softw. Eng. 5(4), 120–123 (2015)
14. Patil, R.R.: Heart disease prediction system using Naive Bayes and Jelinek-Mercer smoothing. Int. J. Adv. Res. Comput. Commun. Eng. 3(5), 6787–6792 (2014)
15. Kharya, S., Agrawal, S., Soni, S.: Naive Bayes classifiers: a probabilistic detection model for breast cancer. Int. J. Comput. Appl. 92(10), 26–31 (2014). ISSN 0975-8887
16. UCI Machine Learning Repository. http://ics.uci.edu/mlearn/MLRepository.html
17. Hickey, S.J.: Naive Bayes classification of public health data with greedy feature selection. Commun. IIMA 13(2), 87–98 (2013)
18. Ambica, A., Gandi, S., Kothalanka, A.: An efficient expert system for diabetes by Naïve Bayesian classifier. Int. J. Eng. Trends Technol. (IJETT) 4(10), 4634–4639 (2013)

Electronic Circuits for Communication Systems

Design of a Single-Ended 8T SRAM Cell
for Low Power Applications

S. R. Mansore[1(✉)], R. S. Gamad[2], and D. K. Mishra[2]

[1] Ujjain Engineering College, Ujjain, India
srmansore15@gmail.com
[2] S.G.S. Institute of Technology and Science, Indore, India

Abstract. This paper presents a single-ended eight-transistor (8T) static random-access memory (SRAM). The proposed cell achieves enhanced write ability by weakening the pull up transistor during write '0'. Feedback loop cutting approach is employed for successfulwrite '1' operation. Unlike the conventional 6T cell, proposed 8T cell employs separate transistors for read and write operations to eliminate conflicting design requirement on access transistor. Simulation is done on 180 nm CMOS technology on Cadence. Write static noise margin (WSNM) of the proposed SRAM cell is 9% largerthan that of the conventional 6T cell at 400 mV. The proposed cell consumesless leakage power 0.94x as that of the conventional 6T cell at 400 mV.

Keywords: Leakage power · Read disturbance · SRAM · Write ability

1 Introduction

SRAM is one of the critical blocks of modern portable devices such as laptops, biomedical instruments and other handheld devices. These devices strongly require low power dissipation for longer battery life. SRAM is the primary consumer of power of the total chip power as it occupies a significant portion of the silicon chip [1–3]. Hence, designing an SRAM that consumes low power is desirable. An effective technique of lowering power dissipation is to scale down the supply voltage. However, cell stability degrades as supply voltage is scaled down [4]. Also, transistor dimensions continue to scale down for achieving higher integration density. However, down-scaling of MOSFETs to sub nanometre range leads to variation in threshold voltage which results in dramatic reduction in cell stability [5].

Schematic of the conventional 6T bit cell is shown in Fig. 1. The 6T cell offers simple structure but it suffers from read disturbance problem and conflicting read versus write design requirement. Let us assume that logic '1' (Q = '1') is stored in the cell. During read operation, access transistor tries to raise voltage at node QB towards VDD while pull- down transistor tries to maintain QB at '0'. Thus, there is contention between pull-down and access transistors. The bit flip can take place if, access transistor wins the fight. This is referred to as read disturbance problem. To mitigate the read disturbance problem, access transistor is required to be weaker than the pull-down transistor. However, stronger access transistor and weaker pull-up transistor is required

© Springer Nature Singapore Pte Ltd. 2019
S. Verma et al. (Eds.): CNC 2018, CCIS 839, pp. 499–508, 2019.
https://doi.org/10.1007/978-981-13-2372-0_44

for a successful write operation [6]. Therefore, it is difficult to operate conventional 6T cell at lower supply voltage due to conflict design requirement on access transistor.

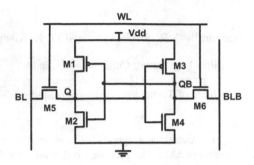

Fig. 1. Conventional 6T cell

To overcome the problems of the conventional 6T cell, various SRAM cell structures are proposed by the researchers. SRAM cell proposed in [7–9] offer enhanced RSNM but these cells use more control signal which results in increased switching power and area. In [10], a separate read buffer is used to eliminate the read disturbance but this cell has poor write '1' ability as this cell employs two series NMOS write access transistors. Since an NMOS passes a logic '1' weakly. In [11, 12], successful write operation is performed by weakening pull-up and pull-down network of the cells. A single ended read disturb-free 8T SRAM cell is proposed which is based on cells proposed in [11] and [12]. The proposed design offers enhanced write ability and consumes lesser switching power as it employs single bit line.

2   Proposed 8T SRAM Cell

Figure 2 depicts the schematic of the proposed 8T bit cell. Transistor M2–M4 and M5–M6 form the latch. The write word line (WWL) and word line (WL) control transistors M1 and M3, respectively. The write access transistor M7 passes data from bit line BL to storage node Q when enabled by WWL. The read access transistor M8 is controlled by RWL. Table 1 gives the Truth table of the proposed 8T bit cell.

2.1   Read Operation

To read the cell content, bit line BL is precharged to VDD. RWL is raised to high while WWL and WL are forced to ground. The bit line BL is discharged conditionally through M6 and M8. For instance, if Q = '0', then M6 is OFF which keeps BL at its precharged level VDD. However, high Q turns ON transistor M6 which discharges bit line BL through transistors M6 and M8.

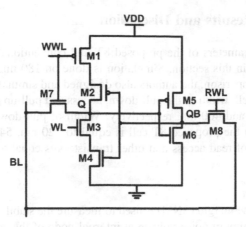

Fig. 2. The proposed cell

Table 1. Truth table of the proposed 8T cell

Operation	WWL	WL	RWL	BL
Read	'0'	'0'	'1'	'1'
Write '0'	'1'	'1'	'0'	'0'
Write '1'	'1'	'0'	'0'	'1'
Hold	'0'	'1'	'0'	'1'

2.2 Write Operation

To write a '0' in the cell, BL is pulled down to the ground. Control signals WWL and WL are forced to VDD while RWL is forced to ground. As a result, transistor M1 is turned OFF which weakens the pull up transistor M2. Consequently, node Q discharges quickly to ground through ON transistor M7. At the same time M5 is turned ON to raise the voltage at node QB. Thus, node Q holds data '0' when the cell returns to hold mode by forcing WWL to ground. For writing a '1' in the cell, BL is loaded with data '1'. Now, WWL is forced to VDD while WL and RWL are pulled down to ground which results in flow of current from BL to node Q through M7. Low WL turns OFF transistor M3 which allows charge accumulation at node Q resulting in voltage hike at Q. As a result, M6 is turned ON and QB is discharged to ground (QB = '0'). Consequently, node Q = '1' when the cell returns to standby mode (WWL = '0' WL = '1').

2.3 Hold Mode

In the hold or standby mode WWL and RWL are forced to ground while WL is raised to VDD. The cross-coupled inverters hold the stored data if supply is ON.

3   Simulation Results and Discussion

Important design parameters of the proposed 8T and conventional 6T cells are simulated and compared in this section. Simulation is done on 180 nm CMOS technology on Cadence. For comparison, the authors also designed and simulated the conventional 6T cell. For the 6T cell, width of the pull-down, access and pull-up transistors is chosen as 800 nm, 600 nm and 400 nm, respectively. Width of pull-down, write access and pull-up transistors in the proposed 8T cell is equal to 720 nm, 540 nm, and 400 nm, respectively. Width of read access and other transistors is equal to 400 nm.

3.1   Hold Stability

The metric static noise margin (SNM) is used to measure the stability of a bit cell. SNM is defined as the minimum noise voltage at internal node of the cell that can alter the cell content. SNM during hold mode is referred to as the Hold SNM (HSNM). Figure 3 shows the graphical method for finding the HSNM. It is the side length of the largest square fit inside the lobe butterfly curve. Higher value of the HSNM is desirable for better cell stability. The proposed cell shows HSNM = 142 mV at 0.4 V.

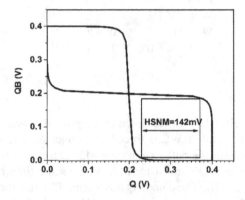

Fig. 3. Butterfly curve during hold mode

3.2   Read Stability

Read stability is expressed in terms of RSNM. RSNM indicates the ability of the cell to retain the stored data during read operation. The conventional 6T cell shows poor stability due to degraded RSNM (Fig. 4). During read operation, a non- zero voltage is developed at the '0' storing node due to voltage division action between access and driver transistors. This rise in voltage can alter the contents of 6T cell. In the proposed cell, transistor M3 cuts off the feedback loop dynamically during read operation. Therefore, node Q is isolated from BL and therefore, the cell content does not altereven if voltage at node QB becomes equal to the trip point voltage of the left inverter [12]. Thus, the proposed cell offers higher read stability and is free from read disturbance.

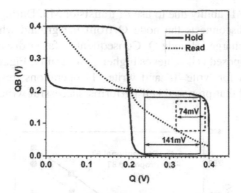

Fig. 4. HSNM versus RSNM of the conventional 6T cell

3.3 Write Ability

Metric WSNM is used to measure write ability. WSNM indicates the ability of a SRAM cell to pull down the voltage of the inverter storing logic '1' below the trip point voltage of inverter storing logic '0'. Figure 5 shows the voltage transfer curves of the cell during write '0' operation. In Fig. 5 two curves intersect at only one point. This means that the proposed cell exhibits monostable behaviour during write operation [12]. Thus, successful write '0' operation is performed.

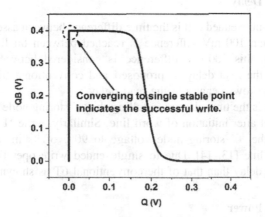

Fig. 5. Write '0' VTC of the proposed cell

Figure 6 shows the variation in the WSNM with the supply voltage for conventional 6T and proposed cells. From Fig. 6 it is observed that our cell offers 9% larger WSNM than that of the conventional 6T cell. Higher value of the WSNM means the proposed cell has better write ability than the conventional 6T cell. Enhancement in WSNM of the proposed cell is due to the use of power gated transistor M1 which weakens the pullup transistor M2 during write '0' operation. The proposed cell also exhibits higher write '1' ability due to use of transistor M3. During write '1' operation, OFF transistor M3 disconnects the node Q from the ground which results in faster accumulation of the charge sat node Q. Consequently, faster discharge of node QB to ground. Thus, the proposed cell achieves higher write ability. Figures 7 and 8 show the simulated waveforms for write '0' and write '1' operations, respectively. From the graphs, it is observed that proposed cell performs successful write operation at 0.4 V.

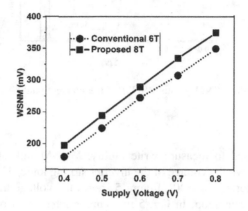

Fig. 6. WSNM (write '0') versus supply voltage

3.4   Read/Write Delay

Read delay for a double ended cell is the time difference between assertion of word line and the instant when 100 mV difference is reached between bit lines. For a single-ended SRAM cell, this 100 mV difference is considered between BL and VDD. Table 2 compares the read delay of proposed and conventional 6T cells at VDD = 400 mV. Our cell shows penalty in the read delay.

Write '0' delay is the time elapsed in falling the '1' storing node voltage to 10% of its initial high level after initiation of word line. Similarly, write '1' delay is the time elapsed in rising the '0' storing node voltage to 90% of its initial low level after initiation of word line [13, 14]. Due to single ended write operation, proposed cell shows larger write delay than that of the conventional 6T as shown in Table 2.

3.5   Read/Write Power

Because of the single ended structure, bit line in the proposed 8T cell is discharged only if Q = '1' (or QB = '0'). For Q = '0' (or QB = '1') bit line BL remains at its precharged level. Therefore, our cell consumes less switching power as compared to double ended 6T bit cell in which one of the bit lines is always discharged [15]. Table 3 shows the power consumption of the proposed cell during read operation. This power consumption is the average of read '0' and read '1'. From the Table 3, it can be observed that the read power consumption of the proposed 8T cell is 0.63x of the conventional 6T cell. Proposed 8T cell employs single bit line for the write operation. Therefore, low power is consumed in charging and discharging of single bit line as

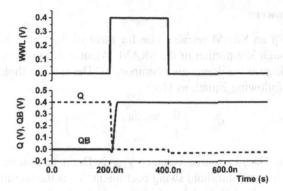

Fig. 7. Simulated waveform during write '0'

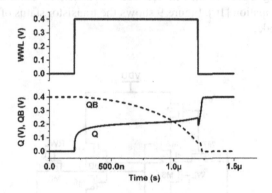

Fig. 8. Simulated waveform during write '1'

Table 2. Read and write delay at VDD = 0.4 V.

Operation	Conventional 6T cell (ns)	Proposed 8T cell (ns)
Read	155	580
Write	15	22

compared to differential bit lines [16]. Table 3 records the write power consumed by the proposed 8T cell. It is observed that the proposed cell consumes lesser power during write operation.

Table 3. Read and write power consumption at VDD = 0.4 V.

Operation	Conventional 6T cell (nW)	Proposed 8T cell (nW)
Read	72.33	45.4
Write	74.7	50

3.6   Leakage Power

A major portion of an SRAM remains idle for most of the times. However, leakage current flows through idle portion of the SRAM. Among various leakage currents, the sub-threshold leakage is the dominating component. The sub-threshold leakage current can be found by following equations [16]:

$$I_{Sub} = k\frac{W}{L}e^{\frac{V_{GS}-V_{TH}}{nV_T}}\left(1 - e^{\frac{-V_{DS}}{V_T}}\right) \tag{1}$$

Where, V_{GS} is Gate to source voltage, V_{DS} is Drain to Source voltage, V_{TH} is threshold voltage n is sub-threshold swing coefficient, V_T is the thermal voltage and W and L are the channel width and length, respectively. In the proposed 8T cell, left inverter consists of series combination of the four transistors M1, M2, M3 and M4. Therefore, stacking effect results in reduced subthreshold current and hence low leakage power dissipation [16]. Figure 9 shows the transistor status of the proposed cell in the hold '0' mode.

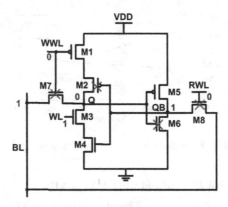

Fig. 9. Leakage current during hold '0' mode

As shown in the figure, BL leakage current flows through stack of the three transistors M7-M3-M4 resulting in reduced leakage current. Also, drain and source of transistor M8 are at the same potential ($V_{DS} = 0$) which results in zero leakage current through M8. Thus, total leakage current due to the cell is reduced. Leakage power of the proposed and conventional 6T cells is illustrated in Fig. 10. It can be noticed that leakage power of the proposed 8T cell is 0.94x lesser as compared to the conventional 6T cell.

3.7   Area

The layouts of the conventional and proposed 8T cells using 180 nm design rules is shown in Figs. 11 and 12, respectively.

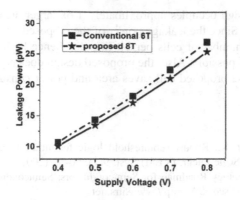

Fig. 10. Leakage power versus supply voltage

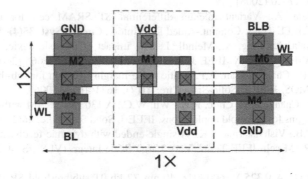

Fig. 11. Layout of conventional 6T cell

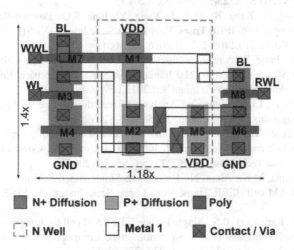

Fig. 12. Layout of proposed 8T cell

The proposed design occupies approximately 1.6x larger area as compared to the conventional 6T cell. Since the leakage power of the proposed 8T cell is lesser than 6T cell therefore, more number of cells per bit line and hence higher density of SRAM using proposed cell is possible. Also, the proposed design does not use additional write assist circuit hence the proposed cell saves area and power consumption.

References

1. Soeleman, H., Roy, K.: Robust subthreshold logic for ultra-low power operation. IEEE Trans. Very Large Scale Integr. (VLSI) Syst. **9**(1), 90–99 (2001)
2. International Technology Roadmap for Semiconductors: Semiconductor Industry Association (SIA), SanFrancisco, CA. http://www.itrs.net
3. Lin, S., Kim, Y., Lombardi, Y.: A highly-stable nanometer memory for low-power design. In: IEEE International Workshop on Design and Test of Nano Devices, Circuits and Systems, pp. 17–20 (2008)
4. Pal, S., Islam, A.: Variant tolerant differential 8T SRAM cell for ultralow power applications. IEEE Trans. Comput.-Aided Des. Integr. Circuits Syst. **35**(4), 549–558 (2016)
5. Bhavnagarwala, A., Tang, X., Meindl, J.: The impact of intrinsic device fluctuations on CMOS SRAM cell stability. IEEE J. Solid-State Circ. **36**(4), 658–665 (2001)
6. Calhoun, B.H., Chandrakasan, A.P.: Static noise margin variation for sub-threshold SRAM in 65-nm CMOS. IEEE J. Solid-State Circ. **41**(7), 1673–1679 (2006)
7. Chang, M.F., Chang, S.W., Chou, P.W., Wu, W.C.: A 130 mV SRAM with expanded write and read margins for threshold applications. IEEE J. Solid State Circ. **46**(2), 520–529 (2011)
8. Kushwah, C.B., Vishvakarma, S.K.: A single-ended with dynamic feedback control 8T sub threshold SRAM cell. IEEE Trans. Very Large Scale Integr. (VLSI) Syst. **24**(1), 373–377 (2016)
9. Lu, C.Y., et al.: A 0.325 V, 600-kHz, 40-nm 72-kb 9T subthreshold SRAM with aligned boosted write word line and negative write bit line write-assist. IEEE Trans. Very Large Scale Integr. (VLSI) Syst. **23**(5), 958–962 (2015)
10. Oh, T.W., Jeong, H., Kang, K., Park, J., Yang, Y., Jung, S.O.: Power-gated 9T SRAM cell for low-energy operation. IEEE Trans. Very Large Scale Integr. (VLSI) Syst. **25**, 1183–1187 (2017). https://doi.org/10.1109/TVLSI.2016.2623601
11. Pasandi, G., Fakhraie, S.: A new sub-threshold 7T SRAM cell design with capability of bit-interleaving in 90 nm CMOS. In: 21st Iranian Conference on Electrical Engineering (ICEE) (2013). https://doi.org/10.1109/IranianCEE.2013.6599738
12. Wen, L., Duan, Z., Li, Y., Zeng, X.: Analysis of read disturb-free 9T SRAM cell with bit-interleaving capability. Microelectron. J. **45**, 815–824 (2014)
13. Noguchi, H., et al.: Which is the best dual port SRAM in 45 nm process technology?-8T, 10T single ended, and 10T differential. In: IEEE International Conference on Integrated Circuit Design and Technology (ICICDT), pp. 55–58 (2008)
14. Ahmad, S., Gupta, M.K., Alam, N., Hasan, M.: Single-ended Schmitt-trigger based robust low power SRAM cell. IEEE Trans. Very Large Scale Integr. (VLSI) Syst. **24**(8), 2634–2642 (2016)
15. Madiwalar, B., Kariyappa, B.S.: Single bit line 7T SRAM cell for low power and high SNM. In: International Mutli-Conference on Automation, Computing, Communication, Control and Compressed Sensing (iMac4s), pp. 223–228 (2013)
16. Pasandi, G., Fakhraie, S.: An 8T low voltage and low-leakage half selection disturb-free SRAM using bulk-CMOS and FinFETs. IEEE Trans. Electron Devices **61**(7), 2357–2363 (2014)

Y-Shaped Cantilever Beam RF MEMS Switch
for Lower the Actuation Voltage

Aamir Saud Khan[1] and T. Shanmuganantham[2(✉)]

[1] Pondicherry University, Pondicherry 605014, India
aamir.105023@gmail.com
[2] Departments of Electronics Engineering,
Pondicherry University, Pondicherry 605014, India
shanmuga.dee@pondiuni.edu.in

Abstract. In today's world one of the major concerns for the electronics engineers and scientists is how to reduce the power consumption of the electronics devices. To overcome this problem we come across different technologies. Radio Frequency (RF) Microelectromechanical (MEMS) switches are one of the leading technologies for past two decades. But the main concern with RF MEMS switches is its high actuation voltage and high switching time. This paper generally concentrates on the simulation of RF MEMS contact switch having Y-shaped cantilever beam to obtain low actuation voltage with less switching time. The simulation and results are obtained by the Intellisuite 8.7v software. The actuation voltage depends on the air gap, Young's modulus, thickness of the beam etc. The "pull-in" voltage is found to be 1.2 V and the switching time is about 52.3 µs.

Keywords: RF MEMS · Cantilever beam · Actuation voltage
Air gap · Young's modulus

1 Introduction

Micro Electro Mechanical system or Micro system is a multidisciplinary topic which generally comprises of electronics, mechanical, biomedical etc., it generally miniaturize the device. By miniaturization we mean reducing the value, reducing the cost, reducing the size etc., but there should not be any effect on the function of the device i.e., functionality should be constant. The RF MEMS switch is one of the most studied and one of first in RF MEMS technology. The physics behind the RF MEMS switch is similar to as 'mechanical relay', but on size it resembles with semiconductor switches [1]. The RF MEMS based switches out-shine the traditional semiconductor switches such as PIN diodes, HEMTs, FETs. The main problem with RF MEMS switches are its high switching time, its power handling capacity is less, its actuation voltage is high, and its reliability is less as compared to solid state counterpart [2]. In 2017, Raman, Shanmuganantham design a serpentine spring structure RF MEMS switch whose actuation voltage comes around 4 V [3]. In 2015, Attaran and Rashidzadeh, proposed a novel design to reduce the actuation voltage and the switch structure is helical and its actuation voltage is as low as 0.5 V [4]. In 2017, Khan and Shanmuganantham design an arc shape cantilever beam RF MEMS switch and its actuation voltage is about 1.4 V

© Springer Nature Singapore Pte Ltd. 2019
S. Verma et al. (Eds.): CNC 2018, CCIS 839, pp. 509–517, 2019.
https://doi.org/10.1007/978-981-13-2372-0_45

[6], in this paper the main focus is to reduce the actuation voltage. This paper generally discusses about the Y- shaped cantilever beam for lower the actuation voltage and decreases the transient response of the switch.

2 Proposed Design

The RF MEMS switches are generally divided into two parts: Static analysis and Dynamic analysis. It is a Y-shape cantilever beam which is anchored at one end and another end is freely hanging over the CPW transmission line. The design parameter of the beam such as its length, width, thickness, air gap and width of lower electrode is given in Table 1.

Table 1. Parameters of dimensions

Design parameters	Measurements
Length of beam, l	300 μm
Width of beam, w	100 μm
Thickness of beam, t	1 μm
Width of lower electrode, W	100 μm
Air gap, g_0	1 μm

Whereas the silicon substrate thickness is 50 μm and a bias voltage is given between the lower electrode and the cantilever beam as the cantilever beam gets deflects by 1 μm we get the actuation voltage. The material used for making the switch is aluminum (Al) [5] (Figs. 1, 2 and 3).

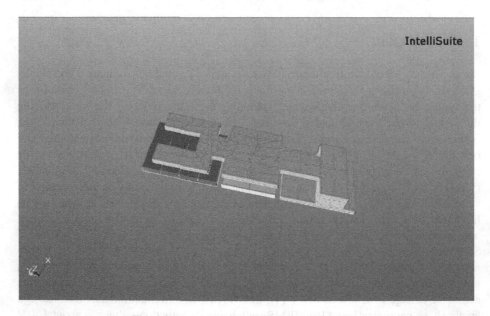

Fig. 1. Top view of Y shaped cantilever beam

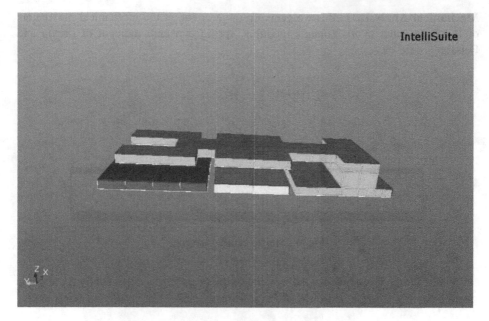

Fig. 2. Side view of Y shaped cantilever beam

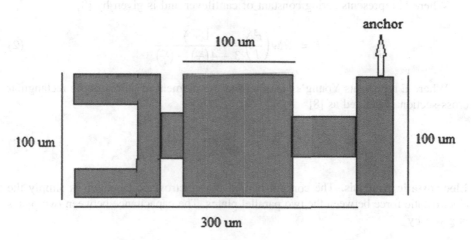

Fig. 3. Schematic representation of cantilever beam

3 Mathematical Modeling

3.1 Static Analysis

In the static analysis we generally give attention to the mechanical behavior of the beam and the physics behind the electrostatic actuation of the beam (Fig. 4).

Mechanical Analysis. In this we generally give attention the mechanical parameters of the beam such as its Young's modulus, spring constant, moment of inertia and Poisson's ratio etc.

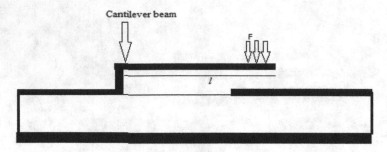

Fig. 4. Simple cantilever beam

When a force F is applied at the free end of the beam it gets deflected by Δx and it is given by

$$F = K \Delta x \tag{1}$$

Where K represents spring constant of cantilever and is given by [8]

$$K = 2Ew\left(\frac{t^3}{l}\right)\frac{1 - \frac{x}{l}}{3 - 4\left(\frac{x^3}{l}\right) + \left(\frac{x^4}{l}\right)} \tag{2}$$

Where E represents Young's modulus and the moment of inertia of the rectangular cross-section is defined as [8]

$$I = \frac{wt^3}{12} \tag{3}$$

Electrostatic Analysis. The concept behind the electrostatic actuation is simply the electrostatic force between the two parallel plates. The capacitance between two plates is given by

$$C = \frac{\mathcal{E}Ww}{g} \tag{4}$$

Where g represents beam height above the lower electrode and $\mathcal{E}$ represents the permittivity of the medium. The electrostatic force is given by the [9]

$$F_e = -\frac{\varepsilon W w V^2}{2g^2} \tag{5}$$

Where V represents the applied bias voltage between the beam and the lower electrode and F_e represents electrostatic force. So when we equate the electrostatic force with the spring force we get

$$\frac{\varepsilon W w V^2}{2g^2} = k\left(g_0 - g\right) \tag{6}$$

Where g_0 is the beam height for zero bias voltage. By solving Eq. (6) for voltage we get

$$V = \sqrt{\frac{2kg^2(g_0 - g)}{\varepsilon W w}} \tag{7}$$

At $\left(\frac{2}{3}\right)$ g_0 mechanical restoring force becomes more than the electrostatic force resulting cantilever beam becomes unstable then beam collapse to down state position. By putting the value of g in the Eq. (7) we get [9]

$$V_p = V\left(\frac{2g_0}{3}\right) = \sqrt{\frac{8kg_0^3}{27\varepsilon W w}} \tag{8}$$

Where V_p is known as "pull-in voltage" or "actuation voltage".

3.2 Dynamic Analysis

The dynamic analysis of the switch is generally used to find out the transient response of the switch i.e., the switching time. The frequency of the beam is given by

$$w_0 = \sqrt{\frac{K}{m}} \tag{9}$$

Where m is mass of the cantilever beam and quality factor of the beam is given by

$$Q = \frac{K}{w_0 b} \tag{10}$$

Where b is the damping coefficient and it can be reduce by using holes in the cantilever beam. It is found from experiments that if $Q \leq 0.5$ then shows slow switching time and if $Q \geq 2$ then it shows long settling time when it released. So for better performance Q = 1. For $Q \leq 0.5$ the switching time is given by the [10]

$$t_s = \frac{9V_p^2}{4w_0QV_s^2} \text{ for } V_s >> V_p \tag{11}$$

Now when the $Q \geq 2$ and damping coefficient is very small (b = 0) then the switching time is given by the [10]

$$t_s = 3.67\frac{V_p}{V_sw_0} \text{ for } V_s \geq 1.3V_p \tag{12}$$

4 Fabrication Process

The virtual surface micromachining process is used here for fabrication in Intellisuite 8.7v software in Intellifab module. First silicon is defined then three masks are used for building the device. First aluminum is deposited by conformal deposition for making lower electrode and CPW transmission line. Second anchor is build by depositing a sacrificial layer then last cantilever beam is mounted on the anchor and the sacrificial layer which is used for providing air gap is completely removed [7].

5 Simulations and Results

The simulation has been done in the Intellisuitev8.7 software in the thermo electromechanical (TEM) module. First of all simulation is set then material is selected then boundary conditions were applied for fixing the anchor and the substrate. Then load is given in terms of voltage between the lower electrode and the beam so as to get pull-in voltage. From the Fig. 5 it can be seen that switch shows a deflection of 1.0526 μm and from the Fig. 6 it can be seen that mises stress is about 2.1962 Mpa. From the simulation we get the vertical displacement of the cantilever with applied voltage is shown in the Fig. 7 and it is found to be about 1.2 V. From Fig. 8 it is clear that the switching time is about 52.3 μs.

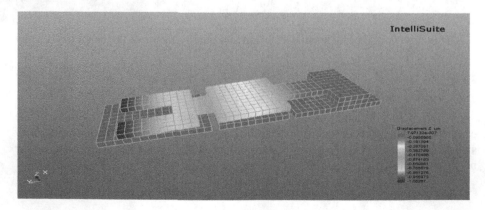

Fig. 5. Switch displacement

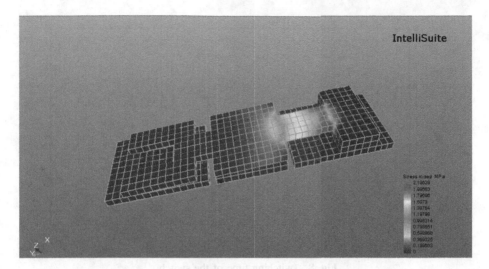

Fig. 6. Mises stress

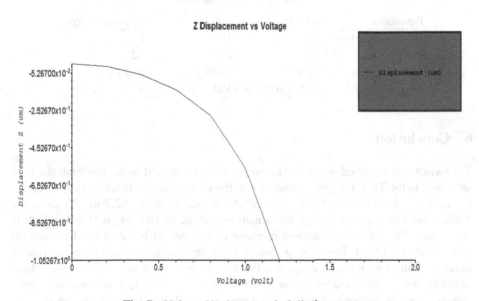

Fig. 7. Voltage V/s beam vertical displacement

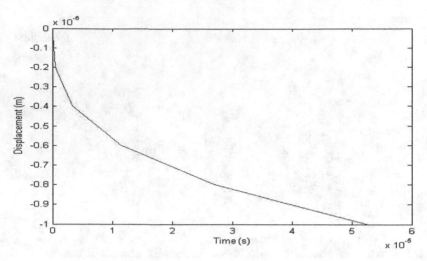

Fig. 8. switching time of the switch

Table 2. Comparison table

Parameters	Ref. [4]	Ref. [6]	Proposed design
Displacement (μm)	1.5	1	1
Pull in voltage (V)	0.5	1.4	**1.2**
Switching time	0.5 ms	56.04 μs	52.3 μs
Size	1264 × 635 μm²	350 × 100 μm²	350 × 100 μm²

6 Conclusion

The switch was designed in the 2-D layout then it is fabricated in the Intellifab and then simulated in the TEM analysis module. From the simulated results we can say that pull-in voltage is found to be 1.2 V and switching time is about 52.3 μs. So from the Table 2 we can say that though the actuation voltage of Ref. [4] is 0.5 V, which is better than this design but transient response of this design is far better than Ref. [4] which is about 0.5 ms. From the analysis we can say that some parameters are crucial in determining the pull-in voltage and the switching time of the switch. Since these switches show very good results so it is widely used as defense and research applications. We can further wok on its S-parameters, reliability, power handling etc., for overall better performance.

References

1. Raman, R., Shanmuganantham, T.: Conjoined rectangular beam shaped RF micro-electro-mechanical system switch for wireless applications. Int. J. Adv. Microwave Technol. (IJAMT) **1**(1) (2016)
2. Raman, R., Shanmuganantham, T.: Design and modeling of RF MEMS metal contact switch for wireless applications. In: International Conference on Control, Instruments, Communication and Computational Technologies (ICCICCT) (2016)
3. Raman, R., Shanmuganantham, T.: Frequency reconfiguration of microstrip patch antenna with serpentine spring shaped RF MEMS switch. Int. J. Adv. Microwave Technol. (IJAMT) **2**(1) (2017)
4. Attaran, A., Rashidzadeh, R.: Ultra low actuation voltage RF MEMS switch. Micro Nano Syst. Lett. **3**(7) (2015)
5. Raman, R., Shanmuganantham, T.: Design and analysis of RF MEMS switch with π shaped cantilever beam for wireless applications. In: IEEE International Conference on Emerging Technological Trends (ICETT) (2016)
6. Khan, A.S., Shanmuganantham, T.: Arc-shaped cantilever beam RF MEMS switch for low actuation voltage. In: IEEE International Conference on Circuits and Systems (2017)
7. Khan, A.S., Shanmuganantham, T.: Simulation and analysis of RF MEMS cantilever switch for low voltage actuation. In: IEEE International Conference on Circuits and Systems (2017)
8. Rebeiz, G.M., Muldavin, J.B.: RF MEMS switches and switch circuits. IEEE Microwave Mag. **2**, 59–71 (2001)
9. Varadan, V.K., Vinoy, K.A., Jose, K.A.: RF MEMS and Their Applications. Wiley, New York (2003)
10. Rebeiz, G.: RF MEMS Theory, Design and Technology. Wiley, New York (2003)

Concentric Circular Ring Arc Antenna at Dual Band for Ku Band Applications

T. Srinivasa Reddy[✉], S. K. Nannu Saheb, P. Koteswara Rao,
and Ashok Kumar Balijepalli

Department of Electronics and Communication Engineering,
Universal College of Engineering and Technology, Guntur, India
srinivasareddy.reddy5l@gmail.com

Abstract. In this paper, the concentric circular ring arc patch antenna is presented. The circular ring slots and arc slot is presented in circular patch. The proposed antenna is resonated at two frequencies are 13 GHz, 16.6 GHz with return loss −24.9 dB and −27 dB for Ku band applications. The maximum gain of resonant frequencies are 3.84 dB, 3.94 dB. The co polarization and cross polarization of E plane and H plane and impedance bandwidth of proposed antenna measured at resonant frequencies.

Keywords: Circular ring antenna · Arc shaped slot
Co polarization and cross polarization

1 Introduction

Now a days the dual band multi band antenna configurations are increased due to their attractive features like less cost, low complexity, easy to design for Ku band and satellite applications. The microstrip antenna are essential design in communication and radar systems used in ultra wide band applications (3.1 GHz–10.6 GHz).

[1] Karli proposed a rectangular patch antenna for dual band antenna with bandwidth of 0.4 in upper band and lower band and used for wireless communications. [2] Guha proposed circular patch with arc shaped defected ground structure (DGS) for improve the suppressing the XP (cross polarization). [3] The parasitic stubs and slots are slots in rectangular antenna for wide bandwidth and wireless local area networks. [4] A circular feed circular ring slot antenna was designed for wide bandwidth and gain of 5.7 dBi, the circular ring microstrip patch antenna with coupled-fed stacked microstrip for dual-frequency has considered. The researchers proposed different antennas for improve the bandwidth of the circular antenna [4, 5]. [4] A center fed circular ring patch with annular ring introduced for monopole radiation pattern, gain of 5.7 dB at resonant frequency 5.8 GHz. The researchers are proposed different types of split ring resonator (SRR) [6], aperture coupled annular ring [7], annular ring slot antenna [8] for circular polarization.

Coupled-fed stacked microstrip monopolar patch antenna for monopole like radiation pattern are obtained in the dual bands (2.28–2.55 GHz, 5.15–5.9 GHz) for wireless local area network (WLAN) applications [9]. Soodmand [10] proposed breach

S. Verma et al. (Eds.): CNC 2018, CCIS 839, pp. 518–527, 2019.
https://doi.org/10.1007/978-981-13-2372-0_46

coupled circular ring patch with four port dual band dual polarized for global system for mobile communication (GSM) and distributed control system (DCS) applications. Compact circular ring patch antenna for dual and triple band antennas resonate at fourth generation (4G) band [5]. The two appended coin shaped patches with ring shaped feed strip for Ultra-high frequency (UHF) radio frequency identification (RFID) applications [11].

The traditional antennas like rectangular patch antenna, circular, square and semi circle antennas has less bandwidth, low radiation characteristics. The proposed antenna has operated at dual frequencies and used for Ku band applications. The maximum gain is 3.94 dB, 3.84 at two operating frequencies and co polarization and cross polarization of E plane and H plane are designed.

2 CCAP Antenna Design

The Fig. 1 depicts the Concentric Circular ring Arc Parch (CCAP) for Ku band applications. The substrate of CCAP is designed with FR4 epoxy material and relative permittivity (ε_r) is 4.4. The substrate is designed with length (L_1) and width (W_2). The copper coated metallized circle is placed on top of the substrate with radius (R_1) The outer ring (R_2) and inner ring (R_3) radii has thickness of t_1 and outer ring (R_4) and inner ring (R_5) radii has thickness t_2. The inner ring slot (t_1) and outer ring slot (t_2) are slotted on circle (R_1) for improve the bandwidth of the CCAP antenna. The 10^0 of arc (a_1) is slotted on circle (R_1) with input impedance of CCAP is 50 Ω and feed line is connected to circular ring with length (L_2), width (W_2). The optimized parameter values of CCAP are shown in Table 1.

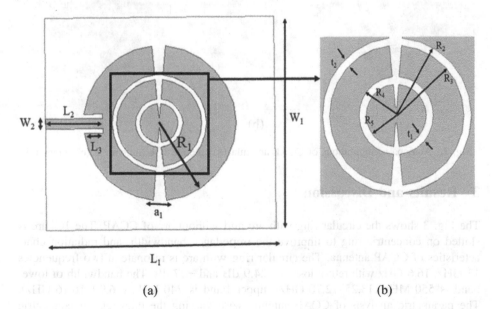

(a)   (b)

Fig. 1. (a) The concentric circular ring arc patch antenna (b) concentric circular slots

Table 1. The parameter values of proposed CCRA patch antenna

Parameter	Values (mm)	Parameter	Values (mm)
L_1	48	W_3	1
W_1	44	R_1	16
L_2	12	R_2	10
W_2	2	R_3	9
L_3	3.8	R_4	5
a_1	10^0	R_5	4

2.1 Antenna Configuration

The antenna configurations of the concentric circular arc patch is shown in Fig. 2. The design begin with single circular patch with feed line, the concentric circular slots are added to the circular patch to improve the impedance bandwidth of the proposed antenna. The 10^0 of arc is placed on the concentric circular slot antenna to improve the radiation characteristics of E plane and H plane of the proposed antenna. The cross polarization is reduced by the arc is slotted on circular ring patch.

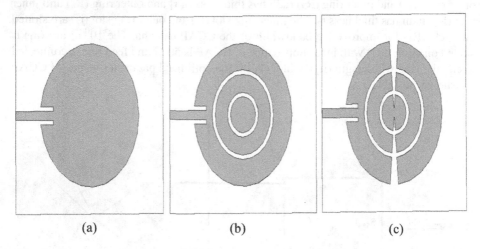

(a)   (b)   (c)

Fig. 2. Antenna configurations of CCAP antenna (a) antenna 1 (b) antenna 2 (c) antenna 3

3 Results and Discussion

The Fig. 3 shows the circular ring with arc and without arc of CCAP. The 10^0 arc is slotted on concentric ring to improve the impedance bandwidth, and radiation characteristics of CCAP antenna. The circular ring with arc is resonate at two frequencies 13 GHz, 16.6 GHz with return loss of -24.9 dB and -27 dB. The bandwidth of lower band is 550 MHz (13.25–12.70 GHz), upper band is 740 MHz (16.90–16.16 GHz). The parametric analysis of CCAP antenna with varying the thickness of concentric rings are t_1 and t_2 are shown in Fig. 3 and comparison of antenna 1, antenna 2 and antenna 3 shown in (Figs. 4 and 5).

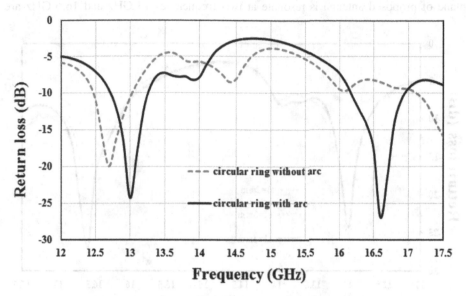

Fig. 3. Circular ring with arc and without arc of CCAP

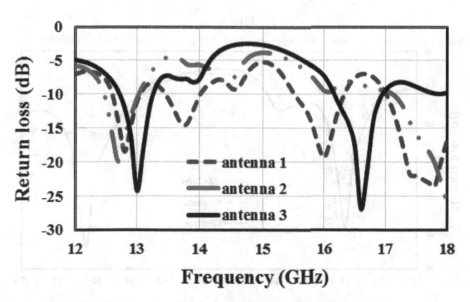

Fig. 4. Comparison of proposed antenna 1, antenna 2, antenna 3.

3.1   Parametric Analysis and Radiation Patterns of CCAP Antenna

The radiation characteristics of co polarization and cross polarization of E plane and H plane of proposed antenna is resonate at two frequencies 13 GHz and 16.6 GHz are

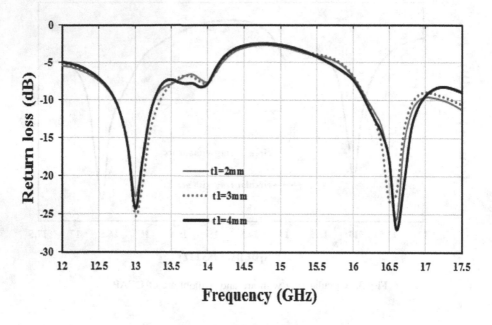

(a)

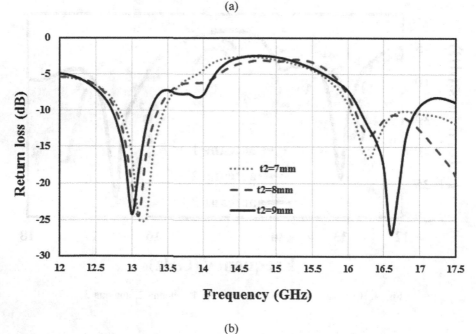

(b)

Fig. 5. Return loss of CCAP antenna for different values of (a) t_1 (b) t_2

shown in Fig. 6. The co polarization of E plane radiates in omnidirectional and cross polarization is quasi omnidirectional at resonant frequency 13 GHz. The co polarization of H plane in quasi omnidirectional and H plane has radiates bi directional at 13 GHz. At resonant 16.6 GHz the cross polarization of E plane has very low compared to cross polarization of E plane at resonant frequency 13 GHz.

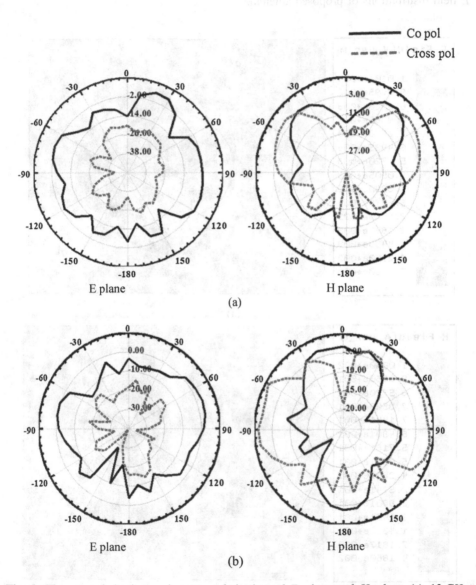

Fig. 6. The co polarization and cross polarization of E plane and H plane (a) 13 GHz (b) 16.6 GHz.

3.2   Field Distributions of CCAP Antenna

The field distributions of the concentric circular arc patch antenna at E field, H field and J field is shown in Fig. 7. The maximum E field distributions of the proposed antenna at feed line of 101 V/m. The maximum magnetic field and J field of proposed antenna observed has 10 A/m, the arc shape of slot on circular ring has improve the maximum E field distributions of proposed antenna.

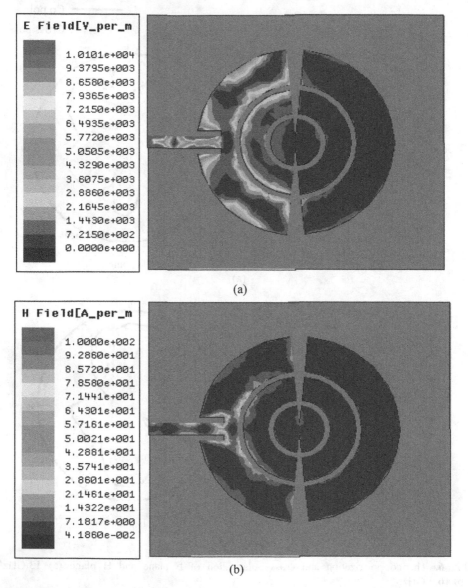

(a)

(b)

Fig. 7. Field distributions of concentric circular arc patch antenna at (a) E field (b) H field (c) J field.

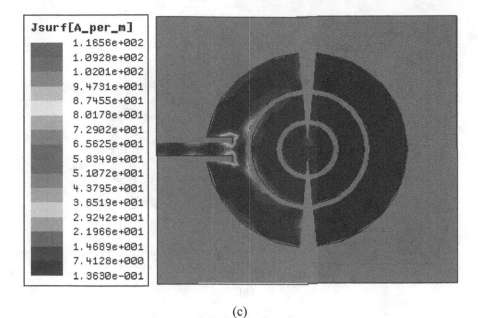

(c)

Fig. 7. (*continued*)

3.3 Maximum Gain

The maximum gain of CCAP at two resonant frequencies are shown in Fig. 8. The gain is 3.84 dB at resonant frequency 13 GHz and 3.95 dB gain at 16.6 GHz. The arc shape of slot is improve the maximum of proposed antenna. The proposed antenna has improve the maximum gain, impedance bandwidth and reduce the cross polarization.

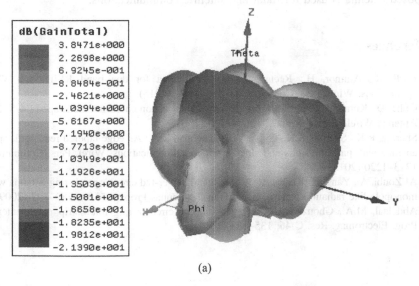

(a)

Fig. 8. The maximum gain at resonant frequencies (a) 13 GHz (b) 16.6 GHz.

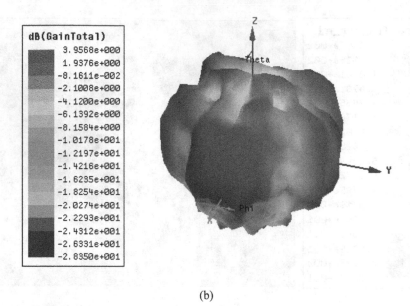

(b)

Fig. 8. (*continued*)

4   Conclusion

The concentric circular ring arc patch antenna designed for dual band and Ku band applications. The proposed antenna has operated at two resonant frequencies are 13 GHz, 16.6 GHz with maximum gain of 3.84 dB, 3.94 dB. The co polarization and cross polarization of E plane and H plane of proposed antenna is measured. The proposed antenna is used for radar and satellite communications.

References

1. Karli, R., Ammor, H.: Rectangular patch antenna for dual-band RFID and WLAN applications. Wirel. Pers. Commun. **83**, 995–1007 (2015)
2. Guha, D., Kumar, C., Pal, S.: Improved cross-polarization characteristic shaped DGS. IEEE Antenna Wirel. propag. Lett. **8**, 1367–1369 (2009)
3. Sharma, R.K., Sharma, S.K., Gupta, A., Chaudary, R.K.: An edge tapered rectangular patch antenna with parasitic stubs and slot for wideband applications. Wirel. Pers. Commun. **86**, 1213–1220 (2016)
4. Al-Zoubi, A., Yang, F., Kishk, A.: A broadband center-fed circular patch-ring antenna with a monopole like radiation pattern. IEEE Trans. Antennas Propag. **57**(3), 789–792 (2009)
5. Abdelaal, M.A., Ghouz, H.H.M.: New compact circular ring microstrip patch antennas. Prog. Electromag. Res. C **46**, 135–143 (2014)

6. Rahimi, M., Maleki, M., Soltani, M., Arezomand, A.S., Zarrabi, F.B.: Wide band SRR-inspried slot antenna with circular polarization for wireless application. Int. J. Electron. Commun. (AEU) **70**, 1199–1204 (2016)
7. Row, J.S.: Design of aperture-coupled annular-ring microstrip antennas for circular polarization. IEEE Trans. Antennas Propag. **53**(5), 1779–1784 (2005)
8. Zhang, J.L., Yang, X.Q.: Integrated compact circular polarization annular ring slot antenna design for RFID reader. Prog. Electromag. Res. Lett. **39**, 133–140 (2013)
9. Liang, Z., Liu, J., Li, Y., Long, Y.: Dual-frequency broadband design of coupled-fed stacked microstrip monopolar patch antenna. IEEE Antenna Wirel. Propag. Lett. **15**(15), 1289–1292 (2016)
10. Soodmand, S.: Circular formed dual-band dual-polarized patch antenna and method for designing compact combined feed networks. Int. J. Electron. Commun. (AEU) **65**, 453–457 (2011)
11. Liu, X., Liu, Y., Tentzeris, M.M.: Novel CP antenna with coin shaped patches and ring shaped strip. IEEE Antenna Wirel. Propag. Lett. **14**, 707–710 (2015)

Design of Spider Shaped Microstrip Patch Antenna for IoT Application

S. K. Vyshnavi Das and T. Shanmuganantham[✉]

Department of Electronics Engineering, Pondicherry Central University,
Pondicherry 605014, India
vyshnadassk@gmail.com, shanmugananthamster@gmail.com

Abstract. A Spider shaped microstrip patch antenna has been designed for IoT application. The evolution of the spider shape from a hexagonal structure microstrip patch antenna is analyzed here. The Defected Ground Structure (DGS) is introduced to enhance the bandwidth of the antenna. The simulated impedance bandwidth is found to be 280 MHz at every resonant band. The proposed multiband antenna has the resonant frequencies at 1.48 GHz, 2.5 GHz and 3.72 GHz with S_{11} = −31.14 dB, −11.7 dB, −16.1 dB respectively which found in the working ranges of GPS, Bluetooth and WiFi hence enables the IoT application.

Keywords: Spider shaped microstrip patch antenna · Hexagonal structure Defected ground structure (DGS) · IoT

1 Introduction

Recent research works are concentrating on incorporating more than one wireless technology due to the high demand for the virtual world. Now a day the concept of the communication between the physical world to the virtual world and vice versa is defined by the term Internet of Things (IoT). Internet of Things (IoT) is the combination of more than one technology which makes the virtual world in to reality [1]. The components of IoT are categorized as per intelligence, sensing and communication. It is a smart network interconnection of wireless sensor network, software and wireless communication network [2]. The wireless communication is enabled by antennas which could have multiband of resonant frequencies. The proposed antenna is a multiband antenna and which works in the frequency ranges of different wireless communication modules. Since IoT promotes only low data rates, so the bandwidth of the multiband antenna is restricted to the range which less than 1 GHz.

2 Antenna Design

The substrate of the proposed antenna is FR4 material of dielectric constant 4.4 and dimension 29 mm × 40 mm × 1.6 mm. The antenna is fed by microstrip line feed method of width of 4 mm. The principle of area equivalent is taken for the design of the Spider shaped antenna. The design of the resonant frequency depends on the surface area of the microstrip patch antenna. Since the antennas which have same resonant frequency will be having same equivalent area and vice versa.

Initially the rectangular microstrip patch antenna is designed for 3.6 GHz and the total surface area is calculated. Then the microstrip patch antenna of hexagonal shape of equivalent area that of rectangular patch is taken for analysis. The next step is to divide the area of the hexagonal microstrip patch in to different shapes which evolved in to the spider shape microstrip patch antenna. The design of these antennas is done by the aid of the following equations.

$$W = \frac{v_0}{2f_r}\sqrt{\frac{2}{\varepsilon_r + 1}} \tag{1}$$

$$\varepsilon_{reff} = \frac{\varepsilon_r + 1}{2} + \frac{\varepsilon_r - 1}{2}\left(\frac{1}{\sqrt{1 + \frac{12h}{W}}}\right) \tag{2}$$

$$\frac{\Delta L_{eff}}{h} = 0.412\frac{(\varepsilon_{reff} + 0.3)\left(\frac{W}{h} + 0.264\right)}{(\varepsilon_{reff} - 0.258)\left(\frac{W}{h} + 0.8\right)} \tag{3}$$

$$L = \frac{v_0}{2f_r\sqrt{\varepsilon_{reff}}} - 2\Delta L_{eff} \tag{4}$$

$$A_r^2 = \frac{3\sqrt{3}}{2}A_h^2 \tag{5}$$

$$A = \frac{3\sqrt{3}}{2}a_{1h}^2 + \frac{3\sqrt{3}}{2}a_{2h}^2 + 8a_{1r}^2 + 8a_{2r}^2 \tag{6}$$

W – width of the rectangular patch	V_o – the light velocity in free space
ε_r – dielectric constant of the medium	ε_{reff} – effective dielectric constant
h – thickness of the substrate	ΔL_{eff} – effective change in the length of the patch
L – Actual length of the patch	A_r – area of the rectangular patch
A_h= side length of hexagonal patch	A – The total area of the proposed antenna
a_{1h}, a_{2h} – the side length of the hexagons	a_{1r}, a_{2r} – the side length of the rectangles

The equations from (1)–(4) is used for the design of rectangular patch antenna. After calculating its width and length, we can find its area. This area made to equal with the hexagonal patch area (5) and finding its dimension. The total area of the hexagonal patch is divided into the sum of area of two hexagons and sixteen rectangles (6). Introducing different shapes in the geometry of the antenna alters the phase of the surface current flow and hence enables multi-band response [3, 4]. By introducing Defected area in the ground structure disturbs the surface wave distribution in the substrate material and which in turn enhances the bandwidth [5, 6]. As well as introducing slots and parasitic stubs in the surface geometry of the antenna results improved gain of the antenna [7]. The development of surface geometry of the proposed

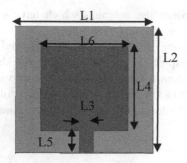

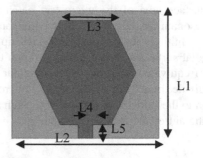

Fig. 1. Rectangular microstrip patch antenna   **Fig. 2.** Hexagonal microstrip patch antenna

microstrip patch antenna from the rectangular to the Spider shape is given in the following figures.

Initially rectangular microstrip patch antenna in Fig. 1 is selected for the development of the proposed antenna at 3.6 GHz and the surface area of the antenna is calculated. Using the area equivalent principle, the side length of the hexagonal microstrip patch antenna in Fig. 2 is designed (Tables 1 and 2).

Table 1. Dimension of the rectangular microstrip patch antenna (mm)

L1	L2	L3 (mm)	L4	L5	L6
40	29	4	19.4	5	25.35

Table 2. Dimension of the hexagonal antenna (mm)

L1	L2	L3	L4	L5
40	29	13.76	4	3

The total area of the hexagonal microstrip patch antenna is divided in to the sum of two hexagons and 16 rectangles area and the shape of spider shape is developed for the proposed microstrip patch antenna in Fig. 3. Making truncations in the effective area of the antenna changes the normal distribution of the surface current thus changes the phase of the current flow. The dependency of the resonant frequency to the phase of the current distribution enables multiband response of the antenna (Fig. 4 and Table 3).

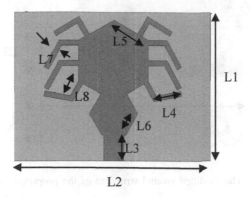

Fig. 3. Rectangular microstrip patch antenna

To improve gain and reflection coefficient of the developed antenna, introduced slots of hexagon and rectangle shapes in the surface of the microstrip patch antenna (Table 4).

Table 3. Dimension of the hexagonal antenna (mm)

L1	L2	L3	L4	L5	L6	L7	L8
29	40	5	6	8	4.79	1	4

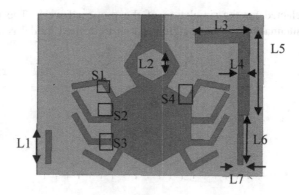

Fig. 4. The proposed antenna microstrip patch antenna

Table 4. Dimensions of proposed microstrip patch antenna (mm)

L1	6	L4	2	L7	1	S3	0.2 × 0.2
L2	3	L5	13	S1	0.3 × 0.3	S4	0.2 × 0.2
L3	10	L6	9	S2	0.2 × 0.2	-	-

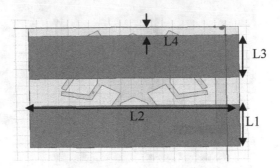

Fig. 5. The modified ground structure of the proposed antenna

The Defected Ground Structure (DGS) introduced in the proposed antenna, disturbs the distribution of the surface wave in the substrate of the antenna and which in turn enhances the bandwidth of the antenna (Fig. 5 and Table 5).

Table 5. Dimensions of the modified ground structure of the developed antenna (mm)

L1	L2	L3	L4
10	40	10.4	2

3 Simulation Results and Discussion

HFSS 15.0 is selected for the simulation of the proposed work. The gradual development of the antenna from the rectangular patch to desired model is analysed using this software.

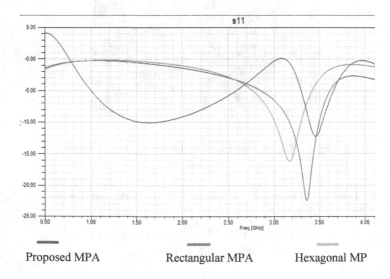

| Proposed MPA | Rectangular MPA | Hexagonal MP |

Fig. 6. S parameter of the developed antennas

The variation of the resonant frequencies in the different structure of the MPA is shown in the Fig. 6. Since the rectangular microstrip patch antenna gives the designed resonant frequency response. Coming to hexagonal shape resonant frequency variation starts and multi band response is achieved in the proposed antenna without modification in the developed structure (Fig. 7).

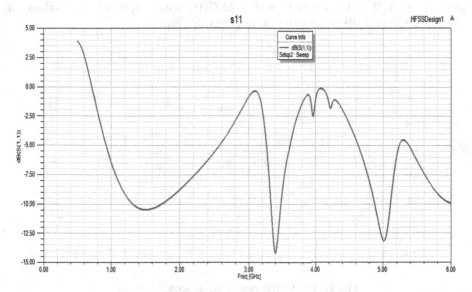

Fig. 7. S parameter of the proposed MPA without ground modification

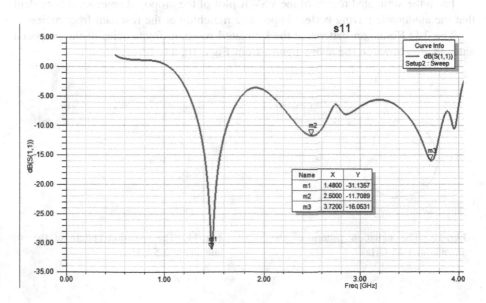

Fig. 8. S parameter of the developed antenna with DGS

After introducing slots and parasitic stubs in the surface geometry of the proposed antenna structure gives multiband response with better reflection coefficient is given in the Fig. 8.

Since the introduction of defected ground structure in the developed model of the antenna results better reflection coefficient as well as better gain of performance.

According to the simulation results, the proposed antenna is having resonant frequencies at 1.48 GHz, 2.5 GHz and 3.72 GHz with improved S_{11} values of -31.135 dB, -11.7 dB and -16.05 dB respectively (Fig. 9).

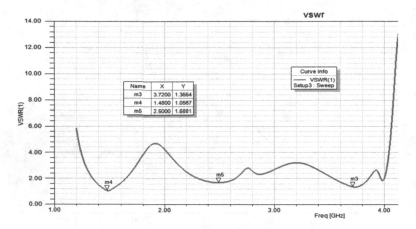

Fig. 9. The VSWR plot of the proposed antenna

From the simulated results of the VSWR plot of the proposed antenna, it is evident that the antenna is having perfect impedance matching at the resonant frequencies.

The 2-D Radiation patterns at the simulated resonant frequencies of the proposed antenna are shown in the above figures from Figs. 10, 11, 12.

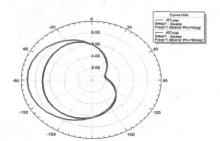

Fig. 10. The radiation pattern of the antenna at 1.48 GHz

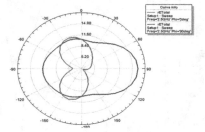

Fig. 11. The radiation pattern of the antenna at 2.5 GHz

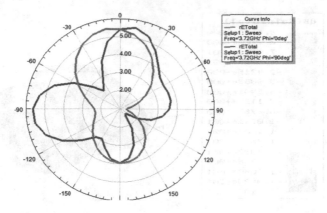

Fig. 12. The radiation pattern of the antenna at 3.72 GHz

The simulated gain of the proposed antenna in 3-D is given in the figures from Figs. 13, 14 and 15. According to these results of the proposed antenna, for every resonant frequency the antenna is having the gain of more than 2 dBi and it exhibits maximum gain of 6.337 dBi at 2.5 GHz (Table 6).

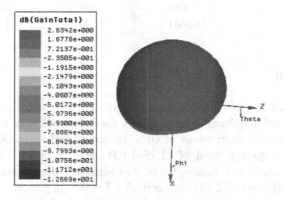

Fig. 13. The 3-D plot of the gain of the antenna at 1.48 GHz

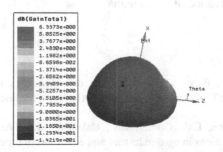

Fig. 14. The 3-D plot of the gain of the antenna at 2.5 GHz

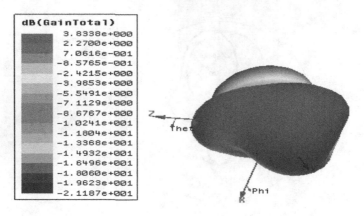

Fig. 15. The 3-D plot of the gain of the antenna at 3.72 GHz

Table 6. The overall performance of the antenna

No.	Resonant frequency (GHz)	Reflection coefficient (dB)	Bandwidth (MHz)	VSWR	Gain (dBi)
1	1.48	−31.1357	280	1.0587	2.6342
2	2.5	−11.7089	280	1.6881	6.3373
3	3.72	−16.0631	280	1.3654	3.8338

4   Conclusion

The Spider Shaped Microstrip Patch Antenna (SSMPA) is gradually developed in this work. The designed multiband antenna fulfills the requirements of Internet of Things which incorporates the applications of GPS, Bluetooth and WiMAX. The antenna is working in the frequency band of (1.35–1.63) GHz, (2.35–2.63) GHz and (3.55–3.83) GHz with impedance bandwidth of 280 MHz and the resonant frequencies at 1.48 GHz, 2.5 GHz and 3.72 GHz respectively. The design principle of the antenna is based on the dependency of frequency to the surface area of the antenna as well as the equal area concept. The Defected Ground Structure as well as parasitic patches enhances better performance of the antenna.

References

1. Cervanres-Solis, J.W., Baber, C.: Towards the definition of a modeling framework for meaningful Human-IoT interactions. In: British Human Computer Interaction Conference (2017)
2. Talaverra, J.M., Tobon, L.E., Gomez, J.A., Culaman, M.A., Aranda, J.M., Parra, D.T.: Review of IoT applications in agro-industrial and environmental fields. J. Comput. Electron. Agric. **142**, 283–297 (2017)

3. Elevarasi, C., Shanuganatham, T.: SRR loaded CPW-fed multiple band rose flower shaped fractal antenna. Microw. Opt. Technol. Lett. **59**(10), 2518–2525 (2017)
4. Elavarasi, C., Shanmuganantham, T.: CPW fed SGF TSRR antenna for multiband applications. Int. J. Microw. Wirel. Technol. **9**, 1–6 (2017)
5. Dileepan, D., Madhuri, V., Kumar, S.A., Shanmuganantham, T.: A high efficient Compact CPW fed hexagonal slot antenna for diversified applications. IEEE International Conference on Electromagnetic Interference and Compatibility (2016)
6. Kiruthika, R., Shanmuganantham, T., Gupta, R.K.: A fan shaped triple microstrip patch antenna with DGS for X-band application. In: Control, Instrumentation, Communication and Computational Technologies (ICCICCT) (2016)
7. Dileepan, D., Madhuri, V., Kumar, S.A., Shanmuganantham, T.: A high efficient compact CPW fed hexagonal slot antenna for diversified applications. In: IEEE International Conference on Electromagnetic Interference and Compatibility (INCEMIC) (2016)

Design of Microstrip Polygon Shaped Patch Antenna for IoT Applications

S. K. Vyshnavi Das and T. Shanmuganantham[✉]

Department of Electronics Engineering, Pondicherry Central University,
Pondicherry 605014, India
vyshnadassk@gmail.com, shanmugananthamster@gmail.com

Abstract. A Microstrip polygon shaped patch antenna is proposed in this work for Internet of Things (IoT) application. The antenna has multiband response at 2.39 GHz, 4.39 GHz, 5.8 GHz and 6.56 GHz with bandwidth of 230 MHz, 380 MHz, 390 MHz and 350 MHz respectively. The partial ground structure is developed for bandwidth enhancement of the proposed model. The FR4 material is selected as the substrate of the antenna. The antenna operates over the frequency ranges of Bluetooth and WiFi as well as RF Devices and Radio Location applications.

Keywords: Microstrip polygon shaped patch antenna · Partial ground structure
Bluetooth · WiFi · RF devices · Radio location · Internet of Things (IoT)

1 Introduction

Internet of Things (IoT) is an emerging sprawling set of technology. The working frame of IoT consists of network connected devices which is embedded in the physical environment. The advantage of IoT simply improves some existing process or enables new scenario which was not previously reliable. The sensors, actuators and software together bring the IoT in to reality. Each component which can be accessed through IoT is identified by a unique IP address [1, 2]. The interconnection between the devices to the host and vice versa is done by various wireless communication modules like WiFi, WiMax, Bluetooth etc.

For a smart scenario, the combination of more than one wireless communication technology is required. So the antenna that used for IoT applications should be a multiband antenna and the resonant frequencies should be in the ranges of prerequisite frequency bands. The IoT module prefers the compact size for the components, so that the power consumption and memory of the devices should be reduced [3, 4]. As well as the low rate of data transfer is currently possible through this virtual communication. Hence the antennas that required having the limits of bandwidth less than 1 GHz. Thus the requirements of the antenna that using in IoT technology is should have multiband response and bandwidth less than 1 GHz.

© Springer Nature Singapore Pte Ltd. 2019
S. Verma et al. (Eds.): CNC 2018, CCIS 839, pp. 538–547, 2019.
https://doi.org/10.1007/978-981-13-2372-0_48

2 Antenna Design

The designed antenna should be fabricated on a grounded substrate of FR4 material, which has the dielectric constant of 4.4. The Microstrip line feeding mechanism is selected for the feeding of the antenna. The analysis of the antenna for the prerequisite resonant frequencies is gradually emerged from the simple circular shaped Microstrip patch antenna (CSMPA). The calculation of the dimensions of the CSMPA is done by using the following equations.

$$F = \frac{8.791 \times 10^9}{f_r \sqrt{\varepsilon_r}} \tag{1}$$

$$a = \frac{F}{\left\{ 1 + \frac{2h}{\pi F \varepsilon_r} \left(ln\left(\frac{\pi F}{2h}\right) + 1.7726 \right) \right\}^{0.5}} \tag{2}$$

$$a_e = a \left\{ 1 + \frac{2h}{\pi \varepsilon_r a} \left[ln\left(\frac{\pi a}{2h}\right) + 1.7726 \right] \right\}^{0.5} \tag{3}$$

$$\varepsilon_{reff} = \frac{1}{2}(\varepsilon_r + 1) + \frac{1}{4}\left(\frac{\varepsilon_r - 1}{\sqrt{1 + \frac{12h}{a}}} \right) \tag{4}$$

The parameter f_r is the resonant frequency, ε_r is the dielectric constant, h is the substrate height and a is the radius of the CSMPA. ε_{reff} is the effective dielectric constant and a_e is the effective radius of the CSMPA [5]. Since the surface area of microstrip patch antenna is inversely proportional to the resonant frequency. Thus for a defined area, there should be a fixed resonant frequency. So for a particular resonant frequency response can be obtained by changing the planar geometrical shapes of the antenna which shares same equivalent surface area. A Hexagonal shaped Microstrip patch antenna (HSMPA) is evolved from the CSMPA by this equal area concept.

$$\pi a_e^2 = \frac{3\sqrt{3}}{2} a_h^2 \tag{5}$$

Where a_h is the side length of the HSMPA. Then the proposed polygonal shape is introduced as the combinations of six rectangles with a single hexagon. The area of the HSMPA is made to the equivalent of sum of area of six rectangles and the area of single hexagon.

$$A_H = A_h + A_r \tag{6}$$

A_H is the area of HSMPA and A_h and A_r are the area of single hexagon and six rectangles respectively in the proposed structure. The evolution of the proposed Microstrip polygonal shaped patch antenna from the CSMPA is given in the following figures.

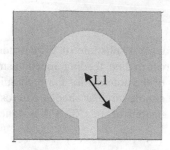

Fig. 1. The circular shaped microstrip patch antenna with L1 = 15.94 mm

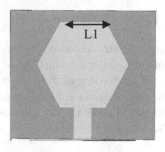

Fig. 2. The hexagonal shaped MPA with L1 = 17.5 mm

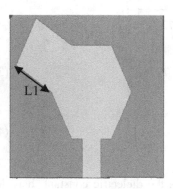

Fig. 3. The derived geometry of the MPA with L1 = 14.9 mm

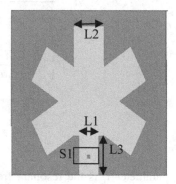

Fig. 4. The proposed antenna structure

The substrate dimension of the Microstrip patch antenna is 45 mm × 55 mm 1.6 mm. The Figs. 1, 2, 3 and 4 gives the gradual development of the proposed antenna for same equivalent area. Figure 1 represents CSMPA is considered the basic antenna structure for the evolved antenna. The HSMPA in the Fig. 2 has the same equivalent surface area of CSMPA. The prior stage of the proposed antenna structure is given in Fig. 3 and the proposed antenna with slotted structure for gain enhancement [6, 7] is shown in Fig. 4 (Table 1).

Table 1. Dimensions of the proposed antenna (mm)

L1	L2	L3	S1
7	11	10.8	1 × 1

The modified ground structure is also introduced in the proposed antenna which is shown in the following figure (Fig. 5).

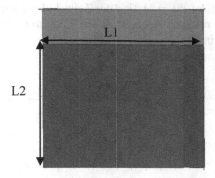

Fig. 5. The partial ground structure of the proposed antenna With L1 = 55 mm and L2 = 35

The partial ground structure in the proposed antenna gives improved impedance bandwidth as well as reflection coefficient due to the disturbance in the distribution of surface waves in the substrate of the antenna.

3 Simulation Results and Discussion

The simulated results of the each stages of the antenna is discussing here. The change in the resonant frequencies and the reflection coefficient of each stage of the antenna is shown in the given figure (Fig. 6).

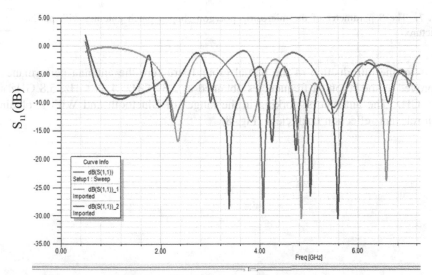

— The proposed antenna without ground modification
— The derived structure of the MPA
— The hexagonal MPA

Fig. 6. The S parameter of the antenna

The simulated results of the reflection coefficient of the each stage of the antenna gives the changes in the resonant frequencies according to the geometry. The tuning of the resonant frequency in to the prerequisite frequencies is done by the each evolvement stage of the proposed antenna (Fig. 7).

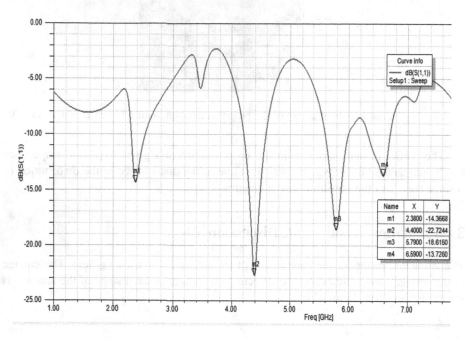

Fig. 7. The S parameter of the microstrip polygon shaped patch antenna with partial ground structure.

After the introduction of the partial ground structure the antenna performance is improved as the resonant frequencies obtained at 2.39 GHz, 4.39 GHz, 5.8 GHz and 6.56 GHz. The antenna is working in the ranges of Bluetooth and WiFi is obtained with relevant reflection coefficient (Fig. 8).

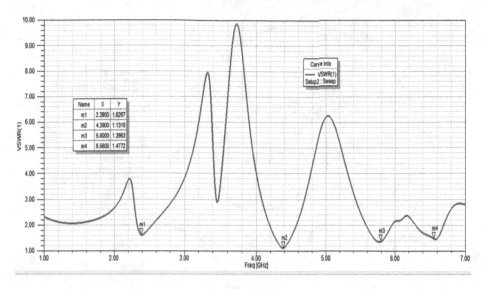

Fig. 8. The VSWR plot of the proposed antenna

The VSWR values of the respective resonant frequencies are simulated as less than 2 which indicate that perfect impedance matching at the simulated resonant frequencies.

The 2-D radiation pattern of the antenna is simulated with the values of azimuthal angle (phi) at zero and 90° respectively is given in Figs. 9 and 10.

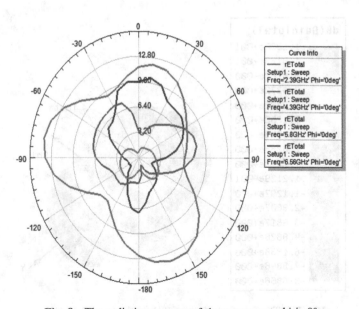

Fig. 9. The radiation pattern of the antenna at phi is 0°

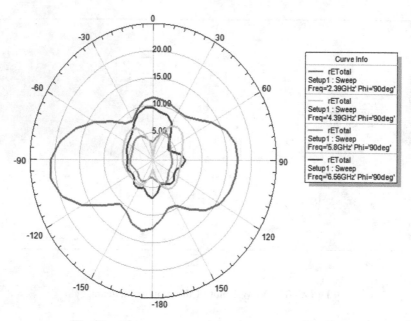

Fig. 10. The radiation pattern of the antenna phi is 90°

The simulated gain result of the proposed antenna at each resonant frequency is given in the figures from Figs. 11, 12, 13 and 14. These results show that the maximum gain of the antenna is obtained 11.3 dBi at 2.39 GHz.

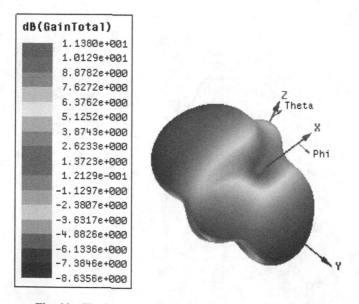

Fig. 11. The 3-D plot of gain of the antenna at 2.39 GHz

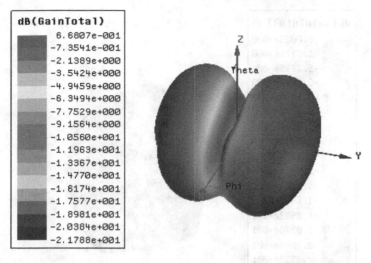

Fig. 12. The 3-D plot of gain of the antenna at 4.39 GHz

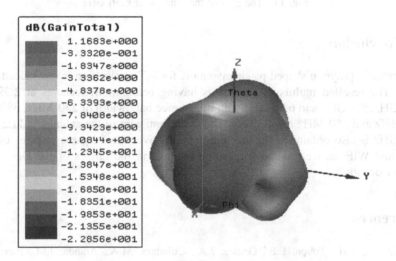

Fig. 13. Gain of the antenna at 5.8 GHz

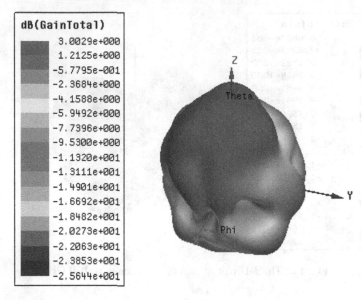

Fig. 14. The gain of the antenna at 6.56 GHz

4 Conclusion

A Microstrip polygon shaped patch antenna is for IoT application is introduced in this work. The resulted multiband antenna is having resonant frequencies at 2.39 GHz, 4.39 GHz, 5.8 GHz and 6.56 GHz with impedance bandwidth of 230 MHz, 380 MHz, 390 MHz and 350 MHz respectively. The maximum gain of the antenna is 11.3 dBi at 2.39 GHz is also obtained. The antenna operates over the frequency ranges of Bluetooth and WiFi as well as the application extends in the ranges of RF Devices and Radio Location.

References

1. Talaverra, J.M., Tobon, L.E., Gomez, J.A., Culaman, M.A., Aranda, J.M., Parra, D.T.: Review of IoT applications in agro- industrial and environmental fields. J. Comput. Electron. Agric. **142**, 283–297 (2017)
2. Katoch, S., Jotwani, H., Pani, S., Rajawat, A.: A compact dual band antenna for IoT applications. In: International Conference on Green Computing and Internet of Things (ICGCIoT) (2015)
3. Vikram, N., Kashwan, K.R.: Design of ISM band RFID reader antenna for IoT applications. In: IEEE International Conference on Wireless Communication, Signal Processing and Networks (2016)
4. Cervanres-Solis, J.W., Baber, C.: Towards the definition of a modeling framework for meaningful Human-IoT interactions. In: British Human Computer Interaction Conference, (2017)

5. Kiruthika, R., Shanmuganantham, T., Gupta, R.K.: A fan shaped triple microstrip patch antenna with DGS for X-band application. In: Control, Instrumentation, Communication and Computational Technologies (ICCICCT) (2016)
6. Elavarasi, C., Shanmuganantham, T.: CPW fed SGF TSRR antenna for multiband application. Int. J. Microw. Wirel. Technol. **9**, 1–6 (2017)
7. Dileepan, D., Madhuri, V., Kumar, S.A., Shanmuganantham, T.: A high efficient compact CPW fed hexagonal slot antenna for diversified applications. In: IEEE International Conference on Electromagnetic Interference and Compatibility (2016)

A Novel Microstrip Patch Antenna with Single Elliptical CSRR for Multiband Applications

V. Priyanka, T. Shanmuganantham[✉], and Daisy Sharma

Department of Electronics Engineering, Pondicherry Central University,
Pondicherry 605008, India
mtechpu23@gmail.com, shanmuga.dee@pondiuni.edu.in,
daisy28nov@gmail.com

Abstract. An Elliptical CSRR patch antenna has been proposed. Analysis for this antenna has been carried out in each stage of the antenna design. The U-Shaped patch along with two circular rings on the patch resulted in Quad-Band resonance. The analysis result proved that replacing the two elliptical rings by a single ring elliptical CSRR in ground plane resulted in a multiband resonance at 1.4 GHz, 3.2 GHz, 3.9 GHz, 5 GHz, 7.1 GHz, 8.6 GHz, 11.1 GHz, 12.9 GHz, 14.7 GHz which are used as an application for WiMax, WLAN, RFID, earth exploration satellites, microwave communication and space research.

Keywords: Elliptical · CSRR · U-Shaped · Multiband · Microwave
Space research

1 Introduction

The microstrip patch antennas are the customarily used antennas due to their Eloquent features such as reduced size, cheaper cost, enhanced gain and better radiating features [1, 2]. One of the salient features of these antennas is their multiband operation along with compatible design [3–5]. These antennas are used in various applications like passive earth exploration satellites, reduced range wireless devices, aeronautical radionavigation, fixed microwave communication [6, 7]. The Proposed elliptical metamaterial based Complementary Split Ring Resonator (CSRR) antenna is a multiband antenna capable of producing nine bands of resonance covering almost all the devices in wireless application, as well as satellite and radar communication.

2 Antenna Design

The proposed antenna is a 30 mm × 40 mm antenna with a Microstrip feed line width of 3 mm. The customarily used FR4 substrate with an increased thickness of 3.2 mm is employed. A pair of Elliptical CSRR rings are introduced in the ground plane to widen the narrowband. The U-Shaped patch produced a single band resonance (Figs. 1, 2 and Tables 1, 2).

© Springer Nature Singapore Pte Ltd. 2019
S. Verma et al. (Eds.): CNC 2018, CCIS 839, pp. 548–556, 2019.
https://doi.org/10.1007/978-981-13-2372-0_49

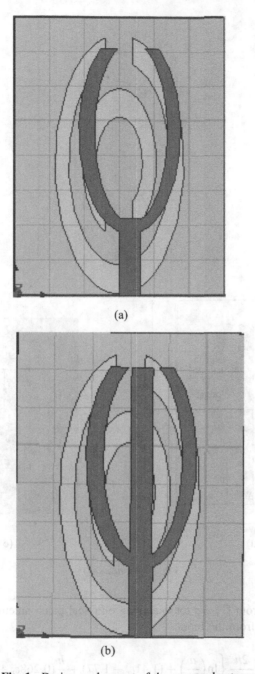

(a)

(b)

Fig. 1. Design evolvement of the proposed antenna

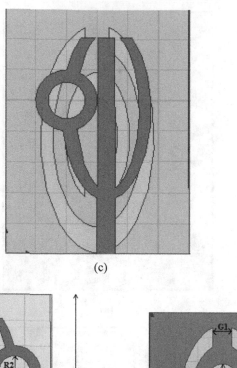

(c)

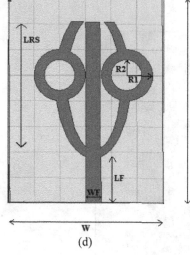

(d)

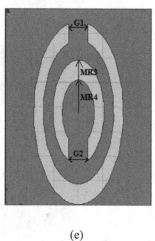

(e)

Fig. 1. (*continued*)

The equations from [7] are for analyzing elliptical patch antenna to find resonant frequencies (fe, fo) from the input:

$$a_{eff} = a\left[1 + \frac{2h}{\pi\varepsilon_r a}\left\{\ln\left(\frac{a}{2h}\right) + (1.41\varepsilon_r + 1.77) + \frac{h}{a}(0.268\varepsilon_r + 1.65)\right\}\right]^{1/2} \quad (1)$$

$$q_{11}^e = -0.0049e + 3.7888e^2 - 0.727e^3 + 2.314e^4 \quad (2)$$

$$q_{11}^0 = -0.0063e + 3.8316e^2 - 1.1351e^3 + 5.2229e^4$$

$$f_{11}^{e,0} = \frac{15}{\pi e a_{eff}} \sqrt{\frac{q_{11}^{e,0}}{\varepsilon_r}} \tag{3}$$

Where,

a-semi-major axis
h-height of dielectric substrate
ε_r-Permittivity of dielectric substrate
a_{eff}-effective semi-major axis
e-eccentricity of elliptical patch
$f_{11}^{e,0}$-dual-resonance frequency
$q_{11}^{e,0}$-approximated Mathieu function of the dominant $TM_{11}^{e,0}$ mode

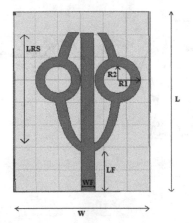
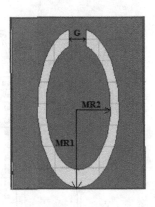

Fig. 2. Patch and ground design of single elliptical CSRR antenna

Table 1. Dimensions of antenna (mm)

L	W	LF	WF	LRS	R1	R2
40	30	9	3	24.5	5	3

Table 2. Dimensions of CSRR (mm)

MR1	MR2	MR3	MR4	G/G1	G2
9.3	7.3	5.3	3.3	4	4

Further by adding the rectangular string to this U-Patch a dual band was produced. The feeding to this antenna is given uniformly at the centre of the patch. While the metamaterial is introduced beneath the substrate to widen the narrowband. The metamaterial employed is a pair of Elliptical rings and the inner ring is spaced 4 mm away from the outer ring. Now by using a rectangular strip at centre of the U-Patch along with two circular rings on it and removing a CSRR from it produced multiband resonance.

3   Simulation Results and Discussion

A stage by stage analysis for the Elliptical CSRR antenna is performed and as in the above figure the design A is a U-Shaped patch with a pair Elliptical CSRR in the ground plane which resulted in a single resonance at 9.2 GHz (Fig. 3).

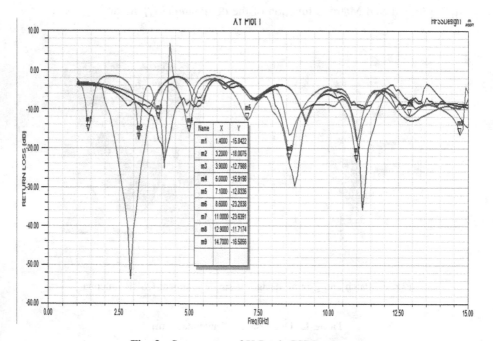

Fig. 3. S parameter of U-Patch CSRR antenna

In the design B, a rectangular strip added to the patch was responsible for the resonance at 2.9 GHz, so it produced a dual band resonance.

In the design C, a single circular ring was introduced in the U-Patch, which resulted in a triple band resonance at 4.1 GHz, 8.8 GHz, 11.2 GHz. In the design D, another circular ring added produced a Quadband resonance.

In the proposed design, the two elliptical CSRR rings were replaced by a single larger Elliptical ring which improved the band performance to nine resonance bands at 1.4 GHz, 3.2 GHz, 3.9 GHz, 5 GHz, 7.1 GHz, 8.6 GHz, 11.1 GHz, 12.9 GHz, 14.7 GHz.

The VSWR of the proposed antenna is minimum at the resonant frequencies, indicating perfect impedance matching of the antenna (Fig. 4).

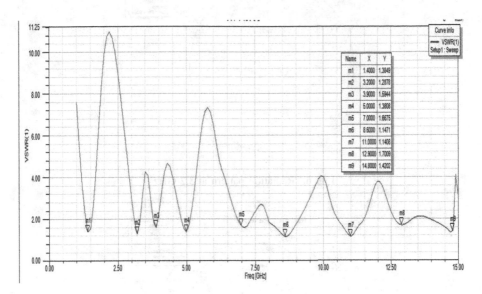

Fig. 4. VSWR graph of proposed single elliptical CSRR U-Patch antenna

The radiation pattern of the antenna was observed at the resonant frequencies in which it exhibited a bidirectional radiation pattern at the lower frequencies, and has the frequency increased its bidirectional pattern was changed (Figs. 5, 6, 7, 8, 9, 10, 11, 12, 13 and 14).

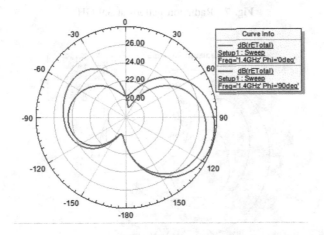

Fig. 5. Radiation pattern at 1.4 GHz

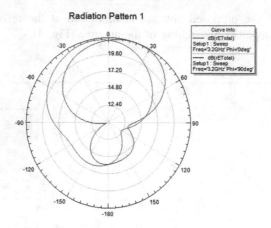

Fig. 6. Radiation pattern at 3.2 GHz

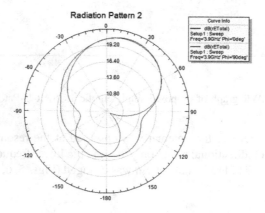

Fig. 7. Radiation pattern at 3.9 GHz

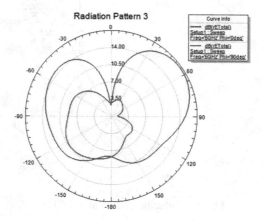

Fig. 8. Radiation pattern at 5 GHz

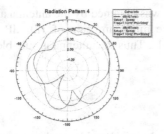

Fig. 9. Radiation pattern at 7.1 GHz

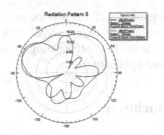

Fig. 10. Radiation pattern at 8.6 GHz

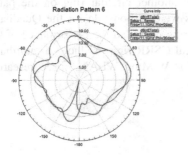

Fig. 11. Radiation pattern at 11.1 GHz

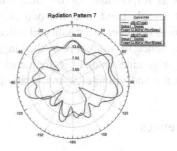

Fig. 12. Radiation pattern at 12.9 GHz

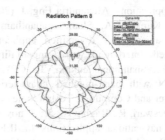

Fig. 13. Radiation pattern at 14.7 GHz

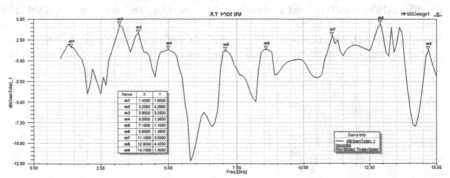

Fig. 14. Gain vs frequency graph of proposed single elliptical CSRR U-Patch antenna

The gain of 4.25 dB was the maximum gain that was obtained by the antenna at the higher resonating frequency of 12.9 GHz while the minimum gain of 1.02 dB was obtained at the lower resonating frequency at 1.4 GHz. Thus the antenna is suitable for multiband applications.

4 Conclusion

The elliptical U-Shaped CSRR antenna was initially designed and by making stage by stage analysis of the antenna certain conclusions were made such as the U-Shaped patch produced a single band resonance and the rectangular strip added at centre of the patch was responsible for the dual band further another circular ring on the patch created a triple band, thus the two circular rings were responsible for the Quadband resonance, however the smaller Elliptical CSRR ring degraded the performance of the antenna hence by removing it, the single Elliptical CSRR ring produced a multiband profile with nine resonating frequencies ideal for WiMax, WLAN, space research, microwave and satellite communication.

References

1. Vinodha, E., Raghavan, S.: Double stub microstrip fed two element rectangular dielectric resonator antenna for multiband operation. Int. J. Electron. Commun. **78**, 46–53 (2017)
2. Kumar, S.A., Raj, M.A., Shanmuganantham, T.: Analysis and design of CPW fed antenna at ISM band for biomedical applications. Alexandria Eng. J. (2017, in Press)
3. Dileepan, D., Madhuri, V., Kumar, S.A., Shanmuganantham, T.: A high efficient compact CPW fed hexagonal slot antenna for diversified applications. In: IEEE International Conference on Electromagnetic Interference and Compatibility (2016)
4. Thakur, R.K., Pandey, R.K., Shanmuganantham, T.: CPW-fed bull head shaped UWB antenna for Wimax/WLAN with band-notched characteristics. In: IEEE International Conference on Circuit, Power and Computing Technologies (2016)
5. Jha, N., Tirkey, S.R., Pandeeswari, R., Raghavan, S.: A novel patch antenna with C shaped slots for GSM, WiMax and navigational applications. In: IEEE International Conference on Wireless Communications, Signal Processing and Networking, pp. 1585–1589 (2016)
6. Rajeshkumar, V., Raghavan, S.: SRR-based polygon ring penta-band fractal antenna for GSM/WLAN/WiMax/ITU band applications. Microw. Opt. Technol. Lett. **57**, 1301–1305 (2015)
7. Josan, S.K., Sohal, J.S., Dhaliwal, B.S.: Design of elliptical microstrip patch antenna using genetic algorithm. In: IEEE International Conference on Communication Systems (2012)

Analysis of Circular Ring Patch Antenna for Enhancement of Wide Bandwidth with Defected Ground Structure

T. Srinivasa Reddy[✉], Ashok Kumar Balijepalli, P. Koteswara Rao,
and S. K. Nannu Saheb

Department of Electronics and Communication Engineering,
Universal College of Engineering and Technology, Guntur, India
srinivasareddy.reddy5l@gmail.com

Abstract. The circular ring antenna patch with defected ground structure for triple band applications. The concentric circular rings introduced to improve the impedance bandwidth, high gain. The proposed antenna operate at three different frequencies are 8.3 GHz, 11.8 GHz and 14.5 GHz with 10 dB return losses are −24.48 dB, −35.50 dB and −21.90 dB. The co polarization and cross polarization (XP) are observed and XP are found at is 0^0, −15 dB (co pol) and −33 dB (cross pol) at 8.3 GHz. The radiation patterns are observed at is 0^0 and is 90^0 in xz and yz plane for three resonance bands. The co and cross polarization has presented and cross polarization is found below 20 dB at one plane of each angle and operating frequency. The simulation results measured results have good agreement.

Keywords: Defected ground structure · Circular ring patch antenna
Slots in ground plane

1 Introduction

The microstrip patch antennas (MSPA) is a essential device in the modern communication and radar systems. The provocative characteristics of MSPA are low cost, easy to design and conformability of the object. However the multi-band antennas has widely used in wireless and satellite communications.

A center fed circular ring patch with annular ring introduced for monopole radiation pattern, gain of 5.7 dB at resonant frequency 5.8 GHz [1]. Coupled-fed stacked microstrip monopolar patch antenna for monopole like radiation pattern are obtained in the dual bands (2.28–2.55 GHz, 5.15–5.9 GHz) for wireless local area network (WLAN) applications [2]. Soheyl Soodmand [3] proposed breach coupled circular ring patch with four port dual band dual polarized for global system for mobile communication (GSM) and distributed control system (DCS) applications. Compact circular ring patch antenna for dual and triple band antennas resonate at fourth generation (4G) band [4]. The two appended coin shaped patches with ring shaped feed strip for Ultrahigh frequency (UHF) radio frequency identification (RFID) applications [5]. [6–11] the different shape of defected ground structures (DGS) at ground plane to improve the

© Springer Nature Singapore Pte Ltd. 2019
S. Verma et al. (Eds.): CNC 2018, CCIS 839, pp. 557–567, 2019.
https://doi.org/10.1007/978-981-13-2372-0_50

impedance bandwidth, integration of microstrip lines and reduce the cross polarization. Liu proposed the planar monopole antenna with inverted L shaped DGS for wireless local area networks (WLAN) 2.4/5.2/5.8 GHz, WiMAX 3.5/5.5 GHz applications [6]. The spiral shape of the defected ground structure for dual polarized isolation, high input impedance 75 Ω, 150 Ω, and 100 Ω effectively [7], the monopole antenna with double U shaped DGS for improve impedance bandwidth of 112.4% over the traditional design [8]. The arc shape of DGS [9] and rectangular patch of asymmetric DGS [10] for reduce the cross polarization. The Zig Zag shaped rectangular patch with circular DGS for 2.45/5.28-GHz WLAN bands and the 3.5-GHz WiMAX and resonate at three resonant frequencies with gain of 4–6 dB [11]. Liu et al. [11] has reported tri-band monopole antenna with protrudent strips cross-shaped DGS for operate at UWB, WiMAX, WLAN and using for low pass filters [12–14].

In the view of that the ring antennas has been proposed to operate with high gain. But the ring patch has cross polarization problem. So, to improve that two concentric rings has been consider in this proposed design. The proposed concentric circular patch antenna with geometric series DGS has operated with triple bands are 8.3 GHz, 11.8 GHz and 14.5 GHz with return loss of −24.48 dB, −35.50 dB, −21.90 dB at three resonant frequencies. This triple bands are very much useful at WLAN, WiMAX applications to protect the cross polarization.

2 Antenna Design

Figure 1 shows the proposed concentric circular patch with geometric series factor DGS. The substrate dimensions has consider length (L_1) and width (W_1) are 30×30 mm^2 shown in Fig. 1. The substrate dielectric constant Fr4 epoxy ($\varepsilon_r = 4.4$) with thickness is 1.6 mm. The top layer of substrate is patch and ground patch with geometric series defected ground structure.

The concentric circles are patch with outer circle and inner circle of radius (R_1) 10 mm, radius (R_2) 5 mm, radius (R_3) 1.6 mm, radius (R_4) 1.6 mm, width of the ring. The input impedance of feed line is 50 ohms and length (L_2) and width (W_2) of feed line is 5×2 mm^2. The ground patch has equally subdivided into three parts with length (L_3) 9.993 mm, width (W_3) 9.993 mm is shown in Fig. 1(b), again second part and third part equally subdivided into three parts with length (L_4) and width (W_4) are 3.324×3.324 mm^2. To improve bandwidth, reduce size of antenna, again the third part is equally subdivided into three part with length (L_5) 1.101 mm and width (W_5) 1.101 mm shown in Fig. 1(b) for equally subdivided the ground plane. The with DGS and Without DGS are shown in Fig. 2.

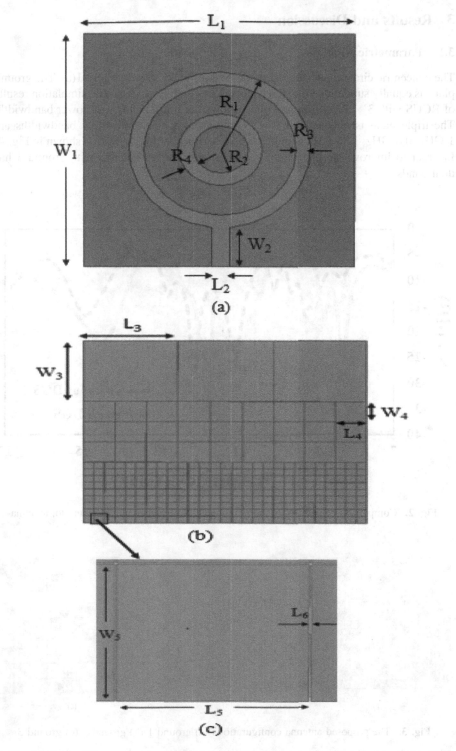

Fig. 1. (a) Patch of the concentric circular ring (b) Ground patch of geometric series factor DGS

3   Results and Discussion

3.1   Parametric Analysis

The concentric circles patch with geometric series DGS shown in Fig. 1(a). The ground plane is equally subdivided into three parts is shown in Fig. 3(a). The simulation results of RCUS with 3 × 3 cells ground plane shows the multi bands with lower bandwidth. The triple band is obtained for 9 × 9 cells ground plane and triple bandwidths are 1 GHz, 0.6 GHz, 1.86 GHz with lower gain at resonant frequencies is shown in Fig. 4. In order to improve the bandwidth and gain of proposed antenna with ground 3 has dual bands.

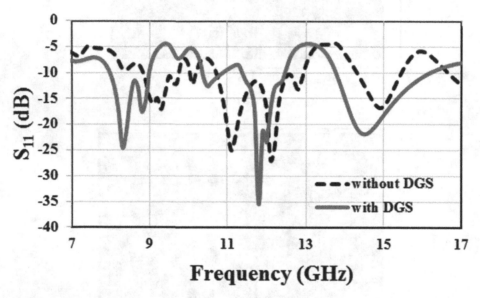

Fig. 2. Comparison of with DGS and without DGS of rectangular circular slot antenna

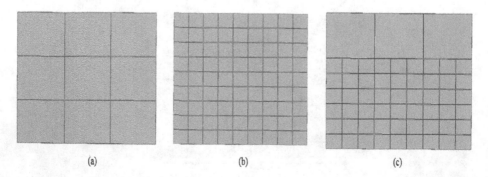

Fig. 3. The proposed antenna configurations (a) ground 1 (b) ground 2 (c) ground 3

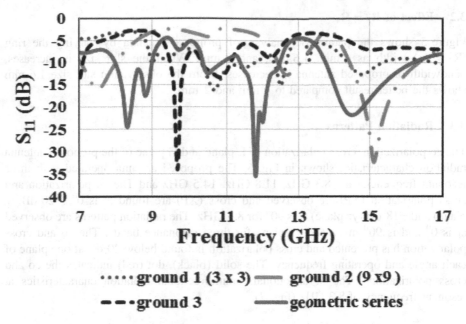

Fig. 4. Return loss of proposed antenna for different ground planes.

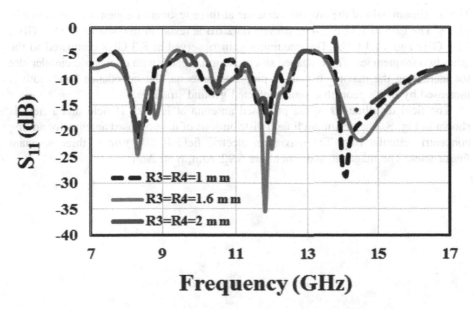

Fig. 5. Parametric analysis of proposed antenna by varying $R_3 = R_4$

3.2   Effect of $R_3 = R_4$

Figure 5 shows the parametric analysis of proposed antenna by varying the ring $(R_3 = R_4)$ width as 1 mm, 1.6 mm, and 2 mm. When the slot size is increases, bandwidth of proposed antenna is decreases. From the observation slot size 1.6 mm shows the better result compared to 1 mm and 2 mm.

3.3   Radiation Patterns

The co polarization, cross polarization of E plane and H plane of the proposed antenna radiation characteristics shown in Fig. 6. The proposed antenna operated with three resonant frequencies are 8.3 GHz, 11.8 GHz, 14.5 GHz and The co polarization and cross polarization (XP) are observed and cross (XP) are found at is 0^0, -20 dB(xz plane) and -18 dB (yz plane) at is 90^0 for 8.3 GHz. The radiation patterns are observed at is 0^0 and is 90^0 in xz and yz plane for three resonance bands. The co and cross polarization has presented and cross polarization is found below 20 dB at one plane of each angle and operating frequency. The solid (black), dot (red) indicates the co and cross polarizations. The bi directional, omnidirectional radiation characteristics at resonant frequency of 8.3 GHz (Fig. 7).

3.4   Field Distributions and Maximum Gain of Proposed Antenna

The maximum gain of the proposed antenna at three resonant frequencies are shown in Fig. 8. The gain of 7.42 dB, 4.92 dB and 6.42 dB at resonant frequencies are 8.3 GHz, 11.8 GHz and 14.3 GHz. The maximum gain observed at 8.3 GHz compared to the other two frequencies. The U shaped slot rectangular patch with concentric circular slot for increasing the maximum gain of proposed antenna, the impedance bandwidth is increased by using geometric series defected ground structure.

The field distributions of the proposed antenna at E field, H field and J field is shown in Fig. 8. The maximum E field distributions of the proposed antenna for adding concentric circular ring. The maximum electric field is 206 V/m at three resonant frequencies. The magnetic and J field are 6.92 A/m, 6.60 A/m.

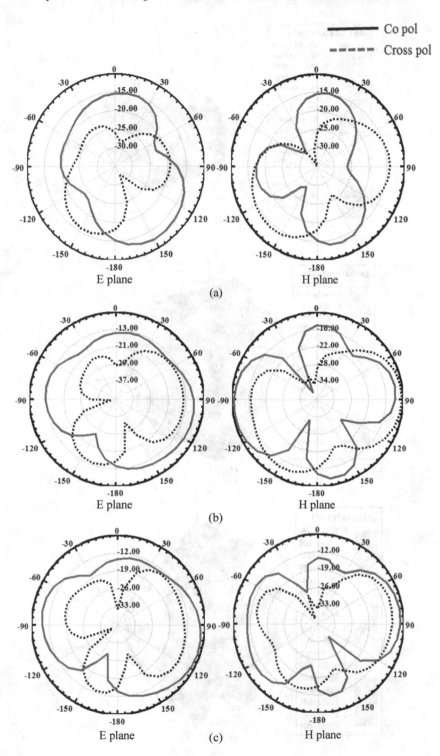

Fig. 6. The co polarization and cross polarization of E plane and H plane (a) 8.3 GHz (b) 11.8 GHz, (c) 14.5 GHz. (Color figure online)

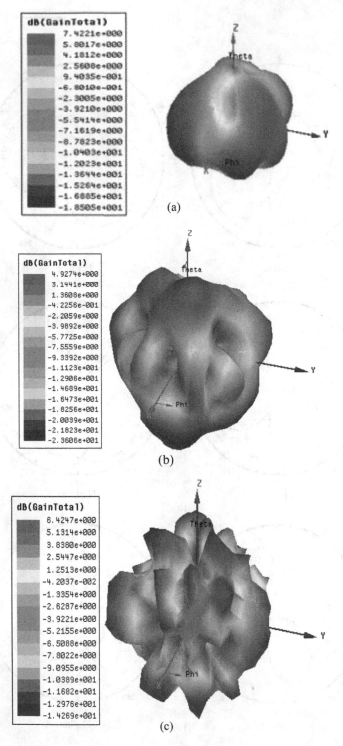

Fig. 7. The maximum gain at three resonant frequencies (a) 8.3 GHz (b) 11.8 GHz (c) 14.5 GHz

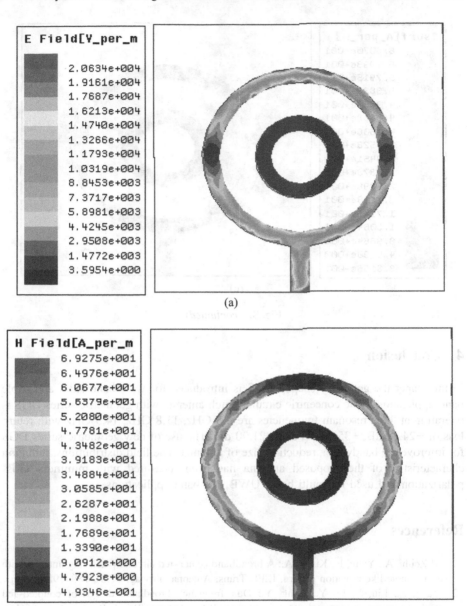

E Field[V_per_m

    2.0634e+004
    1.9161e+004
    1.7687e+004
    1.6213e+004
    1.4740e+004
    1.3266e+004
    1.1793e+004
    1.0319e+004
    8.8453e+003
    7.3717e+003
    5.8981e+003
    4.4245e+003
    2.9508e+003
    1.4772e+003
    3.5954e+000

(a)

H Field[A_per_m
    6.9275e+001
    6.4976e+001
    6.0677e+001
    5.6379e+001
    5.2080e+001
    4.7781e+001
    4.3482e+001
    3.9183e+001
    3.4884e+001
    3.0585e+001
    2.6287e+001
    2.1988e+001
    1.7689e+001
    1.3390e+001
    9.0912e+000
    4.7923e+000
    4.9346e-001

(b)

Fig. 8. The field distribution of star polygon antenna at (a) E field, (b) H field, (c) J field.

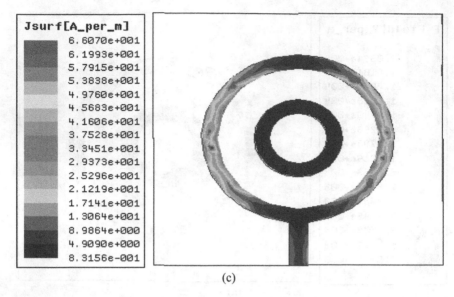

(c)

Fig. 8. (*continued*)

4 Conclusion

In this paper the geometry shaped DGS is introduced for wide bandwidth and triple band applications. The concentric circular patch antenna with geometric series DGS is operating at three resonant frequencies are 8.3 GHz, 11.8 GHz, 14.5 GHz with return loss of −24.48 dB, −35.50 dB and −21.90 dB. The use of new geometric series DGS for improve the bandwidth, reduction size of antenna. The field distributions, radiation characteristics of the proposed antenna has been measured with minimum cross polarization and used for multi band, UWB, Ku band applications.

References

1. Al-Zoubi, A., Yang, F., Kishk, A.: A broadband center–fed circular patch ring antenna with a monopole like radiation pattern. IEEE Trans. Antennas Propag. **57**(3), 789–792 (2009)
2. Liang, Z., Liu, J., Li, Y., Long, Y.: Dual-frequency broadband design of coupled–fed stacked microstrip monopolar patch antenna. IEEE Antenna Wirel. Propag. Lett. **15**(15), 1289–1292 (2016)
3. Soodmand, S.: Circular formed dual-band dual-polarized patch antenna and method for designing compact combined feed networks. Int. J. Electron. Commun. (AEU) **65**, 453–457 (2011)
4. Abdelaal, M.A., Ghouz, H.H.M.: New compact circular ring microstrip patch antenna. Progress Electromagnet. Res. C **46**, 135–143 (2014)
5. Liu, W.-C., Wu, C.-M., Dai, Y.: Design of triple-frequency microstrip-fed monopole antenna using DGS. IEEE Trans. Antennas Wirel. Propag. **59**(7), 2457–2463 (2011)

6. Liu, W.-C., Wu, C.-M., Dai, Y.: Design of triple frequency microstrip fed monopole antenna using defected ground structure. IEEE Trans. Antennas Propag. **59**(7), 2457–2463 (2011)
7. Chung, Y., Jeon, S.-S., Kim, S., Ahn, D.: Multifunctional microstrip transmission lines integrated circuits. IEEE Trans. Micro. Theory **52**(5), 1425–1431 (2004)
8. Chiang, K.H., Tam, K.W.: Microstrip monopole antenna with enhanced bandwidth. IEEE Antenna Wirel. Propag. Lett. **7**(5), 532–535 (2008)
9. Guha, D., Kumar, C., Pal, S.: Improved cross-polarization characteristic shaped DGS. IEEE Antenna Wirel. Propag. Lett. **8**, 1367–1369 (2009)
10. Kumar, C., Guha, D.: Reduce cross polarized of rectangular microstrip with a symmetric DGS. IEEE Trans. Antennas Wirel. Propag. **64**(6), 2503–2506 (2016)
11. Reddy, B.R.S., Vakula, D.: Compact zig zag shaped slit microstrip antenna with circular defected ground structure. IEEE Antenna Wirel. Propag. Lett. **14**, 678–681 (2015)
12. Verma, A.K., Kumar, A.: Design low pass filters using some defected ground structures. Int. J. Electron. Commun. **65**, 864–872 (2011)
13. Guo, X.L., Zhang, G.A., Zhang, Z.J., Yin, H.H., Wang, Z.L.: Tunable low-pass MEMS filter using defected ground structure (DGS). Solid-State Electron. **94**, 28–31 (2014)
14. Yang, J., Wu, W.: Compact elliptic-function low-pass filter using defected ground structure. IEEE Microw. Wirel. Compon. Lett. **18**(9), 578–580 (2008)

The Analysis of U Slotted Rectangular Patch with Geometric Series DGS for Triple Band Applications

T. Srinivasa Reddy(✉), P. Koteswara Rao, Ashok Kumar Balijepalli, and S. K. Nannu Saheb

Department of Electronics and Communication Engineering, Universal College of Engineering and Technology, Guntur, India
srinivasareddy.reddy51@gmail.com

Abstract. In this paper U shaped slotted on rectangular patch with geometric series defected ground structure (DGS) has been proposed. The proposed antenna has operated at three different operating frequencies of 8.3 GHz, 11.8 GHz, 14.3 GHz with return losses are −20.67 dB, −22 dB, −45.23 dB. The triple band has wide impedance bandwidth and maximum gain at operating frequencies. The co polarization and cross polarization of E plane and H plane are measured, the current distributions of U slotted rectangular patch antenna is measured.

Keywords: Defected ground structure · Circular ring patch antenna
Slots in ground plane

1 Introduction

The microstrip patch antennas (MSPA) is a essential device in the modern communication and radar systems. The provocative characteristics of MSPA are low cost, easy to design and conformability of the object. However the multi-band antennas has widely used in wireless and satellite communications.

[1–6] the different shape of defected ground structures (DGS) at ground plane to improve the impedance bandwidth, integration of microstrip lines and reduce the cross polarization. Liu proposed the planar monopole antenna with inverted L shaped DGS for wireless local area networks (WLAN) 2.4/5.2/5.8 GHz, WiMAX 3.5/5.5 GHz applications [1]. The spiral shape of the defected ground structure for dual polarized isolation, high input impedance 75 Ω, 150 Ω, and 100 Ω effectively [2], the monopole antenna with double U shaped DGS for improve impedance bandwidth of 112.4% over the traditional design [3]. The arc shape of DGS [4] and rectangular patch of asymmetric DGS [5] for reduce the cross polarization. The Zig Zag shaped rectangular patch with circular DGS for 2.45/5.28-GHz WLAN bands and the 3.5-GHz WiMAX and resonate at three resonant frequencies with gain of 4–6 dB [6]. The center fed circular ring patch with annular ring introduced for monopole radiation pattern, gain of 5.7 dB at resonant frequency 5.8 GHz [7]. Coupled-fed stacked microstrip monopolar patch antenna for monopole like radiation pattern are obtained in the dual bands

© Springer Nature Singapore Pte Ltd. 2019
S. Verma et al. (Eds.): CNC 2018, CCIS 839, pp. 568–578, 2019.
https://doi.org/10.1007/978-981-13-2372-0_51

(2.28–2.55 GHz, 5.15–5.9 GHz) for wireless local area network (WLAN) applications [8]. Soodmand [9] proposed breach coupled circular ring patch with four port dual band dual polarized for global system for mobile communication (GSM) and distributed control system (DCS) applications. Compact circular ring patch antenna for dual and triple band antennas resonate at fourth generation (4G) band [10]. Liu et al. [11] has reported tri-band monopole antenna with protrudent strips cross-shaped DGS for operate at UWB, WiMAX, WLAN and using for low pass filters [12–14].

In commercial antennas such as rectangular, triangular and other shapes are having low gain. In the view of that the ring antennas has been proposed to operate with high gain. But the ring patch has cross polarization problem. So, to improve that two concentric rings has been consider in this proposed design. The proposed U shaped slotted rectangle patch antenna with geometric series DGS has operated with triple bands are 8.3 GHz, 11.8 GHz and 14.3 GHz with return loss of −20.67 dB, 11.80 dB, 14.3 dB at three resonant frequencies. This triple bands are very much useful at WLAN, WiMAX applications to protect the cross polarization.

2   Antenna Design

Figure 1 shows the proposed U shaped slot on rectangular patch with geometric series factor DGS. The RCUS substrate dimensions has consider length (L_1) and width (W_1) are 70×50 mm^2 shown in Fig. 1. The substrate dielectric constant Fr4 epoxy ($\varepsilon_r = 4.4$) with thickness is 1.6 mm. The top layer of substrate is patch and ground patch with geometric series defected ground structure.

The rectangular patch length (L_2) is 40 mm and width (W_2) is 30 mm and concentric circles are slotted on the rectangular patch with outer circle and inner circle of radius (R_1) 13 mm, radius (R_2) 11.5 mm, radius (R_3) 6.5 mm, radius (R_4) 5.5 mm, width of the ring $(d_1 = d_2)$ 1.5 mm. The U shaped slots are placed at corners of rectangular patch for improve the bandwidth of proposed antenna and length (L_4), width (W_4) of U shape are 3.8 mm, 3.8 mm and thickness (d_3) of slot is 0.5 mm is shown in Fig. 1(a). The input impedance of feed line is 50 ohms and length (L_3) and width (W_3) of feed line is 20×2 mm^2. The ground patch has equally subdivided into three parts with length (L_5) 23.2 mm, width (W_5) 16.53 mm is shown in Fig. 1(b), again second part and third part equally subdivided into three parts with length (L_6) and width (W_6) are 7.6×5.38 mm^2. To improve bandwidth, reduce size of antenna, again the third part is equally subdivided into three part with length (L_7) 2.40 mm and width (W_7) 1.66 mm shown in Fig. 1(b). Slot $(S_1 = S_2)$ of 0.2 mm for equally subdivided the ground plane. The each rectangle is connected to another rectangle with equal dimensions $(S_3 = S_4 = S_5 = S_6)$ of 0.2 mm. The with DGS and Without DGS are shown in Fig. 2.

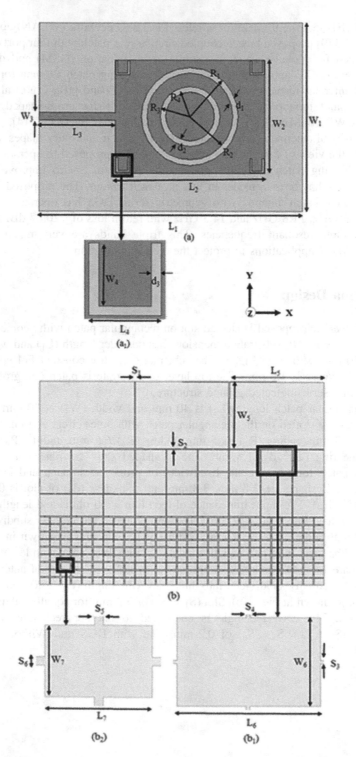

Fig. 1. (a) Patch of the rectangle circular with U shaped slots (b) Ground patch of geometric series factor DGS

3   Results and Discussion

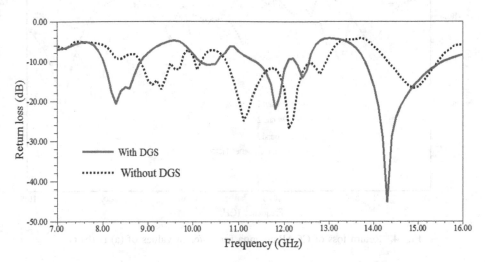

Fig. 2. Comparison of with DGS and without DGS of rectangular circular slot antenna

3.1   Parametric Analysis

The rectangular of concentric circles and U shaped slots (RCUS) patch shown in Fig. 1 (a). The ground plane is equally subdivided into three parts is shown in Fig. 3(a). The simulation results of RCUS with 3 × 3 cells ground plane shows the multi bands with lower bandwidth. The triple band is obtained for RCUS with 9 ×9 cells ground plane and triple bandwidths are 1 GHz, 0.6 GHz, 1.86 GHz with lower gain at resonant frequencies is shown in Fig. 4. In order to improve the bandwidth and gain of proposed antenna with ground 3 has dual bands. The reflection coefficients of ground 3 are −37.5 dB (7.8 GHz), −15.8 dB (15.2 GHz) with lower bandwidth compare to ground 1 and ground 2 is shown in Fig. 4.

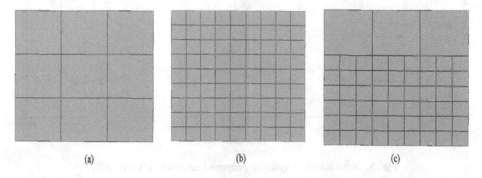

Fig. 3. The proposed antenna configurations (a) ground 1 (b) ground 2 (c) ground 3

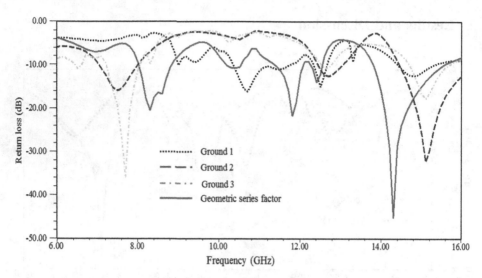

Fig. 4. Return loss of CCAP antenna for different values of (a) t_1 (b) t_2

3.2   Effect of S_1

Figure 5 shows the parametric analysis of proposed antenna by varying the slot (S_1) width as 0.2 mm, 0.3 mm, and 0.4 mm. When the slot size is increases, bandwidth of proposed antenna is decreases. From the observation slot size 0.2 mm shows the better result compared to 0.3 mm and 0.4 mm.

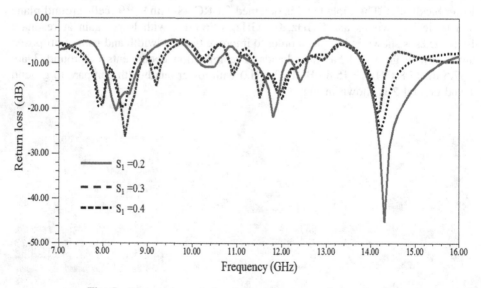

Fig. 5. Parametric analysis of proposed antenna by varying S_1

3.3   Effect of D_1

The width of ring (d_1) is decreases, bandwidth and gain of proposed antenna decreases. The parametric analysis on proposed antenna by varying ring (d_1) width as 1.1 mm, 1.3 mm and 1.5 mm. From the observation ring size of 1.5 mm shows the better result compare to 1.1 mm and 1.3 mm is shown in Fig. 6.

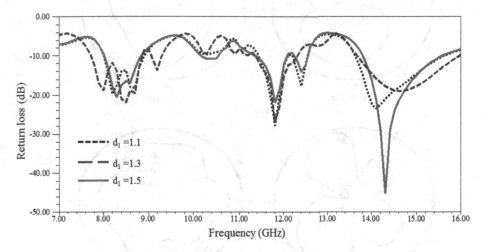

Fig. 6. Parametric analysis of proposed antenna by varying d_1

3.4   Radiation Patterns

The co polarization, cross polarization of E plane and H plane of the proposed antenna radiation characteristics shown in Fig. 7. The proposed antenna operated with three resonant frequencies are 8.3 GHz, 11.8 GHz, 14.3 GHz and The co polarization and cross polarization (XP) are observed and cross (XP) are found at is 0^0, -20 dB(xz plane) and -18 dB (yz plane) at is 90^0 for 8.3 GHz. The radiation patterns are observed at is 0^0 and is 90^0 in xz and yz plane for three resonance bands. The co and cross polarization has presented and cross polarization is found below 20 dB at one plane of each angle and operating frequency. The solid (black), dot (red) indicates the co and cross polarizations. The bi directional, omnidirectional radiation characteristics at resonant frequency of 8.3 GHz.

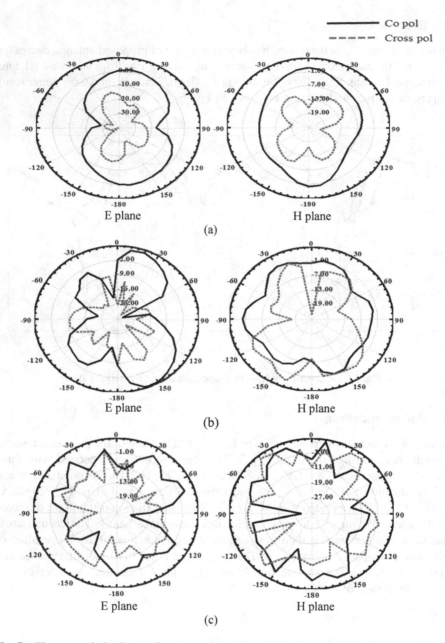

Fig. 7. The co polarization and cross polarization of E plane and H plane (a) 8.3 GHz (b) 11.8 GHz, (c) 14.3 GHz. (Color figure online)

3.5 Field Distributions of Proposed Antenna

The field distributions of the proposed antenna at E field, H field and J field is shown in Fig. 8. The maximum E field distributions of the proposed antenna for adding

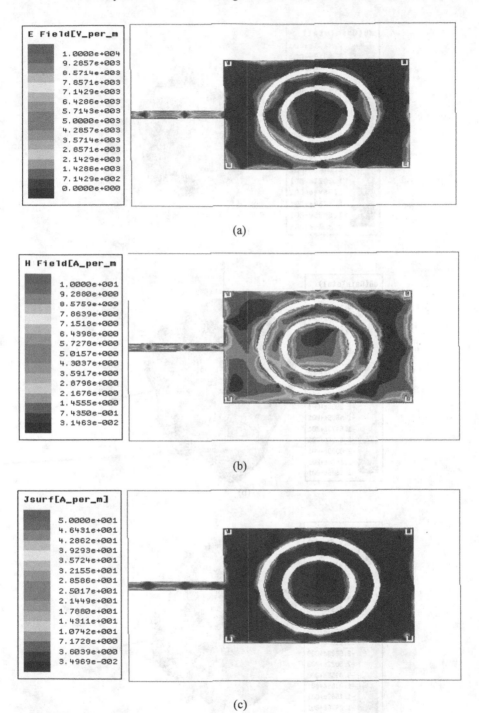

Fig. 8. The field distribution of star polygon antenna at (a) E field, (b) H field, (c) J field.

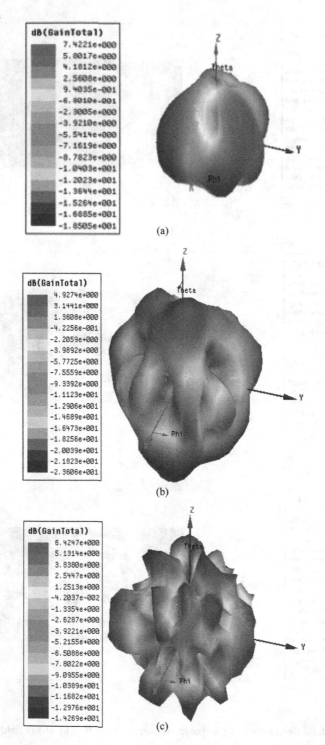

Fig. 9. The maximum gain at three resonant frequencies (a) 8.3 GHz (b) 11.8 GHz (c) 14.3 GHz

concentric circular slot, U shaped slots. The maximum electric field is 101 V/m at three resonant frequencies. The magnetic and J field are 10 A/m, 50 A/m.

3.6 Maximum Gain

The maximum gain of the proposed antenna at three resonant frequencies are shown in Fig. 9. The gain of 7.42 dB, 4.92 dB and 6.42 dB at resonant frequencies are 8.3 GHz, 11.8 GHz and 14.3 GHz. The maximum gain observed at 8.3 GHz compared to the other two frequencies. The U shaped slot rectangular patch with concentric circular slot for increasing the maximum gain of proposed antenna, the impedance bandwidth is increased by using geometric series defected ground structure.

4 Conclusion

In this paper the geometry shaped DGS is introduced for wide bandwidth and triple band applications. The U shaped slot on rectangular patch antenna with geometric series DGS is operating at three resonant frequencies are 8.3 GHz, 11.8 GHz, 14.3 GHz with return loss of −20.67 dB, −22 dB and −45.23 dB. The use of new geometric series DGS for improve the bandwidth, reduction size of antenna. The field distributions, radiation characteristics of the proposed antenna has been measured with minimum cross polarization and used for multi band, UWB, Ku band applications.

References

1. Liu, W.-C., Wu, C.-M., Dai, Y.: Design of triple frequency microstrip fed monopole antenna using defected ground structure. IEEE Trans. Antennas Propag. **59**(7), 2457–2463 (2011)
2. Chung, Y., Jeon, S.-S., Kim, S., Ahn, D.: Multifunctional microstrip transmission lines integrated circuits. IEEE Trans. Micro. Theory **52**(5), 1425–1431 (2004)
3. Chiang, K.H., Tam, K.W.: Microstrip monopole antenna with enhanced bandwidth. IEEE Antenna Wirel. Propag. Lett. **7**(5), 532–535 (2008)
4. Guha, D., Kumar, C., Pal, S.: Improved cross-polarization characteristic shaped DGS. IEEE Antenna Wirel. Propag. Lett. **8**, 1367–1369 (2009)
5. Kumar, C., Guha, D.: Reduce cross polarized of rectangular microstrip with a symmetric DGS. IEEE Trans. Antennas Wirel. Propag. **64**(6), 2503–2506 (2016)
6. Reddy, B.R.S., Vakula, D.: Compact zig zag shaped slit microstrip antenna with circular defected ground structure. IEEE Antenna Wirel. Propag. Lett. **14**, 678–681 (2015)
7. Al-Zoubi, A., Yang, F., Kishk, A.: A broadband center–fed circular patch ring antenna with a monopole like radiation pattern. IEEE Trans. Antennas Propag. **57**(3), 789–792 (2009)
8. Liang, Z., Liu, J., Li, Y., Long, Y.: Dual-frequency broadband design of coupled–fed stacked microstrip monopolar patch antenna. IEEE Antenna Wirel. Propag. Lett. **15**(15), 1289–1292 (2016)
9. Soodmand, S.: Circular formed dual-band dual-polarized patch antenna and method for designing compact combined feed networks. Int. J. Electron. Commun. (AEU) **65**, 453–457 (2011)
10. Abdelaal, M.A., Ghouz, H.H.M.: New compact circular ring microstrip patch antenna. Progress Electromagnet. Res. C **46**, 135–143 (2014)

11. Liu, W.-C., Wu, C.-M., Dai, Y.: Design of triple-frequency microstrip-fed monopole antenna using DGS. IEEE Trans. Antennas Wirel. Propag. **59**(7), 2457–2463 (2011)
12. Verma, A.K., Kumar, A.: Design low pass filters using some defected ground structures. Int. J. Electron. Commun. **65**, 864–872 (2011)
13. Guo, X.L., Zhang, G.A., Zhang, Z.J., Yin, H.H., Wang, Z.L.: Tunable low-pass MEMS filter using defected ground structure (DGS). Solid-State Electron. **94**, 28–31 (2014)
14. Yang, J., Wu, W.: Compact elliptic-function low pass filter. IEEE Microw. Wirel. Compon. Lett. **18**(9), 578–580 (2008)

A Dual Band Coplanar Concentric Ring Patch Antenna for Ku Band Applications

T. Srinivasa Reddy$^{(\boxtimes)}$, Ashok Kumar Balijepalli, S. K. Nannu Saheb, and P. Koteswara Rao

Department of Electronics and Communication Engineering,
Universal College of Engineering and Technology, Guntur, India
srinivasareddy.reddy51@gmail.com

Abstract. The coplanar concentric ring patch (CCRP) to operate at dual band for ku band applications. Two concentric rings has considered on the patch with ground plane. The proposed antenna has worked at 13.98 GHz and 16.54 GHz with 8.15 dB, 8.44 dB gain. The radiation patterns are observed at θ is 45^0 and is 90^0 at two operating bands. The co polarization and cross polarization (XP) are observed and XP are found at is 45^0, -50 dB(xy plane) and -60 dB (xz plane) at is 90^0 for 13.98 GHz. For 16.54 GHz, the XP at is 45^0, -40 dB (xy plane) and 90^0, -40 dB (xz plane). The radiation patterns are observed at is 45^0 and is 90^0 in xy, yz and zx plane for two resonance bands. The co and cross polarization has presented and cross polarization is found below 40 dB at one plane of each angle and operating frequency. The measurement has been carried out with simulation results of return loss of proposed antenna.

Keywords: Concentric ring circular patch antenna · Ground plane
Ku band

1 Introduction

The microstrip patch antennas (MSPA) is a essential device in the modern communication and radar systems. The provocative characteristics of MSPA are low cost, easy to design and conformability of the object. However the multi-band antennas has widely used in wireless and satellite communications.

A center fed circular ring patch with annular ring introduced for monopole radiation pattern, gain of 5.7 dB at resonant frequency 5.8 GHz [1]. Coupled-fed stacked microstrip monopolar patch antenna for monopole like radiation pattern are obtained in the dual bands (2.28–2.55 GHz, 5.15–5.9 GHz) for wireless local area network (WLAN) applications [2]. Soodmand [3] proposed breach coupled circular ring patch with four port dual band dual polarized for global system for mobile communication (GSM) and distributed control system (DCS) applications. Compact circular ring patch antenna for dual and triple band antennas resonate at fourth generation (4G) band [4]. The two appended coin shaped patches with ring shaped feed strip for Ultra-high frequency (UHF) radio frequency identification (RFID) applications [5]. Guha [6] proposed circular patch with arc shaped defected ground structure (DGS) for improve the suppressing the XP (cross polarization). The researchers are proposed different

© Springer Nature Singapore Pte Ltd. 2019
S. Verma et al. (Eds.): CNC 2018, CCIS 839, pp. 579–589, 2019.
https://doi.org/10.1007/978-981-13-2372-0_52

types of split ring resonator (SRR) [7], aperture coupled annular ring [8], annular ring slot antenna [9] for circular polarization. [10] Karli proposed a rectangular patch antenna for dual band antenna with bandwidth of 0.4 in upper band and lower band and used for wireless communications. [6] Guha proposed circular patch with arc shaped defected ground structure (DGS) for improve the suppressing the XP (cross polarization). [11] The parasitic stubs and slots are slots in rectangular antenna for wide bandwidth and wireless local area networks. [1] A circular feed circular ring slot antenna was designed for wide bandwidth and gain of 5.7 dBi, the circular ring microstrip patch antenna with coupled-fed stacked microstrip for dual-frequency has considered.

In commercial antennas such as rectangular, triangular and other shapes are having low gain. In the view of that the ring antennas has been proposed to operate with high gain. But the ring patch has cross polarization problem. So, to improve that two concentric rings has been consider in this proposed design. The proposed coplanar concentric ring patch has operated with dual bands are 13.98 GHz and 16.54 GHz with 8.15 dB, 8.44 dB gain at two resonant frequencies. This dual bands are very much useful at Ku band applications to protect the cross polarization.

2 Antenna Design

Figure 1(a) shows the proposed structure of coplanar concentric ring patch antenna (CCRP) with ground patch is shown in Fig. 1(a). The proposed antenna is designed with FR4 as substrate material with dielectric constant (ε_r) 4.3. The dimensions of the

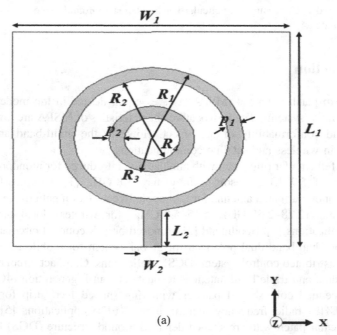

(a)

Fig. 1. (a) Geometry of the proposed coplanar concentric ring patch antenna.

substrate is $30 \times 30 \times 1.6$ mm³. The outer ring patch thickness is p_1 with radius R_1 and R_2. Similarly, inner ring patch thickness is p_2 with radius R_3 and R_4. A feed line of length L_2 and with W_2 is added to the outer ring patch. The prototype of the proposed antenna top and bottom view is shown in Fig. 2(a)–(b). The optimized dimensions of the proposed antenna is listed in Table 1.

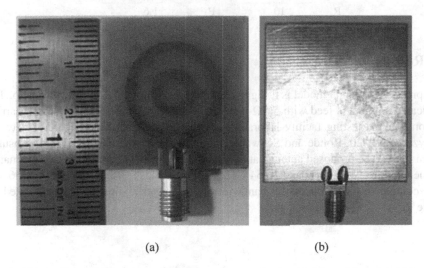

(a)   (b)

Fig. 2. Fabrication of the proposed coplanar concentric ring patch antenna (a) Top view (b) Bottom view.

2.1 Antenna Configuration

See Fig. 3.

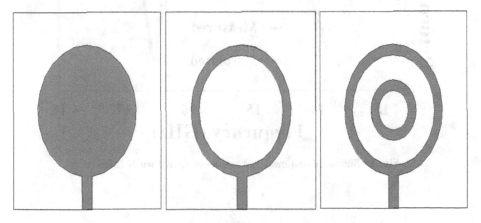

Fig. 3. Antenna configurations of CCRP antenna

Table 1. The optimized CCRP antenna parameters.

Parameter	Values (mm)	Parameter	Values (mm)
L_1	30	R_2	8.4
W_1	30	R_3	6.6
L_2	5	R_4	5
W_2	2	P_1	1.6
R_1	10	P_2	1.6

3   Results and Discussion

The proposed antenna model is designed and simulated in CST Microwave studio. The fabricated antenna is feed with 50 Ω impedance. The measurements have been carried out on antenna testing facility laboratory with anechoic chamber and vector network analyzer (ZNB-20, Rohde and Schwarz). Figure 4 shows the simulated and measured return loss of the proposed antenna at two resonant bands. The observed two resonance frequencies are 13.98 GHz and 16.54 GHz with return loss −18.68 dB and −21.56 dB. The comparison of impedance bandwidth with respect simulated is tabulated in Table 2.

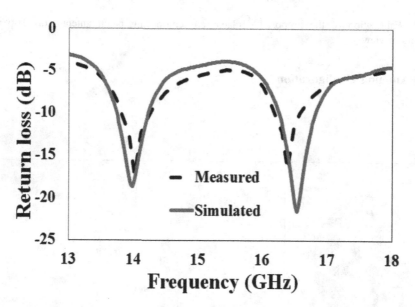

Fig. 4. Simulated and measured results of CCRP patch antenna.

Table 2. Simulated results data

Frequency (GHz)	Return loss (dB)	Simulated bandwidth (MHz)	Measure bandwidth (MHz)	Gain (dB)	VSWR
13.98	−18.68	490 MHz (13.724– 14.214 GHz)	484 MHz (13.74– 14.224 GHz)	8.15	1.25
16.54	−21.56	491 MHz (16.22– 16.64 GHz)	350 MHz (16.23– 16.58 GHz)	8.44	1.20

3.1 Parametric Analysis

The parametric study of the proposed antenna is carried out by varying the thickness of the two concentric rings. Figure 5(a) to (c) shows the return loss plot of the proposed antenna by varying the thickness as 1.4 mm, 1.6 mm, 1.8 mm at three conditions as p_1, p_2, and p_1&p_2. The results are shown in Fig. 5(a) to (c) for these three conditions. However, the proposed model thickness 1.6 mm has optimum return loss (Table 3).

3.2 Radiation Patterns and Field Distributions of CCAP Antenna

The radiation pattern plots of the designed antenna are shown in Figs. 6 and 7. The radiation pattern with respect to X-Y plane, X-Z plane and Y-Z plane is shown in Fig. 6 at θ is 45^0 and 90^0. From these plots the coplarization and cross polarizationhas presented three planes. Elevation angle 45^0 the cross polarization has observed below 60 dB at XY plane and 90^0 the cross polarization has observed −50 dB at XZ plane. The radiation pattern is shown in Fig. 7 at 16.54 GHz for three planes. The co and cross polarization has observed −40 dB at 45^0 in XY plane and 90^0 in XZ plane.

The field distribution of the proposed antenna at two resonant frequency is shown in Fig. 8. Where the maximum field distribution is observed at outer ring patch. The field distributions of 115A/m and 80.8 A/m are observed at two resonance frequencies.

3.3 Maximum Gain

The maximum gain of CCAP at two resonant frequencies are shown in Fig. 9. The gain is 8.15 dB at resonant frequency 13.98 GHz and 8.44 dB gain at 16.54 GHz. The proposed antenna has improve the maximum gain, impedance bandwidth and reduce the cross polarization.

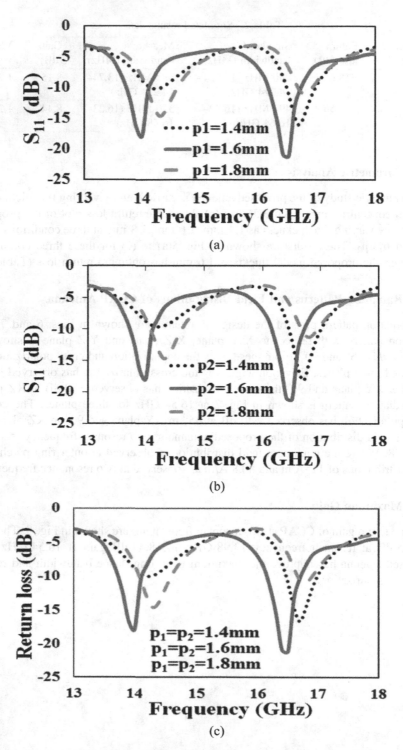

Fig. 5. S_{11} (dB) for CCRP antenna for different values of (a) ring (p_1) (b) ring (p_2) (c) ring ($p_1 = p_2$).

Table 3. parametric results of CCRP antenna

Variable	P1	P2	P1 = p2
1.4 mm	−10.23 dB (14.25 GHz)	−9.65 dB (14.2 GHz)	−10.06 dB (14.2 GHz)
	−16.03 dB (16.69 GHz)	−18.15 dB (16.7 GHz)	−16.71 dB (16.7 GHz
1.6 mm	−18.68 dB (13.98 GHz)	−18.68 dB (13.98 GHz)	−18.68 dB (13.98 GHz)
	−21.56 dB (16.54 GHz)	−21.56 dB (16.54 GHz)	−21.56 dB (16.54 GHz)
1.8 mm	−14.68 dB (14.3 GHz)	−14.63 dB (14.3 GHz)	−14.68 dB (14.3 GHz)
	−10.63 dB(16.70 GHz)	−11.21 dB(16.8 GHz)	−11.01(16.80 GHz)

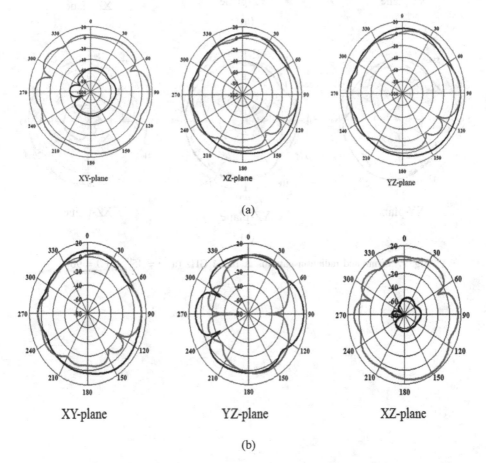

(a)

XY-plane   YZ-plane   XZ-plane

(b)

Fig. 6. Simulated radiation pattern at frequency 13.98 GHz (a) $\theta = 45^0$, (b) $\theta = 90^0$.

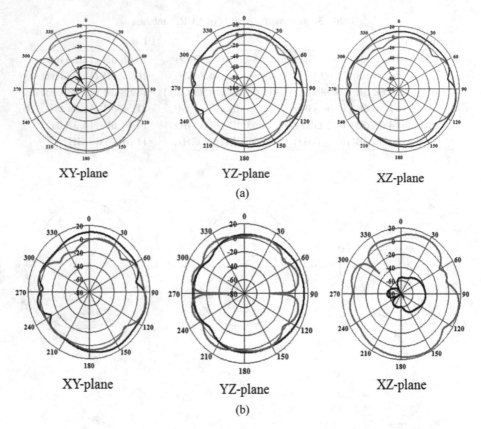

XY-plane   YZ-plane   XZ-plane

(a)

XY-plane   YZ-plane   XZ-plane

(b)

Fig. 7. Simulated radiation patterns at 16.54 GHz (a) $\theta = 45^0$, (b) $\theta = 90^0$.

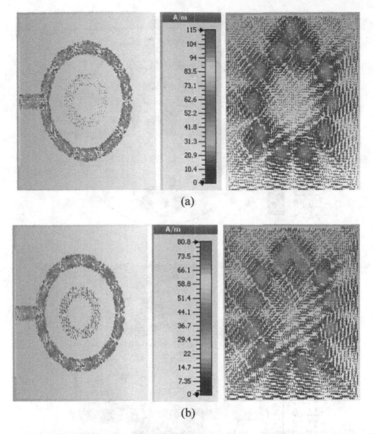

(a)

(b)

Fig. 8. The field distributions of CCRP antenna at (a) 13.98 GHz, (b) 16.54 GHz.

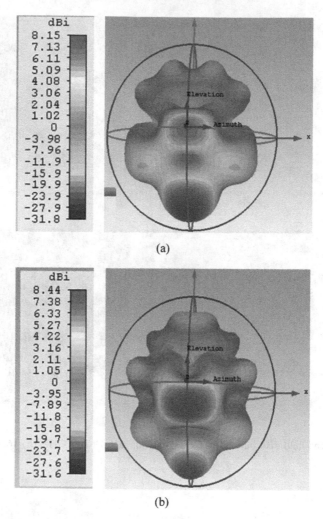

Fig. 9. The maximum gain at resonant frequencies (a) 13.98 GHz (b) 16.54 GHz.

4   Conclusion

The proposed antenna has work at two operating bands with 8.15 dB and 8.44 dB gain. The cross polarization is observed at 45^0 and 90^0 for these bands and found that less than −40 dB on the one plane only. So, this analysis is very much useful for satellite applications to transmitter and receiver the signals.

References

1. Al-Zoubi, A., Yang, F., Kishk, A.: A broadband center–fed circular patch ring antenna with a monopole like radiation pattern. IEEE Trans. Antennas Propag. **57**(3), 789–792 (2009)
2. Liang, Z., Liu, J., Li, Y., Long, Y.: Dual-frequency broadband design of coupled–fed stacked microstrip monopolar patch antenna. IEEE Antenna Wirel. Propag. Lett. **15**(15), 1289–1292 (2016)
3. Soodmand, S.: Circular formed dual-band dual-polarized patch antenna and method for designing compact combined feed networks. Int. J. Electron. Commun. (AEU) **65**, 453–457 (2011)
4. Abdelaal, M.A., Ghouz, H.H.M.: New compact circular ring microstrip patch antenna. Progress Electromagnet. Res. C **46**, 135–143 (2014)
5. Liu, X.Y., Liu, Y., Tentzeris, M.M.: Novel CP antenna with coin shaped patches and ring shaped strip. IEEE Antenna Wirel. Propag. Lett. **14**, 707–710 (2015)
6. Guha, D., Kumar, C., Pal, S.: Improved cross-polarization characteristic shaped DGS. IEEE Antenna Wirel. Propag. Lett. **8**, 1367–1369 (2009)
7. Rahimi, M., Maleki, M., Soltani, M., Arezomand, A.S., Zarrabi, F.B.: Wide band SRR-inspried slot antenna with circular polarization for wireless application. Int. J. Electron. Commun. (AEU) **70**, 1199–1204 (2016)
8. Row, J.S.: Design of aperture-coupled annular-ring microstrip antennas for circular polarization. IEEE Trans. Antennas Propag. **53**(5), 1779–1784 (2005)
9. Zhang, J.L., Yang, X.Q.: Integrated compact circular polarization annular ring slot antenna design for RFID reader. Progress Electromagnet. Res. Lett. **39**, 133–140 (2013)
10. Karli, R., Ammor, H.: Rectangular patch antenna for dual-band RFID and WLAN applications. Wirel. Pers. Commun. **83**, 995–1007 (2015)
11. Sharma, R.K., Sharma, S.K., Gupta, A., Chaudary, R.K.: An edge tapered rectangular patch antenna with parasitic stubs and slot for wideband applications. Wirel. Pers. Commun. **86**, 1213–1220 (2016)

Optimal Design of CMOS Amplifier Circuits Using Whale Optimization Algorithm

M. A. Mushahhid Majeed$^{(\boxtimes)}$ and Patri Sreehari Rao

Electronics and Communication Engineering Department,
National Institute of Technology Warangal, Hanamkonda, Telangana, India
mushahhid17@gmail.com, patri@nitw.ac.in

Abstract. A metaheuristic search algorithm named Whale Optimization Algorithm (WOA) is presented in this paper to optimally design most commonly used yet important analog circuits i.e., Complementary metal-oxide semiconductor (CMOS) differential amplifier circuit and two-stage CMOS operational amplifier circuit. The WOA algorithm is the basic impersonation of the hunting and foraging mechanism observed in humpback whales' natural behavior. Searching for, encircling and bubble-net attacking method are the three main steps of hunting, which are implemented in this algorithm. The sizes of transistors are optimized using WOA to improve the design specifications of the circuit by reducing the area occupied by the transistors. The simulation results and convergence plots demonstrate the superiority of WOA over some of the other algorithms such as Particle Swarm Optimization (PSO), Sine Cosine Algorithm (SCA), for analog circuit design.

Keywords: CMOS circuit sizing · Electronic design automation
Whale Optimization Algorithm · Operational amplifier

1 Introduction

An Integrated circuit comprises of analog, digital and mixed signal circuits. Analog circuits form one of the prominent blocks in modern electronic systems that serve as an interface between the signals from real world and digital realm. The importance of analog circuits cannot be neglected as the large size of the analog circuits in ICs imposes a major restriction on the design performance and overall cost. The automation of digital circuits has become a successful attempt as a result of the research since few decades, but analog circuit automation is challenging due to perplexed design [1]. Analog circuit automation is a complex, monotonous, time consuming, iterative, composite and tedious process, due to three degrees of design freedom i.e., channel width, channel length and drain current. Hence, new strategies need to be introduced to assure optimal solutions in terms of design specifications such as gain, Unity Gain Frequency (UGB), Slew Rate (SR), area, etc., for an amplifier.

A typical analog circuit design process comprises of three phases: topology selection, component sizing and layout extraction [2]. Simple circuits, constituting less number of components, can be designed by utilizing the experience and perception of expert designers [3]. However, in the case of complex circuits with large search space,

© Springer Nature Singapore Pte Ltd. 2019
S. Verma et al. (Eds.): CNC 2018, CCIS 839, pp. 590–605, 2019.
https://doi.org/10.1007/978-981-13-2372-0_53

it is one of the time consuming and difficult tasks for designers to generate an optimal solution. In optimization of transistor sizes, the ability to design analog circuits with high performance is one of the important issues [4]. The reliability and smoothness of an optimization technique depends on the aspect ratios of the transistors in CMOS analog circuit design. Hence, effective optimization techniques are important in optimal sizing of analog circuits. In the recent past, several methods have been proposed for the automation of analog circuits which utilize a set of rules depending on the knowledge of the circuits for automated designing with respect to specification set [5]. Since, creation of new set of rules for different topologies requires lot of labor, these methods are proven less fruitful. As an advancement, many other tools and techniques have been proposed for analyzing analog circuit design problem, which include ANACONDA [6], APE [7], geometric programming [8], equation engines based on symbolic analysis [9], optimization engines based on evolutionary algorithms [10], etc. Geometric programming uses additional computational steps before having the input at the optimization engine, for deriving specific set of mathematical equations [11]. In equation based symbolic analysis, circuit topology is used for the translation of analog circuit design problem into function based optimization problem at an expense of additional computational steps and accuracy. On the other hand, heuristics based evolutionary algorithms that mimic the behavior of natural entities are employed to derive optimal solution. Metaheuristic algorithms have gained significant interest in the field of optimization due to four reasons: derivation free mechanism, avoidance of local minima, simplicity and flexibility.

Metaheuristics are classified as single solution based and population based [12]. Single solution approach involves iteration of one parameter to achieve the target specifications. Whereas, a population based approach uses a set of solutions which are initialized randomly and the same population is enhanced through iterations. Population based metaheuristics enjoy the advantages of information sharing, avoidance of local minima through proper coordination and greater exploration, over single solution based metaheuristics. One of the interesting derivatives of metaheuristics is Swarm Intelligence (SI), whose origin is from natural behavior of swarm of entities such as colonies, schools, herds and flocks. Some of the advantages of swarm intelligence are: less number of operators, ease in implementation and few parameters to adjust. One of the properties in SI is that it saves the best solution obtained so far, unlike evolutionary algorithms, before searching the new best solution.

This paper deals with the second phase of the circuit design process i.e., component sizing. For the validation of the performance of the proposed optimization technique, two of the most commonly used analog circuits i.e., CMOS differential amplifier (CMOSDA) and two-stage CMOS operational amplifier (CMOSOA), with reduced MOS area, lower power consumption and higher gain. The application of WOA to obtain optimal design parameters is considered as a design problem with given technology parameters. The optimal sizing of CMOS transistors yielding minimum area is considered as the major objective of this work. In literature, different heuristic algorithms were applied for analog circuit design problem, but to the best of the authors' knowledge this is the first time that the WOA algorithm is applied to analog circuit design problems. The results obtained verify that the application of WOA for designing amplifiers yield less area, lower power consumption and higher gain when compared to those reported in recent literature. This proves that applying WOA to analog circuits is proven to better than using some other optimization algorithms for analog circuit design problem.

The organization of the paper is as follows: Sect. 2 gives the overview of WOA algorithm. In Sect. 3, design of CMOS amplifiers and formulation of cost function is discussed. Section 4 discusses the comprehensive and demonstrative results and their validation is presented followed by conclusion in Sect. 5.

2   Whale Optimization Algorithm

In this section, the inspiration of the proposed method is first discussed. Then, the mathematical model is provided.

Whales are considered to be the largest mammals in the world weighing around 180 tons. They are assumed to be one of the highly intelligent animals on earth and most attentive predators. The social behavior observed in humpback whales is interesting that deals with foraging and hunting their favorite prey such as, small fish and krill herds. The special hunting method observed in humpback whales is bubble-net feeding method. This process starts with diving into ocean up to 12 m deep and creating bubbles with spiral and upward movement towards the prey. The following maneuver includes coral loop, lobtail and capture loop which are explained in [13]. The mathematical modelling, for optimization, is done based on the spiral bubble-net maneuver in humpback whales.

The hunting process or exploitation phase starts with encircling the prey after recognizing its position as a target or close to optimum solution. After defining the best search agent, search agents update their positions towards the best solution, which is mathematically represented as follows:

$$\vec{D} = \left| \vec{C} \cdot \vec{X}_p(t) - \vec{X}(t) \right| \tag{1}$$

$$\vec{X}(t+1) = \vec{X}_p(t) - \vec{A} \cdot \vec{D} \tag{2}$$

where t is current iteration, $\vec{X}_p$ is the best solution position vector obtained, $\vec{X}$ is position vector and $\vec{A}$, $\vec{C}$ are coefficient vectors. The position $\vec{X}_p$ must be updated in each iteration to obtain better solution. The vectors $\vec{A}$ and $\vec{C}$ are calculated using following equations:

$$\vec{A} = 2\vec{a} \cdot \vec{r_1} - \vec{a} \tag{3}$$

$$\vec{C} = 2\vec{r_2} \tag{4}$$

where r_1, r_2 are random vectors within range [0, 1] and $\vec{a}$ has its components decreased linearly from 2 to 0 during the iterations.

The mathematical modelling of the bubble-net behavior is done based on two approaches i.e., shrinking circles mechanism and spiral position update. The behavior of shrinking circles mechanism is obtained by reducing the value of $\vec{a}$ as shown in (3) which eventually reduces the fluctuation range of $\vec{A}$ i.e., $\vec{A}$ is a random value in a range $[-a, a]$. If the value of $\vec{A}$ is set randomly between $[-1, 1]$, the new position is anywhere between current best position and original position of an agent. The spiral position update firstly calculates the distance between whale and prey. Then a spiral equation is created whale and prey to mimic the helix-shaped movement as shown below:

$$\vec{X}(t+1) = \vec{D'}.e^{bl}.\cos(2\pi l) + \vec{X_p}(t) \tag{5}$$

where $\vec{D} = |\vec{X}_p(t) - \vec{X}(t)|$ is the distance between the prey and ith whale, b is the logarithmic spiral defining constant and l takes any random number in range $[-1, 1]$. Both of these phenomena are merged to depict the behavior of the humpback whales which is modelled as follows:

$$\vec{X}(t+1) = \begin{cases} \vec{X_p}(t) - \vec{A}.\vec{D} & \text{if } p<0.5 \\ \vec{D'}.e^{bl}.\cos(2\pi l) + \vec{X_p}(t) & \text{if } p\geq0.5 \end{cases} \tag{6}$$

Besides bubble-net method, the humpback whales follow random search, according to each other's position, for searching prey. This process depends on the value of $\vec{A}$ i.e., when $\vec{A}$ is less than -1 or greater than 1, the search agent is forced to move away from the reference whale. Here in exploration phase, the position update is done according to the randomly chosen search agent instead of best search agent so far. The exploration phase is mathematically modelled as follows:

$$\vec{D} = |\vec{C}.\vec{X}_r(t) - \vec{X}(t)| \tag{7}$$

$$\vec{X}(t+1) = \vec{X}_r(t) - \vec{A}.\vec{D} \tag{8}$$

where $\vec{X}_r$ is a random search agent from current population.

The pseudo code for WOA algorithm is shown in Fig. 1. Similar to most of the algorithms, WOA starts with a set of random search agents. A search agent updates its position according to best solution obtained so far or randomly selected search agent. The exploration and exploitation are decide using the parameter which is reduced from 2 to 0. When $|\vec{A}| > 1$, random search agent is selected and when $|\vec{A}|<1$, best solution obtained so far, are selected for updating the position of search agents. The movement of the whale i.e., circular or spiral is decided using the parameter 'p'. Finally, the WOA algorithm is terminated when the termination criteria is satisfied.

Initialize the whales population Xi (i = 1, 2, ..., n)
Calculate the fitness of each search agent
X$_p$=the best search agent
while (t < maximum number of iterations)
    for each search agent
        Update a, A, C, l, and p
        if (p<0.5)
            if (|A| < 1)
                Update the position of the current search agent by using (1)
            else if (|A| ≥ 1)
                Select a random search agent (X$_r$)
                Update the position of the current search agent by using (8)
            end if
        else if (p ≥ 0.5)
                Update the position of the current search by using (5)
        end if
    end for
    Check if any search agent goes beyond the search space and amend it
    Calculate the fitness of each search agent
    Update X$_p$ if there is a better solution
    t=t+1
end while
return X$_p$

Fig. 1. Pseudo code for Whale Optimization Algorithm [12].

3   Design of Analog Circuits

The design of CMOSDA and CMOSOA, using WOA as an optimization algorithm, is presented in this paper. The design specifications considered for designing CMOSDA and CMOSOA are unity gain bandwidth (UGB), voltage gain (A$_v$), power dissipation (P$_d$), input common mode range (V$_{ICmin}$ and V$_{ICmax}$), and slew rate (SR). Besides design specifications, we also have design parameters i.e., aspect ratios (W/L) of all the transistors in circuits and load capacitance (C$_L$), which are crucial in designing an analog circuit. The schematics for CMOSDA and CMOSOA are shown in Figs. 2 and 3, respectively.

The performance specifications for designing CMOSDA are SR, f$_{3dB}$, V$_{ICmin}$, V$_{ICmax}$ and P$_d$. The variables that are initialized before starting the iterative optimization process include: power supply (V$_{dd}$), threshold voltage inputs for NMOS and PMOS (V$_{tn}$ and V$_{tp}$), gate to source voltage (V$_{GS}$) of MOS transistor, drain to source voltage (V$_{DS}$) of MOSFET, transconductance parameter of PMOS and NMOS ($K'_p = \mu_p.C_{ox}$, and $K'_n = \mu_n.C_{ox}$), mobility of charge carriers (μ_n for electrons and μ_p for holes), gate oxide capacitance (C$_{ox}$), channel length modulation parameters (λ_p for PMOS and λ_n for NMOS), transconductance (g$_m$), output conductance (g$_{ds}$), output

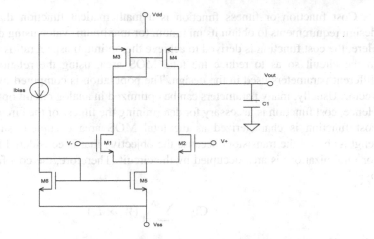

Fig. 2. Schematic for CMOS differential amplifier.

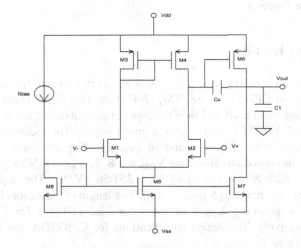

Fig. 3. Schematic for two-stage CMOS operational amplifier.

resistance (R_{out}) and drain current (I_D). The design flow for both circuits is done using the methodology in [14] as shown in Appendix A.

The initial population size for the WOA algorithm is considered to be a matrix of size ($P \times Q$), where $P = 60$ and $Q = 7$, where P is number of particles and Q is the particle vector. The particle vectors for the CMOSDA and CMOSOA are as follows:

$$X_{diffamp} = A_V, C_L, SR, V_{ICmin}, V_{ICmax}, f_{3dB}, P_d] \qquad (9)$$

$$X_{opamp} = [A_V, C_L, SR, V_{ICmin}, V_{Icmax}, UGB, P_d] \qquad (10)$$

Cost function or fitness function is a mathematical function that evaluates the design requirements to obtain its minimum (or maximum) value using design variables. Here, the cost function is derived to achieve the optimum aspect ratios of all transistors in the circuit so as to reduce the total MOS area, using the relationships between different parameters used in the design. The population is computed by fitness of each vector. Usually, many parameters can be optimized in analog circuit optimization tasks. Hence, cost function is necessary for determining the fitness of the circuit. In this paper, cost function is characterized as the total MOS area occupied (sum of widths × lengths) by all the transistors because the objective that is considered for optimization (or minimization) is area occupied by the circuit. Therefore, the cost function is given by

$$CF = \sum\nolimits_{i=1}^{N} (W_i \times L_i) \tag{11}$$

where, N is the total number of transistors in a circuit whose desired value is less than 300 μm^2 for both the circuits. Hence, the WOA algorithm is used to obtain the optimal value of the cost function.

4   Simulation Results

The WOA algorithm is used to find the optimal aspect ratios of all the transistors using MATLAB 2014a on CPU Intel core (TM) i7-4790 at 3.60 GHz. These amplifiers are implemented using MATLAB and then the aspect ratios obtained are used to simulate the amplifiers in CADENCE analog design environment. The technology parameters are chosen from 180 nm CMOS standard process. The constants considered for designing above discussed amplifiers are V_{DD} = 1.8 V, V_{SS} = 0 V, V_{tp} = −0.4523 V, V_{tn} = 0.3215 V, K_p = 80.6 $\mu V/A^2$ and K_n = 351.56 $\mu V/A^2$. The aspect ratios are considered to be in the range (0.5 μm, 10 μm). The length of transistors is fixed as 0.75 and 0.54 ($\geq$3 × minimum length of transistor i.e., 180 nm) for CMOSDA and CMOSOA, respectively. The design specifications for CMOSDA and CMOSOA are summarized in Table 1.

The ac performance of the CMOSDA is shown in Fig. 4. The CMOSDA achieves a gain of 46.06 dB and a phase margin of 89.54°. The amplifier has a CMRR of 85.495 dB, PSRR of 92.12 dB and slew rate of 14.79 V/μsec, as shown in Figs. 5, 6 and 7 respectively. Similarly, the ac response of CMOSOA shows the DC gain of 80.13 dB and phase margin of 62.66° with UGB of 4.293 MHz as shown in Fig. 8. The CMRR and PSRR of 91.29 dB and 80.07 dB, obtained through the ac analysis, are shown in Figs. 9 and 10, respectively. The slew rate of 13.44 V/μsec obtained through transient analysis is shown in Fig. 11.

The design parameters, including the aspect ratios of transistor and load capacitor (C_L), attained after the optimization of CMOSDA and CMOSOA using WOA algorithm are illustrated in Table 2.

The convergence plot for the differential amplifier using WOA algorithm is shown in Fig. 12, which is also compared with convergence plots of SCA and PSO algorithm.

Table 1. Target specifications for the design of differential amplifier and two-stage operational amplifier.

Parameters	Differential amplifier	Operational amplifier
Av (dB)	> 40	> 70
P_d (μW)	≤ 200	≤ 500
SR (V/μs)	≥ 10	≥ 10
UGB (MHz)	≥ 4	≥ 4
C_L (pF)	≥ 3	≥ 7
Phase Margin (°)	≥ 45	≥ 60
CMRR (dB)	≥ 60	≥ 70
PSRR (dB)	≥ 70	≥ 80
Area (μm²)	≤ 50	≤ 150

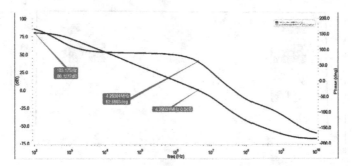

Fig. 4. DC gain of CMOS differential amplifier.

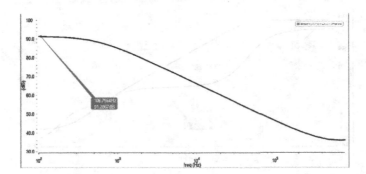

Fig. 5. CMRR of CMOS differential amplifier.

Similarly, the convergence plot for two-stage operational amplifier and its comparison with convergence plots of PSO and SCA are shown in Fig. 13. These plots show the convergence to globally optimal solution which is much faster than other competing algorithms. The number of iterations considered for all the three algorithms is 500 (termination criteria) with the population size of 60 and vector size of 7.

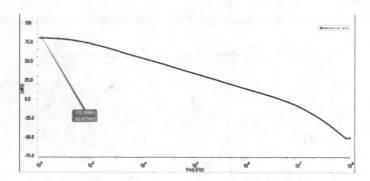

Fig. 6. PSRR of CMOS differential amplifier.

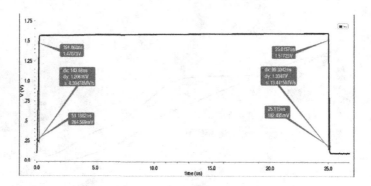

Fig. 7. Slew rate of CMOS differential amplifier.

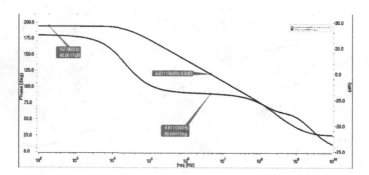

Fig. 8. DC gain of two-stage CMOS operational amplifier.

These plots show that the WOA algorithm converges much faster than SCA and PSO algorithms i.e., at 72 iterations and 115 iterations for CMOSDA and CMOSOA, respectively. The minimum area after optimizing the CMOSDA using WOA is 19.83 μm^2 and after optimizing the CMOSOA is 33.442 μm^2.

Tables 3 and 4 summarize the results obtained after circuit level implementation in CADENCE SPECTRE environment using the aspect ratios shown in Table 2, for

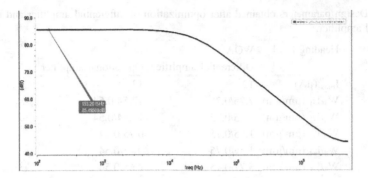

Fig. 9. CMRR of two-stage CMOS operational amplifier.

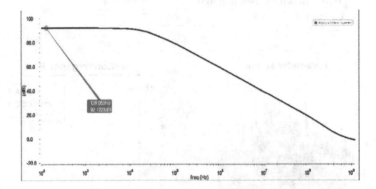

Fig. 10. PSRR of two-stage CMOS operational amplifier.

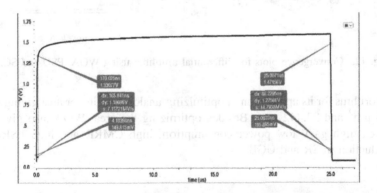

Fig. 11. Slew-rate of two-stage CMOS operational amplifier.

CMOSDA and CMOSOA, respectively. These results are also compared with those from the recent literature [14–16] using PSO, [17] using Artificial Bee Colony (ABC) and [18] using Convex Optimization (CO) and Geometric Programming method. It is observed from the comparison that the performance of WOA is better than

Table 2. Design parameters obtained after optimization of differential amplifier and two-stage operational amplifier.

Heading level	WOA	
	Differential amplifier	Operational amplifier
I_{bias} (µA)	12	13
W_1/L_1 (µm/µm)	7.25/0.75	17.54/0.54
W_2/L_2 (µm/µm)	7.25/0.75	17.54/0.54
W_3/L_3 (µm/µm)	1.55/0.75	0.75/0.54
W_4/L_4 (µm/µm)	1.55/0.75	0.75/0.54
W_5/L_5 (µm/µm)	5.27/0.75	2.65/0.54
W_6/L_6 (µm/µm)	3.12/0.75	6.20/0.54
W_7/L_7 (µm/µm)	Not required	16.50/0.54
W_8/L_8 (µm/µm)	Not required	0.95/0.54
C_L (pF)	3	7

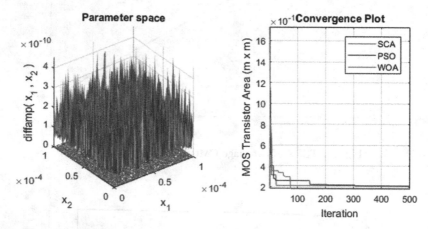

Fig. 12. Convergence plots for differential amplifier using WOA, PSO and SCA.

other algorithms for its application in optimizing analog circuits for area giving the area of 19.83 µm² and 33.442 µm². Besides optimizing the area, WOA also gives better results i.e., high gain, low power consumption, high CMRR and high PSRR, with slight reduction in SR and UGB.

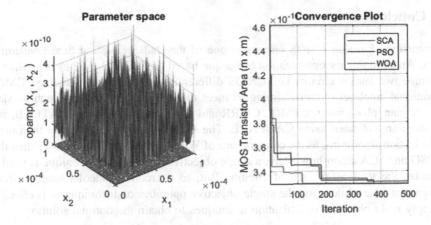

Fig. 13. Convergence plots for two-stage operational amplifier using WOA, PSO and SCA.

Table 3. Comparison of design parameters for CMOS differential amplifier

Design criteria	ABC [15]	PSO [16]	PSO [17]	WOA
C_L (pF)	5	5	14.83	3
SR (V/μs)	15.67	22.40	49.06	14.79
P_d (μW)	830	1260	408	70.20
Phase Margin (°)	91.24	83.80	90.20	89.544
F_{-3dB}(KHz)	112	100	-	153.87
Gain (A_V)	42.045	42	29.11	46.06
CMRR (dB)	79.67	84.2	46.47	85.492
PSRR (dB)	68.42	68	-	92.12
MOS area (μm²)	-	296	46.43	19.83

Table 4. Comparison of design parameters for CMOS two-stage operational amplifier

Design criteria	CO [18]	PSO [16]	PSO [19]	WOA
C_L (pF)	3	10	-	7
SR (V/μs)	88	11.3	18	13.44
P_d (μW)	5000	2370	184	266
Phase Margin (°)	60	66.55	63.53	62.66
UGB (MHz)	86	5.526	20.03	4.293
Gain (A_V)	89.2	63.8	59.19	80.13
CMRR (dB)	92.5	83.74	67.08	91.29
PSRR (dB)	98.4	78.27	63.84	80.07
MOS area (μm²)	8200	265	28.52	33.44

5   Conclusion

Automation of analog CMOS circuits is one of the challenging and time consuming tasks. An evolutionary optimization technique based on WOA algorithm is applied to optimize two analog circuits i.e., CMOS differential amplifier and two-stage CMOS operational amplifier circuits, aiming to meet the design specifications such as slew rate, dc gain, phase margin, PSRR, CMRR and power consumption in MATLAB, and the same are validated using CADENCE. The WOA is proved to be better than other optimization algorithms, as the convergence of WOA algorithm is much faster than that of PSO and SCA algorithms. Here, a single objective optimization technique is used to optimize the total MOS area of circuits. But, to overcome tradeoffs analog circuit design that arise while using the single objective optimization technique, it is effective to apply multi objective optimization techniques to obtain the optimal solution.

Appendix: A

The design process considered for the design of amplifier circuits is as follows:

(1) CMOS Differential Amplifier:
  (a) The range of I_{D5} is obtained to satisfy SR.

$$SR = \frac{I_{D5}}{C_L} \tag{1}$$

$$f_{3dB} = \frac{1}{R_{out}C_L} \tag{2}$$

  (b) S_1 ($=S_2$) is determined in order to satisfy A_V, where

$$A_V = \frac{\sqrt{4K_n'S_1}}{(\lambda_n + \lambda_p)\sqrt{I_{D5}}} \tag{3}$$

  (c) Determine S_3 ($=S_4$) to satisfy the maximum value of V_{ICmax}.

$$V_{ICmax} = V_{DD} - V_{SG3} + V_{tn1} \tag{4}$$

$$S_3 = \frac{2I_{D5}}{K_p'(V_{SG3} + V_{tp})^2} \tag{5}$$

  (d) The value of S_5 is determined to satisfy minimum V_{ICmin}.

$$V_{ICmin} = V_{SS} + V_{DS5sat} + V_{SG1} \tag{6}$$

$$S_5 = \frac{2I_{D5}}{K'_n(V_{DS5sat})^2} \tag{7}$$

(e) The current I_{D5} is determined to satisfy P_d, where

$$P_d = I_{D5}(V_{DD} + |V_{SS}|) \tag{8}$$

Where $S_i = W_i/L_i$

(2) Two stage CMOS Operational Amplifier:
  (a) The small value of C_C is chosen such that the second pole is placed about 2.2 times greater than the UGB and to get the phase margin of 60°; the right-hand plane zero is assumed to be about ten times beyond UGB.

$$C_C > 0.22C_L \tag{9}$$

$$p_2 = -\frac{g_{m6}}{C_L} \tag{10}$$

$$z_1 = \frac{g_{m6}}{C_C} \tag{11}$$

  (b) The range of ID5 is obtained to satisfy SR

$$I_{D5} = SR.C_C \tag{12}$$

  (c) The input transconductance of transistors M1 and M2 is determined from UGB and C_C.

$$g_{m1} = 2\pi.UGB.C_C \tag{13}$$

  (d) Determine S_1 (=S_2) using following equation

$$S_1 = \frac{g_{m1}}{K'_n I_{D5}} \tag{14}$$

  (e) Maximum value of ICMR is used to determine S_3(=S_4)

$$S_3 = \frac{I_{D5}}{K'_p(V_{DD} - V_{inmax} - |V_{tpmax}| + V_{tnmin})^2} \tag{15}$$

  (f) Minimum value of ICMR is used to determine S_5 (=S_8)

$$S_5 = \frac{2I_{D5}}{K'_n(V_{DS5sat})^2} \tag{16}$$

where,

$$V_{DS5sat} = V_{inmin} - V_{SS} - V_{inmax} - \sqrt{\frac{I_{D5}}{K'_n S_1}} \qquad (17)$$

(g) To estimate S_6 we have

$$S_6 = \frac{S_4 g_{m6}}{g_{m4}} \qquad (18)$$

Where $g_{m6} \geq 6\, g_{m1}$ and $g_{m4} = \sqrt{K'_p S_4 I_{D5}}$

(h) The current I_{D6} is required for power dissipation (P_d)

$$I_{D6} = \frac{(g_{m6})^2}{2 K'_p S_6} \qquad (19)$$

(i) In order to attain the current ratio between I_{D5} and I_{D6}, we evaluate the value of S_7 as follows,

$$S_7 = \frac{S_5 I_{D6}}{I_{D5}} \qquad (20)$$

(j) The values of gain and power dissipation are estimated using following equations

$$A_V = \frac{2 g_{m2} g_{m6}}{I_{D6}.I_{D5}.(\lambda_n + \lambda_p)^2} \qquad (21)$$

$$P_d = (I_{D5} + I_{D6})(V_{DD} + |V_{SS}|) \qquad (22)$$

References

1. Bashir, M., Rao, S.P., KrishnaPrasad, K.S.R.: 0.5 V, high gain two-stage operational amplifier with enhanced transconductance. Int. J. Electron. Lett. **6**, 1–10 (2017)
2. Stehr, G., Graeb, H.E., Antriech, K.J.: Analog performance space exploration by normal-boundary intersection and by Fourier–Motzkin elimination. IEEE Trans. Comput. Aided Des. Integr. Circ. Syst. **26**, 1733–1748 (2007)
3. Tlelo-Cuautle, E., Duarte-Villasen, M.A.: Evolutionary electronics: automatic synthesis of analog circuits by gas. In: Yang, A., Shan, Y., Bui, L.T. (eds.) Success in Evolutionary Computation. Studies in Computational Intelligence, vol. 92, pp. 165–188. Springer, Berlin (2008). https://doi.org/10.1007/978-3-540-76286-7_8
4. Toumazou, C., Lidgey, F.J., Haigh, D.G.: Analog IC Design: The Current Mode Approach. IET (1990)
5. Gielen, G.G.E., Walscharts, H.C.C., Sansen, W.M.C.: Analog circuit design optimization based on symbolic simulation and simulated annealing. IEEE J. Solid-State Circ. **25**, 707–713 (1990)

6. Phelps, R., Krasnicki, M., Rutenbar, R., Carley, L.R., Hellums, J.: ANACONDA: simulation-based synthesis of analog circuits via stochastic pattern search. IEEE Trans. CAD **19**, 703–717 (2000)

7. Nunez-Aldana, A., Ranga Vemuri, R.: An analog performance estimator APE for improving the effectiveness of CMOS analog systems circuit synthesis. In: Design, Automation and Test in Europe (DATE) Conference, Munich, Germany (1999)

8. Mandal, P., Visvanathan, V.: CMOS op-amp sizing using a geometric programming formulation. IEEE Trans. Comput. Aided Des. Integr. Circ. Syst. **20**, 22–38 (2001)

9. Shokouhifar, M., Jalali A.: Automatic symbolic simplification of analog circuits in MATLAB using ant colony optimization. In: 22nd Iranian Conference on Electrical Engineering (ICEE), Tehran (2014)

10. Kao, Y.T., Zahar, E.: A hybrid genetic algorithm and particle swarm optimization for multimodal functions. Appl. Soft Comput. **8**, 849–857 (2008)

11. Hassan, R., Cohanim, B., de Weck, O., Venter, G.: A comparison of particle swarm optimization and the genetic algorithm. In: 46th AIAA/ASME/ASCE/AHS/ASC Structures, Structural Dynamics and Materials Conference, Structures, Structural Dynamics, and Materials and Co-located Conferences, Austin, Texas (2005)

12. Mirjalili, S., Lewis, A.: The whale optimization algorithm. Adv. Eng. Softw. **95**, 51–67 (2016)

13. Goldbogen, J.A., Friedlaender, A.S., Calambokidis, J., Mckenna, M.F., Simon, M., Nowacek, D.P.: Integrative approaches to the study of baleen whale diving behavior, feeding performance, and foraging ecology. Bioscience **63**, 90–100 (2013)

14. Allen, P.E., Holberg, D.R.: CMOS Analog Circuit Design. Oxford University Press, New York (2002)

15. Vural, R.A., Erkmen, B., Bozkurt, U., Yildirim, T.: Differential amplifier area optimization with evolutionary algorithms. In: Proceedings of World Congress on Engineering and Computer Science, San Francisco USA (2013)

16. Vural, R.A., Yildirim, T.: Analog circuit sizing via swarm intelligence. AEU - Int. J. Electron. Commun. **66**, 732–740 (2012)

17. Prajapati, P.P., Shah, M.V.: Optimization of CMOS based analog circuit using particle swarm optimization algorithm. IPASJ Int. J. Electron. Commun. **3**, 1–8 (2015)

18. Hershenson, M.D., Boyd, S.P., Lee, T.H.: Optimal design of a CMOS op-amp via geometric programming. IEEE Trans. Comput. Aided Des. Integr. Circ. Syst. **20**, 1–21 (2001)

19. Prajapati, P.P., Shah, M.V.: Two-stage CMOS operational amplifier design using particle swarm optimization algorithm. In: IEEE UP Section Conference on Electrical Computer and Electronics (UPCON), Allahabad (2015)

Reliability Analysis of Comparator: NBTI, PBTI, HCI, AGEING

Seelam V. Sai Viswanada Prabhu Deva Kumar[(✉)] and Shyam Akashe

ITM University, Gwalior, MP, India
{betnlec14023_vasavi, shyam.akashe}@itmuniversity.ac.in

Abstract. In this research, we focus on analytical reliability assessment. The reliability of meticulous conditions of voltage, temperature and degradation will be reported to device bounds. Such as the same effect on analogue or digital device performance like Comparator cell and combined circuits. In this research article, we are challenged with some explore methodologies to scrutinize the impact of reliability on comparator circuits. The reliability evaluation under the parameters of "Positive Bias Temperature Instability *(PBTI)*, Negative Bias Temperature Instability *(NBTI)* and Hot Carrier Injection *(HCI)*" are performed. In this analysis, we considered which MOSFET was the utmost pretentious and slightest pretentious by the comparator circuit. Like all analogue and digital circuits, reliability is a major issue has instigated in a circuit that does fades performances because it enhances the trap concerning the source and the drain of every specific MOSFET. Large-scale assessment reliability has shown that the effect of every single MOSFET leads to the misleading conduct of comparator and ultimately causing damages. The precision of the comparator is exposed to this research with varying aspects. The total simulation work is performed using the 45 nm technology cadence virtuoso.

Keywords: Reliability · Comparator · CMOS technology · HCI
NBTI · PBTI and ageing

1 Introduction

A serious threat to the expansion of Bias Temperature Instability (BTI) which alters the execution of the VLSI circuit designed by CMOS Technology. NBTI greatly affects the temperature performance parameters such as reliability problems, and the tolerance voltage of a transistor, and the saturation transconductance of PMOS current. Similarly, NMOS transistors are affected by PBTI, but the effect PBTI, VLSI circuit chip is less important compared to the effect of NBTI, in particular in the Si02 layer case. Including NBTI and PBTI have another reason to compromise the reliability of the Hot Carrier Injector (HCI). Reducing the device reduces the duration of PMOS and NMOS transistors and their functionality is significantly degraded.

As technology grows, the performance of the device is increased by decreasing the size of the transistors that affect the life of design. Reliability involves the capability of methods to preserve distinct behaves in wholly conditions. At this nanometre age, most manufacturing faults are contemporaneous and guilty for the destruction of the useful

© Springer Nature Singapore Pte Ltd. 2019
S. Verma et al. (Eds.): CNC 2018, CCIS 839, pp. 606–619, 2019.
https://doi.org/10.1007/978-981-13-2372-0_54

life of the emblem. The procedure deviation requires changes in the properties of the transistor (length, width and thickness of the oxide in the manufacture of the emblem). In the variant of the process, there are labour constraints because of nanoscale technology identical degradation condition to 250 nm,180 nm and 45 nm, we have to moderate the screen, but we cannot proficient to reduce the screen as it is static by 135 nm screening scale.

This research paper deals with reliability, many problems to be identified mainly by the variation of PBTI, HCI and NBTI. In HCl, mutually PMOS and NMOS are concerned, in PBTI merely NMOS is distressed and PMOS influences traps merely in NBTI. Useful life is greatly reduced by the outflow current generated in the device and maximum of the circuits are confidence in the dispersion temperature. HCl affects the reliability of CMOS devices; causing the voltage rise below the threshold and reducing the carrier mobility, which is additional in NMOS transistor. While device layout is biased high Vds devices, HCI is a very reliant aspect. At NBTI once the voltage is pragmatic to the port of the PMOS designs, the tolerance voltage will increase. It quickens the rise in temperature and rises the dispersion current and the transverse current. PBTI is likewise a problem of reliability, although is less important in the performance of the design.

In technology, VLSI expands portable design applications such as mobile phones, laptops, PDAs, electronic instruments and systems. The comparator means that it is used to compare two binary words for equality. Parameters, such as response speed and maximum bandwidth usage, are paid by operating amplifier architecture. The use of an op-amp as a comparator principal to an inefficient condition where the current transmission fraction is truncated. The reliability analysis has proven that it does contribute towards increasing the sensitivity of the comparator. Reliability has also proven that it could increase the vulnerability of the least sensitive parts of the comparator as disclosed in Fig. 1.

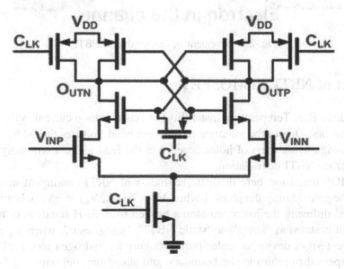

Fig. 1. CMOS design of comparator

2 Impact of PBTI on MOSFET

PBTI mainly occurs in NMOS devices since the operating voltage of the NMOS gate drain is largely positive or we can say that the NMOS device is affected positively (Vgs > 0) and has temperature dependence. PBTI effect is negligible compared to NBTI and HCI. It presents itself as a technology problem and metal gate High-K gate stack.

This problem occurs when negative carriers are trapped in the silicon/ oxide interface because the oxide or the voltage (Vgs > 0), a temperature dependence. You can see the support of negative movements.

PBTI (Positive Bias Temperature Instability) is alike to the simulated (hot-carrier injection) HCI, but there are different sets of model parameters and degradation life. If the parameters defined life PBTI, PBTI then the effects are simulated; On the other hand, they skipped. Both of these effects can be simulated HCI and PBTI together or separately. To stimulate PBTI, the following models are required of the oxide layers (Fig. 2).

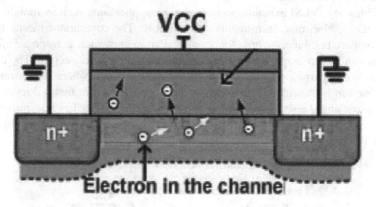

Fig. 2. Movement of carrier due to PBTI

3 Impact of NBTI on MOSFET

NBTI (Negative Bias Temperature Instability) affects the drain current, Vth, etc., of the PMOS transistors. Due to the variance in uniform band voltage, the NMOS transistor devises an insignificant even of holes accessible the feed and consequently, performs not endure from NBTI degradation.

In a PMOS transistor, here dualistic segments of NBTI contingent upon the bias ailment of the gate. During the phase 1 when $V_g = 0$ (i.e., $V_{gd} = -V_{dd}$), boundary traps are generated diffusing the hydrogen atoms broken from Si-H bonds near to the gate. This segment is stated as "stress" or "static NBTI". In segment 2, when $V_g = V_{dd}$ (i.e., $V_{gs} = 0$), the PMOS device is under pure recovery as hydrogen atoms closer to the interface dispersed in return to the boundary and strengthen the wrecked Si-H bonds.

This segment is stated as "recovery" and has a momentous effect on the appraisal of NBTI during the forceful interchanging in digital operations. However, in analogue applications recovery is unlikely to happen as the transistors are always undergoing stress when operating (Fig. 3).

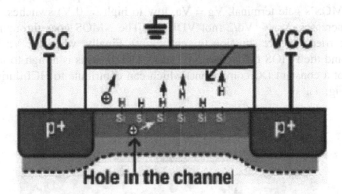

Fig. 3. Movement carrier due to NBTI

Based on this reaction-diffusion model and considering the simplest case, in which the gate is under a constant stress with a DC voltage, the shift of threshold voltage can be given by

$$\Delta V_t = (K_v^2 t)^n \tag{1}$$

where n is the period interpreter for NBTI which indicates the dilapidation rate. For a H_2 centered dissemination standard, $n = 1/6$ and for an H centered ideal, $n = 1/4$. Kv has an exponential necessity dependency on temperature (T) and electric field in the dielectric and this is called the static model.

$$K_v = \left(\frac{qt_{ox}}{E_{ox}}\right)^3 K^2 C_{ox} (V_{gs} - V_{th}) \sqrt{C} \exp\left(\frac{2E_{ox}}{E_0}\right) \tag{2}$$

Where q is electron charge, k is Boltzmann constant, Cox is the oxide capacitance per unit area, Eox is the vertical electric field across the oxide and tox is the oxide chunkiness.

4 Impact of HCI on MOSFET

Hot carrier injection is a further deprivation mechanism perceived in MOSFETs. The main source of heat on MOSFET's channel during circuit operation, rather than "anode", as anode-hole injection models. These powerful carriers can penetrate into the oxidation of the surface and the engendered electrons or holes privileged the channel or heating conductors. In this method, inoculated carriers spawn boundary or bulk oxide deficiencies, and as a result, the MOSFET features such a way of as the initial voltage, etc. are reduced over time.

Hot carrier pressure circumstances are intrinsic in the CMOS circuit operation. Figure 1(a) illustrations the CMOS inverter with feedback terminal A and output terminal. When the Va is increased (VDD), the PMOS off experiences NMOS, TDDB pressure. NMOS's gate terminal, Vg = Va, low to high (= 0 V) switches, canal bias, Vd = Vb, increases. Vg ~ Vd/2 (not VDD/2!), The NMOS goes through the maximum heat carrier pressure situation (given below). Finally, when the Va is low, the NMOS off and the PMOS belongs to NBTI and TDDB. This is a high-to-low low Va (which is not a constant DC component) which can contribute to HCI during inverter operation (Fig. 4).

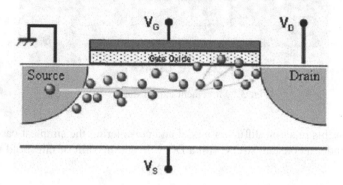

Fig. 4. Flow of carrier due to HCI

The degradation of hot-carrier models in MOS transistors includes:

- A model to calculate the current substrate (NMOSFET, PMOSFET) and gate (PMOSFET).
- A life model that calculates the Hot-carrier circuits that operate under experimental results in accelerated test conditions.
- Ageing model that describes the degradation characteristics of transistors in the voltage function: this model type parameters cadence model for simulation of degraded circuit performance degraded.

5 Simulated Reliability Graphs and Results

Reliability results are simulated for each NMOS & PMOS used in the simulated circuit. In this paper we simulated the parameters like NBTI, HCI and Ageing below the stress circumstances of Voltage, current and temperature. The result of PBTI was negligible so it has been neglected in the paper. Only HCI & NBTI effects are discussed. The circuit of comparator consists of 10 MOSFETS which are of 06 NMOS and 04 PMOS. This designed technology is known as CMOS technology.

5.1 Effect in PMOS Due to NBTI

From Table 1 it can be concluded that increasing supply voltage increases each PMOS transistor Vg & Vd values, which affects the threshold value Vth & saturation value Vsat of the circuit and its transistors (Figs. 5, 6, 7, 8, 9, 10, 11 and Tables 2, 3, 4).

Table 1. Presents the maximum absolute Vgs & Vds values of PMOS used in circuit at 0.7 V, 1 V & 1.5 V supply voltages for transistors under NBTI condition.

	Max Vg (V)			Max Vd (V)		
Volts→	0.70 V	1.0 V	1.20 V	0.70 V	1.0 V	1.20 V
PMOS↓						
PM1	7.01E−01	1.01E+00	1.21E+00	1.62E−01	2.81E−01	3.69E−01
PM2	1.6E−01	2.76E−01	3.62E−01	1.61E−01	2.81E−01	3.69E−01
PM3	1.64E−01	2.81E−01	3.69E−01	1.6E−01	2.76E−01	3.69E−01
PM4	7.01E−01	1.01E+00	1.21E+00	1.59E−01	2.76E−01	3.69E−01

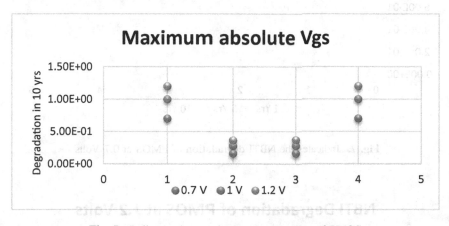

Fig. 5. Indicates the maximum absolute Vgs of PMOS

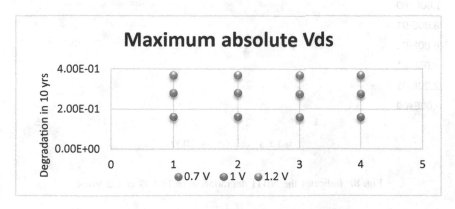

Fig. 6. Indicates the maximum absolute Vds of PMOS

Table 2. Presents the degradation of PMOS used in circuit at 0.7 V, 1.2 V supply voltages for transistors at the duration of 1Y, 5Y & 10Y under NBTI condition.

	0.7 V			1.2 V		
Time→	1Yrs	5Yrs	10Yrs	1Yrs	5Yrs	10Yrs
PMOS↓						
PM1	7.71E−01	4.51E−01	8.2E−01	7.1E−01	1.41E−01	9.2E−01
PM2	4.6E−02	3E−02	1.91E−01	7.32E−02	3.5E−01	5.5E−01
PM3	5.01E−02	4.01E−02	1.9E−01	8.52E−02	3.52E−01	5.71E−01
PM4	7.69E−01	4.51E−01	8.21E−01	7.22E−01	1.5E−01	9.31E−01

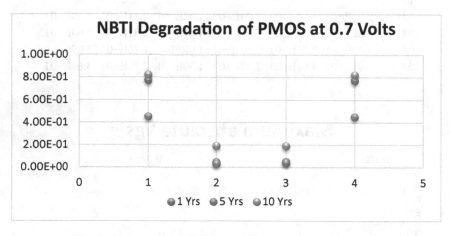

Fig. 7. Indicates the NBTI degradation of PMOS at 0.7 Volts

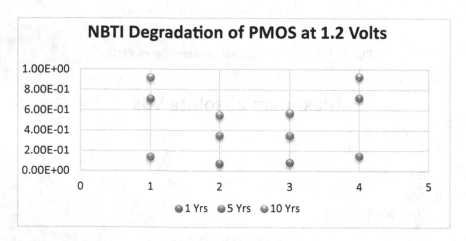

Fig. 8. Indicates the NBTI degradation of PMOS at 1.2 Volts

Table 3. Presents the ageing of PMOS used in circuit at 0.7 V, 1.2 V supply voltages for transistors at the duration of 1Y, 5Y & 10Y under NBTI condition.

	0.7 V			1.2 V		
Time→	1Yrs	5Yrs	10Yrs	1Yrs	5Yrs	10Yrs
PMOS↓						
PM1	2.18E−09	1.09E−08	2.18E−08	8.49E−08	4.25E−07	8.49E−07
PM2	4.60E−02	1.52E−10	3.04E−10	1.13E−10	5.63E−10	1.13E−09
PM3	3.11E−11	1.55E−10	3.11E−10	1.20E−10	5.99E−10	1.20E−09
PM4	3.04E−11	1.09E−08	2.19E−08	8.57E−08	4.29E−07	8.57E−07

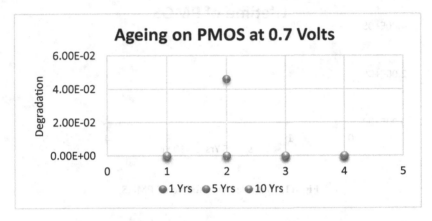

Fig. 9. Indicates the ageing on PMOS at 0.7 Volts

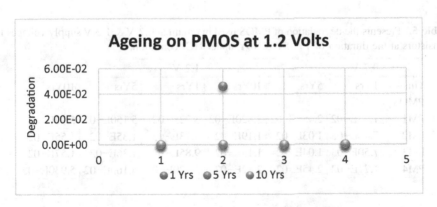

Fig. 10. Indicates the ageing on PMOS at 1.2 Volts

Table 4. Presents the Lifetime of PMOS used in circuit at 1.2 V supply voltages for transistors at the duration of 1Y, 5Y & 10Y under NBTI condition.

Time→	1 Yrs	5 Yrs	10 Yrs
PMOS↓			
PM1	5.210E+03	5.210E+03	5.210E+03
PM2	3.740E+05	3.740E+05	3.740E+05
PM3	3.660E+05	3.660E+05	3.660E+05
PM4	5.200E+03	5.200E+03	5.200E+03

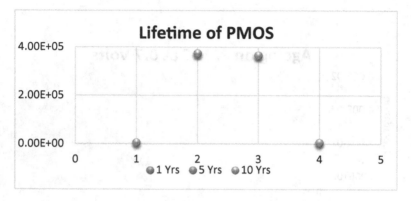

Fig. 11. Indicates the lifetime of PMOS

5.2 Effect in PMOS Due to HCI

See Table 5 and Figs. 12, 13.

Table 5. Presents the degradation of PMOS used in circuit at 0.7 V & 1.2 V supply voltages for transistors at the duration of 1Y, 5Y & 10Y under HCI condition.

	0.7 V			1.2 V		
Time→	1Yrs	5Yrs	10Yrs	1Yrs	5Yrs	10Yrs
PMOS↓						
PM1	1.77E−02	2.450E−02	2.820E−02	3.72E−02	5.150E−02	5.92E−02
PM2	7.46E−03	1.03E−02	1.19E−02	9.73E−03	1.35E−02	1.55E−02
PM3	7.50E−03	1.04E−02	1.19E−02	9.85E−03	1.36E−02	1.57E−02
PM4	1.77E−02	2.45E−02	2.82E−02	3.720E−02	5.160E−02	5.930E−02

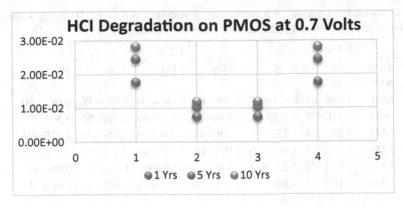

Fig. 12. Indicates the HCI degradation of PMOS at 0.7 V

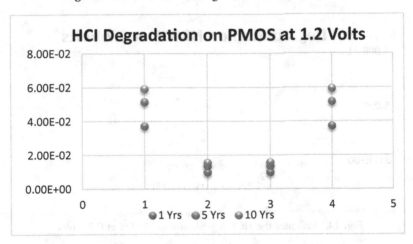

Fig. 13. Indicates the HCI degradation of PMOS at 1.2 Volts

5.3 Effect in NMOS Due to HCI

See Tables 6, 7 and Figs. 14, 15, 16, 17.

Table 6. Presents the degradation of NMOS used in circuit at 0.7 V, 1.2 V supply voltages for transistors at the duration of 1Y, 5Y & 10Y under HCI condition.

	0.7 V			1.2 V		
Time→	1Yrs	5Yrs	10Yrs	1Yrs	5Yrs	10Yrs
PMOS↓						
NM1	8.50E−27	1.59E−26	2.08E−26	0.0E+00	0.0E+00	0.0E+00
NM2	1.22E−29	2.29E−29	3.00E−29	2.17E−27	4.06E−27	5.32E−27
NM3	6.89E−27	1.29E−26	1.69E−26	6.22E−28	1.16E−27	1.53E−27
NM4	1.16E−26	2.18E−26	2.86E−26	5.79E−24	1.08E−23	1.42E−23
NM5	2.60E−29	4.86E−29	6.37E−29	0.0E+00	0.0E+00	0.0E+00
NM6	3.82E−22	7.15E−22	9.37E−22	1.89E−18	3.54E−18	4.64E−18

Table 7. Presents the ageing of NMOS used in circuit at 0.7 V, 1.2 V supply voltages for transistors at the duration of 1Y, 5Y & 10Y under HCI condition.

	0.7 V			1.2 V		
Time	1Yrs	5Yrs	10Yrs	1Yrs	5Yrs	10Yrs
NMOS						
NM1	1.29E−67	6.43E−67	1.29E−66	0.0E + 00	0.0E + 00	0.0E + 00
NM2	6.54E−75	3.27E−74	6.54E−74	3.87E−69	1.94E−68	3.87E−68
NM3	7.50E−68	3.75E−67	7.50E−67	1.57E−70	7.84E−70	1.57E−69
NM4	2.89E−67	1.44E−66	2.89E−66	2.39E−60	1.20E−59	2.39E−59
NM5	4.54E−74	2.27E−73	4.54E−73	0.0E+00	0.0E+00	0.0E+00
NM6	1.12E−55	5.58E−55	1.12E−54	3.36E−46	1.68E−45	3.36E−45

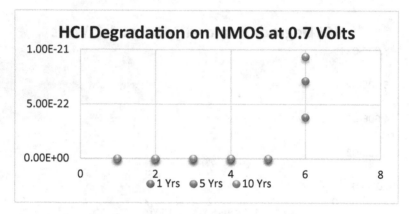

Fig. 14. Indicates the HCI degradation of NMOS at 0.7 Volts

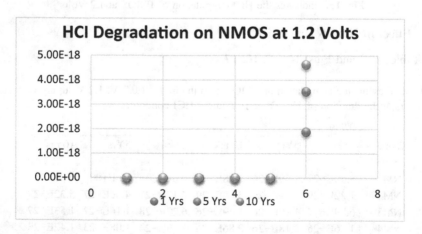

Fig. 15. Indicates the HCI degradation of NMOS at 1.2 Volts

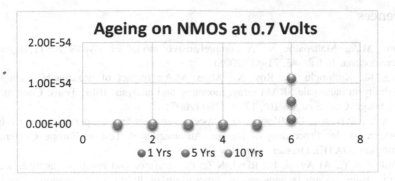

Fig. 16. Indicates the ageing on NMOS at 0.7 Volts

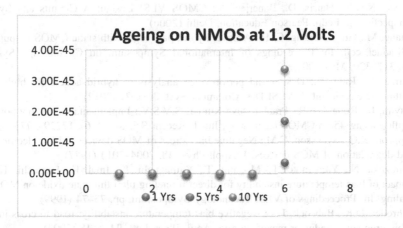

Fig. 17. Indicates the ageing on NMOS at 1.2 Volts

6 Conclusion

Here, PBTI, NBTI and HCI represent a challenge for reliability issues with nano-scale CMOS technologies. Concerning this article we explored the consequences of NBTI, PBTI and HCI on the Comparator under the conditions of degradation, lifetime and aging in the altered years with various stressed voltages. We have concluded that the effect of HCI and NBTI increases the time and voltage output and respectively is an increase in Vth value that reduces the lifetime of PMOS and NMOS transistors and degrades them to some values that say changes in Isub, Ig, and lifetime.

Acknowledgment. I would like to thanks ITM University for providing the Cadence Virtuoso Tool of 45 nm Technology.

References

1. Alam, M.A., Mahapatra, S.: A comprehensive model of PMOS NBTI degradation. Microelectron. Reliab. **45**, 71–81 (2005)
2. Kang, K., Kufluoglu, H., Roy, K., Alam, M.A.: Impact of negative-bias temperature instability in nanoscale SRAM array: modeling and analysis. IEEE Trans. Comput. Aided Des. Integr. Circ. Syst. **26**(10), 1770–1780 (2007)
3. Zhuo, C., Sylvester, D., Blaauw, D.: Process variation and temperature-aware reliability management. In: Proceeding of Design, Automation & Test in Europe Conference & Exhibition (DATE), Dresden, Germany (2012)
4. Rahul, A.K.Y., Al Ayubi, H., Rizvi, N.Z.: Performance and reliability analysis for VLSI circuits using 45 nm technology. In: Proceeding of ICEEOT, International Conference, Chennai, India (2016)
5. Guerin, C., Parthasarathy, C.: New hot-carrier lifetime technique for high- to low-supplied voltage nMOSFETs. In: Proceedings of 14th IPFA, Bangalore (2007)
6. Weste, N.H.E., Harris, D., Banerjee, A.: CMOS VLSI Design: A Circuits and Systems Perspective, 3rd edn. Pearson Education, Delhi (2006)
7. Zhang, M., Gu, J., Chang, C.-H.: A novel hybrid pass logic with static CMOS output drive full-adder cell. In: Proceedings of International Symposium on Circuits and Systems, pp. 317–320, May 2003
8. Sarma, R., Raju, V.: Design and performance analysis of hybrid adders for high speed arithmetic circuit. Int. J. VLSI Des. Commun. Syst. **3**(3), 21 (2012)
9. Nayini, L., Ronald, E.R., Prabhu Deva Kumar, S.V.S.V.: Implementation of low power d-flipflop using 45nm CMOS technology. Int. J. Recent Sci. Res. **8**(6), 17729–17732 (2017)
10. Jeppson, K.O., Svensson, C.M.: Negative bias stress of MOS devices at high electric fields and degradation of MOS devices. J. Appl. Phys. **48**, 2004–2014 (1977)
11. Kimizuka, N., Yamamoto, T., Mogami, T., Yamaguchi, K., Imai, K., Horiuchi, T.: The impact of bias temperature instability for direct tunneling ultra-thin gate oxide on MOSFET scaling. In: Proceedings of VLSI Technology Symposium, pp. 73–74 (1999)
12. Schroder, D.K., Babcock, J.A.: Negative bias temperature instability: road to cross in deep submicron semiconductor manufacturing. Appl. Phys. Lett. **94**, 1–18 (2003)
13. Prabhu Deva Kumar, S.V.S.V., Venkat, P., Nayini, L.: Implementation and designing of low power SR flip-flop using 45 nm CMOS technology. Int. J. Inf. Technol. (IJOIT) **1**(4) (2017)
14. Van Dam, C., Hauser, M.: Ring oscillator reliability model to hardware correlation in 45 nm SOI. In: Reliability Physics Symposium (IRPS), Anaheim, CA, USA (2013)
15. NBTI aging analysis and aging-tolerant design of p-type domino AND gatesp. In: 2015 12th International Conference on IEEE Trans. Electron Devices (2015)
16. Chang, C.H., Gu, J.M., Zhang, M.: A review of 0.18-μm full adder performances for tree structured arithmetic circuits. IEEE Trans. Very Large Scale Integr. (VLSI) Syst. **13**(6), 686–695 (2005)
17. Wairya, S., Singh, G., Nagaria, R.K., Tiwari, S.: Design analysis of XOR (4T) based low voltage CMOS full adder circuit. In: Proceedings of IEEE Nirma University International Conference on Engineering (NUiCONE), pp. 1–7, December 2011
18. Goel, S., Elgamel, M., Bayoumi, M.A.: Novel design methodology for high-performance XOR-XNOR circuit design. In: Proceedings of 16th Symposium on Integrated Circuits and Systems Design (SBCCI), pp. 71–76, September 2003
19. Khandelwal, S., Akashe, S.: Design of 10T SRAM with sleep transistor for leakage power reduction. J. Comput. Theor. Nanosci. **10**(1), 165–170 (2013)

20. Akashe, S., Sharma, S.: Low power SRAM cell design based on 7T configuration. Int. Electron. Eng. Math. Soc. IEEMS **4**, 11–18 (2010)
21. Li, X., Qing, J., Wang, Y.: Prediction of NBTI degradation in dynamic voltage frequency scaling operations. IEEE Trans. Dev. Mater. Reliab. **16**, 9–19 (2015)
22. Wang, W., Reddy, V., Krishnan, A.T., Vattikonda, R., Krishnan, S., Cao, Y.: Compact modeling and simulation of circuit reliability for 65-nm CMOS technology. IEEE Trans. Dev. Mater. Reliab. **7**(4), 509–517 (2007)
23. Dayal, A., Akashe, S.: A novel double gate FinFET transistor: optimized power and performance analysis for emerging nanotechnologies. Comput. Inf. Syst. Dev. Inform. Allied Res. **4**(4), 75–80 (2013)

Sag Calculations in Transmission Line with Different Case Studies

Sandeep Gupta[✉] and Shashi Kant Vij

Department of Electrical Engineering, JECRC University, Jaipur 303905,
Rajasthan, India
jecsandeep@gmail.com, shashikant.vij@jecrcu.edu.in

Abstract. Sag in the transmission line is defined as the different in level between points of supports and the lowest point on the conductor. In order to permit safe tension in the conductor, conductors are not fully stretched; rather they are allowed to have sag. Therefore, sag is mandatory in transmission line conductor suspension. Therefore, this paper focuses on calculating the sag produced by transmission lines under different conditions such as with supports at same level in planes, supports at different levels at mountains, river crossings with and without wind and ice loads etc. for different physical parameters. In this paper, different factors are explained which are affected the transmission line sag. Effect of loading on the development of conductor sag will also be considered in this paper. After this, there are presents the mathematical formulation responsible for sags of parabolic and catenary shape and analyze the difference of magnitude between them using results of MATLAB programming.

Keywords: Sag · Transmission line · Wind zone · Stability and soft computing

1 Introduction

The design of a transmission line has to be satisfactory from electrical as well as mechanical considerations [1]. The line should have sufficient current carrying capacity so that the required power transfer can take place without excessive voltage drop or overheating [2]. The line conductors, supports and cross arms should have sufficient mechanical strength to cope with the worst probable weather condition. The line conductor supports and cross arms must be strong enough to give satisfactory service over a long period of time without the necessity of too much maintenance. The tension in the conductor should be well below the breaking load. Adequate clearance between the lowest point on the line and ground must be maintained.

In the previous research [3–7], we have observed that whenever the conductor is erected between two supports or towers it is impossible to maintain the straight tension between the two supports as the effect of gravitational pull plays its part. Also since the conductors are also very heavy and there is span between the towers ranging 200 m to 800 m depending upon the area in which it is being erected and the high voltage supply which it is carrying; it is impossible to assume a zero sag condition. Hence to safe guard the community, the ground clearance safety norms has been established and implemented.

© Springer Nature Singapore Pte Ltd. 2019
S. Verma et al. (Eds.): CNC 2018, CCIS 839, pp. 620–631, 2019.
https://doi.org/10.1007/978-981-13-2372-0_55

In the simple language sag can be defined as vertical dip or drop in the straight line (imaginary) joining the transmission or distribution towers [2]. When both the towers are at same ground level, the sag is calculated at the centre of the distance between the towers, but when the towers are at different levels (which is generally the case in hilly areas), we consider two sags i.e., the vertical distance from the respective ground levels.

The factors which affect the sag were taken; for example span or the distance between the towers (or line supports), tension in the line, line supports, weight of the conductor, various conductor configuration and its effects [8]. The limits for ground clearance and conductor spacing table were referred as per the Indian electricity rules 1956 [6]. This will be followed by problem formulation for different conditions taking as case studies [9] in which wind speed data was taken from Devgarh, Chittorgarh wind power plant [10]. In one of the case studies requiring different parameters which were not considered earlier this paper has referred Indian standard code of practice for design, installation and maintenance of overhead lines by Indian Standard Institution, New Delhi (copyright 1986) [11] and design data from 132 kV substation Sodala, Jaipur [12].

This paper is discussed the factors on which the sag mainly depends for example weight of the conductor (including the loading due to ice and/or wind), span or the distance between the supports and the conductor tension. Section 2 represents the main factors, which are affected the sag. Section 3 shows the case studies and problem formulation. In this section, it includes the sag calculations under different conditions and parameters, data table for standard conductor and MATLAB graphical output of different cases. Finally, Sect. 4 concludes this paper.

2 Factors Affecting the Sag

The Sag is affected by mainly the following factors:

2.1 Weight of Conductor

Sag is directly proportional to weight per unit length of conductor [12]. It acts downwards due to gravity, hence proper selection of conductor material is very important, it should be mechanically very strong so that it doesn't slack due to its own weight neither it is much affected by the surrounding air/wind, which can not only cause the swinging or dancing conductors but it can also result it the conductors touching among themselves.

2.2 Span

A longer span causes more sag, simple logic behind is that as the span increases the weight of the conductor increases resulting in more sag [12]. But there are unavoidable circumstances due which we are forced to increase the spans which are also mentioned above mainly due to unavailability of land. Also there can be interference due to flying objects aero planes, birds etc. Since sag is proportional to square of span, an increase of 25% in span increase the sag by 56.25% [2].

2.3   Conductor Tension

Sag is inversely proportional to conductor tension. And an increase in conductor tension causes more stresses in the conductor and more load on insulators and towers. In the conventional conductor made of ACSR the tension varies from 3×10^4 to 3.8×10^4N [13]. The maximum tension in the conductor should not exceed half the breaking load (so as to allow the factor of safety as 2) [12].

Binomial theorem and neglecting the higher terms we get the erection tension such that the tension under worst probable conditions will not exceed the safe limit of tension. Using this value of tension, the sag for erection condition can be calculated. Using the normal sag expression and this modified expression the graph of tension vs. temperature and sag vs. temperature can be plotted. Graph is plotted for a fixed span and is known as stringing chart as shown in Fig. 1.

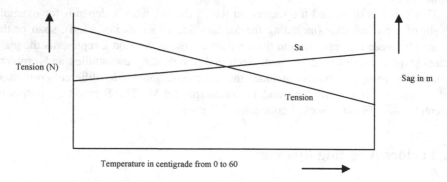

Fig. 1.   Stringing chart.

3   Case Studies and Problem Formulation

In this section, there is calculated sag for different cases considering various arrangements i.e. supports at same and different levels. Effect of loading on the development of conductor sag will also be considered in this chapter. We will also discuss the mathematical formulation responsible for sags of parabolic and catenary shape and analyze the difference of magnitude between them using results of MATLAB programming [14].

3.1   Case1: Sag Calculation Without Any Load for Supports at the Same Level at Given Span

Sag in the transmission line even under congenial conditions could lead to disastrous results so we need to take measures for sag reduction and control which makes it indispensable to go for sag calculation. Given below calculates the sag in transmission line attached between the two supports at same level with no wind or ice loading. Suppose an overhead line suspended between two supports A and B at the same level. The line is assumed to be flexible and sags below the level AB due to its weight. The exact shape of the line is that of a catenary. Except for lines with very-very long span and large sag, it is sufficiently accurate to assume that the shape of the line is that of a parabola $y = ax^2$ where a is constant for a given line, P(x, y) be any point on the curve and O is the origin in the Fig. 2. Required data for sag calculation for this case is given in Table 1. Output of the sag due to the weight of the conductor alone is shown in Fig. 3.

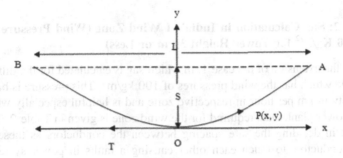

Fig. 2. Sag (without any load) for supports at same level.

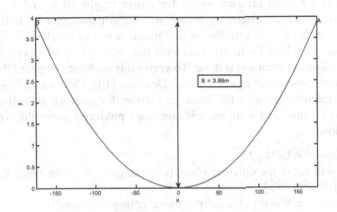

Fig. 3. MATLAB output of the sag due to the weight of the conductor alone.

When sending your final files, please include a readme informing the Contact Volume Editor which of your names is/are your first name(s) and which is/are your family name(s). This is particularly important for Spanish and Chinese names. Authors are listed alphabetically according to their surnames in the author index.

Table 1. Data for sag calculation (without any load) for supports at same level.

S. no.	Input		Output (in m)	
1	Length of span	350 m	Sag between supports at same level	3.8969
2	Conductor tension	33400 N		
3	Conductor weight per unit length	8.5 N/m		
4	Line voltage	220 kV	The spacing between the conductor lines	3.4407

3.2   Case 2: Sag Calculation in India's I Wind Zone (Wind Pressure Is ≤ 100 Kg/M^2 for Tower Height 30 m or Less)

This case is the extension of the case 1, in which sag is calculated for the different wind zone in India which has the wind pressures of 100 kg/m^2. This pressure is based on the wind velocity in km per hour in respective zone and is helpful especially while setting up a wind power plant. Data required for the wind zone is given in Table 2. This data is also helpful in deciding the safe spacing between the conductors as these wind can cause the conductors to touch each other causing a faults in power system such as double line fault or double line to line fault etc. It is the data which is used while erecting the transmission as well as the distribution lines.

These data for wind pressure zones for tower height 30 m and below too are provided to various state electricity boards as design parameters by Indian standard code of practice for design, installation and maintenance of overhead lines by Indian Standard Institution, New Delhi [9]. This wind data is very helpful especially when the survey of wind power plant site is done. To verify this we have compared the wind data as was available from wind power plant at Devgarh [10], Chittorgarh Rajasthan.

Here we calculate the sags for these three zones for catenary as well as parabolic shape as given below and compare with the sags produced under the weight of the conductor alone:

$S = \{H/W\}[\cosh (WL/H) - 1]$

But this sag will act in the different plane (at an angle γ from the vertical load).

where $W = [(W_c)^2 + W_w^2]^{1/2}$

and $W_w = P \times D$ = Weight of wind per metre acting horizontally.

D is the diameter of the conductor.

$P = 0.006 \, V^2$, where P is wind loading in kg/metre^2

V = velocity of wind in km/hr.

H = Horizontal tension.

W_c = Weight of the conductor per unit length.

W = Resultant weight of the conductor per unit length.

L = Half span between the supports.

The conductor take the form of a catenary using above equation in the new plane, although we can get the parabolic shape if we neglect the higher powers on expanding the hyperbolic function as given below:

$$\text{Sag} = \{H/W\}\left[1 + (1/2!) \times \left(W^2L^2/H^2\right) + (1/4!) \times \left(W^4L^4/H^4\right) + \ldots\ldots - 1\right]$$
$$\approx WL^2/2H$$
$$= WL^2/2T \quad \text{(Since T (Tension in the conductor) is very nearly equal to H)}$$

Table 2. Data for sag calculation in India's I wind zone (wind pressure is $\leq 100 \text{ kg/m}^2$ for tower height 30 m or less).

S. no.	Input		Output (in m)	
1	Conductor weight per unit length	0.85 kg/m	Sag with catenary shape (with no wind), Fig. 4(a)	4.7829
2	Diameter of conductor	0.0195 m	Sag with parabolic shape (with no wind), Fig. 4(b)	4.7716
3	Horizontal tension at centre point of curve	2000 kg	Total sag with catenary shape (with wind load)	11.9910
4	Half span length	150 m	Sag with parabolic shape (with wind load)	11.9413
5	Maximum wind velocity (up to 30 m height)	129.1 km/hr	Vertical Sag with catenary shape (with wind load), Fig. 4(c)	4.7914
			Vertical sag with parabolic shape (with wind load), Fig. 4(d)	4.7716

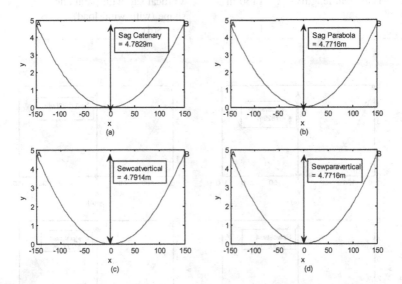

Fig. 4. Outputs of the comparison of sags for I wind zone in India.

MATLAB outputs of this case for the three wind zones are shown in Fig. 4. Figure 4(a) and (b) give the value of sag under the effect of weight of the conductor alone with catenary and parabolic shape respectively. Whereas, Fig. 4(c) and (d) give the value of sag under the effect of weight of the conductor and wind both with catenary and parabolic shape respectively. Outputs of this case are also shown in Table 2.

3.3   Case 3: Sag Calculation in India's II Wind Zone

The regions in India where the wind pressure on the conductor caused by the wind flow is ≤ 150 kg/m^2 for tower height of 30 m or less; is classified as II wind zone. Here we have taken a data of the conductor to calculate the sag in this region as shown in Table 3. This table also shows the outputs of this case. The comparison of sags for II wind zone is shown in Fig. 5.

Table 3. Data for sag calculation in India's II wind zone (wind pressure is ≤ 150 kg/m^2 for tower height 30 m or less).

S. no.	Input		Output (in m)	
1	Conductor weight per unit length	0.85 kg/m	Sag with catenary shape (with no wind), Fig. 5(a)	4.7829
2	Diameter of conductor	0.0195 m	Sag with parabolic shape (with no wind), Fig. 5(b)	4.7716
3	Horizontal tension at centre point of curve	2000 kg	Vertical sag with catenary shape (with wind load), Fig. 5(c)	4.8021
4	Half span length	150 m	Vertical sag with parabolic shape (with wind load), Fig. 5(d)	4.7716

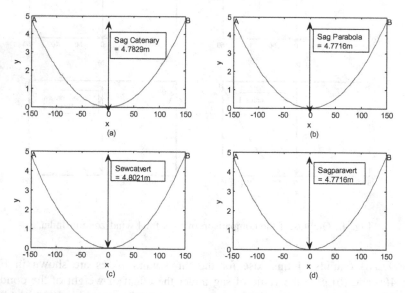

Fig. 5. MATLAB output showing the comparison of sags for II wind zone in India.

3.4   Case 4: Sag Calculation in India's III Wind Zone

The regions in India where the wind pressure on the conductor caused by the wind flow is ≤ 200 kg/m^2 for tower height of 30 m or less; is classified as III wind zone. Here we have taken a data of the conductor to calculate the sag in this region such as given in Table 4. Figure 6 shows the comparison of sags for III wind zone in India. These results are also given in Table 4.

Table 4. Data for sag calculation in India's III wind zone (wind pressure is ≤ 200 kg/m^2 for tower height 30 m or less).

S. no.	Input		Output (in m)	
1	Conductor weight per unit length	0.85 kg/m	Sag with catenary shape (with no wind), Fig. 6(a)	4.7829
2	Diameter of conductor	0.0195 m	Sag with parabolic shape (with no wind), Fig. 6(b)	4.7716
3	Horizontal tension at centre point of curve	2000 kg	Vertical sag with catenary shape (with wind load), Fig. 6(c)	4.8171
4	Half span length	150 m	Vertical sag with parabolic shape (with wind load), Fig. 6(d)	4.7716

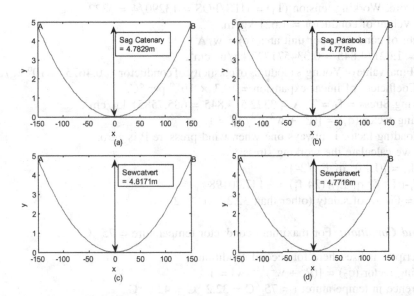

Fig. 6. MATLAB output showing the comparison of sags for III wind zone in India.

3.5   Case 5: Sag Calculation Considering the Parameters like Young's Modulus of Elasticity and Ultimate Tensile Strength with Temperature Change

In this case the sag calculation is done with the different conditions of temperature, considering the parameters like Young's modulus of elasticity, ultimate tensile strength, linear expansion of the given conductor. These are the same design calculations which are carried out in Rajasthan State Electricity Board and are authenticated by Indian Standard Institution, New Delhi (copyright 1986) under the manual of Indian standard code of practice for design, installation and maintenance of overhead lines [11].

For everyday day temperature = 32.2 °C
Let maximum conductor temperature = 75 °C
Let minimum conductor temperature = −2.25 °C

First Condition: For everyday day temperature = 32.2 °C.

Subscript 1 is used for first condition.
L = Basic span between towers = 350 m.
A = Area of cross section of conductor = 4.845 cm^2.
UTS = Ultimate tensile strength of conductor = 13290 kg.
FOS = Factor of safety (at 32.2 °C) = 4.
Therefore, Working tension (T_1) = UTS/FOS = 13290/4 = 3322.5 kg.
w = Weight of conductor = 1.621 kg/m.
Weight of conductor per unit area (δ) = w/A.
or δ = 1.621/4.845 = 0.334571723 kg/m/cm^2.
E_f = Final value of Young's modulus of elasticity of conductor = 0.4675 × 10^6 kg/cm^2.
α = Coefficient of linear expansion = 19.3 × 10^{-6} per °C.
Working Stress = f_1 = T/A = 3322.5/4.845 = 685.75851 kg/cm^2.
Loading factor (q_1) = $[(P^2 + w^2)^{1/2}/w]$ = 1.
The loading factor is always one when wind pressure P is zero.
Now we calculate the working stress:
$f_1^2[f_1\text{-}k]$ = $[(L^2\ \delta^2\ q_1^2\ E_f)/24]$
$k = f_1\text{-}[(L^2\ \delta^2\ q_1^2\ E_f)/(24\ f_1^2)]$ = −147.70198
FOS = Factor of safety (other than 32.2 °C) ≥ 2

Second Condition: For maximum conductor temperature = 75 °C.

Subscript 2 is used here for second condition.
Loading factor (q_2) = $[(P^2 + w^2)^{1/2}/w]$ = 1
Difference in temperature: t = 75 °C − 32.2 °C = 42.8 °C
Working stress = f_2
$f_2^2[f_2\text{-}(k\text{-}\alpha t E_f)]$ = $[(L^2\ \delta^2\ q_2^2\ E_f)/24]$
or f_2 = 555.553321 kg/cm^2
Working Tension T_2 = A × f_2 = 2691.656 kg.
Maximum sag = $[(L^2\ \delta\ q_2)/8\ f_2]$ = 9.22 m.

Third Condition: For minimum conductor temperature = -2.5 °C.

Subscript 3 is used here for third condition.
Loading factor $(q_3) = [(P^2 + w^2)^{1/2}/w] = 1$
Difference in temperature: $t = -2.5 - 32.2 = -34.7$ °C
Working stress = f_3
$f_3^2[f_3 - (k - \alpha t E_f) = [(L^2 \delta^2 q_3^2 E_f)/24]$
or $f_3 = 851.8511701$ kg/cm^2
Working Tension $T_3 = A \times f_3 = 4127.219$ kg.
Therefore, factor of safety = $13290/4127.2 = 3.22$, hence it is OK.
Maximum sag = $[(L^2 \delta q_3)/8 f_3] = 6.01$ m.
Now we can calculate sag of any span,
Sag of any span = Sag at basic span $\times$ [(span length)^2/(basic span)^2]

   Working tension, loading factor, working stress and maximum sag is calculated for different conditions according to the temperature of different places with different parameters, which are given in Table 5. Output result of this case is shown in Fig. 7.

Table 5. Data for sag calculation considering the conductor parameters like E_f, UTS, α and temperature for a given and required span.

S. no	Input		Output (in m)	
1	Basic span	350 m	Sag at the given	9.2217
2	Ultimate tensile strength of conductor	13290 kg	span length	
3	Overall diameter of conductor	28.62 mm		
4	Weight of conductor per metre length	1.621 kg/m		
5	Wind pressure	0 kg/m^2		
6	Co-efficient of linear expansion	0.0000193/°C		
7	Final Young modulus of elasticity of conductor	686000 kg/cm^2		
8	Conductor temperature	75 °C		
9	Everyday temperature	32.2 °C		
10	Area of cross section of conductor	4.845 cm^2		
11	Factor of safety	4	Sag at the span	18.819
12	Second value of span	500 m	length of 500 m	

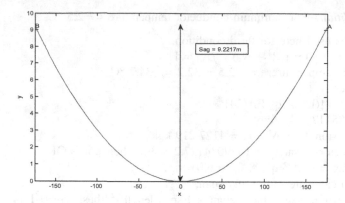

Fig. 7. MATLAB output for sag considering E_f, UTS, α and temperature of the given conductor span.

4 Conclusions

This paper is discussed the factors on which the sag mainly depends for example weight of the conductor (including the loading due to ice and/or wind), span or the distance between the supports and the conductor tension. While calculating the sag for designing any power system; the ground clearance standards, conductor configurations and spacing between the conductors must be met satisfactorily in accordance with the Indian Electricity rules. After that, this paper takes up various case studies in which the sag calculation is done using different conditions such as calculating sag with supports at same level and with supports at different level. Sag calculation using different loading such as ice and wind acting solo or collectively. Sag calculation for different shapes for example parabola and catenary with and without loading conditions. Sag calculation using normal conditions or using different parameters such as Young's modulus of Elasticity, Ultimate tensile strength and linear expansion of conductor under different temperature conditions with and without loading. This paper reaches to a conclusion with respect to the parabolic and catenary shape of the sag developed that the sag produced with parabolic shape is approximately 98%–99% of that due to catenary shape.

References

1. Larruskain, D.M., et al.: Power transmission capacity upgrade of overhead lines. In: ICREQ (International Conference on Renewable Energies and Power Quality), vol. 1, no. 4, pp. 221–227, 2 March 2006. https://doi.org/10.24084/repqj04.296
2. Kothari, D.P., Nagrath, I.J.: Modern Power System Analysis, 4th edn. Tata McGraw-Hill Education, New York (2011). ISBN 978-0071077750
3. Edris, A.: EPRI Project Manager of technical report on High-Temperature, Low-Sag Transmission Conductors, June 2002

4. Raymond Browning, United States Patent Inventor for "Method for controlling sagging of a power transmission cable", Patent Number 2007/0009224 A1, Date of patent 11 January 2007. www.freepatentsonline.com
5. Shirmohamadi, M.: United States Patent Inventor for "Various Sag Compensative Devices", Patent Number 6057508, Date of patent 2 May 2000. www.freepatentsonline.com
6. THE Indian electricity rules 1956, pp. 63–68. www.powermin.nic.in/acts_notification/pdf/ier1956.pdf
7. Gupta, S., Tripathi, R.K.: FACTS modelling and control: application of CSC based STATCOM in transmission line. In: 2012 IEEE Students Conference on Engineering and Systems (SCES), pp. 1–5 (2012)
8. El Dein, A.Z.: The effects of the span configurations and conductor sag on the magnetic-field distribution under overhead transmission lines. J. Phys. 1, 11–23 (2012)
9. Sidorov, A.I., Medvedeva, Y.V., Khanzhina, O.A.: Calculation of settings for the control systems of insulation in power distribution grids with voltage of 6 or 10 kV in conditions of uncertainty. In: IOP Conference Series: Earth and Environmental Science, vol. 44, no. 5, pp. 52–58. IOP Publishing, October 2016
10. Average annual wind speed data from Devgarh, Chittorgarh wind power plant. http://www.indiaenvironmentportal.org.in/files/file/wind%20energy%20Rajasthan.pdf
11. Indian standard code of practice for design, installation and maintenance of overhead lines by Indian Standard Institution, New Delhi (1986). http://www.dgms.net/IErules1956.pdf
12. Satyanarayana, S., Sivanagaraju, S.: Electric Power Transmission and Distribution. Pearson India (2008). ISBN 9789332503410
13. Bakshi, U.A., Bakshi, M.V.: Transmission and Distribution of Electrical Power. Technical Publications (2009). ISBN 8184317107 & 9788184317107
14. Hahn, B.D., Valentine, D.T.: Essential MATLAB for Engineers and Scientists. Butterworth-Heinemann (2007). ISBN 0750684178

Dual Band Slotted Patch Microstrip Antenna Array Design for K Band Application

Ritesh Kushwaha[✉] and R. K. Chauhan

Department of Electronics and Communication Engineering,
Madan Mohan Malaviya University of Technology,
Gorakhpur, Uttar Pradesh, India
`riteshkushwaha08@hotmail.com, rkchauhan27@gmail.com`

Abstract. Proposed array antenna is designed with a rectangular patch antenna with slots made at patch for better result. Its application is in K Band and in X Band frequency range because it is dual band antenna. The design and concept is based on microstrip patch design for radiation.

There is an array designed with the help of single element radiation result and so array of the antenna gives the better result and that is required for the radar application. It gives 6.27 dB gain. The material used for the substrate is FR4 dielectric with relative permittivity 4.4 and loss tangent of 0.02. There is 0.5 GHz bandwidth obtained at 10.75 GHz and 1.5 GHz bandwidth at 18.85 GHz. The proposed antenna has design and simulated using Ansys HFSS tool.

Keywords: Array antenna · Patch antenna · High gain · Bandwidth, dual band Slotted patch

1 Introduction

For getting high gain and high performance from an antenna then array of antenna is preferred over single element of antenna. There is interference phenomenon in the waves of different antenna which are used to make an array, so that a required directional gain and result as needed is obtained.

There is a problem of mutual coupling for required antenna performance [3]. For improved loss, narrow bandwidth, polarization distortion, multi patches in array are used for this purpose, there will be problem of scan blindness action and scattering. This problem can be countered by using thick substrate and more separation between ground and patch.

To minimize collateral negative effects, defected ground structure can be used for this ground plane irregularity and etching because of this the current distribution will be disturbed. So, by using modification in the characteristics of transmission line and DGS, also inductive and capacitive characteristics increment will give better result [1].

© Springer Nature Singapore Pte Ltd. 2019
S. Verma et al. (Eds.): CNC 2018, CCIS 839, pp. 632–641, 2019.
https://doi.org/10.1007/978-981-13-2372-0_56

2 Antenna Design

The proposed antenna is an array antenna of slotted patch. The patch of the antenna has been designed by creating different slots. The circular slot of radius 1 mm has been cut from patch and rectangular slot of different dimensions has been cut in the patch. The excitation given to the antenna is lumped port. The line feeding technique is used for feeding the antenna.

For the array of the antenna, there are different single elements has been used. The spacing used between these elements is λ/4. The proposed antenna is array of 2x2 size. Each element of array are given different excitation. Lumped port is given to each and every element and line feeding is given to every element (Fig. 1).

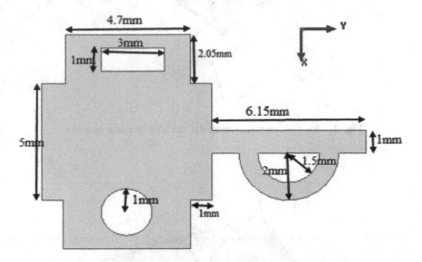

Fig. 1. Slotted patch element of microstrip array antenna

As shown in the above figure, it represents array element of microstrip slotted patch array antenna, which consists of FR4 substrate of dielectric constant of 4.4. As shown, patch element is slotted with different structure that is circular and rectangular in shaped (Fig. 2).

A Single rectangular patched antenna is described in figure. This structures consists of slotted rectangular patch with line feeding. Material used for substrate is FR4 with dielectric constant of 4.4 (Fig. 3).

As shown above, 2x2 array antenna elements are combine to form microstrip array antenna. λ/4 spacing is given between array elements. Line feeding is provided to each and every elements of the proposed array antenna design (Table 1).

The different parameters that are used for the design of antenna is described in the table. The above table also describe the corresponding values of corresponding parameters of the proposed microstrip patch array antenna.

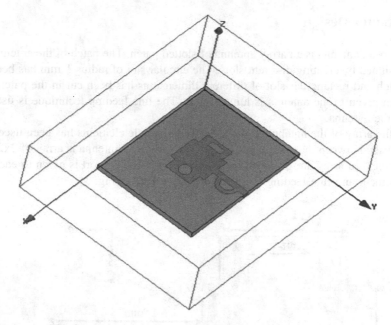

Fig. 2. A single slotted rectangular microstrip patch antenna

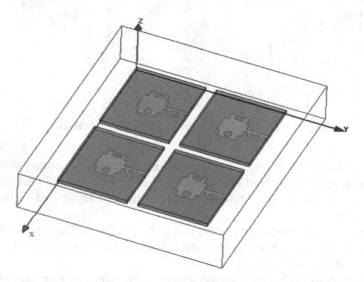

Fig. 3. A 2x2 slotted rectangular patch microstrip array antenna

Table 1. Design considerations for proposed array antenna

Parameters	Values
Dielectric constant (substrate)	4.4
Substrate length	23 mm
Substrate width	19 mm
Substrate height	1.57 mm
Size of array	2x2

3 Result and Discussion

As shown in the figure for the proposed single patched antenna, dual band in X-band and in K-band as well with good bandwidth of 0.5 GHz and 1.5 GHz respectively is obtained (Figs. 4 and 5).

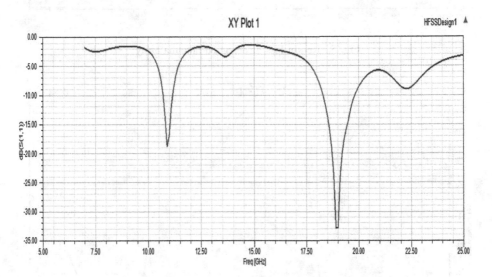

Fig. 4. Return loss of designed single patch antenna

As shown in above figure, 2x2 rectangular patch microstrip array antenna's return loss is shown. The return loss obtain is very high for the K band. 41.3 dB is the return loss obtained at 18.8 GHz frequency with having a bandwidth of 1.5 GHz in K-Band range and return loss obtain in X-band is 20.5 dB at 10.75 GHz with band-width of 0.5 GHz.

VSWR plot for the designed single patched antenna and for the antenna array has been shown in the given plot (Fig. 6).

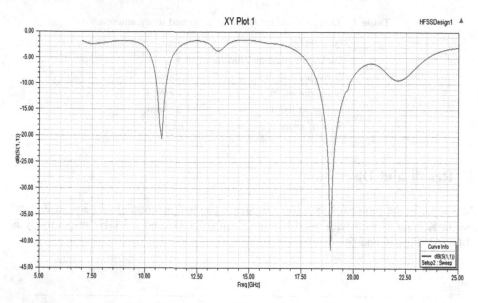

Fig. 5. Return loss of designed antenna array

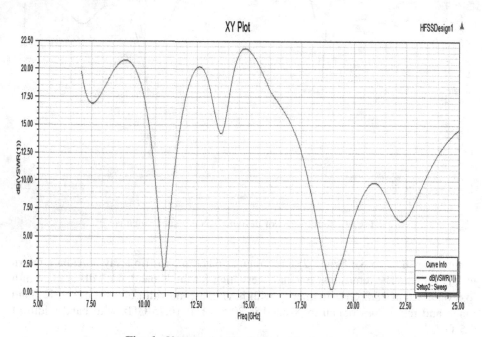

Fig. 6. VSWR plot for single patched antenna

The radiation pattern is shown in figure for both single patched antenna and for designed antenna array at different degree is shown below (Figs. 8, 9, 10, 11 and 12).

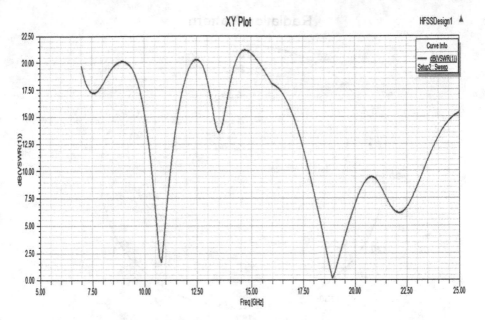

Fig. 7. VSWR plot for designed antenna array

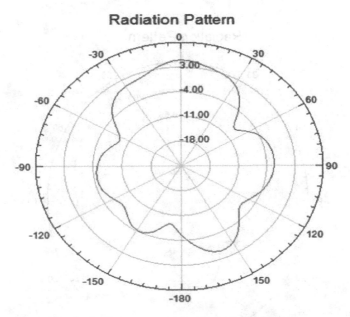

Fig. 8. Radiation pattern for single patched antenna

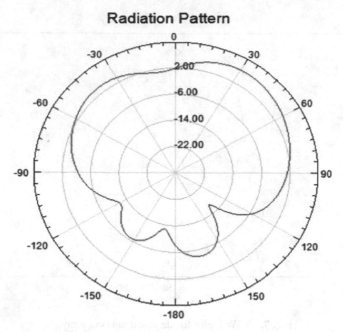

Fig. 9. Radiation pattern for single patched antenna

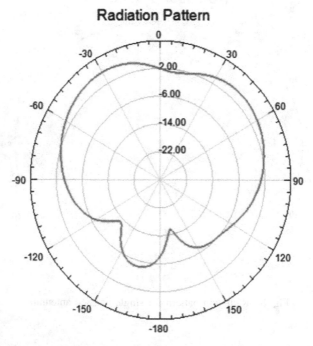

Fig. 10. Radiation pattern for designed antenna array

Radiation Pattern

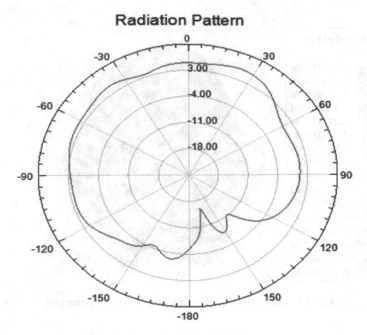

Fig. 11. Radiation pattern for designed antenna array

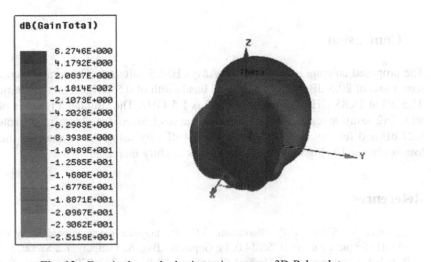

Fig. 12. For single patched microstrip antenna 3D Polar plot

The 3D polar plot for single rectangular patched antenna for proposed design as shown in the figure is described and the gain obtained for the proposed antenna is 6.27 dB (Fig. 13).

As shown above in Fig. 7, it shows the 3D polar plot of array antenna design. For the proposed microstrip array antenna obtained a high gain of 6.4 dB. By using 2x2

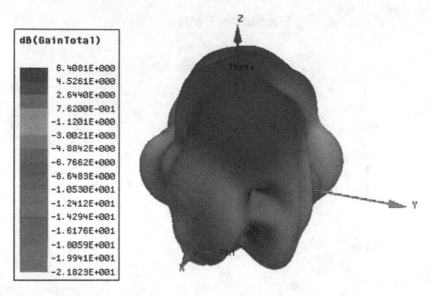

Fig. 13. For microstrip array antenna design 3D polar plot

array, the results in terms of bandwidth of 1.50 GHz in K band and 0.5 GHz in X-band is obtained.

4 Conclusion

The proposed antenna is simulated on Ansys HFSS software. The array antenna has a return loss of 20.5 dB at 10.75 GHz and bandwidth of 0.5 GHz. Also the return loss is 41.3 dB at 18.85 GHz and the bandwidth is 1.5 GHz. The simulated result is obtained with 2x2 array antenna design. The total gain obtained for single patch antenna is 6.27 dB and for the array antenna it was 6.4 dB. By using Array antenna, the return loss is obtained is high and gain obtained is slightly increased.

References

1. Midasala, V., Siddaiah, P., Bhavanam, S.N.: Rectangular patch antenna array design at 13 GHz frequency using HFSS 14.0. In: Gupta, S., Bag, S., Ganguly, K., Sarkar, I., Biswas, P. (eds.) Advancements of Medical Electronics. LNB, pp. 263–270. Springer, New Delhi (2015). https://doi.org/10.1007/978-81-322-2256-9_24
2. Herd, J.S., Fenn, A.J.: Design considerations for space-based radar phased arrays. In: Proceeding IEEE MTT-S International Microwave Symposium Digest, p. 4 (2005)
3. Alexopoulos, N.G., Rana, I.E.: Mutual impedance computation between printed dipoles. IEEE Trans. Antennas Propag. **29**(1), 124–128 (1981)
4. Clark, T., Jaska, E.: Million element ISIS array. In: IEEE International Symposium on Phased Array System Technology, pp. 29–36 (2010)

5. Sego, D.J.: System and methods for radar and communication applications. U.S. Patent 7,782, 255 (2010)
6. Pozar, D.M., Kaufman, B.: Increasing the bandwidth of a microstrip antenna by proximity coupling. Electron. Lett. **23**(8), 368–369 (1987)
7. Prasad, T.D., Kumar, K.V.S., Kumar, V.S.: Comparisons of circular and rectangular microstrip patch antennas. Int. J. Commun. Eng. Appl. **2**(4), 187–197 (2011)
8. Garg, R., Bhartia, P., Bahl, I., Ittipiboon, A.: Microstrip Antenna Design Handbook. Artech House (2001)

A 6-Bit Low Power SAR ADC

K. Lokesh Krishna[1]($\boxtimes$) (iD), K. Anuradha[2], and Alfakhri M. Murshed[3]

[1] S.V. College of Engineering, Tirupati, Andhra Pradesh, India
kayamlokesh78@gmail.com
[2] L.B.C.E.W., Visakhapatnam, Andhra Pradesh, India
[3] S.V.C.E.T., Chittoor, Andhra Pradesh, India

Abstract. The design of a 6-bit, 100 MHz successive approximation register (SAR) analog to digital converter (ADC) is presented in this paper. The implemented SAR ADC is realized by using SAR logic, a 6-bit DAC, a sample and hold circuit and a comparator circuit. The fully realized system is measured under different input frequencies with a sampling rate of 100 MHz and it consumes 36.7 µW from a 1.8 V power supply. The ADC implemented in 130 nm CMOS technology exhibits signal-to-noise plus distortion ration SNDR of 64.2 dB and occupies a die area of 0.14 mm^2.

Keywords: Data converter · High linearity · Low power · Time-interleaving
Comparator · Amplifier

1 Introduction

Physically most data in the real world is described by analog signals. In order to control/process the data using a microprocessor or microcontroller, a data converter circuit is very much indispensable. A data converter is a microelectronic circuit that is used to transform analog signal to digital signal or a digital signal to analog signal. Currently, there has been rapid progress in the design of electronic systems for various applications. The prominence of data converter circuits in the implementation of digital computers and signal processing in communications, image processing, instrumentation and industrial control systems is increasing by leaps and bounds. Hence data converter circuits are extensively used as interface between analog and digital circuits. In general there are two different types of data converter circuits. They are (i) Analog to Digital Converter (ADC) and (ii) Digital to Analog Converter (DAC). Analog to Digital Converter converts an analog signal (continuous time and continuous magnitude) into digital signals (discrete time and discrete magnitude).

ADCs are used in various applications such as Wireless Telecommunication circuits, Medical Imaging technologies, Audio and Video Processing Systems, Software radio and Instrumentation. Broadly there are numerous ADC architectures available to be used for these applications. But selection of an ADC is determined by the application and its specifications. However no single ADC architecture is found to be appropriate for all these applications. At present the major advances in consumer electronics are reflected in smart phones, notebook computers, camcorders, tablets and portable storage devices. All these devices employ various wireless technologies. Also

© Springer Nature Singapore Pte Ltd. 2019
S. Verma et al. (Eds.): CNC 2018, CCIS 839, pp. 642–652, 2019.
https://doi.org/10.1007/978-981-13-2372-0_57

wireless infrastructural systems such as satellite communication systems, cellular base stations, and various electronic warfare systems require the direct digitization of analog signal in the giga-hertz range. High resolution, High speed and low power consumption are the essential requirements in many wireless portable applications.

Different ADC architectures such as Flash type, Two-step flash type, Integrating type, Sigma-Delta, Pipeline and Interleaving are being used to deliver these requirements for various applications. The performance of an ADC is often affected by the nature of the input signal they process. Because the input analog signal is continuous in nature, ADCs suffer numerous problems such as clock jitter, nonlinear input impedance, number of bits, signal and clock skew, number of components, chip size, power dissipation etc. These problems limit the use of ADC architectures for various applications. Flash ADCs are very fastest converters and are well suitable for large bandwidth applications. But the main problem is that they consume lot of power as the resolution of the converter increases which in turn reflects in the increase in the size of the chip. Also as the chip size increases, more problems associated with signal and clock routing becomes noticeable.

Two step ADCs also well known as subranging converters is a cross between a flash ADC and pipeline ADC can be used to realize higher resolution and small power. Pipelined ADC architecture is a more specialized application of the two-step architecture and has been developed to be the most popular architecture for sampling rates from a few mega samples per second (MS/s) to 500 MS/s, with resolutions ranging from 8 bits to 12 bits.

Sigma-Delta ($\sum$-Δ) ADC architecture are used in low speed applications with resolution ranging from (12–24) bits. Integrating ADCs provide increased resolution and can offer good line frequency and noise rejection. Time interleaved ADCs uses several identical analog to digital converters to process regular sampled data series at a faster rate than the operating rate of each individual ADC. Time inter leaving technique will relax the power-speed tradeoffs of ADC and minimizes metastability error rate while increasing the input capacitance.

Presently Successive Approximation Register (SAR) ADCs are being used in many applications, due to the innovations in architectural design and process scaling techniques of the transistors, which in turn lead to the improvements in low power consumption and high speed operation. SAR analog to digital converters are highly power efficient. Also in recent years, time interleaving of SAR ADCs have led to operate in the giga hertz range. One of the reasons SAR ADCs are doing better is because they use simple logic circuitry (both analog and digital) that tend to scale well and benefit from the evolving newer technologies day by day.

Lai et al. [1] presented a SAR analog-to-digital converter implemented in TSMC 0.18-um CMOS process which can be used as a part of the biological signal acquisition system. It employs single-sided switching method that reduces DAC switching energy, thereby achieves low power consumption. Yan et al. [2] proposes a two channel interleaved 6-bit 2GS/s SAR ADC design, that employs different comparators using small sized capacitor for each stage, which eliminates digital control delay. Zhu et al. [3] presents a high-speed and low-power SAR ADC, that uses a common-mode based charge recovery switching method. Kull et al. [4] presents a single-channel SAR ADC which operates at high-speed by converting each sample with two alternate comparators clocked asynchronously and a redundant capacitive DAC with constant common mode to improve the accuracy of the comparator. Kuo *et al.* [5] propose a new structure namely the charge redistribution DAC to reduce the area cost and power consumption and to enhance the bandwidth. Yang *et al.* [6] proposed an asynchronous ADC realized by time interleaving two ADCs based on the binary successive approximation (SA) algorithm using a series capacitive ladder circuit. Lee *et al.* [7] implemented an ultra-low power SAR ADC for biosignal acquisition systems which utilized a passive sample-and-hold circuit, and an op-amp free, capacitor-based DAC. Compared to the previous related works, a 6-bit low power and medium resolution successive approximation register ADC is designed and simulated in this work.

The outline of the work is as follows. Section 2 discusses the theoretical background of successive approximation register ADC architecture and various parameters associated with the proposed work. Section 3 describes the implementation of the proposed SAR ADC. The simulation results are presented in Sect. 4. Finally conclusions are provided in Sect. 5.

2 Successive Approximation Register ADC Architecture

An SAR analog to digital converter works on the principle of binary search algorithm. This algorithm requires exactly N steps for converting the analog input voltage to an N-bit digital output. Figure 1 shows the block diagram of 6-bit SAR analog to digital converter. It includes a SAR control logic block which is realized using D-flip flop with set and reset controls, a sample and hold circuit, 6-bit digital to analog converter and a comparator circuit [8]. Initially the most significant bit of 6-bit control logic block has been set to 100000. The output of the SAR logic block is connected to 6-bit DAC. This in turn produces equivalent analog output voltage. The output of the 6-bit DAC is compared with the output of the Sample and Hold (S/H) circuit. If the DAC output is higher than the sample and hold output, then the comparator produces a logic zero output, else the comparator produces logic high.

Based on the output of comparator circuit, the SAR control logic will remains the same or reset the control logic block [9]. Recently the design of SAR ADCs has been enhanced considerably in terms of speed, power, resolution, signal to noise ratio and dynamic performance. The important specifications considered in this design are resolution = 6 bits, power supply voltage = 1.8 V, input bandwidth = upto 1 GHz, sampling rate = 100 MHz, power dissipation less than 2 mW and fabricated in 130 nm CMOS technology.

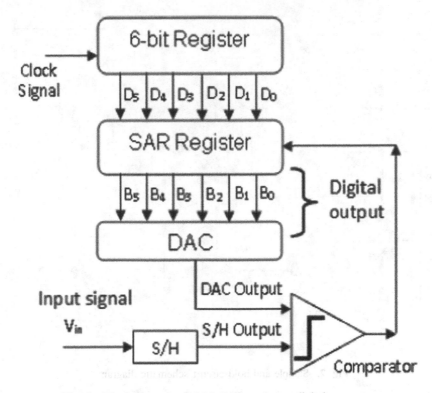

Fig. 1. Block diagram of 6-bit SAR analog to digital converter

3   System Implementation

This section discusses the design of the individual building blocks of the SAR ADC. The performance of these blocks will govern the performance of each stage and then finally the performance of the 6-bit converter. All these blocks are implemented on the HSPICE and Cadence schematic editor.

3.1   Sample and Hold Circuit

The S/H circuit is a key analog building block in many applications. The purpose of the sample and hold circuit is to sample an input analog signal and hold the analog input value over a certain interval of time for sub sequent processing. Here input signal is sampled based on the clock frequency. Figure 2 shows the schematic diagram of sample and hold circuit. It consists of a transmission gate circuit and a sampling capacitor. As long as the clock signal is high i.e. V_{DD} output voltage is same as the input voltage. When the clock signal becomes low, the input signal is sampled and the output voltage is same as the voltage across the sampling capacitor. The input to the sample and hold circuit is a sine wave having amplitude of 1.2 V_{p-p}, power supply is ±1.8 V, and clock frequency is 100 MS/s. A voltage follower circuit is connected at the output side, in order to avoid the loading effect.

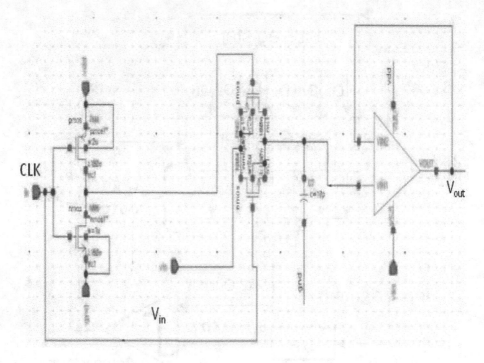

Fig. 2. Sample and hold circuit schematic diagram

3.2   Comparator Circuit

A CMOS Comparator circuit is used for comparing the input voltage with a known reference voltage. If the input voltage is greater than reference voltage the comparator output is one, else if the input voltage is less than reference voltage the comparator output is zero. Here transistors M_1 and M_2 act as a differential pair. The source of transistors M_1 and M_2 are connected with the current sink for biasing. The transistors M_3 and M_4 are PMOS based current mirror, used to realize the load. The transistor M_8 is connected in common source configuration which helps to improve the gain of the complete stage. The comparator schematic is shown in Fig. 3.

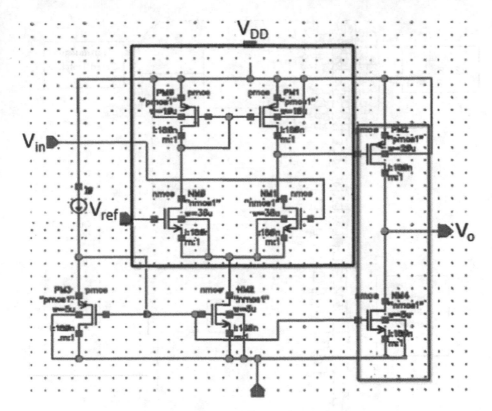

Fig. 3. Comparator schematic

3.3   6-Bit Digital to Analog Converter Circuit Using Transmission Gates

The Fig. 4 shows the 6-bit DAC circuit implemented using resistive ladder network and transmission gates. The resistive ladder network consists of 64 resistors. Based on the values of SAR registers, the distributed voltage is compared with the sample and hold circuit output by comparator.

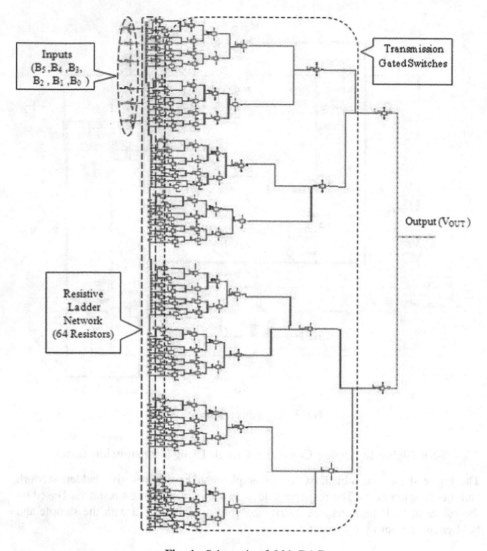

Fig. 4. Schematic of 6-bit DAC

4 Simulation Results

The performance of the proposed 6-bit SAR ADC was simulated using Cadence spectre. The entire SAR ADC is designed in 130 nm CMOS technology. The simulation results of sample and hold circuit is shown in Fig. 5. The input to the sample and hold circuit is a sine wave having amplitude of 1.0 Vp-p, power supply is ±1.8 V, and clock frequency is 800 MHz. The input signal is sampled based on the clock signal frequency.

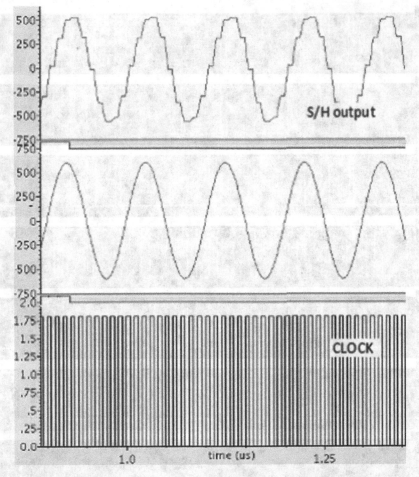

Fig. 5. Simulation results of sample and hold circuit

The final simulation results of 6-bit SAR ADC are shown in Fig. 6. The entire design of the SAR ADC is carried out using 130 nm CMOS technology.

The results obtained are summarized in Table 1.

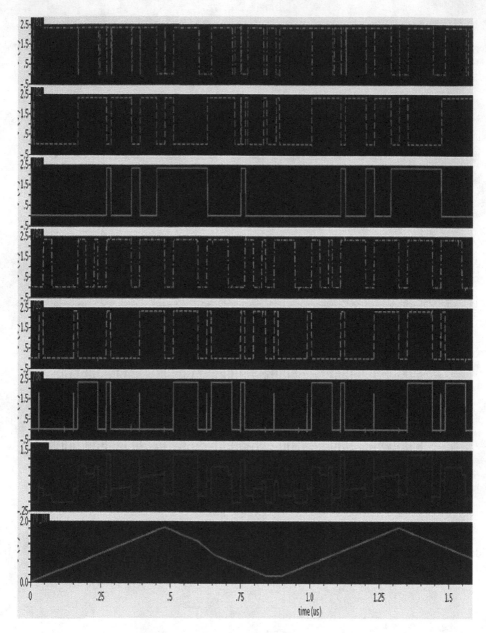

Fig. 6. Simulation results of 6-bit SAR ADC

Table 1. Summary of the 6-bit SAR ADC

Resolution	6 bits
Technology	CMOS 130 nm
Power supply	+1.8 V
Sampling rate	100 MHz
Input signal frequency	upto 1 GHz
Input voltage range	1.0 V_{P-P}
Power dissipation	36.7 µW
Area	0.14 mm^2
SNDR	64.2 dB

5   Conclusion

In this paper, a 6-bit 100 MHz successive approximation register ADC is designed and implemented in a 130 nm CMOS process technology. The ADC is operated at a power supply of 1.8 V and the simulated power consumption is only 36.7 µW. The sampling rate of the proposed ADC is 100 MHz. The ADC with an active die area of 0.14 mm^2 shows a maximum signal to noise distortion ratio (SNDR) of 64.2 dB. The designed SAR ADC can be used in applications requiring lower power dissipation, resolution requirement is medium and speed required is also not high which is MHz to KHz range such as in ultrasonic medical imaging and wireless transmission sensor networks.

References

1. Lai, W.C., Huang, J.F., Hsieh, C.G., Kao, F.T.: An 8-bit 2 MS/s successive approximation register analog-to-digital converter for bioinformatics and computational biology application. In: 2015 IEEE 12th International Conference on Networking, Sensing and Control, Taipei, pp. 576–579 (2015)
2. Yan, F., Libing, Z., Liyuan, L., Dongmei, L.: A 2GSPS 6-bit two-channel-interleaved successive approximation ADC design in 65 nm CMOS. In: 2013 International Conference on Computational and Information Sciences, Shiyang, pp. 1640–1643 (2013)
3. Zhu, Y., et al.: A 10-bit 100-MS/s reference-free SAR ADC in 90 nm CMOS. IEEE J. Solid-State Circ. **45**(6), 1111–1121 (2010)
4. Kull, L., et al.: A 3.1 mW 8b 1.2 GS/s single-channel asynchronous SAR ADC with alternate comparators for enhanced speed in 32 nm digital SOI CMOS. IEEE J. Solid-State Circ. **48**(12), 3049–3058 (2013)
5. Kuo, H.L., Lu, C.W., Lin, S.G., Chang, D.C.: A 10-bit 10 MS/s SAR ADC with the reduced capacitance DAC. In: 2016 5th International Symposium on Next-Generation Electronics (ISNE), Hsinchu, pp. 1–2 (2016)
6. Yang, J., Naing, T.L., Brodersen, R.W.: A 1 GS/s 6 bit 6.7 mW successive approximation ADC using asynchronous processing. IEEE J. Solid-State Circ. **45**(8), 1469–1478 (2010)
7. Lee, S.Y., Cheng, C.J., Wang, C.P., Lee, S.C.: A 1-V 8-bit 0.95 mW successive approximation ADC for biosignal acquisition systems. In: 2009 IEEE International Symposium on Circuits and Systems, Taipei, pp. 649–652 (2009)

8. Krishna, K.L., Ramashri, T.: VLSI design of 12-Bit ADC with 1 GSPS in 180 nm CMOS integrating with SAR and two-step flash ADC. J. Theor. Appl. Inf. Technol. **68**(1), 27–35 (2014)
9. Baker, R.J.: CMOS Circuit Design, Layout and Simulation, 3rd edn. Wiley-IEEE Press, Hoboken (2010)

Author Index

Abhishek, 443, 466, 476
Agarwal, Arun 76, 223
Agrawal, Aayushi 411
Agrawal, Animesh Kumar 286
Ahmed, Hasib 365
Akashe, Shyam 606
Akhtar, Md. Amir Khusru 133
Alam, Md. Ashraful 365
Andola, Nitish 49
Ansari, Mohd Ali 422
Anuradha, K. 642
Arakeri, Megha P. 351

Balijepalli, Ashok Kumar 518, 557, 568, 579
Bhogal, Rosepreet Kaur 411
Burange, Anup 273, 298

Chakraborty, Bodhi 262
Challa, Rama Krishna 165
Chaturvedi, Anshu 432
Chaturvedi, Arti 452
Chauhan, Nisha 223
Chauhan, R. K. 632
Chaurasia, Brijesh Kumar 110

Dargad, Sweta 340
Das, Purnendu 400
Dhamecha, Maulik 215
Dhiman, Ashish 308
Dixit, Nitin 385
Dwivedi, Rajendra Kumar 142

Elhence, Ashima 466

Gamad, R. S. 499
Gautam, Savita 3
Golla, Monika Rani 317
Gupta, Manjari 452
Gupta, Sandeep 620
Gupta, Sanjay Kumar 452
Gupta, Saurabh 385
Gupta, Vishal 308

Hassan, Fazal Mahmud 365

Jadhav, Bhushan 24
Jain, Ruchi 191
Jain, Shushant Kumar 13

Kannojia, Suresh Prasad 373
Kaur, Navdeep 165
Kewat, Anil 485
Khan, Aamir Saud 509
Khatri, Pallavi 286
Khurana, Anu 165
Koteswara Rao, P. 518, 557, 568, 579
Krishna, K. Lokesh 642
Kumar Singh, Binod 37
Kumar, Bhupendra 286
Kumar, Binod 37
Kumar, Dinesh 133
Kumar, Jasvant 373
Kumar, Mohit 133
Kumar, Sanjay 191
Kumar, Suraj 329
Kushwaha, Ritesh 632

Lakshmi, Napa 351

Maharana, Madhu Sudan 64
Majeed, M. A. Mushahhid 590
Malhotra, Shubhi 13
Mangaraj, Biswa Binayak 64
Manoria, Manish 153
Mansore, S. R. 499
Misalkar, Harshal 273, 298
Mishra, Bharat 153
Mishra, D. K. 499
Mishra, Guru Prasad 64
Mistry, Krupali 340
Modak, Sumon 64
Murshed, Alfakhri M. 642

Nagwani, Naresh Kumar 121
Nannu Saheb, S. K. 518, 557, 568, 579
Nikam, Umesh 273, 298

Pandey, Nikhil   329
Pandey, Raksha   329
Pandey, Sudhakar   191
Patalia, Tejas   215
Patankar, Archana B.   24
Patil, Kalpak   121
Prabhu Deva Kumar, Seelam V. Sai
      Viswanada   606
Prakash, Sourabh   49
Priyanka, V.   548
Purohit, Antra   476

Raghav,   49
Rahman, Tanvir   365
Rajawat, Bhairo Singh   110
Rajesh, Akula   89
Raju, B. L.   89
Rakesh,   476
Rathore, Poonam   99
Reddy, K. Chenna Kesava   89
Roy, Bir Ballav   365

Sadhya, Debanjan   262
Saluja, Avneet   340
Samad, Abdus   3
Sengar, Hirendra Singh   432
Shanmuganantham, T.   509, 528, 538, 548
Sharma, Aman   286
Sharma, Arvind Kumar   485
Sharma, Ashutosh   235
Sharma, Bishakha   76
Sharma, Daisy   548

Sharma, Mayank Satya Prakash   110
Sharma, Poonam   317
Sharma, Prachi   142
Shekhar, Chandra   181
Shrivastava, Laxmi   99
Shrivastava, Vineet   13
Shukla, Prashant   443
Singh, Damanbir   308
Singh, Dushyant Kumar   422
Singh, Krishna Pratap   262
Sreehari Rao, Patri   590
Srinivasa Reddy, T.   518, 557, 568, 579
Srivastava, P. N.   485
Suman, R. R.   37

Tomar, Ranjeet Singh   110, 201
Tripathi, Krishnavijay   235
Tripathi, Sarsij   121
Tyagi, Manoj   153

Vats, Hitender   201
Venkatesan, S.   49, 251
Verma, Abhishek   443
Verma, Shekhar   49, 251, 262, 443, 466, 476
Vij, Shashi Kant   620
Vyshnavi Das, S. K.   528, 538

Yadav, Pradeep   385
Yadav, Vijay Kumar   251

Zakir, Shamma Binte   365

Printed in the United States
By Bookmasters